Design in Depth

Unique Projects Created,
Visually Explored
and Analyzed by Fifty-One
Leading Design Firms

Organized by
DK Holland
William Drentell
Michael Beirut

Written by
DK Holland

Essays by
DK Holland
Larry Keeley
Laura Shore
Eric Smith
Ellen Lupton

Designed by
Whitehouse & Company

Published by
Rockport/Allworth Editions
Rockport Publishers, Inc.
Allworth Press

Design in
Depth

Ta

First published in the United
States by Rockport/Allworth
Editions, a trade name of
Rockport Publishers, Inc. and
Allworth Press.

Rockport Publishers, Inc.
146 Granite Street
Rockport, Massachusetts
01966
Telephone: 508.546.9590
Facsimile: 508.546.7141

Allworth Press
10 East 23rd Street
New York, NY
10010
Telephone: 212.777.8395
Facsimile: 212.777.8261

Distribution to the book
and art trade in the United
States by:

Consortium Book Sales
& Distribution, Inc.
1045 Westgate Drive
Saint Paul, MN
55114
Telephone: 612-221-9035
800-283-3572

Distributed to the book and
art trade throughout the rest
of the world by:
Rockport Publishers, Inc.
Rockport, Massachusetts
01966

ISBN: 1-56496-091-9
Printed in China

Table of Contents

Acknowledgem

It was Tad Crawford of Allworth Press who conceived of the idea of a unique series of books of the work of graphic designers. The first book, published in 1992, was named Graphic Design: New York-The Work of 39 Great Graphic Design Firms from the City That Put Graphic Design on the Map. We are publishing volume two of that book this year. GDNY's success in creating a high visibility for graphic design led us to conceive of Graphic Design: America-The Work of Twenty-eight Design Firms from Across the United States and Canada (volume two is coming out this year as well), and Signs and Spaces-A Survey of the Environmental Graphic Design Work of Twenty-two Major International Graphic Design Firms. And, of course, the next natural step was to think of the need to educate the world about graphic design, hence this book.

Tad had the vision to include Rockport Publishers as co-publishers of the book. Rockport Publishers' Stan Patey and Arthur Furst lent their invaluable publishing and sales expertise and wisdom throughout the project.

Ted Gachot copy edited this book, including each of the fifty-one introductions DK Holland wrote. Shannon Roach, while a graduate communications design student at Pratt Institute, helped contact the design firms in the beginning. Kim Sceili devoted many hours working with the designers to help them feel comfortable with their sections. Rebecca Horowitz came in at the last leg of the race to get this book out and we are grateful for her compassion and diligence in helping us make it to the finish line.

There were three designers over the four years it took to create this book—

all working under the watchful and artful eye of Roger Whitehouse. Kanchen Rajanna, Jonathan Posnett and Harriet Spear. Harriet, like Rebecca, came in at the final moments of the project, contributed her fine eye and labored over every detail, no matter how small, to make the book as perfect as humanly possible.

By the end of the third year of working on the book we had changed the working title from Design in Depth to Design in Debt. By year four it was called Design in Death. It was truly the perseverence of a small number of people like Harriet and Rebecca we have to thank for seeing this book through to publication. Finally, we wish to thank Regent Printing in Hong Kong for their artful handling of the printing process.

Ab

Dedication

Walter Landor was a graphic designer, a gentleman and a good business man. He didn't start a business, he embraced a profession. Designers were his friends and colleagues, not his competitors.

This book is dedicated to the memory of a generous man, who was also a visionary in the profession of graphic design. Walter Landor, (1913-1995) Chief Executive Officer of Landor Associates; San Francisco.

ents

out this Book

This book fulfills a need: The need to make the world aware of the creative and intellectual abilities that graphic designers bring to our lives. Specifically, the need to express the importance of graphic design to the business world, the value of the design process and its resulting expressions.

Design in Depth was conceived by Michael Bierut of Pentagram Design, William Drenttel of Drenttel Doyle Partners and myself. We had approached Rockport/Allworth Editions about the notion that design is paradoxical—both invisible and omnipresent. Design enters into practically all projects, for better or worse.

Unfortunately (or fortunately, depending on how you look at it), the sales force or Rockport didn't get what we meant. We realized we could end up only preaching-to-the-converted. So, since we wished to attract a much broader audience than designers or design mavins, we gave the book design an editorial look and feel—the results of which you hold in your hands.

There are fifty one sections and design firms in the book: one project from each design firm each totally unique from the other. If, when you're looking through the book, you think of graphic design as *anything* that helps express a thought or concept visually, you got the gist of what we were thinking—design is (or could be) an important component of just about everything in the world.

The designer and client form a partnership. I say "partner" loosely since, more often than not, the designer does not share in the economic gains of the client. Rather, they become familiar with the client's goals, the value of the client's offering (retail store, catalog, promotions, product line), and move forward together to develop the graphic approach required by the client to allow the product or service to reach its fullest potential.

When deciding how to choose the designers in the book, one thing was clear: We needed to express the complement of designers and clients in the United States today. We went to great lengths to show a complete range from individual creators who design to large design firms, from Fortune 500 clients to entrepreneurs.

DK Holland
The Pushpin Group

Mapping Our Approach to Design for the Next Millenium

Everything is changing. Everything needs to be re-designed, re-thought, re-tooled. Few times in history has this statement been true. Futurist Paul Saffo and environmentalist Paul Hawken independently observed this in the Fall of 1994 at the AIGA's first Business Conference in New York. What compelled pundits Saffo and Hawken to address this relatively small group of designers? Perhaps from Saffo's point of view, education and information are the hope of democracy. Then what will the role of the designer become—graphic designers whom Saffo refers to as "idea embalmers?" Are graphic designers, as Saffo infers, people who take live ideas and freeze them on the printed page like a butterfly collector pins down carcasses of magnificent specimens?

If so, doesn't it further suggest that the second millennium challenges graphic designers to consider a new perception of the value that they add to the world? Do they not need to do some fresh thinking? If successful, this rebirth could put designers in an excellent position to make important contributions in education and business.

Embellishing Saffo's "idea embalmer" analogy, it is often the client, quite ironically, who holds the formaldehyde bottle aloft, impatient to pour, while the graphic designer painstakingly and lovingly prepares the cadaver for embalming. (Note: in *my* version of this analogy, the designer's favorite part is, after all, applying the make-up on the corpse.) So much for keeping design alive. Sadly, it is the client's funeral—and such funerals are so wasteful.

The message of the designer's responsibility to ecology (as creators of 75 percent of all landfills), was keenly felt when Hawken made a convincing and eloquent plea calling for a new world ethic: what you create, you own forever. Make it so it is able to return to the earth without harm to the environment, or make it so it is worth keeping for good, but take responsibility, in all cases. This philosophical change is not an option—from Hawken's point of view, it is an imperative.

It is unusual to find a designer/client team in the business world who appreciate the responsibilities and goals of one another. As a colleague of mine often puts it, "Clients make the worst clients." Often this is because they are ill equipped to work on a design team. In the same vein, "Designers make the worst communicators." This is because the language they use is often self-referential and narrow while they ironically scratch their heads wondering why people don't get it. Ask 10 people who are not versed in graphic communication for their view about a design shown to them and I guarantee you 10 different answers. Perhaps some only slightly different, but all the same—as unique as our finger prints, as singular as our

by
DK Holland

interpretations of the world around us.

Because of the client's bottom-line concerns, most design professionals can correlate the decline in their revenues with the amount of work the client's taken back inhouse for the past five years. Paying for funerals gets expensive.

The term graphic design has, itself, accumulated such a bad reputation that professionals, including Clement Mok of San Francisco and Richard Saul Wurman of Newport, Rhode Island, no longer refer to themselves as graphic designers, but as information architects. This moniker may seem contrived and circuitous, but they have a point, and I say this rhetorically: What is the accepted definition of a graphic designer? Is there one? As the old story goes, the graphic designer's mother walks into the studio, "So tell me" she says, "You make the pik cha?" "No ma," the designer says. "You make the woids?" "No ma."

She appears more and more frustrated as the conversations goes on, which further confuses her understanding of just what exactly it is her boy does for a living. Finally, after a lengthy pause a lightbulb turns on. She says, "Keep this job. It's a *good* job."

There are those who have but a vague and dangerous notion of what the graphic designer does. For instance, I was in a meeting with my colleague Roger Whitehouse. We were referred by a client to discuss a major signage and identity project with another potential client, a New York restaurateur who was opening a fast food store in the World Trade Center. The project sounded like a good fit for us until we told the client what we did (i.e. environmental graphic design, strategic positioning and identity development). He threw his hands up and in exasperation said, "I asked for a graphic designer." What he clearly meant was a $35 an hour Mac whiz. That is what he meant by graphic designer, and it was clear there was no way to dissuade him: he knew what he needed. Since graphic designers seem a dime a dozen, don't clients have a legitimate reason to be confused?

On a more positive note, many successful graphic design professionals are shifting from being single-disciplinary print designers to multimedia/multi-disciplinary design strategists. This is good news for those who are up for the challenge, especially since the last half-dozen years have been chock-o-block full of bad news for this profession. But, this is more evidence of doomsday for those one-note-Johnnie-designers who are still affixed on the future and job description they bought into when they decided to become a graphic designer 10 years-or-more ago.

On the following pages are 51 projects — all created within the past few years during the rise of the high-tech, environmentally conscious bottom-line driven era.

Regardless of the business objectives of the project, these designers, their teams and their clients have much in common. Each worked in an exemplary way, combining intuition and rational abilities towards the objectives of the project. Each will help realize a better future, perhaps the future Saffo and Hawken envision.

While leafing through this book, pause to consider the role of the designer and the ability to apply design in infinite ways, to infinite audiences, for infinite purposes in a world that would, as a result of incorporating design, be infinitely enriched. It is for you, the reader — whether you have only a spector's interest in design or are an avid viewer — that design exists. That is something that the designer (and client) can never forget.

The client and designer relationship need not end in a funeral, but can be happy marriage of talents and skills that both may benefit from. Design can make the world a far better place to live in.

DK Holland is a partner in The Pushpin Group in New York and an Editor of Communication Arts magazine. This essay was also the introduction for a feature in CA called The Client Designer Partnership.

From left to right:
Tom Kluepfel, William
Drenttel, Stephen Doyle.

Since its founding in 1985, the written word has been pivotal to the work of Drenttel Doyle Partners. This editorial orientation is evident in the work created for the National Design Museum (formerly named the Cooper-Hewitt). Working closely with the museum, Drenttel Doyle Partners created a new identity program which emphasizes the word "Design," visually restating the main point of the museum's mission statement: that design is a process of shaping matter to a purpose. The firm also created installations, exhibition graphics and collateral materials for the museum. Other recent clients include: Champion Paper, Princeton University, Wamsutta and Springmaid home fashions, the Edison Project, the New York Zoological Society and the New York Transit Authority. The principals are William Drenttel, Stephen Doyle and Tom Kluepfel.

Drenttel Doyle Partners
1123 Broadway
New York, NY 10010
212/463-8787

66 The new logo presents us as a proactive institution involved with all aspects of the built environment. Our programs aren't tied to our location, but reach out into the city and the world. **99**

Diane Pilgrim, Director
National Design Museum

Reprinted from
Design In Depth.
Printed in Hong Kong.

COOPER-HEWITT.
NATIONAL DESIGN MUSEUM,
SMITHSONIAN INSTITUTION,
IS THE ONLY MUSEUM IN
THE UNITED STATES DEVOTED
EXCLUSIVELY TO HISTORICAL AND
CONTEMPORARY DESIGN.
THROUGH ITS PROGRAMS,
THE MUSEUM SEEKS TO EDUCATE
ALL PEOPLE BY EXPLORING
HOW DESIGN AFFECTS
OUR DAILY LIVES.

▼ *Temporary exhibition signage on the Fifth Avenue fence. Colorful planks are cantilevered off the museum's stately fence at jaunty angles—visual confetti that announces things are happening inside.*

▲ *The Mission Statement of the National Design Museum is displayed in the foyer of the museum. Silkscreened directly on the wall, a frame is hung on top of it. The presentation playfully alludes to the context of the museum and the process of design.*

Designer and Client:
Drenttel Doyle Partners
for Cooper-Hewitt,
National Design Museum,
Smithsonian Institution

National Design Museum

▼ The schedule of events
and newsletter were
transformed into a
comprehensive magazine,
highlighting the range and
diversity of the programs
offered by the museum.

◀ The kiosk at the National
Design Museum's entrance
proclaims the new name and
updated look. The circular
sign at top is permanent;
the posters on the kiosk
are seasonal.

A design is a plan. Drenttel Doyle created the ultimate design: a graphic identity for a museum of design. And this museum, the Cooper-Hewitt, has a special locale: Manhattan's magnificent museum mile. The museum's mission as a national advocate for design into the twenty-first century provided the firm with the appropriate posture for the identity. With Stephen Doyle providing creative direction, Drenttel Doyle Partners' masterful and distinctive style explores language as typography. The identity uses no mark, no logo, no image beyond type and color. In fact, DDP's primary focus in designing the new identity was to create a new name for the former Cooper-Hewitt, a staid and aloof name which clarified little about the museum's purpose or intent. Stephen Doyle says, "With the new name, design becomes a process and not just a class of objects. Design is an activity that affects every aspect of our daily lives—that's the essence of the museum's mission."

▲ *An exhibition about the museum's new identity is separated into discrete areas by inexpensive fluorescent construction fencing.*

▼ *Cognizant of the enormous banners just blocks away at the Metropolitan Museum, Drenttel Doyle Partners created a unique scale for the Cooper-Hewitt by using the museum's fence to announce the 1992 "A Design Resource" show. Since then, changing exhibitions have been posted on the fence. The practice forms the basis for a proposed new name sign.*

◀ Sign and symbol are combined in this multi-lingual "Coat Check" sign, a wool overcoat with silkscreened type.

▼ Exhibition signage in the museum's Great Hall lets the paneled walls become part of the signage program. White gatorfoam letters sit atop the dado ledge and lean against the wall, providing a contrast to the baroque room and directional indicators to shows.

13

▼ Drenttel Doyle Partners' earlier signage for the 1992 "A Design Resource" show.

The stationery and press ▶ kit for the National Design Museum playfully wrap the name from front to back, inside to outside. Envelopes are lined with architectural drawings of the Carnegie Mansion, an homage to Ivan Chermayeff's previous identity for the museum.

THE
A DESIGN
COOPER·HEWITT
RESOURCE
COLLECTIONS

"With many paper promotions, clients get carried away by the design and production values. What intrigued me about the Ugly promotion was that clients got carried away by the paper"

Laura Shore, Mohawk Paper Mills, Inc.

From left to right: Laura Shore, Mohawk Paper Mills, Inc., and Jilly Simons, Concrete;
Portrait: Peter Rosenbaum

Concrete, a firm of 4 1/2, was founded in 1987. Mohawk Paper Mills came to Jilly Simons as a politically-astute industry leader whose design methodology is meticulous yet imaginative. Ironically, for all of Concrete's awareness of paper waste, the process ended with a mile high stack of proposals, memos, faxes and miscellaneous documents. These documents, a haunting reminder of the volume of paper we consume, had helped shape and articulate Simons' approach to the process of solving Mohawk's design needs. Other contributors to the project included Cindy Chang, Designer; Deborah Barron, Copywriter; François Robert, Photographer; David Robson, Photograms; Active Graphics, Inc., Pre-Press and Printer.

Concrete
The Office of Jilly Simons
Jilly Simons, Principal
633 South Plymouth Court, Suite 208
Chicago, IL 60605
312/427-3733

This work in progress ▶ shows how attention to each detail is key to uplifting the familiar or average to perfection.

Reprinted from
Design In Depth.
Printed in Hong Kong.

Things Are Going to Get Ugly

Designer and Client:
Jilly Simons, Concrete
for Laura Shore,
Mohawk Paper Mills, Inc.

In an industry deluged with paper, promotions from paper mills are received by designers with mixed emotions. As gorgeous as they tend to be, paper promotions notoriously employ an excess of production techniques to show off the printability of the paper. This excess, often covers up the lack of an actual solid design concept in the promotion, and says nothing about the paper.

Jilly Simons used this knowledge to create a meaningful, humorous and artful promotion for Mohawk Paper Mills. The deliberately ironic interplay of familiar industrial landscapes as precious miniatures, "ugly" text, and meticulous printing of the promotion demonstrates the beauty that can be found in the commonplace while focussing attention on the practical virtues of the paper line.

Designers chuckled upon receiving "Things Are Going to Get Ugly," realizing this alternately laughable and ominous prediction was aimed at them. After taking it all in, they undoubtedly added it to their personal permanent collections of inspired design.

WARNING
Mohawk has determined that exposure to the enclosed papers may produce altered perception of the familiar.

This paper promotion contains a WARNING

▲ *This is a detail of Natural Parchment showing the light coming through onto the next page, made of Splendorlux paper.*

◄ *This dummy, with actual copy in place, was presented to Mohawk for approval.*

Things Are Going to Get Ugly

This direct mail "teaser" ▶
was used in select markets
to request the promotion.

The creation of the bindery ▼
and die-cutting dummy
(using actual press sheets)
involved an unusually
intricate process to insure
accuracy in the final product.

The concept of "ugly," that ▶
Simons pursued, translated
into wonderful copy and
inspired images of the
familiar. Familiar as the paper
was, the use of it was inspirational.

This is an example▶
of some early structural
exploration.

▲ The dummy (comprehensive) shown on the actual paper.

W A R N I N G
Mohawk has
determined
that exposure
to the enclosed
papers may
produce altered
perception of
the familiar.

PULL

UNLOCK THE SAFE Pop the cork DEBUNK THE MYTH
Expand the horizon TIP THE SCALES Stretch the point
KICK THE HABIT Jump the fence BUCK THE TREND
Override the veto DESTROY THE MOLD Jerk the chain
CHANGE THE CHANNEL Strike the set UP THE ANTE
Ditch the date DUCK THE COPS Snap the thr
BREAK THE ENGAGEMENT Split the infiniti
THE MIDDLE Raise the stakes TURN TH
Smash the glass PERISH THE THOU
bullet SCRATCH THE SURFACE Der
SHUFFLE THE CARDS Beat t
POTATOES Paint the town BR
skin RIP THE SEAM Bre
Toot the born HALT TH

You've found yourself face to
face with something basic,
something familiar. A bridge,
perhaps. What does it look like?
Wait! Before you describe it, ask:
What time of day is it? Am I in
love? Is it raining? How well do I
swim? Does this bridge remind me of
Venice? Do I like surprises? Would other
people call ugly the things I'd defend as
beautiful? What happened at work today? What
is a bridge, anyway? An extension of the road, or an
end in itself? Because it's you, looking at the world
through your eyes, from your unique point of view, no
bridge is familiar. There's no such thing as your your
basic bridge. Now it's time to put pen to paper and show
the world what the bridge looks like to you. If you're of a
classical temperament, you'll search for papers that are
frightfully elegant. If you're a romantic, only appallingly
lovely paper will do. And if you're practical (we're sorry), you'll
want your sheer hardworking and accessible as well as terribly
extraordinary. Your search for the peculiarly, unique paper begins at your
own, at your unique point of view. Your search ends at Mohawk.

W A R N I N G
Mohawk has
determined
that exposure
to the enclosed.
papers may
produce altered
perception of
perception of
familiar.

"I knew what I wanted the customer to know walking out of the showroom, but I had absolutely no idea how to achieve it. In the initial meeting with the Vignellis I was enchanted by how quickly and thoroughly they grasped the objectives and started working towards a perfectly simple solution."

Christine Albertini
Steelcase Design Partnership

From left to right:
Lella Vignelli, Vignelli Associates; George Beylerian, Christine Albertini, Steelcase Design Partnership; Massimo Vignelli and Sharon Singer, Vignelli Associates. ©1995 Luca Vignelli.

Lella and Massimo Vignelli had cultivated a long term relationship with Partnership consultant George Beylarian when he introduced the Vignellis to Christine Albertini, marketing director of the Steelcase Design Partnership Grand Rapids showroom. Lella Vignelli says, "Christine had a very strong, clear vision. She was the driving force behind the project. The objectives were all derived from our mutual clarification of the marketing concept of the Partnership." She adds, "Grand Rapids is to contract furnishings what High Point is to home furnishings." In other words, the epicenter for office furnishings.

The project team included: Massimo Vignelli, Vignelli Associates/Jennifer Sliker, David Perkins Associates, graphic designers; David Perkins Associates, graphic coordination; Massimo Vignelli/Lella Vignelli/Sharon Singer, Vignelli Associates, interior designers; Xibitz, general contractor/exhibit fabricator.

Massimo Vignelli
Lella Vignelli
Sharon Singer
Vignelli Associates
475 Tenth Avenue
New York, NY 10018
212/244-1919

Reprinted from
Design In Depth.
Printed in Hong Kong.

Designer and Client:
Lella Vignelli, Massimo Vignelli and Sharon Singer, Vignelli Associates for Steelcase Design Partnership

Steelcase Design Partnership Showroom

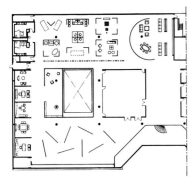

▲ *Floor plan of the Steelcase Design Partnership showroom.*

The Steelcase Design Partnership is an amalgam of eight separate companies that were acquired by Steelcase with the purpose of complementing its office furniture activities and offering its clients a complete and coordinated line. When facilities managers of larger corporations flock to Grand Rapids to shop for their office furniture needs, they can now complete their tasks all in one place by stopping at the Steelcase Design Partnership Showroom.

When Steelcase chose to communicate the capabilities and roles of the Partnership,

◄ *Cover and spreads from the product brochure.*

they found that Vignelli Associates, well respected in the international worlds of interior, industrial, graphic and environmental graphic design, was a perfect fit.

The Vignellis, who think and design simultaneously in two- and three-dimensions, worked closely with Partnership marketing director, Christine Albertini, and quickly came to the mutual conclusion that the showroom and the brochure should reflect the strategy undertaken by Steelcase in creating the Partnership. Since the budget for the showroom redesign was limited, Vignelli Associates embraced these limitations and created a simple product theater of moveable partitions. Lella Vignelli observes, "When thinking through an environmental design, we always work in three-dimensions right away. It saves a lot of time and energy because we understand the space for what it is, and, therefore, what it's capable of becoming." Massimo Vignelli adds, "The Partnership showroom became four acts of the same play. Of course, the protagonist in all cases was the product." Sensible and sublimely understated, the Vignelli system is both timeless and adaptable: it offers a perfect stage on which the Partnership's offerings may evolve and grow.

Steelcase Design Partnership Showroom

*Detail of fabric display ▶
in the Design Resource
Center/Library.*

*Perforated steel display▲
walls and a moveable
hanging arcade made of
anodized aluminum function
as a proscenium in the
Product Theater.*

*One of the individual com- ▶
pany vignette areas, featuring
products from each company
within the Partnership.*

Vecta is dedicated to the principles of performance, innovation and the concept of industrial elegance for the office environment.

◄ The Design Resource Center/Library for samples and cut-sheet catalogs.

VECTA

Seating

Contemporary

Transitional

Traditional

Executive Seating   Side Seating

▲ Sand-blasted glass panels with individual company presentation.

◄ Back-lit product display wall: the complete product offering is grouped by category and price range (parallel to the product brochure).

▲ The Brainfood program begins with a morning of interactive audience participation and role playing with various theatrical, dance and musical groups, like Robert Faust and the Faust Maskworks Theatre. The activities are interrupted by the surprise entrance of African dancers moving to the beat of tribal drum rhythms and distributing lunch—circular food packaged in recycled tubes. This is part of a two day kickoff event that encourages observation and discovery skills and provides a relaxed atmosphere for the launch of the program.

From left to right:
James Sakamoto, Wayne Sakamoto, Mark Sackett
Photo: Christiana Ceppas

Designer Mark Sackett, who surrounds himself with magical toys, antique dolls, circus posters and board games, is himself the quintessential product of Brainfood. Sackett's forte is a combined focus on marketing and collaborating with clients to arrive at design solutions that increase their visibility, market share and sales. Brainfood program clients have included Hallmark and the Creative Division of Mervyn's, a large U.S. retailer.

Sackett Design Associates has offices in San Francisco and Kansas City.

Reprinted from
Design In Depth.
Printed in Hong Kong.

Photo: Roger Paperno

❝The Brainfood program has worked a minor miracle. It has taken a cynical and overworked group and pumped some spirit back into it.❞
Genia Service
Graphics Manager, Mervyn's

Designer and Client:
Sackett Design Associates for
Brainfood Creative Programs

Brainfood

▶ Mason jars containing
over a hundred items from
various sources, are handed
out during the second day
of the kickoff event. Games,
gum, baseball cards, peanuts,
crayons, dolls, toys, and
unusual foreign coins and
stamps evoke childhood
memories and engage the
participants' senses of
taste, smell and touch.
Strong memories, from
a time in life when newness,
exploration and discovery
were everyday occurrences,
help reinvigorate the participants' imaginations.

▼ The Brainfood poster was
designed to be cut into
various shapes and used as
the program's basic marketing
materials. Cards, with the
words "info," "Brain" and
"food," can be trimmed out
from the poster, imprinted
and distributed via corporate
inter-office mail systems,
providing event information
and inspirational messages.

Sackett Design Associates realizes that, now
and then, every creative or marketing person
needs to find fresh motivation, inspiration and
resources. "Brainfood" is a program designed
to provide a creative jump-start for corporations with in-house marketing and creative
departments or for anyone who could benefit
from fresh and interesting ways to stay
abreast of visual and marketing trends.

Brainfood's basic premise is to provide a
venue which allows for the inspiration and
motivation of creative individuals and

ultimately, an improved creative product.
A questionnaire allows Sackett Design
Associates to conduct a needs analysis and
to then tailor the program to those needs and
the interests of the participants. The program
is flexible and includes seminars, cognitive
re-training and weekly meetings. The goal is
simple: to help creative individuals who are
blocked, frustrated, stale or uninspired find
the tools that will allow them to re-energize
their creativity however and whenever they
have the need.

Brainfood

▲ Since opening their offices in San Francisco, Sackett Design Associates has taken out-of-state clients on shopping trips in the Bay Area as a way of doing immediate and impression- able retail and trends research. For Brainfood, they refined these trips and created "Bay in a Day," a day of shopping, research, discovery and visual stimuli. Photos: Roger Paperno

◄ ▶ The core of the pro- gram is the Brainfood note- book that each participant receives during the kickoff event. Each notebook and its dividers are handmade and assembled in limited editions. They become the participants' central creative and motivational resource, providing a wealth of inter- esting and relevant informa- tion and imagery.

Eleven different sections contain materials on trends, resources, reading files, typography, the environment and other important topics. Participants are encouraged to submit pages relating to any of the subjects in the notebook. These pages are reproduced and "fed" to the participants during weekly meetings.

The notebooks contain over six hundred pages of information on a wide vari- ety of topics and become an evolving resource for the participants, which can be referred back to whenever necessary. A subscription series that would allow anyone to subscribe to the Brainfood resource notebook is currently being planned. Photos: Rick Der

◄ ▶ Instead of visiting obvious locations, like museums and tourist attractions, "Bay in a Day" focuses on small, interesting boutique store and retail concepts, murals, graffiti, galleries and restaurants. Careful observation of the unique ways these locations utilize texture, color and materials in the presentation of retail concepts, helps par- ticipants see how effective sometimes ground-breaking concepts are possible on extremely small budgets or in limited space.

The "Bay in a Day" excursion helps individuals sharpen their abilities to recognize emerging retail trends and isolate important visual concepts within often cluttered environments. The blend of locations provides a varied cultural and visual experience, which becomes a rich memory of a full and exciting day.

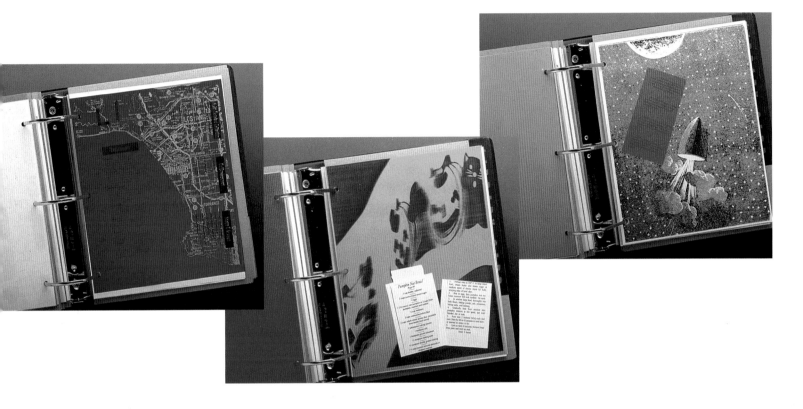

Reprinted from
Design In Depth.
Printed in Hong Kong.

From left to right: Naomi Mizusaki, designer; Andrea Codrington, editor; David Sterling, editorial and creative direction; Mark Randall, editorial and creative direction; Chika Azuma, designer; (not pictured: Calvin Chu, designer). Photo: Kelly Campbell

❝A much needed voice in the design community. Even with all the good intentions of so many individuals and organizations—this is one of the first examples I can recollect of a design publication addressing social issues on this broad a scale. ❞

Peter Comitini

World Studio Foundation was established in 1993 as an organization that would serve as the impetus for increasing the involvement of the creative professions in socially responsible actions. Observations were made at its inception about the lack of people of color in the design disciplines, in part exacerbated by increasing art and design school tuitions. Furthermore, existing professional organizations have focused mainly on assisting the profession's insular needs and concerns. These facts, World Studio's founder believes, have created a "design elite," further alienating the general public from the creative professions. World Studio Foundation has a different mission: its core belief is that creativity can be a prime tool for social change, and that its restorative nature should be available to all. The Foundation's goals, therefore, are to increase diversity in the creative professions, and to stimulate social awareness among its members, who are primarily creative professionals.

World Studio Foundation
New York, NY
212/366-1317

◀ *The World Studio logo (left) by Mark Randall and John Pirman; and (right) the cover of the first issue of Sphere, photocollage by Frank W. Ockenfels 3, illustrates a sign showing the international symbol for information.*

Sphere Magazine

Designer and Client:
David Sterling, founder and
president, Mark Randall,
vice-president, World Studio
Foundation and editorial and
creative directors of *Sphere*.

▲ *Seeking to arouse a
sleeping design community
to action in a variety of
social agendas, Sphere's
graphics are bold and
provocative and aim for
the heart as much as
the mind. Peter Hall reports
on how hemp and other
non- wood fibers could be
the basis for paper in the
twenty-first century.*

Noting that paper companies are one of the worst contributors to paper waste—perhaps most evident in expensive paper promotions—World Studio Foundation approached Su McLoughlin at Gilbert Paper with the idea of doing a "paper promotion with a purpose." Gilbert loved the idea, and gave the Foundation carte blanche to begin. The concept evolved into *Sphere*—a publication featuring people and projects that engage social agendas around the world. The maga-

zine was subsequently mailed gratis to 20,000 designers nationwide. The development of *Sphere* took on the collaborative nature that the foundation embraces: an advisory board of editors from noted publications was assembled to provide advice; Andrea Codrington, senior editor at *ID Magazine*, acted as editor; three recent graduates from School of Visual Arts in New York acted as the design team, with World Studio, Inc. as design director; and the masthead was designed by Erik Spiekermann, noted type designer in Germany. In addition, all pre-press services were donated by Typogram in New York, and Gilbert Paper provided paper and funding for the project.

28

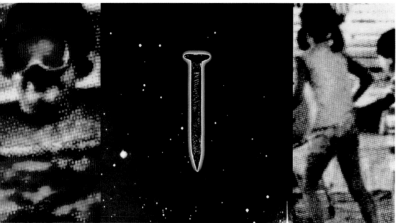

Each issue of Sphere ▲ contains a call-to-action card on a timely social or environmental topic. In this issue readers were encouraged to respond using this postcard on the subject of "Who are the architects of society? What should an American design council do?" Reply card design by Tom Bonauro, San Francisco.

The article, "Second Lives: ▶ Recycling in India," is a visual review of cups, bags bowls and boxes made of second hand materials that illustrate the practical beauty found in India's reincarnated objects.

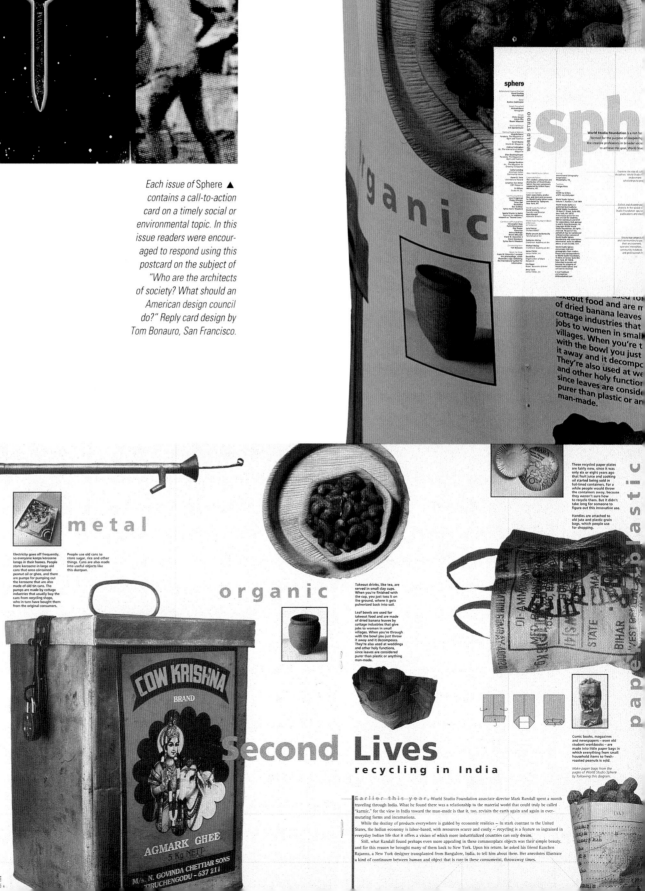

metal

Electricity goes off frequently, so everyone keeps kerosene lamps in their homes. People store kerosene in large old cans that once contained peanut oil or ghee, and there are pumps for pumping out the kerosene that are also made of old tin cans. The pumps are made by cottage industries that usually buy the cans from recycling shops, who in turn have bought them from the original consumers.

People use old cans to store sugar, rice and other things. Cans are also made into useful objects like this dustpan.

organic

Takeout drinks, like tea, are served in small clay cups. When you're finished with the cup, you just toss it on the ground, where it gets pulverized back into soil.

Leaf bowls are used for takeout food and are made of dried banana leaves by cottage industries that give jobs to women in small villages. When you're through with the bowl you just throw it away and it decomposes. They're also used at weddings and other holy functions, since leaves are considered purer than plastic or anything man-made.

These recycled paper plates are fairly new, since it was only six or eight years ago that fruit juice and cooking oil started being sold in foil-lined containers. For a while people would throw the containers away, because they weren't sure how to recycle them. But it didn't take long for someone to figure out this innovative use.

Handles are attached to old jute and plastic grain bags, which people use for shopping.

Comic books, magazines and newspapers – even old student workbooks – are made into little paper bags in which everything from small household items to fresh-roasted peanuts is sold.

Make paper bags from the pages of World Studio Sphere by following this diagram.

Second Lives
recycling in India

Earlier this year, World Studio Foundation associate director Mark Randall spent a month traveling through India. What he found there was a relationship to the material world that could truly be called "karmic," for the view in India toward the man-made is that it, too, revisits the earth again and again in ever-mutating forms and incarnations.

While the destiny of products everywhere is guided by economic realities – In stark contrast to the United States, the Indian economy is labor-based, with resources scarce and costly – recycling is a feature so ingrained in everyday Indian life that it offers a vision of which more industrialized countries can only dream.

Still, what Randall found perhaps even more appealing in these commonplace objects was their simple beauty, and for this reason he brought many of them back to New York. Upon his return, he asked his friend Kanchen Rajanna, a New York designer transplanted from Bangalore, India, to tell him about them. Her anecdotes illustrate a kind of continuum between human and object that is rare in these consumerist, throwaway times.

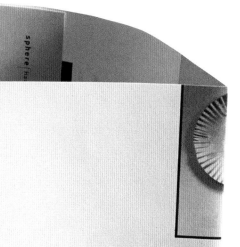

◀ *Comic books, magazines and newspapers—even old student workbooks—are made into little paper bags in which everything from small household items to fresh roasted peanuts are sold. The article on recycling in India came complete with instructions on how to turn the pages of* Sphere *into paper bags.*

you are here

Latitude and longitude – the who, what, where and how. In this section World Studio looks at people around the globe who have created a place for themselves on the edge with border-expanding projects.

I got the children to make personal guardian angels. I didn't want them to think of pretty little angels with wings, I wanted...

Welcome to the premier issue of Sphere...

▲ *Spreads from* Sphere *showing the editorial page, an article on designers working worldwide and a look into an inner-city oasis in Philadelphia created by resident guardian angel, Lily Yeh.*

WORLD STUDIO

sphere

▲ *Masthead design by Erik Spiekermann, MetaDesign, Berlin.*

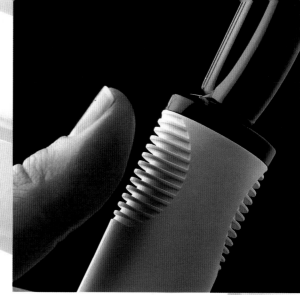

Good Grips' basic design ▶ principle is the large oval handle and the soft finger-print for control. Adding a few fins made the products fun and inviting. Realizing that people change and that ergonomics are in flux, Smart Design extends the useful life of both the object and the user.

From left to right: Davin Stowell, Sam Farber and Tucker Viemeister.

Good Grips have set a new standard for kitchen gadgets because they fit everybody's needs. By making things better, they make people happier and that makes the world better.

The Smart Design Good Grips team included: Davin Stowell, project director; Dan Formosa, ergonomics; Tucker Viemeister, designer; Michael Callahan, designer; Steve Russak, designer; Stephan Allendorf, designer; Scott Bolden, designer/engineer; Vanessa Sica, designer; Rie Norregaard, graphic designer, Evelyn Teploff, graphic designer; Kenneth Willardt, photographer.
Portrait by Jarrod Linton.

Smart Design Inc.
7 West 18th Street
New York, NY 10011
212/807-8150

66Smart Design broke new ground by applying innovative universal design principals to simple kitchen tools.99
Sam Farber, OXO International

Kitchen Trio OXO

handy Measuring Spoons on a jail house ring

Swivel Peeler
Measuring Cups
Measuring Spoons

GOOD GRIPS

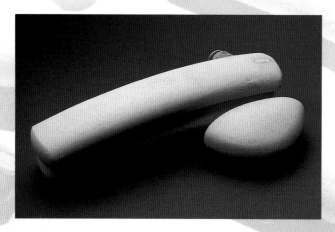

◀ Quick styrofoam test models, like this one of a can opener and the prototypes shown in the background, help the designer resolve issues while testing ease of handling. After the basic design is refined, detailed and working prototypes can be made before injection molding tools are machined for mass production.

Reprinted from
Design In Depth.
Printed in Hong Kong.

Good Grips

Designer and Client:
Davin Stowell, president;
Tom Dair, executive vice
president; Tucker Viemeister,
vice president design; Tamara
Thomsen, vice president
graphics; Smart Design Inc.
for Sam Farber, president,
OXO International, General
Housewares division

▲ *A product's shape can communicate more concretely than its name or description; by integrating product and graphic design a clear message can be sent. The panoramic arrangement of the faces of the Kitchen Trio gift package dramatically displays all the features of the products.*

Many of the tools the world needs have yet to be redesigned for modern living. Sam Farber, the housewares magnate and gourmet cook, realized this quite profoundly as he watched his wife, who had a mild case of arthritis, attempt to peel potatoes with a standard peeler. Since, for the Farbers, cooking was synonymous with entertainment, drudgery was contradictory to the joy of cooking.

Sam Farber's response was to seek out Smart Design to develop a line of hand held kitchen tools that were ergonomically tested and that could be manufactured and sold at a reasonable price to the mass market.

Smart restated the objectives by asking some simple questions: why can't a kitchen tool be comfortable, easy to use, good quality, aesthetically pleasing, easy to maintain and reasonably priced?

Good Grips is sold in mass market retail outlets and has accomplished its stated objectives with flying colors while continuing to expand its line and win awards at an equally rapid pace.

◀ *The Good Grips Sierra Club trowel is made of the same soft material with the patented fins, but the shape and size of the handle conform to the different ways the hand moves when gardening. Part of the proceeds from the sale of these tools goes to the Sierra Club to help preserve and protect the environment.*

◀ Since Good Grips were introduced, a dozen or more imitators have entered the market. Smart Design and OXO keep ahead of the competition by introducing new products. The new Good Grips Basics handle is contoured to achieve the same results as the original Good Grips soft handle at half the price.

▲ Smart Design's goal is to create environments, objects and graphics that will be sympathetic to the range of human abilities—for everybody. Not only did Smart Design create the universal kitchen gadgets, the logo, packaging, displays and tradeshow booth, but Davin Stowell helped introduce the products at the Gourmet Show.

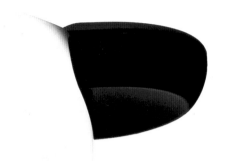

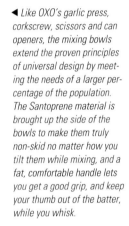

◀ *Like OXO's garlic press, corkscrew, scissors and can openers, the mixing bowls extend the proven principles of universal design by meeting the needs of a larger percentage of the population. The Santoprene material is brought up the side of the bowls to make them truly non-skid no matter how you tilt them while mixing, and a fat, comfortable handle lets you get a good grip, and keep your thumb out of the batter, while you whisk.*

▲ *Smart Design created the OXO logo and packaging. By reversing the packaging orientation (conventionally the tools hang down), the hanging card pack invites customers to feel the rubber handle.*

◀ *A holistic approach to design, engineering, marketing and distribution ensures that every opportunity, like this gift pack concept, is explored. This elegant set-up box and fancy display transforms a bunch of kitchen gadgets into a gift fit for a king.*

❝We approached Studio W to help us reposition ourselves as an agency and to redesign our identity because of how impressed we were with how they used photography❞
Robert Fox, Impact Visuals

from left to right:
Donna Binder, Fo Wilson,
Robert Fox. Photo ©
1994 Christopher Smith,
Impact Visuals.

Studio W, Inc., nationally recognized for its work in magazine development and its annual reports, promotion and packaging for national clients, found the collaboration with Donna Binder and Robert Fox of Impact Visuals refreshing. "So much of the job of a designer is to clarify the mission of any given assignment," says Fo Wilson, president and creative director. "What was great about working with Impact was that they had already clarified what they needed the design to do, so we could spend most of our time developing affordable tools to help them reach their objectives."

Wilson feels the role of today's graphic designer needs to be redefined and enrolled in New York University's Executive MBA program to broaden her skills. "I could not stay in business justifying pieces simply by aesthetics. Design has to work even harder at being effective in today's technologically advanced environment. I'm looking to the program to help me, among other things, incorporate more sophisticated marketing and strategic planning concepts with my twenty years of experience in the communications field."

Studio W, Inc.
17 Vestry Street
New York, NY 10013
212/274-8744

Designer and Client:
Studio W, Inc.
for Impact Visuals

Remaking an Impact

The new logo not only ▶ underscores the most critical tool for any photographer, their eye, it also represents the photo agency's concern with pressing global issues.

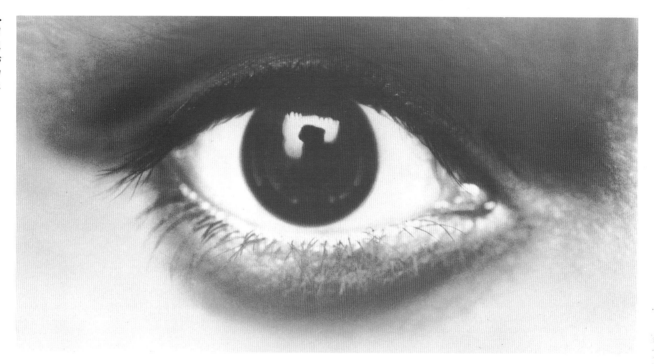

Impact Visuals is an alternative source of photography focusing on social issues, an area outside of the mainstream of what is available from stock photo houses. Donna Binder and Robert Fox, the former managing editor and general manager, wanted "to attract new clients without alienating the ones we already have."

"We approached Studio W to help us reposition ourselves as an agency and to re-design our identity because of how impressed we were with how they used photography," says Fox. "We were a little nervous because our budget was tight and were quite surprised when they agreed to do it pro bono."

"I felt the pro bono relationship was the proper way to maintain the integrity of both parties," says Fo Wilson, president and creative director of Studio W. Wilson also enlisted the help of Ken Gobel of Enterprise Press in New York and Laura DesEnfants, a rep with Mohawk Paper Company. "Ken was not only willing to be more than reasonable with his prices, he contributed ideas that brought printing costs down while adding quality to the project, " says Wilson. Mohawk graciously donated a significant amount of paper after seeing the comps.

The studio offered Impact Visuals several solutions built on components that could be produced as the company developed its resources. "Even though we offered them workable options that were less expensive, we were taken when they opted for the most complete package and took out a loan to produce everything at once," says Wilson. "They saw the value of effective design without any convincing."

▲ *Before Studio W redesigned its identity, Impact Visuals presented an image appropriate to an agency serving underground, alternative and non-profit organizations but which limited their credibility in the mainstream media.*

▲ *Studio W proposed a simple, cost effective packaging system that could be used to send out requested stock, promotional materials and other mailings.*

IMPACT
a cooperative photo agency
VISUALS

IMPACT
a cooperative photo agency
VISUALS

David Friend, Director of Photography
Life Magazine
1271 Avenue of the Americas
New York, N.Y. 10020

January 1, 1995

Dear David,

What a wonderful usage of our photo by Andrew Litchenstein on the cover of your year-end special issue. Andrew was elated! Having followed the conflicts in Haiti for over five years now, he is so close to what is going on. His timing is impeccable and so is yours.

Could we please get copies of the issue and/or tearsheets as we discussed. This is a real big break for our agency. We appreciate your faith in us and your support as we've been growing. I'll send over Marie von Dickerson's work in Germany on the Neo-Nazi eruptions, as soon as she gets back from an assignment in London.

What a wonderful usage of our photo by Andrew Litchenstein on the cover of your year-end special issue. Andrew was elated! Having followed the conflicts in Haiti for over five years now, he is so close to what is going on. His timing is impeccable and so is yours.

Could we please get copies of the issue and/or tearsheets as we discussed. This is a real big break for our agency. We appreciate your faith in us and your support as we've been growing. Could we please get copies of the issue and/or tearsheets as we discussed. This is a real big break for our agency. We appreciate your faith in us and your support as we've been growing.

What a wonderful usage of our photo by Andrew Litchenstein on the cover of your year-end special issue. Andrew was elated! Having followed the conflicts in Haiti for over five years now, he is so close to what is going on. His timing is impeccable and so is yours.

Sincerely,

Robert Fox
General Manager

24 WEST 25TH STREET 12TH FLOOR NEW YORK, N.Y. 10010 USA 212 807-6422

**IMPACT
VISUALS**

*▼ The second solution, a
proposed folder, with a
brochure incorporated into it,
created a flexible system
that would accommodate
future promotional materials.*

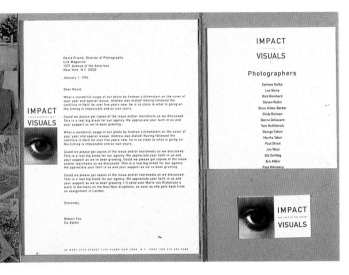

*◄ The final Impact Visuals
folder was the most sophisticated, comprehensive
and expensive to produce,
with type letterpressed
onto the cover, two pockets
and a letter held in place by
an elastic band.*

*Studio W also created a
new promotional brochure
that could be sent to old,
new and prospective clients
either on its own or as part
of the folder.*

"Working with Eric Baker and his staff on *500 Nations* was one of the happiest collaborations I've ever had with a designer.

The book was planned to accompany an 8-hour CBS documentary about American Indians, which was produced by Kevin Costner's company TIG Productions. The text written by Alvin M. Josephy, Jr., a leading historian and one of Knopf's treasured authors.

Almost immediately Eric came up with a jacket and a book design that not only met our expectations but added an extra dimension to the project. Throughout the year he solved brilliantly whatever problems arose and there were many because the art came in erratically and often not at all.

In short, Eric made what was a difficult project with difficult time restraints fun and rewarding, producing in the end a truly beautiful, one-of-a-kind book. "

Ann Close, Senior Editor
Alfred A. Knopf, Publishers

Reprinted from
Design In Depth.
Printed in Hong Kong.

From left to right:
Eric Baker, Rymn Massand,
Jason Godfrey, Karen
Kautzky, Robert Hudson,
Mathieu Araud.

Eric Baker Design Associates, Inc. produces a wide range of work in the field of publishing and corporate communications, especially in the area of illustrated books and specialty publishing projects. The book project, 500 Nations, was the result of a longstanding relationship with Alfred A. Knopf, for which they had designed promotional items, store displays and cover designs. Their first full book for the publisher, 500 Nations was created as a companion to a television series produced by Jack Luestig and Kevin Costner.

Working in concert with editor Anne Close and art director Peter Anderson, Eric Baker Design Associates created a flexible design for a classic book telling American history from the Native American point of view.

Eric Baker Design Associates, Inc.
11 East 22nd Street
New York, NY 10010
212/598-9111

▲ *Eric Baker Design Associates designed the packaging for the audio book to coordinate with the illustrated edition.*

Designer and Client:
Eric Baker Design Associates
for Alfred A. Knopf

500 Nations

Alfred A. Knopf, Inc. approached Eric Baker Design Associates to design *500 Nations,* a book illustrating the diversity of Native American cultures. The 460 page, large-format book was written by Alvin M. Josephy, Jr. as a companion to an eight-part television documentary. The visual nature of the project meant the book would include 485 paintings, woodcuts, drawings, photographs and artifacts illustrating the civilizations of the pre-Columbian Mayas, the Anasazis and the Temple Mound Builders of the Mississippi Valley, the Toltecs and Aztecs, Pueblos and Hopis, Navahos and Apaches, Creeks, Natchez and Choctaws— and those hundreds of other Indian groups who first inhabited North America.

Eric Baker Design Associates created a grid and typography system that would allow a great degree of flexibility within the framework of a classically designed book. Their goal was to design a book that would not become dated or ephemeral, but rather establish a quiet structure that would enable the reader to enjoy both the text and illustrated matter.

Eric Baker Design Associates also designed the book's cover and binding, the companion audio book and display poster as well as the logotype used for the video presentation to work together and create harmony between the various pieces.

▲ *500 Nations is a story of leaders, customs, political systems, and ways of life— of men and women told in their own words or resurrected from memory, memoir, and ancient documents.*

CHAPTER 3

CLASH OF CULTURES

▲ Eric Baker Design
Associates grid allowed them
to create a classic design
with a great deal of flexibility
in response to a wide
variety of images. The book
integrates imagery from a
wide variety of sources into
a timeless homage to the
Native American way of life.

KNOPF

◀ The display poster captures the spirit of the book: rich in color, imagery and message.

Reprinted from
Design In Depth.
Printed in Hong Kong.

Donovan and Green, a firm of 45, was founded in
1974. Well-known for its environmental graphic
projects, it has won many awards for work in exhibition, graphic and multimedia design.
Donovan and Green has had a longstanding working relationship with Corning. Other contributors
to the Corning Wall of Light project included partner Susan Berman and designer Allen Wilpon.

Donovan and Green
Michael Donovan and Nancye Green, Principals
71 Fifth Avenue, New York, NY 10003
212/989-4050

**Michael Donovan and
Nancye Green,**
Donovan and Green.

**❝The chairman, Jamie Houghton,
recognized at our first presentation
the value and significance of the
metaphor, 'light as Corning's ally'.❞**

Designer and Client:
Michael Donovan and Nancye Green, Donovan and Green; James Houghton, Chairman; Fred Murrell, Design Director; Chris Hacker, Design Director; Corning, Inc.

Corning Wall of Light

◀ *The entrance to Corning's new international headquarters is a wall of light. Using basic optical principles of science and state-of-the-art technology, Donovan and Green articulated Corning's cutting-edge technological advances. In addition, the presentation created a memorable visual experience.*

In the 1850s, Corning Glass Works moved to Corning, New York, to manufacture red and green glass lenses for railroad signal lights. A century and a half later, the altered transmission of light is a major component of Corning's business. Fiber optics, the next century's communication medium, is a product Corning helped invent and will continue to develop in the future.

Corning is best known by the general public for its vast product lines of glass home accessories—casseroles and other storage containers that can go from freezer to oven because they are adaptable to extreme heat and cold.

Donovan and Green was asked to develop an entry to Corning's new international corporate headquarters in New York City. Extensive knowledge of the company's current products and direction led them to propose that the properties of glass and light would make a dramatic and appropriate vehicle to reinforce the company's image and identity.

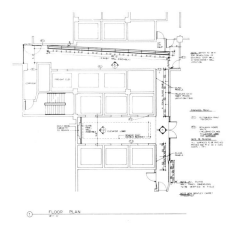

▲ Using dichroic filters, prisms, and optical mirrors combined with pure white, point source lighting, a rotating pattern of spectral light is focussed on 50 feet of wall.

Corning Wall of Light

◄ *Dichroic filters separate light into the various colors of the visible light spectrum. By carefully selecting dichroic filters and aiming them through mirrors and prisms, the color palette becomes an ever-changing array.*

▲ *Light sources are programmed by computer so that the light show constantly provides a variety of color patterns and a memorable visual experience.*

> **"The first time I met Doug Harp,
> I knew that he would be perfect for
> the re-design of the *Serious Fun!*
> brochure for that season. He had
> exactly the right energy level and
> sense of humor which captured in
> print the spirit of the festival. It
> was a very good collaboration."**
> Susan Panetta, Lincoln Center
> for the Performing Arts

From left to right: Douglas
G. Harp, Linda E. Wagner,
Harp and Company; and
Susan Panetta, Lincoln Center
for the Performing Arts.

*At the suggestion of a client who liked Harp and
Company's work, Douglas Harp wrote to Lincoln
Center offering to do overflow work once a new
art director was hired. To call attention to the fact
that he was not applying for the new position, he
circled that paragraph with his rainbow pencil.
When Harp spoke to David Rivel, the director of
marketing at Lincoln Center, Rivel said he'd put
Harp's letter aside out of over 500 he'd received.
Shortly after meeting with Susan Panetta, the
newly-hired art director, Harp and Company was
asked to design the Serious Fun! brochure.*

*Harp and Company
5 Prospect Street
Hanover, NH 03755
603/643-5144*

*Robert Barker, designer photo;
Eric Van Den Brulle, client photo*

Harp and Company used ▶
*an uncomfortable grid
and odd color combinations
to capture the spirit of
Lisa Kron's "101 Humiliating
Stories."*

Reprinted from
Design In Depth.
Printed in Hong Kong.

Designer and Client:
Douglas Harp, Principal, Harp
and Company for Susan Panetta,
Art Director, Lincoln Center
for the Performing Arts, Inc.

Variations at the Center

▲ *The Kipper Kids' faces were a layout in themselves. Yellow squares on each page were the one constant used throughout the brochure. They announce the critical information for each act: date, time, title and a brief synopsis.*

Lincoln Center, the performing arts mecca in New York, is commonly thought of as the home of opera, ballet and classical music. Serious Fun! is a plucky, audaciously experimental cultural program designed to draw the radically less conservative market that lurks in the metropolitan area.

Douglas Harp was selected to design the promotion for Serious Fun!, Susan Panetta, art director at Lincoln Center, commented, primarily because of his affinity for poster design and his portfolio, which sparkles with vitality and youthful energy—exactly the

graphic tone they needed. Harp adds, "This project actually ended up becoming a wonderfully disparate assortment of poster designs."

Douglas Harp and his associate Linda Wagner whipped together a promotional brochure comprised of 15 "posters" of programs that ranged from live video acts performed by the Emergency Broadcast Network, to performance art by Pomo Afro Homos. Harp and Company worked exclusively from available art and photography supplied by Lincoln Center, and from whatever inexpensive means and methods were available around the studio. Since this project was for a nonprofit organization, the budget and time frame were tight; yet at the same time, Lincoln Center's expectations were great. Harp says, "There was really no time to overanalyze anything; we had less than 30 days to complete the project, and this included three presentation trips to New York. This built-in imperative forced us to design from the gut. The process was a delightful mixture of anxiety and pure adrenaline-pumping fun, and the end product offered an appropriately crazy, spontaneous glimpse of what Serious Fun! was all about."

The brochure was a great success for both designer and client, and Serious Fun!'s increased attendance was attributed, in part, to Harp and Company's efforts.

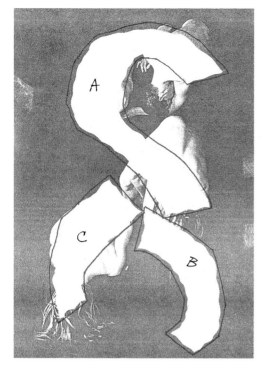

The sinewy dancers' ▲ bodies of la Compagnie Marie Chouinard seemed a perfect fit for the S in the Serious Fun! title.

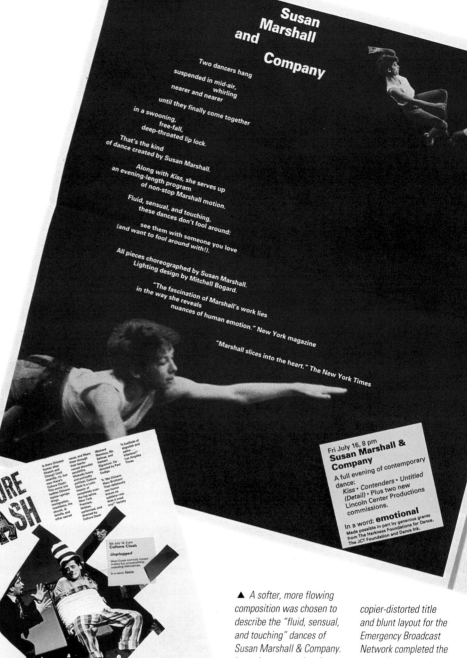

Susan Marshall and Company

Two dancers hang
suspended in mid-air,
whirling
nearer and nearer
until they finally come together
in a swooning,
free-fall,
deep-throated lip lock.

That's the kind
of dance created by Susan Marshall.

Along with *Kiss*, she serves up
an evening-length program
of non-stop Marshall motion.

Fluid, sensual, and touching,
these dances don't fool around:
see them with someone you love
(and want to fool around with!).

All pieces choreographed by Susan Marshall.
Lighting design by Mitchell Bogard.

"The fascination of Marshall's work lies
in the way she reveals
nuances of human emotion." New York magazine

"Marshall slices into the heart." The New York Times

Fri July 16, 8 pm
Susan Marshall & Company
A full evening of contemporary
dance:
Kiss • *Contenders* • *Untitled
(Detail)* • Plus two new
Lincoln Center Productions
commissions.

In a word: **emotional**
Made possible in part by generous grants
from The Harkness Foundations for Dance,
The JCT Foundation and Dance Ink.

▲ A softer, more flowing composition was chosen to describe the "fluid, sensual, and touching" dances of Susan Marshall & Company. In stark contrast, the photo-copier-distorted title and blunt layout for the Emergency Broadcast Network completed the unsettling spread.

▼ The small-scale faces on the Twisted Roots page provide visual steppingstones to the full-bleed portrait of La Monte Young. The lenses of Young's glasses are knocked out of a photo of his band on stage.

Harp's notes to Susan ▶ Panetta describing how the i in the title would be created.

NOTE:
what shows as white here prints as the same red b'ground as on the Diamanda Galás page (p 2 or I.F.C.)

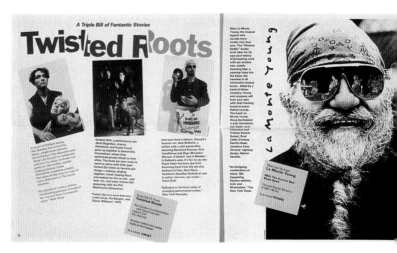

Serious Fun

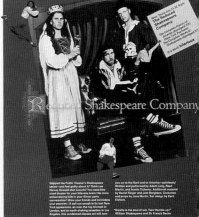

Harp felt that Lisa Kron's ▶ cracking-up face had to somehow be included in the "Serious" portion of the title.

▼ *The intensity of La Compagnie Marie Chouinard and the inanity of the Reduced Shakespeare Company made them natural bedfellows on this spread.*

**Sat July 17, 8 pm
Emergency
Broadcast Network**
Live video acts.
In a word: **scrambled**

...could be too insane even ...TV? EBN, the Emergency ...cast Network, that's ...EBN is three video heads ...earson, Gardner Post, ...n O'Donnell) who will ...u on the virtual reality ...our life! Their full-force ...o performance includes ...mpling ("found" TV ...rom broadcast, ...and cable feeds) and ...ideo, tapes that are

barrages of scrambled images set to blasting hip-hop beats. EBN comes straight at you from the telepodium, an entertainment enhancement device equipped with two giant pivoting color monitors, a smoke generator, and revolving gun turrets; three of the largest video screens in existence are the backdrop. EBN is muscular entertainment for a pumped-up country!

"Like watching CNN on acid heavily laced with speed." The Washington Post

"Blindingly fast cut edits, loops, fades, laps, F/X—similar to channel surfing at high tide, all tracked to a stuttering techno assault of beats and grunge guitar." Creem

La Compagnie Marie Chouinard

Reduced Shakespeare Company

7

▼ *Thumbnail sketch showing the conceptual direction for the Megadance '93 page. Most of the final layouts closely resemble the first* round of thumbnails that were presented to Panetta, as there was little time for anything other than a swift, intuitive approach.

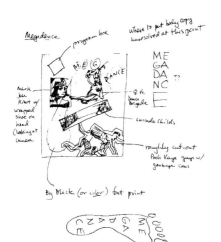

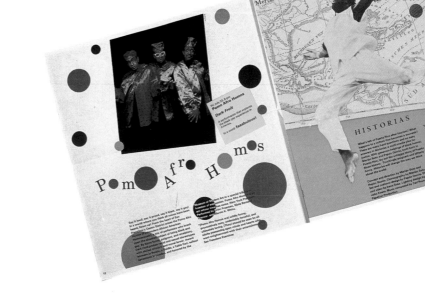

HISTORIAS

Pomo Afro Homos

by
Larry Keeley

Designers who know it tend to love D'Arcy Thompson's book Growth and Form, an extraordinary scientific treatise on how animal shapes change at varying stages in life. It is from this book that we learn that creatures tend to be round and lovable while young, and more angular as they age. There are exceptions, of course, but even these have a logic: baby alligators are not nurtured while young, and they are fierce looking from birth.

Lately it's been fun to ponder a parallel. Imagine being able to draw forms that capture the nature of the times we live in, and show how they might change with age. You would draw shapes that are simple for any year that ends 00 through about 12; the forms would get wilder at the end of each century, and truly weird by the end of each millennium. No one knows why this particular cycle reoccurs, but it is customary for societies to experience big, often disconcerting changes at the end of a century, with some attendant social upheaval.

So while societies go through a period of upheaval every hundred years, human lives average around eighty years. It is logical, then, that we do not get a lot of direct, personal advice from ancestors that pre-date us by five generations. In the absence of personal stories from our great, great, great grandparents to help us recognize the syndrome, we tend to assume that the times we inhabit are somehow unique, and could not possibly have been experienced before. Then too, perhaps the end of a millennium, not merely a century, may amplify the oddities.

So we suddenly see ourselves as wrestling with tectonic shifts, and just maybe this instinct is correct. But, in the main, we cannot truly see the patterns, and instead focus on superficial aspects of change. So a reckless attempt will be mounted here to identify some of the design challenges that matter most going forward. Such a grandiose ambition for a short essay is preposterous of course, so feel free to disagree or dismiss it entirely.

Argument 1: Few designers understand the sheer scale of modern business transformation. The corollary here is important too: few designers think it matters to them. But what separates design from fine art is its interdependence with commerce, so it's actually vital that designers both understand and care about these shifts.

Designers should be conversant with at least two sweeping themes: One is the shift to a networked economy. This term describes how once separate and distinct businesses have suddenly become interdependent with one another in ways that few truly understand. It's as if businesses are suddenly attached to one another with rubber bands: sometimes they cooperate, often they compete; occasionally it's planned, but more often it's accidental. But now the actions that one firm takes may ripple through other firms, often creating new businesses and industries along the way.

A second major shift has occurred in innovation velocity. Caused in part by the networked economy—using digital systems and telecommunications as an accelerant—we are experiencing a time where new ideas spawn others at a remarkable speed. What's more, these derivative innovations occur in ways that are unknown and unknowable, no matter how much data market-research firms might throw at issues and markets.

These two trends make switched-on designers highly valuable. Among other sources of value, helping business understand and cater to end-users is a key. This helps designers make innovations easy to understand, delightful to experience, and culturally connected. These advances, in any combination, help to make novel things important and hip—help-

Wicked, Weird,

De

ing people embrace artifacts and attach them to their everyday lives.

Argument 2: We need to understand what it means to live and work in revolutionary times. There are always conflicts at the core during unusual times. We are witnessing conflicts between large established companies and small start-ups; between corporations as shapers of society and other institutions like church, school or government; and between governments and the people they govern. New technologies come faster and faster, adding to the tension and fueling these revolutions.

For some people revolutions are exciting: researchers immersed in the Human Genome Project or people involved with say, Netscape, are having the time of their lives because every moment matters. Others find themselves thrown out of work, perhaps after decades of loyal service to a major company. Still others become extremists: producing cults, Una-bombers, neo-Nazis and arsonists.

Here again, there's a special place for design and designers. Designers are more comfortable with change than most people as they can help others see what the future might hold. A vital design skill is prototyping. When it is combined with a common value that designers cherish—to continually make the world a better place—this can help make

the future easier to understand and accept. Indeed, it can help the future show up somewhat ahead of its regularly scheduled arrival.

Argument 3: Designers can play a pivotal role in resolving the contradictions between business and societal needs. It's a sad fact that corporations today are the most vital force for societal change. Corporations have become the educators of the last resort, they play crucial roles in the support of communities and the arts, and they pay to manage the health of their workers and retirees. Virtually everywhere people are seeing that not only is government an ineffectual force for a time of revolutionary change, but churches and schools are even less effective.

Yet in a global, networked economy, few people can expect corporations to do everything needed for the success and well being of individuals. Corporations need perpetual innovation; society needs stability. Corporations need global competitiveness; societies need a common good. In the zeal to be efficient, agile, and flexible, corporations will not always support local communities and maintain loyalties to them. Meanwhile, individuals are taking on increased personal responsibility for managing everything from health, to finance and investment, to education, family care, and career planning.

These conflicts are huge and, candidly, often bigger than design's view of itself. Nonetheless, thoughtful designers can help corporations understand how valuable it is to motivate people, support their needs in balanced ways, and access what they need to know to make effective personal decisions. In this way designers can help corporations understand the value beyond money in creating healthy cultures inside an enterprise and healthy communities outside of them.

The French term, *fin de siècle*, captures the notion that the end of the century is typically a strange period. It departs from conventional morals or social traditions. Designers can step up to some very exciting challenges in ways and levels not seen since at least the industrial revolution. In partnership with corporations, and leveraging other specialties like strategy, anthropology and sociology, designers can help make the breakthroughs that change our world. But fasten your seat belt, it's going to be a wild ride.

Larry Keeley is President of Chicago-based Doblin Group, a leading design planning firm. He also teaches at IIT's Institute of Design. This essay appeared in a modified form in the Design Issues column of Communication Arts magazine.

sign in a Time of & Wild Change

Roger Whitehouse, trained as an Architect in the UK, founded Whitehouse & Company in New York with the particular mission of designing information equally responsive to function and aesthetics. In designing from the user's point of view and in pioneering the application of user based research, Whitehouse emphasizes the obligation of the design professional to the public. Whether in the form of identity programs, publications, exhibits, or environmental graphics and wayfinding systems, his work is characterized, on the one hand, by a clear and elegant directness of form, typography, and image, and on the other, by the identification of a common ground on which diversity of need, ability and culture can meet.

Whitehouse & Company
18 East 16th Street
New York, NY 10011
212/206-1080

Reprinted from *Design In Depth*. Printed in Hong Kong.

Infinity, BraiIleRail, and *TacTile* are trademarks of ASI Sign Systems, Inc.

▲ Working with a blind staff member of The Lighthouse, Roger Whitehouse conducts tests to determine ideal letterforms and spacing for tactile reading.

▼ These seemingly simple signs incorporate unique features that were developed as a result of user testing. The large color-coded shapes respond to the needs of individuals with reduced visual or tactual acuity, or cognitive impairments. The high contrast reversed-out lettering provides the highest level of legibility, particularly for users with clouded vision. The tactile ledge presents both Braille and custom-designed raised characters at the most comfortable angle for reading with the fingertips; it also houses the downward-pointing Infra-red LED "talking sign" transmitters.

The Lighthouse Inc.'s new headquarters building in New York City, acclaimed as a model of accessibility, was designed by Mitchell/ Giurgola Architects with whom Roger Whitehouse collaborated throughout the design process.

Designer and Client:
Whitehouse & Company for
The Lighthouse

Redefining Accessibility

23 Accounts

BrailleRail is a concept developed by Whitehouse to provide a continuous trailing rail which presents information in an easily located manner. It features low visual acuity color-coded arrows, and audible, visible and tactile directional and room identification. Only partially employed at the Lighthouse, it is currently being developed as a stand-alone system.

Elevator

When The Lighthouse – the world's leading organization providing services for those with low-vision or blindness – joined forces with Roger Whitehouse to develop a wayfinding system for their new headquarters building in New York City, their collaboration became the cornerstone of an even more far-reaching endeavor. Roger Whitehouse seized the opportunity to undertake in-depth user research as the basis for developing a

solution that could serve as a benchmark of universal design and for creating a system responsive to the widest possible spectrum of user needs: not only of those with impaired vision, but of individuals with hearing, cognitive, and mobility disorders as well. After a wide-ranging series of tests into the visual and tactual legibility of different typeforms and mapping systems, Whitehouse proposed a comprehensive system incorporating

high-contrast visual signs, a tactile ledge, combined tactile and visual maps, and infra-red "talking signs." So successful is the program, now installed throughout The Lighthouse's headquarters, that the principles Whitehouse established are serving as the foundation for revised standards for both the American National Standards Institute and the Americans with Disabilities Act.

As a result of work at The ▶ Lighthouse, Roger Whitehouse is currently developing a series of audio-visual landmarks which, as well as having a strong visual identity, create soothing, non-intrusive sounds and act as universal wayfinding devices. The designs include a series of balls rolling down a cone-shaped spiral, an airborn sphere, a pendulum clock, and a perpetual waterfall.

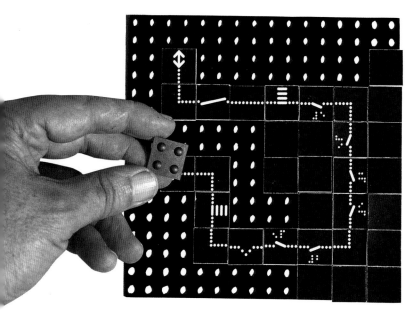

◄ Developed as a tool for creating modular tactile route-and-event diagrams, TacTiles are based on Roger Whitehouse's patented Infinity sign system and feature modular magnetic tiles depicting standard building features.

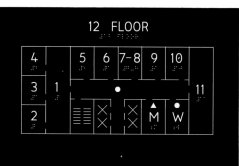

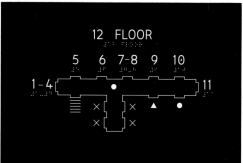

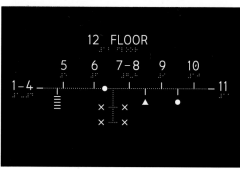

▲ To create tactile maps for The Lighthouse, three concepts were tested: a "full spatial" map showing the outline of all architectural features; a "partial spatial" map showing only the out-line of the corridors, with doors and other destinations leading from it; and a "route and event" diagram showing preferred paths of travel with destinations and events located along it.

ABCDEF123
ABCDEF123

◀ Six iterations of the tactile maps were used to develop the final design. Continuous user feedback enabled Whitehouse to establish the most effective formats and details.

▲ Discovering through research that conventional typefaces were difficult to read by touch, Whitehouse developed a series of custom tactile letterforms. The upper example is based on the premise of tracing the character as a single path.

The lower example, Haptic Light, which was finally used, focuses on the overall form and employs a distinct cross-section, large open counter-spaces, and the exaggeration of unique individual letterform characteristics.

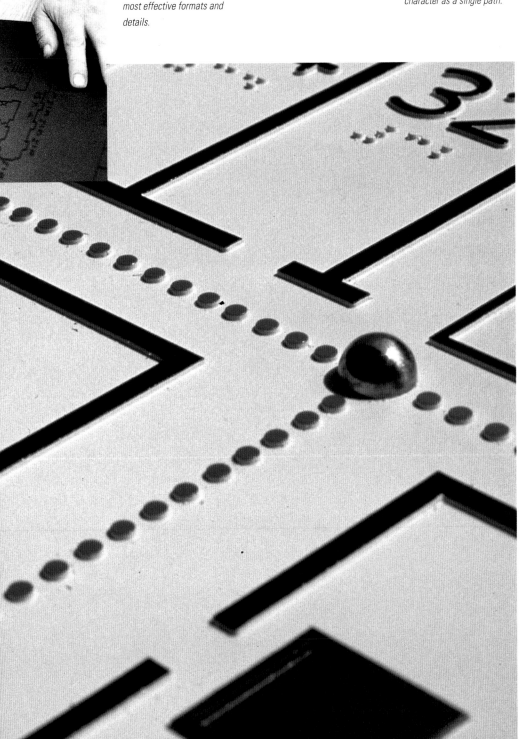

▲ Mounted in a consistent place on each floor of The Lighthouse, the tactile maps are positioned at an angle so they can be easily read. Their location at the reception desk allowed them to be used either independently or as a communications tool for the staff.

◀ Because of the blind user's inability to "scan" a map as a sighted user does, Whitehouse developed a super-tactile "you are here" locator that can be quickly identified with a sweep of the hand. Tactile/visual symbols coordinated with those on the wall signs enable quick location of key features and destinations.

▼ *Issue Five,* Rogers vs. Koons, *focused on a significant copyright infringement case between an artist and a photographer, written by James Traub. Designer Chip Kidd addressed the mirror-image by creating a book which reads two-ways.*

❝It was a collaborative effort from the start. We put together a team with a designer, a literary thinker and a project facilitator. The traditional role for the 'client' was shouldered by all three of us, making for very interesting/ creative reviews.❞

Tony McDowell,
Champion
International Corporation

The Subjective Reasoning *series sets out to tackle what few publications dare to; the issues and ideas that accompany shifts in our ever-changing world. The authors and designers of the series break free from traditional barriers and confront topics from a personal perspective. Although the design is instrumental to the message, the series relies on editorial content because, as the* Subjective Reasoning *thesis states, "today, and in the future, authored perspective must not be ignored."*

Champion International Corporation
One Champion Plaza
Stamford, CT 06921
800/348-1770

Left to right: Paula Scher of Pentagram, William Drenttel of Drenttel Doyle Partners and Tony McDowell of Champion International Corporation.

Reprinted from
Design In Depth.
Printed in Hong Kong.

▲ *Issue Three,* The View From the Mirror, *presents photographer Duane Michals' exploration of the intangible aspects of life and old age.*

Subjective Reasoning on Champion Kromekote®

Designers and Client:
William Drenttel of
Drenttel Doyle Partners and
Paula Scher of Pentagram
for Champion International
Corporation.

What's the first thing you think about when you hear the words *paper promotion*? How about outrageous design? Or tired swatch-books? Since its debut, one paper promotion has broken the mold and earned the praise of both designers and editors worldwide. Why? Because it focuses on provocative content, not excessive design.

When Paula Scher, of Pentagram; Bill Drenttel, of Drenttel Doyle Partners; and Champion teamed up to create a meaningful demonstration of Kromekote paper, they chose subjects outside the professional interests of graphic designers, like human rights, ethics, sports and culture. And by all accounts, they've hit on a good formula. Suffice it to say that several of the publications in the series resulted in major articles, acting as further publicity for Champion and either condemning or extolling the message of that particular issue. At least one of the publications in the series was tossed in the trash by indignant designers. Such high emotion was just the kind of exposure they were looking for.

The books stray from the traditional recipe of a promotion by combining excellent design and serious writing in the presentation of contemporary subjects. For instance, the first issue was a hand-lettered reprint of a speech on the end of communism given by Vaclav Havel, the former president of the Czech Republic. And the latest issue, the tenth in the series, titled *Moneyball*, is an uncompromising look at the disturbing relationship between money and sport. When it comes to proving the performance of Kromekote, a product familiar to most designers, nothing works better than showing it in action. So, despite a flood of mailings from paper companies to designers, *Subjective Reasoning*, love it or hate it, has become a must read.

▼ *Designer Steven Doyle, of Drenttel Doyle Partners, chose* The End, *to start the series.*

◄ *Issue Eight,* Muddy Waters on Nantucket and Other Tales, *is a compilation of 14 stories by Peter Watrous on an immense 12" x 72" fold-out book designed by Alex Isley.*

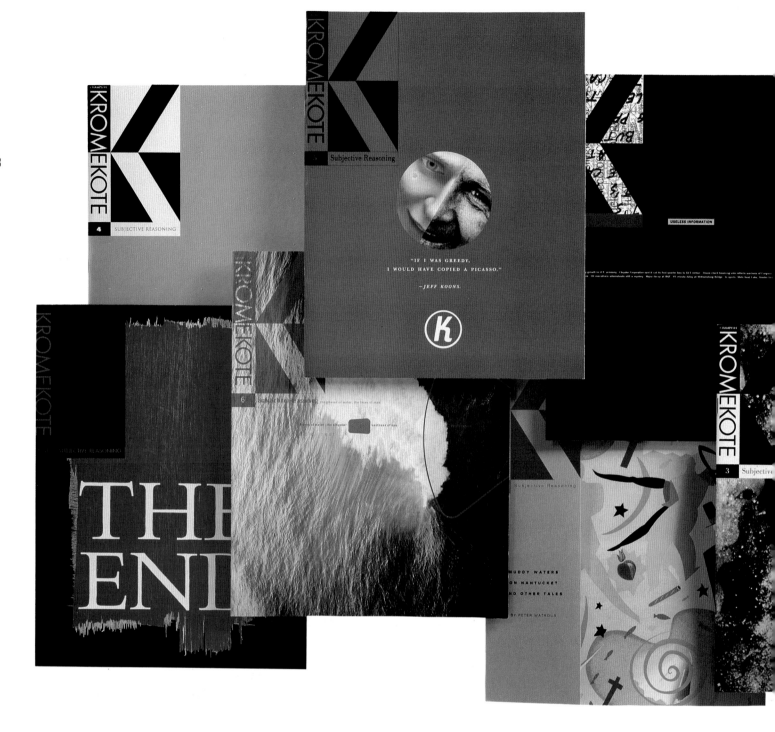

◀ Masterminded by Hard Werken, Issue Six, *Equilibrium Vessel*, presents a neoteric combination of design and copy to explore— at one level— the disparity of humanity and humane-ness.

The Subjective Reasoning *series has been recognized for its innovative design and content by organizations around the world.* Adweek, Magazine Week, Eye, Graphic Design: USA, *the* Village Voice Literary Supplement, *and* Portfolio, *a Japanese design magazine, have all featured the promotion.* Subjective Reasoning *was the sole paper promotion to win an award— and one of only 17 winners in the graphics category— in* IDs *1993 Annual Design Review.*

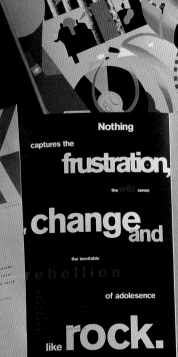

"A sharp, clean blast in a roomful of frippery."
Michael Manwaring, Beaux Arts Ball Judge

◀ The inspiration for the centerpiece was the Man Ray photograph "Compass" (1920), which depicts a gun attached to a large magnet. As Fox explains, "I was struck by this juxtaposition because it is both logical and illogical. I wanted to create a similar tension with the vise and flowers." [The Metropolitan Museum of Art, Ford Motor Company Collection, Gift of the Ford Motor Company and John C. Waddell, 1987. (1987.1100.40)]

Mark Fox, who founded BlackDog in 1986, takes a bold and often wry approach to corporate identity. "I want to engage people with my work, and letting design create a narrative—tell a story—is one of the best ways to accomplish this. I find it difficult to engage anyone with abstraction." Stylistically, Fox's work is deceptively simple: he favors a limited color scheme, reductive geometric forms, and the use of typography as illustration. "I prefer working with two or three colors; there is an inherent graphic power in limiting your palette. Likewise, I prefer simple, massive forms to delicate or intricate designs. Haight/Ashbury and Cranbrook are probably the antithesis of my aesthetic." Silk screen and fabrication for the project by Jeff Wasserman, Kevin Giffen and Kevin Murphy of Wasserman Silk Screen Co., Santa Monica.

BlackDog
Mark Fox, Principal
239 Marin Street, San Rafael, CA 94901
415/258-9663

Mark Fox, BlackDog

Reprinted from
Design In Depth.
Printed in Hong Kong.

Beaux Arts Ball

Designer and Client:
Mark Fox, BlackDog
for San Francisco Museum of
Modern Art

▶ *The hand-painted tablecloth reads "We declare art and its priests illegal."*
Quote: Konstantin Medunetskii, Vladimir Stenberg, Georgii Stenberg, 1922.
▼ *An early rough sketch for the centerpiece. "It took me weeks to figure out what to put in the vise," says Fox. "I tried an old window, a No Trespassing sign, roses—even job folders."*

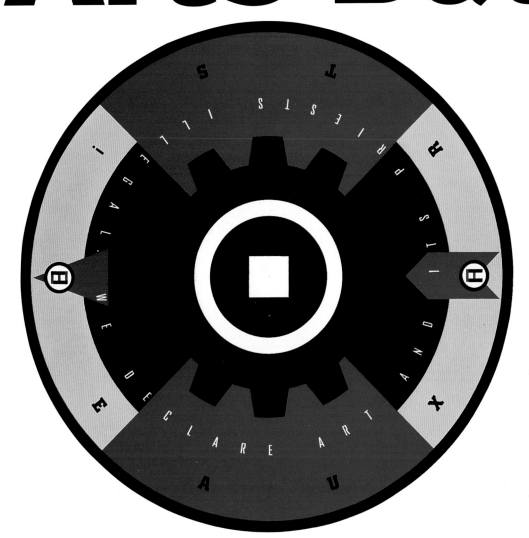

When Kit Hinrichs of Pentagram asked BlackDog to create a table setting for a San Francisco Museum of Modern Art Fundraiser, Mark Fox turned to some of his favorite 20th century artists for inspiration. "At first I was interested in creating a monument to some of my heroes, like Rodchenko and Stepanova, Karl Schulpig and Lucian Bernhard. One sketch for the mask, in fact, depicted Rodchenko's shaved head with a halo—Saint Rodchenko!" The focus shifted, however, when Fox decided to excerpt Constructivist writings and manifestos. "I wanted to highlight the ideas of this movement rather than the personalities. And these ideas are so dogmatic, so unwavering in their contempt of art, that I thought it would be amusing to voice them in the context of a museum fundraiser." Fox's one-man design studio competed against 39 other design and architectural firms. His table design won first prize.

62

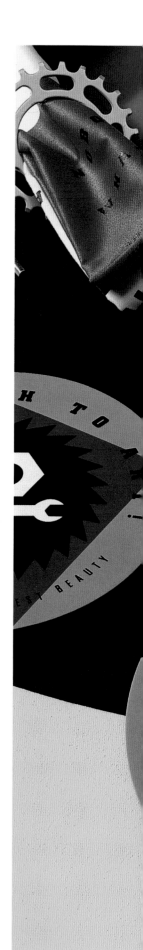

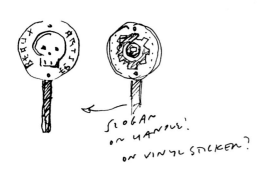

SLOGAN
ON HANDLE!

ON VINYL STICKER?

DEATH TO ART!

EFFICACIOUS EXISTENCE IS THE HIGHEST BEAUTY

◄ Ten masks were created, one for each table guest. "These masks amuse me because they lack eye holes. They mask both the guest and the event," said Fox. The B.A.B. monogram shown on the handle was also developed for the event. Quote: Aleksei Gan, 1922; Naum Gabo and Noton Pevsner, 1920.

▼ The table setting uses bicycle sprockets as napkin rings and replaces the utensils with a file, wrench, and drill bit. The service plate reads "In the final analysis, art is falsehood, an opiate, and unnecessary.

Work for life, and not for palaces, churches, grave-yards, and museums." Quote: Karl loganson, 1922; Aleksandr Rodchenko, 1921. [Photography: Kirk Amyx]

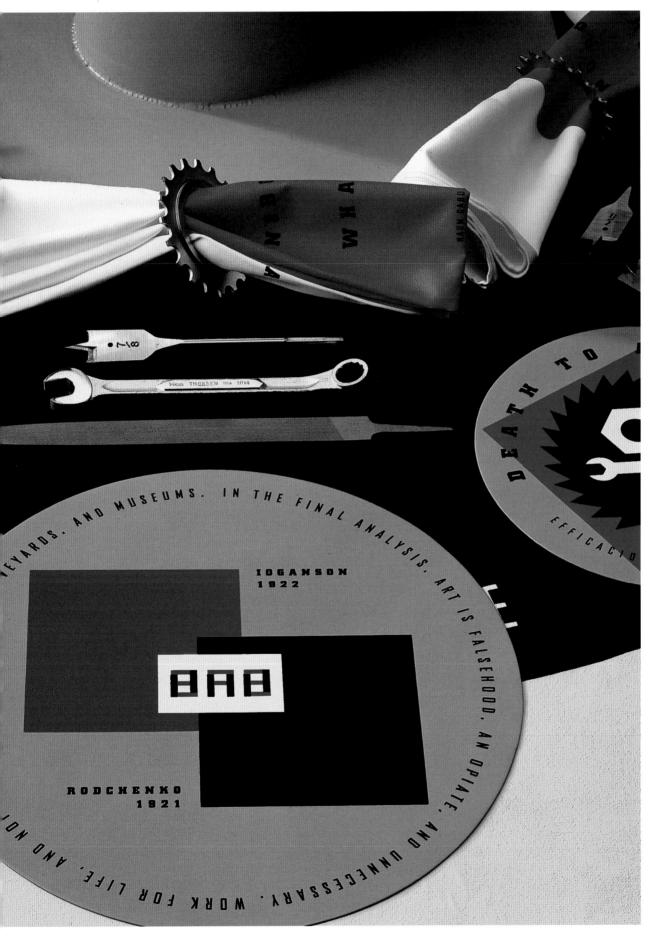

▲ The napkin, also pictured in the table setting, proclaims "Nobody can tell us what the future is and what utensils does one eat it with." Quote: Naum Gabo, Noton Pevsner, 1920.

> **"The design team not only created one of the most visually interesting calendars we've ever done, but also managed the logistical nightmare of coordinating the many functions needed to produce it on time."**
>
> Hank Sandbach, Nabisco

Reprinted from
Design In Depth.
Printed in Hong Kong.

From left to right: John Manfredi, Nabisco Senior Vice President, External and Governmental Affairs; Dave Stivers, Nabisco Senior Manager Administration/ Archivist; Janice Fudyma, Iris A. Brown, Bernhardt Fudyma Design Group; Craig Bernhardt; Hank Sandbach, Nabisco Vice President, Public Relations.

Other designers for the project were Iris Brown and Jane Sobczak. Picture research, Natalie Goldstein; historical research, Joe White; copywriting, Stan Hironaka; cover typography, Gerard Huerta; printing, L.B. Thebault; Nabisco Archivist, Dave Stivers.

Bernhardt Fudyma Design Group, Inc.
Janice Fudyma and Craig Bernhardt, Principals
133 East 36th Street
New York, NY 10016
212/889-9337

Designer and Client:
Bernhardt Fudyma Design
Group for the Nabisco
Foods Group

Nabisco Bicentennial Calendar

◄ *The calendar works as a timeline tracing Nabisco's history through world events. Nabisco was founded in 1792, the same year the Republican Party was formed and the New York Stock Exchange opened.*

Few American companies can attest to a continuing corporate heritage that spans two centuries. One such company is Nabisco Foods. 1992 marked the bicentennial anniversary of the founding of the bakery that eventually became the company we now know as Nabisco. Since its founding hearkens back to 1792, Nabisco has a rich and nostalgic relationship with American culture, and is the source of memorable associations for most Americans—Oreo cookies, Life Savers, Animal Crackers and Fig Newtons.

To commemorate the event, Nabisco selected Bernhardt Fudyma to design an important promotional item—a calendar to be distributed to 100,000 employees, suppliers and key commercial buyers.

Although they developed several concepts, Bernhardt Fudyma recommended a dynamic timeline approach that would parallel important Nabisco manufacturing achievements, product introductions and company milestones with corresponding world events. Each calendar month presents the reader with a graphic time capsule created by the design firm, and brought to life by the collaborative efforts of the Nabisco archivist and in-house photographers, historical and image researchers and the copywriter.

Nabisco Bicentennial Calendar

The result: an award-winning chronicle of one of America's best known companies—that was celebrated all year long.

66

▲ *This order form was also designed to be used by salesmen when requesting calendars for distribution to their customers.*

Producing the calendar was a logistical as well as a design effort, involving the Nabisco archivist, a historical researcher, a photo researcher, a copywriter, Nabisco's in-house photog rapher, a type designer and the Bernhardt Fudyma design team working simultaneously, on a tight schedule, to create the parallel histories in words and images.

APRIL

SUNDAY	MONDAY	TUESDAY	WEDNESDAY	THURSDAY	FRIDAY
			1	2	3
5	6	7	8	9	10
12 Palm Sunday	13	14	15	16	17 Good Friday Passover
19 Easter Sunday	20	21	22	23	24
26	27	28	29	30	

MARCH

The world readied for the turn of the century. Zeppelins took to the skies. And a new company, The National Biscuit Company, emerged to set a standard of excellence.

1892
Americans welcomed new NABISCO Shredded Wheat, as Americans-to-be surged through the country's new front door, Ellis Island.

1893
Faced with tough market conditions and the start of a four-year depression, farmers throughout the Wheat Belt were warmed by a legendary Nabisco product, CREAM OF WHEAT. So were rural delivery men riding the range.

1897
Canadians turned to AYLMER for fine canned fruits and vegetables and a new baking aid, MAGIC Baking Powder. Americans met The Katzenjammer Kids.

1898
The founding of the National Biscuit Company ushered in a new era in reliable, branded consumer goods. The yellow-slickered child reminded consumers of UNEEDA's moisture-proof package. Count Ferdinand von Zeppelin built his first airship.

The world was heading toward war. And the world's fastest luxury liner, thought to be unsinkable, headed into the Atlantic on a fateful voyage. And in the U.S., a flow of new products, major new facilities and new technologies were adding to the foundation of the National Biscuit Company. Among the decade's introductions were products that still satisfy American — and world — appetites today.

1912
Who would have known that the new OREO would be far more than just another cookie... or that the Titanic would never finish its Atlantic crossing. There were two other new Nabisco brands that year that would become household names: LIFE SAVERS and LORNA DOONE.

1913
A chocolate-covered marshmallow and cake combination, called MALLOMARS, became an instant national favorite. And in ballrooms around the country, Americans began dancing the newest craze, the "fox trot."

1914
From fox trot to fox holes war began in Europe. On the home front, progress continued in the U.S. as National Biscuit Company converted to gasoline trucks in Chicago, where new bakeries opened.

JULY

SUNDAY	MONDAY	TUESDAY	WEDNESDAY	THURSDAY	FRIDAY	SATURDAY
	JUNE	AUGUST	1 Canada Day (Canada)	2	3	4 Independence Day
5	6	7	8	9	10	11
12	13	14	15	16	17	18

NOVEMBER

WEDNESDAY	THURSDAY	FRIDAY
	1	2
7	8	9
14	15	16
21	22	23
28	29	30

NABISCO FOODS GROUP
200 Years of Excellence

66 When you deal with surfaces and spaces as in a remodel, we always believe that the graphics are integral to the design. In fact they become one of the most important means by which the design is lifted to its objective. We are pleased with the success of the graphics and feel that they are a critical part of the success of the space. **99**

Len Adams, Director,
The Yarmouth Group

From left to right:
Debra Nichols, President
William Comstock, Vice President
Debra Nichols Design
Photos: Phil Toy and Wes Thompson

For the renovation of a 1.5 million square foot development of two towers, food court, retail space and concourse in San Francisco, the owners assembled a team of professionals who were compatible and shared a dedication to bringing about their objectives. Debra Nichols, leading the firm, has over two decades of experience at seeking solutions alongside an architectural team— in this case Cesar Pelli and Associates— to create signage that integrates architecture and graphics and brings artistic imagination into the realm of business and commerce.

Debra Nichols Design
486 Jackson Street
San Francisco, CA 94111
415/788-0766

The entrance to the ▶ parking garage is marked with a 12 foot vertical sign composed of stacking bars and perforated metal panels. Three dimensional letters are traced in white neon.

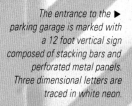

▲ Retail signage was developed for the Service Court to echo architectural "street trees" in the con-course. Logos for most of the tenants were designed by Debra Nichols Design.

Designer and Client:
Debra Nichols Design
for IBM; The Yarmouth
Group; CB Commercial
Real Estate Group; Equity
Office Properties, Inc.

One Market

▲ The main building entrance identification signs are 7-foot square glass panels floating in front of perforated metal panels which cantilever over the sidewalk above each door. The logotype is a combination of carved glass and three dimensional gold leaf letters.

Debra Nichols Design ▶ developed an architectural model based on their lattice pavilion logo which was delivered as a gift along with the announcement/party invitation.

▲ The logo was implemented on a series of gifts which were provided to tenants ranging from umbrellas to champagne glasses.

The goal for Debra Nichols Design at One Market was to raise the potential of this 70's era property. For this major architectural renovation the strategy was to design signage which was an integral part of the architecture in order to extend the spirit of the setting— a form of communication through art born of functional necessity.

The client inspired a sense of team work, where each discipline was called upon to contribute their full potential. The architects—Cesar Pelli and the design team led by Turan Duda—orchestrated the efforts of the various design disciplines, but by no means defined their scope or restricted their efforts. In fact, in many areas of the project the architects turned to Debra Nichols Design to take the lead, such as the Food Court storefront identity system, building entrance identities and retail canopies. The individual "bursts of energy" from the various members of the design team enrich and enliven the character of the project, infusing it with a very human spirit.

Throughout the design phase, members of the design team met every week and worked together, constantly tackling the major issues and refining the details. These work sessions were well managed by the owners and maintained the momentum and high energy level. One Market was an unusual and invigorating immersion for firms accustomed to balancing several projects at once.

One Market

▲ *Monthly newsletters updated One Market tenants on the renovation with news about the design process and design team.*

Three canopies cantilevering ▶ over the sidewalk mark the entrance to Bayside Cuisines, each with a different abstract food sculpture composition. The 40 foot high vertical signs become landmarks visible from San Francisco Bay and the Embarcadero.

The Bayside Cuisines logo ▶ and food sculpture is carried by a metal bar structure at the main interior entrance.

▼ *The logo for Bayside Cuisines continues the theme of light transparent images over solid ones and the colors reflect San Francisco Bay. Debra Nichols Design created promotional pieces to announce the opening of the food court to the office building teants.*

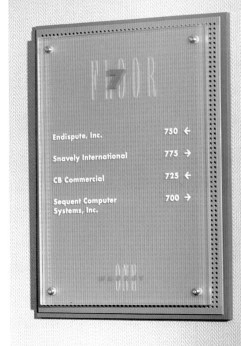

◀ *Typical tower lobby directory, tenant door signs and code signs continue the theme of layering transparent materials.*

▼ *The stationery system designed for the project supports the new identity.*

▲ *The signature logotype identity of each tower is implemented in the portal entrances off the central concourse in carved marble and gold leaf letters.*

Elevator bank ▶ identification flanks each elevator lobby and reiterates the spirit of the logotype: solid sans-serif gold leaf numbers overlay the elegant vertical serif type, classically carved in marble.

"So, tell me about this virtual Telemetrix Company."
Unidentified, Stock Broker

John Bielenberg is a friend to his fellow designers. And it is as a colleague, not an adversary, that he has designed this campaign to talk to professionals about their responsibilities. Bielenberg Design, a firm of six, was founded in 1990. Other collaborators on the Virtual Telemetrix Annual Report were Erik Adigard, Dana Arnett, Michael Cronan, Jilly Simons, Rick Valicenti and John Watson.

Bielenberg Design
421 Tehama Street
San Francisco, CA 94103
415/495-3371

2004 8th Street
Boulder, CO 80302
303/473-0757

Reprinted from
Design In Depth.
Printed in Hong Kong.

The second component of ▶ the campaign confronts the issues of waste and lack of content. The hard bound book, shown against one of its pages, exists only to announce that it has been produced on recycled paper. A book marker is even provided as a final statement.

This book is printed on recycled paper! This book is printed on recycled paper! This book is printed on recycled paper! This book is printed on recycled paper! This book is printed on recycled paper! This book is printed on recycled paper! This book is printed on recycled paper! This book is printed on recycled paper!

This book is printed on recycled paper! This book is printed on recycled paper! This book is printed on recycled paper! This book is printed on recycled paper! This book is printed on recycled paper! This book is printed on recycled paper! This book is printed on recycled paper! This book is printed on recycled paper! This book is printed on recycled paper! This book is printed on recycled paper! This book is printed on recycled paper! This book is printed on recycled paper! This book is printed on recycled paper! This book is printed on recycled paper! This book is printed on recycled paper! This book is printed on recycled paper! This book is printed on recycled paper!

This book is printed on recycled paper! This book is printed on recycled paper! This book is printed on recycled paper! This book is printed on recycled paper! This book is printed on recycled paper!

This book is printed on recycled paper! This book is printed on recycled paper! This book is printed on recycled paper! This book is printed on recycled paper! This book is printed on recycled paper! This book is printed on recycled paper! This book is printed on recycled paper! This book is printed on recycled paper! This book is printed on recycled paper! This book is printed on recycled paper! This book is printed on recycled paper! This book is printed on recycled paper! This book is printed on recycled paper! This book is printed on recycled paper! This book is printed on recycled paper! This book is printed on recycled paper! This book is printed on recycled paper! This book is printed on recycled paper!

This book is printed on recycled paper! This book is printed on recycled paper! This book is printed on recycled paper! This book is printed on recycled paper! This book is printed on recycled paper! This book is printed on recycled paper! This book is printed on recycled paper! This book is printed on recycled paper! This book is printed on recycled paper! This book is printed on recycled paper! This book is printed on recycled paper! This book is printed on recycled paper!

This book is printed on recycled paper! This book is printed on recycled paper! This book is printed on recycled paper! This book is printed on recycled paper! This book is printed on recycled paper! This book is printed on recycled paper! This book is printed on recycled paper!

This book is printed on recycled paper! This book is printed on recycled paper! This book is printed on recycled paper! This book is printed on recycled paper! This book is printed on recycled paper! This book is printed on recycled paper! This book is printed on recycled paper! This book is printed on recycled paper! This book is printed on recycled paper! This book is printed on recycled paper!

Designer and Client:
John Bielenberg, Bielenberg
Design for John Bielenberg,
Bielenberg Design

The Practice of Graphic Design Campaign

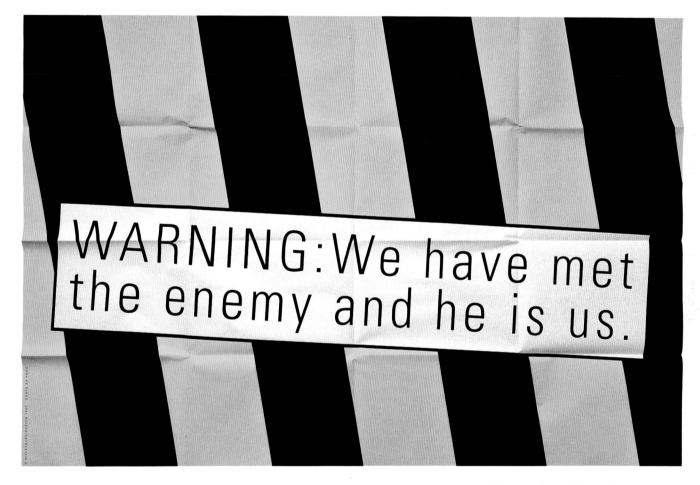

WARNING: We have met the enemy and he is us.

▲ *The poster was the first part of the campaign mailed to designers and design publications. The yellow bars and warning label were borrowed from vernacular icons to grab attention. The large scale also played an important role in the success of the poster.*

The creation of a huge four by six foot poster was the first political statement of many to come from John Bielenberg on the subject of indulgent design. Bielenberg has created a campaign to send to his fellow designers to warn them that they are responsible. Responsible for what? For authorizing and encouraging waste, for contributing to deceitful promotion. In his words, "Why does everything that's real have to be made into something fancier and bigger?" The answer may well be, "Because we can." Bielenberg would like designers to reconsider their priorities, avoid over-indulgences, and accept the fact that clients will follow our lead to design not decorate; communicate not confuse the message.

▼ *The third element of the campaign addresses the form and content of the annual report, poking fun at both the designer and corporate America. Bielenberg says that it will not be the last piece of* *the campaign, considering the production of a video as a fourth component.*
The spread below is the "consolidated balance sheet" which lacks the traditional list of dizzying numbers.

CONSOLIDATED BALANCE SHEET

VIRTUAL
TELE
METRIX
1993
ANNUAL
REPORT

FINANCIAL INFORMATION NOT INTERESTING AT TIME OF PUBLICATION.

◄ The "report of independent auditors" spread states, "Financial information not interesting at time of publication."

▲ The top spread indicates that the design process results in a migraine and a therapist, while the lower one makes fun of the traditional presidential shot. The blowup of the woman's heel comes from beneath the president's desk.

"We have offices around the world. This disciplined and practical system has given us a consistant image that reflects our professional attitude: careful, considered and straightforward."

Mary Anne Costello
Louis Dreyfus

It was important for Louis Dreyfus to develop a foundation for presenting word and image that clearly communicates in an informative and provocative way. The identity and communications program is an on-going commitment by Louis Dreyfus to address functional and aesthetic objectives. Consolidation of information, effective use of technology and centralized production translate into significant efficiencies.

Wood Design
135 West 16th Street
New York, NY 10011
212/989-5295

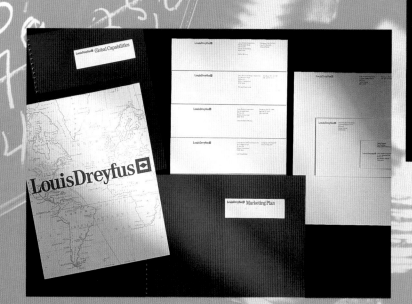

Binders for Louis Dreyfus Energy, shown in the background, are an extension of the presentation system and provide an alternate format for employee manuals, pocket-folders and proposals.

Designer and Client:
Wood Design for the
Louis Dreyfus Group

Simplifying a Complex Identity

▼ *Presentations and brochures range from case bound books to computer generated documents, depending on the client's needs and budget.*

▶ *The leasing brochures capture the essence of each property through the use of abstract photography of materials, textures or light.*

With services and products ranging from real estate to natural gas, Louis Dreyfus needed an appropriate image reflecting the culture and dignified 140-year history of its global network of companies. The identity system had to simplify and unify materials that represented Louis Dreyfus and Louis Dreyfus Energy and their diverse businesses. At the same time, it had to accommodate and define the hierarchy and the particular requirements of the markets in which the companies operate.

One disciplined and flexible system was created for the voice and vision to be clearly expressed. Each of the identities has been established with the creation of a unique signature. Louis Dreyfus uses an original typeface created by Wood Design that combines the elegance of Bodoni, the warmth and readability of Century and the strength of Fenice. The symbols were developed from the original Louis Dreyfus nautical flag. The Louis Dreyfus logotype emphasizes the company name and strength of the family heritage. The Louis Dreyfus Energy signature reflects its own progressive and industrial personality.

LouisDreyfus ◨

LouisDreyfusEnergy
◇

▲ *The Louis Dreyfus Energy
signature distinguishes the
company as a separate entity
with its own personality
while sharing an identity and
literature system. The symbol
for energy retains the diamond,
or the "seed," signifying the
creation of a new corporation.*

▲ *The literature system
allows for typographic and
layout experimentation.
The brochures maintain the
continuity and integrity of* *the system through format,
typography, photography,
color palette and unusual
use of materials.*

SALES COLLAR

This is a reciprocal option with no cost to either party giving both of them an obligation and an option at the outer range of two prices. If market prices rise to the high price strike, the Buyer declares that Louis Dreyfus Energy will deliver natural gas at that price. If prices fall to the low price, Louis Dreyfus Energy declares it will sell at that low price. The high and low price are sometimes referred to as, cap and floor. If prices fall between the high and low price so that neither party exercises its options, two things may happen. The Buyer and Louis Dreyfus Energy may negotiate their contract with a spot gas delivery, if a supply contract is important, or the contract may be negotiated so there is no physical delivery. This is an attractive risk management tool because the Buyer is protected against rising prices and can acquire gas at low prices. There is no premium cost for this price protection as there is in a cap. A sales collar is also available for a long-term contract.

FINANCIAL SWAP

This financial transaction allows two parties to fix price without physical delivery. They can maintain spot market or index contracts with current customers and still manage price risk by fixing the price with each other. Because this is a financial hedge, the end user can purchase fuel which is most economical at the time of procuring the supply. The two parties agree to a fixed price, location, natural gas publication delivery point, quantity and period. There is a monthly settlement price, which is the difference between the fixed price of the contract and the index price in the publication for that month's date. If the index price for the delivery period is higher than the fixed price of the swap contract, then Louis Dreyfus Energy pays the Buyer the difference. This helps finance the Buyer's purchase of fuel in the physical market. If the index price for the delivery period falls below the fixed price of the swap contract, the Buyer will pay Louis Dreyfus Energy the difference. While paying, the Buyer is also purchasing fuel at lower prices. The net effect of the financial swap is that the Buyer locks in a fixed price to hedge the cost of his fuel supply. If market prices rise or fall, he has still locked in the price of the financial swap.

MULTI-BTU

This is a supply contract for Buyers who have dual or multiple fuel capabilities. The parties negotiate a price per MMBtu for the specific volume, the delivery period and the fuels and specifications applicable under the contract. They agree to a notification period so the Buyer's plant can arrange to accept an alternate fuel. The number of fuel switches allowed during the delivery term is also specified. The price of the multi-Btu contract is less expensive than a standard natural gas supply contract. Each contract is individually designed depending on plant locations and fuel requirements. Prices vary subject to availability of local storage and fuel specifications.

Louis Dreyfus Energy, as part of the Louis Dreyfus Group, benefits from over 140 years of experience merchandising diverse commodities in all international markets. That experience added to the operation of physical assets in the production, refining and distribution of energy products makes us unique as an energy supplier. Louis Dreyfus Energy is a production company with expertise in risk management, combining marketing experience with innovative hedging strategies.

TRANSPORTATION CONTRACTS ON ALL MAJOR PIPELINES link SUPPLIES FROM PRODUCING AREAS TO MARKETS NATIONWIDE.

Louis Dreyfus Energy is a creative energy supplier able to adapt a variety of risk management products to meet customers' specific needs.

marketing and distribution

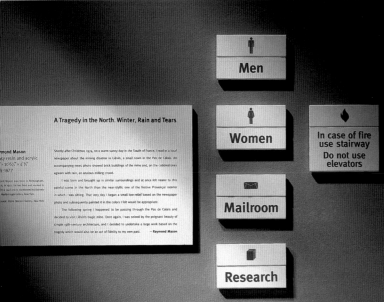

A Tragedy in the North. Winter, Rain and Tears

Raymond Mason
...xy resin and acrylic
...× 10 6⅜" × 4 ¾"
...6-1977

Shortly after Christmas 1974, on a warm sunny day in the South of France, I read in a local newspaper about the mining disaster in Liévin, a small town in the Pas de Calais. An accompanying news photo showed brick buildings of the mine and, on the cobblestones again with rain, an anxious milling crowd.

I was born and brought up in similar surroundings and at once felt nearer to this painful scene in the North than the near-idyllic one of the festive Provençal interior in which I was sitting. That very day I began a small low-relief based on the newspaper photo and subsequently painted it in the colors I felt would be appropriate.

The following spring I happened to be passing through the Pas de Calais and decided to visit Liévin's tragic mine. Once again, I was seized by the poignant beauty of simple 19th-century architecture, and I decided to undertake a large work based on the tragedy which would also be an act of fidelity to my own past.   — Raymond Mason

---

◀ Part of an extensive interior and exterior signage program for Louis Dreyfus, these modular signs are practical, easy to read and can be used in any of the company's offices.

▼ Pictograms used for internal publications were designed to provide a bit of humor within the communications program.

Men
Women
Mailroom
Research
In case of fire use stairway Do not use elevators

"We needed a unifying graphic representation that instantly communicated a new design concept to the industry: a visual vocabulary of multicolored coordinated patterns, interpretations of materials of nature, from sand-like particles to gradually increasing earthy configurations.**"**

Allessandro De Gregori,
Formica Corporation

From left to right:
Lisa Ballard, Allessandro
De Gregori, Lori Siebert.
Photo: Brad Smith.

Lori Siebert and Lisa Ballard met with a team at Formica whose task it was to launch a new product line, Formations. The input from the product's designer, Allessandro De Gregori, helped Siebert Design to communicate his vision for the product graphically.

Siebert Design Associates
1600 Sycamore
Cincinnati, OH 45210
513/241-4550

FORMATIONS

▲ *Siebert Design assisted in brainstorming names for the product line. The name was intended to tie into the archeological theme. The type used for the selected name, "Formations," was inspired by letterforms found on an Egyptian mummy case.*

◄ *The Formations laminate itself became the background for the cover of the second promo, adorned with swatches sent by the participating architects.*

Reprinted from
Design In Depth.
Printed in Hong Kong.

Designer and Client:
Lori Siebert, Lisa Ballard,
Siebert Design Associates
for Allessandro De Gregori,
Formica Corporation

Formica Formations

▲ The initial mailing was a
folder that expanded into
a poster featuring a spiral
chart showing how the
product colors and textures
were interrelated.

Formica had created an innovative line of brand laminates and wanted a direct mail piece which explained and positioned the high-end product line.

Formations, which featured laminates reminiscent of natural materials buffered by time, was targeted to architects and interior designers. The promotion needed to inspire these professionals to consider specifying Formations for residential and commercial projects.

Siebert Design chose a geological spiral as the central image for the entire project. The spiral was a logical organization for the chart showing the colors and textural choices.

For the second Formations promotion, Siebert sent crates to four top architectural/interior design firms, to fill with materials that created a design scheme around Formations. Lori Siebert says, "When they sent back the crates, we got everything from a plastic lobster to exquisite silks." Siebert Design used these elements to compose photographs around the Formations products. The end result was a successful launch that communicated the product's versatility and theme.

Formica Formations

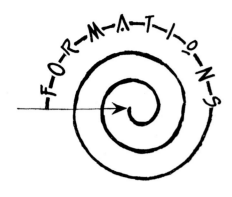

◀ The spiral became a
unifying element to all
Formations promotions.
The spiral chart was used
as a key wall graphic in the
Formica trade show exhibit.

Each texture level was ▶
represented by an individual
insert. The die cut edges and
primitive, rusted photo props
reinforced the product and its
resemblance to materials
buffered by time.

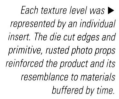

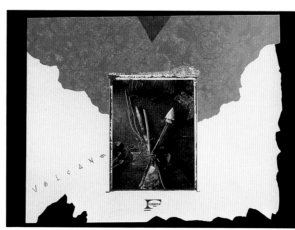

ANDRE PUTMAN

◀ A series of initial concept boards were presented along with verbal statements. The chosen direction involved participation from four nationally known architectural firms.

▼ This archaic disk was "unearthed" while gathering information and inspiration. The idea of using the spiral as a key graphic came from images like this one.

◀ Each architect's submissions were presented on a spread. Siebert Design styled the props into graphic photographs paired with testimonial quotes.

"I used to think of designers as the people who set type, created logos, and got the annual report printed. Now I realize—with the right chemistry, of course—that designers are able to help build companies and add elements most CEOs might never dream of pursuing on their own."

David Gustafson, President
Four Corners Paper Company

▶ Trademark for Le Desktop, a catalog group which supports Four Corners products and assists in defining marketing strategies for new products.

From left to right:
Stewart West., Debra Traylor, Victoria Seegers, Valerie Richardson, Forrest Richardson, David Gustafson, Christi Ballard, Tami West

Early on in their relationship, designers Richardson or Richardson started to help create a whole new company. As Forrest Richardson says, "We actually helped define the company's philosophy, the categories of products it would carry and even its name. The end result is a good example of what we mean by the term 'design DNA.' To us, design DNA is a way to express the structure that can be created by using design to affect how a company is positioned and how it is perceived. In essence, design is able to tell a story, communicate an idea and create an attitude."

Richardson or Richardson became design and product development partners with Four Corners, directing the creation of ten new families of papers within a year while paying attention to such minute but telling details as the design of the company's "on hold" telephone recordings.

Richardson or Richardson
1301 East Bethany Home Road
The Old Hess Farmhouse
Phoenix, AZ 85014
602/266-1301

▲ EarthCast Post paper colors were selected by the designers to provide a range from bright white to greys, in both warm and cool shades.

Designer and Client:
Richardson or Richardson for
Four Corners Paper Company

Four Corners Paper Company

Initial work for Four ▶ Corners involved the development of a color palette for LaserCast, a coated and colored paper for use in laser printers. This retail display rack was created with a single sheet of galvanized metal and two threaded rod supports.

With computer technology came the ability to churn out magnificent and meticulous printed materials—in quantities from one to one million. Along with desktop publishing came the opening of another market: one for papers that allowed for the highest quality to be printed even in the lowest quantity.

Paper is more than a surface for printing or writing to designers Forrest and Valerie Richardson, who showed Four Corners the depth and breadth to which they could go with the product offerings.

Richardson or Richardson started by developing a line of papers compatible with laser printers. As designers, they understood the range of possibilities for papers all too well and explored color, textures and coatings that allowed the end-user a rich range of choice. This was an auspicious start of what was to become a long and bountiful relationship for the Richardsons and Four Corners.

◀ EarthCast is the brand name for several lines of recycled papers including Post, Kraft and Sandstorm. A green tint supports the environmental orientation of the unbleached kraft packaging.

ImageCast, defined by its rust colored pattern, includes a variety of cut sheet papers sold in 50-, 100-, or 500-sheet boxes.

OverCast is the name developed for a system of compatible envelopes that can be used with all Four Corners papers. The designers worked closely with the manufacturing side of the company to create each detail, down to the flavor of the gum adhesive.

▼ Golf Paper Stationery Sets contain letterpressed stationery, matching envelopes and a set of golf balls with matching golf icons. The sets are sold to exclusive retail stores and golf proshops for seasonal sales, such as Father's Day and Christmas.

Tradeshow exhibit furni-▶
ture was custom designed
to house literature and computer equipment needed to
demonstrate the products.
At tradeshows, Japanese
Origami artists craft paper
swans and other animals out
of the Four Corners paper as
a remembrance for visitors
to take with them.

▼ These color boards, prepared before paper colors
are chosen and manufac-
tured in huge quantities, are
made up of color references
taken from actual paper
samples, industrial papers
and old books. Once a specific color and texture is
identified, designers work
with the mill experts to create small hand samples.

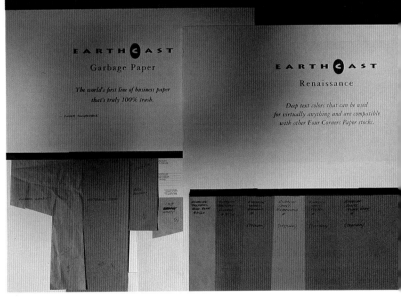

◀ Structural "towers" were
engineered to display paper
in retail environments. The
displays could not take up
more than four square feet of
floor space and had to hold
up to 400 pounds— about
$2000 worth of product—to
be cost effective. Each tower
can be shipped in a small box
about 15 inches in height
when disassembled.

Above, from left to right:
Catherine Ann Schmeltz and Crit Warren.
Below: Katherine Williams Wright.

Schmeltz + Warren, were a logical choice to work with the Ohio College Association. For client Katherine Wright, the strategy was to choose an avant garde designer to pull their sleepy and dull publication out of stagnation. "We believe this strategy is working. Annual sales jumped from less than 45,000 to over 64,000 at a time when demographic numbers had declined and despite printing costs and sales price having more than doubled. A survey of counselors who use it indicates that the booklet's design has made the difference in stimulating interest in our subject." Furthermore, Wright adds, "Realizing that TCIO must also be 'user friendly' to parents and counselors, we may have felt that some of the graphics and text design were a bit 'far out'. We are willing to forego personal likes and dislikes because the evidence indicated that the design is working."

Schmeltz + Warren
74 Sheffield Road
Columbus, OH 43214
614/262-3055

▼ Four types of images were used in the brochure: videograbs from Hi 8 video, scans from Polaroids and 35mm chromes and photo CD stock images.

Reprinted from
Design In Depth.
Printed in Hong Kong.

Designer and Client:
Catherine Ann Schmeltz
and Crit Warren, co-partners,
Schmeltz + Warren for
Katherine Williams Wright,
executive director and
managing editor,
Ohio College Association

Toward College in Ohio 89 1995-1996

"You are not your parents," is the opening line on the cover of *Toward College in Ohio* — an all too obvious statement except in this context, when addressed to 16 year olds who are thinking (or not thinking) about their futures. Together with the edgy, layered, nineties design, the opening line suggests the next line might be, "Furthermore, we are not your parents either, so it's cool to read on."

It's a difficult task, communicating with an audience of another generation. Not true, however, for Schmeltz + Warren, who have the beat of this younger generation. Schmeltz + Warren have, for ten years running, designed this overview, reinventing the subject each year with a fresh view of the higher educational opportunities offered by the fair state of Ohio.

Any 16 year old who may have passed on the options in the quiet and seemingly non-descript state has to think twice when they see, and read, *Toward College in Ohio*.

▲ *The* Toward College in Ohio *brochure treats each page as a mini poster, allowing the copy to be bite-sized and appealing to high school students.*

To stimulate interest ▶ in the diversity of educational possibilities available in Ohio, Schmeltz + Warren and the Ohio College Association had to make lots of dry, factual information lively and interesting.

90

▼ A sampling of the fonts used throughout the brochure. Schmeltz + Warren worked with Katherine Wright to get away from an expected "institutional look".

▲ The brochure also acts as a detailed guide to the approximately 115 colleges and universities that belong to the Ohio College Association.

◄ *Schmeltz + Warren always begin with massing scribbles in thumbnail form before moving to the computer for roughing out.*

▼ ▲ *TCIO is 100% digital, which not only reduced the production budget, but allowed for a more visually interesting and up-to-date look than would have been possible by traditional and more costly methods.*

Getting

As a paper mill's communications manager exploring this brave new world of TQM (Total Quality Management) and cross-functional teams, one challenge is coaxing great design solutions from a process that seems to put a greater value on consensus rather than creativity.

by
Laura Shore

As corporations reinvent themselves to become more competitive, we are all being asked to work in new ways. Cross-disciplinary teams replace traditional departments—a product development or marketing task force may have members from manufacturing, marketing, product testing, customer service and research. But with the right strategic focus, an approach that blurs the distinctions between disciplines can lead to a wider buy-in, resulting in rapid product development and implementation.

Sounds like business heaven, doesn't it? As a paper mill's communications manager exploring this brave new world of TQM (Total Quality Management) and cross-functional teams, one challenge is coaxing great design solutions from a process that seems to put a greater value on consensus rather than creativity.

For many years we have relied on designers to help us compete in a marketplace full of parity products. The projects that emerged in the days before TQM were highly creative and executed efficiently with a minimum of meddling by upper management. And we succeeded in achieving the goal of raising

Great Design...

our profile in the design community. Unfortunately, these projects had little measurable effect on sales and profits. Recently the use of "total quality" techniques has increased opportunities for communication within the company, allowing us to work in new ways and integrate the design function more closely with corporate strategy.

In the process, I have thought a lot about how designers and clients can better work together. It is often said that clients don't know what designers do. Actually, that's probably true. As a client who's worked with designers for over 10 years, I can safely say that I still don't know what designers do. What I do know is that design can be an effective competitive tool if used correctly. It's designers who provide the link between a great marketing idea and a real product. It's designers who create a visual expression of who we are. It's designers who create a unique voice in the marketplace.

Today we work together on various teams. The process is often laborious as we strive to communicate our ideas back and forth to each other. And though it often feels slow and unproductive at first, it has resulted in some unbelievable product breakthroughs.

For me, the result has been that I don't get to single-handedly execute every cool, quirky idea that comes along. But because the design projects are linked to the larger goals of the company, I have been able to work on larger projects with bigger paybacks. In turn, these projects started raising the perceived value of design within the company. But it wasn't easy getting there.

The change in my company started about a year ago. A new president was hired whose primary mission was to reverse a slide in our core markets and sweep the company into the twenty-first century. So, like most of corporate America today, the company is in the midst of reinventing itself. Old job descriptions no longer apply. Old ways of working are no longer relevant. Of course, people were hesitant to change: everyone, including myself, thought they had all the answers. Our technical guys thought their new "foo-foo juice" would save the company. The production guys thought all we had to do was limit our line to one product in order to make it efficient at a really low cost. The sales guys even thought we should turn the advertising budget over to them in the form of higher salaries.

I, too, suffered from job-induced myopia. It first became apparent to me when we hired a new marketing guy. I was initially put off by his "rows and columns" approach. I had always worked instinctively and creatively, but after working together for a while, I noticed that my new colleague listened intently as I rambled on — later translating my verbal hand-waving into outline form — draining all my ideas of its emotion. Using strange words like "zero-based budgeting" and "maximize," he molded my pure experience and intuition into logic. Soon I realized that others in my company were much more receptive to his approach. An idea that had seemed just a little bit goofy when I presented it suddenly seemed reasoned and informed. He was an IBM to my Macintosh: together we make one good brain.

While changing the way I communicated within the company, I also attempted to change the way we work with designers. I realized that it wasn't enough for me to be passionate about design. I had to find a way to translate that passion to others within the organization. Therefore, I've tried to multiply the opportunities for interaction with designers in order to get management lined up behind a good design concept. The challenge, of course, when involving number-crunchers is that many of them are what I call design-blind. Like color blindness, design-blind individuals usually let their spouses pick out their ties. They truly can't tell if something is well designed, or they don't care. This is where it makes sense to involve the right designer. I look for people who can survive the team meat grinder, as well as those who — besides being good designers — are good at sales. These highly articulate business-minded individuals can then work at a strategic level to make a difference for my company.

Slogging through a recent product development/launch program, we began to implement this new approach. After forging the design brief in the committee, I deleted the jargon, found the essence and translated it back to the design firm. As the project started to take shape, some committee members were invited to participate in client meetings at the design firm. We then invited the senior designer from the firm to the mill for a comprehensive presentation to a cast of thousands, which included people from the product development team, marketing, finance, manufacturing, engineering, upper management, sales, etc. A very small group of senior management were invited to participate in a work discus-

sion over lunch. (A good strategy to control the nitpicking, since we're all taught not to speak with our mouths' full).

While it's important to build an internal consensus and enthusiasm for a new product launch, it is also essential to build enthusiasm in the marketplace. Before the design presentation all we had was a collection of words and ideas — some paper tests and printing trials. After the presentation I sensed a palpable wave of enthusiasm among my normally stoic colleagues. We now had a product with a name and a visual story. Something we could all fall in love with.

When the project was finally ready to launch, the senior designer was invited to return (along with the printer and a client-user), and present the results of "beta testing" to our sales force and a group of highly influential customers. The response was unbelievably positive. In two hours the group moved from polite skepticism to an almost scary level of enthusiasm. While there are a variety of reasons for a successful product launch (not the least of which is having a great product), I'm pleased to say that for the first time the design firm received significant share of the credit.

From the personal to the political — I've given up a lot during this transition. I used to like working on my own with just the designer, coming up with focused solutions.

Working on a team is hard, and I hate all the jargon that seems to come bundled with the total-quality- movement. Now our projects have a much broader focus with less quirky solutions, and are more mainstream. But the payback — in terms of closer cooperation between departments and greater sales — are more than worth the effort it has taken to change.

Just as I've had to learn to translate my ideas and values into a language others in my company could understand, designers and clients today still need to see the world from each other's perspective. We've often heard the phrase: to do great design, get a great client? The flip side is: to get great design you have to become a great client.

Even the best design program won't sell a flawed or poorly positioned product. Yet, because design is so visible it can easily be blamed for bad performance. Of course, if the product is a raging success then management will claim it was the strategy... Hey, at least designers will get more work.

Laura Shore is the Communications Manager of Mohawk Paper Mill. This essay appeared in a modified form in the Design Issues column of Communication Arts magazine.

A Great Client

Knows their own capabilities and can communicate them to the design firm..

Knows what customers want and need.

Puts customers first.

Has a clear sense of the problem they want solved—whether it's a communications,

marketing or advertising problem.

Is open to fresh ideas.

Evaluates the ideas presented based on company needs.

Has clout internally or the ability to sell design internally.

Is able to allocate the resources to do good work.

Has carefully researched the design firm's capabilities, and can identify

the right designer for the job.

Client-oriented Designers

Need to see through the client to the customer.

Can talk to the client's customers.

Remember that design-blind individuals tend to react to content rather than visuals.

Remember that professional project management enhances

credibility among client management.

Never bring up Deconstructionism unless they're prepared to define it

in the same sentence.

Find someone in the organization who can tease out the issues that

allows you to create great visual solutions.

Take heed: If the client's problem requires a business consultant rather than a

graphic designer, proceed at your own risk.

The art of postage stamps,

depicting people, places,

and events of America's

two hundred year history ~

collectible and now wearable.

▲ *The Postmark brand message.*

Reprinted from
Design In Depth.
Printed in Hong Kong.

66 As full-service licensing agency, Hamilton works closely with our clients and licenses in selecting creative agencies. We have known Parham Santana for several years and have long admired their work. Parham Santana immediately understood the vision we had for the Postmarks Original apparel and developed a brand identity program that reflected that vision perfectly. **99**

— Debra Joester, President
of Hamilton Projects

The Postmark Team
Parham Santana, Inc.
Left: John Parham, President;
Maruchi Santana, Creative
Director. **Right:** Rick Tesoro,
Senior Art Director.
Photographs: Bart Gorin

Hamilton Projects, the official licensor, and American Eagle Apparel Group, the official licensee of the U.S. Postal Service, turned to Parham Santana, a firm with extensive experience in licensing and consumer product categories as a natural choice. Parham Santana's clients have included Anheuser Busch, Guess Eyewear, MTV Networks and Swatch. A natural design team to help tell the Postmark story.

*Parham Santana, Inc.
7 West 18th Street
New York, NY 10011
212/645-7501*

POSTMARK *American Wear*

PRODUCED UNDER LICENSE BY
AMERICAN EAGLE APPAREL GROUP

Designer and Client:
Parham Santana, Inc.
for American Eagle
Apparel Group

The Postmark Story

◀ Graphics designed by American Eagle Apparel Group were inspired by U.S. Postal Service stamps. The Postmark logo evokes comforting familiarity, while sparking new excitement. The concept "collectible," which has become a hallmark for the USPS, is reinforced through the use of special hangtags designating limited editions of selected Postmark products.

A great wealth of honorable American design exists in the archives of the United States Postal Service. Historically, philatelists have collected rare and beautiful stamps and lovingly kept these treasures in albums to be squirreled away. But in our contemporary, fast-paced world of licensing, postage stamps are now applied to apparel and accessories.

The strength of Parham Santana is their ability not only to develop a graphic identity and all the attendant merchandising materials, but to strategically position a branded identity. Through research, and by working closely with American Eagle Apparel Group, Parham Santana helped to define the unique attributes of this licensing opportunity, and to position Postmark American Wear as "Wearable. Collectible."

The team visited various post offices and the U.S. Postal Museum in Washington D.C., looking at thousands of stamps going back to the 1800s. Maruchi Santana explains, "We immersed ourselves in the subject matter, so we could process it into a look that's evocative of the past but reflecting a contemporary lifestyle."

Using functional, utilitarian materials in fresh ways, Rick Tesoro, Senior Art Director, created a marriage of tradition and newness throughout the entire Postmark program. The emphasis is on subtlety and simplicity: subdued colors, familiar patterns and closures. The result is a rich, elegant look, that speaks with authority and without hype.

98

▲ Teaser postcards used to introduce the line asked: "What would you say if we told you the newest look in clothes today is over 100 years old and came from a square?"

▲ The Postmark Information Kiosk is a two-sided display unit on wheels. One side introduces the Postmark concept with free brochures and posters and a Look Book showing the entire season's collection. The other side highlights new graphics based on stamps from the U.S. Postal Service.

▲ Parham Santana, Inc., together with Alpha 20/20, a retail consulting firm, created the Postmark American Wear retail concept. Each freestanding store was designed to house three Postmark American Wear divisions: Men's, Women's and Kid's". The design was inspired by Postal Service industrial materials and fixtures and integrated with an up-to-date simplicity of space and color.

Signage and merchandising fixtures were rendered with simple materials and utilitarian shapes. ▶

Point-of-sale materials ▶ show how the stamp graphics evolved into lifestyle apparel graphics and into the Postmark American Wear concept: "Wearable. Collectible."

▲ Parham Santana created the corporate identity for American Eagle Apparel Group and all of its business collateral materials. The Postmark brand message appears on the back of each business card.

◀ The Look Book is designed to showcase collection graphics and explain the significance and history of the stamp that inspired each graphic. The stand allows the easily-updated Look Book to be displayed on countertops.

◀ IDEO's design of electric vehicle charging systems included not only the charge station, but also the charging port on the car. The two elements need to fit visually and physically in order to make a simple, efficient connection.

IDEO's Mark Biasotti, John Lai, Sigi Moeslinger and Mark Roemer were brought in by Dick Bowman and Fred Silver of Hughes Power Control Systems in Tustin, California, to develop the design of the Electric Vehicle Charging System. Hughes needed to package its groundbreaking technology in a consumer-oriented, easy-to-use format that would appeal to a wide range of users and lifestyles. This challenge was successfully addressed based on research and input from IDEO's human factors and industrial design specialists.

IDEO Product Development
151 University Avenue
Palo Alto, CA 94301
415/688-3400

Above and below: Mark Biasotti and Jane Fulton Suri.

◀ Unlike gasoline-powered vehicles, electric cars will get most of their power at home, recharging in the garage at night from units like these to take advantage of off-peak hours for electricity usage.

❝IDEO has created a very clean, nonthreatening design, resulting in a device that is intuitive to use. This design is truly a high mark of the electric vehicle recharging market.❞

Dick Bowman,
Hughes Power Control Systems

Electric Vehicle Charging System

Designer and Client:
Mark Biasotti, Jane Fulton
Suri, IDEO Product
Development for Hughes
Power Control Systems

▼ *The convenience charger is small enough to fit in a car trunk and light enough to be portable. Like jumper cables or spare tires, it is not intended for everyday use, but is always there when needed.*

The world has long awaited a practical alternative means to power motor vehicles. IDEO and Hughes Power Control Systems took on this challenge by creating a handheld charger for electrically powered vehicles. The resulting design—ergonomic, compact and handsomely housed—makes ultimate economic and environmental sense.

Hughes had developed a safe, convenient and adaptable charging method by transferring energy through electric induction, without any exposure of conductive metal elements. However, they needed to refine this concept to accommodate a broad range of user behavior. IDEO's human factors specialists and industrial designers teamed up to investigate these issues. IDEO and Hughes determined that four types of chargers were needed to meet the level of convenience required for an electric vehicle (EV) operator: a wall-mounted 220-volt residential module, a 220-volt curbside column for use in parking garages or at homes without garages, a kiosk-style energy station and a 110-volt adapter unit that would be included with the vehicle and stored in the trunk. The first active charging station is an unattended installation in Walnut Creek, California. Users can park their EV commuter vehicle for the day and let it charge while they take light rail to the office. The station's streamlined, geometric forms convey the cleanliness, efficiency and simplicity of electric "fuel."

Electric Vehicle Charging System

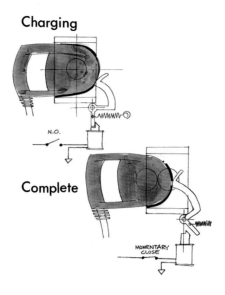

Charging

Complete

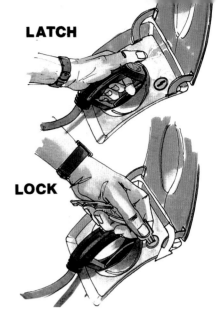

LATCH

LOCK

▼ The large, high-voltage Public Charge Stations will be visually similar to today's gas stations. Without gasoline fumes or spillage, however, these stations will be much cleaner than the ones we are accustomed to today.

▲ Since the charging port uses an induction scheme for transferring electrical energy to the vehicle, contaminants that would normally ruin electrical contacts can easily be washed through. This is a key safety feature when considering the tremendous amounts of energy that are necessary to facilitate quick, efficient charging.

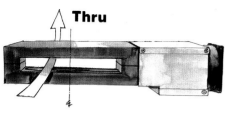

Thru

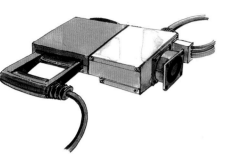

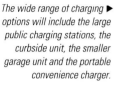

INDICATORS

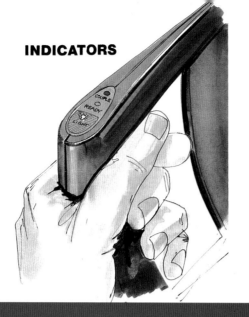

◀ The charging "paddle" is designed with an aerodynamic metaphor that not only relates to the vehicle it charges, but also conveys an efficient, safe and convenient aesthetic. Since the entire scheme of induction charging centers around safety, it was important that the key element of interface, the charge paddle, be given this attention to detail. Pictured is an early concept that incorporates built-in indicators for the charge condition.

The wide range of charging ▶ options will include the large public charging stations, the curbside unit, the smaller garage unit and the portable convenience charger.

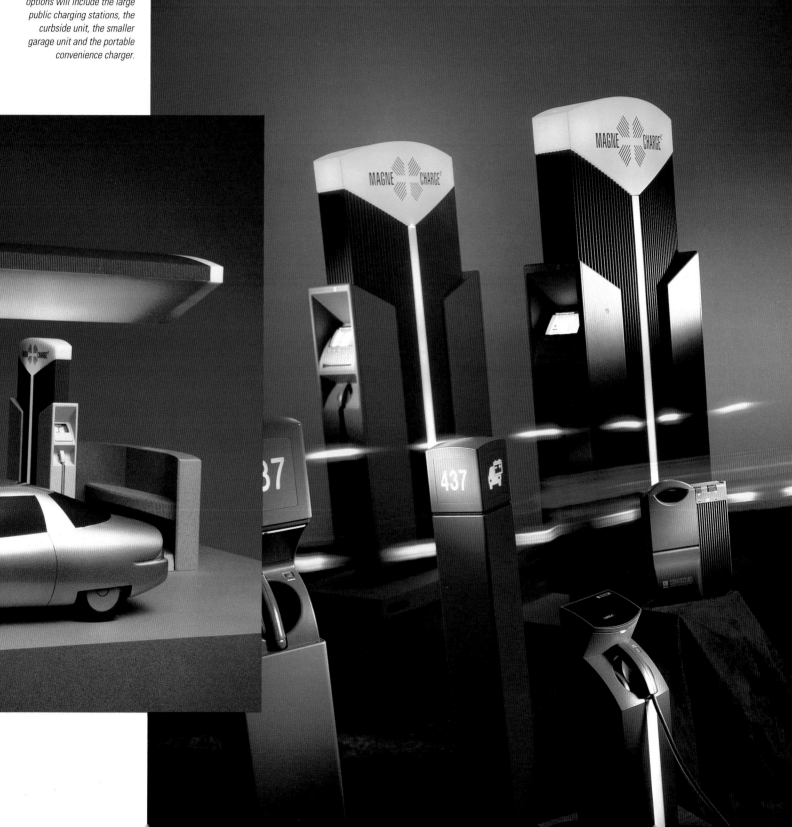

From left to right: Frank Todaro, Kent Hunter, Robert Wong and Brian Buckley (standing). Andreas Combuchen, Aubrey Balkind and Kim Yuen (seated).

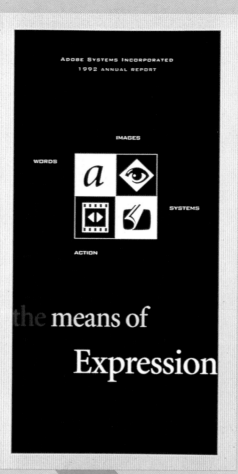

ADOBE SYSTEMS INCORPORATED
1992 ANNUAL REPORT

IMAGES

WORDS

SYSTEMS

ACTION

the means of

Expression

◄ The annual report cover uses "the means of Expression"— type, image, video and systems— to communicate that Adobe provides the standard for ways people express themselves through computers.

Frankfurt Balkind is a "Strategic Communications Agency," made up of recognized experts from all segments of the communications industry, with the express purpose of developing core marketing strategies and executing them in innovative ways across disciplines. The award-winning Adobe annual report is an example: it was approached like an advertising medium, and strategically repositions Adobe to the financial community as a visionary company that solves universal communications problems (rather than a niche player in the software marketplace).

Frankfurt Balkind Partners
244 East 58th Street
New York, NY 10022
Aubrey Balkind, 212/421-5888

369 Pine Street
Penthouse
San Francisco, CA 94104
Philip Durbow, 415/677-9525

6135 Wilshire Boulevard
Los Angeles, CA 90048
Peter Bemis, 213/965-4800

❝Adobe was seen as a specialty software marketer. Here was a broad-based product that we could use to reposition Adobe, the corporation.❞
Linda Prosser, Adobe

adobe acrobat

▲ Proposed product packaging emphasized the new symbol, as Adobe believed it best conveyed the software's importance as ground-breaking technology.

Reprinted from
Design In Depth.
Printed in Hong Kong.

Designer and Client:
Frankfurt Balkind Partners
for Adobe Systems, Inc.

Adobe Acrobat

Howdy.

PROBLEM:

MOST COMPUTERS CAN'T
EXCHANGE DOCUMENTS WITH
EACH OTHER.

Huh?

SOLUTION:

INTRODUCING ADOBE ACROBAT

The Adobe corporation and its Postscript software are commonly known among graphic designers, but Adobe had created a revolutionary new product whose success required broader appeal. This new software allowed, for the first time, different computer operating systems to exchange visually sophisticated documents with everything intact. Its audience included everyone from senior MIS decision-makers to department managers and their employees.

Frankfurt Balkind established three objectives for moving forward: first, opportunistically relate the new product's identity to Adobe corporation (as Postscript had not); second, convey this new software's revolutionary character so that it could become a communications standard; third, emphasize its friendliness so that a mass market viewed it as accessible.

To accomplish these goals for the new software, Frankfurt Balkind created the positioning, name and identity of Adobe Acrobat; print marketing materials; an introductory video for use at COMDEX and later sales efforts; trade advertising strategy and package design. For Adobe corporation, new corporate positioning was developed and introduced first in the corporate annual report and later expressed in a new corporate identity.

The office of the '90s.

Does this sound like the ideal way to work?

Didn't think so.

Adobe *Acrobat*

▲ ▶ *To introduce the Acrobat family of software at COMDEX, the national computer trade show, Frankfurt Balkind produced a video that humanly and humorously dramatized Acrobat's potential role in business communications, showing the folly of current business practices and the benefits Acrobat offered.*

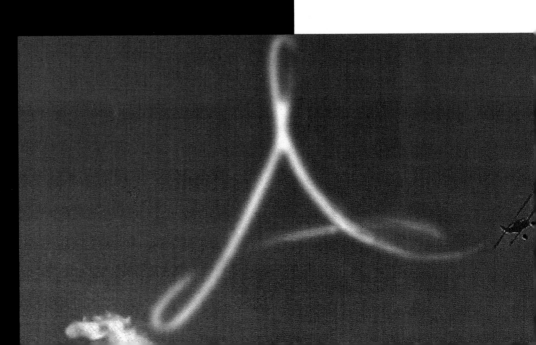

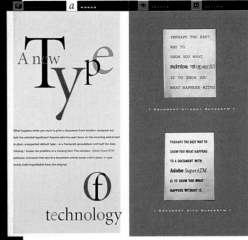

Actually, it is a computer. But when it only crunches numbers or processes words and inserts them into featureless spreadsheets or reports, it's only doing half its job. The other, more important half is to communicate all that data in an effective, meaningful way. Before Adobe introduced the PostScript page-description language, personal computer users had almost no access to the richness of format, typography and illustration that adds expressiveness to digital communication. Without these capabilities, computers can only compute – often just adding to the rising tide of information, cluttering more than they communicate.

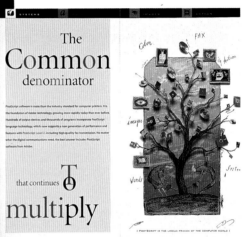

▲ At the top of each annual report spread are icons delineating whether the featured product involves type, image, video and or system software. The spreads are treated like ads, focusing on the unique benefit each product offers.

◄ The selected symbol best communicated "amazing feats between platforms" by conveying continuity (infinity), motion and flexibility (a triple loop) and an A for Adobe and Acrobat.

◀ Primo Angeli Inc. worked ▶ in collaboration with four other design firms, including architects and urban planners, to develop the "look" of the Centennial Olympic Games.

Reprinted from
Design In Depth.
Printed in Hong Kong.

"This is the celebration of the first 100 years of the modern Olympic Games. This is the biggest Olympic Games, and it will be the most spectacular. A once-in-a-lifetime experience that will never come again. I want you to knock the socks off the world for this one."

Billy Payne,
President and CEO, ACOG

From left to right:
Paul Acocella, director creative services; Christine Donovan, manager look of the games; Ginger Watkins, managing director of corporate services; Andrea Pavone-Said, manager design services.
Below: Primo Angeli, PAI creative director.

Primo Angeli Inc. worked with Copeland Hithler/Murrell, Favermann Design, Turner Associates/ Architects & Planners, Jones Worley Design Inc. and Malcom Gear Designers, Inc. as partners in designing the overall graphic program for the 1996 Centennial Olympic Games in Atlanta. The de facto *Creative Decision Maker was Ginger Watkins, Managing Director of Corporate Services for the Atlanta Committee for the Olympic Games. Angeli says, "We were specifically chosen because of the multifaceted team situation, a diverse group of people, a diverse talent, a diverse background. We had the ability to communicate and reach a global audience rather than apply a personal style to an esoteric few. That's why we were chosen and, in sum, that's how we work."*

Primo Angeli Inc.
590 Folsom Street
San Francisco, CA 94105
415/974-6100

The objective of the ▶ project is to create the appropriate, basic visual symbols and to apply this family of symbols throughout the entire spectrum that constitutes the "look" for the 1996 Atlanta Olympic Games.

Designer and Client:
Primo Angeli Inc.
for the 1996 Atlanta
Olympic Games

1996 Atlanta Olympic Games

◀ *The integrated leaf pattern expresses the passage of time—100 years, Athens and Atlanta—in visual cues familiar to the Georgian landscape.*

Centennials are a symbol of consistency and survival, and as such hold a special meaning for us. Primo Angeli Inc. (PAI) was given the challenge to coordinate the design of the 1996 Atlanta Olympics; the 100-year anniversary of the modern-day Olympic Games. Angeli observes, "In expressing the micro and macro relationship between time and distance, we developed the integrated small and large leaf pattern, a subtle symbolism that expresses the passage of time." Representing both the Greek and Georgian landscapes, the leaf motif expresses the commonalty between the past and present, the Greek Games of antiquity and the Olympics of today.

PAI's multifaceted tasks in this project included the coordination of a large creative team made up of five design firms from around the country. The most successful solutions were obtained when the team was fully integrated with the client, where openness and flexibility existed between design, management and message.

PAI is a master of design management, naming, positioning, and packaging, and this project called on all of the firm's resources. From the onset, the team focused on establishing a clear positioning statement; as Angeli says, "essentially, a statement that we could hit with an arrow rather than a sawed off shot gun." Totally appropriate for an event that celebrates human precision and accuracy.

110

▲ The "Quilt of Leaves" is the basis for the "Look of the Games" as applied to all environmental graphics. Interwoven into the design is another identity element, the Atlanta Olympics torch trademark. The quilt is native to the South and suggests the combining of many constituents into one. The leaves are an allusion to the lush greenery of the American South and to the bay leaves of victory associated with the Olympic Games of ancient Greece. Quilting is a traditional communal art; celebration of the Olympics is a traditional communal art of worldwide proportions.

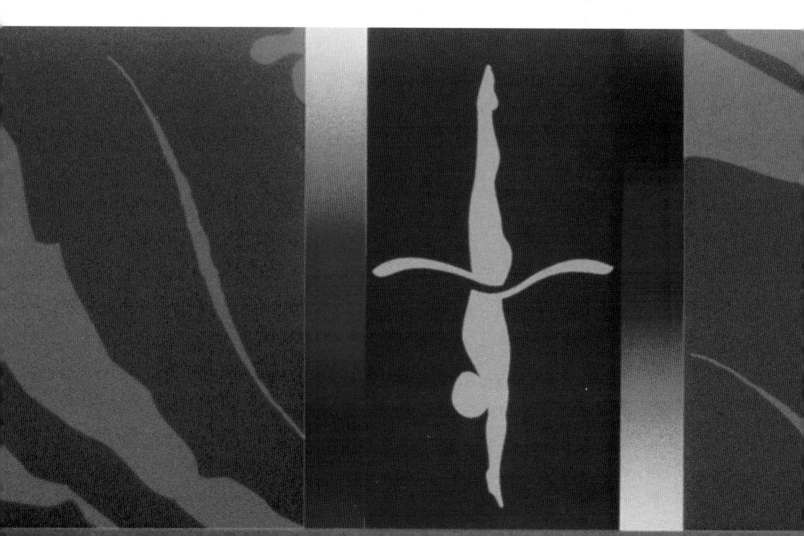

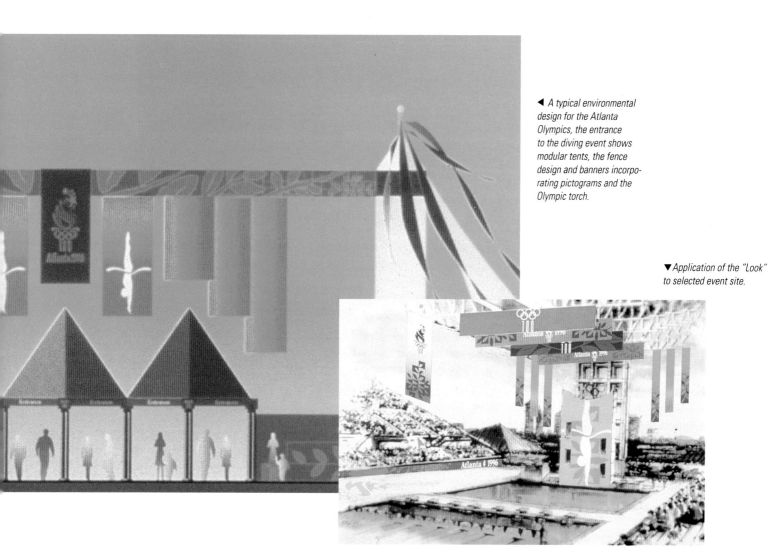

◀ A typical environmental design for the Atlanta Olympics, the entrance to the diving event shows modular tents, the fence design and banners incorporating pictograms and the Olympic torch.

▼ Application of the "Look" to selected event site.

◀ In the Atlanta Olympics, as in the Lillehammer Olympics, pictograms not only form a nonverbal language but also become part of the family of identities. The pictogram identities were mainly Malcolm Grear's contribution, though we all had input.

▶ The Atlanta Committee for the Olympic Games commissioned PAI to design this official poster. In celebration of the centennial anniversary of the modern-day Olympic Games, the androgynous athletic figure at the center of the poster takes on the characteristics of a classic Greek sculpture through the use of the Atlanta Olympics torch logo shown in shadow across the torso.

Reprinted from
Design In Depth.
Printed in Hong Kong.

❝With sweats on the market ranging from athletic to preppy, we needed a marketing position that Levi Strauss & Co. could own.❞
Stacey Bovero, Levi Strauss & Co.

Dennis Crowe and Neal Zimmermann worked with Stacey Bovero at Levi Strauss & Co. to develop the launch of Levi's Sweats. Zimmermann, formerly art director at LS & Co., and Crowe formed ZCD in 1988 and quickly became a valued, enduring resource for Levi's. David Peterson photographed and filmed the sweats project.

*Zimmermann Crowe Design
Neal Zimmermann and Dennis Crowe, Principals
90 Tehama Street, San Francisco, CA 94105
415/777-5560*

From left to right: Stacey Bovero, Dennis Crowe, Neal Zimmermann.

ZCD worked with Levi ▶ Strauss & Co.'s product development department on fit, color and embroidered graphics for the Sweats line.

Designer and Client:
Neal Zimmermann and
Dennis Crowe, Zimmermann
Crowe Design for Stacey
Bovero, Levi Strauss & Co.

Levi's Sweats

THE *american* UNIFORM IS COMPLETE

◀ A sweatshirt and a pair of jeans is a combination worn by almost everyone in the country, thus ZCD introduced the tagline "The American Uniform is Complete" on the hangtag. The irregularly shaped hang-tag is printed in one color on plain chip board so that the tag is simultaneously basic and current.

The sweats pin, a promo-▶ tional accessory, was distributed to the Levi's sales force to keep them excited about the product launch. It was eventually sold in stores direct-ly to consumers. The "sweats man" displays an attitude consistent with the program.

Zimmermann Crowe Design is stretching the limits of the role traditional graphic design plays in corporate America. Highlighted here is the program they created for Levi's Sweats. Their work illustrates a diversity in mediums and yet a consistency in image which puts their firm into a new creative category.

Levi's Men's jeans Marketing Director, Stacey Bovero, brought in ZCD at the very beginning of the project. She had a solid marketing position, a progressive product manager and an open mind.

Together, Bovero and ZCD created a street smart, gritty image for Levi's sweats that was a stark contrast from the competition's "athletic" or "preppy sweater alternative" positioning. ZCD worked closely with product developement to ensure that the product and image gelled into a synergistic presentation.

This kind of creativity and collaboration is necessary in providing the focus and unity essential for a product to rise to the top of the retail fashion world.

Levi's Sweats

TRUE VALUES

STREET TRIBE

▼ The sell-in brochure acted as an image piece as well as a sales tool (at Left) featuring tipped-in fabric swatches. It also included a product line list, order information and a reference for visual merchandising.

The sell-in video developed ▼ by ZCD to explain product positioning to the Levi's sales force was so successful that they were asked to produce an in-store image video as well as a :30 TV spot. ZCD casted, directed, edited, scored and created the animated titles for the video projects. David Peterson, the sole still photographer for the campaign, also shot the motion picture film. Grain and contrast were accentuated to create a gritty urban atmosphere.

LEVI'S SWEATS

HOODS

FIVE ZERO

▲ To support a "sweats for jeans" strategy, the Levi's Sweats logo borrows from Levi Strauss & Co.'s rich heritage. The double arc shape pays homage to the trademarked stitching pattern on the back pocket of all Levi's Jeans.

▲ ZCD created co-op outdoor advertising including billboards and bus shelter kiosks (like the one above). Radio spots (:60 and :30) were also created to supplement the ad campaign.

" In initiating a summer graphics program it was important that the designs reflect a personalized style—that they should have an individual, one-of-a-kind quality, yet hold together in content and style throughout each piece. "
Tim Dittmer, The Limited Too

Above and below: *Kirk Richard Smith (foreground), Terry Alan Rohrbach (behind) and Tim Dittmer.*

Firehouse 101 Art + Design is a graphic design studio specializing in full-service design and illustration including: logo and identity systems, brochures, posters, CD packaging, direct mail, annual reports, animation and fashion wear. Their goal is to go beyond simple problem solving and to take advantage of the intrinsic elements of emotion, spontaneity and passion within communication. Clients include Nickelodeon, The Limited Too, Structure, Levi Strauss & Company, Bantam Doubleday Dell, and CompuServe.

The Limited Too is a retail clothing division of The Limited, offering fashion for girls. For the Summer Wear Graphics Project, The Limited Too asked Firehouse 101 to interpret styles and concepts rather than to simply emulate a current trend in developing this line of summer wear graphics for girls.

Firehouse 101 Art + Design
492 Armstrong Street
Columbus, OH 43215
614/464-0928

Reprinted from
Design In Depth.
Printed in Hong Kong.

The main objective of the ▶ project was to design clothes for girls that communicated universal expressions of summer and the feelings and concerns children have for the world.

The Limited Too Summer Wear117

Designer and client:
Kirk Richard Smith, designer/
illustrator and principal,
Firehouse 101 Art + Design
for Tim Dittmer, art director,
The Limited Too.
Photography: Will Shively

The Limited Too offers fashion for girls ages four to sixteen. Tim Dittmer, art director of The Limited Too says, "We believe that girls make their own choices about the clothes they wear. Often they're making a personal statement about the things that are important to them."

With this in mind, Firehouse 101 Art + Design set about designing a graphic system that girls could relate to with content that reflected statements of universal sentiment.

Understanding and embracing the child's perspective was interesting and liberating for designer/illustrator Kirk Richard Smith.

Buyers from The Limited Too provided market research that guided the design team towards color palettes, textures and graphic influences that allowed for a rich variety of directions and resulted in a delightful and highly successful line of summer clothing.

▲ The Limited Too Summer Wear Graphics Project included a series of designs incorporating illustration and calligraphy for a summer season promotion involving T-shirts, tank tops and biker shorts. The overall goal of the project incorporated respect for the integrity of a child's imagination and their instinctual ability to understand forms, colors and subjects.

▲ Firehouse 101 Art + Design created images that were fun and summer-like in attitude while at the same time having the sophisticated and direct emotional quality of a Picasso or Matisse—primitive and innocent but also universal.

The goal was not to underestimate children's creativity and understanding. The result was subject matter reflecting universal concerns: saving the animals, loving the earth, celebrating the seasons, peace, friendship and love between all races.

The Limited Too Summer Wear

▼ *"We tried to return to the essence of freedom associated with a child's perspective of the world and incorporated this essence within the designs. All of us maintain our own child's point of view of life, but often forget how wonderful it is to incorporate this perspective into the professional design world." Kirk Richard Smith, Firehouse 101 Art + Design.*

◄ *Symbols such as hearts, flowers, stars, globes, hippies, fish and spirals all relate to sixties imagery of freedom but with a nineties twist in style. The brush work has a fine arts attitude which is appealing to both kids and adults. The bright color palette and simplistic line quality convey optimism and the feelings of summer.*

From left to right: Lance Wyman and Mark Fuller.

Lance Wyman, Principal of Lance Wyman Ltd., is a master of iconography. Trained as an industrial designer he integrates expressive visual icons with physical materials to create functional objects.

Mark Fuller, Principal of MTFuller is a designer and fabricator of environmental graphic systems. Trained as an architect he combines sensitivity to design issues with the skill for applying the right production processes to the best materials.

Lance Wyman Ltd.
118 West 80th Street
New York, NY 10024
212/580-3010

MTFuller
109 South Olive Avenue
West Palm Beach, FL 33401
407/659-2933

"The ram and the wolf create the perfect setting in my Southampton garden. I enjoy the serenity of these beautiful chairs as my three fleet footed Staffordshire pups, clearly sensing no competition, run under and around them with a measure of contempt."

Wilson McLean
Artist/Illustrator

Camelsticks are ▶ assembled like a puzzle from three flat pieces of steel.

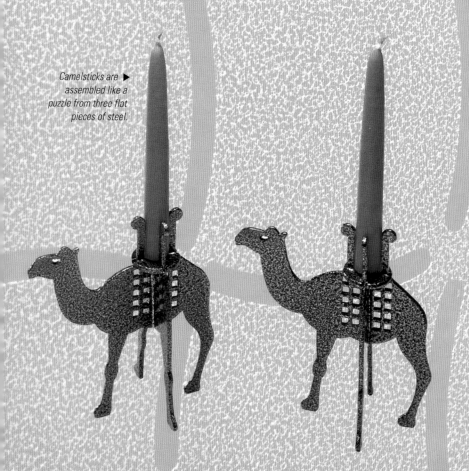

Animates

Designer and Client:
Lance Wyman and
Mark Fuller for Animates
© copyright 1992

Animates is a company with a vision of bringing more animal forms into our living spaces by combining current technology and silhouettes of animals such as bears, wolves and alligators, to create a collection of furniture and accessories. The collection was designed by Lance Wyman and produced by Mark Fuller. Wyman & Fuller also own Animates

tion comes from stories my grandfather told me as a child.

A railroad engineer who lived in the Pocono Mountains, he often reminisced about talking to the animals on his daily walks to work and how he would stop his freight train, climb down and "give a deer a boot" to get him off the tracks so the train wouldn't hit him. His tender attitude toward animals has rubbed off on me. As a designer I enjoy the challenge of capturing the personality and spirit of an animal in minimal form."

We started with the Tablegator," Fuller recalls. "Lance made pencil drawings, small paper study models, and then sent a full size pattern for me to plot on the computer for laser cutting in steel. Now all the designing is done on computer and e-mailed directly to me to plot for the laser cutter, and output as small study

models in steel, or full size pieces."

Wyman and Fuller have collaborated before as designer and producer, most notably on the wayfinding system for the American Museum of Natural History in New York, where museum floor numbers are integrated with animal icons on directories and signs. Prior to that Wyman designed the animal icons which identify the trails and exhibits at the National Zoo in Washington DC. and the Minnesota Zoo in Apple Valley, Minnesota.

"People have a need to relate to animals," Wyman reflects. "They play an important role in the mythological stories of every culture and are used to represent strength, speed and cunning in today's corporate logos. For me however, a deeper fascina-

▲ *The chairs & tables designed include the Tablegator (shown above), Beavertable, Wolfchair, Ramchair, Bearchair and Pumachair.*

◄ Fish silhouettes are folded once and can be used heads or tails up to hold books in place. Photos: Lance Wyman

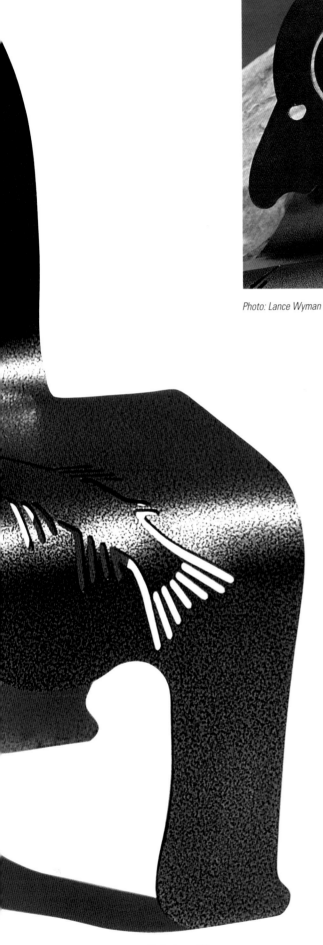

Photo: Lance Wyman

Each chair and table is made by laser cutting a full body silhouette of an animal out of a single sheet of steel and forming it into the contour of a table or chair while still maintaining a recognizable posture of the animal. Cut through patterns allow light to pass through the steel creating shadow images.

Photo: Tom Shelby

Photo: Lance Wyman

Reprinted from
Design In Depth.
Printed in Hong Kong.

"Peterson & Company turned to the earth and sky for inspiration, paired with a review of product ingredients as they appear in nature. The final design visually communicates purity, naturalness, earth-friendliness and innovation — the foundation of Earth Preserv's marketing messages."

Keith Waldon
CEO, Earth Preserv, Ltd.

From left to right: Keith Waldon, Bryan Peterson, Jan Wilson

In a true example of positive client-designer collaboration, after Peterson & Company approached Earth Preserv, Ltd. with several preliminary ideas, the client became very active in steering the look of the project. The design team was initially worried that the look of the project might become compromised, but was delighted to find that Earth Preserv had such a well-defined vision of their product that the collaboration resulted in a look that both has design integrity and is exactly right for the product line.

The design team at Peterson & Company included: Jan Wilson, Bryan L. Peterson, Nhan T. Pham, Scott Ray, David Eliason, Scott Paramski; with illustrations by Amy Bryant.

*Peterson & Company
2200 North Lamar
Suite 310
Dallas, TX 75202
214/954-0522*

This guide to natural ▶ and synthetic ingredients designed by Nhan T. Pham is one of several peripheral items designed for in-store displays and buyer incentives.

The Earth Preserv products ▶ were designed for three sizes of product marketed in aluminum bottles including: shampoo, hair vitalizer, bath crystals, nourishing body bath, sunscreen.

Earth Preserv

Designer and Client:
Peterson & Company for
Earth Preserv, Ltd.

▲ *Other buyer incentives include this travel set, gathering the Earth Preserv products packaged in one ounce aluminum bottles. The Earth Preserv symbol evolved through 15 steps, beginning with an idea by Scott Ray and finally being refined by Bryan Peterson.*

Bathing is a ritual enjoyed by many for its ability to comfort, relax and cleanse the body. Earth Preserv is a body-care product line with this sense of comfort and the environment very much in mind. The graphic image, developed by Peterson & Company, integrated the ecological concerns of much of the enlightened world with the convictions and vision of the client through the use of materials, graphic imagery and typography.

This timely packaging, made of durable aluminum, juxtaposes (and tones down) its slick image with soft and earthy illustrations. The promotion has a recycled look and contains real, hard-hitting information about the environment meant to educate as well as entice the consumer.

The message to the consumer is clear: being good to the environment can be fun. The message to business is that it can also be profitable.

▼ *This "blow-in insert," designed by Jan Wilson, was inserted in the JC Penney section of Sunday papers nationwide to announce the launch of Earth Preserv.*

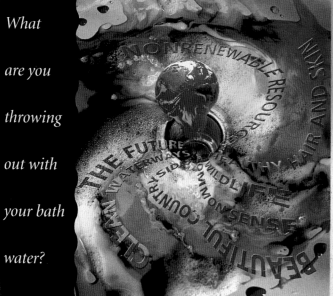

What are you throwing out with your bath water?

Jan Wilson refined Bryan ▶ Peterson's basic bottle design to appeal to the client while maintaining the original integrity of the design. Realistic illustrations of fruit were replaced with stylized illustrations—like this one of the sun for Earth Preserv sunscreen.

earth preserv

sunscreen

aloe vera gel; rapeseed; palm oil; coconut oil; chamomile extract; balm mint extract; calendula extract; cornflower extract; ginseng extract; alfalfa extract; matricaria extract; vitamin E; avo oil; jojoba oil; mountain ash berries; beta-carotene; chamomile; xanthan plant gum; vitamin E; milk enzymes; benzoin

bathe the body...

Earth-Friendly Bath, Hair & Skin Care.
Typical bath, hair & skin care products pollute our bodies with potentially damaging synthetic chemicals, and those same chemicals pollute our waterways, endangering wildlife. Likewise, most products are packaged in plastic, which is filling our landfills and littering our countryside. Now there's a solution: **earth preserv's** purely natural products packaged in 100% recyclable aluminum bottles and wraps.

and hair, and they don't pollute our waterways like the synthetic chemicals used in many products. No animal by-products are used, and **earth preserv** products are never tested on animals.

Pamper Your Body & Protect Our Waterways.
Each of **earth preserv's** ingredients is harvested from nature. Every ingredient is proudly listed on the front of each container in terms you can understand. These natural ingredients pamper your skin

Zero-Garbage Packaging To Save Our Countrysides.
Billions of pounds of plastic are produced each year, and less than 3% is recycled annually because plastic recycling is unprofitable, damaging to the environment and a logistical nightmare. Nearly 70% of all aluminum cans are recycled annually, so **earth preserv** created bottles and soap wraps made of 100% recyclable aluminum. Now you can bathe without polluting the earth.

A reusable shopping bag ▶
was among the buyer incentives designed by Jan Wilson.

127

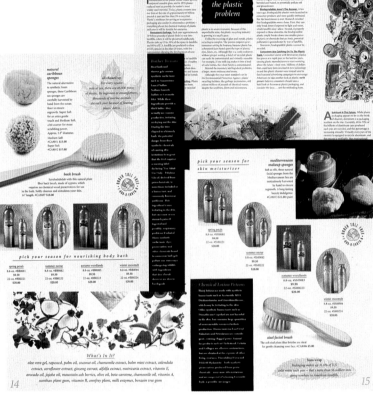

▲ A catalog was mailed to
150,000 potential buyers,
offering the Earth Preserv
products along with an
array of bath accessories.

◀ The insert announcing
Earth Preserv opened up to
offer a complete introduction
to the all-natural and envi-
ronmentally-friendly line
of products.

66*FuturePresent* was perfect. The strategy was on target and inspired. The execution exceeded my expectations. The graphic design for each phase of the project enriched the concept and expanded our vision of what would have otherwise been somewhat routine objectives. *"FuturePresent"* defined an industry in transition. Steve Wedeen gifted our leadership and the rest of the team, with a handle on a rapidly evolving future. It's a handle that we continue to grasp.**99**

From left to right:
Michele Obermeier, U S WEST;
Steve Wedeen, Rick Vaughn, Richard
Kuhn, Vaughn Wedeen Creative.

Vaughn Wedeen Creative has enjoyed a satisfying and mutually beneficial relationship with U S WEST for over ten years. The strategic partnership role they play with this client is one that extends beyond the traditional definition of the design firm-client relationship. In most cases, U S WEST involves Vaughn Wedeen in projects from the beginning, during the planning stages. In that way multiple goals and objectives can be addressed and incorporated into all projects. This allows for highly creative and unusual executions that fulfill both short and long term positioning needs. Strategic messaging is combined with high entertainment value to provide a program that is fun and engaging while delivering important and relevant content. Optimum economy is also achieved through careful planning. This project, like many others done for U S WEST started with a smaller set of objectives and grew as the collaborative process progressed.

Vaughn Wedeen Creative, Inc.
407 Rio Grande NW
Albuquerque, New Mexico 87104
505/243-4000

FuturePresent

▼ *Six foot robots were placed around the hotel, welcoming participants and directing them to various meeting sites.*

Designer and Client:
Vaughn Wedeen Creative
for U S WEST

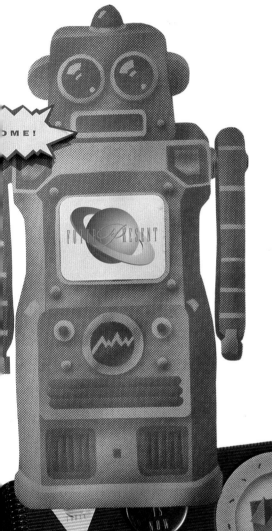

This project for U S WEST Communications started with a directive to develop a theme for a four day event for the company's top performers. A combination of celebration and motivation was required because these employees were being rewarded for their previous year's performance but also needed to walk away from the event with direction, enthusiasm and motivation for stellar performance in the coming year. The initial meeting yielded the vague direction of "We want something to do with the future." With knowledge of U S WEST's needs and culture, as well as existing market conditions, and with further input from the client, it was determined that the task was to create a program that would define "the future" as something other than "something out there, out of our control", but something that is "very much in our control, and taking place all the time, right under our nose". FuturePresent was coined as a new "tense", not past or present or future, which sent a message of self empowerment and excitement. As a provider of "future" technology in the form of telecommunications products and services, U S WEST genuinely makes the FuturePresent for its customers. This theme and positioning was enthusiastically adopted by the client and quickly became the overall theme for the Small Business Group for that year. As a result, the scope of the project grew.

Identities and materials needed to be generated for two different events as well as ongoing collateral. The first 'launch' featured a predominantly silver with black and purple look, with a stacked typographic treatment for the logo. The second unveiling was dominated by a black background with silver, purple and aqua accents. At this point the logo had evolved with script embellishments and a saturn-like symbol.

Every point of communication from the invitations and pre-arrival kits, to the signage, conference collateral and media presentation carefully integrated the look and content of FuturePresent. The events and campaign were enormously successful and well received. Participants left with the optimum combination of having had a great time and having had their time well spent.

◄ *This FuturePresent President's Club Prearrival Kit was sent out to participants to create excitement and give information about the event. Dress requirements were printed on the back of the "Robot," hotel information on the "Space Station," meals on the "Future Plate" and the little "Space Cars" are luggage tags.*

SMALL BUSINESS MARKET UNIT

THURSDAY

SEP 23

JUEVES

"EMPIRES OF THE FUTURE ARE EMPIRES OF THE MIND."

Winston Churchill

USWEST COMMUNICATIONS

A desk calendar given ▲ to all U S WEST Small Business Group employees features daily quotations to stimulate thought about taking hold of your future. The calendar keeps the theme alive on a daily basis.

FUTURE PRESENT

Welcome to your future. Do you consider the future some distant time or place? Tomorrow, next June, the year 2000? Well, surprise. The future has arrived early. (It has a sneaky habit of doing that.) In fact, it's here right now. The future is present; it is in our midst. Or if you prefer, we are in its midst. What to do now? Call Jeanne Dixon? Brace ourselves for

▲ The FuturePresent identity was created to evolve. The silver "box" logo used for materials at the annual meeting was printed with black and purple accents for this subsequent event.

Shirts and other materials ▶ were handed out throughout these events. The packaging was meticulously thought out and most everything was personalized with a hang tag.

THE FUTURE IS NOW

◀ Instead of the hotel "mint" on the pillow, this teaser was placed in the rooms of all recipients. The instructions asked the participants to dim the light, gaze into the crystal ball and imagine themselves in six months and in 2010: Where are they? What are they doing? What does the world look like?

This limited-edition metal ▶ covered book was a gift and remembrance of the four day event. It summed up the content and philosophy of FuturePresent. The dual spine and mixture of metal, paper and plastic pages allowed pictures and copy to be juxtaposed in different ways for new and unexpected interpretations.

Diana Graham

Diana Graham is founder of Diagram Design and Marketing Communications which has strengths in financial, entertainment and real estate. A \graduate of the School of Visual Arts, Diana has over 25 years experience in the field. Honored in 1980 as the first recipient of the "Women in Design International Award", Ms. Graham has won awards and judged competitions for the Type Directors Club, Art Directors Club, AIGA and Communication Arts. Her work has appeared in major design publications and these magazines choose her as the subject of feature articles. She is much in demand as a lecturer and has addressed design organizations both nationally and internationally. Recently, she closed her New York office and is now residing and working in Munich, Germany.

Diana Graham
Diagram Design
Weisser Berg #15
82266 Inning, Germany
49-8143-94139

Reprinted from *Design In Depth*.
Printed in Hong Kong.

❝We need to address problems in the workplace between men and women.❞

Caroline Hightower
Former President, AIGA,

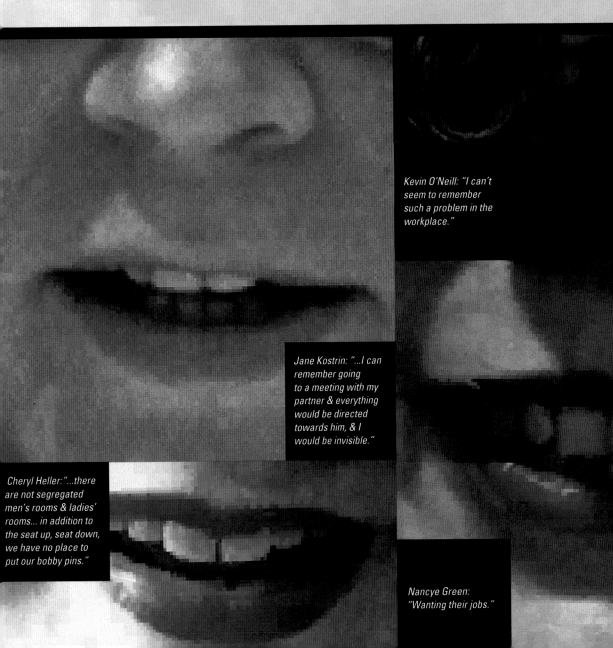

Kevin O'Neill: "I can't seem to remember such a problem in the workplace."

Jane Kostrin: "...I can remember going to a meeting with my partner & everything would be directed towards him, & I would be invisible."

Cheryl Heller:"...there are not segregated men's rooms & ladies' rooms... in addition to the seat up, seat down, we have no place to put our bobby pins."

Nancye Green: "Wanting their jobs."

Designers and Client:
Diana Graham of Diagram
Design for the American
Institute for Graphic Arts

Men & Women & the Business

◄ *The rewards of participating in the survey included a set of these plastic chattering teeth, customized by Graham.*

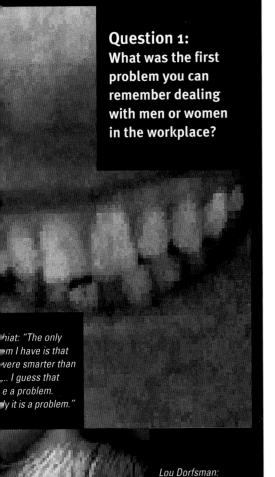

Question 1:
What was the first problem you can remember dealing with men or women in the workplace?

hiat: "The only ...m I have is that ...vere smarter than ... I guess that ...e a problem. ...y it is a problem."

Lou Dorfsman: "I never had a problem."

Diana Graham, a confident and seasoned professional designer, was asked to revisit the age old subject of men and women working together in business for the National AIGA Conference. Embracing the happy coincidence of the emerging computer technology and the availability of innumerable outspoken New York designers and art directors, Graham artfully cropped her subjects in the video frame, and, using a computer as her tool, created a toothy view of the opposite sexes. Focussing solely on the mouth (a symbol of both communication and sex) Graham asked a large number of well-known faces, all opinionated men and women, to accept the challenge of meeting the subject of sex head on, so to speak.

"Good afternoon and thank you all for coming..." Graham narrates, "We're going to look at a vintage question: Are men and women really different? How do men and women differ in their reactions to real-life commonplace business situations?" She went on, never to show her own face, but to address each question to the speakers.

After the video was aired to an enthusiastic audience at the AIGA Conference, Graham graciously presented each speaker with a pair of dime store plastic talking teeth, after, of course, customizing the packaging to "Thank you for chatting."

Graham's video is a time capsule. The speakers were anywhere from their 20s to 60s in age, a cavernous range considering that it represented both a generation who gave birth to the industry of graphic design and advertising and, the profession's progeny, a generation for whom the business of graphic design represents the far future.

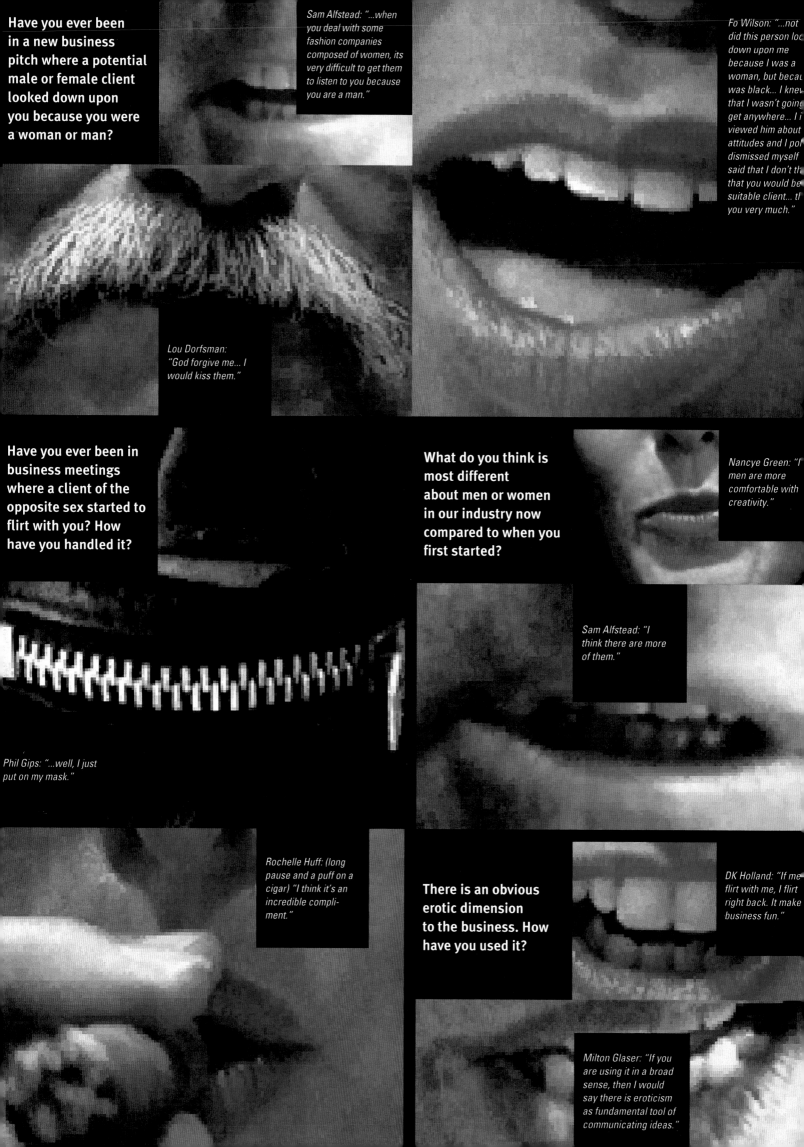

Have you ever been in a new business pitch where a potential male or female client looked down upon you because you were a woman or man?

Sam Alfstead: "...when you deal with some fashion companies composed of women, its very difficult to get them to listen to you because you are a man."

Fo Wilson: "...not did this person loo down upon me because I was a woman, but becau was black... I knew that I wasn't going get anywhere... I i viewed him about attitudes and I pol dismissed myself said that I don't th that you would be suitable client... tl you very much."

Lou Dorfsman: "God forgive me... I would kiss them."

Have you ever been in business meetings where a client of the opposite sex started to flirt with you? How have you handled it?

What do you think is most different about men or women in our industry now compared to when you first started?

Nancye Green: "I men are more comfortable with creativity."

Sam Alfstead: "I think there are more of them."

Phil Gips: "...well, I just put on my mask."

Rochelle Huff: (long pause and a puff on a cigar) "I think it's an incredible compliment."

There is an obvious erotic dimension to the business. How have you used it?

DK Holland: "If me flirt with me, I flirt right back. It make business fun."

Milton Glaser: "If you are using it in a broad sense, then I would say there is eroticism as fundamental tool of communicating ideas."

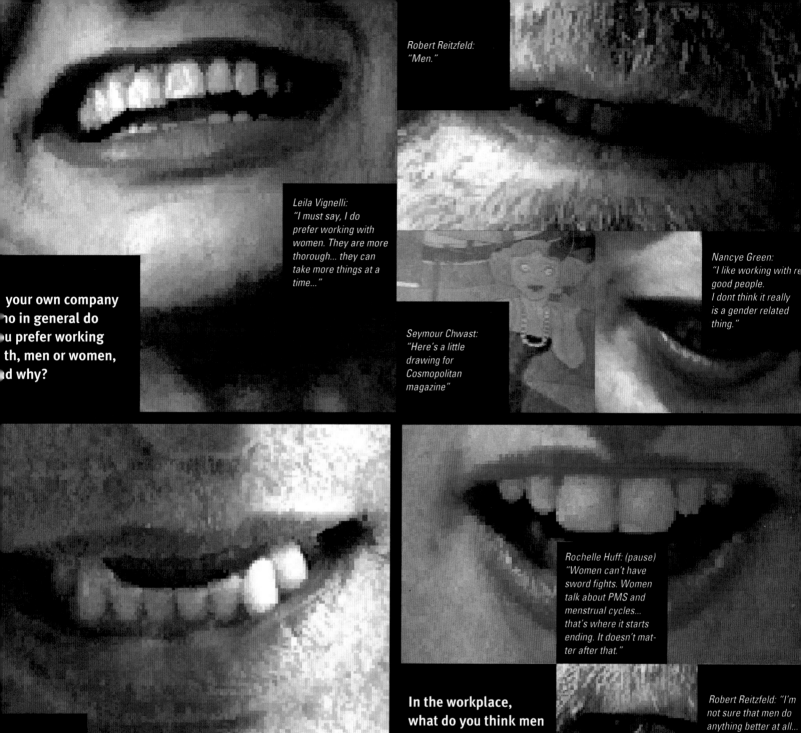
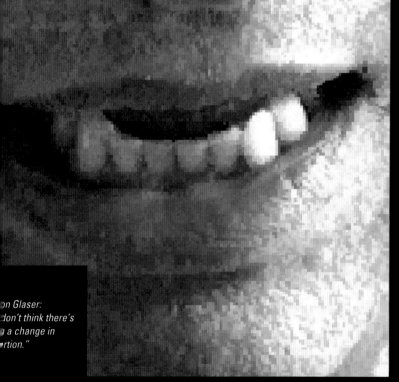
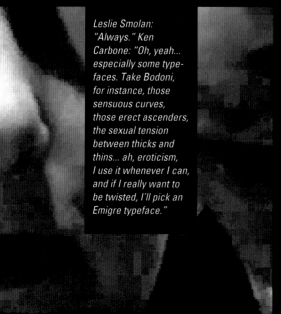
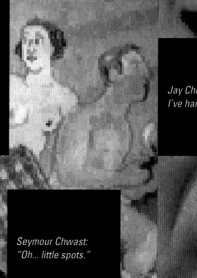

Robert Reitzfeld:
"Men."

Leila Vignelli:
"I must say, I do prefer working with women. They are more thorough... they can take more things at a time..."

Nancye Green:
"I like working with re good people. I dont think it really is a gender related thing."

your own company ho in general do u prefer working th, men or women, d why?

Seymour Chwast:
"Here's a little drawing for Cosmopolitan magazine"

Rochelle Huff: (pause)
"Women can't have sword fights. Women talk about PMS and menstrual cycles... that's where it starts ending. It doesn't matter after that."

In the workplace, what do you think men do better than women? And what do you think women do better than men?

Robert Reitzfeld: "I'm not sure that men do anything better at all... in fact quite the revers is true."

on Glaser:
don't think there's a change in rtion."

Leslie Smolan:
"Always." Ken Carbone: "Oh, yeah... especially some type-faces. Take Bodoni, for instance, those sensuous curves, those erect ascenders, the sexual tension between thicks and thins... ah, eroticism, I use it whenever I can, and if I really want to be twisted, I'll pick an Emigre typeface."

If you have an employee that you are attracted to, how do you handle it?

Jay Chiat: "Lately, I've handled it well."

Aubrey Balkind: "It's a difficult question..."

Seymour Chwast:
"Oh... little spots."

by
Eric Smith

Whenever I'm asked what I do for a living, I always get this lump in my throat. Not that I am embarrassed about what I do, but it's more of a fear of labeling myself with a title that restricts rather than expands my perception of my career pursuits. In a nutshell: I design, sell, and market socks and tights. But the job requires a closet full of different "hats" that I need wear to accomplish this. Yes, I own as well as administer the financial and operational aspects of a small business. But I hate calling myself "President." It makes me feel so constricted, like I should be wearing a tie. So, I opened my thesaurus for some input and my business card now says: "Top Banana."

But still, it is impossible to define the creative work I do in one word. Sure, it would be easy to just call myself a "designer," but that was not my training in school. Like a good Jewish boy from Long Island, I went to law school, not design school—attempting to avoid the family business of selling tube socks to the mass market. But socks just seemed to be in my jeans/genes! So, after I passed the bar exam I incorporated my business and opened EG SMITH Socks.

I can't draw or sketch, but I do have an eye for things. I see ideas for products and I have concepts for packaging and marketing. I have a good sense of style and color, but please don't call me a designer. Still... what do I call myself: Attorney at Socks? I need some help on this one!

I have always felt that my right brain and left brain were both of equal capabilities. However, although I mastered the operational aspects of running a business, the reasons for my company's success lay more in the creative side. And I envy the creative talent of those

What

who have the natural gift to realize their vision with their own hands. I guess I'm an artist who lacks the skills of a painter, graphic designer or photographer. So, when I went into the fashion business, I worked closely with creative artists to help me develop, visualize and execute product, packaging and marketing.

Sometimes this simply requires hiring an artist to sketch a definite design I have in mind for a sock, such as rendering a Vasarely-style optical pattern; or graphing the MONA LISA for our Art Gallery Sock Collection. Other times I collaborate with illustrators, photographers and graphic designers to help explore and ultimately execute ideas for sales brochures or new packaging concepts. I guess this makes me an "Art Director."

A sock, is a sock, is a sock.....or is it? And for the last 13 years I have looked at this ordinary and mundane item of clothing and attempted to knit it, package it, display it, image it, promote it, advertise it and sell it. Being in a "creative business," especially where a product is produced, requires the collaboration from other specialists at every level: From working with a machine technician capable of executing a complex design to working with corporate clients who execute the day to day business operations.

While the 1980's were all about the self-made entrepreneur, the 1990's seemed to require a new way of doing business. Doing everything on my own no longer seemed to work. The more successful my business became, the more time I had to devote its operations. Eventually I had to acknowledge my limitations in being CEO to make time for the creative role that both drove the business and made me happy.

So, in 1990 I decided to search for a "Partner." Not being successful at finding the knight-on-the-white-horse type, I sought partnership in the form of another corporation through licensing. Licensing seemed to make sense: find a company that has the financial resources and the experienced internal operational structure, but lacks in the creative vision and direction that EG SMITH has to offer. Licensing would create the opportunity for me to "rent" my name and ideas to a company in return for a percentage of sales.

In theory, this licensing partnership is a dream come true. I could become a design studio, solely focusing my energies and resources on developing new and innovative products, packaging to enhance the products, and even an advertising budget to expand the product's personality to a wider audience — all without the day-to-day headaches and responsibilities of owning inventory, managing a sales force and office staff.

Twice I tried licensing as the solution to my personal and business needs for a collaborative partnership. Twice I got my business back after a short period of time. So what went wrong? In short... a lack of synergy between the "Partners." These two failed experiences through licensing, however, taught me that it is not productive to hand over a business to "strangers" who are disconnected from the brand's personality: We spoke two different languages. Therefore, when it came time to make decisions requiring investments in product, packaging and promotions, they didn't understand each other. Inhibited communication resulted in the ultimate "watering down" of the brand's personality. So much of what made my business successful in the 1980's

(before licensing) was a combination of new ideas in product, packaged and promoted in unconventional ways combined with the stability and predictability of running the day-to-day operations. As separate as these two factors appeared, its interdependent balance was a key factor to its success.

I learned that it is critical to be true to your vision, as well as work with people who support and inspire that vision. Money doesn't buy that. "Success" comes when you have an idea and you work with others who create the vision on every level. After all, isn't success measured, ultimately, when what you intended to create is understood and acknowledged by the viewer?

My licensing ventures have ended and I have my business back: presidential duties, inventory, office, staff and all. I am glad, once again, to be able to work freely with people who easily understand, believe, and expand the vision for my company as I do. And as new people come into different areas of expanding that vision, the "synergy" of thinking is the first thing that I look for.

There is no textbook formula for "success." Listen to the voice inside that speaks your own truth. Then look around and listen to those that share your truth. Labels are for canned products, not for evolving human beings. But, for those who do need to label me, you'll find a Top Banana: President, Lawyer, Designer, Art Director, Performer... and even Psock-ologist.

Eric Smith owns EG Smith in New York.

Am I?

"The rev-x wheel's sophisticated design and proven performance created excellent market exposure and dealer awareness. The rev-x wheel proves that good design is good business."

Martin Connolly, CEO, Spinergy, Inc.

CSD Team, from left to right:
Jeff Breidenbach, Designer;
Robin Perkins, Principal;
Clifford Selbert, President.
Photo: Anton Grassl

Spinergy, a sports and fitness technology firm based in Wilton, Connecticut, was founded in 1990 by entrepreneurs Martin Connolly, Ted Kutrumbos and engineer Raphael Schlanger. Its **rev-x** wheel has been used in top bicycling competitions and has scored numerous wins for world-renowned racers. Both company and wheel have won an array of design industry awards including: a Silver Industrial Design Excellence Award (IDEA), a New American Logo award for **rev-x** and an American Corporate Identity Competition award for Spinergy. The **rev-x** wheel graphics were also featured in Communication Arts 1994 Design Annual, and the HOW Magazine International Annual of Design. The success of both the company and its **rev-x** wheel has come from the combination of cutting-edge product and identity design.

Clifford Selbert Design Collaborative (CSD) is a multidisciplinary design firm specializing in strategic corporate identity design, print and environmental communications design, product and package design, environmental design, and multimedia production. Among its many clients, CSD has recently developed identity programs for the National Park Service, Stream International, Stride Rite and the World Cup '94 USA Games.

▼ CSD's innovative **rev-x** product packaging boldly promotes the wheel, protects against damage during shipping, provides an attractive presentation for in-store storage and is simple and economical to manufacture.

Clifford Selbert Design Collaborative
2067 Massachusetts Avenue
Cambridge, MA 02140
617/497-6605
FAX 617/661-5772

2016 Broadway
Santa Monica, CA 90404
310/453-1093
FAX 310/453-9491

Photography by Gregory Wostrel, except where noted.

Reprinted from
Design In Depth.
Printed in Hong Kong.

Designer and Client:
Clifford Selbert Design Collaborative
for Spinergy, Inc.

Spinergy

◀ *Examining the product and the intended message, CSD named the wheel **rev-x** and designed its identity to evoke the revolutionary and distinctive x-shaped spoke structure.*

▲ *CSD designed a series of advertisements that targeted bicycling enthusiasts. The ongoing campaign has been placed in internationally-distributed bicycling magazines and has had a tremendous response.*

◀ *CSD effectively targeted Spinergy's market in **rev-x** promotional literature. Testimonials from competitors and enthusiasts were combined with clearly designed technical and performance information. These promotions built strong customer and media interest in Spinergy and **rev-x**.*

This revolutionary sports and fitness technology company hit the road running with an innovative identity program designed by Clifford Selbert Design Collaborative.

Three entrepreneurs, Martin Connolly, Ted Kutrumbos, and Raphael Schlanger, had a vision — using innovative design, engineering and materials from the aerospace industry, they set out to make the fastest, strongest and most aerodynamic wheel on the market. But they had no name or identity for their company and product. They knew that a strong identity and distinctive graphics would connect them with their target market — the world's best competitive racers and bicycle enthusiasts. They turned to CSD, a multidisciplinary design firm specializing in strategic corporate identity design.

The project presented CSD with the opportunity to develop a comprehensive graphic identity — to completely define both company and product. Connolly, CEO, and Kutrumbos, VP of Marketing, wanted to develop strong brand recognition that would help their company become an industry leader. Understanding the target market, CSD had to create an identity that was sophisticated, elegant, hi-tech and cutting edge.

Since their introduction, Spinergy and the **rev-x** wheel have been great successes. For CSD, this meant designing more product literature, print advertising, apparel, product packaging and a promotional video. The project exemplifies the power of strategic corporate identity design and the advantages of unified multidisciplinary design services.

140

▲ CSD designed the **rev-x** owners manual to complement the campaign and to stand alone as a technical data piece. Campaign graphics were fused with product blueprints. The blueprints simplified instructions, while the simple blueprint color scheme made for inexpensive printing.

▼ CSD launched Spinergy and **rev-x** with a distinctive bi-fold direct-mail piece. When folded, its bold graphics focus on the company. Inside, its simple color and copy explain the new company and its new technology. Unfolded, more dramatic color and exaggerated logos introduce **rev-x** with specs and initial test results. It was an easy and cost-effective direct-mail solution.

Photography by Gregory Wostrel, except where noted.

Spinergy utilized CSD's ▶
multidisciplinary design
services in developing the
rev-x promotional video.
"Our vision was successfully
adapted to this exciting
medium," says Robin Perkins,
CSD Principal. "We evoked
our initial concepts of speed,
sophistication and a cutting-
edge attitude through exaggerated angles, bold graphics
and fast-cut editing."

▲ During the early brain-
storming meetings,
CSD noticed that the words
"spin," "energy" and
"motion" kept appearing.
Out of these discussions
came the company name,
Spinergy, Inc., and its
logo which features an
attenuated "S" seemingly
in motion.

▲ The x-rated campaign was
targeted at Spinergy **rev-x**
dealers. Those who offered
customers test rides on **rev-x**
wheels were designated
official x-rated dealers. The
promotion was launched with
an oversized brochure that
featured a centerfold which
doubled as a poster.

▼ CSD designed a full range
of product collateral
which included the **rev-x**
wheel bag, Spinergy and
rev-x merchandise,
and a trade show booth
featured at the International
Cycling Show.

> **"Monterrey Tech University's 50th anniversary celebration was multipurpose: To celebrate the university's illustrious past, to promote and market the university and to showcase the university's vision of the future. The Hill Group's design and applications fulfilled the university's objectives for the anniversary celebration. A complex problem was solved simply."**
>
> Enrique Silva, Director of
> Promotions and Communications
> Monterrey Tech University

Reprinted from
Design In Depth.
Printed in Hong Kong.

From left to right: (back row) Jeff Davis, Meredith Nordquist, Tom Berno, (front row) Lisa Butler, Chris Hill, Laura Menegaz.

Monterrey Tech University was seeking an American designer to work with them in creating a new image for the school through the design and production of exciting, up-to-date promotional and recruitment materials. They saw the Hill Group's work in several design annuals and contacted them. Because they already had several clients in Mexico, the Hill Group was able to reassure the university that they understood their culture and their marketing needs. They have worked with the university on its various marketing and recruitment programs for the last five years.

For the Hill Group, working with foreign clients is no different than working with American clients once you understand and appreciate the cultural differences. Each client has an image it wants to project—a message they want to get across. Communicators and problem solvers, the Hill Group finds creative solutions to match each client's unique needs.

Hill, A Marketing Design Group
Chris Hill, Principal
3512 Lake Street
Houston, TX 77098
713/523-7363

▲ *Monterrey Tech University, a leader in the development of advanced technology in Mexico, is located on a metropolitan campus in the north central state of Nuevo Laredo.*

◀ *Illustrator Linda Bleck created an updated version of Monterrey Tech University's centerpiece mural to represent the university's current areas of study and campus landmarks.*

Designer and Client:
Chris Hill, principal of Hill/
A Marketing Design Group,
for Monterrey Tech University

50th Anniversary of Monterrey Tech University

◀ One of the most important parts of the 50th Anniversary materials was a leatherbound program holder given to dignitaries and special guests.

It was important to embody cultural references to art and literature in the celebration of the anniversary of this great university. Hill Design Group looked for images that would show an appreciation of the past while looking to the future.

In the center of this metropolitan campus, where the 50th anniversary celebration was held, is a giant mural created for the original dedication of the University in 1943. Symbolic of Mexico's heritage, the mural depicts the courageous and powerful vision of Mexico's future of half a century before. Hill Design Group worked with illustrator Linda Bleck to reinterpret this work of art to reflect a new vision. Thus this art became the centerpiece of the anniversary.

Don Quixote was also chosen to represent the spirit of the people of Mexico because the Spanish author Miguel de Cervantes is greatly admired and loved throughout Mexico.

*Color-coded name tags ▶
served as a convenient way
of controlling access to
restricted events.*

◀ *An illustrated book of
quotes from Don Quixote
was given to dignitaries and
special guests. Illustrations
are by Jack Unruh of Texas.*

ROGRAMA PARA

ALUMNOS

DE CAMPUS

DE ZONA

ANIVERSARIO

DEL ITESM

1943·1993

ROGRA

DIRECTIVOS

PROFESORES

DE LOS CAMPUS

MONTERREY

Y EUGEN

GARZ

NOS

MPUS

RREY

GENIO

ZA SADA

ANIVERSARIO

DEL ITESM

1943·1993

CINCU

▲ A paper program holder
was given to all attendees.
The holder contained one
of six color-coded programs,
a fold-out campus map
and a note pad.

◀ Linda Bleck's illustration
was printed in a variety of
colors on the invitations to
various events.

Above: Louise Fili, principal,
Louise Fili Ltd.

Reprinted from
Design In Depth.
Printed in Hong Kong.

Louise Fili Ltd.
71 Fifth Avenue
New York, NY 10003
212/989-9153

◀ *Book jacket for* The Lover,
the bestselling novel by
Marguerite Duras.

Designer and Client:
Self-promotion for
Louise Fili Ltd.

Louise Fili Ltd. Promotional Booklet

*Front of the book jacket, ▼
printed on Fabriano
Roma stock, in letterpress,
with tip-on.*

When faced with the problem of how to promote her design office, Louise Fili capitalized on her celebrity. Known as a designer of thousands of book jackets for Pantheon Books (where she was an art director for eleven years) and other publishers, she did not want to be pigeon-holed in that discipline. So Fili decided to create a limited edition book that combined her award-winning book jackets with new work, including posters, logos, package and label design and restaurant identities.

The miniature book was the perfect vehicle for it did not merely show off her samples, it was itself a splendid example of design and ingenuity. What's more, it was done primarily in letterpress which, in this era of digitalization, has its own special allure. Fili had all the pages, including the separate jacket, printed in hot metal type by a small letterpress printer in Massachusetts. All the color illustrations were printed offset at another printer in Illinois. The color proofs were then meticulously cut and hand-tipped on to the letterpress pages by interns at Fili's studio. It has been an arduous and time consuming process, with each book taking a long time to print and assemble. "The printer delivers about ten copies a month," says Fili, who numbers each one before sending them to prospective clients.

Yet for Fili, ten promotion pieces a month is enough. "I know exactly the kind of work I do best," she says. "My audience is naturally quite limited, and that's fine with me."

Modernism & Eclecticism ▶
poster for the School of
Visual Arts. Double
page tip-on.

A HISTORY OF AMERICAN GRAPHIC DESIGN NUM

MODERN
ECLECT

SATURDAY, FEBRUARY 22ND & SUNDAY, FEBRUARY

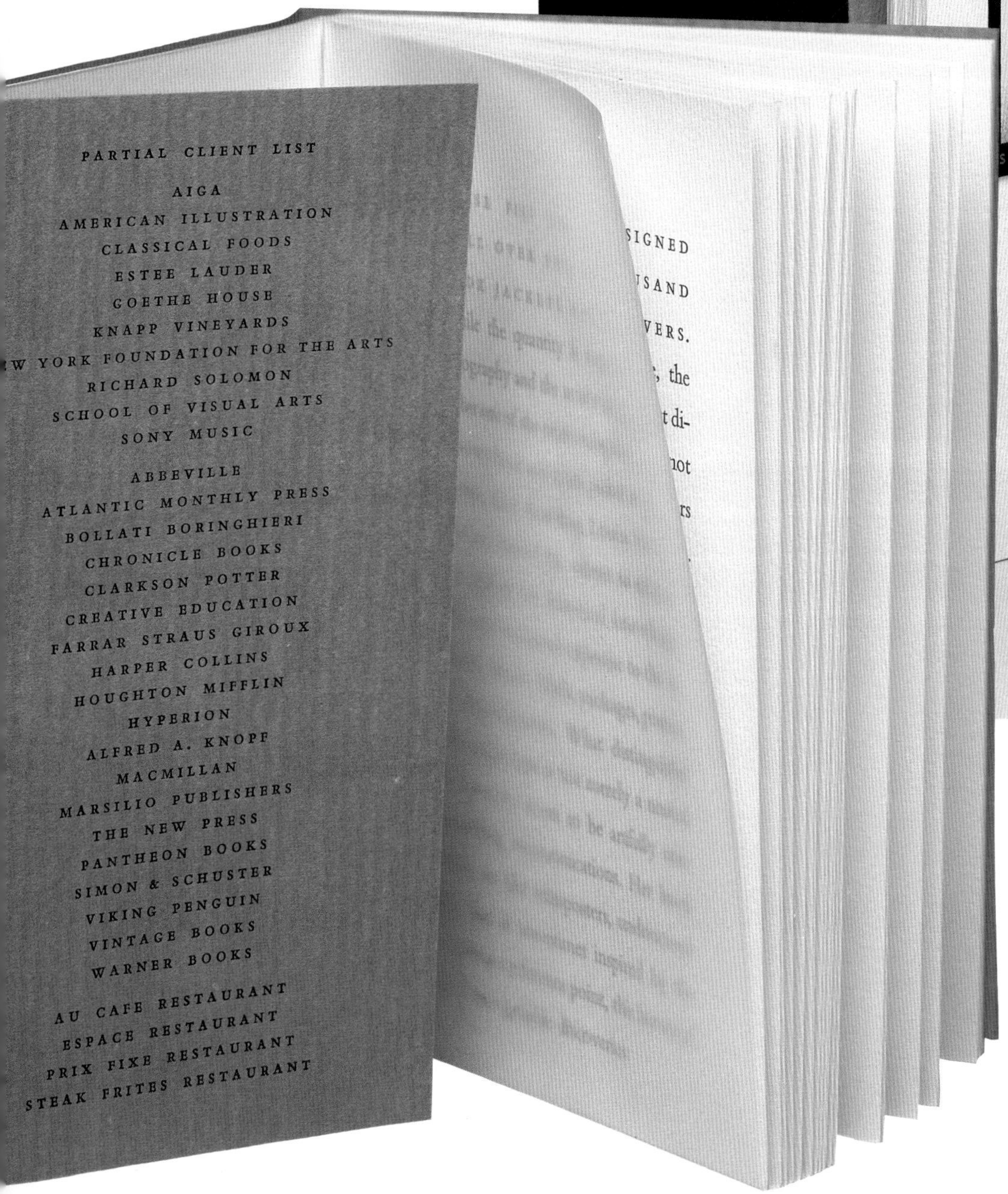

PARTIAL CLIENT LIST

AIGA
AMERICAN ILLUSTRATION
CLASSICAL FOODS
ESTEE LAUDER
GOETHE HOUSE
KNAPP VINEYARDS
NEW YORK FOUNDATION FOR THE ARTS
RICHARD SOLOMON
SCHOOL OF VISUAL ARTS
SONY MUSIC

ABBEVILLE
ATLANTIC MONTHLY PRESS
BOLLATI BORINGHIERI
CHRONICLE BOOKS
CLARKSON POTTER
CREATIVE EDUCATION
FARRAR STRAUS GIROUX
HARPER COLLINS
HOUGHTON MIFFLIN
HYPERION
ALFRED A. KNOPF
MACMILLAN
MARSILIO PUBLISHERS
THE NEW PRESS
PANTHEON BOOKS
SIMON & SCHUSTER
VIKING PENGUIN
VINTAGE BOOKS
WARNER BOOKS

AU CAFE RESTAURANT
ESPACE RESTAURANT
PRIX FIXE RESTAURANT
STEAK FRITES RESTAURANT

▲ Inside flap (showing
partial client list)
with vellum flyleaf.

▼ *Messinia Olive Oil
package design for
Classical Foods, Inc.*

THE SCHOOL OF VISUAL ARTS

SM&
CISM

AT THE LOEWS SUMMIT HOTEL

MESSINIA

EXTRA
VIRGIN
OLIVE OIL

MESSINIA OLIVE OIL, CLASSICAL FOODS
ILLUSTRATOR: MELANIE PARKS

RICHARD
SOLOMON

PROMOTIONAL BOOKLET, RICHARD SOLOMON,
FRONT AND INSIDE COVER

◄ *Front cover and inside page
of a promotional book for
Richard Solomon, an artist's
representative. The red eyes
of the front cover turn to the
O's in the client's name when
the book is opened.*

66HADW got to the soul of Starbucks Coffee Company and produced a packaging design that was an emotional fit.99
Derrick Chasan, Starbucks
Vice President of Brand Marketing

Reprinted from
Design In Depth.
Printed in Hong Kong.

The "7-1/2-minute ▶ display" depicts Starbucks' French press coffee making process and merchandises its products.

From left to right:
Jack Anderson, HADW,
Derrick Chasan, Starbucks

HADW believes that at the heart of every great design is a partnership relationship with the client, a solid understanding of the client's business and an unwavering commitment to the relationship's success. The firm's history with Starbucks Coffee Company is an excellent example of this philosophy in action.

Beginning with the creation of a bean bag for Starbucks' array of coffee blends, HADW's work has extended to include the merchandising and imaging of the company throughout its packaging, mail order catalogs, annual reports, collateral materials, truck graphics and in-house corporate facilities display. HADW created the image now recognized as Starbucks, and the look continually evolves as new applications are developed and the need for freshness and creativity continues.

Hornall Anderson Design Works, Inc.
1008 Western
6th Floor
Seattle, WA 98104
206/467-5800

◀ A whimsical pattern and the Starbucks logo create a rich background texture for the granola packaging.

Starbucks Coffee

Designer and Client:
Hornall Anderson Design
Works for Starbucks Coffee
Company

▼ *Starbucks' new identity was developed by incorporating the company's existing logo with a new graphic kit-of-parts: an intimate illustration style, steam patterns, a warm organic color palette and recycled materials.*

In a company culture where "everything matters," one of the contributing elements credited for Starbucks' popular appeal is the graphic image created by Hornall Anderson Design Works (HADW). The design solution is a direct reflection of who Starbucks is. The artistic use of elements from within the coffee industry presents a rich, warm, coffeehouse image. The look captures the company culture and visually projects Starbucks' commitment to high quality products, premium service, environmental sensitivity and long-term value for its people and customers.

The graphics encourage Starbucks' customers to learn about its bean-to-cup story and support the company's leadership position as the coffee experts. Maintaining a leadership role allows Starbucks to educate consumers on coffee classifications and what goes into making an excellent cup of coffee. This information clarifies the company's point of difference and increases the customers' appreciation of Starbucks' commitment to quality. Together, this strategy and the graphics created by HADW position Starbucks as premium in an otherwise commodity category.

Starbucks Coffee

▼ *Leveraging the Starbucks image, a new and distinct brand personality evolved for Mazagran sparkling coffee. Program components include a proprietary bottle shape and merchandising graphics.*

Delivery trucks were ▶ *given a new identity to reinforce Starbucks' presence in the cities it serves.*

◀ *Mail order catalogs bring the store experience to customers. Covers alternate between natural Kraft and color for differentiation and freshness.*

The third annual report highlighted in-store photographs to satisfy requests from investors who had never seen a Starbucks store.

Starbucks' packaging consists of a distinct family of colors, images, typestyles and materials. The combination of these elements varies from application to application, but the branded look remains consistent.

The initial direction for American Crew incorporated a substantial amount of photography to help build the image of the brand. After establishing the balance between product and image-oriented photography, rough layouts for the book were sketched on tissue.

❝We accomplished the unexpected. Usually it takes two to three years to get coast-to-coast distribution. With these marketing tools American Crew achieved that goal in six months.❞

**David Raccuglia,
American Crew**

American Crew is a manufacturer and marketer of salon hair care products for men. The company was founded in 1992 by hair stylist David Raccuglia after spending several years developing exclusive product formulas. With first-hand knowledge of the salon industry, he had a strong sense of the qualities that his products needed to possess as well as how the brand should be marketed. Liska and Associates' role was to make the American Crew identity visible, reflecting the brand's unique character through all of its communication materials.

Liska and Associates, Inc.
676 North Saint Clair
Suite 1550
Chicago, IL 60611
312/943-4600

526 West 26th Street
Suite 604
New York, NY 10001
212/627-3200

Reprinted from
Design In Depth.
Printed in Hong Kong.

The primary marketing tool ▶ created for American Crew— a coffee table-style book— is unique for the salon industry in its subtle approach to product promotion

American Crew

Designer and Client:
Liska and Associates, Inc.
for American Crew

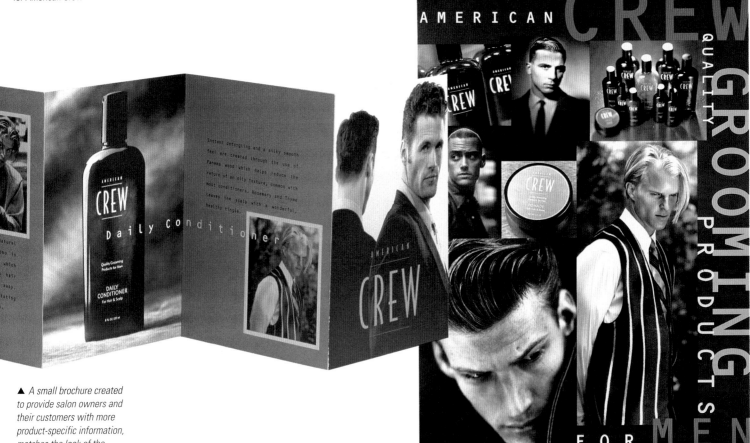

▼ *Realizing that many hair salons—even those with a substantial male client base—project a predominantly female image, Liska and Associates created in-store marketing materials featuring men.*

▲ *A small brochure created to provide salon owners and their customers with more product-specific information, matches the look of the packaging and the book, continuing to reinforce the American Crew image.*

Traditionally, women have gone to salons and men have gone to barber shops. The sexes have different hair care needs requiring different services and products. In the 1970s, when unisex became the vogue, salons began to service both men and women, and have continued to do so today. But the hair care products available in professional salons still only reflect the preferences and needs of their female clientele.

David Raccuglia, founder of American Crew, Inc., created a high-end line of grooming products specifically designed for men. Liska and Associates, Inc. was chosen to develop an image of American Crew which communicated the brand's character, favoring quality and utilitarian traits over sheer fashion. Additionally, a cohesive image needed to be established among the various marketing and promotional materials which would gain the interest and loyalty of male salon customers.

◄ Design is used as a core part of American Crew's marketing strategy, not only to draw attention and reinforce the stature of the products, but also to reflect positively on the salons which carry them.

◄ ▲ Black and white photography is a significant design element in the 40-page American Crew book. It is used somewhat abstractly to communicate a visual story about the brand as well as to connect imagery with the American Crew products. The book was edited from over 500 photographs by Mark Havriliak of New York.

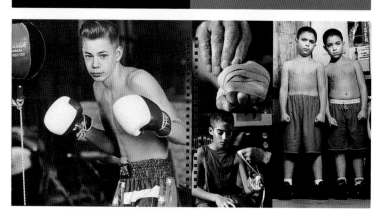

◀ *Budget and quality were important issues during the conceptual stage of the American Crew book. Consideration was given to finding an approach that would maintain high-quality production standards within the limited budget of a start-up business.*

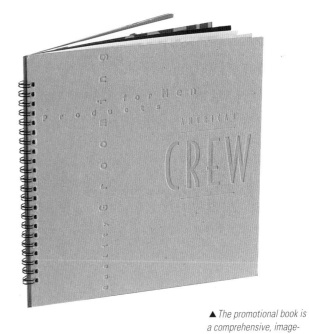

▲ *The promotional book is a comprehensive, image-building tool intended to capture the interest of visually-sophisticated salon owners and customers alike.*

◀ *Different approaches for a point-of-purchase display were explored, with an emphasis on visual appeal and cost-efficient production.*

> **"Earl's solution brought a message of the spirit and personality we had become known for in our books. It was eclectic, visual and exciting—definitely not what one normally sees."**
>
> Michael Carabetta, Chronicle Books

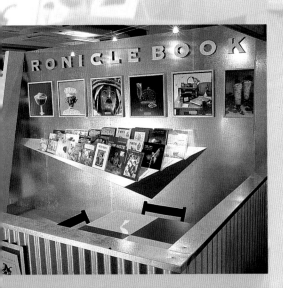

Earl Gee met Michael Carabetta when Gee was a designer at Landor Associates in San Francisco. Gee went out on his own to form Earl Gee Design in 1990 and Carabetta later became the Design Director of Chronicle Books, San Francisco, one of the most respected publishers of trade and general audience books in the country. Of their collaboration, Carabetta credits Gee with creating "an environment that people really wanted to spend time in, circulating and examining books. The unusual architectural features made people want to see what it was all about." Earl Gee Design, a firm of five, was founded in 1990. Other contributors to the project were Barr Exhibits, fabrication, and Andy Caulfield, photography.

Earl Gee
Designer, Earl Gee Design

Earl Gee Design
Earl Gee, Principal
38 Bryant Street, Suite 100
San Francisco, CA 94105
415/543-1192

In contrast to the horizontal ▲ rows of shelving of typical bookselling booths, the Chronicle booth features pockets of interest: different areas for different functions. Visitors can bounce off one area of interest to another but still stay in the booth, as opposed to walking right through, as is common with cross-aisle designs. Small pockets of interest, such as the two pictured, serve as conference areas with seating for two to six people.

Reprinted from
Design In Depth.
Printed in Hong Kong.

Chronicle Books Tradeshow

▼ Chronicle's corporate logo—a pair of reading glasses—is utilized as an oversize three-dimensional icon inviting visitors to "take a look" at Chronicle Books, a company that "sees things differently."

One of the reasons industry veteran Michael Carabetta of Chronicle Books selected Earl Gee as the designer of their American Booksellers Association exhibition was because Gee had never designed an ABA booth before, nor attended an ABA Show. Gee says, "I was armed with a powerful tool — ignorance." Once briefed on the objectives of the project, Gee saw the exhibit environment as a unique opportunity for Chronicle. Gee redefined the problem saying, "Rather than seeing the problem as the design of a trade show exhibition, I created an innovative way to display books. By using strong metaphors for growth, upward progression and attainment — a gear, a ladder and a staircase, each display fixture said something about the company while functioning as a unique display environment. " The muted shades of galvanized steel and natural wood allowed the books to take center stage. The results? Chronicle drew far larger crowds to its exhibit and has proceeded to expand its size this year. The effort was a tremendous success for Chronicle, as the ABA is one of the most important tradeshows in the world for the book publishing industry.

VISIT OUR CHILDREN'S BOOK DISPLAY IN BOOTH 1314

This free-standing shelving ▶ unit resembles a standing figure, incorporating the human element into the Chronicle exhibit. It displays a sampling of children's books in an appropriately whimsical manner, while directing exhibit attendees to the Chronicle children's booth in an adjacent hall.

Designer and Client:
Earl Gee, Earl Gee Design for Michael Carabetta, Chronicle Books

Chronicle Books Tradeshow

▼ The exposed-construction wall contains interior-illuminated alcoves which provide a private viewing area for featured titles.

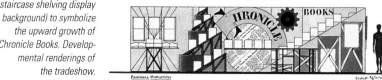

Gee utilizes the massive ▶ staircase shelving display (in background) to symbolize the upward growth of Chronicle Books. Developmental renderings of the tradeshow.

The industrial cog helps to ▲ create an engaging and innovative "machine" for the display of Chronicle's highly-illustrated books.

◀ The oversized ladder serves as a metaphor for Chronicle's growth. Gee's exhibition is expected to last for five to seven more years. Gee says, "We created many built-in storage spaces. The large staircase houses a rear projection unit, while functioning as a storage space for thousands of Chronicle catalogs."

▲ Alternating dark and light grey carpet effectively joins together the two halves of the cross-aisle configuration exhibit.

A rotating gondola ▶ provides a space-efficient and accessible shape to house a large number of backlist titles.

▲ *Romero says, "Sony couldn't give away its posters and premiums to teenage boys. Now they steal the banners. This thrills Sony. We've since created a line of products for Sony Autosound from T-shirts to bum bags."*

From left to right:
The design team for Autosound
(Javier Romero, far left,
not pictured, Marty Homlish)

Marty Homlish, now Senior Vice President of Audio Products at Sony, selected Romero after interviewing several firms. Romero recalls, "Marty knew he had to take a risk in order to break into the teen boys' market, he had to do something daring. While other companies told Marty what he ought to do, I listened to what Marty knew he had to do. Also, when Marty asked who he'd be working with, I told him I would be the designer. Other firms seemed to be planning to delegate the responsibility down."

Today Romero has an office in New York and another in Madrid. He illustrates as well as designs. "I love to illustrate and besides, I feel I have to keep my connection with art." Javier Romero Design Group, Inc., a firm of eight, was founded in 1987.

Javier Romero Design Group, Inc.
Javier Romero, Principal
24 East 23rd Street
Third Floor
New York, NY 10010
212/420-0656

Reprinted from
Design In Depth.
Printed in Hong Kong.

Designer and Client:
Javier Romero, Javier Romero
Design Group, Inc. for Marty
Homlish, Sony Autosound
Division

Sony Autosound

▲ The most recent Autosound tour was entirely contained within this semi truck. This enabled the tour to unfold directly in front of electronic stores that featured Sony systems.

Teenage boys cruise in their sport cars soaking up the coolest sounds on their car stereo system. When Sony realized they were missing out on this segment of the automotive electronics market, they had to find a way to talk to this most elusive and inscrutable market. Added to the complex problem is the intangibility of the product—sound.

Javier Romero was selected by then president of Sony's Mobile Automotive Electronics division, Marty Homlish, to form a team with him to meet this objective.

The result was a traveling show covered in Romero's aggressive, youthful graphic statement, contained in a truck that toured the United States. Teen boys eagerly came to hear the explosive Sony sounds in tents that set and controlled just the right mood. The market turned up for Sony and sales rose dramatically.

Three years later, the Autosound traveling display that Romero designed for Homlish underwent an evolution as younger boys emerged to form Generation X. Romero was called on to respond to this shift in sensibilities and to modify his original design to make

the Autosound look more organic and tactile. The results also included a rethinking of the logistics of the plan and dealt with the cumbersome complexity of setting up and breaking down tents.

Today, the new Sony Autosound truck travels with the Sony Autosound Beach Volleyball Team on the Bud Light tour. The truck literally blossoms, unfolding to become a dynamic display adding to the event. The music fills the air as sales rise dramatically, reportedly upwards of 400 percent.

164

▲ This logo is the updated version for the young, hip Generation X audience and appears on all the touring vehicles like the van below.

◄ Autosound Poster, inviting potential customers to check out the sound quality of Sony car stereo systems. The logo is the earlier version, used before the Generation X logo above

▲ The semi truck would park, open, and spin out to become an all-in-one concert sound stage and product display area.

▲ The initial Autosound tour required considerable space and set-up time, and was more like a small carnival. The second Autosound tour was more efficient for electronics stores that did not have a vast, open field for set-up.

The van, known as the ▶ "Jaminator," was used to demonstrate Autosound products and toured with the truck.

AUTOSOUND TO

Reprinted from
Design In Depth.
Printed in Hong Kong.

From left to right:
David Eyman, principal industrial design, Firehouse Design Team; Stephen N. Joffe, M.D., president, LCA Inc., Laser Centers of America; Sandra Joffe, LCA Inc., Laser Centers of America; Robert Probst, principal graphic design, Firehouse Design Team; Gary Long, vice president technology development, LCA Inc., Laser Centers of America.

Dr. Stephen Joffe is a design-sensitive and environmentally-conscious individual. He, and Gary Long, head of technology development, drew Firehouse Design Team into every aspect of the product development process. A recycling code is etched into all of their plastic parts, and they have a vision to eventually get all discarded handpieces back to recycle them into new tools. Probst and Eyman say, "There are new breakthroughs every three months or so. Dr. Joffe and his partner/wife Sandra Joffe, still present us with new challenges, and we appreciate working with a client of such caliber."

*Firehouse Design Team
2701 Vine Street
Cincinnati, OH 45219
513/221-2295*

66We have great respect for Robert Probst and David Eyman. They're educated, clever and thinking professionals. All these factors helped things get off on the right foot with our relationship.**99**

Sandra Joffe,
Laser Centers of America

▲ *Inner packaging for the Neos handpiece fits into the shipping cartons.*

▼ *Offset posters from a promotional portfolio. "I wanted to create a series of icons that related to the company's philosophy," Robert Probst explained. The laser beam is a hot stamp metallic foil. Each piece was wrapped in mylar which was silkscreened and placed in a linen portfolio.*

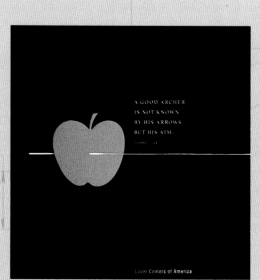

A GOOD ARCHER
IS NOT KNOWN
BY HIS ARROWS
BUT HIS AIM.

Laser Centers of America

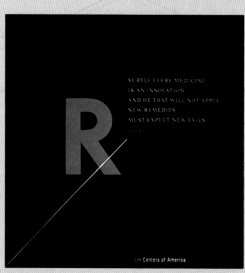

SURELY EVERY MEDICINE
IS AN INNOVATION
AND HE THAT WILL NOT APPLY
NEW REMEDIES
MUST EXPECT NEW EVILS.

Laser Centers of America

HEALING IS
A MATTER OF TIME
BUT IT IS
SOMETIMES ALSO
A MATTER
OF OPPORTUNITY

Laser Centers of America

Laser Centers of America

Designer and Client:
Robert Probst and David
Eyman, Firehouse Design
Team for Dr. Stephen Joffe;
Sandra Joffe; Gary Long,
Laser Centers of America, Inc.

LCA VISION

▲ *The logo and symbol Probst developed for Laser Centers of America.*

▶ *The Contact Laser Scalpel is ergonomically designed to perfectly fit the human hand so that it becomes an extension of it. The scalpel is used in general surgical procedures where it is necessary to activate the button with the index finger.*

Some years ago, Dr. Stephen Joffe, a renowned surgeon who was instrumental in the introduction of lasers to the medical field, shifted his goal to establishing centers for minimally invasive surgical procedures, training and education services at hospitals around the United States. He approached designer Robert Probst to develop promotional materials for his company, Laser Centers of America.

Joffe's Laser Centers expanded rapidly. "We moved to create an identity program for the company which included the naming of products, logotypes, coloring, packaging and finally the design of equipment including contact laser scalpels," Probst says.

Probst and his Firehouse Design Team partner, industrial designer David Eyman, traveled the country visiting hospitals to research equipment and procedures. Eyman says, "We were surprised at the high level of professionalism and also the emotions present in the operating room." The two designers were allowed to be on scene during several operations, standing "right next to the bed," says Probst, who was looking closely at how the doctors held their tools, and studying what sorts of moves the doctors made with them. Probst and Eyman realized that the tools they were seeing demonstrated were not ergonomically designed; they often lacked balance and a comfortable form for the hand to grasp with confidence.

Probst says, "It was clear that they take their responsibilities very seriously, for their actions may be decisions of life and death." Commensurately, the designers emerged from their own experience aware of their responsibilities when designing tools used for such important work.

168

◀ *Symbol developed for Research and Development Divsion of LCA.*

ZOË

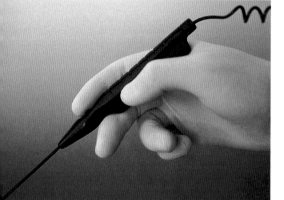

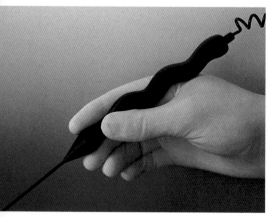

▲ *Form studies from the Contact Laser Scalpel prototype series.*

Shipping cartons for Neos ▶ *products. Labels include icon system to identify content.*

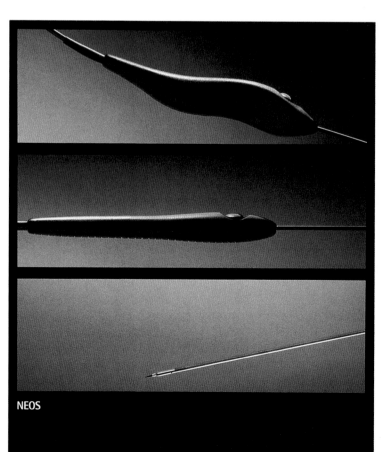

NEOS

◀ *Promotional sales sheet introducing the two selected handpiece shapes for the NEOS Conact Laser Scalpel series.*

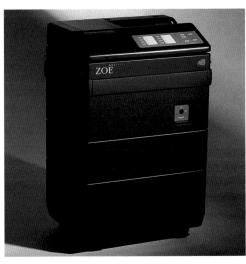

◄ The Zoë Laser, center, flanked by two prototype studies for the next generation Zoë Laser. The prototype on the right has a curved rubber bumper stripe on the front, interface panel in warm beige wood with backlit Information Stripe (black) inserted and stainless steel buttons.

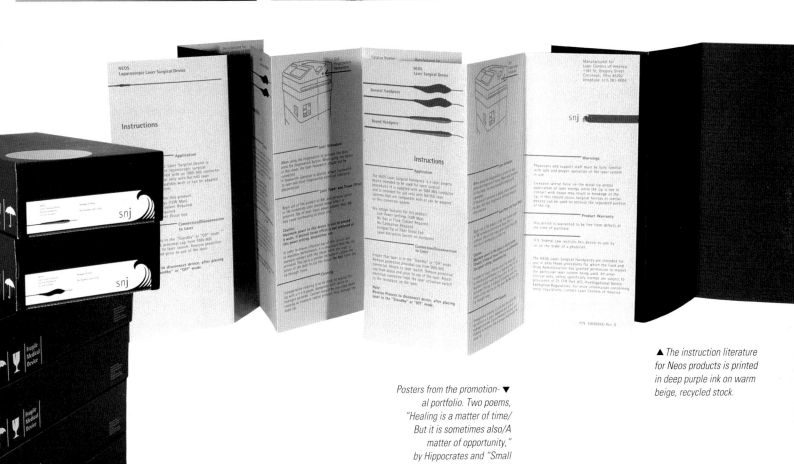

▲ The instruction literature for Neos products is printed in deep purple ink on warm beige, recycled stock.

Posters from the promotion- ▼
al portfolio. Two poems,
"Healing is a matter of time/
But it is sometimes also/A
matter of opportunity,"
by Hippocrates and "Small
opportunities are often/
The beginning of great
enterprises," by Demosthenes,
inspired the direction and
attitude of the posters' design.

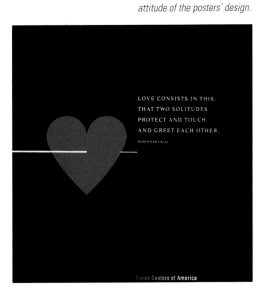

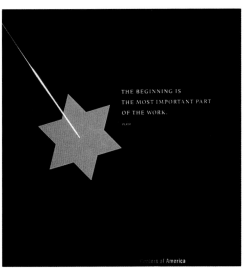

Pentagram, an international design consultancy founded in London in 1972, was originally established by five partners: an architect, a product designer and three graphic designers. Today, there are 15 partners and a total support staff of about 130 in five offices who handle projects for a broad range of national and international clients. Each partner manages his or her own design team and projects but shares financial and administrative staff with others. The goal is to retain the entrepreneurial spirit and creative freedom necessary for producing fresh, original work, while receiving the interdisciplinary support of a larger organization.

Michael Bierut joined Pentagram's New York office as a partner in 1990. He and Pentagram designer Esther Bridavsky worked with Eric Smith and John Boyce from E.G. Smith World Love and a team at Hanes Hosiery headed by Jessica Chereskin and David McBride over the six-month process of creating the work shown here.

Pentagram Design
204 Fifth Avenue
New York, NY 10010
212/683-7000 telephone
212/532-0181 fax

From left to right: Partners Michael Bierut, Michael Gericke, Paula Scher, Peter Harrison, James Biber and Woody Pirtle at Pentagram's New York office. Photo: Ray Charles White

❝With this project, we needed to marry corporate with personalized quirkiness. Pentagram did the impossible.❞

Eric Smith,
E.G. Smith World Love

Reprinted from
Design In Depth.

Designer and client:
Michael Bierut, art
director and Esther
Bridavsky, designer;
Pentagram Design for
E.G. Smith World Love
and Hanes Hosiery

EG Smith

▲ *This mailer announced the
new line to buyers. Through
clever folding, Pentagram
exploited the low-tech,
interactive functionality
of old-fashioned "cootie-
catcher" technology.*

Eric Smith is a successful New York based entrepreneur who had the distinction of being the first sock designer elected to the prestigious Council of Fashion Designers of America. Indeed, Smith's self-described mission when taking over the family tube sock business was to "glamorize the sock," a quest that he has managed to artfully achieve through his company E.G. Smith World Love. Smith micro-manages every conceivable detail of his six-million-dollar-in-sales company from product development to distribution.

Hanes Hosiery approached Smith and suggested a joint venture: Smith would design a new line of socks and bodywear for the twenty-something audience and Hanes would take over the manufacturing and marketing. Then the partners turned to Pentagram to commission an identity for the new brand and extend it to packaging, literature and showrooms.

The challenge was to reconcile two points of view about how the product should be marketed. Smith wanted to communicate with his audience in a private language he had invented exclusively for them; Hanes' goal was to maximize the brand's exposure to the mass market. Pentagram achieved both goals while providing an expansion of Smith's language which enriched the identity development.

EG Smith

◀ *Pentagram satisfied both parties in the Hanes/E.G. Smith partnership by centering the identity on an intricate monogram that was either brash and aggressive or mysterious and hard to read, depending on your point of view.*

172

▲ *Used on packaging including "cigar band" labels and insert cards, the monogram continues Eric Smith's tradition of communicating with his audience in a private language invented exclusively for them, while also maximizing the brand's exposure to a mass market.*

◀ Pentagram also produced this printed catalog and color chart for distribution to buyers.

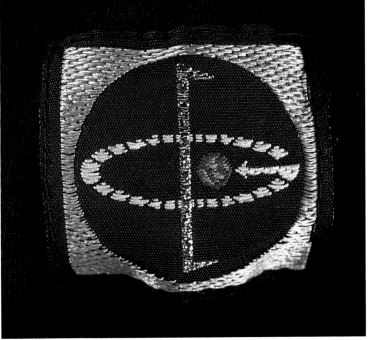

▲ The new monogram used on a woven garment label.

◀ Inexpensive materials like colored paper, photostats and foamcore were used by Pentagram to transform a nondescript showroom at Hanes headquarters in Manhattan into "E.maginationland" for men's fashion week.

"Knowing what it is you really want to do, understanding the problems you're facing and making sure to craft the tool around the job at hand, a solution — not just something clever"
Jim Brouwer
president and founder of CollegeView

Reprinted from
Design In Depth.
Printed in Hong Kong.

CollegeVie

A NETWORK OF DISCOVER

CollegeView, an interactive publishing network, was founded in 1990 in Cincinnati, Ohio. With the high volume of information and complexity of this project, Clement Mok was the natural choice to create CollegeView's new service. Mok, who helped launch and explain Hypercard technology for Apple, was one of the first designers to become immersed in computer technology. He is well-known for his intelligent and highly methodical approach to problem solving both in two dimensions and in the digital world.

Clement Mok designs, Inc.
600 Townsend Street
Penthouse
San Francisco, California 94103
415/703-9900

Clement Mok, Top,
Bottom, **Jim Brouwer**,
president, CollegeView

*Working on several screens ▶
at one time, Mok and his
colleague, designer
Steve Simula, brainstorm
on the content flow of
the prototype design.*

CollegeView

CollegeView

Click anywhere to begin...

▲ *The clean, simple folder (an icon of the Macintosh), adds ordinary tools like pencils and pads as props, and puts the audience at ease. The message is clear: this is organized and not going to be a high-tech-video-game experience. College-View is sophisticated but down to earth.*

Designer and Client:
James R. Brouwer, College-View and Clement Mok of Clement Mok designs, Inc.

Days were, when determining which college was best for your needs required the acquisition of a mass of bewildering books and taking endless campus tours. Computers have made it possible to economize, compact and animate the process. And Clement Mok, the master computer designer, has added good, intuitive design and humor — in short, the human touch. The result is CollegeView, a subscription-based online database system.

Clement Mok designs created four characters to help guide the student, counselor and parent through the maze of information compiled on each school. When a user needs help, they ask a character. Dr. Hartman, for instance, is an imaginary counselor, a some-

what hip and very likeable big brother. He waves on the screen to the computer user and, as the user chooses one of the many categories that can be assessed through an interactive network, walks and talks as they go through the category together. Mok says, "Understanding and breaking down the content allows a designer to create intelligently for each individual situation."

The prototype debuted at the National Association of College Admissions Counselors (NACAC) National Conference in 1993 — at which the guidance counselors and admissions professionals gave CollegeView rave reviews. Dartmouth College and Phillips Exeter Academy are two schools that signed up immediately to be part of the system.

CollegeView had brought the basic concept to Clement Mok, who recognized the potential. He says, "It was obviously a good idea that simply lacked structure." People don't read manuals, so whatever he designed had to be user-friendly to the nth degree. Using the Chromakeying (a.k.a. Blue Screen) technique, Mok and his team created the digital moving characters, blended into the applications, that bring the whole program to life.

◄ *"The dog ate my homework,"
the cliché line from a high
school student, is in this case
true. Murphy, CMd's mascot did
eat Mok's homework.*

Pacing and organization ▶
*were a collaboration between
Mok and Murphy.*

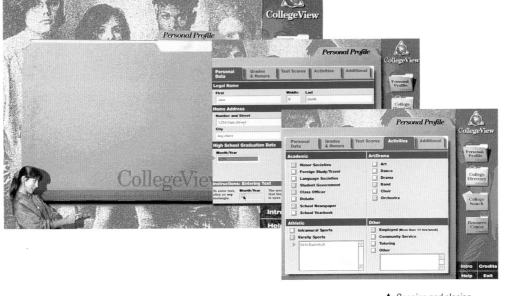

▲ Opening and closing folders allows the viewer to clear their mind of the complex information they have just confronted before going on to another subject. Again, the character in the frame adds human interest and extends the attention span for the viewer.

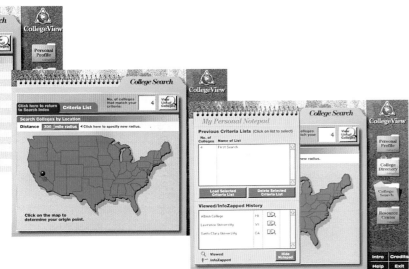

Some of the complex-▶ made-easy folders that Mok created are shown here. Note the characters that peek around corners and appear in front of folders.

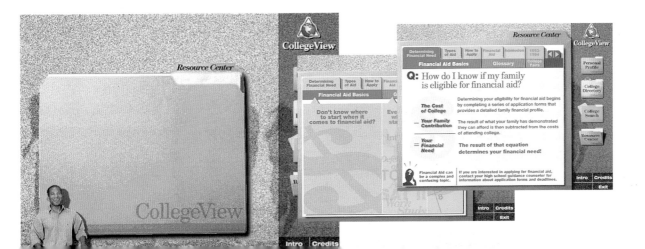

**by
Ellen Lupton**

Graphic design's respectability as a profession is indebted to the rise of the corporate identity in the 1950s. Led by proselytizers like Paul Rand, Lester Beall, and Raymond Loewy and brand-building empires like Landor Associates and Lippincott & Margulies, the builders of corporate image lifted graphic design out of its lowly origins in artistic bohemia and the blue-collar trades. Design became both a science and a service.

Modernist designers rejected the ornamental detail, literal illustrations, and centered typography found in traditional business communications. The printer's vernacular at mid-century can be seen in the work of the William T. Manning Company, a Connecticut photoengraver that produced stationery for businesses across the country. Between 1940 and 1965, in-house designer Joel Anderson created meticulous renditions of factories, corporate headquarters, and industrial equipment that exploited the ability of the photoengraving process to reproduce minutely-detailed photographs on soft bond paper. [figures 1 and 2]

The new science of corporate identity rejected such literal representations in favor of the consistent use of bold, direct symbols and logotypes, applied in a rigorously controlled manner to objects and environments large and small. The grandest ambition of design for corporate identity was to encompass an entire architectural setting with a coordinated language of colors, materials, symbols and typography. The corporate headquarters of companies like IBM and Westinghouse — designed by Rand and architect Eliot Noyes — became landmarks in the culture of business, symbols for the sophistication and stability of the management community, as well as for the professionalization of the design field.

Several identity programs designed by Chermayeff & Geismar Associates in the early 1960s maintain their essential elements today. The firm's logotype for Mobil, typeset in blue with a round red o, is familiar around the world. Even in languages written in non-Roman characters — in Arabic, for example, a flash of red calligraphy still stands out from its blue surroundings. Chermayeff & Geismar Associates had designed the Chase Manhattan bank logo in 1960. Even after the merger of Chase Manhattan and Chemical banks — which yielded one of the nation's largest banking companies — the Chase name and logo was retained to identify the new conglomerate, even though Chemical was the larger and stronger institution.

While such classics of corporate identity are directed largely at the business community, product identities speak to consumers. The logo for Betty Crocker, introduced by Lippincott & Margulies in 1954, uses handwritten letters on a red spoon to invoke the spirit of home cooking in the context of packaged foods. And what would a cake mix be without the box? It would sit there, gray and lifeless in its waxy bag, a mere sack of pre-measured powders. But the crisp, rectilinear package offers an alluring four-color rendition of the cake-to-be. Betty Crocker herself is a fictional personality, embodied at the corporate headquarters in a series of oil paintings that have evolved to reflect changing images of the housewife, who, in her 1965 and 1980 renditions, was permitted to be a little bit sexy as well as sensible. [figures 3 and 4]

fig. 1,2

Andy Warhol tapped into the energy contained in supermarket vernacular when he started making paintings and objects in the late 1950s based on nationally-branded products. He bypassed quaint and folksy forms of packaging — charming fruit-crate labels and cheerful biscuit tins — in favor of blandly-contemporary consumerism. A brand name is often a company's most valuable asset serving to distinguish generic goods such as detergent, toilet paper or peanut butter with the mystical rune of the trademark. A Kraft ad published in 1989 shows its famous red, white and blue package erupting from within a block of cheese. The ad showed how packaging — normally viewed as an external, protective shell for the product wrapped inside — is, in the experienced reality of the marketplace, the driving motor of sales. Any cheese will do, as long as it's Kraft. [figure 5]

The omnipresence of corporate identity has generated a heightened literacy of the eye. To be literate in contemporary culture means not only to know the letters of the alphabet but to recognize a vast range of logos, brand names and product images. This vocabulary of corporate symbols constitutes a "second alphabet," a set of symbols

fig. 3

that we thoroughly internalize, that becomes second nature. When the Walt Disney Corporation bought ABC Television in 1995, the New York Post put mouse ears on Paul Rand's 1962 logo for ABC, creating a visual "sentence" in the alphabet of corporate image. [figure 6] In New York's East Village, the band Lotion has made street posters that recast familiar product identities with the band's own name, meticulously designed by band member Tony Zajkowski in 1992. These posters exploit the use of the vernacular "second alphabet". *[figure 7]*

What is happening at the higher end of design for corporate identity today? I see a move away from the monolithic programs of the 1950s, 60s, and 70s, which sought to clean up the illustrative character of conventional business printing in favor of flatness, abstraction, and a reduction to essential forms. Landor Associates' 1994 redesign of the Federal Express corporate image overturned the tortured, abstracted letterforms the company had used since the early 1970s. Some may dismiss the new design as "non-design," but its genius lies in embracing the phrase "FedEx," a piece of international slang whose clipped, telescopic form is familiar around the world. Landor Associates preserved the equity of the purple and orange color scheme, making the transition to the new design smooth and nearly unnoticeable to the general public.

Recent logos created by Siegel & Gale have introduced depth into the realm of corporate trademark design. For New York's Metropolitan Transit Authority (MTA), the firm created a logo that recedes into space, suggesting a moving train or bus. In 1995 the firm picked a new name for Northern Telecom—NORTEL—and turned the letter o into a "globemark" that, according to a promotional brochure, communicates "strength, dynamism, and global reach." In contrast with the abstractly suggestive sphere designed by Bass & Yager Associates for AT&T in 1984, the NORTEL mark is an overtly figurative reference to a globe, yet it employs a subtle, visually sophisticated vocabulary of arcs and curves that hovers between two-and three-dimensional modes of representation. *[figures 8 and 9]*

A figurative globe also enlivens the graphic identity created by Lippincott & Margulies for Continental Airlines in 1990. The new corporate symbol—a gold and white wire-frame drawing of a globe floating in a deep blue ground—finds its most dramatic setting on the tail of an airplane, where its complexity and dimensionality is an astonishing surprise amongst the drab, dreary, and obsessively "safe" context of most airline identities.

Contemporary graphic designers use the term "vernacular" to refer to popular styles of typography and layout generated outside the profession. As an institution in search of legitimacy, design has long defined itself in opposition to commonplace commercial styles and do-it-yourself printing and publishing. Today, the lines between official and vernacular codes are becoming increasingly blurred. As a corporate identity or product image gains currency throughout the culture, it becomes open to appropriation and reuse. At the same time, the creators of major identity programs are allowing forms of everyday communication—from verbal slang to illustrative icons—to enter into their own languages.

Ellen Lupton is curator of contemporary design at Cooper-Hewitt, National Design Museum, Smithsonian Institution. She is organizer of the book and exhibition Mixing Messages: Graphic Design in Contemporary Culture.

fig. 4

fig. 5

fig. 6

fig. 7

fig. 8

fig. 9

Thoughts on Identity at the Century's End

From left to right: Joël Desgrippes, principal of Desgrippes Gobé-Paris and Marc Gobé, principal of Descrippes Gobé-New York in the firm's New York retail architecture studio.
Photo: Ray Charles White.

❝The Gillette Series is the union of our heritage and our future.❞
Peter Hoffman, Vice President Business Management, The Gillette Company

Desgrippes Gobé & Associates was selected by Gillette to mastermind the design development of a revolutionary new product line, scheduled for simultaneous launch in Europe and the United States. Specifically, Gillette wanted to leverage the success of Sensor, the world's best-selling shaving system, into the larger arena of male grooming. Following a comprehensive audit and analysis of the global market, and with the support of Gillette's in-house engineering team, Desgrippes Gobé developed a set of strategically driven designs that fit Gillette's worldwide leadership position, increasing its brand equity and capitalizing on the company's reputation for quality and innovation.

The design team included: Marc Gobé, Kenneth Hirst, Chris Freas and Tim Robinson. The Gillette team included: Peter Hoffman, Michelle Stacy, Julie Krupa and Pamela Parisi.

Desgrippes Gobé & Associates
411 Lafayette Street
New York, NY 10008
212/979-8900

◀ *Gillette Series packaging incorporates silver, black and grips to recall Gillette's highly successful Sensor razor. Silver plastics were developed to produce an unprecedented "steel" look.*

Reprinted from
Design In Depth.
Printed in Hong Kong.

Gillette Series

Designer and Client:
Desgrippes Gobé &
Associates for The
Gillette Company

▼ *The unique effectiveness of the shaving gel's push-button dispensing system lies in its one-piece actuator shroud that has a bellows appearance. The color blue evokes water and communicates a clean shave.*

At Desgrippes Gobé & Associates, design begins with a unique visual research process called SENSE. An acronym for Sensory Exploration plus Need States Evaluation, SENSE helps identify a product's equities, profiles the customer, analyzes the competition and develops an emotionally charged visual vocabulary that serves as the foundation for the design process.

For the Gillette Series, a line of 14 high-performance toiletry products for men, an analysis of competitive lines in North America and Europe revealed a dichotomy between the two markets. In America men usually buy toiletries individually from different manufacturers. In mass outlets, dated containers and conventional logos compete for the customers attention. In Europe men's toiletries have an elevated status. Often displayed as part of an upscale system, they cater to a man's special needs. The graphics and packaging send a visual message that is more than what a product does. It's how a man feels, acts, carries and conducts himself.

Using SENSE, Desgrippes Gobé & Associates were able to look at the brand's inherent values, the way it interacts with its customers, who those customers are and what role the product plays in their life. An astute assessment set Desgrippes Gobé on the right path. The design of the Gillette Series speaks to men around the world.

Gillette Series

◄ *Structural designs are proportioned to fit a man's hand, whether sleek and cylindrical or ribbed and reminiscent of a man's broad shoulders.*

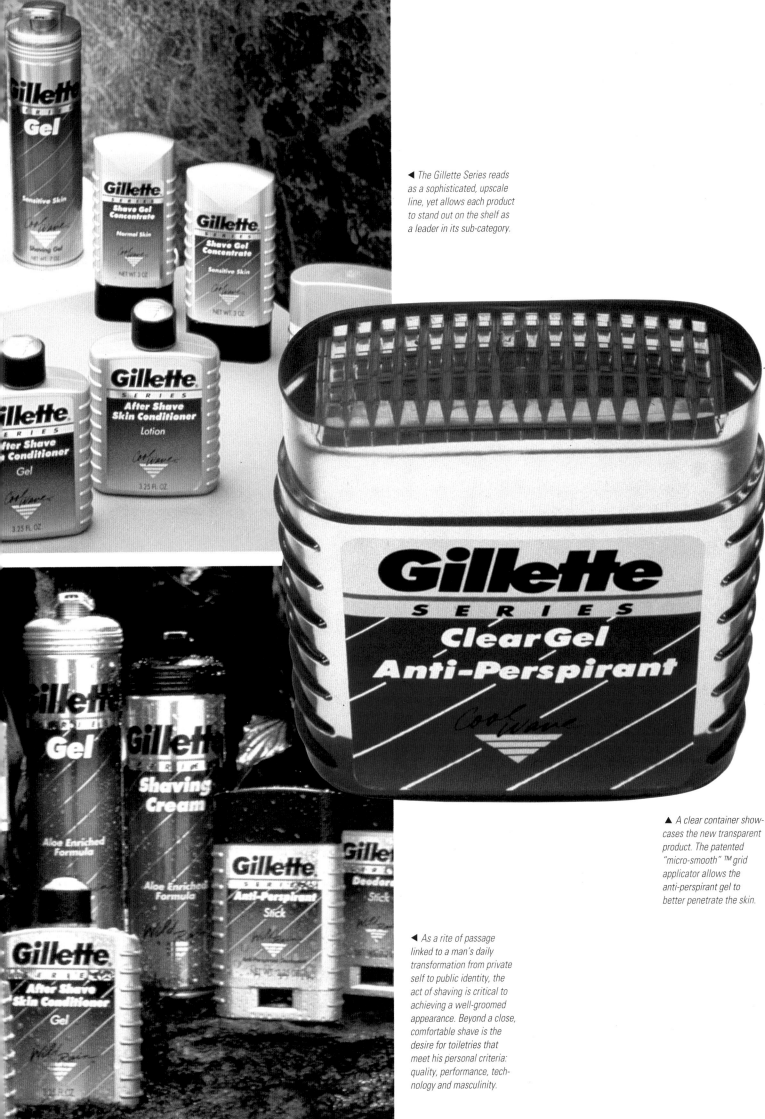

◄ The Gillette Series reads as a sophisticated, upscale line, yet allows each product to stand out on the shelf as a leader in its sub-category.

▲ A clear container showcases the new transparent product. The patented "micro-smooth" ™ grid applicator allows the anti-perspirant gel to better penetrate the skin.

◄ As a rite of passage linked to a man's daily transformation from private self to public identity, the act of shaving is critical to achieving a well-groomed appearance. Beyond a close, comfortable shave is the desire for toiletries that meet his personal criteria: quality, performance, technology and masculinity.

❝The benefits to us aren't just cosmetic. They are tangible and practical. We've leveraged the impact of our brand to its fullest potential.❞

Gayle Christensen,
Managing Director, Corporate Marketing,
FedEx

For more than 50 years, Landor Associates has crafted strategic and creative solutions for a range of identity, image and branding issues. Clay Timon is Chairman, President and CEO of Landor. "Our clients come to us with branding issues of every scope and complexity," says Timon. "With FedEx, we've involved all aspects of our business—consulting, research, naming and design—to create a comprehensive corporate identity program that works for FedEx's global needs."

Landor Associates
1001 Front Street
San Francisco, CA 94111
415/955-1400

Delivering the FedEx Identity

Designer and Client:
Landor Associates for FedEx

According to Clay Timon, ▶ Landor's Chairman and CEO, "The new FedEx identity derives its elegance and power from its simplicity and ability to work globally; to transcend cultural and linguistic barriers."

The company once known as Federal Express by American consumers has become known worldwide simply (and affectionately) as FedEx in 21 short years. Federal Express invented overnight delivery service just as industry was developing facsimile machines, computers and other high-speed conduits. Over the years, competition inevitably developed in the overnight delivery market, and Federal Express faced the need to modernize and streamline its image.

Once Landor Associates was charged with evolving the Federal Express identity, worldwide research and analysis revealed Federal Express possessed strong equities in its familiar name, impeccable reputation and distinctive purple and orange colors. But while customers gave high marks to Federal Express for reliability, speed and service, many were unaware that it delivered to 187 countries, or that it delivered large freight shipments in addition to small packages. Also, some customers associated "Federal" with government, and for many non-English speaking customers "Federal" is difficult to pronounce.

The simplicity of the new FedEx wordmark is testimony to its high visibility. But the older logo stacked the two words Federal and Express, creating a bullet effect which, set on an angle, had a feeling of lift-off. Wanting to retain this sense of speed, Landor connected the d and E, creating an arrow to connote movement.

The world has gotten smaller and commerce more global, so Landor created an important tag line: "The World on Time," as part of the brand identity system. It's a friendly reminder to customers and employees alike that FedEx stands for worldwide reliability and speed.

186

▼ The bold new logo will help FedEx generate more and better brand visibility and awareness. The new identity features letters that stand almost twice the height of those on the old "stacked" logo, making it easier to spot both on vehicles and mail order catalogs, where it is normally allotted only a small amount of space.

The new identity allows ▶ the fuselage of FedEx's planes to be painted white rather than purple. Purple absorbs heat, making the plane's climate control systems work harder to cool the cabin. Under the new identity system, only the tail remains purple, making the planes more fuel efficient and saving FedEx a considerable sum on fuel.

▼ *The FedEx identity can now be consistently and effectively staged across all applications, from planes to trucks to drop boxes.*

Left to right: Mark Anderson and Patrice Eilts-Jobe.

EAT Design was brought in by Gulfstream Aerospace's advertising agency Eidson Speer Watson & Dickerson to help in the development of a strategy and concept for the Gulfstream IV direct mail program. EAT Design ultimately designed, produced and executed the total package of materials. The partners, Patrice Eilts-Jobe and Mark Anderson are award-winning graphic designers with a great deal of experience in corporate and retail communication design and advertising. The project was art directed by Mark Anderson and Patrice Eilts-Jobe; designers were Eilts-Jobe, Anderson and Kevin Swanson; illustration by Michael Weaver and Mark English; writing by Daniel Bucheit.

EAT Design, LLC
Patrice Eilts-Jobe and Mark Anderson, Principals
2 West 39th Street, Suite 204
Kansas City, MO 64111
816/931-2687

Reprinted from
Design In Depth.
Printed in Hong Kong.

▲ Because the direct mail materials needed to be attention-grabbers, "giftable" items were decided upon. Since many companies have policies that gifts not exceed a unit cost of $25, they needed to be inexpensive yet appeal to corporations capable of purchasing a $35 million aircraft. The first mailing was a crystal globe with an etching of the world on its surface. It came packaged in a box showing a map of the world as Columbus knew it.

Designer and Client:
Mark Anderson and Patrice
Eilts-Jobe, EAT Design, for
Eidson Speer Watson &
Dickerson and Gulfstream
Aerospace

New Global Market Discovery

The Gulfstream IV, a $35 million private jet that functions as a flying office, is a tool for opening new global markets. Gulfstream's jets are primarily purchased by foreign heads of state and major corporations as the flagship of their aviation transportation fleet.

A short-term campaign, targeted to CEOs and flight administrators of certain Fortune 500 corporations, was proposed by Gulfstream's agency, Eidson Speer Watson & Dickerson. EAT Design focused on the identity of a romanticized Christopher Columbus, the entrepreneur, adventurer and world traveler, in order to capture the attention and imagination of this sophisticated audience. An additional, tantalizing offer accompanied the promotion: a trip anywhere in the world for the decision-maker accompanied by a Gulfstream representative.

With 44 general responses, 23 requested trips and 3 sales, the response more than satisfied Gulfstream's objectives. Plus, the promotion has endured as a gentle reminder in the form of a globe on the desks (or print on the wall) of many CEOs who might yet decide on Gulfstream as their flagship aircraft.

▲ *The second mailing contained a portrait of Columbus, a signed and numbered limited-edition print, by illustrator Mark English. At the same time this was sent to CEOs, an accompanying package arrived on the desk of the corporations' Flight Administrators with technical information about the Gulfstream IV so that they would be prepared to field questions from the CEOs.*

190

◀ *Carefully researched and painted by Michael Weaver, the map became the continuity element in the graphics for the program.*

▶ *The Gulfstream IV is a tool for opening new global markets for business worldwide. EAT Design's strategy was to create an emotional and physical link between Columbus the great explorer and the CEOs. The idea that these corporate heads viewed themselves as discoverers and explorers in their quest for new global markets was the core around which the entire direct mail program was developed.*

▼ The last package arrived on Columbus Day. The familiar map graphics and wrapping revealed a leather-bound book, created especially for the occasion, containing written excerpts and drawings from the log Columbus kept on his journey to the New World. A card was enclosed extending an invitation to take a "test flight" in the Gulfstream IV—a free business trip to anywhere in the world.

Above: Ellen Shapiro, principal, Shapiro Design Associates Inc.

With increasing competition from innumerable credit card companies, American Express Travel Related Services Company, Inc. uses design strategically to maintain the American Express® Card's market position as the preferred payment method for over 25 million Cardmembers worldwide.

Shapiro Design Associates Inc. has produced over 100 projects for American Express, including conventional and electronic reproduction art and guidelines for American Express Card logos, a communications manual for the Establishment and the Service Establishment Handbooks, which pictorially demonstrate to merchants how to process charges and credits.

Ellen Shapiro, principal of Shapiro Design Associates, characterizes her firm as a "boutique alternative" to the global advertising agencies. "We bring the same strategic knowledge of the company and creative talents to any size project," she says, but are able to work with marketing managers on a more personal level."

Shapiro Design Associates Inc.
10 East 40th Street
New York, NY 10016
212/685-4095

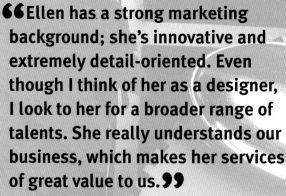

❝Ellen has a strong marketing background; she's innovative and extremely detail-oriented. Even though I think of her as a designer, I look to her for a broader range of talents. She really understands our business, which makes her services of great value to us.❞
Anna Li, American Express Travel Related Services Company, Inc.

At *family-style* restaurants in the ATLANTA area:

At *fine dining* restaurants in NORTHERN NEW JERSEY:

The American Express Card can bring more money to your bottom line.

Here's how:

◀ Still-life photography by Peggy Barnett for the cover of The American Express® Guide to Grammy Week Dining in New York. AmEx published the guide solely for music industry executives and artists who came to town for the Grammy Awards. Shapiro wrote a "sell-in" letter to 500 Manhattan restaurants; over 300 sent or faxed back participation agreements, many offering discounts to parties of two or more who purchased meals with the Card.

Reprinted from *Design In Depth.* Printed in Hong Kong.

American Express

Designer and Client:
Shapiro Design Associates Inc.
for American Express Travel
Related Services Company, Inc.

Ellen Shapiro is a champion of American Express and a believer that its products offer superior service to merchants and customers. In the last ten years, Shapiro Design has played a major role in a strategic campaign that presents the benefits of Card acceptance—the ability to attract consumers who come back often and spend more. The restaurant industry segment of the American Express® Card's market has given Shapiro an exceptional opportunity to combine her personal interest in food with her firm's marketing communications capabilities, and it's yielded some tasty results.

American Express marketing managers usually begin a new project by defining program objectives for Shapiro and supplying a list of targeted establishments. Then they give her an unusual amount of autonomy. Shapiro begins by creating a program tag line and logo. The logo's first application is in a "sell-in letter," which explains how the promotion will work. "We want to create enthusiasm," says Shapiro, "so I might begin the letter with something like: 'Over 8,000 music industry artists and executives will be in town for the Grammys next month, and they'll be looking for interesting places to have breakfast, lunch, dinner and late night snacks. We'd like to direct them to *your* restaurant.'"

The sell-in letter contains a response vehicle designed to most efficiently bring date like cuisine type and average dinner cost into the directory or mailer format. Shapiro writes the copy, art directs the illustrations and photography, and manages every detail of the project including coordination with mailing houses to get the most favorable postal rates and ensure that the promotions "drop" on the right date.

According to managers of regional marketing at American Express, a current campaign, "The Perfect Setting for Business Entertaining," is generating the desired response. "Restaurateurs are commenting that they're seeing good new Corporate Card business and higher average checks."

▲ *Using electronic production techniques, Shapiro Design produced 42 customized versions of a brochure that explains to restaurateurs across the country why welcoming American Express makes good business sense. Facts and figures relate to each market segment. With stacks of research conducted by Price Waterhouse as the point of departure, Shapiro identified and put into plain English key reasons AmEx acceptance can make a restaurant more profitable.*

For use by the American Express sales force, the brochures are addressed to three market segments: fine dining, adult contemporary and family-style—both nationwide and in thirteen U.S. cities. Each version incorporates specific facts and figures relating to a particular market segment, for example: fine dining in Atlanta or family-style dining in San Francisco. Illustrations: Nigel Holmes

194

DINING

IN NEW YORK

▲ Logo used for event-related marketing of restaurants to members of the National Academy of Recording Arts and Sciences in New York for the Grammy Awards. Lettering: Alex Acker

▲ Mailers offering discounts at retail establishments to New York City Cardmembers (above), and at restaurants to Small Business Corporate Cardmembers (below). Versions were produced for five Manhattan neighborhoods and six regions in Southern California.
Illustrations, above: Monica Ragne, below: Michael Witte.

THE AMERICAN EXPRESS GUIDE TO BOSTON AREA RESTAURANTS

◀ *Platinum Card® Fine Hotels & Resorts Worldwide Directory features world maps, photographs and detailed descriptions of dining, recreational and business amenities at over 250 upscale establishments that extend special privileges to Platinum Card members. The Hotel icon logo was drawn by Shapiro and illustrator Javier Romero after the style of Renaissance architect Andrea Palladio. Maps: Martin Haggland*

This "sales presenter" ▶ portfolio allows a salesperson to make a polished presentation with a "deck" that shows how a partnership with American Express will make good economic sense. The portfolio includes a specially designed cover sheet for decks generated in house. Photo: Lisa Stone

◀ *Beginning with a list of restaurants accepting American Express in Boston and Washington, DC, Shapiro Design developed comprehensive directories including maps, tip tables and restaurant listings by neighborhood, cuisine type and price range. Photo: Lisa Stone*

From left to right: Miguel Sole, James Tung, Mitchell Mauk, Allyson Ely.

> **"The projects' result was a flexible merchandising system that was user friendly even in the technological branch environment"**
> James Tung, Charles Schwab & Co.

Mauk Design was chosen for the Charles Schwab & Co. Branch Expansion Program based on the firms extensive experience in combining marketing messages with three dimensional environments. Schwab wanted to provide a high quality branch experience in a market segment known mostly for its "discount" look. Extensive branch surveys and research preceeded the design phase, ensuring a focused design process. Customers needed to feel comfortable in the branch and feel the integrity of the brokers who were handling their money.

Design team: Mitchell Mauk, Tim Mautz, Susie Leversee-Miller, Francis Packer, Julie Bernatz, Christine Lashaw, Lucia Matiolli, Joe Harvard. Charles Schwab Architecture: Miguel Sole, James Tung. Charles Schwab Marketing: Allyson Ely, Randy Goldman, Jennifer Winn. Frieze Photography: Hugh Kretschmer.

Mauk Design
636 4th Street
San Francisco, CA 94107
415/243-9277

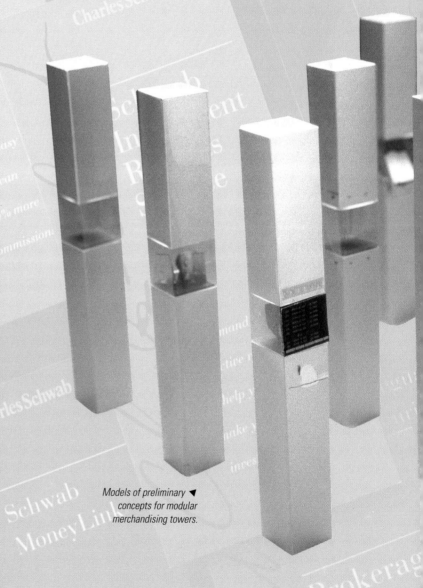

Models of preliminary ◀ concepts for modular merchandising towers.

Cover of the brochure- ▶ standards manual. The graphics developed for the family of financial products include color-coding, a customized Charles Schwab signature and metallic inks.

Reprinted from
Design In Depth.
Printed in Hong Kong.

Charles Schwab

Designer and Client:
Mauk Design for
Charles Schwab & Co.

Charles Schwab invented discount stock brokerage. For those investors without the luxury of a broker who is at the ready to consult on investments nor the wealth to attract financial consultants, the walk-in retail environment provides a unique opportunity. Mauk's task was to humanize Charles Schwab's identity so that the average-man-on-the-street would feel less daunted about stock investment in general.

Mauk capitalized on the strength, honesty and openness of Schwab's signature. When entering the environment, the interior display kiosks allow customers to review literature and learn about stock investing at their own pace, a multimedia display "talks" customers through the investing process thus humanizing through familiarizing.

◄ *This literature tower contains 24 brochures. The configuration of the literature holders, which are secured with magnets, is interchangeable. The tower is on wheels allowing it to be moved to clear lobby space for evening seminars.*

Charles Schwab

Merchandising towers in ▶
use at the prototype branch
in Washington, DC. The pho-
tographic frieze overhead,
portraying various aspects
of modern business, was
screenprinted on wallpaper.

▲ An 80 foot-long Charles
Schwab signature mounted
on the branch windows. The
signature is made of vinyl
which replicates the look
of sandblasting.

◄ *Preliminary concept for an investor information "totem pole". It included time zone clocks, date, world globe, stock ticker, and front page of Wall Street Journal.*

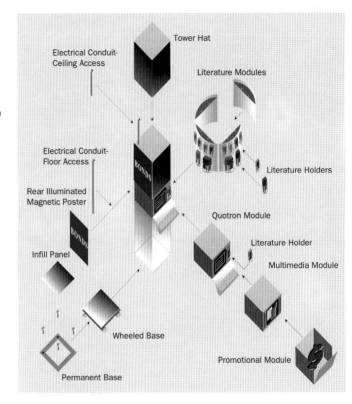

Tower Hat

Electrical Conduit-Ceiling Access

Literature Modules

Electrical Conduit-Floor Access

Literature Holders

Rear Illuminated Magnetic Poster

Quotron Module

Infill Panel

Literature Holder

Multimedia Module

Wheeled Base

Promotional Module

Permanent Base

▲ *This is a diagram of the modular merchandising system used in the branch. By adding function specific elements to a single base unit, a wide array of towers could be acheived.*

▼ *A Trans-Lux Stock Quote sign integrates the company logotype and a board displaying stock quotes in a single boat-shaped overhead unit.*

"BoundSound™ is real multimedia publishing for right now"
Nicholas Callaway, Callaway Editions

Reprinted from
Design In Depth.
Printed in Hong Kong.

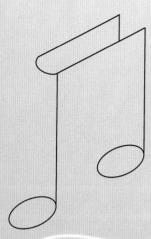

BoundSound™

Callaway Editions, Inc., a firm of twelve, was founded in 1980. Headed by Nicholas Callaway, the publishing and book packaging company has made a name for itself by creating exquisite large-format visual books such as the award-winning Eiko *by* Irving Penn, Sex *by* Madonna *and* Georgia O'Keeffe: One Hundred Flowers. *Through simultaneous international co-editons, Callaway's books are distributed world-wide. Callaway's BoundSound™ multimedia series includes* Ferrington Guitars, *designed by Nancy Skolos and Tom Wedell of Skolos & Wedell;* Malcolm X Speaks Out, *designed by Roger Gorman of Reiner Design; and* Buckaroo: Visions and Values of the American Cowboy, *designed by Toshiya Masuda, staff designer at Callaway.*

Callaway Editions, Inc.
Nicholas Callaway, President
70 Bedford Street,
New York, NY 10014
212/929-5212

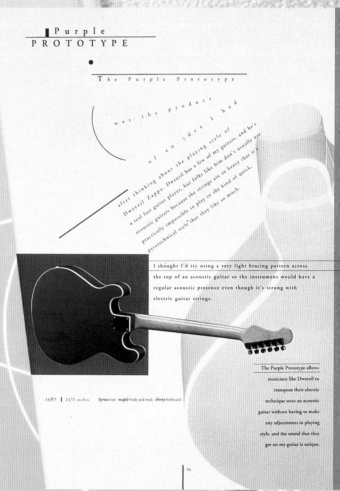

Purple PROTOTYPE

The Purple Prototype

was the product of an idea I had after thinking about the playing style of Dweezil Zappa. Dweezil has a few of my guitars and he's a real fast guitar player, but folks like him don't usually use acoustic guitars because the strings are so heavy that it's practically impossible to play in the kind of quick, pyrotechnical style that they like so much.

I thought I'd try using a very light bracing pattern across the top of an acoustic guitar so the instrument would have a regular acoustic presence even though it's strung with electric guitar strings.

The Purple Prototype allows musicians like Dweezil to transpose their electric technique onto an acoustic guitar without having to make any adjustments in playing style, and the sound that they get on my guitar is unique.

1987 | 25½ inches *Spruce* top *maple* body and neck *ebony* fretboard

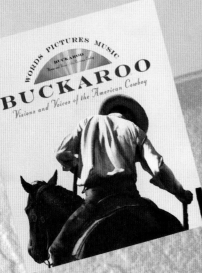

WORDS PICTURES MUSIC
BUCKAROO
BUCKAROO
Visions and Voices of the American Cowboy

◄ *From Albuquerque to Calgary a movement has emerged emulating the life and fables of the cowboy.* Buckaroo *is a slight departure for BoundSound™ in that it's a compendium of folk humor, poetry, ballads and swing music. What fits for Callaway's cultural theme is that the buckaroo has credibility as a poet, performer and musician.*

BoundSound™

◀ Ferrington Guitars *is a
multimedia introduction to
the extraordinary work of
America's legendary guitar
maker, Danny Ferrington.*

Designer and Client:
Nicholas Callaway, Callaway
Editions, Inc. for Andrews &
McMeel, HarperCollins and
Simon & Schuster

BoundSound™, an innovative multimedia
publishing series, integrates text and images
with an audio compact disc which is bound
into a book. This facilitates and enriches the
comprehension of a subject that's three
dimensional. Nicholas Callaway had the vision
to commission nationally renowned designers
Nancy Skolos and Tom Wedell to design the
first BoundSound™—*Ferrington Guitars*—as
an asymmetrical trapezoidal format with a
compact disc imbedded right in the cover.
This spectacularly dramatic graphic statement
created unusual manufacturing requirements,
pushing the envelope in the worlds of printing
and binding and creating what is sure to
become a collector's item. *Ferrington Guitars*:
what better way to teach guitar but to hear,
see and interact with the instrument?

Callaway went further with this cutting
edge technology to extend the series of
BoundSound™ books that allowed a visual
and audio format to define—and refine or
evolve— the image of an artist or personality,
including a book called *Malcolm X Speaks Out*
and *Buckaroo: Visions and Voices of the
American Cowboy*.

Cultural enrichment is a clear theme in
the long list of Callaway's visual books, books
which have created forums for some of
the world's most rarefied and revered artists.
Callaway's leap into the world of multimedia
through the creation of BoundSound™ is a
natural and perspicacious direction for
Callaway Editions.

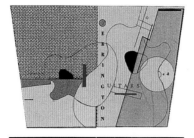

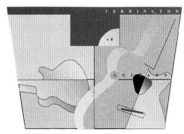

The Ferrington Guitar is ▲
featured throughout the book.
Top pickers Elvis Costello,
Jackson Browne and
J.J. Cale play on Ferringtons.

▲ Nancy Skolos and Tom
Wedell lay out the book on
the floor of their studio.

Nancy Skolos studied the ▶ physical attributes of the Ferrington in order to bring it to life graphically in the book, Ferrington Guitars.

▼ The second in the BoundSound™ Series, Malcolm X Speaks Out, is a compilation of the words, images and voice recordings of one of the most controversial and seminal figures of the twentieth century. Ossie Davis, in his eulogy said, "...our own Black shining prince—who didn't hesitate to die, because he loved us so."

"This stuff makes me very nervous—but that's good. I wanted to push the boundaries and this really does it."

Celia Currin,
Marketing Services Director
The Wall Street Journal

Today's Wall Street Journal provides business readers with the most comprehensive and concise package of news, information and statistics available in print and other media. The marketing initiatives are equally comprehensive, with regional marketing managers and numerous sales reps around the country. The Journals' search for a company that could understand and respond to their complex identity needs led quickly to Waters Design.

A leader in the use of electronic technologies for communications efficiency, Waters has been recognized in major design exhibits, competitions and communications journals throughout the United States, Europe and Japan. The systematic but creative approach Waters takes to complex communications programs has been well received by such other companies as Coopers & Lybrand, EDS, IBM, Merrill Lynch, and NationsBank.

Working closely with Mitchell Engelmeyer, Waters provided the Journal not only creative thinking, but intelligent architecture, hardware and software recommendations, and the training necessary to make it all work.

The Adventures of the WSJ advertising sales team may be found on the Web @adsales.wsj.com. The Waters Edge may be explored @ waters design.com.

Waters Design Associates, Inc.
3 West 18th Street
New York, NY 10011
212/807-0717

From left to right:
Mitchell Engelmeyer, Creative Services Manager, The Wall Street Journal; Colleen Syron, VP New Media, Waters Design; and John Waters, Design Director.

THE WALL STREET JOURNAL

w h e r e

financial

marketing begi

Designer and Client:
John Waters, Waters
Design Associates for
The Wall Street Journal

The Wall Street Journal Case Study

◀ The WSJ sales reps now use Macintosh PowerBooks for sales presentations, shown here with the Marketing Image Standards Guide and the first printed piece in the new program.

Redefining The Wall Street Journal as ideas in motion rather than ink on paper, Waters Design developed visually rich, multiple media, image standards for the Journal's marketing materials.

Waters was asked to evaluate existing materials and internal capabilities (human, computer, & print production) within the Marketing Services department at The Journal, and develop a design scheme and architecture for new materials. The objective was to establish a market oriented design scheme that would provide consistency, uniformity and synergism between elements. The program was to be compatible with the installment of a computer network, linking the marketing services group in New York with regional marketing managers and sales offices around the country. With the new scheme in place, sales people carry laptop computers, and are able to transmit/receive, give presentations, leave printed pieces behind, and connect to the Web without losing image continuity. The new standards reflect a unified strategy that is emphatic, information rich, and resonates across five market segments in any media. Waters Design is widely known for this comprehensive, integrated approach to corporate communications design.

A single screen from ▶ the opening animated sequence. For The Premiere Advertising Vehicle.

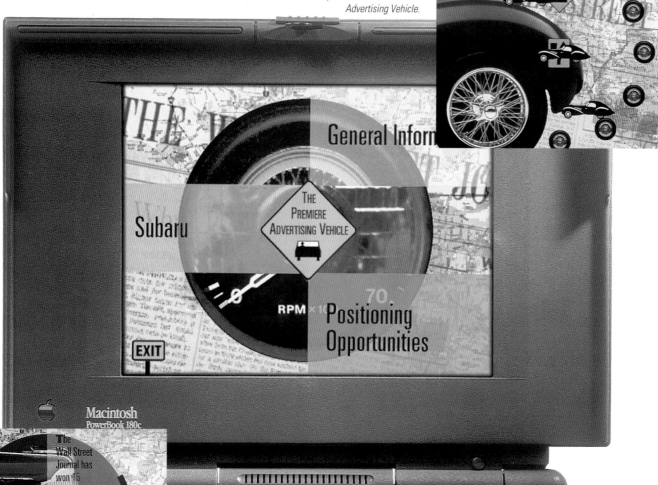

General Inform

Subaru

THE PREMIERE ADVERTISING VEHICLE

Positioning Opportunities

70.

RPM ×1

EXIT

Macintosh
PowerBook 180c

The Wall Street Journal has won 15 Pulitzer Prizes

Excellence

SUBMEN
MENU

According to the annual survey, The People & The Press, The Wall Street Journal is the "most believable" publication in the country.

Most Believable

Source: 1992 Times Mirror

◀ ▲ Title screens for The Premiere Advertising Vehicle, an interactive sales presentation for the automotive market. The presentation is easily customized for potential customers from different car manufacturers.

Subaru Owner Defection Rates

Honda	10.1%
Toyota	8.5
Nissan	4.7
Mazda	3.4
Mitsubishi	1.7

MENU

Source: R.L. Polk, 1992

A viewer may look at ad ▶ space availability on any page in sections A, B, or C.

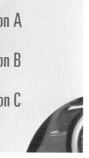

Section A

Section B

Section C

▲ The road signs on the screens are the main navigation buttons, and the headlines are also active buttons leading to wells of information.

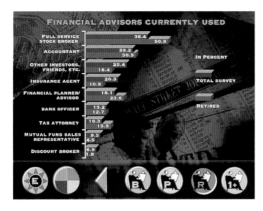  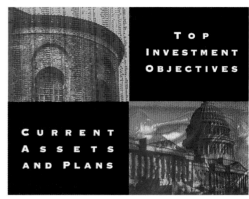

▲ ▶ Screens from The
Affluent Investor. The three
buttons on the bottom left
take the viewer to: exit, main
menu, or previous page.

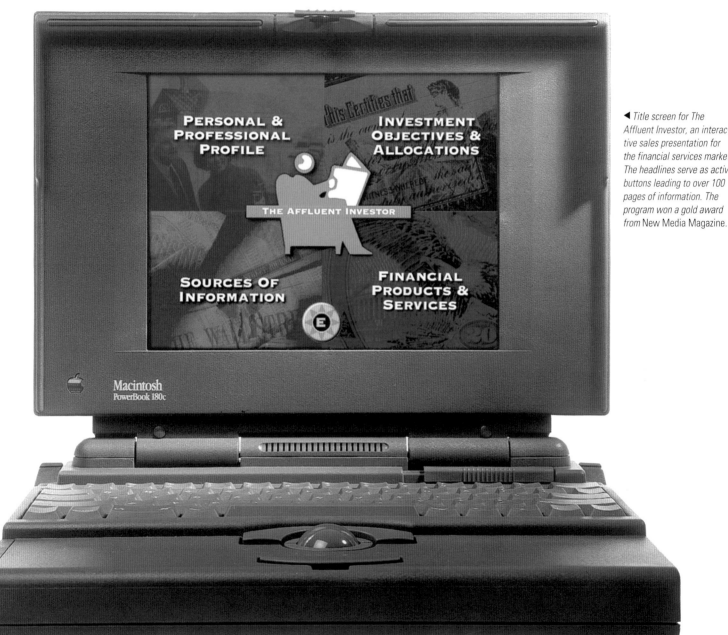

◀ Title screen for The
Affluent Investor, an interactive sales presentation for
the financial services market.
The headlines serve as active
buttons leading to over 100
pages of information. The
program won a gold award
from New Media Magazine.

"With esenzia, we are formulating what we call a new textureality, a total blending of science and art. It's the future of fabric... esenzia allows us to expand our thinking and our markets."

Alex Neely,
Executive Vice President
Burlington Industries

▲ *Every surface, shadow and silhouette in the showroom—even the undulating doorpull—conveys the sensual character of esenzia. Slover [AND] Company worked with architect David Rush to create an intimate space that encourages a softer sell.*

Burlington Industries, leading in market share but lagging in innovation, wanted to shake up a sluggish market. Slover [AND] Company, used to attracting clients who want to be taken in new directions, saw an opportunity to differentiate Burlington from the rest of the market. The result: esenzia is Burlington's most successful product launch in the last decade.

The design team at Slover [AND] Company included: Sarah Allen, Diana Jewell, Cliff Morgan, David Rush and was led by Alessia Usai.

Slover [AND] Company
584 Broadway
Suite 903
New York, NY 10012
212/431-0093

Designer and Client:
Slover [AND] Company for
Burlington Industries

Burlington Luxe

When Burlington Industries was ready to launch an entirely new collection of luxe fabrics, management fully realized that they would be working against market perceptions. Buyers felt they knew what this major American wool/worsted resource had to offer, but Burlington had something entirely different in mind: a totally new fabric collection designed and developed for the global marketplace. Through proprietary technologies and the Italian imagination of textile designer/producer Marco Lucchesi, Burlington was ready, after three years of research and development, to offer unique fabric technology at a price point no other fabric house in the United States could match.

Only by selecting a design firm with a reputation for the unexpected could this American leader convey their extraordinary departure to an accustomed (and sometimes jaded) marketplace. But Susan Slover Design—recently renamed Slover [AND] Company—tends to take clients left when the others are going right, and does it with such determination and detail that clients know it's the shortest way there.

Slover [AND] Company began at the beginning. They named the collection *esenzia*, then developed selling tools and a selling environment that visually—and viscerally—reinforced the character of the collection. The result was a soft selling approach that produced cold, hard sales in a flattened market.

▲ ▶ *The collection's preview invitation included Craig Cutler's macro photographs of thimbles, spools and needles that rotate on die cut shapes that were connected by textured fiber and hand-finished with a bone button.*

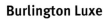

210

Many designers ▶ commented that the swatchbook design was a more immediate method to review and compare colors. The oversized grommet allows the fabrics to spill into a waterfall con-figuration, then fold flat for storage.

▲ *Hand-rubbed boxes made of curly maple—one of the four materials used throughout the showroom—display, like soft sculpture, the 28 esenzia colorways.*

◀ *esenzia capcards tied with hemp are slipped into corru-gated sheets that fold up into neat little carriers. Thus, all esenzia fabrics leave the showroom "in style."*

Functional and memor- ▶
able tools for the trade,
like swatch boxes, steel
scissors and natural wood
pens, assured Burlington
that the esenzia name and
logo would soon be
seen in the design studios
of fashion's top five.

Touch kits were given to ▶
fashion editors and
designers to reinforce the
essential selling message.
These kits were hand-sewn
from textured papers
and closed with a button
and leather thong.

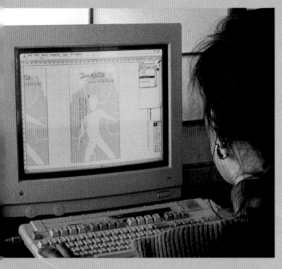

> **"Our mission was to think differently for IBM and express this new human centric technology with the same level of innovation promised from the product."**
> Tim Girvin, Tim Girvin Design, Inc.

Tim Girvin Design, Inc., a firm of forty, was founded in 1977. Internationally renown as a master calligrapher, Girvin has an intense interest in the written word. He says, "There is a magic link between speech communication and writing. In fact, carefully executed writing (i.e. typography, calligraphy) becomes a kind of illustration of language." IBM was impressed by Girvin's assertiveness when they interviewed him for the Power Personal Systems project, "I surprise some clients by advising them about what their competition is up to. I keep up on what's going on beyond design and let the client know what I know; I don't wait to be asked."

Other contributors on the Power Personal Systems project were Chris Spivey, TGD, Senior Designer; Bonnie Zinn, IBM, Project Administration; Jordan Warren, IBM, Exhibit Project Manager; Carl Andrews, Carl Andrews and Associates/Austin, Video Development and Implementation; Live Marketing/Chicago, Theater Lighting, Stage Design, and Live Presentation Production; Design South/Atlanta, Exhibit Engineering, Fabrication, Lighting and Installation; Kristy Lindgren, Photography; and John Gallone, Tim Girvin's Portrait.

Tim Girvin Design, Inc.
Tim Girvin, Principal
1601 Second Avenue, The Fifth Floor,
Seattle, WA 98101
206/623-7808

Tim Girvin draws the Power Personal logo with light.

The brochure given out at ▶ the exhibition served to introduce the concept of the product as well as provide a map of the exhibit. The cover features the icon chosen to identify the product, emulating the product's human-centric design.

Reprinted from
Design In Depth.
Printed in Hong Kong.

IBM Power Personal Systems

Designer and Client:
Tim Girvin, Tim Girvin Design, Inc. for Lineene Krasnow, IBM Power Personal Systems

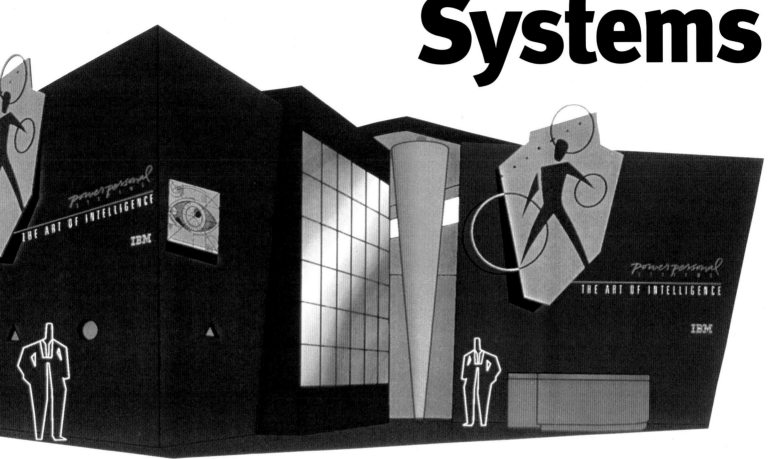

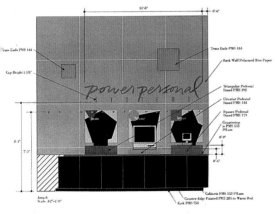

▲ *Enclosing the exhibit added an air of mystery to the display and was a radical departure from conventional exhibition design, which is usually designed an open format. A "store window" gave the audience a chance to peek in.*

▼ *A horizontal rendering showing some of the computer workstations on display inside the exhibit.*

It didn't even have a name when IBM approached Tim Girvin to discuss the promotion of its new hot product which was due to be released in eighteen months. What was known was that the new Power PC chip technology, a joint creation of IBM/Motorola/Apple, would revolutionize the computer industry. And IBM wanted to introduce this technology in a new computer workstation environment in four to six months, a very accelerated rate by any standard.

Girvin says, "We needed to think outside the box. Most other computer products are staid and corporate. This product's identity needed to be fresh, new, left of center." Since there was no name, only a definition, Girvin

created style boards that aided the team in defining the correct direction. Girvin says, "For instance, Green, a new term that refers to environmentally friendly concepts like energy efficiency and recyclability, was one direction. Hot, Cool, Hard, Soft, and Warm (suggesting user friendly) were others. We ended up with a combination of Green and Warm." This agreement of style and image allowed Girvin to proceed quickly, even without a product name. He was then asked to create the Power Personal Systems identity and icon, the division of IBM that was launching this exciting new computer.

The Power Personal Systems computer environment is an example of "human centric"

214

*Graphic and exhibit ▶
design were crucial communication vehicles used to
create drama and interest for
the attendees.*

technology or, technology designed with
the human in mind. While "linked to the
mother ship of IBM," Girvin points out,
"its development incorporated non-linear
thinking and new ideas one doesn't usually
associate with IBM."

The exhibition design Girvin developed used
unconventional, daring and disarming
approaches, such as tilted walls that created
an enclosed feeling (conventionally avoided by
exhibit designers as claustrophobic) and a
bright, painterly palette. Girvin adds, "People
were engaged. They lingered in the booth. The
response was far greater than anticipated. We
were in harmony with the product, which is
amazingly fast and enclosed in handsomely
designed hardware."

*Even the clothing of those ▶
who greeted the attendees
was considered in the
creation of a cohesive and
forceful look for the Power
Personal System.*

Beside the script logo for ▶ Power Personal Systems, Girvin designed an entire typeface which is used in conjunction with the Power PC logo.

PowerPC™

Once inside the exhibition ▲ space, the focus was on the hardware that houses the Power PC chip. "The store window," recommended by Design South, part of the exhibit design team, can be seen in the top photo.

▲ Once inside the exhibit, a multimedia presentation explained the Power Personal System in greater depth. Stage design and lighting by Live Marketing, Chicago.

> **"The night before entering the space the enormity of my self-imposed task overwhelmed me. It became the moment of truth."**
>
> Seitaro Kuroda

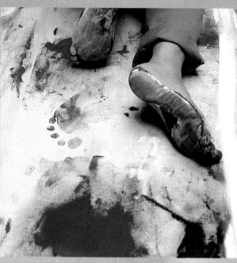

From left to right: Keitsuke Nagatomo, Tamotsu Yagi, Kuroda's assistant, Seitaro Kuroda and Brian Collentine.

Brian Collentine is a graphic designer whose work includes primarily consumer related packaging and retail design. AXO Design Studio, a firm of three, was founded in 1990. Other contributors to the project were Misa Awatsuji, Christian Bentley, Emiko Kaji, Del Rae Roth, and Akira Yagi. All photos by Sharon Risedorph.

AXO Design Studio,
Brian Collentine, Principal
423 Tehama Street, San Francisco, CA 94103
415/543-8712

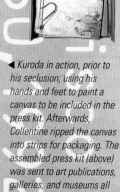

◄ *Kuroda in action, prior to his seclusion, using his hands and feet to paint a canvas to be included in the press kit. Afterwards, Collentine ripped the canvas into strips for packaging. The assembled press kit (above) was sent to art publications, galleries, and museums all over the world.*

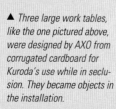

▲ *Three large work tables, like the one pictured above, were designed by AXO from corrugated cardboard for Kuroda's use while in seclusion. They became objects in the installation.*

Reprinted from
Design In Depth.
Printed in Hong Kong.

Designer and Client:
Brian Collentine, AXO Design
Studio and Tamotsu Yagi,
Tamotsu Yagi Design for
Seitaro Kuroda and Keitsuke
Nagatomo, K2

504 Hours

◀ The exterior of 264
Ninth Street where Seitaro
Kuroda was in seclusion for
504 hours.

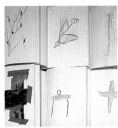

◀ These sample journals are
from some of the 21 journals
that Kuroda kept while in
seclusion.

The Japanese artist Kuroda wished to be secluded, to create, to test himself, to attain a new state of spirituality, a dream he shared with graphic designers Brian Collentine and Tamotsu Yagi on a visit to San Francisco. Kuroda was a friend of the Native American, Dennis Banks and this notion of creation, spirituality through isolation came from Native American culture. Captivated by this idea, Collentine developed a plan to help Kuroda realize his wish. Together they identified and rented an appropriately simple one room warehouse South-of-Market in San Francisco. Collentine created a model of the space and proposed outfitting it with lights, so Kuroda could work at any time he wished,

and corrugated cardboard tables. Kuroda, Yagi and Collentine refined the plan further in Tokyo and made a commitment to undertake the project. Kuroda's only contact with the 'outside world' would be through his assistant. They devised a daily ritual of knocking on the wall to communicate. Collentine says, "We shared the concern that the solitude could drive him nuts."

Kuroda painted his identity K2 on the garage door and, at the appointed hour, the door to the warehouse closed, Kuroda and his supplies inside. At 4 pm on September 20th, 504 hours later, Collentine raised the garage door, for the start of an exhibition of Kuroda's creation. With the press at hand, Kuroda told of the first 336 hours and that he had decided to reject and destroy everything he had created to that point and start over completely. In the final hours he worked feverishly to completely transform the room anew.

Collentine says, "The experience was, besides a unique opportunity to help a friend, an amazing event in my life. The journals are spectacular in their chronicling of Kuroda's days."

218

The 1200 square foot stu-▶ dio space before, during, and after installation by Collentine and Yagi. The view pictured opposite was the result of Kuroda's seclusion after three weeks.

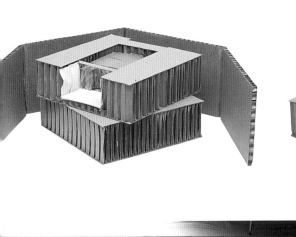

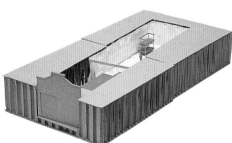

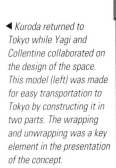

◀ Kuroda returned to Tokyo while Yagi and Collentine collaborated on the design of the space. This model (left) was made for easy transportation to Tokyo by constructing it in two parts. The wrapping and unwrapping was a key element in the presentation of the concept.

◀ AXO designed four rolling halogen light fixtures like the one pictured that could be strung together to light an entire wall.

Reprinted from
Design In Depth.
Printed in Hong Kong.

A collapsible modular panel ▶
was designed by Peter Good
to announce the new sea-
son's programming schedules
to Aetna employees.

Peter Good founded Peter Good Graphic Design
in 1971. Since then the client base of the firm has
grown to include The Wadsworth Atheneum,
Strathmore Paper and the United States Postal
Service (for which Good designed four postage
stamps). Cultural aesthetic is a major theme in the
Good portfolio. Aetna's Christine Farley recognized
this depth of interest and acumen, and wisely
chose Peter Good Graphic Design to guide the
television series promotion campaign for "The
American Experience" in the right direction.
Gordon Bowman was the writer on the team while
Janet Cummings Good and Susan Schaffer-
Beaumier co-designed the project with Peter Good.

Peter Good Graphic Design
Peter Good, Susan Schaffer-Beaumier,
Janet Cummings Good, Principals
3 North Main Street
Chester CT 06412
203/526-9597

**❝Peter Good Graphic Design created visuals
as exuberant as the historical stories on which
'The American Experience' is based. They
provided Aetna with a very effective way of
promoting its support of the series❞**
Christine Farley

From left to right: Gordon
Bowman, Susan Schaffer-
Beaumier, Janet Cummings
Good (front) Christine Farley
(rear) and Peter Good

Biggest ever. The third season of The

*All images for the campaign
were supplied by
historical societies or the
Library of Congress.*

*◀ To stimulate viewer
interest, tent cards were
placed through Aetna's
offices, conference areas
and cafeterias.*

The American Experience

Designer and Client:
Peter Good, Peter Good
Graphic Design for Christine
Farley, Aetna

221

ce tells great stories of people and places from our nation's history. Tune in Mondays at 9 p.m.⁽ᴱᵀ⁾ beginning October 1 on public television. Made possible by Aetna. Ætna

◀ *A sequence from the introduction to the TV series
showed a grid of bold stars
and stripes interspersed with
historical images from the
programs, giving the viewer
an idea of the wide range of
content within the series.*

History tends to generate publicity. The preservation of culture and the "American Way" are of concern to all good citizens of the United States: people can relate to their own history. Aetna's service, insurance, is an intangible; and the nature of the benefits are difficult to advertise.

Hence, when Aetna decided to sponsor "The American Experience, a documentary television series, a campaign to support the series was brought to Peter Good to develop. Good, recognizing the vastness of subject matter, looked for a self-limiting but emotionally-charged factor. Using historical research, Good delved into accessible visuals featuring the American flag in interesting formats.

Good recognized that an important message for Aetna is the pride of America; that translates out into celebrities, celebrations, wars and disasters. All these subjects relate to insurance in the abstract. Preparedness is the essence of insurance and the subtext "protect that which is yours" came across in the visuals that Good developed.

Some first season tune-in ads, using provocative headlines relating to the content of the program.

SEVENTH LYNCHING THIS WEEK

Headlines told the horrid truth to the rural South after the Civil War and well into this century: shocking numbers of African Americans were lynched by white mobs — often with the blessing of civic leaders.

Hosted by David McCullagh, "A Passion for Justice" is the story of Ida B. Wells. Born into slavery in a small Mississippi town, she lost three of her friends to a lynch mob and dedicated the rest of her life to a fearless crusade to fight racism.

Passionate, blunt, uncompromising, she clashed with presidents and social leaders alike. Booker T. Washington saw her as a dangerous radical.

But Ida B. Wells persisted and added a courageous chapter to our nation's history.

The American Experience

Made possible by Aetna

Tonight at 9 pm on Channel 24

Ætna

STOWAWAYS SENT BACK TO EUROPE

It wasn't easy becoming an American citizen if you were an immigrant in the late 19th and early 20th century. First, there was the ocean trip, which was often terrifying. Then, there were Ellis Island, where as many as 10,000 people a day were housed and processed. A dozen reasons, including discovery as a stowaway, could cause rejection and a return to the homeland.

Still, enough of these "poor and huddled masses" made it so that almost one-half of all Americans have an ancestor who came here from the Old World between 1890 and 1920.

Original footage captures the determination of these travelers as they made their way through Europe, across the Atlantic, and into the heart of America.

Hosted by David McCullagh, "Journey to America" tells the story of the greatest immigration wave in our history.

The American Experience

Made possible by Aetna

Tonight at 9 pm on Channel 24

Ætna

NATIONAL PARK COULD BE LOVED TO DEATH

Yosemite National Park is a protected preserve, and one of the glories of the American landscape. In "Yosemite – The Fate of Heaven," hosted by David McCullagh, you can see how stunningly beautiful this breathtaking photography reveals the fragile wonder of the place naturalist John Muir called "a great temple reigned from above."

But, as Robert Redford explains in his film narration, there is a dark side to the park's beauty. So attractive is it to campers, hikers, and sightseers from all over the world, the onslaught of nature lovers threatens to kill the joys of wilderness and solitude that are so much a part of Yosemite's heritage. Fortunately, today, rangers and others work mightily to keep the park from being completely smothered by affection.

Tonight's film won the Blue Ribbon Award at the American Film Festival.

The American Experience

Made possible by Aetna

Tonight at 9 pm on Channel 24

Ætna

▼ *One of the programs portrayed three of the nation's most powerful presidencies. This ad artfully juxtaposed poignant images of the three men. In the case of Kennedy, he's shown as a boy surrounded by the cause for his destiny, his powerful family.*

222

Get ready for an unforget... *Experience.*

The fifth season of *The ... Experience* begins Sun... 20th, with an extraordi... programs which will ... through Thursday, Sep...

The series will present ... unforgettable portraits ... Kennedy family, of Lyn... Johnson, and of Richar...

The Kennedys tells the ... family so powerful, so... them to royalty. Certain... American family has so... shape of politics in Am... Airing Sunday and Mon... 8 p.m.–10 p.m.ET

LBJ is the story of a ma... poverty in the Texas hi... become one of the mos... in all of American polit... only to end his career i... of his commitment of A... in Vietnam. Airing Tue... Wednesday from 8 p.m...

Nixon chronicles the lif... one of the most controv... modern America. Airin... 8 p.m.–11 p.m.ET

Tune in to 11 unforgett... on your public televisio... your local listing.

The American Exp...

Ætna

Made pos...

Thumbnails were used by Peter Good to explore potential layouts.

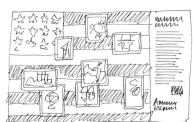

FLAG BACKGROUND WITH PHOTOS. (SEPIA-TONES) OLD PHOTOS - OLD FLAG

N.P. FOR "COLOR OF JUSTICE"

SPUTNIK

STAT. OF LIB.

PROHIB.

AIR RACES

SEARS.

WWI

JAPANESE INTERNMENT.

SYMBOLS AND ARTIFACTS AND PHOTOS TO EXPRESS THE 8 SHOWS.

COULD WORK FOR POSTER ALSO

Hearts And Hands
(rebroadcast)
Monday, December 24, 9:00 p.m.
(Check local listings.)

"Hearts And Hands" is a film that explores the art of quilting, used throughout the nineteenth century as an expression of everything from family histories to political beliefs.

Patterns like Underground Railroad Slave Chain and Job's Tears were used by Northern women to champion the abolitionist cause. When the country moved westward, women stitched the record of their journeys into their quilts. These hand-sewn masterpieces, describing how life was lived in another age, will be featured in this story, along with archival photographs and film.

Bonus Army (wt)
Monday, January 7, 9:00 p.m.
(Check local listings.)

"Bonus Army" looks at the most desperate year of the Great Depression - 1932, when eighty percent of the national workforce was unemployed. Twenty-thousand veterans and their families set up camps in Washington D.C. to claim the cash bonuses promised by Congress and Herbert Hoover. President Hoover loaned them tents, cots, and rations. But when Douglas MacArthur's Army troops attacked the protesters the country became convinced that their President had no compassion for the dispossessed.

▼ Peter Good recognized that the bigger the stars and stripes, the better the sense of nationalism; so one of his research goals was to locate the largest American flags ever created.

▲ An essay contest for secondary-school students required invitations and award programs to coordinate with the stars and stripes theme.

The fifth season of *The American Experience* brings you more glorious stories of people, places and events from America's past. Starting September 20th on public television. Made possible by Aetna.

Cicuic

Axa

Zangar

Tiguas

Coco

Quimechas

Tamaca

LE.SETE.
CITA

Cazones
Madalena

Tabursa

TROPER
PRO:

B. Canoa

Cipola

Vicicila

Loat
S. Michi

S. Alad

B. d'S. ✝

Chiamatlam

Balo
uas

S. pablo
Xalico

Villa
ricca

Acapulco

Tiunstitam

Tutatipeg

C. d's
Higna
Guatuleo

L. al

Guatima
lla

Historical Atlas
of the
North Pacific Ocean

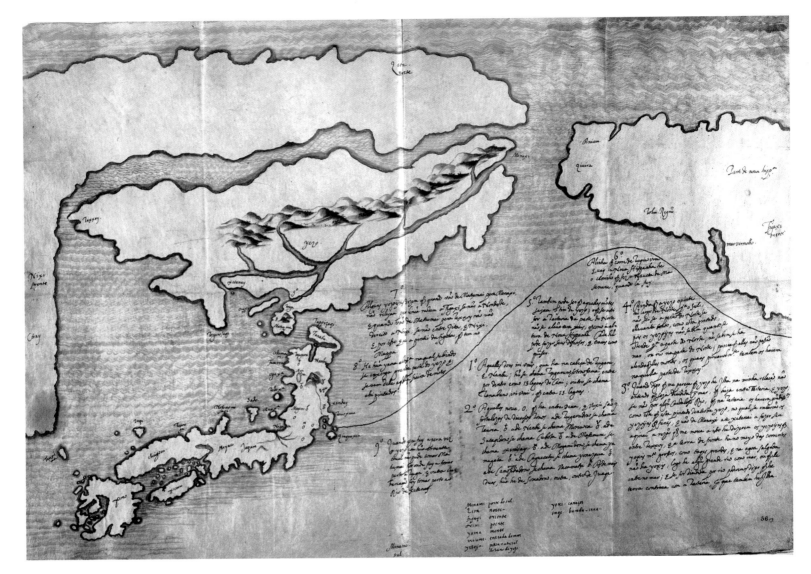

Map 1.
What today appears to us as a bizarre interpretation of the geography of the North Pacific Ocean was based on the latest information available at the time. Drawn in 1621 by a Jesuit missionary in Japan, Girolamo de Angelis, the map shows Japan, to the north of which is a grossly exaggerated Hokkaido, which was not at this time part of Japan. Asia is correctly shown separated from America even though the strait was as yet unexplored by Europeans. On the west coast of North America the peninsula of Baja California is shown; this was known from Spanish explorations from the previous century, but the rest of the west coast is essentially a blank. It would not be explored by Europeans until 1774.

Historical Atlas
of the
North Pacific Ocean

Maps of Discovery and Scientific Exploration
1500 – 2000

Derek Hayes

THE BRITISH MUSEUM PRESS

Originated and published in Canada by Douglas & McIntyre Ltd

Published in Great Britain in 2001 by The British Museum Press
A division of The British Museum Company Ltd
46 Bloomsbury Street, London WC1B 3QQ

British Library Cataloguing in Publication Data
A catalogue record for this book is available from the British Library

ISBN 0-7141-2560-1

Copy editing by Naomi Pauls
Design and layout by Derek Hayes
Printed and bound in Hong Kong, P.R.C., by C&C Offset
Printed on acid-free paper

Derek Hayes
www.derekhayes.ca
derek@derekhayes.ca

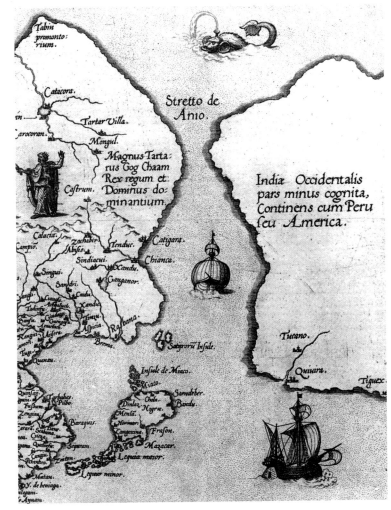

Map 2.
The Pacific Ocean as portrayed on a map from 1578 by Gerard de Jode. The ocean was commonly shown as a relatively narrow sea in the sixteenth and seventeenth centuries.

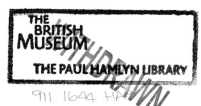
Published under the auspices of the
North Pacific Marine Science Organization (PICES)

With financial assistance from the
National Marine Fisheries Service,
National Oceanic and Atmospheric Administration,
U.S.A.

Acknowledgments

First of all I would like to thank PICES, the North Pacific Marine Science Organization, for commissioning this book.

Many people have assisted in its compilation and writing. In particular I would like to thank the following: Alexander Bychkov, Executive Secretary, PICES, and Robert Wilson and John Garrett of 2WE Associates, Victoria; Skip McKinnell, Assistant Executive Secretary, PICES; Edward Redmond and John Hebért, Geography and Map Division, Library of Congress; Tony Campbell and his staff in the Map Library at the British Library; Andrew Cook and Graham Hutt (Curator, Chinese Section), Oriental and India Office Collections, British Library; Jeffrey Murray at the National Archives of Canada; Adrian Webb and Sharon Nichol at the United Kingdom Hydrographic Office; Brian Tynne at the National Maritime Museum, Greenwich; Alice Hudson (Map Librarian), New York Public Library; Michel Brisebois, Rare Book Curator at the National Library of Canada; Richard Smith, Maps and Plans, National Archives and Records Administration, Washington; Sjoerd de Meer, Map Curator at the Maritiem Museum Prins Hendrick, Rotterdam; Father Joseph de Cock, Archivum Romanum Societatis Iesu, Rome; Catherine Hoffmann, Bibliothèque nationale, Paris; Marina Smyth, Notre Dame University; Carol Urness, Map Curator at the James Ford Bell Library, University of Minnesota; Lincoln Pratson, Earth and Ocean Sciences, Duke University, Durham, NC; Shingo Kimura, Ocean Research Institute, Tokyo University; James Gower and Howard Freeland, Institute of Ocean Sciences, Sidney, BC; Warren Wooster, University of Washington; Walter Smith, NOAA, and Davis Sandwell, Scripps Institution of Oceanography; Alfred Mueller, Beinecke Library, Yale University; Fred Musto, Yale University Library; Susan Snyder, Bancroft Library, University of California; Susan Danforth, John Carter Brown University, Providence, RI; Herman Stapelkamp, Algemeen Rijksarchief, Den Haag; Diane Shapiro, Wildlife Conservation Society, Bronx Zoo, New York; the staff of the British Columbia Archives, Victoria, BC; and the staff at the Vancouver Public Library Special Collections Division. In addition I would like to express my thanks to Naomi Pauls for her superlative editing; and Scott McIntyre of Douglas and McIntyre, Vancouver, and Joan Gregory of Sasquatch Books, Seattle, for their continuing support.

Contents

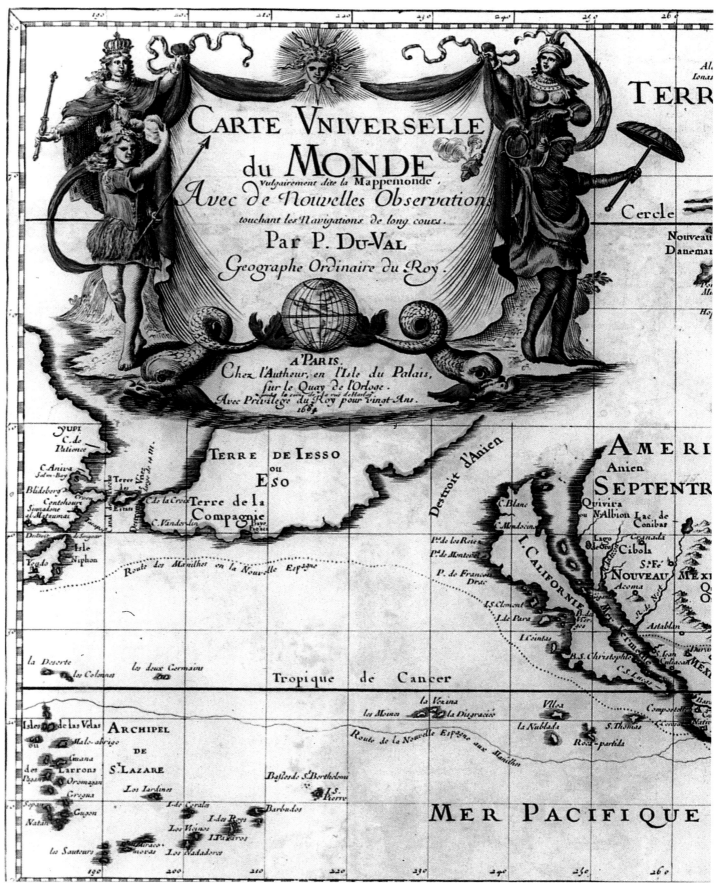

Map 3.

In many early views, the North Pacific Ocean was depicted as half land. In this 1684 map, part of a map of the world by French geographer Pierre du Val, a large continent, "Iesso" or "Eso," is a confusion with Hokkaido, the northernmost large island of Japan. "Company Land" ("Terre de la Compagnie") is one of the Kuril Islands seen by Dutch explorer Maerten Vries in 1643, but not defined on its eastern end. Some mapmakers interpreted this to mean it stretched to North America. The Strait of Anian ("Detroit d'Anien") separates Asia, or Jesso, from America, and California is shown as an island. In the west, Cape Patience, in reality on the island of Sakhalin, is shown as part of the Asian continent.

Historical Atlas
of the
North Pacific Ocean

MAGELLAN

Magnum
MARE del ZUR
cum Insula
CALIFORNIA.

De Groote
ZUYD — ZEE
en 't Eylandt
CALIFORNIA.

Gedruckt 't Amsterdam by R.&I.Ottens

Cartouche from a 1750 map of the
Pacific Ocean by Dutch mapmakers
Reinier and Joshua Ottens. The map
is shown on page 85 (Map 122).

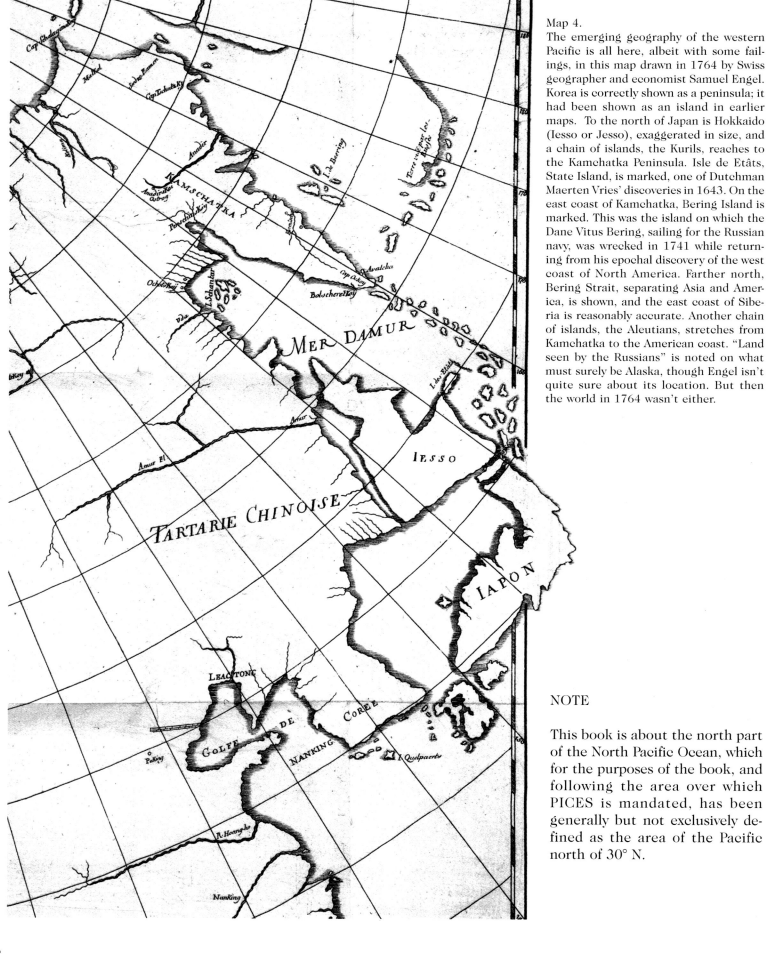

Map 4.
The emerging geography of the western Pacific is all here, albeit with some failings, in this map drawn in 1764 by Swiss geographer and economist Samuel Engel. Korea is correctly shown as a peninsula; it had been shown as an island in earlier maps. To the north of Japan is Hokkaido (Iesso or Jesso), exaggerated in size, and a chain of islands, the Kurils, reaches to the Kamchatka Peninsula. Isle de Etâts, State Island, is marked, one of Dutchman Maerten Vries' discoveries in 1643. On the east coast of Kamchatka, Bering Island is marked. This was the island on which the Dane Vitus Bering, sailing for the Russian navy, was wrecked in 1741 while returning from his epochal discovery of the west coast of North America. Farther north, Bering Strait, separating Asia and America, is shown, and the east coast of Siberia is reasonably accurate. Another chain of islands, the Aleutians, stretches from Kamchatka to the American coast. "Land seen by the Russians" is noted on what must surely be Alaska, though Engel isn't quite sure about its location. But then the world in 1764 wasn't either.

NOTE

This book is about the north part of the North Pacific Ocean, which for the purposes of the book, and following the area over which PICES is mandated, has been generally but not exclusively defined as the area of the Pacific north of 30° N.

A Pacific Ocean?

The Pacific Ocean as it is now defined did not exist in human mind before about 1500. Certainly the Chinese and Japanese knew that there was a vast ocean stretching far to the east, and similarly Europeans knew that there was an equally vast ocean to the west.

Those on the shores of Asia did not know how far the ocean extended, and those in Europe thought it extended to the east Asian shore. The idea that the sea all the way from Europe to Asia was "navigable in a few days if the wind is favorable" was the same idea that led Christopher Columbus in 1492 to sail westwards, as he thought, to the Indies. But even after having made a landfall he continued to think he was on the shores of Asia.

It required the European discovery of North America for there to be a Pacific Ocean. After Columbus, Cabot and many others thought they were sailing to the Indies, to Cathay, to Zipangu (or Chipangu, Marco Polo's name for Japan), and the Spice Islands by sailing westwards; but America "got in the way."

The Spaniard Balboa in 1513 crossed the isthmus at Panama and became the first European to confirm that another ocean lay to the west of America. There followed attempts to find a way through or round this inconvenient continent, a pathway finally being found by Magellan in 1520.

The Martin Behaim globe, famous as being the last European concept of the world before Columbus –

Behaim completed it while Columbus was still at sea in 1492 – shows well the Pacific and Atlantic as one sea extending westwards from Europe. The map shown here is a copy of the globe drawn on paper in 1730 by Johan Doppelmayer. If you look carefully, you can see that it is a map of a 360° globe; the Azores appear on the right-hand side of the "Pacific," as well as in their more correct position off the coast of Spain.

After Columbus and Cabot, many maps showed their discoveries as an extension of Asia. In particular, Newfoundland was considered to be at the far eastern tip of an Asian continent.

This view is well shown in the world map of Giovanni Contarini, drawn in 1506. On what to modern eyes is North America, he has clearly

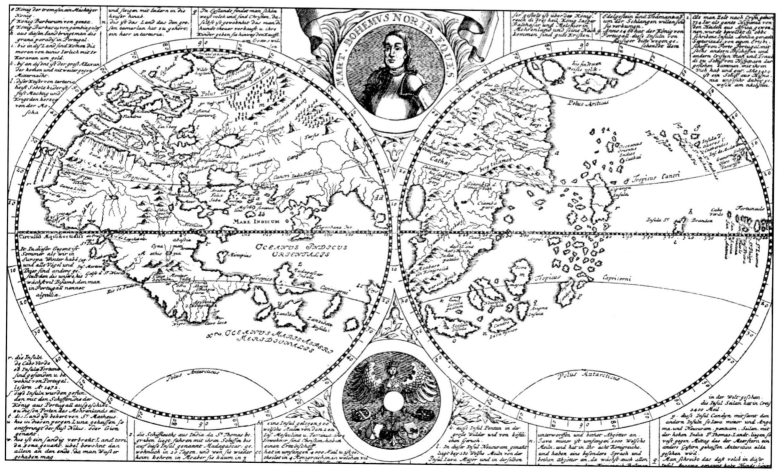

Map 5.
Map of the world according to the Martin Behaim globe, 1492, drawn by Johan Doppelmayer in 1730.

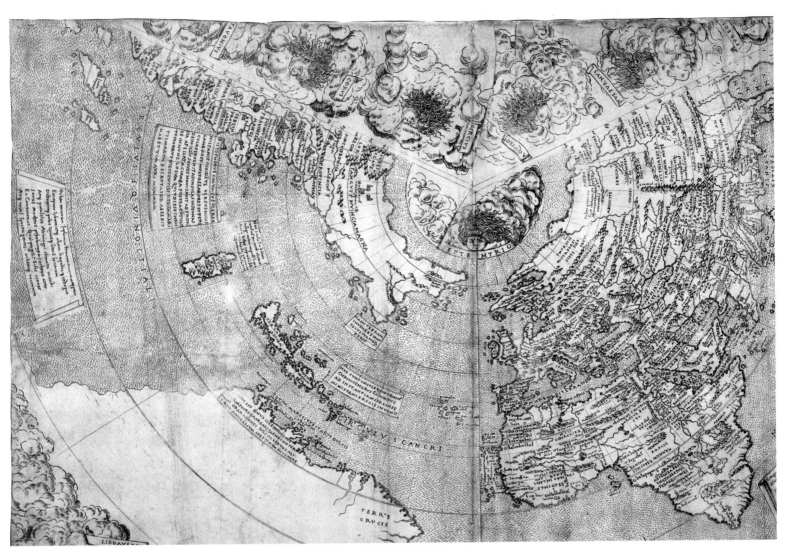

Map 6.
Giovanni Contarini's world map of 1506. The continents of North and South America are conspicuously missing, and the Pacific and Atlantic Oceans are one. Those parts of North America discovered by Europeans at this point are assumed to be an eastward extension of Asia. Ziapan – Japan – is in the middle of the pseudo-Pacific. This was the first printed map to show any part of North or South America. This map shows why Columbus thought he could sail westwards to the Indies. The map was engraved by Francesco Rosselli and is often referred to as the Contarini–Rosselli map.

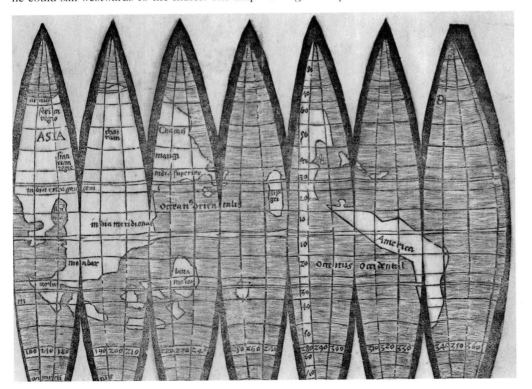

Map 7.
A world map by Martin Waldseemüller in 1506 was the first cartographic depiction of a Pacific Ocean. These are the gores for a globe drawn by Waldseemüller the following year, 1507. The depiction of an American continent necessarily broke the single ocean shown in maps like that of Contarini (above) into two: an Atlantic, and what would later come to be called the Pacific. Waldseemüller was the first to use the name "America" on a map, for South America.

marked Cathay; the island Zipangu is in midocean.

The first, and unusually early, portrayal of the Pacific Ocean along the lines of which we know it today was in a map drawn in 1506 by Martin Waldseemüller. It depicted the North and South American continents in perceptively reasonable form based on information available to him up to that time, and in particular the voyages of Amerigo Vespucci (after whom he coined the name "America"). In so doing, Waldseemüller's map, which has been called an inspired guess, showed a Pacific Ocean virtually by default. No matter that the west coast of his North America was almost a straight line, or that it must have been based on no more than an in-

tuitive guess; it stands as the first mapping of a Pacific Ocean. Apart from a huge Japan – Zipangu – again in the middle of the ocean, the map is a remarkably good delineation of an unknown sea.

Waldseemüller's map was a woodcut, a printed map, and as such was much more widely seen than previous manuscript maps. About 1,000 copies were produced. Thus it was relatively easy for other cartographers to copy Waldseemüller's ideas. The transcription of the Schöner globe, dating from 1520, shows a similar North American continent and Pacific Ocean

In 1529, a major cartographical step was taken in the map of the world drawn by Diogo Ribeiro. His

map is generally considered to be a copy of the secret official *Padrón general*, a large map that Spain constantly updated to make it the most complete map at any given time. Ribeiro was the chief cartographer of Spain and charged with its updating.

The breakthrough that Ribeiro showed on his map was the width of the Pacific Ocean. After two decades of Spanish exploration, Ribeiro finally reasonably correctly calculated the width of the ocean from the amount of longitude that must remain after all else was accounted for. This well-ornamented map has faded badly over the years, and a map redrawn for the Library of Congress in 1886 or 1887 is shown here.

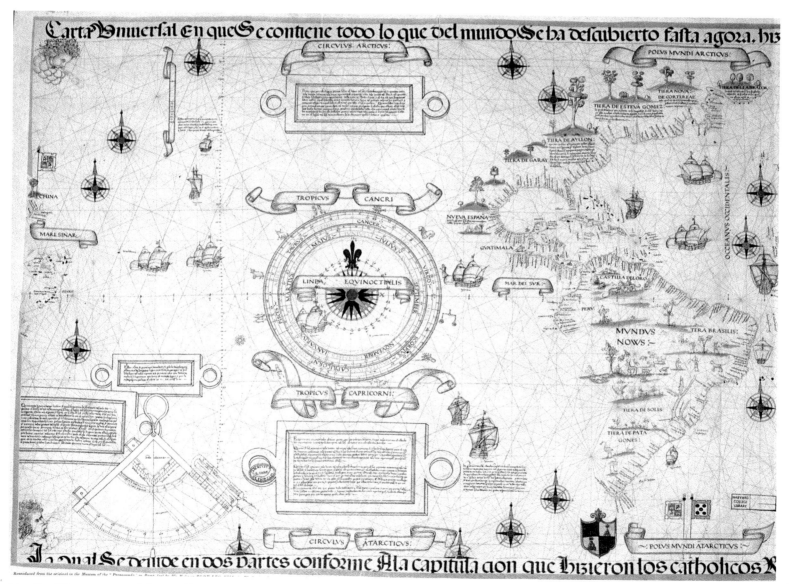

Map 8. Western part of the world map by Diogo Ribeiro, 1529. This was the first map to show the width of the Pacific Ocean with reasonable accuracy. This is a copy made in 1886 or 1887. It is clearer than the original, which has faded.

Map 9.
Sebastian Münster's world map of 1546 showed a large island of Japan in the middle of a new Pacific Ocean and many other smaller, imaginary islands.

Map 10 (below).
The globe made by Nürnberg astronomer and mathematician Johannes Schöner in 1520 showed the imposition of a new continent – Cuba, not America – splitting the medieval world ocean into Oceanus Occidentalis and Orientalis Oceanus – the Pacific. Schöner was a bit liberal with his Pacific islands, the largest of which was Zipangi – Japan.

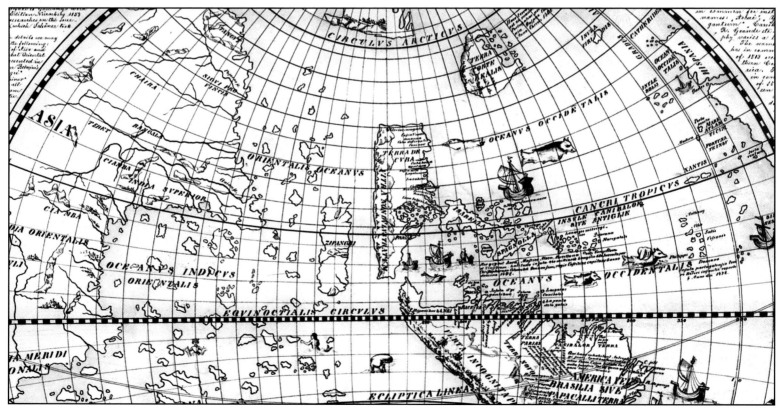

Triumphant Visions of the Boundless Ocean

The earliest recorded Chinese concepts of the world envisioned China at the center of the world surrounded by oceans. The oceans were the limits of the universe.

Early Chinese exploration of the Pacific was likely occasioned by religious motives. In 219 B.C. Hsu Fu was sent with several thousand men to search for a herb said to make one immortal, on "the great immortal island of the Eastern Sea," which has been interpreted to mean Japan. One Chinese theory – not generally accepted in Japan – is that Hsu Fu settled in Japan and set himself up as an emperor.

The most famous Chinese maritime explorer without a doubt was Cheng Ho, or Zheng He. In 1405 he was chosen as the leader of a large exploring expedition to the Indian Ocean. Cheng Ho was to lead six more expeditions after that, the seventh and last not returning to China until 1433. This final expedition was a massive affair, with 26,755 sailors, soldiers, and craftsmen. His expeditions reached Java, India, Arabia, Africa, and, some say, Australia. All were essentially westward expeditions, but all had to traverse the Pacific Ocean first.

As a result, Chinese knowledge of the Pacific and the other oceans he explored was immensely expanded, as were navigational techniques and experience.

Cheng Ho made maps, and one series in particular has survived, at least in a copy from 1621. Generally thought to have been drawn by some of Cheng Ho's men, this series of maps was reproduced in a book entitled *Wu Pei Chih* (literally "Notes on Military Preparation"), and are essentially navigational charts.

Twenty-four pages of maps cover an area from Nanking to the east coast of Africa, with 500 place names, including 200 in China itself. Perhaps not surprisingly, the maps of the coast of China are more detailed than other regions, presumably because Cheng Ho traversed the coastal seas twice for each of his seven expeditions. The tracks taken by his ships are shown as dotted lines, often accompanied by characters giving compass directions.

Cheng Ho's voyages gave rise to a number of early books in China, one of which, *Ying Yai Shêng Lan,* written in 1451, translates wonderfully as "Triumphant Visions of the Boundless Ocean."

Illustrations of ships contemporary with Cheng Ho from *Wu Pei Chih.*

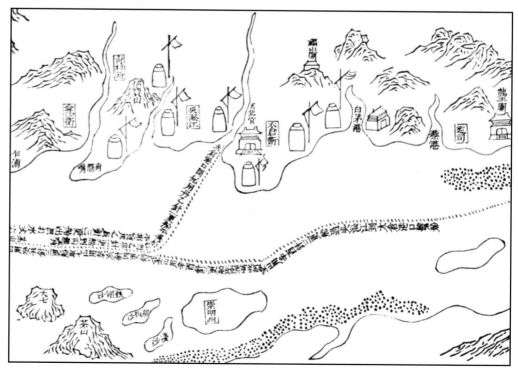

Map 11. Two sections of Cheng Ho's map, showing the coast of China at the mouth of the Yangtze River and part of the East China Sea. The dotted lines are Cheng Ho's tracks, and the Chinese characters give compass directions.

That Exceedingly Vast Sea – Balboa and Magellan

Late in 1512, the Spaniard Vasco Núñez de Balboa, an adventurer in the new Spanish colony of Darién, heard from the natives of a "land of gold, washed by a vast sea" a short distance to the west. In September 1513 Balboa crossed the Isthmus of Panama in search of gold and found a sea.

An allegorical portrait of Magellan entering the Pacific Ocean, from Theodor de Bry's *Voyages*, 1592.

On 25 September 1513 Balboa and his men emerged from the jungle onto a mountaintop and beheld foaming breakers on a curving sandy shore, beyond which was an apparently boundless ocean. Thus he became the first European to see the Pacific Ocean.

Balboa named it the Mar del Sur, the South Sea, because he had followed a southward route across the isthmus and it lay to his south from the point at which he arrived on the coast. Four days later, they were at the water's edge, where, tasting the water and finding it salt, he realized that he had found a new ocean and not just a large lake. He waded into the sea and ceremonially took possession of the ocean *and any coasts that it might wash* in the name of Spain, an action which would be cited later as evidence that the entire Pacific coast of North America belonged to Spain. This action of Balboa's was to mean that for centuries the Span-

ish would regard the Pacific as theirs: a Spanish lake.

When news of Balboa's discovery reached Spain it was received with great excitement. It was instantly recognized that this new sea would give Spain a chance at an even wider-flung empire. If Spanish ships now sailed westwards, the Spice Islands might be reached in a way that would circumvent the Portuguese claims to the East Indies, particularly if the islands lay farther east than thought. They might prove to be east of the Tordesillas line defining the boundary of Spanish and Portuguese spheres

of influence. Better yet, the new sea might lead to Terra Australis Incognita, the fabled Southern Continent that was considered at the time be required to balance the northern continents of the Earth.

After his discovery, Balboa made further plans for exploration, and in 1517 and 1518 two ships were built, *San Cristóbal* and *Santa Maria de la Buena Esperanza,* and began to coast the shores of the Gulf of Panamá in October 1518. Thus they became the first European ships to sail on the waters of the Pacific Ocean.

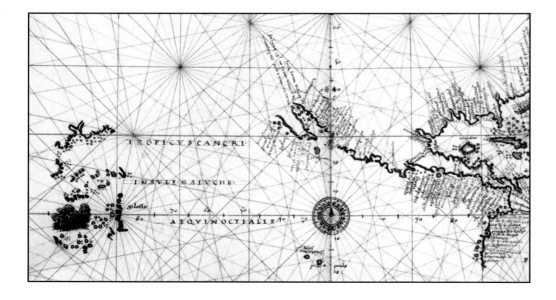

Map 12.
Part of a world map by Battista Agnese, 1542. This Venician map shows Balboa's isthmus and the Moluccas, the Spice Islands reached by Magellan. They had already been discovered by the Portuguese from the east. The Pacific Ocean is shown much narrower than it is in reality.

Fernão de Magalhães, better known by his anglicized name of Ferdinand Magellan, was a Portuguese navigator who was the first to act on the notion that although there was a continent blocking the way from Europe to the Spice Islands or Cathay, it might be possible to find a passage through the land and emerge into the ocean Balboa had seen.

The king of Portugal was uninterested in westward voyages because they would impinge on the territories given to Spain under the Treaty of Tordesillas in 1493 and 1494, when the two countries carved up the world as though it were theirs to carve. But the king of Spain, naturally enough, was interested when Magellan proposed a voyage to take possession of the Moluccas – the Spice Islands (now part of Indonesia) – for Spain by sailing west. He convinced the king that there was a good chance that the islands were on the Spanish side of the demarcation line. In fact it was difficult for either country to determine their position accurately as it involved calculation of longitude. Magellan was given command of five ships, which left Spain in 1519.

Magellan, of course, discovered a way around the southern tip of South America via the straits that today bear his name. Having emerged into the new ocean on an unusually peaceful morning in November 1520, after a long struggle to get through the Strait of Magellan, he named it Mar Pacifica – the Pacific Ocean.

We are fortunate to have the narrative of Antonio Pigafetta, an Italian nobleman who was, quite literally, just along for the ride. Pigafetta's narrative recorded:

Wednesday, November 28, 1520
We debouched from that strait [the Strait of Magellan] *engulfing ourselves in the Pacific Sea. We were three months and twenty days without getting any kind of fresh food . . . We sailed about 4,000 leagues . . . through an open stretch of that Pacific Sea. In truth it was very pacific, for during that time we did not suffer any storm . . . Had not God and His blessed mother given us such good weather we would all*

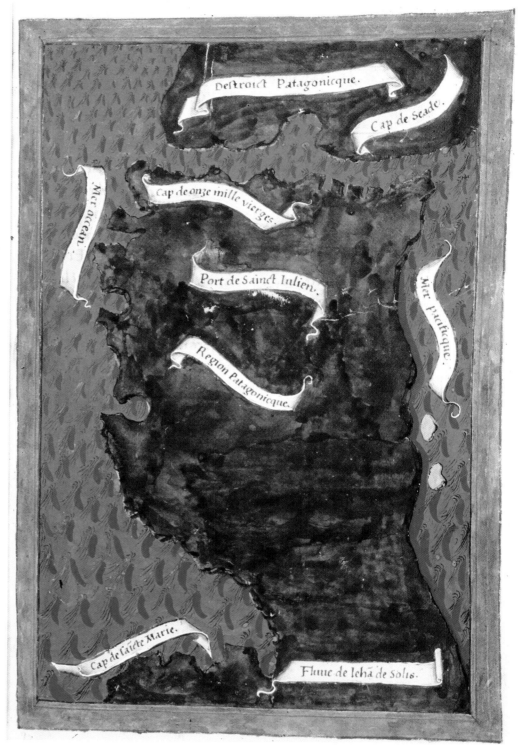

have died of hunger in that exceedingly vast sea. In truth I believe no such voyage will ever be made again.

In that prediction Pigafetta was wrong, but the vastness of the ocean would remain a critical factor in exploration and commerce until the age of steam, and sailors would soon learn that a knowledge of winds and currents was essential.

Magellan made it to the Moluccas, where he was killed by natives, but his

Map 13. The name Pacific Ocean first appears on a map. This "Chart of the Patagonian Region" is from the French edition of Antonio Pigafetta's book. South is at the top, with "Mer oceean," the Ocean Sea, the Atlantic, on the left, and "Mer pacifique," the Pacific Ocean, on the right. On the map in the Italian edition Latin is used; the Pacific is "Mare pacifico."

ship the *Vittoria* (*Victoria*), the sole survivor of the original five ships, continued westwards under Juan Sebastián del Cano and arrived in Seville on 8 September 1522, becoming the first to circumnavigate the world.

Voyage in Search of Gold

In the years after Balboa crossed the isthmus at Panama, the Spanish extended their explorations both north and south along the Pacific coast, their motivation, most of the time, being a search for wealth and riches. Peru was subjugated in 1533, and a Basque pilot, Fortún Jiménez, explored the coast of Baja California in 1533.

Spanish explorer Alvar Núñez Cabeza de Vaca arrived in Mexico City in 1536 with reports of pearls and emeralds to the north on the shores of the South Sea, and other tales of seven golden cities of Cibola

arrived with a Franciscan friar, Marcos de Niza.

In 1539 Hernando Cortés felt it worthwhile to investigate and sent Francisco de Ulloa in three ships north. Ulloa explored the head of the Gulf of California and rounded Cabo San Lucas and sailed north, discovering Isla Cedros, off the west coast of Baja, in January 1540. Ulloa only got as far as Cabo del Engaño, at 30° N, not finding gold or other wealth, but he did show that California was a peninsula, a fact that was to be overlooked by many mapmakers, who

would still insist on depicting it as an island (see page 45).

In 1542, Ulloa was followed by Juan Cabrillo, who got as far north as San Francisco. None of his maps have survived.

Map 14. Part of the fabulously illustrated wall map of Sebastian Cabot, drawn in 1544 and showing the discoveries of the Spanish in the Pacific up to and including that of Francisco de Ulloa in 1539–40. Spanish knowledge of the west coast of the Americas had proceeded faster southwards to Peru than northwards at this time, driven by the pursuit of gold. Nevertheless, a lot has been revealed since Balboa first saw the Pacific Ocean. Text and ornament fills the unknown Pacific.

Spanish Galleons Find Their Way across the Pacific

As early as 1522, when they had first arrived in the western Pacific, the Spanish had found it difficult to sail eastwards across the Pacific. One of Magellan's original fleet, *Trinidad*, under Gonzalo Gomez de Espinosa, left Tidore, one of the Moluccas, in April 1522 to attempt to sail east to Panama. He reached 42° N, seeing large whales and many flocks of birds, but could not make any headway eastwards and had to return to Tidore.

In 1527 Cortés, in Mexico, received directions from the king of Spain to assist ships he had sent to the Moluccas the year before to attempt to secure the islands for Spain. Cortés accordingly dispatched three ships, under Alvaro de Saavedra Ceron. He made it to the Spice Islands, but when he attempted to return by a route almost directly east, he was not able to do so. The following year he tried again, this time to the north, reaching 31° N, but the winds were always contrary and once again the ship had to return to Tidore.

In 1529 the king of Spain pawned any "rights" he may have had to the Spice Islands to the king of Portugal in return for a loan. In any case, by this time the Portuguese were in possession of the most important islands; but they could approach them and return by sailing east from Europe. Looking for other possible sources of wealth, the Spanish decided that the Philippines were within the Tordesillas-defined sphere of Spain and expeditions were mounted.

Sailing west across the Pacific at about 10° N was not a problem, but getting back again was a different matter.

Several unsuccessful expeditions were sent out, and then in November 1564 four ships commanded by Miguel López de Legazpi set sail from Navidad, on the west coast of Mexico, to take possession of the Philippines *and* solve the problem of getting back again. The pilot of the expedition was a friar, Brother Andrés de Urdaneta, a veteran of Pacific sailing, having

been with Juan Sebastián del Cano, the surviving circumnavigator of the Magellan expedition. In fact, Urdaneta had organized the whole expedition, even choosing the commander, a position a cleric was not allowed to hold.

Urdaneta had by this time formulated ideas about the circulation of the winds and currents of the Pacific Ocean, correctly realizing that there were both clockwise and counterclockwise rotations of air. He thus postulated that in order to pick up westerlies a ship would have to sail to higher latitudes, north or south. The question was: how far north or south?

Soon after sailing, one of the ships, *San Lucas,* separated from the rest of the fleet. Its captain, Alonso de Arellano, apparently wanted to reach the Philippines first and steal the glory and the choice spices; the real reason is not known. Whatever the reason, Arellano pulled ahead, reached the Philippines, and, fearing the arrival of the rest of the fleet, filled his ship's holds with cinnamon

Map 15.
A map of the Pacific and Atlantic Oceans made by Antonio de Herrera y Tordesillas. It was copied from a manuscript map of Juan López de Velasco, made about 1575 (see next page), and published in 1601. This map is from an edition of 1622. The Tordesillas demarcation line, the result of a treaty between the Spanish and the Portuguese to divide the world between them, runs through Brazil and also the Malay Peninsula. Spanish territory was supposedly west of the Brazil line and east of the Malay line. The Malay line was drawn as far west as possible by the Spanish (and this is a Spanish map) so as to include the Spice Islands in their domain, but at the time, no one really knew where it should be located.

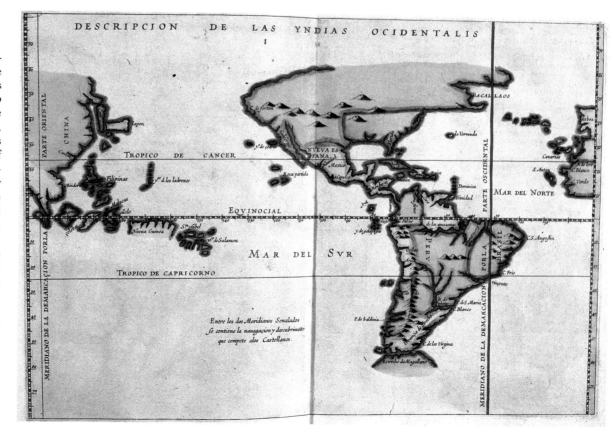

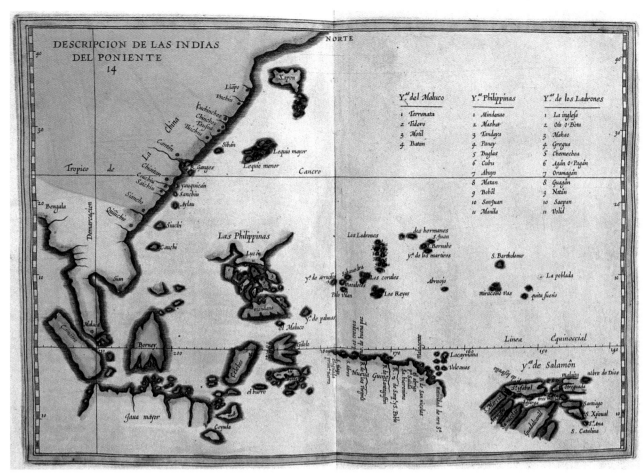

DESCRIPCION DE LAS INDIAS
DEL PONIENTE
14

Y.ᵃˢ del Maluco	Y.ᵃˢ Philippinas	Y.ᵃˢ de los Ladrones
1 Terrenata	1 Mindanao	1 La inglesa
2 Tidoro	2 Mazhat	2 Otis o' Bota
3 Motil	3 Tandaya	3 Mahao
4 Batan	4 Panay	4 Greguia
	5 Buglas	5 Chemechoa
	6 Cubu	6 Agán o' Pagán
	7 Abuyo	7 Oramagán
	8 Matan	8 Guagán
	9 Bohōl	9 Natán
	10 Sanjuan	10 Saepan
	11 Manila	11 Volid

Map 16. A map of the western North Pacific made by Antonio de Herrera y Tordesillas in 1601 (1622 edition). It was copied from the manuscript map of Juan López de Velasco, made about 1575. The supposed location of the Tordesillas demarcation line runs through the Malay Peninsula.

and headed back. Arellano had been briefed by Urdaneta about his theory of wind circulation, so he headed north, hoping to pick up the westerlies.

At about 43° N, he found them. Triumphantly, he tacked east, and for twelve weeks ran before the westerly winds, reaching the North American coast at 27° 45´ N, in Baja California, on 16 July 1565. Turning southward, Arellano reached Navidad in August.

The rest of the fleet had in the meantime reached the Philippines, taking possession of the island of Cebu for Spain. The *San Pablo,* with Urdaneta on board, was sent back to Mexico to urge that reinforcements be sent to Cebu. Sailing north, the westerly winds were picked up at about 35° N, and again after sailing east for about twelve weeks, the coast of North America was sighted at 33° 45´ N, at Santa Barbara. Arellano had hoped, perhaps, to claim glory by being the first of the fleet to reach the Philippines; but he

reaped a lasting place in history by becoming the first to sail across the Pacific Ocean from east to west.

Urdaneta, however, did not go unrewarded. A board of inquiry was established by the Spanish government to determine who was due the credit for solving the wind puzzle, and they decided in Urdaneta's favor. Arellano was disgraced and Urdaneta feted. But Arellano *did* the crossing first.

Soon after the establishment of the Spanish in the Philippines, a galleon made the round-trip every year, to supply the colony and bring back spices and gold to the coffers of Spain.

These galleons sailed every year from the Philippines between mid-June and mid-September, taking a route between 34° and 37° N; being able to quite accurately measure latitude, they could normally keep within these limits, where they knew the winds would be favorable. The passage across the Pacific then took about ninety to a hundred days.

Map 17 (right). Spaniard Juan López de Velasco's map showing the newly discovered sailing track eastward across the Pacific. The westward track is also shown. The map was drawn about 1575, ten years after the discovery of the wind pattern by Arellano and Urdaneta.

Map 18 (right, bottom). Track of the Manila galleon, from a captured Spanish chart. This map appeared in the English translation of the atlas of La Pérouse's voyage, published in 1798 (page 102).

The Manila galleons were not all the same by any means; they ranged from about 78 to 174 feet long. Though reasonably stable, they were not built for fast sailing nor for easy maneuvering. The square sails meant they could not sail into the wind at all, and even with fair winds they sailed at only about five knots. This is why the discovery of winds going in the right direction was so critical.

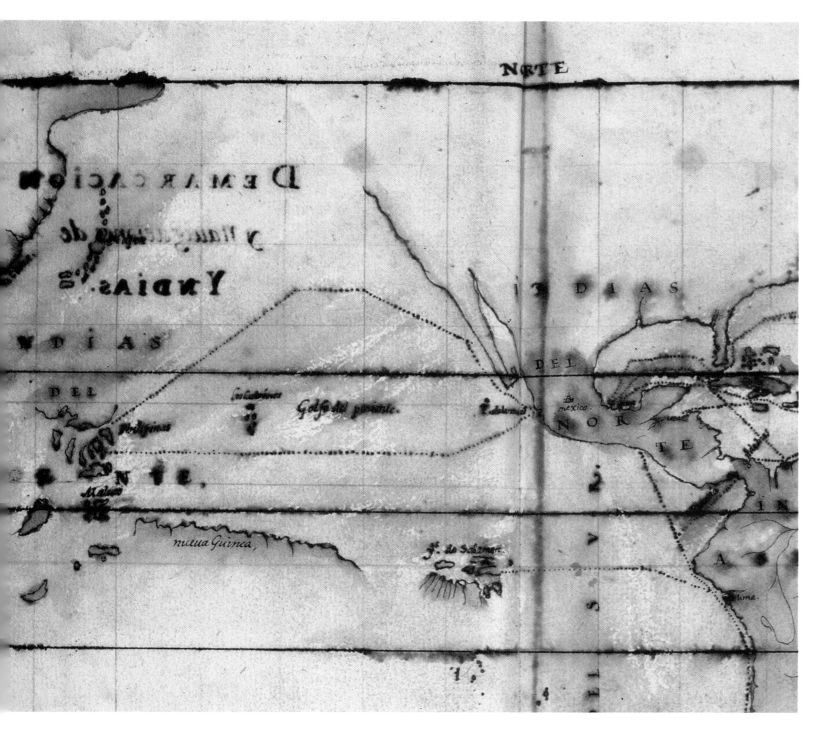

PART OF THE PACIFIC OCEAN BETWEEN CALIFORNIA AND THE PHILIPPINE ISLANDS.

from the Spanish Chart found on board the Galleon taken by Admiral Anson in 1743, which exhibits the state of Geographical knowledge at that period, & the tracks usually followed by the Galleons, in their Voyage between Manilla and Acapulco.

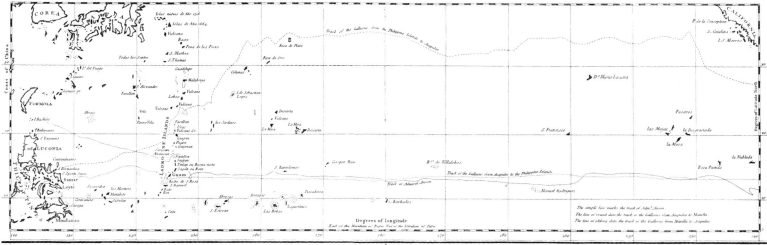

Japan and the Pacific

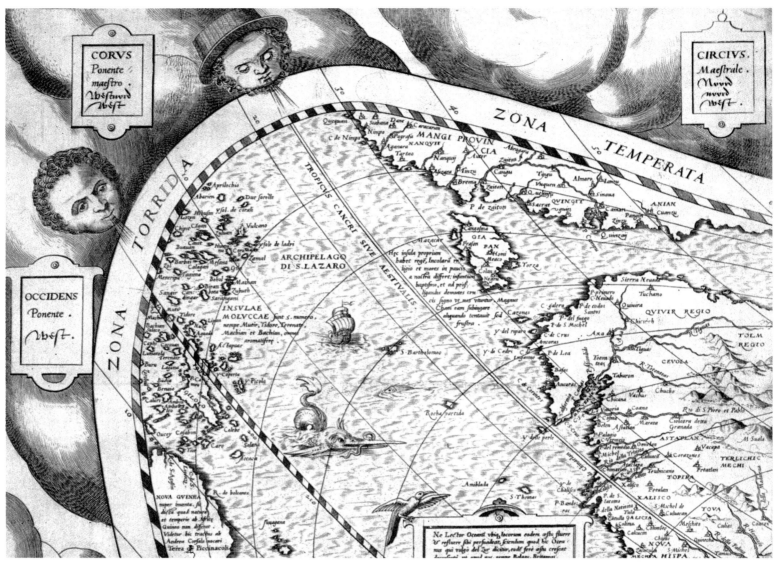

Map 19.
Based on information from Marco Polo, Japan sits in the middle of the ocean in this map, part of a world map drawn by Dutch mapmaker Abraham Ortelius in 1564.

The first European knowledge of Japan was from Marco Polo, who reported in his book, written at the end of the thirteenth century:

Zipangu [or Cipangu; Japan] *is an island far out at sea to the eastward* [of China]*, some 1500 miles from the mainland. It is a very big island . . . they have gold in great abundance.*

This explains why the first depictions of Japan on western maps showed it as a large island right in the middle of the Pacific, as in the map by Abraham Ortelius, drawn in 1564, shown above. Sebastian Münster's map, shown on page 12, likewise positions Japan in the middle of the ocean. Japan remained for many years one of the goals of gold-hungry European explorers.

The earliest surviving Japanese maps are the oldest of any country of the Pacific Rim; the oldest dates from 756, but is a map of landholdings. By the sixteenth century Japanese maps showed islands and terri-

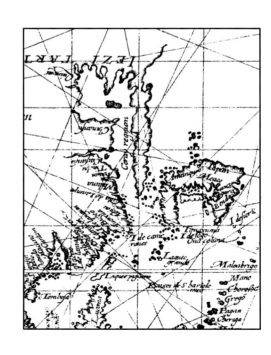

Map 20.
Japan, China, and Southeast Asia on an English map of 1599, drawn by Emery Molyneaux and published in Richard Hakluyt's *Principall Navigations*.

Map 21.
A stunning map of China and Japan drawn by Portuguese cartographer Fernão Vaz Dourado in 1570.

tories outside of Japan, but the maps were very impressionistic; they were works of art as well as maps.

Japanese knowledge of the Pacific was at this time very limited. It took the arrival of Europeans to make the Japanese more aware of the world beyond their shores.

The Portuguese were the first Europeans to arrive. The first documented ship was driven by storms to Tanegashima, just south of Kyushu, in 1542. It didn't take Portuguese traders long to exploit what they saw as an opportunity, for from about 1544 on, Portuguese ships began to frequent Kyushu. Kagoshima, at the southern tip of Kyushu, became a trading port. The Portuguese would trade with the Japanese for almost a century, before being expelled in 1640. The map above is a Portuguese map of Japan, drawn by Fernão Vaz Dourado in 1570.

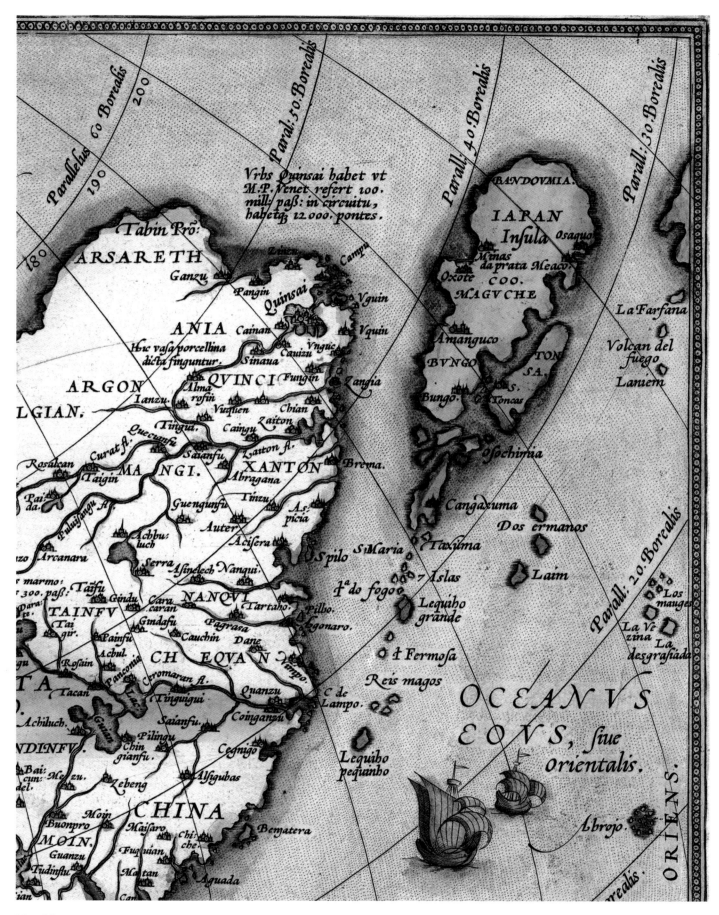

Map 22.
This rather beautiful depiction of Japan and the Chinese coast is from a map of Asia, *Asiae Novo Descriptio*, drawn by Abraham Ortelius in 1570.

The Separation of Asia and America

When Columbus and Cabot first reached North America from Europe, they thought they had reached the Asian continent, and maps of the period reflect this view. The map by Giovanni Contarini, drawn in 1506 and shown on page 10, is typical.

After the discovery of the Pacific Ocean by Balboa and, in the years following, the realization of its immense width, many still assumed that the continents of America and Asia were joined. Maps such as that of Waldseemüller, who was first to show a Pacific Ocean (page 10), were not based on exploration but were merely good guesses.

The Pacific Ocean was assumed to be a kind of large gulf with North America and Asia as its shores. A map by Paolo Forlani, shown below, was published in 1562 and is typical of this school of thought. The ideas in this map were copied from a map by Giacomo Gastaldi published in 1546.

In the middle of the sixteenth century it was widely believed that there must be a northern strait, which would "balance" the Strait of Magellan at the southern tip of the Americas. But then it was realized that for there to be this strait – the Northwest Passage – there would have to be an outlet into the Pacific, which would necessitate that Asia and America *not* be joined. An interpretation of the works of Marco Polo is said to have given rise to the idea of (and the name of) a Strait of Anian,

Map 23.
Part of Paolo Forlani's 1562 map of the world, showing the Pacific Ocean as a gulf between America and Asia. A long "Colorado River" flows into the Gulf of California, not from the American West, but from China.

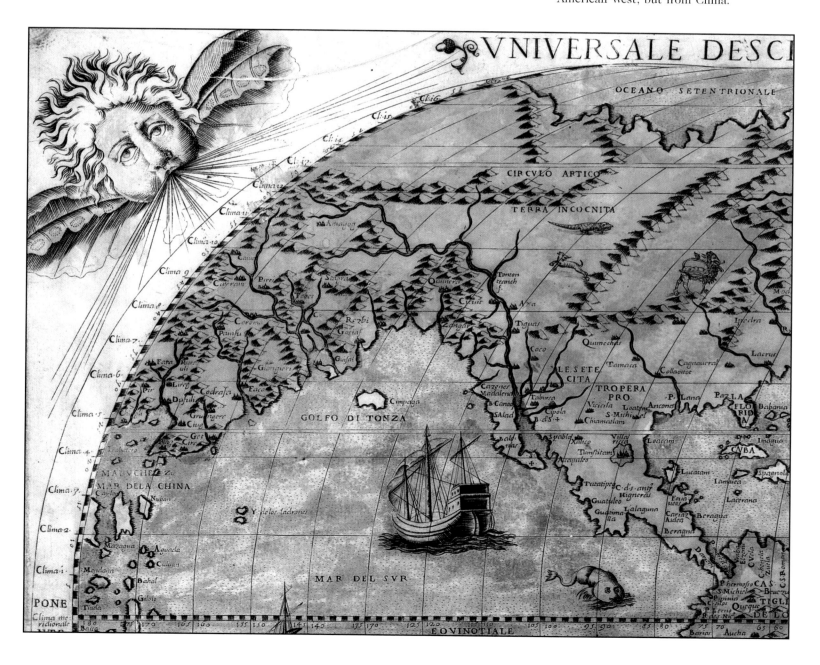

which was probably no better than a guess, but an intriguing one because of its clear resemblance to today's Bering Strait. Giacomo Gastaldi's world map of 1562, a revision of a 1546 map, seems to have been the very first to show this Strait of Anian, and once published, it was much copied, as was normal for the time.

Drawing a map showing a strait is one thing, proving it to exist quite another. It has never been proven that any of the mapmakers who drew a Strait of Anian on their maps derived their information from actual knowledge of what we know today as Bering Strait, yet theirs was a prescient guess.

Map 24.
Part of Giacomo Gastaldi's world map of 1562, showing a "Streto de Anian." This was probably the first depiction of a northern strait on a map.

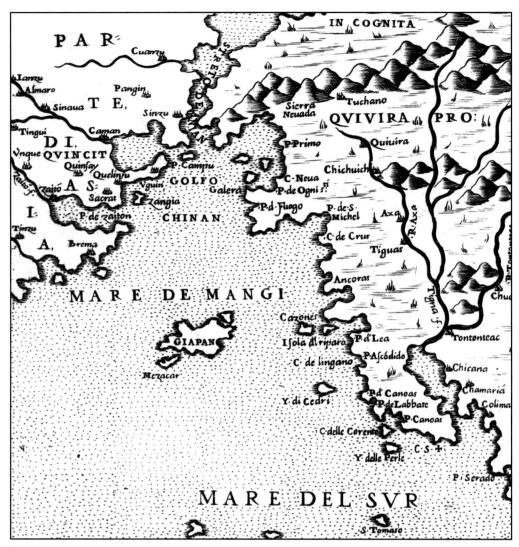

Map 25.
This map by Venetian mapmaker Bolognini Zalterii (but attributed by some to Verona mapmaker Paolo Forlani) was published in 1566 and is one of the first to show the separation of America and Asia. Was it a wild guess, or did he have some information we no longer know about?

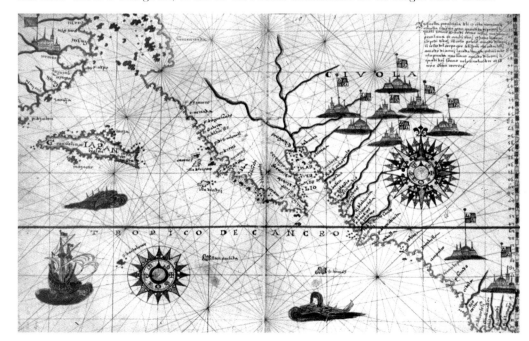

Map 26. A beautiful map of the Pacific Ocean drawn by Sicilian mapmaker Joan Martines in 1578. Japan sits splendidly in the center of the ocean, as Marco Polo's account suggests. Martines shows America and Asia separated, but hedged his bets by conveniently running the Pacific off the top of the map.

Map 27.
By 1570, when Abraham Ortelius published this beautiful map in his new atlas, *Theatrum Orbis Terrarum*, most mapmakers were incorporating the separation of the American continent from Asia into their maps. This map makes "Stretto di Anian" a major northern extension of the Pacific Ocean. Japan is massively out of scale.

Sir Francis Drake – How Far North?

Sir Francis Drake's so-called famous voyage, his circumnavigation of 1577–80, was the first circumnavigation by the English, the second after Magellan's, and the first in which the captain returned with his ship.

After sailing through the Strait of Magellan, Drake headed north, attacking Spanish towns and, in early 1579, attacking and plundering the annual Spanish galleon on its way to Acapulco from the Philippines. He then carried on northwards along the coast of California and, probably, farther north.

For a long time there has been debate about how far north Drake sailed. Some have claimed that Drake's voyage was deemed to have significant strategic value to England and the facts were altered or suppressed as a result, but unless clear archeological or documentary evidence can be found to show where he did get to, these claims will remain theories, albeit intriguing ones.

It does seem likely from the available evidence that Drake reached about 48° N. One recent claim was that he had reached as far north as 56° 40′, at the mouth of the Stikine River in the Alaska panhandle. Part of this hypothesis was based on a document called simply "The Anonymous Narrative," said to be the earliest written account of Drake's voyage; it is now in the British Library. An analysis of the written "48" revealed that it had been altered from 50, being changed to 53 on the way. Unstated, however, was the fact that the alteration had been made *before the ink dried*, making later deliberate change unlikely.

One factor used by some to indicate that Drake got much farther north than California is the evidence of cold temperatures. The account of Drake's voyage, *The World Encompassed*, has a section in it concerning the eastern Pacific Ocean, which may be viewed as the first climatological treatise on the region. It states:

Some of our mariners in this voyage had formerly been at Wardhouse, in 72. deg. of North latitude: who yet affirmed, that they felt no such nipping cold there in the end of Summer, when they departed thence, as they did here in the hottest moneths of June and July.

Drake's book offered a hypothesis to explain the cold:

The large spreading of the Asian and American continent, which (somewhat Northward of these parts) if they be not fully joyned, yet seeme they to come very neere one to the other. From whose high and snow-covered mountaines, the North and North-

Map 28.
Western hemisphere centered on the Pacific Ocean, from the title page to *Purchas His Pilgrimes*, published by Samuel Purchas in 1625. The map shows the explorations of Englishmen, including Drake and his ship in the eastern Pacific. John Saris, the first English East India Company trader to visit Japan, has his name marked on Japan.

west winds (the constant visitants of those coasts) send abroad their frozen nimphes, to the infecting of the whole aire with this insufferable sharpnesse: not permitting the Sunne, no not in the pride of his heate, to dissolve that congealed matter and snow.

Many other navigators on the Northwest Coast have complained of cold, James Cook among them, but nevertheless the degree of cold does seem rather more than would be likely at 48° N; but then again, it also seems too cold for 52° N. And why would Drake, or his chaplain, who was responsible for the book, make a point of complaining about the cold if it showed they were farther north than they were allowed to say, unless they were trying to circumvent the edict in a roundabout way? There is also some evidence (from tree rings) that the climate of the region at this time was considerably colder than the period over which meteorological information has been gathered, and this could have been responsible for the cold. The year 1579 may have been exceptionally cold, but the lower temperatures presumably would have applied both to 48° and 52°.

Map 29.
Part of the "French Drake Map," drawn by Nicola van Sype about 1583. The virtues of ornament for hiding lack of information! Drake's track vanishes behind the cartouche.

There was more at Drake's elusive harbor:

In 38 deg. 30. min. we fell in with a convenient and fit harborough [harbor], and June 17. came to anchor therein: where we continued till the 23. day of July following. During all whiche time, notwithstanding it was the height of Summer, and so neere the Sunne; yet were wee continually visited with like nipping colds . . . we could very well have been contented to have kept about us still our Winter clothes.

And it was difficult to fix their position for, the book noted,

neither could we at any time in whole fourteene dayes together, find the air so clear as to be able to take the height of Sunne or starre.

Drake specifically states that he thinks no Northwest Passage exists:

And also from these reasons we conjecture; that either there is no passage at all through these Northerne coasts (which is most likely) or if there be, that yet it is unnavigable. [Due to ice; correct!] *. . . Though we searched the coast diligently, even unto the 48 deg. yet found we not the land, to trend so much as one point in any place towards the east, but rather running on continually Northwest, as if it went directly to meet with Asia; and even in that height when we had a franke wind, to have carried us through, had there been a passage, yet we had a smooth and calme sea, with ordinary flowing and reflowing, which could not have beene, had there beene a srete: of which we rather infallibly concluded then conjectured, that there was none.*

Long thought to have been located in California near San Francisco, Drake's harbor has more recently been considered by some to be at

Whale Cove, in southern Oregon. Once again, this identification seems reasonable, even probable. But, like the theory that Drake sailed to 52° or 53° N, this idea is reliant on essentially circumstantial evidence. One favorite theory involves comparison of the coastline from Drake-derived maps with the modern coast; a perceived similarity is taken as evidence that Drake sailed past that location.

The "French Drake Map" (Map 29), drawn by Nicola van Sype about 1583, and supposedly seen and corrected by Drake himself, shows Drake's track disappearing behind a convenient cartouche. Four islands are shown on the western coast of America. The same four are shown on the "Dutch Drake Map," a similarly derived copy. These islands have been recently hypothesized to be crude depictions of (from the most northerly) Prince of Wales Island, the Queen Charlotte Islands, Vancouver Island, and the Olympic Peninsula. Of course, they could be, but without corroborating evidence, it is impossible to be definitive.

In 1647, Sir Robert Dudley, the son of one of Drake's financial backers, produced an atlas, *Dell' Arcano del Mare*, which was published in Florence. Some of the coastal features on the map of the northwestern coast of America (Map 30) have been compared to modern coastal features, specifically Cape Flattery, (at the extreme north of the coastline shown); Gray's Harbor (just south of the latter); and the entrance to the Columbia River (the large bay shown between 47° and 48° N).

Map 30.
Robert Dudley's map of western North America, 1647. It was one of the plates in his atlas, *Dell' Arcano del Mare*. Note the tip of Asia shown on the west side of the Pacific. The continuation of this map is shown on page 30 (Map 33), with more on Dudley's monumental atlas.

Drake's ship, *Golden Hind*, from the ornamentation on Hondius' 1589 map.

As one of Drake's financial backers, Dudley's father was in a position to have had direct information from Drake, which makes this map of particular interest. This is most intriguing, but is a similarity of coastal features sufficient to prove the map was drawn from a knowledge of the real coast?

A later printed map, presumed to have been derived from the "Queen's map," the original drawn for Queen Elizabeth I on Drake's return and now lost, is the 1589 world map by the famous mapmaker Joducus Hondius (Map 31). It has an inset map of Portus Nova Albionis in the top left-hand corner. This was derived from Drake's rendering of a harbor in which he careened his ship.

In showing the world as a double hemisphere Hondius created room for decorative devices and pictures. One is a picture of Drake's ship, *Golden Hind*. Hondius marked on the coast of Nova Albion – the name

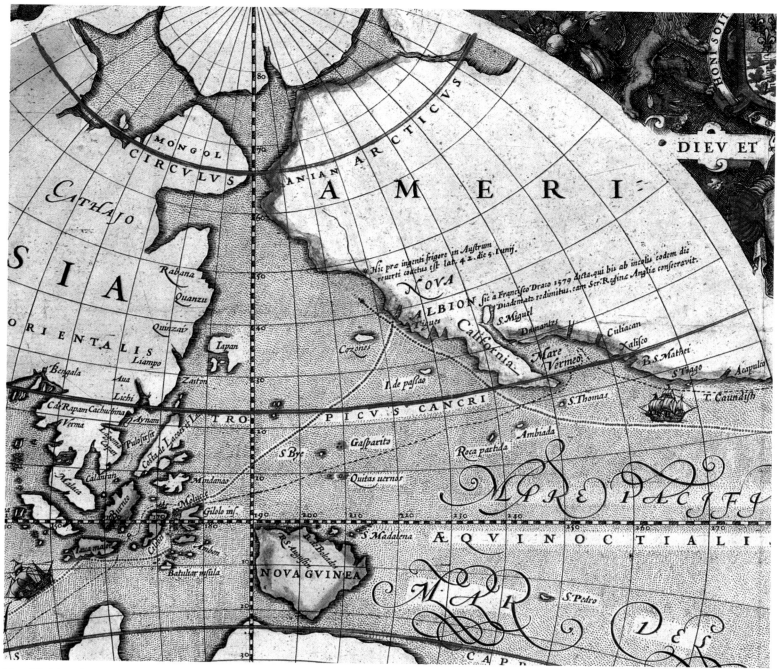

Map 31 (above).

The Pacific Ocean part of Joducus Hondius' world map of 1589. Was the change that seems to have been made on Drake's track the result of deliberate secrecy? Hondius was Dutch, and unlikely to be concerned about English intrigues on his maps (although he was working in England at the time); the map or maps he copied might have been changed, but then why would he have *originally* drawn Drake's track reaching higher latitudes? Unless and until conclusive evidence surfaces, the controversy over Drake's route in the Pacific, and in particular how far north he reached, will likely continue to rage. The track of Thomas Cavendish, the second English circumnavigator, is also shown on this map.

Drake gave to the coast he claimed for England – that Drake turned back at 42° N because of the cold. There are indications on this map that the track was first marked continuing to about 48° N and was then partially deleted from the plate – an interesting correction indeed. Hondius may have corrected it after reading an account of the voyage by Richard Hakluyt, which itself may have been edited at the queen's direction.

Map 32.

Drake's long-sought harbor on the west coast of North America, as depicted on the Hondius map of 1589. The location of this harbor has been the subject of endless debate among Drake aficionados.

Robert Dudley's Sea Atlas

Sir Robert Dudley produced his atlas, *Dell' Arcano del Mare* ("Concerning the Secrets of the Sea"), in Florence in 1647, and another edition in 1661. This huge and heavy tome was nevertheless specifically intended as a hydrographic atlas, to be used for navigation and carried on board ship.

Dudley's work was the first English sea atlas, the first sea atlas of the entire world, and one of the first to use Mercator's projection, on which straight lines are lines of constant bearing, an innovation which was an invaluable aid for mariners. A massive undertaking, the atlas comprised 146 charts, which took master engraver Antonio Lucini twelve years to engrave from Dudley's manuscript copies and utilized 2 270 kg or 5,000 lbs of copperplate!

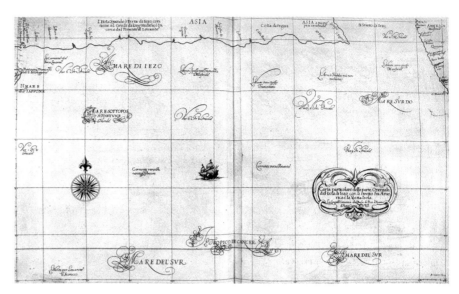

Map 33 (above) and Map 34 (below).
Two plates of the North Pacific Ocean from Robert Dudley's *Dell' Arcano del Mare*. The one below is the continuation westwards of the one above, which in turn is the continuation westwards of the map of the west coast of North America shown on page 28. A vast elongated Hokkaido ("Iezo") is shown extending westwards from the seas just off California. One wonders if Dudley had any knowledge of Maerten Vries' chart of 1643 (page 37), which showed Hokkaido as land with no definite eastward bound, and was to lead to other cartographers mapping a continent right across the North Pacific Ocean. These Dudley maps were first published in 1647 (the ones shown here are from the 1661 second edition of the atlas). On the map of Japan and the surrounding region, below, Korea is shown as an island, as it often was on maps of this period (see page 39).

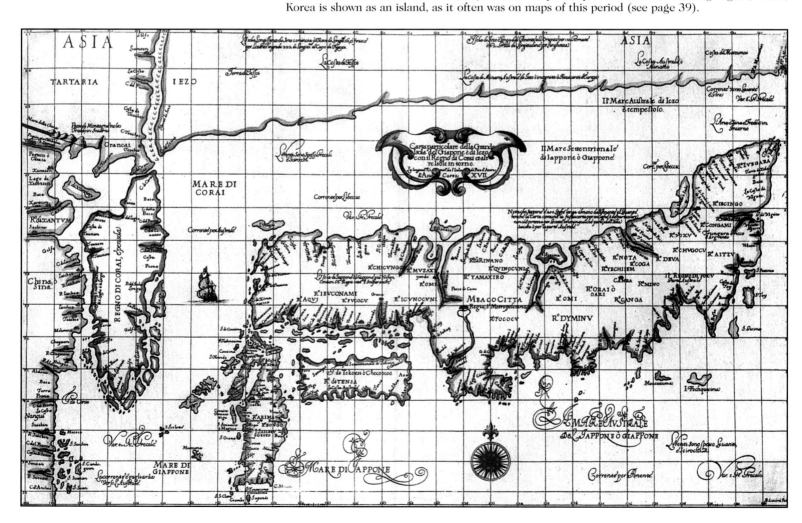

The Voyages of Sebastián Vizcaíno

Towards the end of the sixteenth century, new interest in the unexplored western coast of North America was stimulated by the establishment of the annual Manila galleon route southwards to Acapulco after crossing the Pacific in higher latitudes (see page 18). The appearance in the Pacific of English and Dutch "freelance adventurers" such as Francis Drake and Thomas Cavendish led to the suggestion that a port be established where the galleons could take refuge and where forces could be stationed to defend them.

In 1602 these considerations resulted in the Spanish navigator Sebastián Vizcaíno being given instructions to explore north from Acapulco. Vizcaíno was a merchant who had been involved in the Spanish trade with the Philippines and had sailed in a galleon in both directions across the Pacific; indeed, he had been aboard the galleon *Santa Ana* when it was captured by the English adventurer Thomas Cavendish in 1587.

He was to follow the course taken by Cabrillo some sixty years earlier (see page 16). However, following a common Spanish practice at the time Vizcaíno did not appear to have the previous expedition's charts with him, because he rediscovered San Diego, and the name is that which Vizcaíno gave to the bay. He also discovered the harbor at Monterey, and is again responsible for the name.

Vizcaíno, or at least his pilot or his cosmographer, made charts of the entire coast from Cabo San Lucas to Cape Mendocino, copies of which, made a year later by Enrico Martínez, "cosmographer to his Majesty in this New Spain," have survived.

One section, the northernmost chart of Cape Mendocino, is shown here. It took another two hundred years, however, for the long-lasting Spanish policy of secrecy to be revoked and it was not until 1802 that this summary chart of the entire voyage was published by the Spanish.

The reports of the details of this voyage are often contradictory, but it appears that one of the ships, commanded by ensign Martín de Aguilar, after being separated from the other ships in a storm, was forced northwards beyond Cape Blanco and, on returning southwards, came across a bay with a large river, which they named Rio Santa Ines. This river, because of its strong current and east-west direction, was thought to perhaps be the fabled Strait of Anian.

Many sailors had now succumbed to that scourge of long-distance voyages, scurvy, leaving the ship undermanned, and so no further exploration was carried out. But the reports of the Rio Santa Ines revived interest in a passage from the Pacific to the Atlantic, and this concept was to confuse the cartography of the Northwest Coast for almost two centuries. The "Entrada de Martín Aguilar," or "Opening discovered by Martin Aguilar" on English maps, was to show up on many maps for a long time after. Later, its supposed location somehow became about 43° N, and some thought it might be the Strait of Juan de Fuca.

In 1611 Vizcaíno took a pioneering Japanese delegation from New Spain (Mexico) back to Japan. Again with the idea of identifying potential refuges for the Manila galleon, in 1616 he surveyed several ports and carried out a hydrographic survey of the east coast of the island of Honshu, searching also for the fabled islands of gold and silver, Rico de Oro and Rico de Plata, which the Spanish thought existed in the ocean east of Japan. (These showed up on British Admiralty charts until 1875; see page 59.) Of course Vizcaíno did not find them, and none of the charts he made have survived, although perhaps one day they will be discovered in a Spanish or Japanese archive.

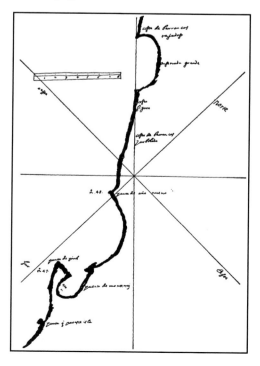

Maps of the coast of California at Santa Barbara and Santa Catalina (Map 35, left) and Monterey Harbor and the coast to Pillar Point (Map 36, right). From Vizcaíno's 1602 voyage, probably by Fray Antonio de la Ascension, copied by Enrico Martínez. These are part of a series of coastal maps drawn soon after the 1602 voyage.

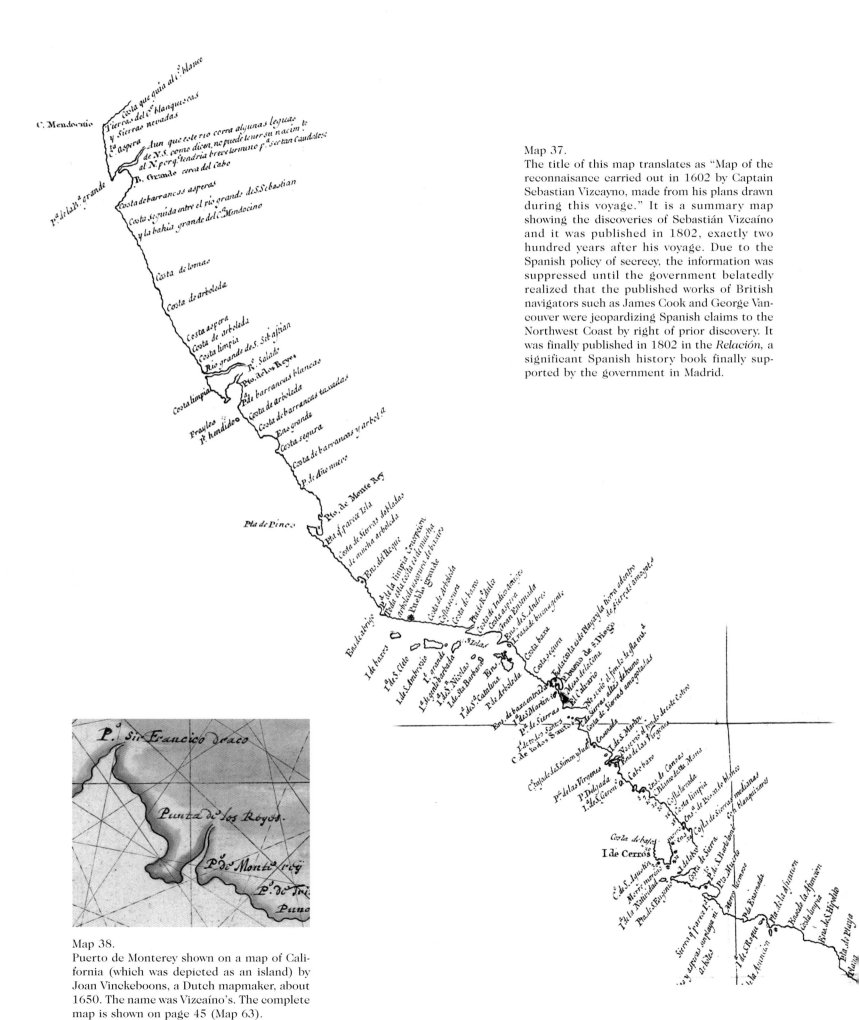

Map 37.
The title of this map translates as "Map of the reconnaisance carried out in 1602 by Captain Sebastian Vizcayno, made from his plans drawn during this voyage." It is a summary map showing the discoveries of Sebastián Vizcaíno and it was published in 1802, exactly two hundred years after his voyage. Due to the Spanish policy of secrecy, the information was suppressed until the government belatedly realized that the published works of British navigators such as James Cook and George Vancouver were jeopardizing Spanish claims to the Northwest Coast by right of prior discovery. It was finally published in 1802 in the *Relación*, a significant Spanish history book finally supported by the government in Madrid.

Map 38.
Puerto de Monterey shown on a map of California (which was depicted as an island) by Joan Vinckeboons, a Dutch mapmaker, about 1650. The name was Vizcaíno's. The complete map is shown on page 45 (Map 63).

The Dutch Reach the Pacific

The Dutch first reached the Pacific Ocean in 1599, when a fleet of five ships from a Dutch trading company sailed through the Strait of Magellan.

One of these ships, *De Liefde* (*Charity*), arrived in Japan in April 1600. The pilot was an Englishman, William Adams, who established himself as an advisor to the shogun Iyeyasu and lived in Japan until his death in 1620.

Close behind this first fleet into the Pacific came Olivier van Noort, sailing on behalf of a rival Dutch company. He made it through the Strait of Magellan, intending to copy the English example and raid Spanish galleons and towns. Van Noort became the fourth to circumnavigate the world, after Del Cano, Drake, and another Englishman, Thomas Cavendish.

And then, in 1619, Jacob Le Maire and Willem Schouten rounded the southern tip of South America, determining that it was not contiguous with a southern continent and naming it Cape Hoorn in honor of their city in the Netherlands.

Dutch merchants had reached the East Indies by late in the sixteenth century and by 1602 had reached the Moluccas. Jan Huijghen van Linschoten published a book called the *Itinerario* in 1596 which summarized the Dutch knowledge of the region; it included the map shown here.

In 1600 the English East India Company was formed, and in 1602, the Dutch East India Company was created to compete with it.

The Dutch traders arrived in Japan first, in 1609, at Hirado, near Nagasaki, and received official trading privileges from the Japanese government, indeed, were encouraged to set up a factory. What a difference from what was to come in future centuries! The first English East India Company trader to arrive in Japan was John Saris, who arrived in Hirado in June 1613 only to find the Dutch already installed. However, with the help of William Adams, the English obtained similar trading rights to those of the Dutch. Saris' name is shown on the map of English explorations on page 26. The English, it seems, tried to sell the wrong goods to the Japanese, and were unsuccessful as a result; the Japanese did not want their woolens, and the English retreated in 1623, leaving the trade to the Dutch, who were destined to control it for more than two centuries.

Good Dutch relations with the Japanese did not continue long, however, and in 1641, the Dutch traders were required to relocate to the man-made island of Deshima, in Nagasaki Bay, where their activities could be monitored. They remained there until the nineteenth century.

Much of the subsequent Dutch exploration and expansion effort in the Pacific was directed to the south, towards Australia, the west coast of which was discovered in 1616.

Map 39

Part of a map of Southeast Asia published by Jan Huijghen van Linschoten in his *Itinerario* in 1596. Japan is shown hook-shaped, as it often was on early maps. Also of note is Korea, shown as a nearly circular island. East is at the top.

In 1638, the governor of the Dutch East India Company, Antonio van Dieman, authorized Abel Tasman to search the Pacific for "islands of gold and silver" rumored to lie east of Japan. Such non-existent islands were shown on maps in that location well into the nineteenth century, and were founded on the belief that silver and gold were most likely to be found in the latitudes of 31° to 42°. The rumor originated with the Spanish, but the Dutch knew of mines in northern Honshu that satisfied this criterion. Tasman, much better known for his later forays to the South Pacific (Tasmania is of course named after him), was captain of one ship, Mathijs Quast of another. They spent the second half of 1639 wandering over vast expanses of the Pacific east of Japan, reaching as far north as about 42° and as far east as about 177° W, finding no islands of silver or gold, and little land beyond the eastern coast of Honshu.

Not discouraged by this lack of results, van Dieman dispatched two ships in 1643, commanded by Maerten Gerritsz Vries. *Castricum* and *Breskens* were to "investigate" the mainland coast of Tartary and carry out yet another search for the fabled islands of silver and gold.

Castricum, with Vries, lost contact with *Breskens* near the northern tip of Hokkaido and continued alone. Vries again of course found no islands of silver and gold, but he did discover some of the Kuril Islands and increased geographical knowledge of the western Pacific.

Vries sailed through a strait (now Vries Strait) between Ostrov Iturup, the Kuril Island immediately to the northeast of Hokkaido, and Ostrov Urup, farther to the northeast. The latter he believed to be not an island but part of a continent, which he named Companies Landt, after his East India Company. This was to add to geographic confusion for a century and a half, for a myriad of maps were later produced that showed Company Land or some variant of it stretching across the North Pacific to a Strait of Anian on a northwest coast of America (see Maps 43–47).

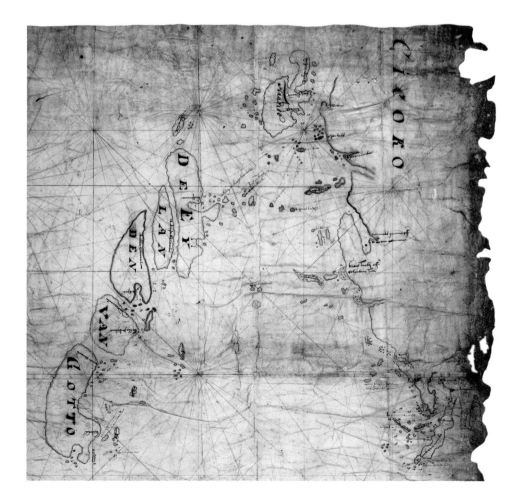

Map 40 (left).
A Dutch map of the westernmost part of Japan and the Gotoretto, the Goto Islands in Korea Strait, between Japan and Korea. Nagasaki is shown at bottom right; this was the location of the Dutch trading station in Japan. The map is undated but is believed to have been drawn about 1680.

Map 41.

Hessel Gerritz's monumental map of the Pacific Ocean, drawn in 1622 and now residing in the Bibliothèque nationale in Paris. It was drawn as the Dutch became more and more interested in the Pacific. The route of Jacob le Maire and Willem Schouten is shown around the southern tip of South America and into the Pacific past Cape Horn, which Schouten named Kaap Hoorn after his hometown in Holland. The fleet shown at the bottom of the map is that of Le Maire and Schouten. Hessel Gerritz was appointed cartographer to the Dutch East India Company in 1617. In this map drawn, or rather painted, in that capacity, the width of the Pacific is reasonably accurate, though longitude is not marked. One legend comments on the "great breadth between the most eastern and western places which are situated far south and north." The navigator portraits at top right are (from left to right) Balboa, Magellan, and Le Maire.

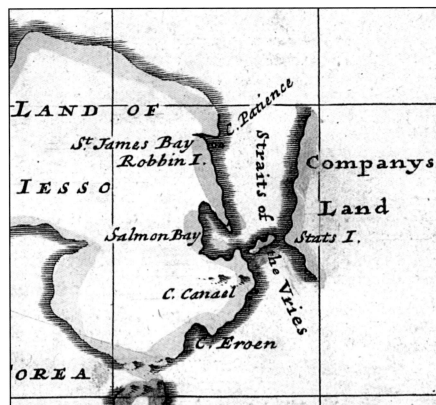

Map 43.
Maerten Vries' discoveries influenced mapmakers for a century and a half after his voyage. Hermann Moll showed a "Strait of the Vries" and "Companys Land" on his world map of 1719. (See also Map 79, page 55.)

Map 42. A Japanese map of the harbor of Nagasaki, drawn about 1680. The artificial island of Deshima, where the Dutch traders were required to live, is clearly shown.

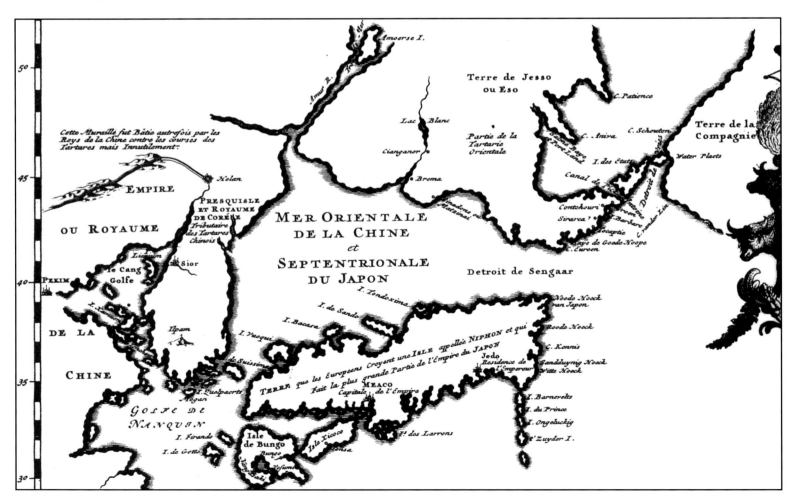

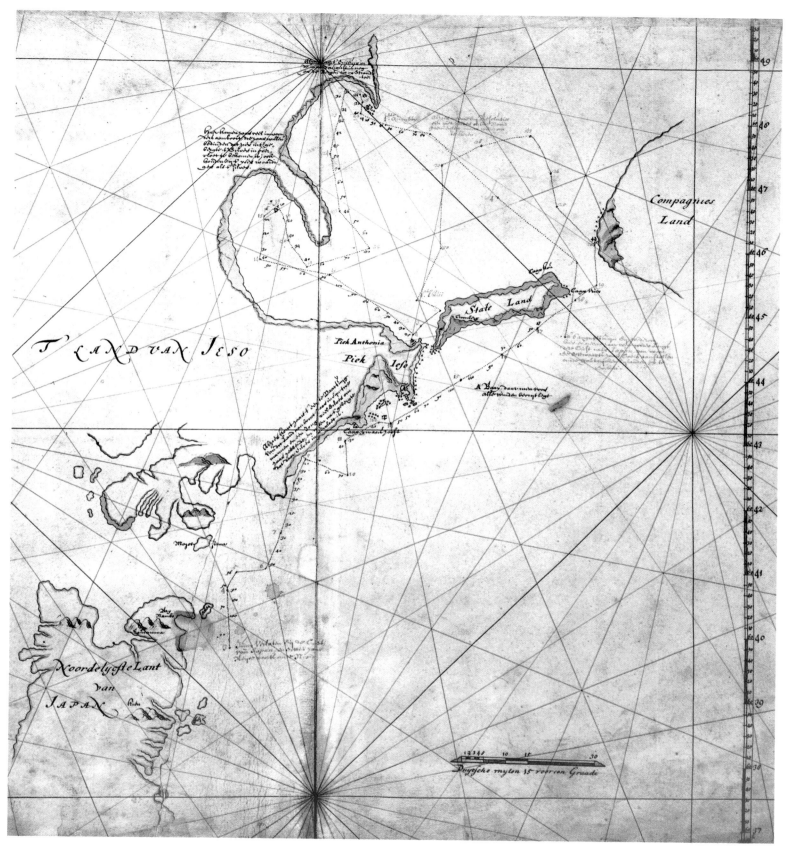

Map 45.
Maerten Vries' map, or at least a contemporary copy, showing his "discovery" of Company Land, actually one of the Kuril Islands. Compagnies Land was named for the Dutch East India Company, his employer. State Land was named for his country, or state, the Netherlands.

Map 44 (left).
This map, drawn by Henri Chatelain in 1719, illustrates the confused geography of the western Pacific at the time. It shows "Terre de la Compagnie" disappearing behind an ornate cartouche, a favorite device of cartographers when they had no idea what was really there. Hokkaido, shown here as "Terre de Jesso ou Eso," curves up to meet Company Land via what in reality are the Kuril Islands.

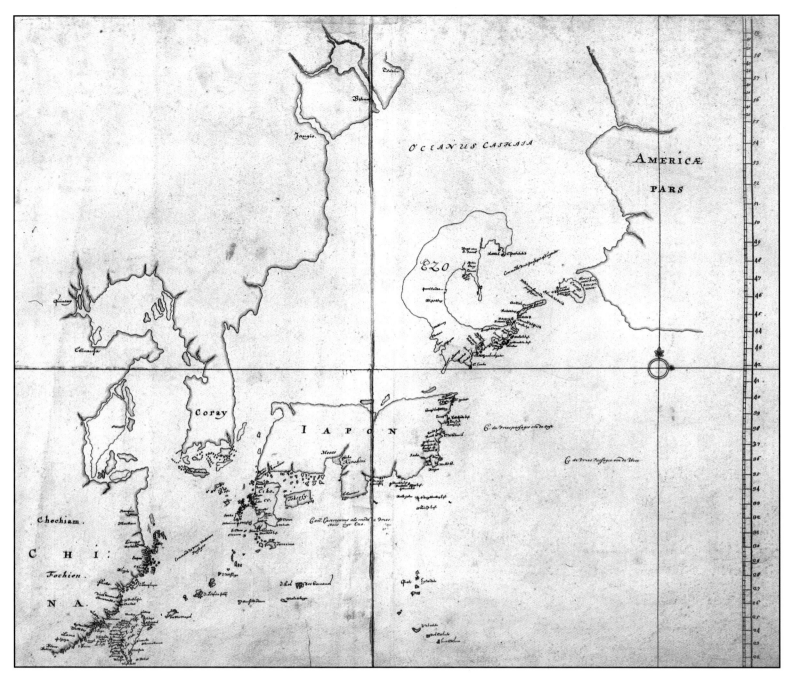

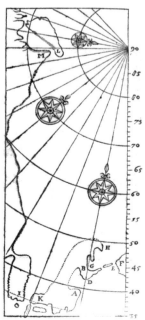

Map 46 (above).
A map contemporary with Vries' drawn about 1644 or 1645 by Isaak de Graaf. Suddenly Vries' Company Land has metamorphosed into "Americae Pars" – part of America. To make this work, mapmakers had to show a continent stretching right across the North Pacific, and many did just that.

Map 47 (left).
A map drawn to illustrate a published account of Vries' voyage. I is Korea; K is Japan; A is also Japan; B is the capital of Jeso (Hokkaido); G is the bay reached by Vries; H is his northernmost point reached; E is "Vries Strait"; and F is "Kompagnies Lant in Amerika." It is easy to see how this idea confused Vries' Company Land with the North American continent. Being a printed book, this presumably had much wider influence than manuscript maps.

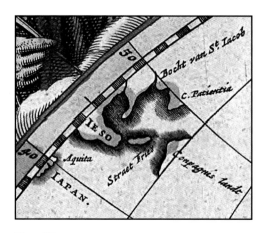

Map 48.
The first atlas depiction of Vries' discoveries was on a world map by Joan Blaeu in 1664. This small part of the edge of the western hemisphere is almost right off the map, literally!

Early Maps of Korea

Early mapmakers couldn't make up their minds as to whether Korea was an island or a peninsula. Because it was a tributary state of China, maps were not usually drawn only of Korea, but of larger areas. Abraham Ortelius' maps of 1570, shown on pages 22 and 25, didn't show Korea at all. Linschoten's map published in 1596 (page 33) showed an "Ilha de Corea" as an almost circular island .

By the middle of the seventeenth century, about half of the maps of the region showed Korea as an island, half as a peninsula, the latter winning out as time went on and geographical knowledge improved.

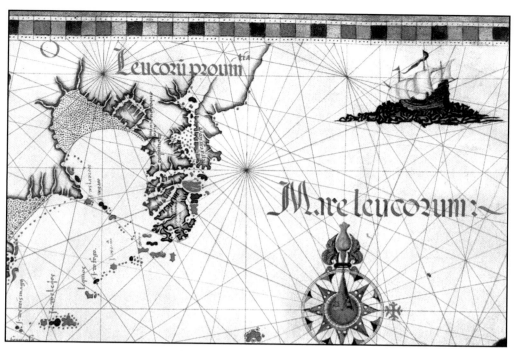

Map 49.
Diogo Homem's beautiful manuscript map of 1558 showed Korea as a peninsula and an archipelago; the large island at the southern end is Japan.

Map 50.
Luis Teixeira's map of Japan and Korea, showing Korea as an island, appeared in an addendum to Abraham Ortelius' *Theatrum Orbis Terrarum*, published in 1595. It was relatively widely circulated and much copied.

Map 51.
Korea as shown on Martino Martini's map of 1655. At this date some cartographers still showed Korea as an island, while others showed it as a peninsula.

Early Maps of China

Until relatively recently, maps in China have had a somewhat different role than those from western cultures. Maps were created as part of a larger intellectual and cultural undertaking that included more than geography and astronomy, encompassing philosophy, literature, art, and religion. Chinese maps often lack a fixed point of reference or change scales from one part of the map to the next, depending on the relative significance of the object being viewed, and often devote much space to text.

The ocean was seen as threatening and depicted with violent waves; more emphasis was given to (presumably less threatening) rivers.

After Cheng Ho's voyages in 1493, the Chinese emperor became increasingly concerned about foreign influences and in 1500 forbade anyone to put to sea on pain of death; foreigners were restricted to certain strictly controlled ports.

Even dynastic change in 1644 to the Manchu did not change the essentially land-emphasized view of the world. Early Chinese maps, then, tend to be depictions of the land, incidentally bordered by the Pacific Ocean. They were maps of the Chinese world, Sinocentric views of the land ruled by the emperor. This attitude, combined with that of the Japanese, meant that the Pacific was left to European powers to fight over.

One important early Chinese map is the *Huatyi tu*, a "Map of China and the Barbarians." It was carved in stone about 1136, though the map itself may date from even earlier: 1040 has been suggested. The 1 m (3 feet) square original is in a Chinese museum, and a paper transcript is shown here (Map 55). The Great Wall is prominent, and much text surrounds the map, describing the foreign countries.

A particularly beautiful example of the cartographic style developed during the Song dynasty (960–1279) is still evident on a world map drawn in 1743. In the section reproduced

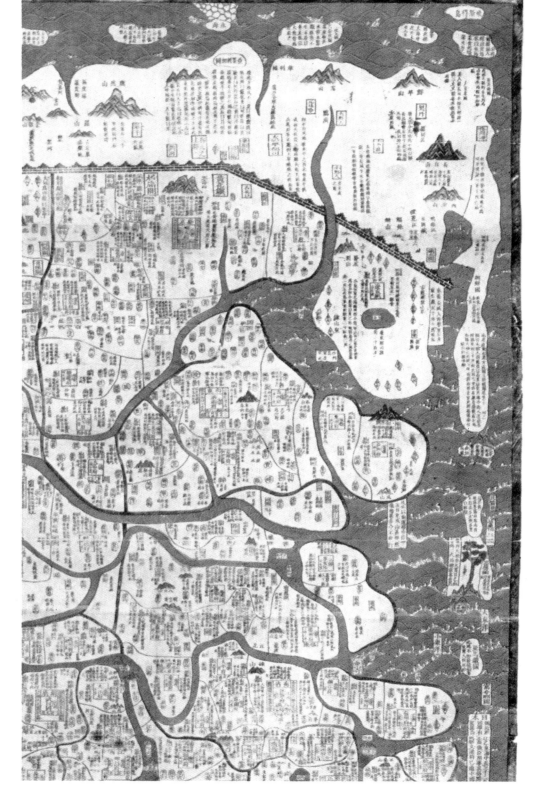

Map 52
Part of an anonymous, untitled Song dynasty Chinese world map, 1743. The map is about 1 200 x 1 370 mm (4 x 4½ feet). A gray-green multitude of "threatening" surf-topped waves uniformly depicts the seas. Rivers are almost as wide as coastal inlets, reflecting their importance.

Map 53. Pacific Ocean portion of a globe made in 1623 in Bejing by two Jesuits, Manuel Dias and Nicolo Longobardi; it is signed in their Chinese names, Yang Ma-no and Lung Hua-min. The globe is made of wood and is painted with lacquer. It is 592 mm (23 inches) in diameter.

here, from the northeastern part of the map, the coast of Asia is shown (Map 52). In the north, the Great Wall is again prominent. The map shows the Liaodong peninsula and then, farther west, a thin Korean peninsula. In reality, of course, the latter is much larger than the former, but it was not part of China, and this is a Chinese map.

The "threatening sea" of the Pacific Ocean is shown in the form of large stylized waves.

The arrival of Jesuit missionaries in China in the late sixteenth century is generally considered to have contributed a great deal to mapping in that country. The pre-eminent missionary was Father Matteo Ricci, who, in response to Chinese interest in Europe, produced a series of maps of the world that combined European techniques with Chinese. In order to please his hosts, Ricci placed China near the center of his maps. His first map has not survived but a close copy is illustrated in a book dated 1613.

The globe shown above was painted in 1623 by two Jesuits, Manuel Dias and Nicolo Longobardi.

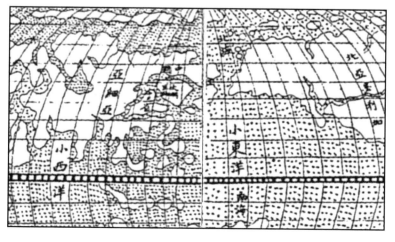

Map 54 (left). *Yudi shanhai quantu,* from Zhang Huang, *Tushu bian,* 1613.

(top left) Father Matteo Ricci, holding a map. From Du Halde's *Description Geographique . . . de l'Empire de la Chine,* 1735.

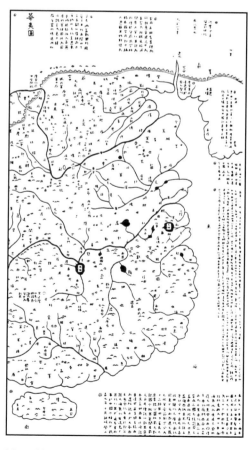

Map 55. *Huatyi tu,* "Map of China and the Barbarians." It was carved in stone about 1136, and probably reproduces a map drawn about 1040. This is a paper representation.

The Russians Reach the Pacific

An ever-expanding search for furs led Russian Cossacks eastwards across Siberia, and in 1639 Ivan Moskvitin reached the shores of the Sea of Okhotsk. In 1643–45 Cossack Vasilii Poyarkov reached the sea via the Amur River.

His exploration was followed in short order by a remarkable voyage by Semen Dezhnev.

The popular perception is that Vitus Bering was the first person to show that Asia was separated from America by a strait; after all, the strait in question is named after him.

However, this is a case of a relatively well documented exploration, that of Bering's first voyage, overwhelming relatively sparse information available about a predecessor. In fact the first (documented) person to sail through Bering's strait was an illiterate Siberian Cossack named Semen Ivanovitch Dezhnev, who in 1648 sailed from the mouth of the Kolyma River, which flows to the Arctic Ocean at about 162° E, round the extreme northeastern tip of Siberia to a point near the Anadyr River, which flows into the Pacific at about 176° E. By so doing he proved, perhaps unwittingly, that Asia and America were separate.

The expedition consisted of seven small *kochas*, roundish-hulled ships that were well designed to deal with ice-filled seas, and ninety men. They left the Kolyma on 20 June 1648. We are not sure how long it took to get to the Anadyr, but we do know that only two ships completed the voyage, that commanded by Dezhnev and that by Fedot Alekseyev.

Because his voyage answered a significant scientific question – in this case whether Asia and America were joined – Dezhnev has been placed by some writers alongside Vasco da Gama, Christopher Columbus, and Ferdinand Magellan.

But Dezhnev did not draw any maps, or if he did, they did not survive; indeed it is far from clear whether any navigational log or other record was ever kept. This is generally a poor way to ensure your exploits are documented for posterity, but Dezhnev was only interested in the gathering of furs, and in survival, and probably did not view himself as an explorer.

Map 56.
The Godunov map of eastern Siberia, named after Petr Godunov, a Russian governor, who commissioned it in 1667. This is probably the earliest map to show the Russian Pacific coast based on actual exploration. The Kolyma and Lena Rivers are shown, incorrectly flowing to the Pacific. The map was drawn with south at the top but is shown here upside down, with north at the top.

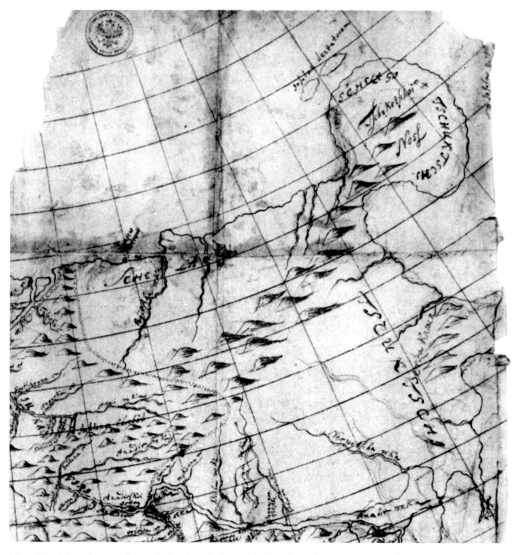

Map 57. Map drawn about 1736 by Gerhard Müller, based on Semen Dezhnev's reports.

It seems likely that Bering knew of his predecessor's achievement, for when the first public notice of Bering's voyage of 1728 (see page 63) was published in the *St. Petersburg Gazette* in March 1730, it contained the information that Bering had "learned from the local inhabitants that fifty or sixty years before a vessel arrived in Kamchatka from the Lena." Inaccurate and incomplete, this appears to have been a reference to Dezhnev's voyage.

In 1736, Gerhard Müller, one of the scientists attached to the Second Kamchatka Expedition, Bering's second voyage (see page 67), found a written account of Dezhnev's voyage in government offices in Yakutsk, in eastern Siberia. This account was sent back to St. Petersburg in 1737, and was published in Russian in 1742, but did not receive much attention until it was published in 1758 by the Russian Academy of Sciences.

By that time the name of Bering Strait had come into use, and Dezhnev Strait was not to be.

The first published information about Dezhnev's voyage appears to be that in a map by a Dutchman, Nicholaas Witsen, in 1687. In 1665 he visited Moscow and obtained geographical information sufficient to create a four-sheet map of Russia. The northeast section of this map appears to show both rivers, the start and end of Dezhnev's voyage, in more or less correct relative positions. Some of Witsen's correspondence also appears to contain knowledge of Dezhnev's voyage. All the information Witsen accumulated makes it hard to believe Dezhnev's voyage was entirely forgotten, at least until the end of the seventeenth century.

With his rediscovery of the voyage in 1736, Gerhard Müller drew a map based on his interpretation of Dezhnev's reports. The map he produced is shown on the previous page. Dezhnev's reports emphasized the Icy Cape, the Chukotskiy Peninsula, and this feature is shown grown large in the Müller-Dezhnev map. Both the Kolyma and Anadyr Rivers are shown.

Russians reached Kamchatka about 1690. Before the end of the

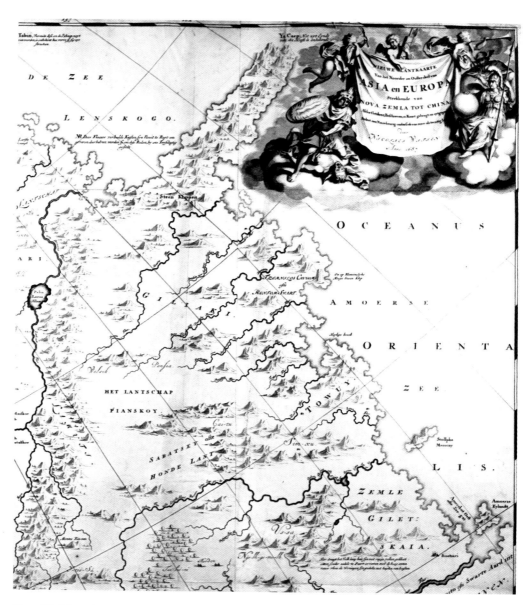

Map 58 (above).
Nicholaas Witsen's 1687 map, likely the first map to show Dezhnev's discovery of the fact that America was not joined to Asia but was separated by a strait, today called Bering Strait rather than Dezhnev Strait. Ironically, the map does not clearly show a strait, with the "Icy Cape" Dezhnev rounded being shown as a peninsula of indefinite length, but the map does show other features noted by the illiterate Dezhnev, notably the Kolyma and Anadyr Rivers, the beginning and end points of his voyage of 1648.

Map 59 (right).
Part of an anonymous map of eastern Siberia drawn in 1701 showing Kamchatka. Oriented unconventionally by modern standards, Kamchatka is the peninsula at the bottom of the map, and the island is Japan.

century, Kamchatka had been subdued by an expedition led by Vladimir
Atlasov, in 1697–99. The first Russian
discovery of Kamchatka has also been
attributed fifty years before to Fedot
Alekseyev, who was with Dezhnev but
was killed by natives. He may have also
been the first to find the northern
Kuril Islands.

The map shown at the bottom of
the previous page, certainly one of
the first if not the first to depict Kamchatka, was drawn in 1701.

Shown at right is a map drawn in
1712 by Siberian mapmaker Semen
Remezov based on information obtained from Vladimir Atlasov. Interesting, but unexplained, is the notation in Russian on the finger of land
shown in the northwest part of this
map: "recently reported land."

Russian explorers began to work
their way south, "island hopping" the
Kuril chain. About 1701 Ivan Golygin
reached the first of the Kuril Islands,
Ostrov Karaginskiy, and by 1712
A. I. Bykov and A. Krestianinov had
reached Ostrov Shiashkotan, the
third of the larger Kurils, going south
from Kamchatka.

In 1682, Peter I ("the Great")
had become tsar. He was interested
in exploration, and in particular what
the extent of his domains might be,
or could be. As we shall see (page 62),
it was he who sent out Vitus Bering
to search for America. But the first

eastward expedition he sent out was
that of Ivan Evreinov and Fedor Luzhin,
to determine the extent of the
Kamchatka Peninsula.

They crossed Kamchatka from
west to east and back again, and in
1721 sailed to, by their calculations,
the sixteenth of the Kurils. Evreinov's
map was the first to show Kamchatka
reasonably accurately, although his
longitudes were incorrect.

Map 60.
Map of Kamchatka based on Vladimir Atlasov's
expedition of 1697–99, drawn by Siberian
mapmaker Semen Remezov between 1712
and 1714. Written on the long peninsula at
top right are the words "recently reported
land." It is tempting to assume that this must
be Alaska, but it is more likely to be a mis-
reported island in the Aleutian chain.

Map 61 (left).
Map of the Kamchatka Peninsula, the Sea of
Okhotsk, and the northern Kuril Islands,
drawn by Ivan Evreinov about 1722.

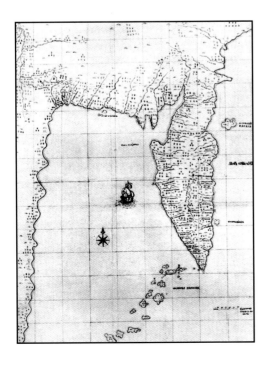

Early Mapping of the American West Coast

The shape of "the backside of America" – the west coast – was shrouded in mystery until the Spanish started to explore northwards from Mexico.

Hernando Cortés sent Francisco de Ulloa north in 1539–40, and he got as far as about 30° N (page 16), showing in the process that Baja California was a peninsula. No matter the facts! As early as 1542 one map (attributed to Alonso de Santa Cruz) showed the lower half of Baja as an island, and from there the myth grew, the depiction of California as an island becoming perhaps the most famous error in the history of the charting of the oceans.

Some mapmakers initially left a tentative opening at the head of the Gulf of California, and this seems to have propelled the concept that the land to the west of the gulf might be an island.

There was not much northward exploration by the Spanish in the latter half of the sixteenth century, and maps of that period still tend to show the California coast as part of mainland North America (for example, maps on pages 24, 25, 27, and 29). But by the seventeenth century the island myth had a resurgence of popularity and showed up in various forms on numerous maps, some of which are illustrated here.

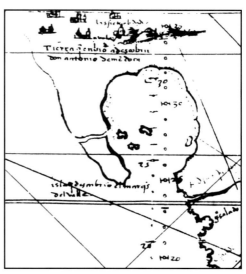

Map 62.
Alonso de Santa Cruz's map of 1542, showing the lower half of Baja California as an island. This seems to be the earliest depiction of any major part of California as an island.

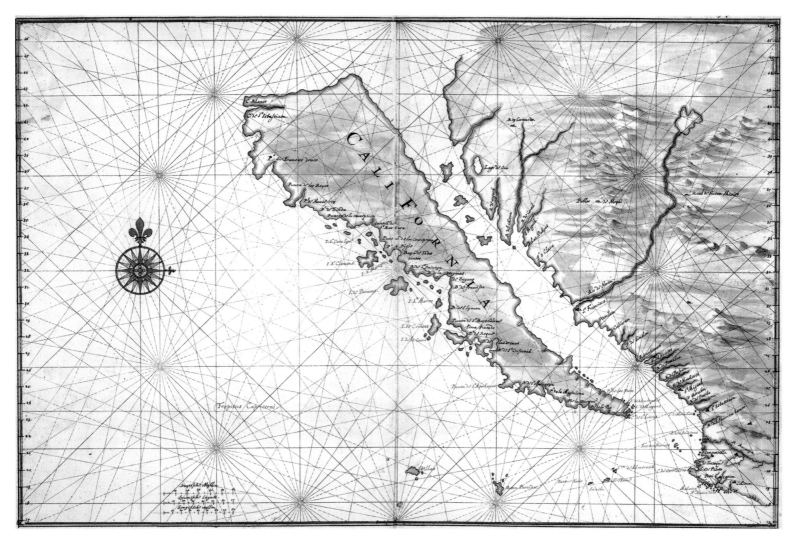

Map 63. A beautiful depiction of California as an island drawn by Dutch cartographer Joan Vinckeboons about 1650.

Now the island of California had become much larger, often encompassing the whole of the coast north to Cape Mendocino or beyond. No one had found a strait at the top of the "island," at about the latitude of Cape Mendocino, going southwards again, which would have been necessary if California really was an island, but this was simply because there was a 172-year hiatus in northward exploration after Sebastián Vizcaíno's 1602 voyage. How convenient for the wayward mapmaker. Just copy someone else's work, and perpetuate the island myth in the process!

In 1700 Jesuit Eusebio Kino explored the head of the Gulf of California and determined that it was a gulf rather than a strait; hence California could not be an island. But

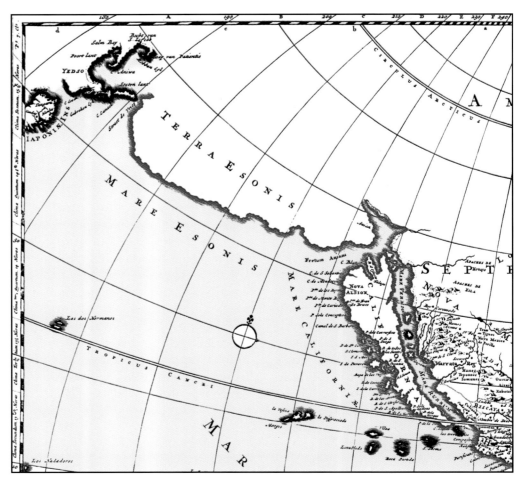

Map 64 (below).
Part of a map published by Henri Chatelain in 1719, from his *Atlas Historique*. The ship's track about a third of the way up the island of California is the eastbound Manila galleon route.

Map 65.
Recentissima Novi Orbis sive Americae Septentrionalis et Meridionalis Tabula, Carolus Allard, 1700. Wonderfully bizarre to modern eyes, this map shows not only an island of California but a continent in the Pacific Ocean, the extension of Maerten Vries' Compagnie Land (see pages 36–37), here named Terra Essonis, from "Yeso" or Hokkaido. Talk about confused geography!

Map 66 (below). Similar geographical ideas on a map by Johann Baptist Homann dated 1731, from a 1737 atlas.

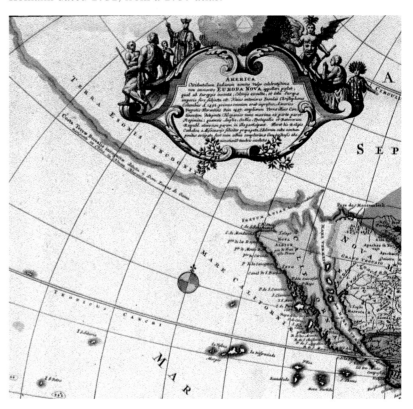

Map 67 (above).
An early depiction of Island California drawn by French mapmaker Nicolas Sanson in 1696.

geographical myths, once established, die hard. Herman Moll, for example (map at right) clung to the island concept. But more scholarly mapmakers, such as Guillaume de L'Isle, did not slavishly copy others but mapped what was known through exploration and left it at that. At the same time as Kino's exploration de L'Isle concluded that California was not an island and showed it on his map of the same date as part of the mainland. During the eighteenth century some maps showed California as an island, others did not, but by the third quarter of the century the myth had finally died, except on the maps of a few regressive mapmakers.

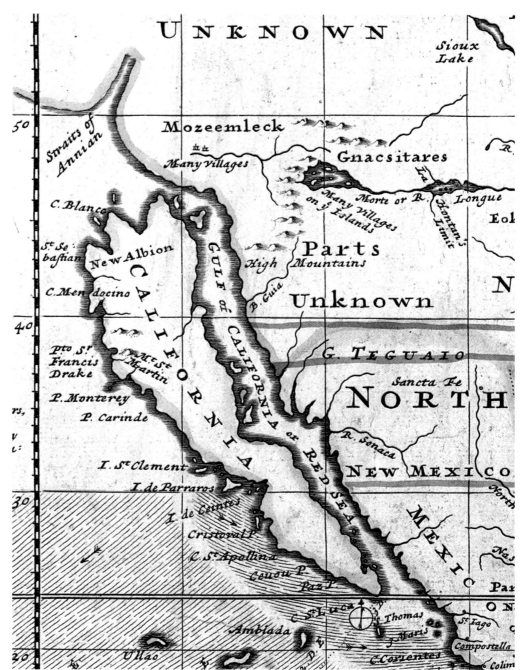

Map 68 (above).
A superb depiction of California as a island by Herman Moll, published in 1719.

Map 69.
In 1752 French mapmaker Philippe Buache published his *Considerations Geographiques et Physiques,* which contained this "consideration" of whether California was an island or not. He seems to have correctly concluded that it was indeed a peninsula.

Van Keulen's Sea Atlases

Johannes van Keulen was a Dutch mapmaker who founded the van Keulen firm in the 1680s, a company that continued producing maps until the 1880s, a two hundred–year span. Van Keulen started his business by buying up all the plates of a friend, Henrik Doncker, who was retiring.

In the late seventeenth and early eighteenth centuries, as the operations of the Dutch East India Company expanded, the Dutch became pre-eminent in the production of maps, especially those used for navigation.

Van Keulen's grandson, also named Johannes, became the hydrographer for the Dutch East India Company and hence was privy to a considerable body of valuable information.

Van Keulen's "sea atlas" was called, aptly enough, *Zee-Fakkel*, or "Sea-Torch," and was a collection of maps intended to be used for navigation rather than just for perusal by armchair geographers.

The practical navigation maps van Keulen and others produced were nevertheless not the spartan affairs they are today. Ornamentation and

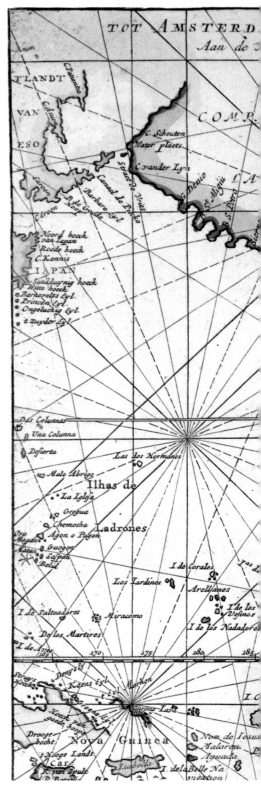

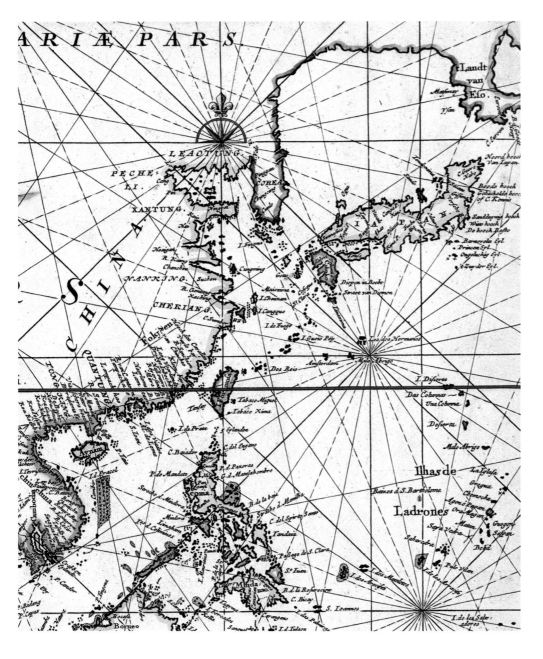

Map 70.
Part of Johannes van Keulen's *Nieuwe Pascaart Oost Indien*, 1680. Korea is shown connected to Hokkaido, as it was on many maps of this period.

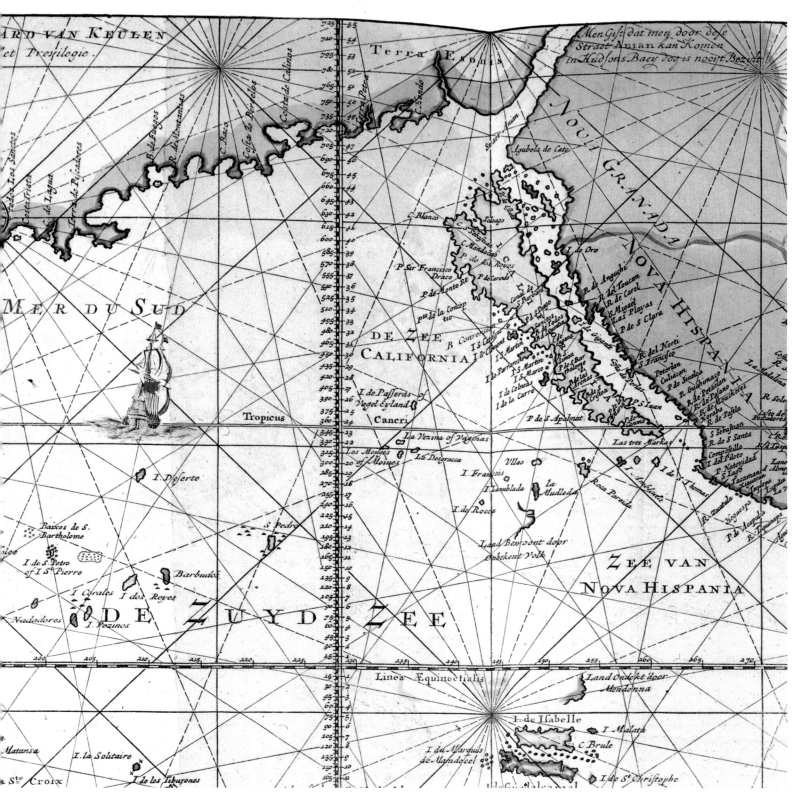

On the map (as labels): RD VAN KEULEN / et Presilegie. · Terra Esonis · Men Gist dat mey door dese Straet Anian kan Komen in Hudsons Baey doo is nooyt Bezuit · NOVA GRANADA · NOVA HISPANIA · Suaet Anian · Agubela de Cato · C. Blanco · MER DU SUD · DE ZEE CALIFORNIA I.S. · Tropicus · Cancri · Linea Æquinoctialis · Land Ondekt door Mendonna · ZEE VAN NOVA HISPANIA · DE ZUYD ZEE · Land Bewoont door Onbekent Volk · I. de Isabelle · I. del Marquis de Mahdocel · C. Brule · I. de St Christophe

color were still seen as essential, so that many of the maps seem to us to be works of art. Shown here are two examples of the van Keulen firm's work.

The map of Japan, Korea, and China is part of a larger map of Southeast Asia published in 1682, a map that was remarkably accurate for its time. The North Pacific was still a mystery,

and this is reflected in the other map, published by Gerard van Keulen, the older Johannes son, in 1728; it seems amazing to modern eyes that this map was actually intended for navigation. Maarten Vries' Compagnie Land stretches across the North Pacific, and California is shown as an island. Difficult navigation indeed!

Map 71.
The North Pacific Ocean as shown on a 1728 edition of van Keulen's atlas published by Gerard van Keulen. This map was published the same year Vitus Bering sailed into the strait separating Asia and America.

Japanese Knowledge of the Pacific

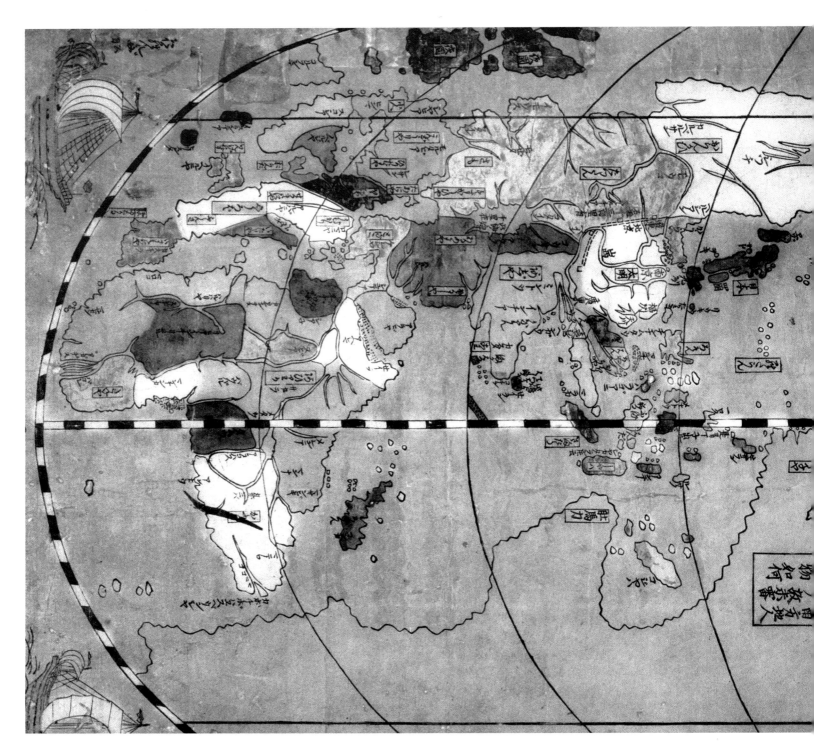

Japanese maps before the 1550s were generally conceptual rather than geographical. In the 1550s Jesuit missionaries arrived in Japan, even before they had reached China, and introduced a completely different view of the world. Japanese ideas of the Pacific Ocean actually came via China rather than directly from Europeans, and the result was a mixture of Western and Oriental concepts. The map shown here, *Bankoku-sozu,* was printed in 1645 from a woodblock in Nagasaki, the most westernized of Japanese cities due to the presence of Dutch traders on an island in the harbor (see Map 42, page 36). The map is centered on the Pacific, as were most Chinese maps. It is not known how widely this map and the geographic knowledge it represents were disseminated; however, those Japanese lucky enough to have seen this map would have had at least some idea that the Pacific was bounded by another continent to the east.

But ordinary Japanese mariners, at least until the 1850s, only got to know the extent of the ocean washing their shores through shipwreck or other mishap.

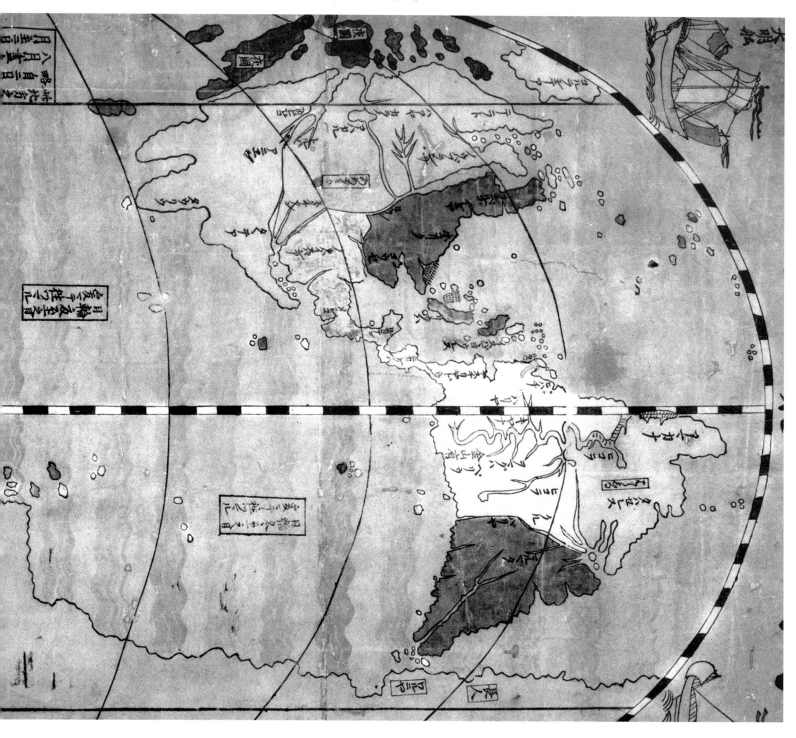

Early Japan was, to say the least, isolationist. An imperial decree in 1636 or 1637 disallowed the return of any Japanese citizen who had been abroad, prohibiting return on pain of death, and the same penalty awaited those who studied foreign languages or introduced foreign customs.

About 1689 the Japanese government ordered all junks to be built with open sterns and large square rudders, deliberately unfit for ocean navigation. They also commanded the destruction of all existing boats built on any foreign model. With these decrees, the government hoped to keep the Japanese people isolated within their own islands.

For, once these ships were forced away from the coast by the weather, their rudders soon washed away and they were soon dismasted. The result was that distressed mariners could only drift, at the mercy of winds and currents.

Thus the distribution of wrecked junks can be expected to tell of the ocean circulation in the Pacific Ocean, and indeed it does. It turns out that almost all of the known wrecks of Oriental boats on the coasts of North America have been Japanese junks.

This is explained by the Kuroshio and other currents that sweep in a northeast direction past Japan towards the Kuril Islands and the Aleutians, then continue east and south along the coasts of Alaska, British Columbia, and Oregon. These currents have swept junks towards North America at the rate of 16 km or 10 miles a day.

There are extensive records of Japanese junks washing up on North American shores, even before the

edicts. One came ashore at Acapulco in 1617; one arrived at Kamchatka in 1694 and a survivor was taken to Moscow; others drifted to Kamchatka in 1710 and 1729. Yet others washed up on the Aleutians in 1782; in Alaska in 1805; on Point Adams, at the mouth of the Columbia, in 1820; on the Queen Charlottes in 1831; and near Cape Flattery in 1833. In the latter instance, three sailors were rescued by the Hudson's Bay Company and sent to England to be returned to an uncertain fate in Japan.

The map below showing the distribution of Japanese junks wrecked and found drifting comes from a book by Charles Brooks published in 1876.

Map 73.
A map of the Pacific Ocean by Tsunenori Iguchi, from a Japanese book published in 1689. It is one of the first printed Japanese maps of the Pacific.

Map 74.
Distribution of Japanese junks found adrift or wrecked in the Pacific Ocean. The ocean currents are also shown, as corrected by George Davidson of the U.S. Coast and Geodetic Survey. From Charles Brooks, *Early Migrations: Japanese Wrecks Stranded and Picked Up Adrift in the North Pacific Ocean*, 1876.

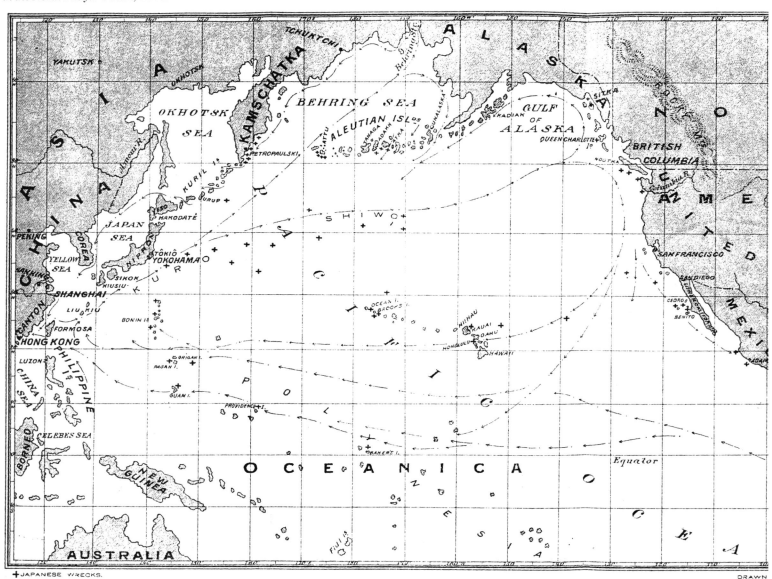

+ JAPANESE WRECKS.

DRAWN

The East Asian Coast before Bering

The Dutch northward effort essentially stopped after Maerten Vries' voyage of 1643; they remained ensconced in Japan, seemingly content with the trade they found there. Then the Russians progressed eastwards in search first of furs and then, two decades into the eighteenth century and at the prompting of Peter the Great, in search of geographical knowledge, undoubtedly intended to later support imperial or commercial designs.

The information collected often was not published, but nevertheless, it often found its way into commercially produced maps and atlases. The pre-eminent commercial firm in this regard was the Homann firm of Nürnberg,

whose founder and principal member was Johann Baptist Homann. After 1702 he was responsible for the creation of many fine maps that incorporated some of the latest information about the east coast of Asia. His maps, and those of others, record with increasing accuracy and detail the emergence of a real geography.

One of Homann's early maps was the one shown below, a map of Muscovy, which records a Pacific coast not much different from that drawn on the Godunov map of 1667 (see page 42). Other mapmakers soon added the peninsula first drawn by Nicholaas Witsen, reflecting knowledge of Semen Dezhnev's voyage in 1648 (see page 43).

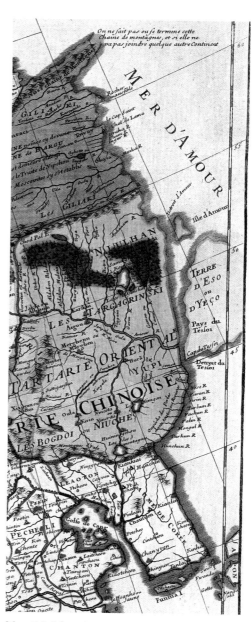

Map 76 (above).
The east coast of Asia as shown on a map published in 1706 by French mapmaker Guillaume de L'Isle.

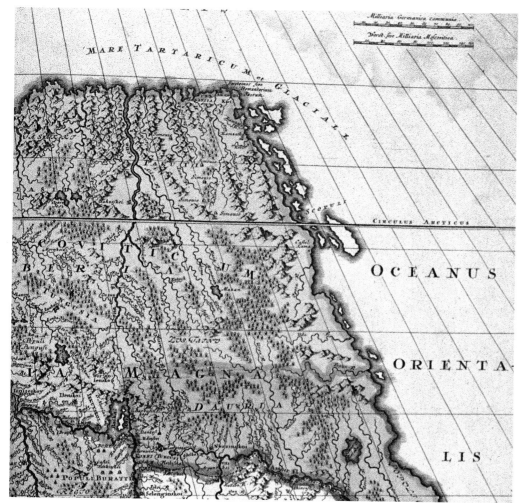

Map 75.
The northeastern corner of Siberia shown on a map of Muscovy by Johann Baptist Homann. The map is dated 1704, although this copy is from a 1731 atlas.

Map 77.
A map by Nicolas Sanson, published by Pierre Mortier in 1708, showing the addition of the Ice Cape peninsula, first drawn by Witsen in 1687 (see page 43).

Map 78.

The northeastern part of Johann Baptist Homann's 1707 map of Asia, *Asiae Recentissima Delineatio*. The Nicholaas Witsen idea of an "Icy Cape" peninsula is well illustrated, corresponding to the Chukotskiy Peninsula of today, opposite Cape Prince of Wales in Bering Strait. Farther south the discoveries of Maarten Vries in 1643 are shown, in particular his "Company Land," stretching eastwards and conveniently off the edge of the map.

Map 79.
Herman Moll's map of 1719 was somewhat regressive, depicting geographical knowledge others knew by that time to be wrong. The coast of Siberia is similar to the Godunov map. The discoveries of Maarten Vries are well shown, complete with the de rigueur undefined "Company Land." Detail of the latter area is shown on page 36.

This peninsula was shown on a map published in 1705 by Guillaume de L'Isle, a respected French mapmaker (page 53). His notation records his uncertainty as to whether it was "joined to another continent." Yeso (Hokkaido) is shown as a landmass going off the edge of the map; all very indefinite.

Homann's beautiful 1707 map of Asia, part of which is shown here (left), also now shows the peninsula, called Ys Caep (Ice Cape), but much smaller. Vries' discoveries are shown, with a large "Terra Yedso" to the north of Japan leading to a huge and indefinite "Compagnie Land" to the east.

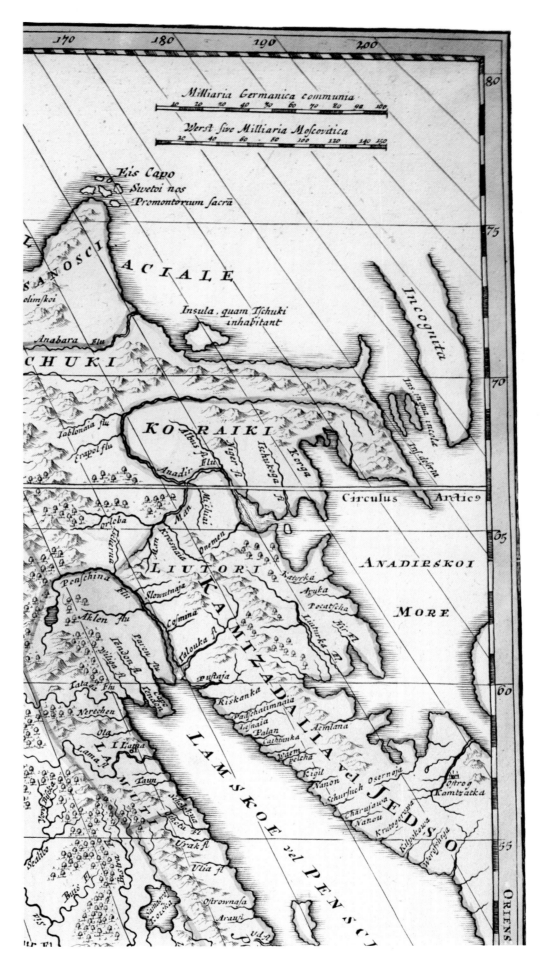

Map 80. Another map by Johann Baptist Homann, this one of Russia, drawn in 1723. The configuration shown, with islands in what might be Bering Strait, together with land marked "Incognita," which might be America, comes from a map by Ivan Lvov drawn in 1710.

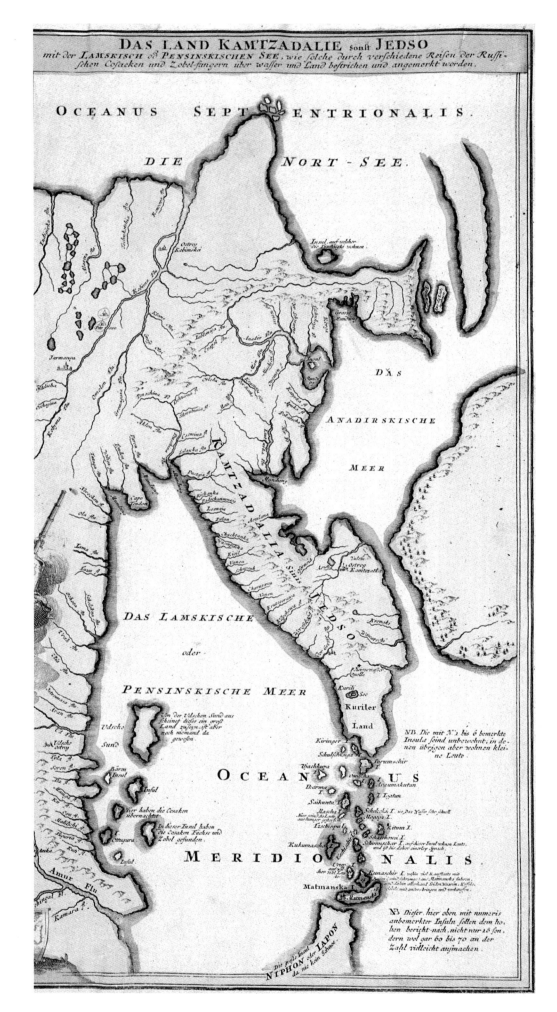

The Homann map of 1723 (Map 80, page 55) shows a considerably changed conception of the coastal outline and may have been based on a map prepared by Ivan Lvov, a Russian geodesist, in 1710; the latter was obtained by Gerhard Müller from a retired Lvov in Yakutsk.

A similar configuration is shown in Homann's regional map of Kamchatka and the adjacent coasts (left), although this one defines Kamchatka as a peninsula instead of merely suggesting it. The significance of the 1723 map is that it is now thought to be the map Vitus Bering was carrying with him when he sailed in 1728 on his voyage to the strait that now bears his name (see page 63).

Map 82.
This map of Kamchatka appeared in Engelbert Kaempfer's *Historia Imperii Japonici,* published in 1727.

Map 81 (left).
This rather beautiful map drawn by Homann in 1725 contains similar information to his 1723 map overleaf, with one important exception: Kamchatka is shown clearly as a peninsula, together with a string of Kuril Islands southwards to Japan. Rather than a part of a larger map, this was specifically a map of Kamchatka and "Jedso" (Hokkaido).

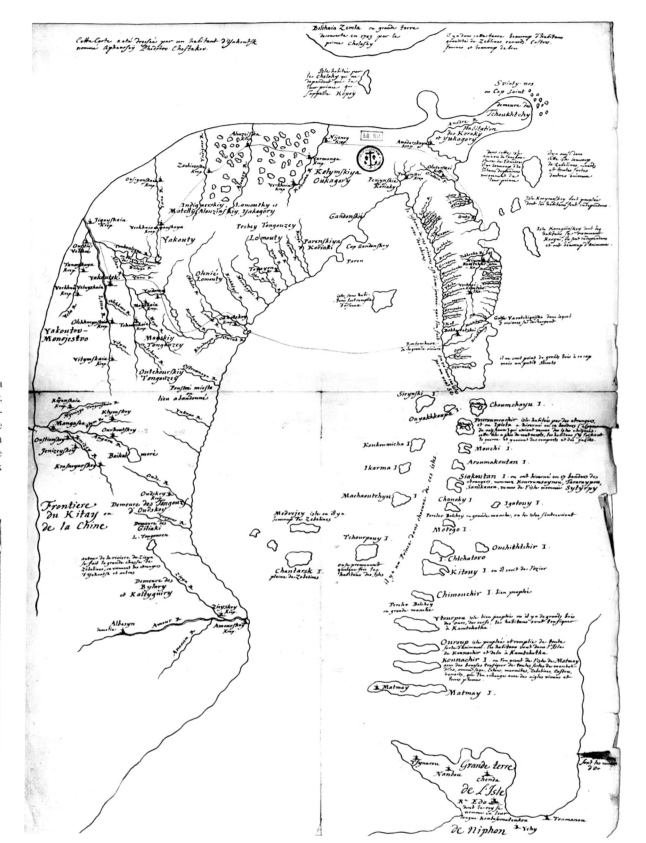

Map 83.
This is a French copy of a map by Afanasii Shestakov, explorer of the Kuril Islands, about 1730. The line drawn across the Sea of Okhotsk shows the supply route from Okhotsk to Bolsheretsk.

An eighteenth-century illustration of a Kamchatka volcano.

Another interesting map is that of Kamchatka, the Sea of Okhotsk, and the Kuril Islands drawn by Kuril Islands explorer Afanasii Shestakov in 1725, a copy of which is shown above.

Shestakov returned to St. Petersburg in 1725 to propose to the Russian government that they subdue the coastal natives of the region and also that he be allowed to search for land which was by this time believed to exist to the east – America. His proposals were welcomed, and he was named head of a special expedition. Two of the specialists assigned to his expedition were Ivan Fedorov and Mikhail Gvozdev, an assistant navigator and a geodesist, respectively.

Shestakov was killed in 1730 during a battle aimed at carrying out part of his first objective. But Fedorov and Gvozdev would achieve his second objective two years later, by finally becoming the first Russians to discover the Great Land – the North American continent (see page 65).

Lost Islands and False Continents

Over the centuries map and chart makers have, for a variety of reasons, often placed land where none exists. There were imaginative lands, exaggerated lands, and mistaken lands.

Until the end of the eighteenth century mapmakers who had poor information about what was in the North Pacific often resorted to filling up the "empty" voids, often with large decorative cartouches. Land was thought to have a "balanced" distribution so as not to disturb the rotation of the Earth, a common misconception leading in its most famous incarnation to the insistence on an unknown Southern Continent, Terra Australis Incognita. And in the North Pacific, the need to map an imagined Northwest Passage led to depiction of land in places it was not.

Land was often placed where mapmakers thought it might be, based on their interpretation of the accounts of voyagers. The depiction of Japan as a large island in the middle of the Pacific was based on a reading of Marco Polo. The Spaniard João da Gama, on a voyage from Macao to Acapulco C1590, reported land in the northeastern Pacific, and "Gama Land" was shown on many maps for two centuries afterwards, leading even Vitus Bering to search for it.

But perhaps the most enduring exaggeration of all in the North Pacific was the depiction of Company Land, actually one of the Kuril Islands, by Maerten Vries in 1643, as shown on page 37. This map led other mapmakers for a long time thereafter to draw what was sometimes a vast continent stretching right across the ocean. Its eastern end formed a suitable west bank for a Northwest Passage, and it was named all manner of

names beyond various permutations of Company Land: Terra Essonis, the land of Yeso, came from a belief that the land was part of Yesso, or Hokkaido, one of the islands of Japan. The mythical continent was also sometimes labeled Gama Land.

And then there were mistakes. Under certain weather conditions it is quite possible to see the mirage of a considerable bulk of land at sea, from squall lines and other cloud for-

Map 84.
This wonderful representation of the North Pacific was drawn by an unknown mapmaker about 1702. Asia is a suitable distance from America, but a huge mythical land mass intervenes where ocean should lie. The "Land of Iesso" derives from Maerten Vries' depiction of an open-ended "Company Land" (see page 37); "Iesso" is one form of the ancient name for Hokkaido, the northernmost major island of Japan. Vries Strait balances the Strait of Anian on the other side of this dubious land.

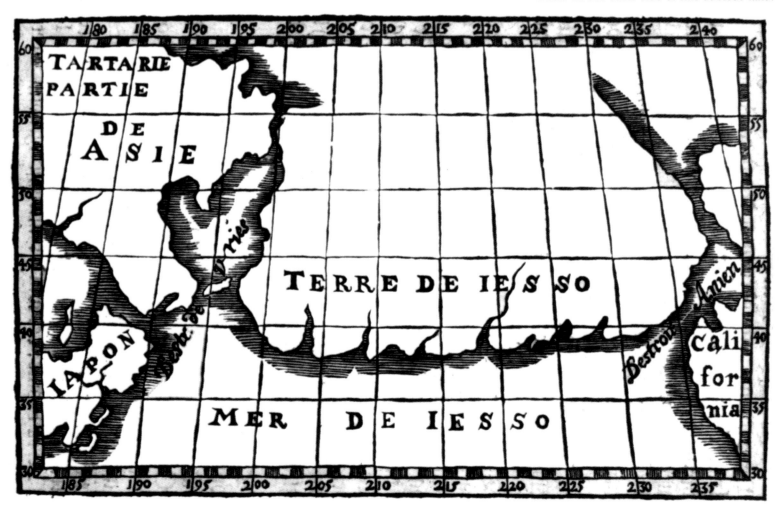

mations. Other sightings resulted from whales, floating seaweed, red tide, or even various debris floating on the surface. In an age of sail it was not usually practical to double back and check, assuming there were any doubts, and many sightings of reefs and islands were by commercial vessels more interested in getting where they were going than in investigating potential islands.

Interestingly, the more traveled the region, the more false islands reported in it; the Pacific north of about 40° suffered less than the zone from the equator to that latitude. For the false islands of the Pacific arose from someone reporting them to be there.

The North Pacific has had in its time hundreds of false islands, reefs or shoals – called *vigias* – mapped even on "serious" government hydrographic office charts, not just those of a commercial mapmaker with a good imagination and too loose with his pen. And many were there until quite recently.

In November 1875 the newly appointed Hydrographer of the Navy in Britain ordered what has been termed a "virtual massacre" of doubtful islands on Admiralty Chart 2683, a single chart that covers the whole Pacific Ocean. With a single stroke of the pen no less than 123 islands were removed, including, hilariously, three that were real and had to be restored again later!

Out went Todos Los Santos, Moor, Weeks, Morrell, Byers, Lots

Wife, Rico de Oro, Rico de Plata, and many more in the Anson Archipelago southwest of Japan; many of these had first found their way onto charts from one captured from a Spanish galleon by Captain George Anson and *Centurion* in 1743. In the eastern Pacific, out went Kentzell, Redfield Rocks, Philadelphia, and Maria Laxar. Exotic names for exotic islands that never existed.

Yet lost islands continued to be shown on charts. As late as 1982 the highly respected American oceanographer Henry Stommel, who wrote a whole book on the lost islands of the world's oceans, found Ganges Island in the Pacific, east of Japan at about 31° N, 134° E, on a globe in a Lufthansa office in Germany. He had originally found this island while leafing through a 1936 edition of the *Oxford Advanced Atlas* and thought it would be a good base for monitoring the Kuroshio Current. Further investigation revealed that the island was not marked on newer atlases, however, dispelling his hopes for a convenient location for his instruments.

Ganges Island had been the subject of numerous reports in the late

"I think I'll throw in a couple of extra islands on this map just for laughs!"

Map 85 (above).
An imaginary island at about 30° N, 140° W, from Thomas Jefferys' *American Atlas*, 1776.

Map 86.
Dutch mapmakers Reinier and Joshua Ottens drew this map in 1745. It shows lands discovered by "Dom Juam de Gama" southeast of Kamchatka. João da Gama was a Portuguese captain who sailed from Macao to Acapulco about 1590. Blown off course, he reported sighting land somewhere in the northwest Pacific. This land appeared on maps for two centuries thereafter!

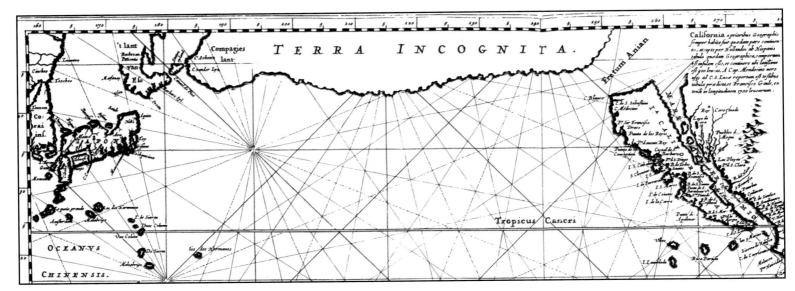

Map 87 (above).
Part of Joannes Jansson's map of the South Sea, 1650. Vries' "Compagies lant" (Company Land) has spawned a massive Terra Incognita continent clear across the North Pacific.

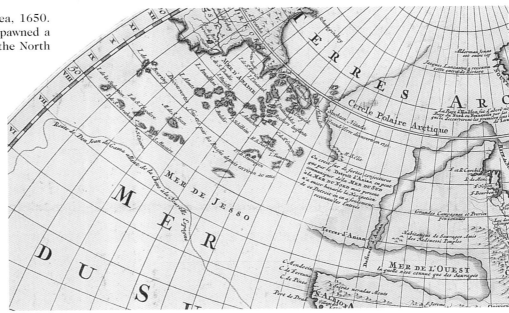

nineteenth century, the multiplicity of which convinced the U.S. Navy Hydrographic Office that they were "surely indicative of the existence of some danger in this region, the establishment of which was important." By 1880 the island was on a list of doubtful dangers to navigation, with the comment that Pacific Mail steamers had repeatedly passed over the position without seeing anything.

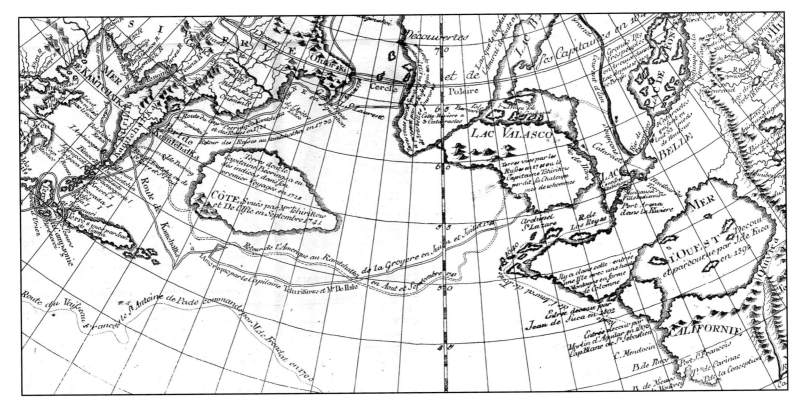

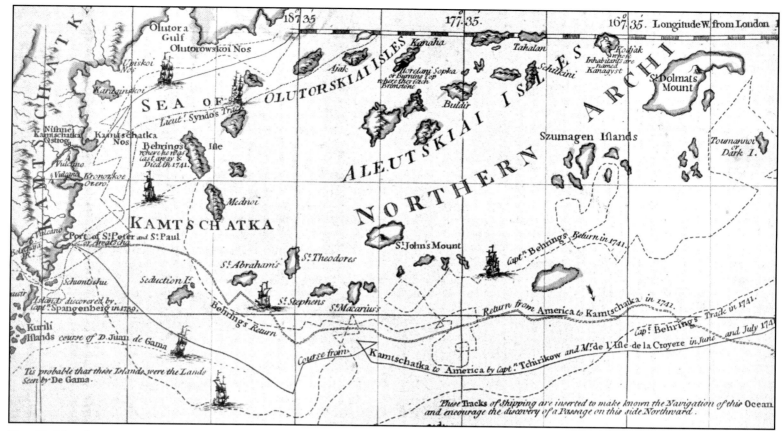

Map 90 (above).
A flurry of islands fills the northwest Pacific in this map by Thomas Jefferys, published in 1775. Some, such as Behring's Isle and Kodiak, are real; most are fictitious. The map is "authenticated" with multiple ship tracks.

Map 88 (left, center).
Jean Covens' and Corneille Mortier's superb map of 1780, showing a huge Sea of the West stretching east to Nebraska and a clear Northwest Passage to Hudson Bay. Alaska is an island.

Map 89 (left, bottom).
One of the most spectacular combinations of fact and fiction in a map of the Pacific Northwest. It was copied by Robert de Vaugondy from a map by Joseph-Nicolas de L'Isle, and published in 1755 in Diderot's *Encyclopedié,* a thirty-volume compilation of what was supposed to be the sum total of all the knowledge in the world. "Land seen by Jean de Gama" is just east of Company Land in the southern Kurils; a huge island attributed to Bering fills the western Pacific; and the coast of North America is a maze of islands, channels, peninsulas, and seas, including a large Sea of the West stretching to the Rocky Mountains. Interestingly, Sakhalin appears as an island off the Russian coast, which it is, but it was not known to be an island at this time. Make enough guesses, and one may turn out to be right!

Map 91 (right).
Part of a Spanish map of North America dated 1802. Large "Islas vistas antiguamente por los Españoles" inhabit the North Pacific Ocean. Also marked are "Dn [Donna] Maria la gorda" just north of Hawaii, and "I. de los Pajaros?" halfway between Hawaii and Baja California.

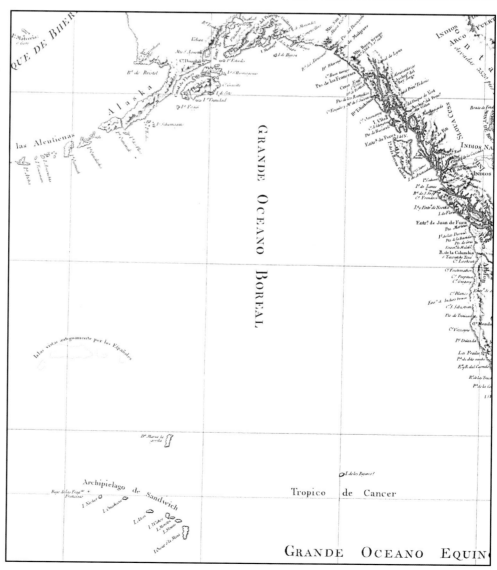

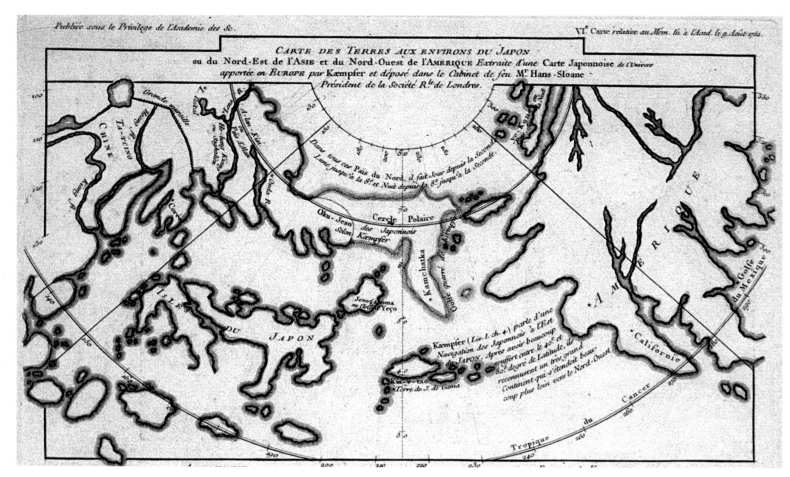

Map 92.
Perhaps the finest imaginary geography of the North Pacific, drawn by Philippe Buache in 1752 after a map belonging to Hans Sloane. All the essential geographical elements are present, however, and this is what makes it such an interesting yet bizarre map; they are almost all misplaced, missized, or misshapen.

Map 94 (right).
This map by Jean Nolin, drawn in 1783, has it all: continents where there are none, and non-existent islands in imaginary seas! In 1783 this nonsense was about to be torpedoed the very next year by the publication of the journals of James Cook's third voyage, spoiling the fun of armchair geographers forever.

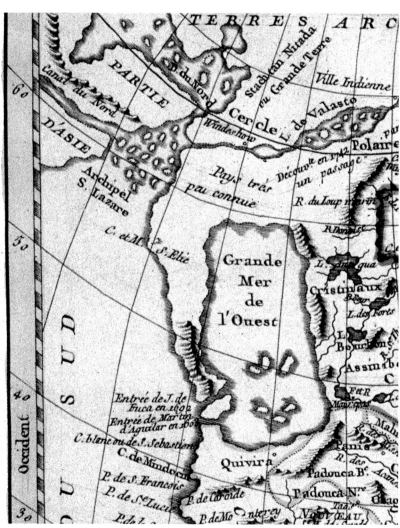

Map 93. Part of another map by Philippe Buache. Company Land, Gama Land, and "land discovered by the Russians" – the Aleutians as a continous coast – are all shown here.

Vitus Bering's First Voyage

The existence of a real Strait of Anian, shown on maps since the middle of the sixteenth century (see page 23), had never been proven when in 1697 the German philosopher-mathematician Gottfried Leibnitz suggested to a visiting Peter the Great that the Russians should be the ones to solve the mystery.

The exploration of the seas to the east of Siberia was a natural enough step for the Russians, who had advanced across Siberia in a relentless pursuit of furs.

As early as 1716 an expedition, called the Great Kamchatka Expedition, had been sent out to determine if there was any land opposite Chukotskiy, the eastern tip of Siberia. This undertaking had failed due to poor logistical planning.

Then, in 1719, the first scientific expedition was organized, that of Ivan Evreinov and Fedor Luzhin, who were sent by Peter the Great to (along with other instructions) "determine whether America is joined to Asia." They did not, but they did map Kamchatka and the Kuril Islands (see map at bottom of page 44).

But the first major scientific expedition to the Siberian Pacific was the First Kamchatka Expedition, initiated by Tsar Peter in 1725 and commanded by a Danish captain in the Russian navy, Vitus Bering.

Peter died a few days after the dispatch of the first detachment, but his wish to send the expedition was honored by Empress Catherine, who succeeded him.

The logistics of the expedition were intimidating. Alexei Chirikov, one of Bering's officers, was the first to leave St. Petersburg, on 24 January 1725, with twenty-five sleds of supplies; but Bering would not sail from Kamchatka until 14 July 1728, three and a half years later. The intervening time was spent in transporting men and supplies overland across an essentially roadless Siberia, dealing with unhelpful local governors, building ships, sailing across the Sea of Okhotsk, transporting everything across Kamchatka to the Kamchatka River, building another ship, more seaworthy than the others, and sailing down the river to – finally – the Pacific.

The new ship was named *Sviatoi Arkhangel Gavriil*. Bering's officers were Alexei Chirikov and Martin Spanberg, and Petr Chaplin was a midshipman, or officer-in-training. They only had eight sailors, but they had soldiers, who had to take over some of the sailors' duties.

They sailed at three in the morning on 14 July 1728, northwards. A careful record of wind directions and the course, speed, and drift of the ship was kept every hour in the watch journal, and at the end of every day the latitude and longitude were recorded, together with the compass variation and the distance computed to have been sailed. Also recorded were all shore reference points, when available, the current, and the weather. This care was to pay off later, enabling Bering to draw a quite accurate map of the Siberian shore.

Peter the Great's Instructions to Vitus Bering

1. You are to build one or two boats, with decks, either in Kamchatka or in some other place.
2. You are to proceed in those boats along the land that lies to the north, and according to the expectations (since the end is not known), it appears that land [is] part of America.
3. You are to search for the place where it is joined to America, and proceed to some settlement that belongs to a European power, or if you sight some European ship, find out from it what the coast is called, and write it down; go ashore yourself and obtain accurate information; locate it on a map and return here.

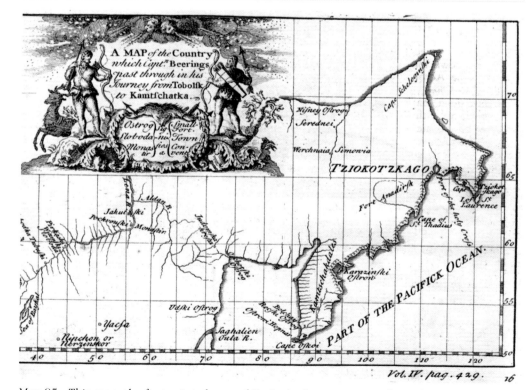

Map 95. This map, the first printed map of Bering's discoveries, was drawn by Joseph-Nicholas de L'Isle and was published in Jean Baptiste Du Halde's *General History of China*, in French in 1735 and in English in 1736. This is from the English edition.

By 27 July they reached Cape Navarin, at the southern extent of the Gulf of Anadyr. On 8 August, near Cape Chukotskiy, opposite St. Lawrence Island, at the very entrance to the strait that was to inherit Bering's name, they were approached by natives, Chukchi, in a hide boat, and through an interpreter were able to determine some features of the geography of the region.

By 13 August they were sailing past the easternmost tip of Siberia and Asia, Cape Dezhnev (East Cape), opposite Cape Prince of Wales on the American side. But they did not see the other shore or even the Diomede Islands, due to poor visibility; the strait is still 80 km or 50 miles wide at its narrowest point.

Now, with the Asian shore turning westwards, Bering requested

from his officers Chirikov and Spanberg their thoughts on what course they should follow. Chirikov suggested they continue northwards in order to eliminate the possibility that a long peninsula (Shelagsk Cape) was connected to America. This peninsula was shown on many maps as continuing indefinitely to the northeast (see, for example, Witsen's map on page 43). Spanberg

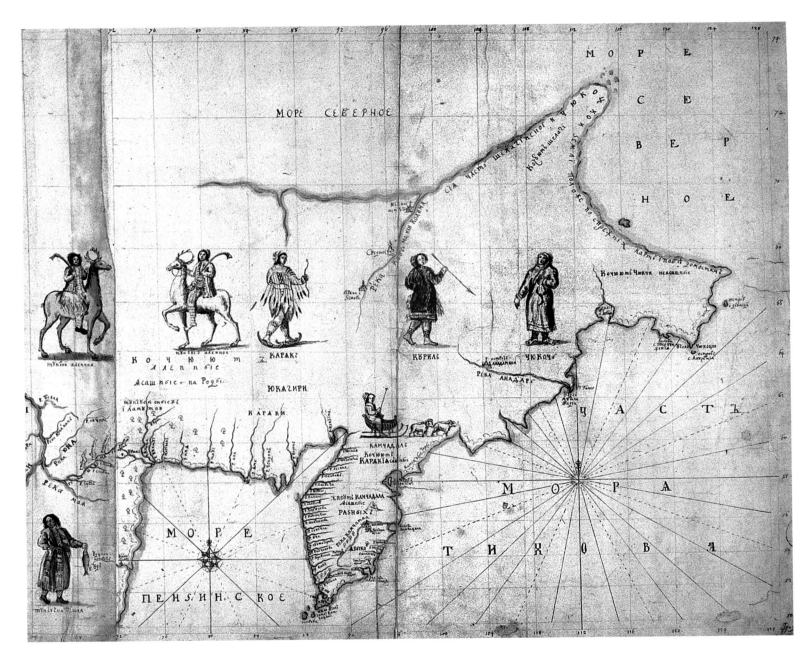

Map 96.
There are about fifteen copies of the map made by Bering of the western shore of the Pacific Ocean and the Bering Sea, which finally delineated Siberia more or less correctly. Because the members of the Kamchatka expeditions were drawn from a number of European countries, and because of the not inconsiderable interest from other nations, these maps found their way into archives and libraries in a number of countries. This one, a particularly handsome example, is from the Royal Library in Stockholm, Sweden. Note the notorious Shelagsk Peninsula, north of Bering's strait, which Bering failed to discredit, and indeed failed to prove it was not connected to North America.

was more conservative, suggesting they turn back in order to avoid the possibility of having to overwinter.

Bering did continue northwards, but only for a few days. On 16 August, pleading broken leeboards and keelboard, he finally decided that the strait had been discovered and gave the order to begin the return voyage. They had reached about 67° 25′ N, just above the Arctic Circle.

Sailing more quickly southwards, by 18 August they passed Cape Chukotskiy again and left Bering's strait.

On 20 August they again met Chukchi, and one of the questions they asked them was "Are there islands or is there land in the sea opposite your land?" But it was too late to be asking such questions; the Chukchi gave an indefinite answer, quite probably because they did not know, it being beyond their territory.

Continuing southwards, Bering reached Kamchatka Bay again on 1 September, entering the mouth of the river the next day. The expedition that had taken three and a half years of land travel (except for crossing the Sea of Okhotsk) was over after only fifty-one days at sea.

For all their care in plotting their route, Bering and his men apparently did not draw a map with their track shown, and as a result, there is still some controversy about specifics, and in particular the location of their most northerly point reached.

Whatever its precise location, the fact remains that Bering did not sail far enough north to conclusively prove the separation of Asia and America by the strait that bears his name today, but this would have been difficult in any case, as however far north he had gone, the connection could always have been at an even higher latitude. He did show that there was a body of water at the location of Bering Strait, but the proof that it was indeed a strait would come later.

It was left to Mikhail Gvozdev to actually sight the American coast, four years later. Even while Bering's expedition was under way, another under Afanasii Shestakov was being organized. Shestakov was in Okhotsk when Bering returned, and it was to him that Bering handed over his ships and provisions. Mikhail Gvozdev and Ivan Fedorov were members of this new expedition, and it was they who sighted the Alaskan coast in 1732.

But it would be Bering again, with Alexei Chirikov, who would lead another expedition, to which is attributed the discovery of the main body of the North American continent from the west, in 1741 (page 67).

Map 97 (right).
Sketch by French geographer Joseph-Nicolas de L'Isle illustrating Bering's voyage in 1728. It was based on a conversation he had with Bering about 1732.

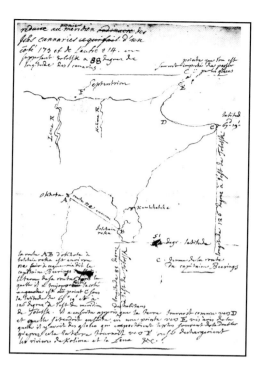

Joseph-Nicolas de L'Isle listed the signs that Bering had observed from which the conclusion could be drawn that he "had not been far from other lands":

1. At some distance from the shore he found the water rather shallow and the waves small just as in straits or arms of the sea.
2. He saw uprooted and other trees which were brought by the east wind, which trees are not seen in Kamchatka.
3. From the natives of the country he learned that an eastern wind brings ice in two or three days, while it takes a western wind four or five days to carry off the ice from northeast Asia.
4. That certain birds come regularly every year about the same month from the east and after having passed several months on the Asiatic shore they return with the same regularity the same season.

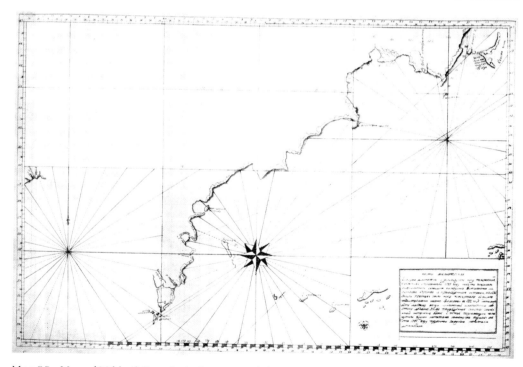

Map 98. Map of Mikhail Gvozdev's discovery of the North American continent, drawn by Martin Spanberg about 1734. The western tip of Alaska is shown in the top right-hand corner of this map, the first time it had been portrayed on a map as a result of exploration rather than conjecture. The Diomede Islands are shown, in Bering Strait.

Martin Spanberg's Voyage to Japan

When Bering presented the results of his first expedition to the Russian government, he also submitted a proposal for a second, more ambitious expedition, which came to be called the Second Kamchatka Expedition. It received preliminary approval in May 1731 but, like all these expeditions, took years to actually get off the ground.

Bering would not sail to America until 1741 (next page), but the Second Kamchatka Expedition also included proposals to explore southwards, to determine the true relationship of Japan to Kamchatka and the Kuril Islands. Martin Spanberg, who had been one of Bering's officers in 1728, was selected to command this effort.

It was June 1738 before they began their voyage to Japan from Okhotsk, in three ships, one of which was commanded by William Walton, an English captain also in the employ of the Russian navy. They had started late due to ice, and as a result got only as far south as about 46° N before the season ran out on them.

The next year they tried again, this time making it to Japan, though Walton became separated from Spanberg and they both made the voyage separately.

Another voyage was attempted in 1741, but a newly built boat leaked so much they didn't get very far. Nevertheless, Spanberg and Walton's voyages did allow them to determine reasonably accurately the position of Japan and most of the Kuril Islands; one of the maps that Spanberg drew is shown here. Russian knowledge of the west Pacific shore was to be more detailed for now than that of the eastern.

Map 99.
Martin Spanberg's map of Kamchatka, the Kuril Islands, and Japan, based on his 1739 voyage and that of William Walton.

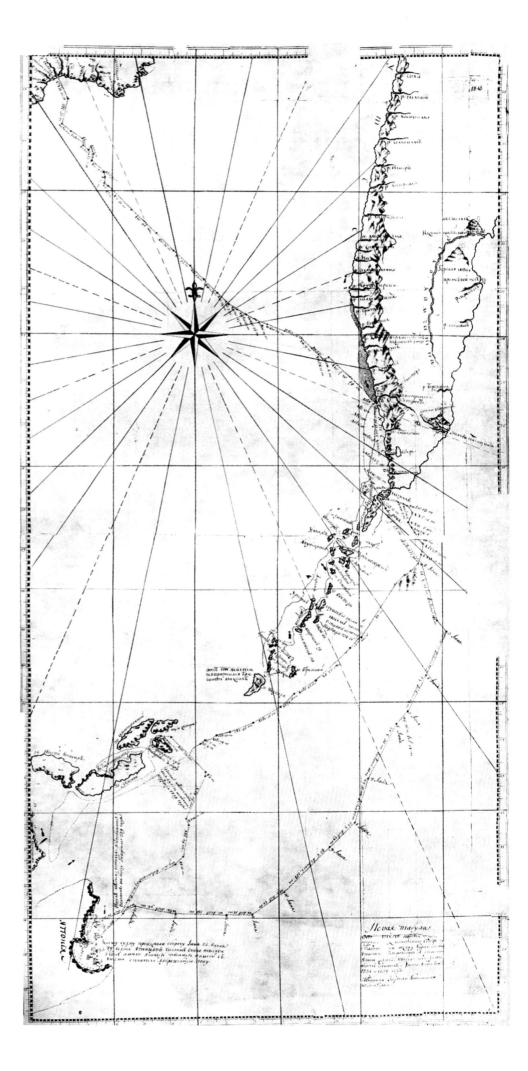

Vitus Bering's Second Voyage

As early as April 1730, when he submitted his report on his first expedition, Vitus Bering proposed to lead another, which would go much farther eastward and discover more exactly the position of North America. Bering clearly recognized that his first expedition had not been definitive in this regard. The proposed new expedition would be part of a larger scientific effort including the exploration of eastern Siberia, so that the whole scheme is often referred to as the Second Kamchatka Expedition; this name appears on some of the maps.

Bering's voyage would also discover whether the previously mapped speculative lands of Eso or Jesso, Gama Land, or Company Land existed. These were lands claimed to have been sighted by various navigators in the seventeenth century, in particular Maerten Vries in 1643 (see page 34), and they showed up on maps now and again either as islands or as part of North America, as cartographers strove to reconcile conflicting accounts.

After much preparation and years getting overland to Okhotsk and then to Kamchatka again, two ships, *St. Peter* and *St. Paul (Sviatoi Petr* and *Sviatoi Pavel),* under the command of Bering and Alexei Chirikov, sailed from Petropavlovsk in the spring of 1741.

When Bering and Chirikov sailed, they used as their guide a largely speculative map that had been prepared by Joseph-Nicolas de L'Isle, who was responsible for some of the worst – or most imaginative – of the speculative maps of the Northwest Coast. The map (below), drawn in 1731 and revised in 1733, was constructed, according to de L'Isle's own memoir, "for the purpose of helping in the discovery of the shortest route between Asia and America."

The map mercifully showed a lot of blank space in the regions that Bering's expedition was about to sail to, blank being better than totally hypothetical. The map did, however, show the speculative Gama Land – land supposedly seen by Jean de Gama – southeast of Kamchatka. De L'Isle's memoir had stated that these lands were "perhaps part of a large continent contiguous to America, joining it north of California."

In seeking these imaginary lands, Bering's officers – including Joseph-Nicolas de L'Isle's brother-in-law Louis de L'Isle de la Croyère –

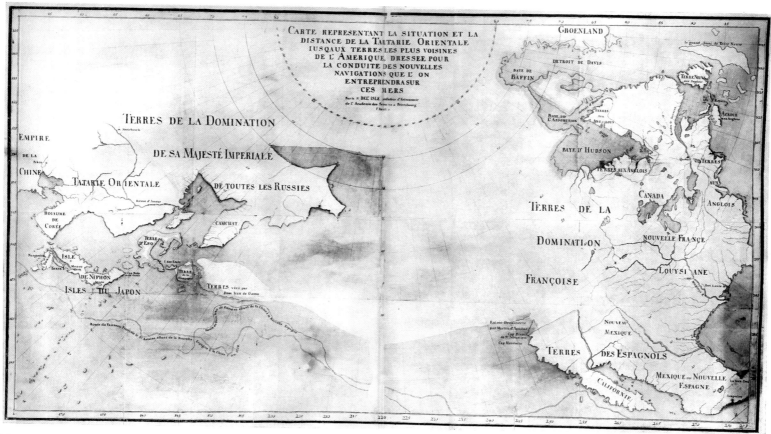

Map 100.

This map by Joseph-Nicolas de L'Isle was drawn in 1731 and was intended to summarize all knowledge of the Pacific Ocean to that date. It was carried by Bering on his second voyage in 1741 – to guide him! De L'Isle presented this map to the Russian senate with a memoir, which stated: "This map represents the true situation and distance of the eastern shores of Asia, known up to the present time, with that part of the continent of North America which is nearest to it. This map was made for the purpose of helping in the discovery of the shortest route between Asia and America."

decided, democratically, as was the custom at that time in such circumstances, to sail southeast towards this "land." The logic was that since the map had been provided to them by the Academy of Sciences, it must be correct.

What faith in government! The famous historian H. H. Bancroft put it succinctly:

The absurdity of sending out an expedition for discovery, requiring it to follow mapped imagination, seems never to have occurred to the Solons of St. Petersburg, and this when they knew well enough (from the first Bering expedition) that the continents were not far asunder toward the north.

Of course, the two ships found nothing, but as a result of this course, they ran into a storm and on 20 June became separated. After finding each other again, the ships once more lost sight of each other, this time for good. Bering's log, which was kept by assistant navigator Kharlam Yushin, recorded on 22 June:

Reef-topsail wind. We could have advanced on our course had we not been obliged to look for the St. Paul.

After wasting valuable time searching for each other, each ship continued by itself towards North America, and at this point we must consider Bering's and Chirikov's voyages separately.

Bering groped his way towards the American coast, beset by fogs, sounding all the time to determine if a coast was being approached. His log (Yushin's) is full of entries like the one for 28 June 1741: "Fog; sounded in 180 fathoms, no bottom" and, later the same day, "Topgallantsail wind, chilly, wet, foggy."

On 17 July 1741 Bering's log recorded sighting high, snow-covered mountains, and among them a high volcano. This was Mt. St. Elias; Bering had finally reached the North American mainland. On 20 July, some of Bering's crew, led by Fleet Master Sofron

Khitrov, were sent in the ship's longboat to land on an island, which Bering named St. Elias Island, as it was that saint's day. (Bering also named the island's most southerly point Cape St. Elias. Mt. St. Elias was given that name later. St. Elias Island is now called Kayak Island.)

Bering's scientist, Georg Steller, also managed a brief foray on shore (see overleaf).

Khitrov made a sketch map in his logbook to show "the position of the bay and the islands and their relation to the mainland." This was the first Russian map to show only part of the North American mainland (Map 101, below). The representation of the mountains, as seen from the side, laid down on the coast, is unusual. The set of cloud-capped mountains shown on the mainland are Mt. St. Elias and adjacent peaks.

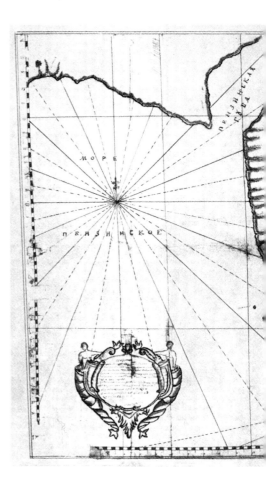

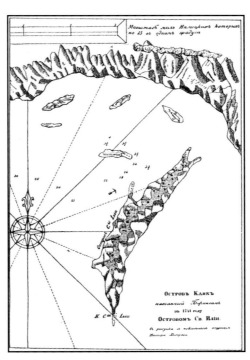

Map 101.
Sofron Khitrov's map of St. Elias Island, now Kayak Island, on the coast of Alaska near Mt. St. Elias.

On the way back towards Siberia, Bering halted at the Shumagin Islands, on the east side of the Alaska Peninsula; again Khitrov drew a map in his logbook.

But the season was drawing to a close and, partly because of the time wasted earlier, they had not arrived back at Kamchatka. The crew were

falling ill with scurvy, and the ship was becoming difficult to handle in poor weather.

Even Yushin, writing the log, noted, "I am altogether exhausted from scurvy, and I stand my watch only because of extreme necessity."

On 4 November, they sighted land: "We think this land is Kamchatka; it lies, however, between N and W, and it seems as if the end of it is not far." It was an island, now called Bering Island, only about 175 km or 110 miles from the Kamchatka coast, and less than three times that to Petropavlovsk, a

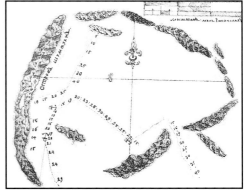

Map 102.
Khitrov's map of the Shumagin Islands.

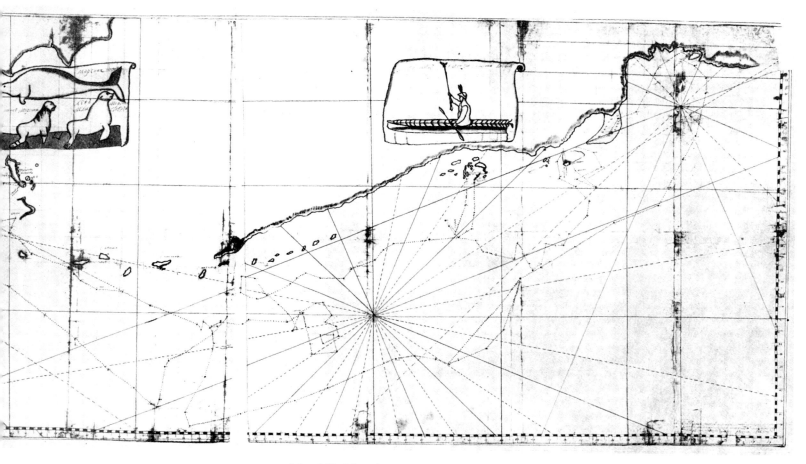

trivial distance compared to the vast space they had already covered.

A decision was made to land, with the intention of trying to save the men from scurvy. Yushin wrote that Bering, who was also ill, met with his officers and crew and decided on this course of action because of the lack of men to sail the ship. Twelve were already dead, and thirty-four completely disabled.

The ship was wrecked on the beach of Bering Island, unable to be properly anchored against the pounding surf. On 8 December 1741 Bering died, and many more of his crew perished over the ensuing winter.

By April, the survivors had determined that they were in fact on an island, and in May they began to build another ship from the wreckage of the first. Now commanded by Lieutenant Sven Waxell, Bering's second-in-command, they finally made it back to the harbor at Petropavlovsk on 5 September 1742.

Map 103 (above).
One of the maps made soon after Bering's voyage, probably by Sven Waxell in late 1742 or early 1743. The relationship of the Alaskan coast relative to Kamchatka is reasonably accurate, but the chain of Aleutian Islands has not been distinguished, so their coasts are plotted as a single shore. Bering Island is shown (close to the Kamchatka coast), and St. Elias Island (Kayak Island), where Bering finally reached North America, is also shown (at top right).

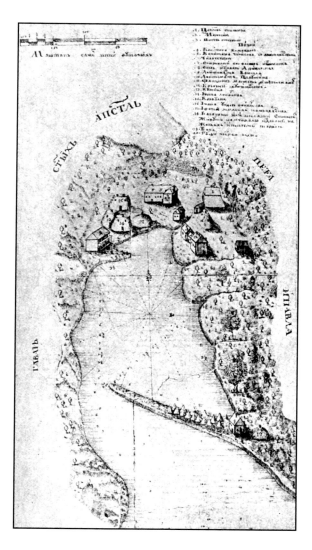

Map 104.
Survey of the harbor of Petropavlovsk, made in 1741, before Bering sailed.

Georg Steller – First Scientist of the North Pacific

Georg Wilhelm Steller was a German scientist who was part of the Second Kamchatka Expedition. This brilliant yet arrogant man was essentially the first scientist ever to be carried on a Pacific voyage, sailing with Bering himself on *Sviatoi Petr* (*St. Peter*).

He was one of Europe's foremost naturalists and was the first to record the unique wildlife of the coasts of Alaska and the islands of the Bering Sea. He was also a physician and a botanist, the multifaceted scientist of course being a common occurrence until well into the nineteenth century.

Steller was employed as personal physician to Archbishop Novgorov in St. Petersburg in 1734 when he heard of Russia's planned expedition to the Pacific. He wanted to be the first to report on the natural history of the region and so applied for a position as a botanist.

Steller wrote many botanical, zoological, and other reports during the expedition, only some of which have survived.

He was the first to describe the life cycle of the anadromous North Pacific salmon, realizing for the first time that this fish migrates from the ocean up rivers into fresh water to spawn and then die. In work with another scientist on the Kamchatka Peninsula, Stepan Krasheninnikov, Steller first identified its five species by the names still used today: *keta*, chum; *nerka*, sockeye; *kisutch*, coho; *tshawytscha*, chinook; and *gorbuscha*, pink.

Steller's name lives on in birds – Steller's jay being perhaps the most well known, but there are others, such as Steller's eider and Steller's eagle. Intriguingly, he also wrote of the Steller's sea monkey, which has never been seen by anyone else; either Steller for once was mistaken (which seems unlikely, as he studied it for two hours), or he saw one of the last of a now extinct species.

Steller is perhaps most remembered today for his descriptions of the also now extinct Steller's sea cow, the northern manatee, an ungainly sea mammal that was quickly hunted out of existence, mostly by Russian fur traders who took a liking to its taste.

Steller's journal, written while he was shipwrecked on Bering Island, describes the sea cow and its habits, notes which are extremely valuable given the extinction of the animal.

These animals, like cattle on land, live in herds at sea, males and females going together and driving the young before them about the shore. They are occupied with nothing else but their food. The back and half the body are always seen out of the water. They eat in the same manner as the land animals, with a slow forward movement. They tear the seaweed from the rocks with the feet and chew it without cessation. However, the structure of the stomach taught me that they do not ruminate, as I had first supposed. During the eating they move the head and neck like an ox, and after the lapse of a few minutes they lift the head out of the water and draw fresh air with a rasping and snorting sound after the manner of horses. When the tide falls they go away from the land to sea but with the rising tide go back again to shore.

Steller also noted the trait that was to doom the sea cow to extinction. "They are not afraid of man in the least," he wrote.

The sea cow must have appeared to the first fur traders to be an inexhaustible resource. Steller wrote:

These animals are found at all seasons of the year everywhere around the island [Bering Island] *in the greatest numbers, so that the whole population of the east coast of Kamchatka would always be able to keep itself more than abundantly supplied from them with fat and meat . . . The weight of this animal with skin, fat, meat, bones and entrails I estimate at 1200 poods.*

It seems that the sea cow provided a unique delicacy:

The meat of the old animals is not to be distinguished from beef; but it has this remarkable property that, even in the hottest summer months and in the open air, it will keep for two full weeks and even longer without becoming offensive, in spite of its being so defiled by the blowflies as to be covered with worms all over . . . All of us who had partaken of it soon found out what a salutary food it was, as we soon felt a marked improvement in strength and health . . . With this sea cow meat we also provisioned our vessel for the voyage [back to Kamchatka].

Steller only spent about ten hours on land once *Sviatoi Petr* reached Alaska, at Kayak Island, which he called St. Elias Island, below Mt. St. Elias. Bering, concerned only about the safety of his ship, sent Sofron Khitrov in the longboat to find a more secure anchorage but would not permit Steller to go with him, fearing that he would interfere with Khitrov's work. Thus there ensued a blistering argument between Steller and Bering in which Steller did finally prevail, as he was permitted to go ashore with a party sent to fill the

water casks. There, working feverishly, he crammed days of work into
his allotted ten hours. And it was
Steller who first detected the presence of other humans, finding a recently used campsite, though no natives were seen. He found

*utensils made of bark, filled with
smoked fish of a species of Kam-
chatkan salmon called nerka [sock-
eye] . . . sweet grass from which li-
quor is distilled . . . different kinds of
plants, whose outer skin had been
removed like hemp . . . for making fish
nets . . . dried inner bark from the
larch or spruce tree done up in rolls
and dried; the same is used as food
in times of famine . . . [and] large
bales of thongs made of seaweed
which we found to be of uncommon
strength and firmness.*

After his return from Bering Island, Steller worked in Kamchatka
and the Kuril Islands. In 1744, returning to St. Petersburg, he was charged
with freeing some Kamchadal prison-
ers, and the stress associated with
this led to his early death, in 1746;
heavy drinking undoubtedly helped.
He was only thirty-seven.

Steller measuring a sea cow on Bering Island. From Leonard Stejneger, in F. A. Golder, 1925.

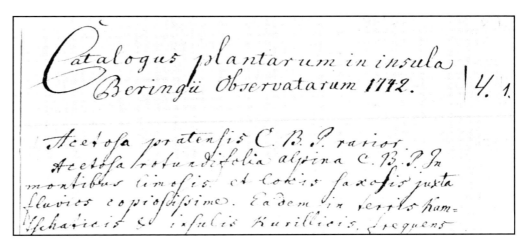

The beginning of the botanical catalog written by Georg Steller, including many plants new to
science he found during his short stay in Alaska. Historian Frank Golder found the manuscript
of Steller's journal, including the botanical catalog, in Russian archives in 1917. The copies he
made are now in the Library of Congress, where this was found in Golder's files.

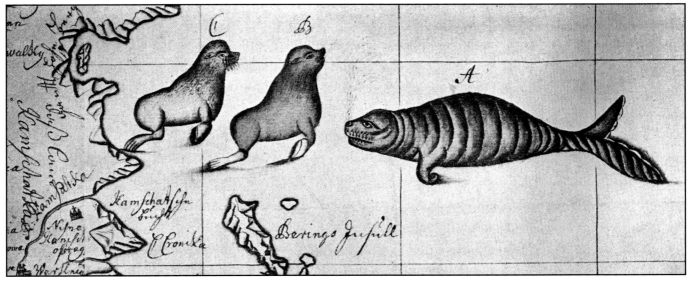

Map 105.
A tantalizing map whose current whereabouts are unknown. This is part of the map, reproduced in 1891. At that time it was in
the Tsar's Library, which was broken up and sold in the late 1930s. The map was drawn by Sven Waxell, hence the Swedish language
used. The animals shown are a fur seal, a sea lion, and a sea cow. Waxell had personally seen the sea cow, and thus his representation
is important because it was drawn from life.

Alexei Chirikov's Voyage

Alexei Chirikov, in his ship *St. Paul*, fared better than Bering, reaching the North American coast ahead of Bering.

On 14 July 1741 Chirikov noted long broad white paths in the water, which he attributed to small fish in large quantities. This would, he thought, mean they were close to shore, and so he ordered systematic soundings to be made. The bottom was not reached at 100 fathoms.

That night, provision was made to be able to drop the anchor in a hurry should this be necessary. They saw ducks and gulls presumably flying from a shore, and they also saw whales and porpoises and three pieces of driftwood. Sure enough, they were at the North American coast; the next day land was seen.

Chirikov had made his landfall at 55° 20´ N, at Baker Island, on the west coast of Prince of Wales Island. The westernmost point of Baker Island is today named Cape Chirikof.

He was sure he had reached America. He had one of Johann Baptist Homann's maps with him. "Several known American places are not very far from this place," he wrote with confidence. He ordered it "placed on the map made of our voyage." Quite where he got his confidence from is a mystery.

They came within 3 km or 2 miles of the shore, and soundings were taken in order to find an anchorage, but none was found, because "everywhere the depth of water was close to 70 fathoms or more." A boat was sent to find a suitable bay and found none, but reports came back of great stands of fir, spruce, and pine on the mountains, and sea lions on the shore. From the *St. Paul* whales, sea lions, and walruses were seen.

Attempting to find an anchorage, Chirikov sailed northwards along the American shore, along the west coast of Baranof Island, past where sixty years later the Russians would establish the headquarters of their American operations, at today's Sitka.

Fleet Master Avraam Dement'ev was finally sent off in the ship's longboat with ten sailors to attempt to find an anchorage, and also to survey the land, as Chirikov had been instructed to do. Dement'ev was given all manner of gifts for any natives he might encounter. But the longboat did not return, and after a difficult week of attempting to stay in the same place, Chirikov and his officers decided that the reason Dement'ev was not returning was that his boat had been damaged. So Chirikov sent off another boat, the only one left, with the ship's carpenter and caulker and two others. But they did not return either.

Two boats did approach *St. Paul*, but they turned out to be natives in canoes, who could not be persuaded to come close.

Eventually, Chirikov could wait no longer; he had by this time concluded that his men had been attacked by natives, but the real reason for their disappearance will probably never be known. They might have been caught in dangerous surf, a whirlpool, or struck a hidden rock, much as a surveying boat from La Pérouse's expedition would do in Lituya Bay some forty-five years later (see page 102).

Now, unable to land and unable to replenish his water supplies, Chirikov reluctantly decided that he had to return immediately to Petropavlovsk, and on 27 July he sailed. Although land was seen at various places, they had no boats and could not land. Fog often constrained their view. Kenai Peninsula was seen, as was Kodiak Island. At Adak, the largest island in the Andreanov group in the Aleutians, natives approached and were given gifts.

Near Kodiak, a rapidly decreasing depth had caused alarm. They cast their lead frequently, and the water depth decreased to 55 fathoms, then 40 fathoms an hour later, then 30 fathoms an hour after that. "Every time the lead was cast," Chirikov recorded,

the soil changed. Sometimes it was fine gravel, sometimes coarse, which did not stick to the lead, and sometimes, fine gray sand, but the shore was not seen at night or in the fog, and even by day when the fog had cleared, it was not seen, and so it is realized that it is a bank far from the shore.

This was Albatross Bank, and Chirikov had discovered it just as surely as he had discovered the American shore.

With their water running critically low, they limped back to Kamchatka, arriving finally in Petropavlovsk on 12 October 1741.

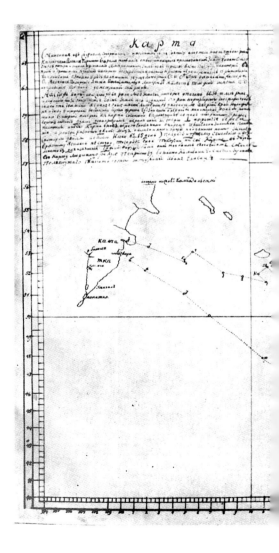

The information gathered by Bering and Chirikov was significant. It allowed a considerable amount of the map of the Northwest Coast to be filled in, and the position of the mainland in relation to Asia was now reasonably fixed, as much as it could be in a time of dead reckoning. Both Bering and Chirikov were out in their calculations of longitude.

It can be seen in Chirikov's map (below) that two American shores are shown. This is because dead-reckoning going eastwards produced a different location for the coast than that plotted going westwards, both positions being drawn from, or to, a known point, determined astronomically on land – that of Petropavlovsk. Currents adding to distance in one direction reduced it in the other. Hence they could not be *exactly* sure where they had been.

In any case, the fixing of points can still be, and was, misconstrued if the mapmaker wishes it. The map of the Northwest Coast copied by Robert de Vaugondy from Joseph-Nicolas de L'Isle and published in 1755 (Map 89, page 60, with caption page 61) marks the tracks of Bering and Chirikov reasonably accurately, but remains an utterly hopeless speculation as far as the west coast of North America is concerned.

Chirikov's maps, such as the one shown on this page, still show speculative geography south of his landfall.

Map 106.
Map of the voyage of Alexei Chirikov drawn by Ivan Elagin, Chirikov's pilot, in 1742. There are two coastlines plotted from Chirikov's track, with the coast on landfall being depicted west of that plotted from the return voyage. Dead reckoning, the method of plotting their position based on estimates of speed and elapsed time, produced different positions for the North American coast on the outbound voyage as compared with the return, both being measured from more accurate positions in Kamchatka. The track of Vitus Bering is also shown, with a North American landfall north of that of Chirikov.

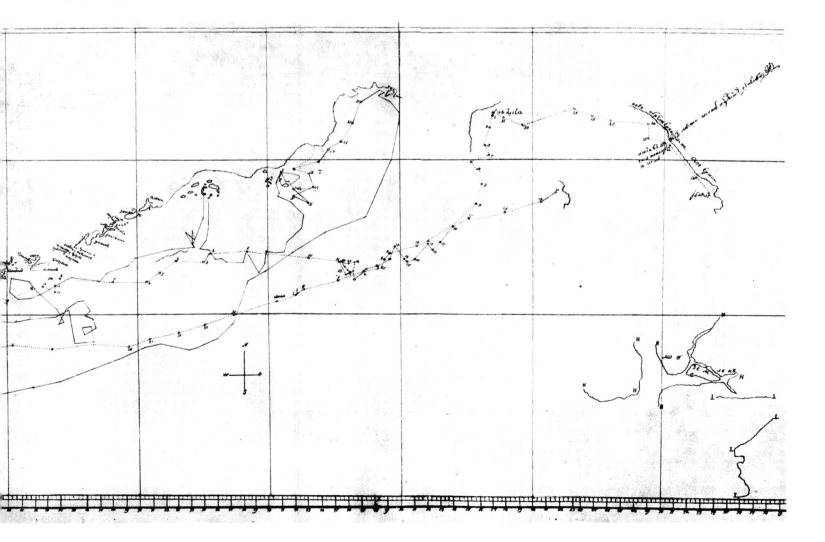

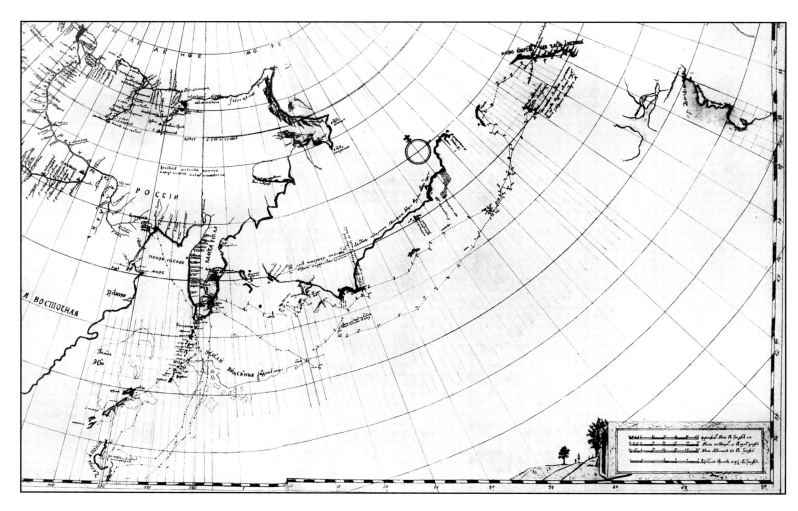

Map 107 (above) and Map 108 (right). Two Russian summary maps produced as a result of the Second Kamchatka Expedition, both drawn about 1742. It is not difficult to see how the sightings of land along the Aleutian chain manifested themselves on maps as a continuous peninsula. This idea would not be corrected cartographically until the arrival of James Cook in 1778, although by that time the Russians had realized that much of the peninsula was composed of islands.

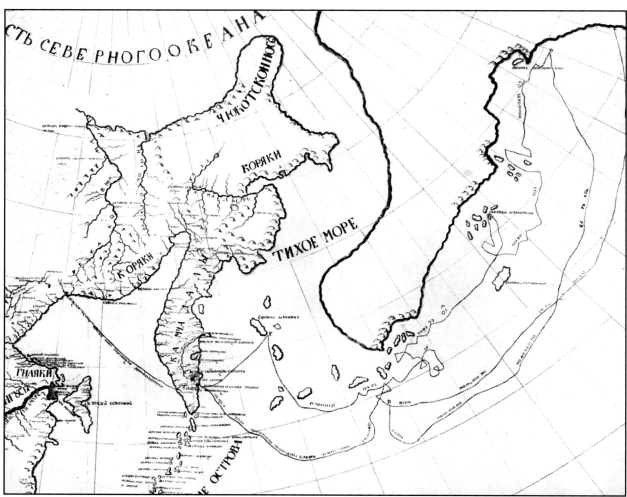

De L'Isle's Fantastic Map

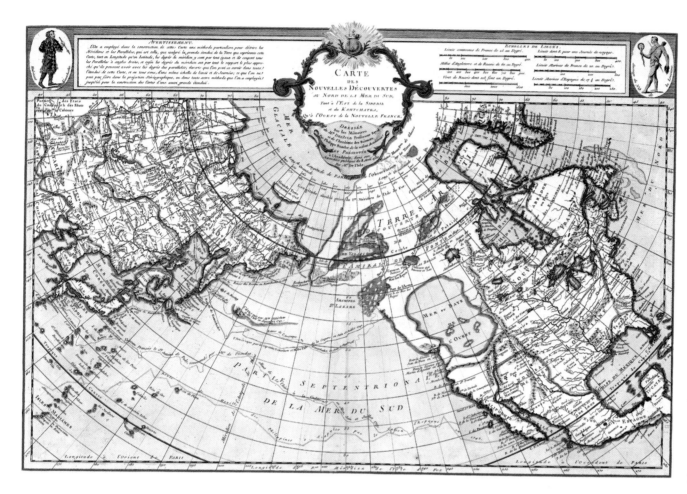

Map 109.
Joseph-Nicolas de L'Isle's 1752 map. Despite its anomalies, the Siberian coast is shown quite accurately; the Russians were annoyed at de L'Isle for stealing their information. A missing continent, Gama Land, has only its south coast marked, in the middle of the North Pacific. A huge Sea of the West covers most of western North America.

Map 110 (below). A similarly bizarre map by Philippe Buache, brother-in-law of de L'Isle and partner in their map publishing business.

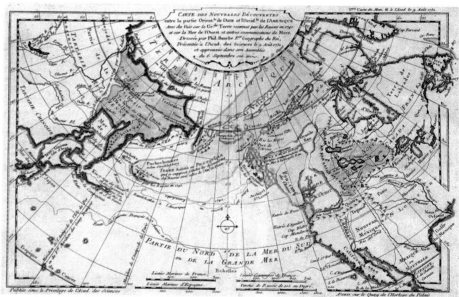

In 1708, a British magazine called *Memoirs for the Curious* published what purported to be a newly discovered account of a 1640 voyage to the northern Pacific Ocean by a Spanish admiral named Bartholemew de Fonte.

In sailing north along the coast, de Fonte was said to have entered a strait that led to a great inland sea and met a ship from Boston, which had supposedly arrived through a Northwest Passage. Inconsistencies in this story plus modern geography show that this voyage was fictitious. Nevertheless, this account was widely read and had an effect on later explorers and mapmakers.

The French geographer Joseph-Nicolas de L'Isle was a proponent of the de Fonte theory. He had spent twenty-one years at the Russian Academy of Sciences. When he returned to Paris to join his brother-in-law Philippe Buache to produce maps, he brought with him some maps he had

acquired from the academy.

In 1752 he published a map which claimed to show the discoveries of the Russians. However, on the Northwest Coast of America he constructed an elaborate speculative map based on the de Fonte account and

his own interpretation of Bering's discoveries. The academy was furious that de L'Isle had removed information to France, was further upset at his geographical speculations, and requested Gerhard Müller to refute them (see page 77).

John Green's Map of the North Pacific

A year after de L'Isle published his map of the Pacific, an Englishman, Bradock Mead, using the pen name John Green, produced a map of North and South America in six large sections in which he attempted to show the most recent discoveries of the Russians in the North Pacific in a much more responsible fashion, and which refuted the de Fonte idea of the geography of the North Pacific.

These important maps were published by Thomas Jefferys in London in 1753. They were an honest attempt to produce maps that only reflected exploration. The northern sheet (right) was the first map to call Bering Strait by that name. Mead had not heard of Semen Dezhnev; otherwise the name might well have been different.

The main North Pacific map (below) finally showed the trend of the North American coast correctly, but due to lack of information was still incorrect in many details, the most notable of which is the large island in the western Pacific "of which Capt. Behring found signs in 1728." Also shown is the strait Juan de Fuca "pretends he entered in 1594 [1592]."

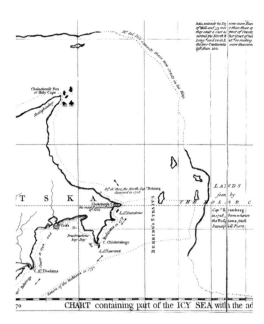

John Green's map of 1753: northern sheet (Map 111, above) and middle sheet (Map 112, below).

CHART, containing the Coasts of CALIFORNIA, NEW ALBION, and *RUSSIAN DISCOVERIES* to the North; with the Peninsula of KAMCHATKA, in ASIA, opposite thereto; And ISLANDS, disperfed over the PACIFIC OCEAN, to the North of the *LINE*.

Gerhard Müller's Famous Map

There were other dissenters to the de L'Isle view of the geography of the North Pacific Ocean.

Gerhard Müller, like de L'Isle, had been a member of the Second Kamchatka Expedition. Acting for the Russians, in 1753 he wrote an anonymous rebuttal, *Lettre d'un officier de la marine russienne*, based on Sven Waxell's journal, and in 1754, Müller constructed a map using information from Vitus Bering's voyages, adding to it other information that he had gathered, such as that about Semen Dezhnev's voyage of 1648. Müller wrote that he had had the map made "on the basis of my data and under my supervision."

He made the map to refute the geographical exaggerations made by de L'Isle on his map of 1752 (page 75). Because the Müller map was the first printed map to show Bering's 1728 and 1741 discoveries to the world in a reasonably accurate fashion, and also information from Dezhnev's voyage, the map assumed considerable significance.

The 1754 map, shown overleaf, had relatively limited circulation, but a 1758 revision was widely disseminated, and was included with a more extensive condemnation of de L'Isle contained in the third volume of a book written by Müller. This map was very influential and was widely copied.

Müller was at the time probably the one individual who knew the most about the geography of the North Pacific, and his map was a vast improvement on anything previously available. Despite this it contained many inaccuracies. The most notable was the enormous semi-tentative peninsula protruding from Alaska. This reflected the official Russian view that the land seen by Bering and Chirikov, which was actually the Aleutian chain, was part of a continent

Map 113.
French mapmaker Jacques Nicolas Bellin's rendering of Müller's ideas. The Aleutian Islands are shown as a peninsula. The tracks of Bering and Chirikov's expedition of 1741–42 are marked.

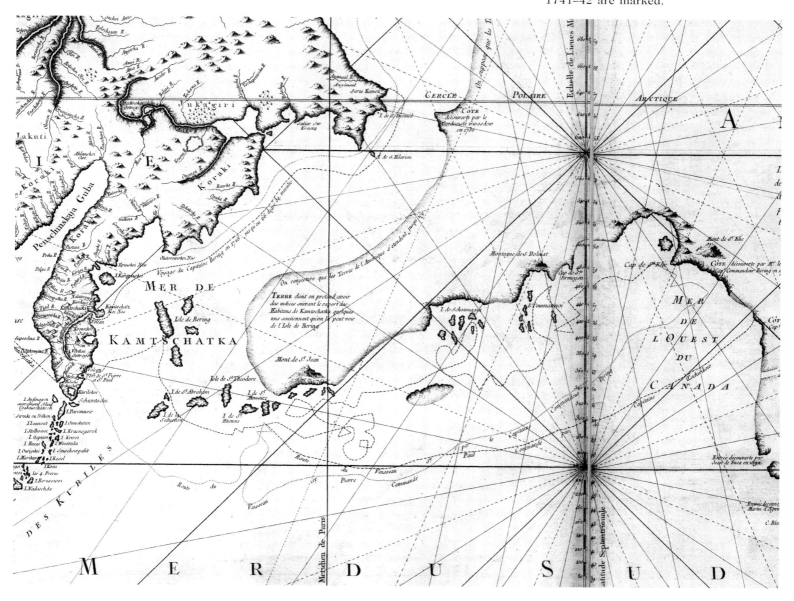

(see map on page 74, bottom). Given the information available, this was not a totally unreasonable assumption; even so, Müller only shows most of the peninsula with dotted lines rather than making bold with geography the way de L'Isle had done.

Another incorrect feature was the troublesome Cape Shelagsk, at the northeastern tip of Siberia, information for which came from Müller's interpretation of Dezhnev's account (see Map 57, page 42). The non-existent cape is shown as a huge mushroom-shaped peninsula extending more than 10 degrees east to west and almost to 75° N. If it had existed, the cape would have been the easternmost tip of Asia.

Müller's concept of the North Pacific remained the authority until James Cook's third voyage. It was modified to incorporate other discoveries, such as those of Ivan Synd (page 81).

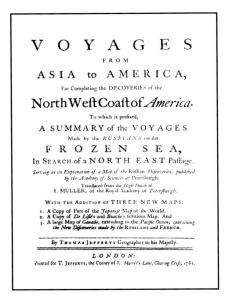

The title page of Müller's book, published in an English translation by Thomas Jefferys in 1761. Müller's map was first published in the 1758 German edition of the book. The 1754 map shown here is much rarer than the 1758 edition, as relatively few copies were printed. It took the publication of the book, and its translations, to widely disseminate Müller's map.

Map 114.
Gerhard Müller's influential map.
This is the original (and now rare) 1754 edition.

NOUVELLE CARTE
S DECOUVERTES FAITES PAR DES
AUX RUSSES AUX CÔTES INCONNUES
MERIQUE SEPTENTRIONALE AVEC LES
PAIS ADIACENTS.
r des memoires authentiques de ceux,
ssisté a ces decouvertes, et sur d'autres
ces, dont on rend raison dans un memoire
separé
t Petersbourg a l'Academie Imperiale
des Sciences. 1754.

BAFFINS BAY

Isle de Jacqud

Détroit de ... Smith

DÉTROIT DE BAFFIN

Isle de Cumberland

Détroit de Cumberland

Isle de bonne Fortune

LABRADOR

Détroit de Alderman Jones

Détroit de Lancastre

HUDSONS BAY

ESQUIMAUX

Mer non entierement decouvert

NOUV SUD WALES

KRIS KRIR ou KILLISTINS

AMERIQUE SEPTENTRIONALE

Pais des Tschuktschi dont on ne connoit pas l'etendue

MER D'ANADIR

CÔTE decouverte par le Geodesiste Gwosden en 1730

Mont de St Elie

CÔTE decouverte par Mr le Capt Commandeur Bering en 1741

Cap de St Elie

CÔTE decouverte par le Capt Tschirikow en 1741

Cap de St Ermogen

Montagne de St Dolmat

Pretendue R. de los Reyes de l'Amiral de Fonte en 1640. suivant Mr Delisle

I de Schoumagin

Bering

Entrée decouv par Mr Martin d'Aguilar en 1603

NOUV ALBION decouverte en 1578 par François Drake

la Capitaine Commandeur

St Paul commandé par le Capt Tschirikow

Entrée decou par Iean de Fuca en 1592

C. Blanc de St Sebastian

C. Mendocin

C. Fortune 1542

Port de François Drake qu'il nomme St Francois

PARTIE DE CALIFORNIE St Pedro

commandé par

DU SUD

The Russians Discover the Aleutians

After Bering there were many enterprising individual fur traders and hunters who sought to exploit the new and rich resources to be found in the islands to the east.

As early as 1743–44, Emelian Basov sailed to Bering Island, site of Bering's demise, and Mednyy Island, close by, was also found by him in 1745. Before the end of the decade, the westernmost Aleutians, Attu, Agattu, and the Semichi group (all the Near Islands), were discovered by M. Nevotchikov. St. Matthew Island was discovered by S. Novikov and Ivan Bakhov in 1748.

Improvements in ship design (up till this point the hunters had been using *shitik,* boats made from wood planks sown together with lengths of twisted willow or fir) and rapid depletion of fur-bearing animals led in the next decade to voyages farther and farther to the east.

Evidence is generally inconclusive, because the fur traders and hunters often did not make maps or determine their positions accurately, but it seems the Andreanof Islands were reached by 1757; Umnak and Unalaska Islands, in the Fox group, by 1761; and the Alaskan mainland

also in 1761, by G. Pushkarev, although he thought it just another island. Kodiak Island was reached by Stepan Glotov in 1763.

These private explorations were supplemented by government-sponsored ones, and it is those that led to the drawing and retention of maps.

In 1762, Catherine II came to power in Russia. She wanted to renew the strength of the Russian navy and was responsible for a renewed interest in discoveries in the

Map 115.
Ivan Synd's map, showing the coast of Siberia from the Sea of Okhotsk to Bering Strait, including the Aleutian islands he discovered.

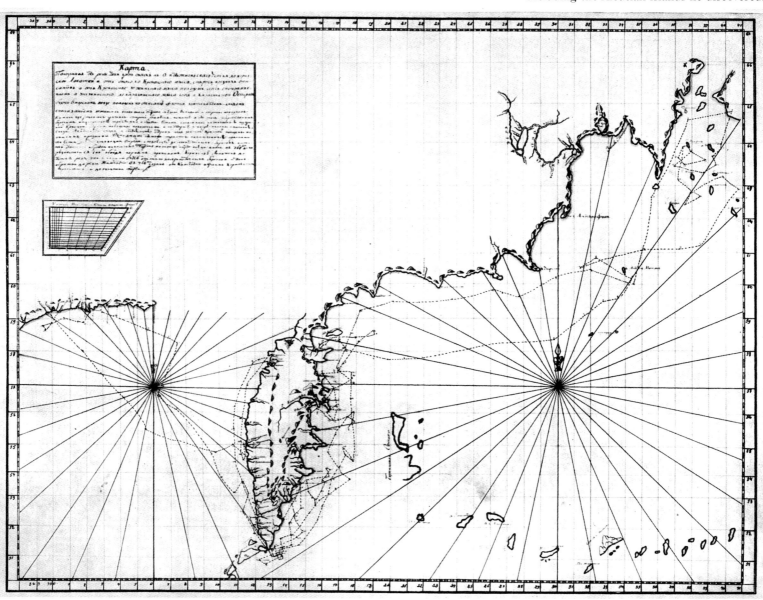

Map 116.
A Russian map from about 1773 showing Alaska as an island. This was Gerhard Müller's map of
1754 (pages 78–79) modified to include Ivan Synd's discoveries.

Map 117. Jacob von Stählin's map of the "New Northern Archipelago discovered by the Russians." Published in a book in 1774, the map was carried by James Cook, causing him to remark on its errors: "What could induce him to publish so erroneous a Map?"

North Pacific. In addition, she heard of the British plan to dispatch Commodore Byron to the North Pacific to seek a Northwest Passage; he sailed to the Pacific, but did not seek the passage.

As a result, in 1764 one of the survivors of the 1741 Bering expedition, Lieutenant Ivan Synd, was sent on a voyage into the Bering Sea.

Although he produced maps and a journal, all but one seem to have been lost. His map showed that there was a strait and showed that there was not a long peninsula from America almost to Kamchatka. The map he drew is shown on page 80.

On the basis of Synd's discoveries, Gerhard Müller's map was modified, and the overly long Alaska

Peninsula was shortened in favor of lots of islands, when reality lay somewhere between the two. The Russian version of this later map, dating from about 1773, is shown on the previous page (Map 116).

Also based on Synd, Jacob von Stählin produced a map in 1774, although it was hardly justified by Synd's own map. The latter showed

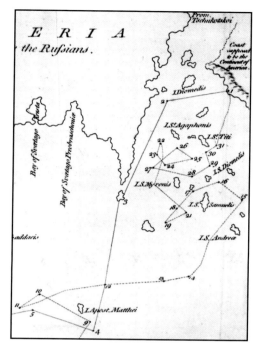

Map 118.
Synd's discoveries in the Bering Sea according to William Coxe, whose book was published in 1780. St. Matthew Island and the Diomedes are identifiable, but the other islands do not exist in the positions given. This map shows St. Matthew Island correctly at about 60° N.

Catherine II was also concerned about possible Spanish designs on "her" northern territories. The voyages of Bering and Chirikov were in her eyes claims of sovereignty based on first discovery. There was also concern about potential British interest in the region following the end of the Seven Years War with France, which resulted in a strengthening of the British position in North America.

Petr Krenitsyn and Mikhail Levashev were ordered to visit the islands to the east in 1764 so that Catherine could find out if there was encroachment by other powers. For secrecy, they were instructed only to build ships if they had no other alternative; otherwise they were to "board a hunting ship or merchant vessel . . . in the general capacity of passengers" so they would attract as little attention as possible.

But there were no ships available, and Krenitsyn and Levashev had to build their own. Taking the maps of Vitus Bering, they explored the North Pacific until 1769, becoming separated a number of times and overwintering three times.

They charted a number of the Aleutian Islands and the western part of the Alaska Peninsula. They produced maps such as one of the Fox Islands, the easternmost of the Aleutians, shown here in a later English edition.

Between 1774 and 1779 Potap Zaikov explored most of the Aleutian Islands, and in 1779 drew the first reasonably accurate and complete map of the entire Aleutian chain (Map 120, overleaf).

Grigorii Shelikov, who would in 1799 be instrumental in the founding of the Russian-American Company; Gerasim Ismailov, who met James Cook at Unalaska in 1778 and exchanged geographical information; and Dimitrii Bocharov added to Russian knowledge of the Aleutians in the 1780s. A summary map by Shelikov, which includes a larger-scale map of Kodiak Island, site of the first permanent Russian settlement in North America, is shown overleaf.

Finally, mention should be made of Gavriil Pribilov, who in 1786–87 discovered the relatively isolated islands of St. George and St. Paul, today named, after him, the Pribilof Islands. These islands would later become economically significant, for they were (and are again) home to vast numbers of fur seals.

fewer and much smaller islands in the northern Pacific. It was von Stählin's map that James Cook would carry with him on his third voyage, the map that would mislead him for some time (see page 98).

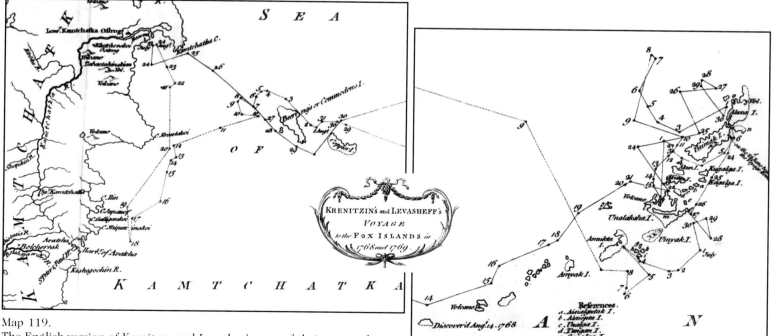

Map 119.
The English version of Krenitsyn and Levashev's map of their voyage from Kamchatka to the Fox Islands, the Aleutian Islands group nearest to the Alaskan mainland. It appeared in a book by Englishman William Coxe in 1780. It is more or less an exact copy of the Russian version, which shows that somehow Coxe, who visited Russia, gained access to the original. The map is long and narrow, with only the track of their ship connecting the detail from the Kamchatka side with that of the eastern Aleutians. The details either side of the map are shown here, and the map title cartouche inset.

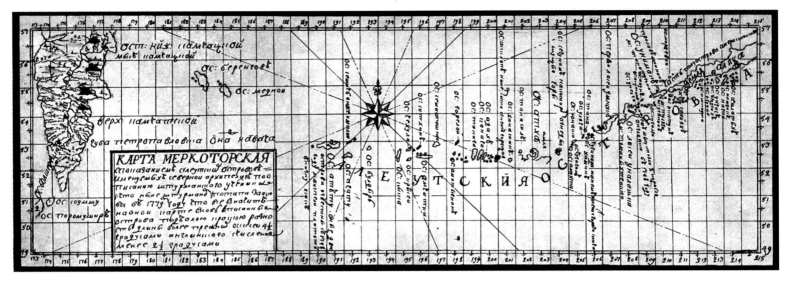

Map 120.
Potap Zaikov's map of the Aleutians, 1779.

Map 121.
A summary map by Grigorii Shelikov, one of the founders of the Russian-American Company.
Drawn in 1787, the map was intended to promote trade possibilities in the North Pacific. It
includes an inset map on a larger scale showing Kodiak Island, site of the first permanent
Russian settlement in North America.

The Spanish Northward Voyages

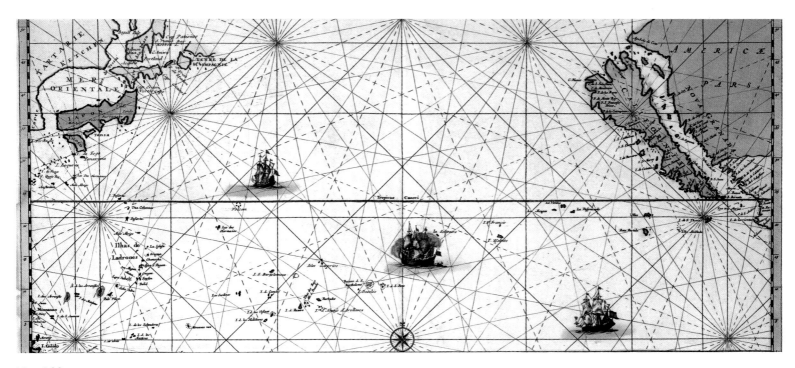

Map 122.
Knowledge of the Pacific Ocean, or South Sea, at the middle of the eighteenth century is shown in this map by Dutch mapmakers Reinier and Joshua Ottens, drawn in 1750. The magnificent cartouche from this map is reproduced on page 7.

Spanish knowledge of the Pacific Ocean north of the Tropics was much less detailed than what they knew of the tropical zone. Their main interest in the sixteenth, seventeenth, and much of the eighteenth centuries focused on the Philippines, and the routes there and back from New Spain. Only when their galleons were blown off course did they learn more, and this was not always interpreted correctly.

João de Gama, actually a Portuguese navigator sailing on a Spanish ship from Macao to Acapulco, is reputed to have seen land in relatively high latitudes in the western Pacific in 1590. Although more likely part of Japan or the Kurils, this gave rise to a "Gama Land" that was persistent on maps for two centuries, and was searched for by Bering and Chirikov in 1741.

Spanish explorations in the North Pacific were largely confined to

the west coast of North America. By about 1768 they had decided to occupy Alta California, the California of today. In 1769 San Diego Bay, which had been found by Sebastián Vizcaíno in 1603, was settled by two overland expeditions meeting two ships which had been dispatched northwards by

sea. One of the ships was commanded by Juan Pérez, who was to lead another northward thrust in 1774. The next year, 1770, Monterey was settled. That year San Francisco Bay was discovered by Gaspar de Portolá, who had led the overland expeditions to San Diego and Monterey.

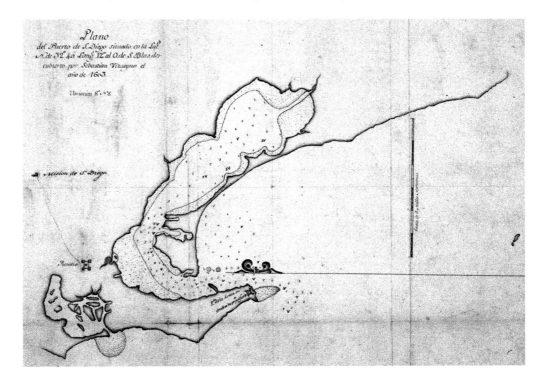

Map 123.
Anonymous Spanish map, about 1779, of San Diego, "discovered by Sebastián Vizcaíno in 1603." North is to the left.

In 1773, the Northwest Coast of North America stood unmapped even in general trend, a major gap in the map of the world; only the polar regions were similarly unmapped. The reason for this state of affairs was a lack of motivation. No European power, up to that point, was really interested. There were no reports of gold to draw men northwards to these often unpleasantly chilly coasts, there were vast distances to cover in any case, and the currents and winds made sailing northwards along the coast next to impossible. Without motivation, no one bothered to try.

The Russian advance eastwards from Kamchatka to the Aleutians changed all that. The Spanish regarded the Pacific Ocean as theirs, and wanted to ensure that no other nation encroached on what they viewed as their own territory.

So in 1773 the Spanish viceroy in New Spain (Mexico) instructed one of his senior naval captains, Juan Pérez, to draw up plans for a voyage to the north to determine once and for all what the Russians were up to in Alaska.

Pérez had been involved with the Spanish advance into Alta California and had been the first Spanish captain since Sebastián Vizcaíno to enter the harbors of San Diego and Monterey, both in 1770.

Now those small settlements seemed reasonably secure, and the Spanish government considered the time ripe for a further northward thrust.

Pérez sailed from the Mexican port of San Blas in January 1774 in the *Santiago,* with a complement of about eighty-six men including, as second-in-command, Estéban José Martínez, and pilot Josef de Cañizarez. Both would feature in later voyages north.

The viceroy instructed Pérez to sail to 60° N. He was, on his southward return, to follow the coast, "never losing sight of it." Not only that, Pérez was to carry tropical spices such as cinnamon and nutmeg to show any natives he might encounter what the Spanish were looking for.

Clearly the Spanish at this time had little concept of the nature of the Northwest Coast!

Pérez reached Monterey on 8 May and finally sailed from this last outpost of Spanish power on 6 June, although adverse winds meant he did not actually leave the bay for another eight days.

Then, sailing offshore, he set a course to the northwest, changing to north at 50°. On 18 July they sighted land, off the northernmost point of the Queen Charlotte Islands, and the following day, near Langara Island (which was named Santa Margarita by Pérez) in Dixon Entrance, they met Haida in canoes, with whom they bartered. But, fearing treachery, they did not venture ashore. It was found that the natives already had some metal, and in particular half a bayonet and a piece of sword beaten into a spoon, which Martínez assumed derived from the abortive landing parties of Alexei Chirikov, just a little farther north, thirty-three years before. A feasible assumption, although the interlinked and far-ranging trading networks of native groups are often overlooked when this sort of "evidence" surfaces; the iron could have migrated a long distance, trading from native group to native group.

Remaining in the area for four days, Pérez was never able to anchor. His latitudes are confused. He maintained that he was at 55° 24´ when he saw and named a cape he called Santa Maria Magdalena; it is marked on the map (right) as Pta de Sta Maria Magdalena. But this has been identified as Cape Muzon, the southern tip of Dall Island, at almost exactly 54° 40´. Not coincidentally, this is also the southern tip of the Alaska panhandle. When the United States inherited the territorial claims of Spain in 1819 under the terms of the Transcontinental Treaty, they claimed the coast up to the magic 54° 40´, and in fact threatened to go to war with Britain in 1845–46 if they didn't get it. As it happened, of course, they settled for 49° instead. But 54° 40´ was accepted as the southern limit of Russian claims, so that when the United States purchased Alaska from the Russians in 1867, this latitude became the boundary between British – now Canadian – territories to the south and American territories to the north.

Pérez gave up at this latitude; although he had been instructed to sail to 60°, he had seen no evidence of Russian encroachment. He tried to keep the coast in view as he returned southwards, without much success until he reached Vancouver Island. There he chanced on the entrance to Nootka Sound, which he named Surgidero de San Lorenzo. Unable to make it into the sound itself, he anchored outside on 7 August and again traded with natives. The latter encounter is significant in that it seems some silver spoons belonging to Martínez were pilfered, and four years later James Cook would trade for those same spoons; Cook mentions in his journal that he regarded them as proof that the Spanish had been at or near Nootka Sound.

The voyage farther south was uneventful and speedy; they arrived back at Monterey on 28 August. Martínez was later to claim that he had seen the entrance to the Strait of Juan de Fuca during this part of the voyage, but nothing in Pérez's account corroborates this claim.

Juan Pérez's voyage did not fulfill his instructions, but it was the first Spanish voyage north, and many others were to follow. The map opposite was drawn by Josef de Cañizarez and is the first map of what is now the coast of British Columbia, Washington, Oregon, and California north of Montery drawn from actual exploration rather than from conjecture.

Map 124.
Map showing the west coast of North America from Monterey to the tip of the Queen Charlotte Islands drawn by Juan Pérez's pilot, Josef de Cañizarez. It is the first map of part of the coast of British Columbia and Washington State to be drawn from actual exploration. Pérez's anchorage off Nootka Sound is shown as "Surgidero de Sn Lorenzo." "Pta de Sta Margarita" is the northern tip of Graham Island in the Queen Charlottes. "Cerro de Sta Rosalia" is Mt. Olympus, Washington.

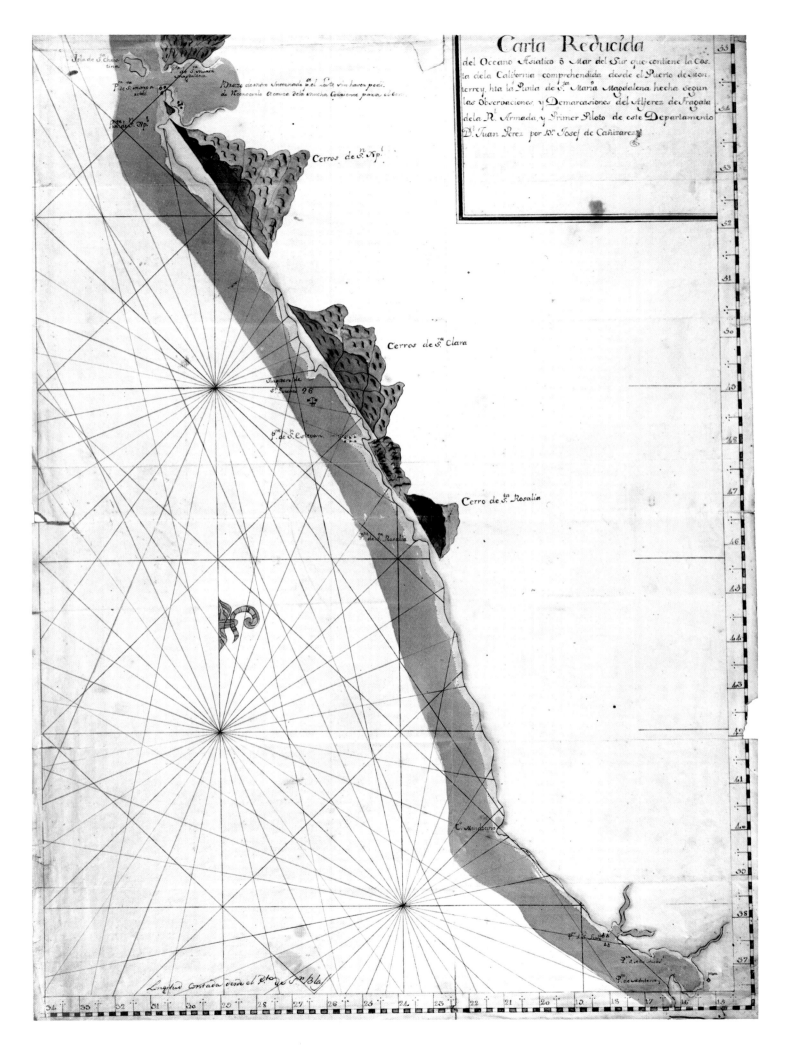

Carta Reducida

del Oceano Asiatico ô Mar del Sur que contiene la Cos.
ta dela California comprehendida desde el Puerto de Mon.
terrey, hta la Punta de S.ta Maria Magdalena hecha segun
las Observaciones y Demarcasiones del Alferez de Fragata
dela R.l Armada y Primer Piloto de este Departamento
D.n Juan Perez por D.n Josef de Cañizares

On 5 August 1775 the first Spanish ship anchored in San Francisco Bay. It was *San Carlos,* commanded by Juan Manuel de Ayala, and with him was pilot Josef de Cañizarez, who had been with Pérez the year before. Cañizarez's map of 1775 was the first of San Francisco Bay from actual survey. When he returned the next year, he drew another map, shown below.

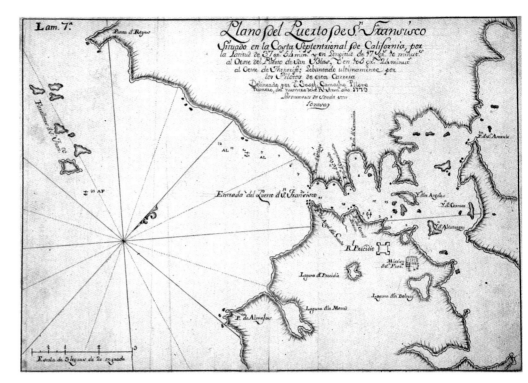

Map 125 (right).
A Spanish map of San Francisco Bay made by Josef Camacho, dated 1779 but probably a later copy.

Map 126 (below).
Part of *Plano del Puerto de Sn Francisco,* a map of San Francisco Bay drawn by Josef de Cañizarez in 1776.

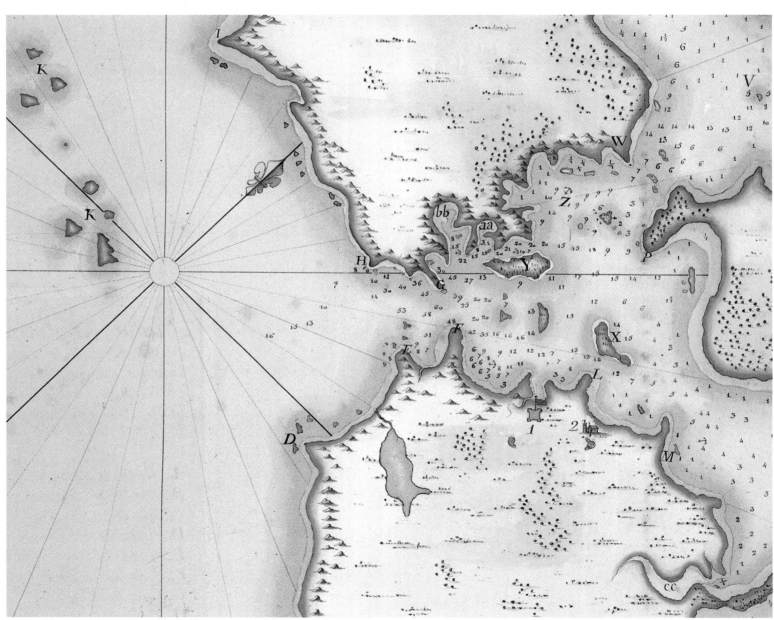

Bruno Hezeta Maps the Northwest Coast

Although it seemed unlikely that the Russians had settlements anywhere where they might threaten the Spanish, a second expedition was sent northwards in 1775, with instructions this time to reach 65° N. Two ships were dispatched: *Santiago*, with Bruno de Hezeta y Dudagoitia commanding the expedition and Juan Pérez now demoted to second officer because of his failure to follow instructions the year before; and *Sonora*, only 38 feet long, commanded by Juan Francisco de la Bodega y Quadra.

Heading offshore to sail northwards, the two ships made a landfall at Trinidad Harbor just south of Cape Blanco, and on 14 July 1775 landed on the Olympic Peninsula near Point Grenville, several miles south of the Quinault River.

Here Hezeta performed a formal act of possession for Spain. Bodega y Quadra sent some of his men ashore again later to fill their water casks, but they were all murdered by natives. Despite this and the short stay, Hezeta made a map of the area, which is shown here. This map is the first known map showing only the coast of Washington.

Leaving the coast and heading out to sea again, the ships were separated in heavy seas. Largely due to an outbreak of scurvy, Hezeta decided to sail the *Santiago* south again, but now he could follow the coast closely.

Map 128.
The first map of the Washington coast, drawn by Bruno de Hezeta y Dudagoitia, July 1775. The map shows today's Cape Elizabeth, the Quinault River, and Point Grenville.

A. Location of the cross (used in an act-of-possession ceremony)
B. Martyrs' Point (after the murdered sailors; now Cape Elizabeth)
C. Landing Island
D. Deceit Island

The river shown is the Quinault, and the dots extending south of Martyrs' Point show a reef on which the *Sonora* was temporarily stranded.

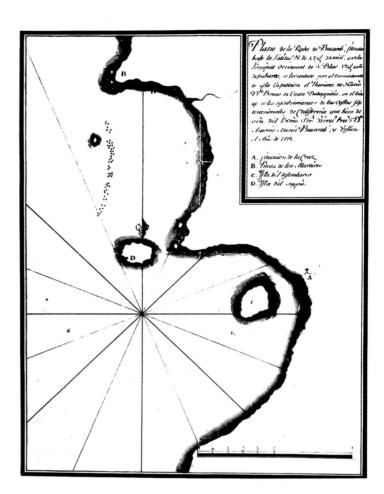

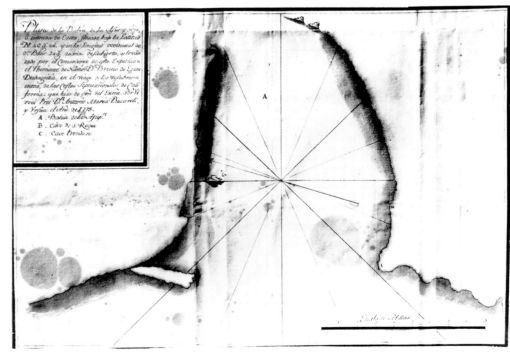

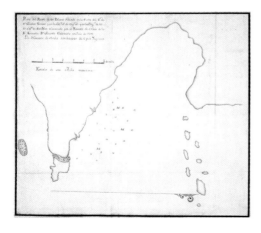

Map 127 (left).
A later Spanish map of part of the coast of Washington (as Map 128, above) either drawn in 1792 by Jacinto Caamaño or copied from him.

Map 129.
Map of Assumption Bay or [H]*ezeta's Entrance.*
Another of Hezeta's maps, drawn in August 1775. This is the first map of the mouth of the Columbia River.

On 17 August 1775, Hezeta came across what appeared to be a large bay, penetrating far inland. Hezeta tried to sail into the bay, but the current was so strong that he could not, even under a full press of sails. "These currents and seething of the waters," he wrote in his diary,

have led me to believe that it may be the mouth of some great river or some passage to another sea.

He decided it was the strait discovered by Juan de Fuca in 1592 and that the latitude had been misjudged. Hezeta named the bay Bahia de la Asunciõn after a holiday two days earlier.

This is the earliest recorded sighting of the mouth of the Columbia River by a European. It was a feature destined to be *missed* by many – including Cook in 1778, Meares in 1788, Malaspina in 1791, and Vancouver in 1792 – until finally being found and entered in 1792 by Robert Gray, in the *Columbia Rediviva,* from whence the river derives its name.

Hezeta was unable to anchor in the bay because he did not by this time have enough fit crew to handle the anchor, and he made directly for Monterey, reaching that port only twelve days later.

Hezeta prepared a map on the basis of what could be seen from outside the Columbia bar, and this is shown on the previous page. This was the first map of the mouth of the Columbia.

Map 130 (top).
Part of a Spanish map drawn in 1787 by Bernabe Muñoz that shows Hezeta's "entrada"; the Columbia now looks more like a river rather than just the bay Hezeta thought it was. It would not conclusively be determined to be a river until the American Robert Gray crossed the bar in 1792.

Map 131 (right).
A 1793 map by Esteban José Martínez shows "Entrada de Ezeta," the mouth of a recognizable Columbia River.

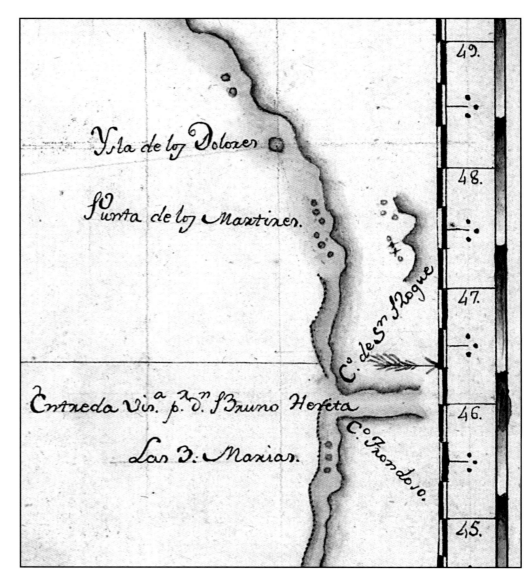

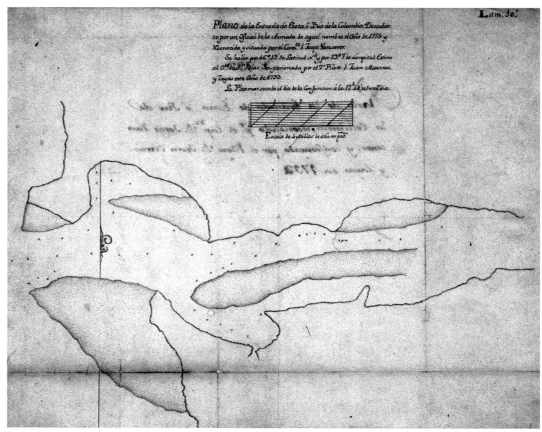

Bodega y Quadra's Epic Voyage

After separating from *Santiago*, Juan Francisco de la Bodega y Quadra in the little *Sonora* had decided to attempt to sail to 65° N, to follow his instructions. Indeed, it is possible that Bodega y Quadra, upset at Hezeta's lack of boldness, had deliberately separated from the other ship in order to be free to continue north. Francisco Antonio Mourelle, the second officer, wrote that they "formulated the temerarious project of separating and dying in their craft rather than return without enlightenment."

It was a brave act to sail from Washington to Alaska on the outer coast in such a small ship, particularly since navigation was little more than guesswork.

Sonora made a landfall on 15 August 1775 at 57° N, near a snow-capped peak they named San Jacinto – today's Mt. Edgecumbe, just west of Sitka. They eventually reached 58° N, just 2° south of the goal set for Pérez the year before.

Bodega y Quadra examined the coast in the area quite extensively, as he expected to find the mythical Strait of Bartholemew de Fonte. They did locate a good anchorage on the west coast of what is now Prince of Wales Island, at a bay they named (and which is still named today) Bucareli Bay, after the Spanish viceroy who had sent them. Francisco Antonio Mourelle performed possession ceremonies there, as Bodega y Quadra was ill that day. Scurvy was beginning to take its toll on the *Sonora*, as it had on the *Santiago*.

They limped back to San Blas via Monterey, arriving on 20 November 1775. A number of the crew died on the voyage, including Juan Pérez.

But enlightenment they found, for Bodega y Quadra was able to draw for the first time a reasonably accurate map of the west coast of North America.

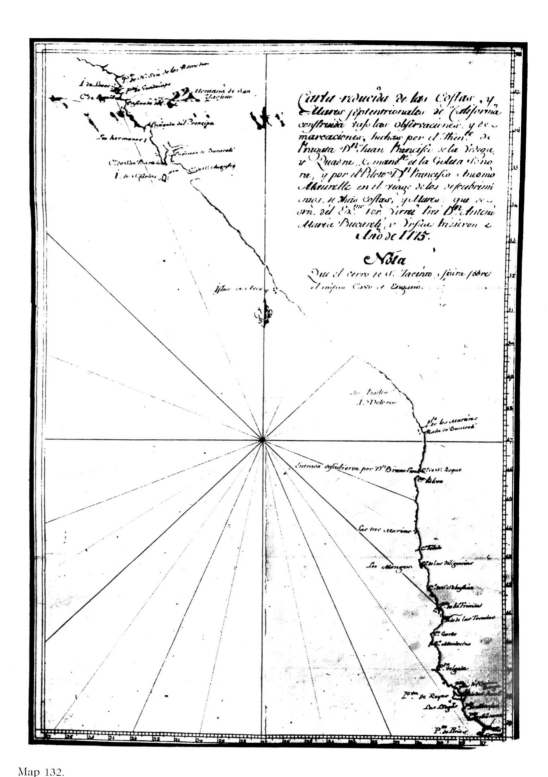

Map 132.
Bodega y Quadra's map of the west coast of North America, based on his discoveries and those of Hezeta. Detail is missing in the central part of the map due to the fact that Bodega y Quadra's ship was offshore at that time. This was a similar situation to that of James Cook in 1778, whose map of the Northwest Coast also shows little detail in the central part. Note the "Entrada descubierta por Dⁿ Bruno Ezeta," the "Entrance discovered by Don Bruno Hezeta," the mouth of the Columbia. Longitude is shown on this map, as it is on all Spanish maps of the period, as degrees west of San Blas, the Spanish naval port on the Mexican coast.

James Cook Defines the Northeast Pacific

The three voyages of James Cook were pivotal in the history of geographical knowledge of the Pacific Ocean. Before Cook there remained vast empty spaces on the map, where continents and straits may or may not have been.

After Cook, the essential outline of almost the entire Pacific Ocean had been mapped in sufficient detail to rule out most hypotheses of Southern Continents and Northwest Passages. Many details remained to be filled in, but the broad dimensions were now known for sure. And positions of islands and coasts had been fixed with remarkable accuracy; not only did Cook have an excellent ability to fix his position astronomically, but on the second and third voyages he carried some of the first examples of the new chronometers.

Cook's mapping of the west coast of North America demonstrated finally the width of the continent of North America, and by extension its corollary, the width of the Pacific Ocean.

Cook's uncanny surveying skills had been learned on the Atlantic coast of Canada and honed to perfection during his first and second voyages to the southern part of the Pacific. On his first voyage he mapped New Zealand and much of the east coast of Australia for the first time; on the second he disproved a popular theory regarding the existence of a Southern Continent by sailing where it was purported to be and in the process reaching beyond 70° S, farther than any had gone before.

In 1776, Cook set off on his third and final voyage, this time to the North Pacific. His instructions were to search for the Northwest Passage – to "find out a Northern passage by sea from the Pacific to the Atlantic Ocean." He was not to bother searching for such a passage below 65° N, as the British Admiralty knew from Samuel Hearne's expedition to the shores of the Arctic Ocean in 1771 that there could be no ocean passage below about that latitude. This is why Cook's maps of the west coast show only the trend of the coastline and not the details. From 65° northwards, Cook was instructed to

very carefully . . . search for, and . . . explore, such rivers or inlets as may appear to be of a considerable extent, and pointing towards Hudson's or Baffin's Bays.

Furthermore, if there should

appear to be a certainty, or even a probability, of a water passage into the aforementioned bays . . . [he was] to use [his] utmost endeavours to pass through with one or both of the sloops.

If he did not find such a passage, Cook was to winter in Kamchatka and then probe northwards to determine if there was a passage yet farther north.

All Cook's actions must be viewed with these instructions in mind.

Portrait of James Cook, painted by Nathaniel Dance between the second and third voyages. This famous painting hangs in the National Maritime Museum in Greenwich, England.

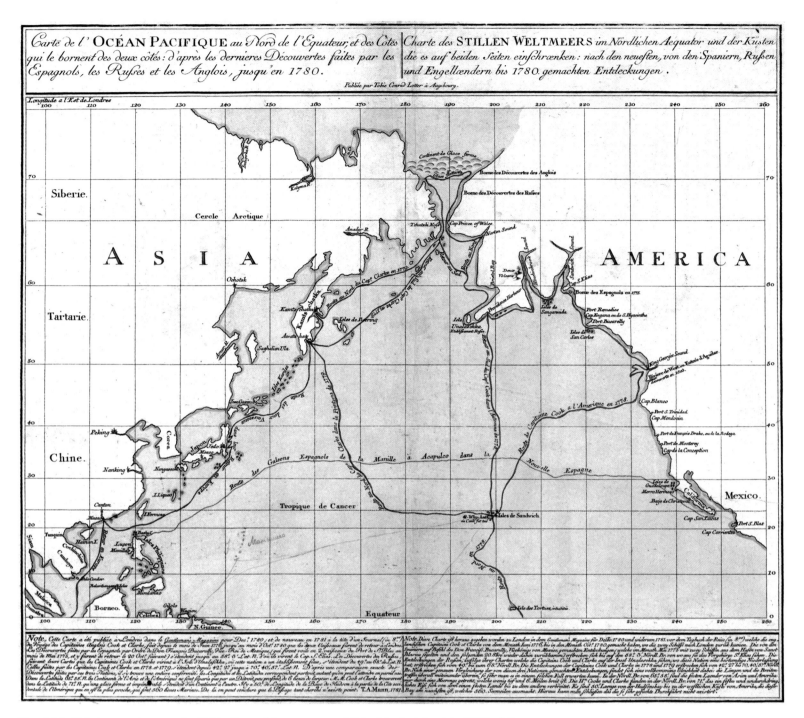

Carte de l' OCÉAN PACIFIQUE au Nord de l'Equateur, et des Côtes qui le bornent des deux côtés: d'après les dernieres Découvertes faites par les Espagnols, les Rußes et les Anglois, jusqu'en 1780.

Charte des STILLEN WELTMEERS im Nördlichen Aequator und der Küsten die es auf beiden Seiten einschrænken: nach den neuesten, von den Spaniern, Rußen und Engellændern bis 1780. gemachten Entdeckungen.

Publiée par Tobie Conrad Lotter à Augsbourg.

Map 133. This interesting map by Tobie Conrad Lotter was published in Augsburg in 1781, fully three years before the appearance of the official edition of Cook's book *A Voyage to the Pacific Ocean*, which was published, posthumously of course, in 1784. There was enormous interest in Cook's third voyage, and the pressure was such that several maps and two books were published before Cook's, with the information coming, often anonymously, from members of Cook's crews.

After discovering and mapping Hawaii for the first time, he arrived on the west coast of North America on 6 March 1778, at a point near Cape Foulweather, in Oregon, at 44° 33´ N. Cook had been instructed to make a landfall at about 45° N, as this was north of any point felt likely to be considered subject to Spanish territorial claims. Britain had no wish to see the voyage cause an international incident. Bad weather did, however,

force the ships southwards to about 43° N before they could begin to work their way northwards.

At about 48° N Cook located a headland south of Cape Flattery, which he so named because it "flattered us with the hopes of finding a harbour," but he failed to find the entrance to the Strait of Juan de Fuca. "It is in the very latitude we were now," Cook wrote in his journal,

in where geographers have placed the pretended Strait of Juan de Fuca. But we saw nothing like it, nor is there the least probability that iver any such thing ever exhisted.

He did record "a small opening in the land" towards dusk. But darkness closed in, the weather deteriorated, and the ships were forced out to sea.

Much has been made of Cook's failure to find the strait, but in fact he was just following his instructions. He had been instructed not to look for a strait in this latitude; if he had,

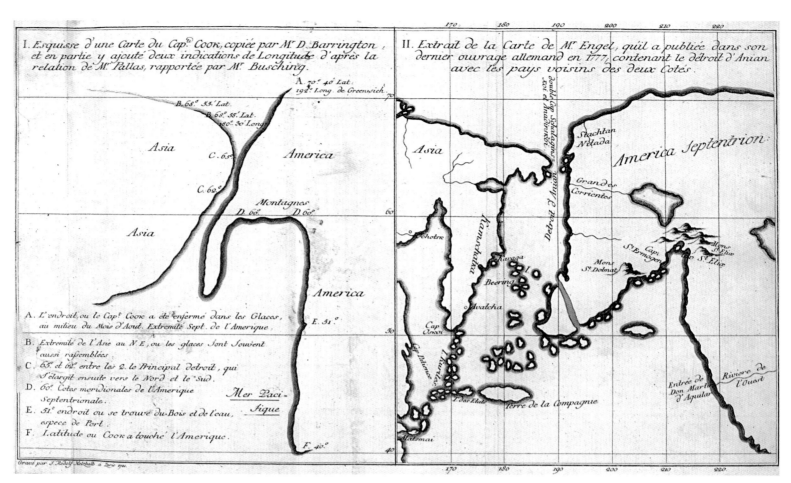

I. *Esquisse d'une Carte du Cap.^e Cook, copiée par Mr D. Barrington, et en partie y ajouté deux indications de Longitude d'après la relation de Mr Pallas, rapportée par Mr Busching.*

A. *L'endroit, ou le Capt Cook a été enfermé dans les Glaces, au milieu du Mois d'Aout. Extrémité Sept. de l'Amerique.*

B. *Extremité de l'Asie au N.E, ou les glaces sont souvent aussi rassemblées.*

C. *65° et 62° entre les 2. le Principal detroit, qui s'élargit ensuite vers le Nord et le Sud.*

D. *60° Cotes meridionales de l'Amerique Septentrionale.*

E. *51° endroit ou se trouve du Bois et de l'eau, espece de Port.*

F. *Latitude ou Cook a touché l'Amerique.*

II. *Extrait de la Carte de Mr Engel, qu'il a publiée dans son dernier ouvrage allemand en 1777, contenant le détroit d'Anian avec les pays voisins des deux Cotés.*

Map 134.
Not everybody got it right! These two maps were included in a book about Cook published in Geneva in 1781 by Swiss geographer and economist Samuel Engel. Clearly the information used was textual not cartographic, and descriptions, one must assume, can mislead. Both of these maps purport to be interpretations of Cook's third voyage. Their claim to fame is that they were apparently the first to be published.

his track record of meticulous exploration of coastlines suggests very strongly that he would have gone back to survey the coast once the weather allowed.

Cook's ships eventually found a harbor farther up the coast of Vancouver Island, at a place they called King George's Sound, later renamed Nootka by the British Admiralty.

Cook anchored his ships on the southeast side of Bligh Island (named after his sailing master, William Bligh, later famous by dint of the mutiny on his ship, *Bounty*) in a cove now named after Cook's ship, Resolution Cove. He stayed there most of the month of April 1778, repairing his ships, surveying, and observing the natives. During this time he surveyed the sound in the ships' boats, producing a map of it. Perhaps more important, he fixed the position of

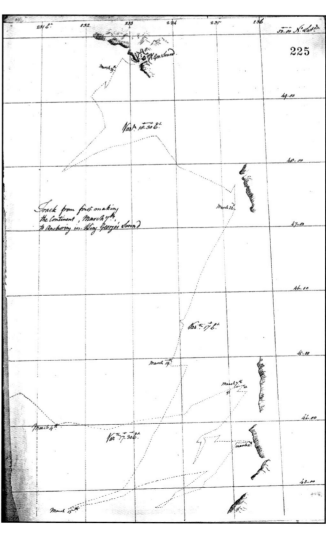

Map 135.
This page from James Burney's journal shows the track of Cook's ships from their landfall on the coast of Oregon northwards to Nootka Sound, Cook's King George's Sound. Clearly it was not all plain sailing! Burney was one of Cook's officers.

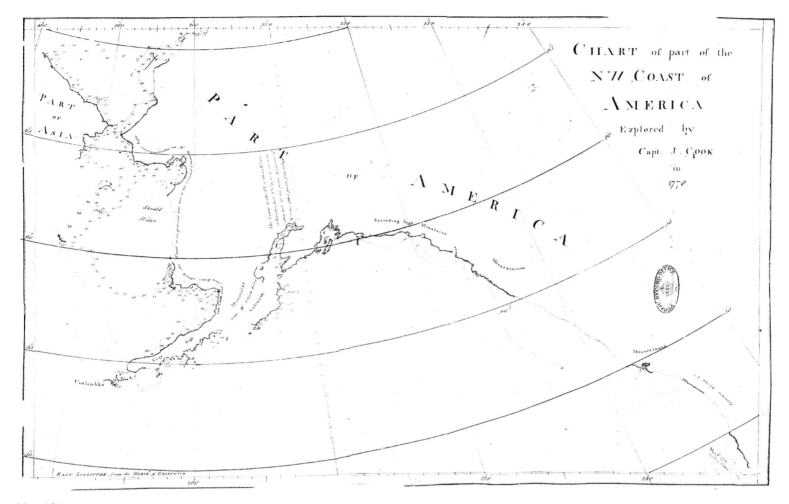

Map 136.
This map was drawn by James Cook and sent in a letter to Philip Stephens, Secretary of the Admiralty. The letter was given to the Russians at Unalaska. It was sent on 20 October 1778 (21 October in Cook's journal; he had sailed east from Britain and thus had gained a day but had not realized it) and arrived in London on 6 March 1780.

Nootka so that henceforth other ships would be able to find it.

At the end of the month, he sailed northwards towards Alaska, where he proceeded to map the coast in far greater detail than had ever been done before.

On his way, passing 50° N on 26 April, Cook noted in his journal that he regretted that again the weather was forcing him to stay away from the land,

especially as we were passing the place where Geographers have placed the pretended Strait of Admiral de Fonte.

Although Cook did not believe that such a strait existed, he wrote,

Nevertheless I was highly desirous of keeping the Coast aboard in order to clear up this point beyond dispute; but

it would have been highly imprudent in me to have ingaged with the land in such exceeding tempestuous weather.

North of about 55° N, Cook began looking for inlets that could be entrances to the Northwest Passage, and this was certainly the thought on his men's minds at this stage, because they would have shared in prize money – twenty thousand pounds – that had been offered by the British government for the discovery of such a passage.

Cook discovered and mapped a very large bay that he named Prince William Sound, and then, a little to the southwest, he found the large opening of Cook Inlet. Surely this was the long-sought Northwest Passage? Cook was not expectant, though many of his men were; naturally enough, they wanted their share of the huge reward.

Bucking the strong tidal rips for which the inlet is well known, they explored the opening: the northern part in two of the ships' boats, one under William Bligh east past the site of today's Anchorage, and the other under James King. They found that the water was turning fresh and the channels narrowing, so after sixteen days in this inlet, and the season running out on them, they gave up and left to resume their explorations westward.

Since Cook did not explore completely the northeastern end of Cook Inlet, and also because he named it Cook's River instead of Cook's Inlet, the possibility remained that a great river entered the sea here that penetrated the interior in such a way as to *still* provide a Northwest Passage, this time by river, and this was postulated by some, notably Canadian fur

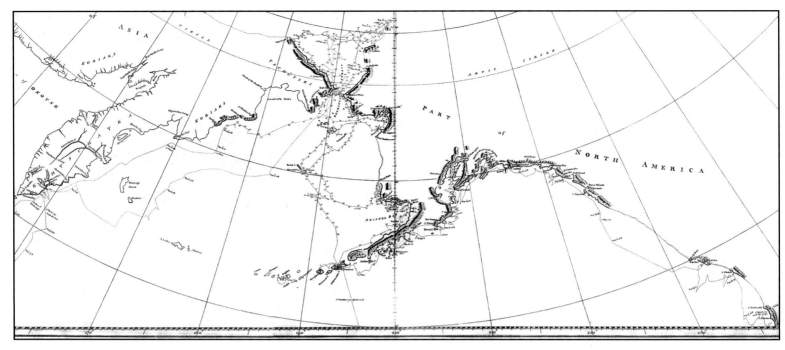

Map 137.
The summary map published in Cook's book in 1784. A coast revealed to the world in the true Cook tradition.

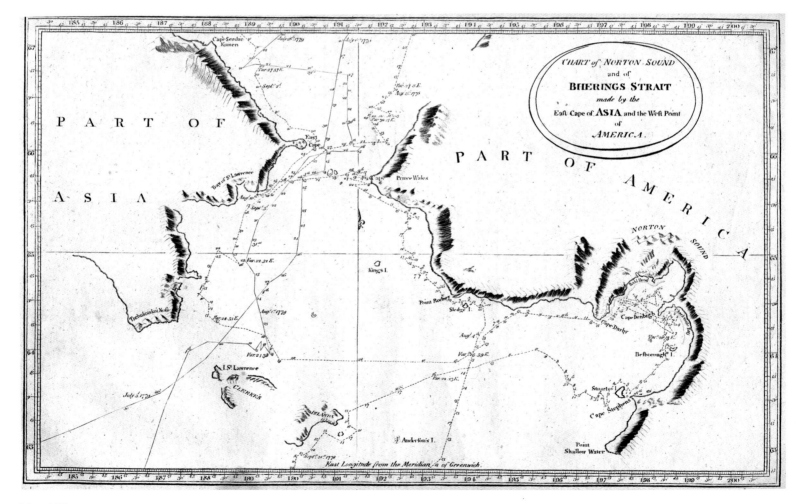

Map 138.
Considered by many to be the most significant map to come out of Cook's third voyage is this one of Bering Strait. Here the correct relationship of Asia and America is accurately laid out for the first time. This is the engraved and published map from the 1784 book.

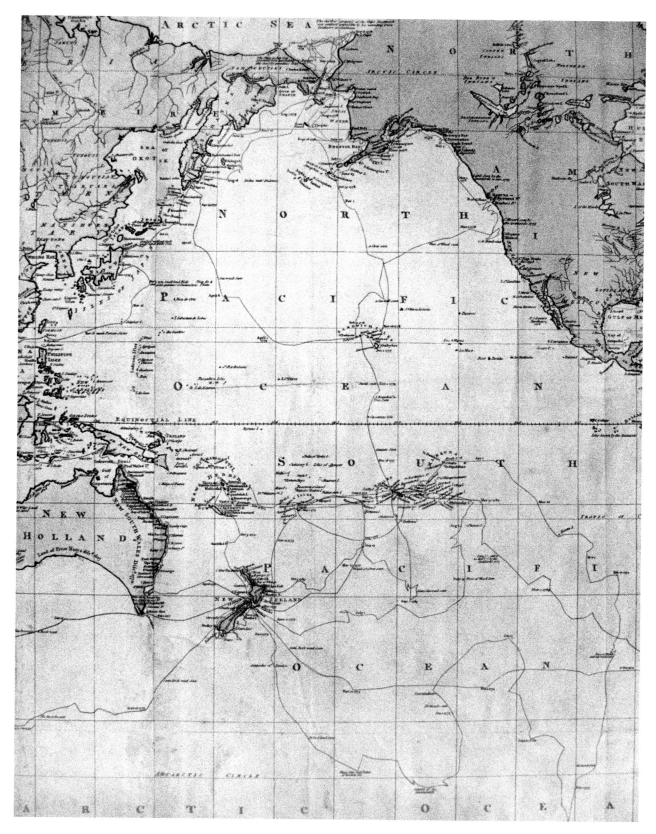

Map 139.
The Pacific Ocean arrives upon the consciousness of the world. This is part of a summary world map entitled *General Chart exhibiting the Discoveries made by Capt. James Cook.* It was published in 1784 by William Faden, but had been painstakingly assembled and drawn by Henry Roberts, who had been Cook's principal mapmaker during the voyage. Roberts had long been charged by Cook with making a world map with the tracks of all his voyages upon it; this was to be Cook's legacy to the world, and even after Cook's death, Roberts continued with this discharge of his instructions. The map attempted to show the relationship between Cook's coastal explorations and those of Samuel Hearne in 1771 and 1772 in the interior. Hearne's discoveries were, however, placed too far north and too far west. Nevertheless, here we have for the first time a reasonably accurate map of all of North America and the Pacific Ocean. Also shown here are the more extensive tracks of Cook in the South Pacific Ocean during his first and second voyages (1768–71 and 1772–75, including the southernmost point of 71° 10´ S reached during the second voyage at the end of January 1773.

trader Peter Pond. It was one of Cook's midshipmen, George Vancouver, who would finally put the myth to rest in 1794, changing the name from Cook's River to Cook's Inlet in the process.

Continuing to the southwest, they found a gap through the eastern end of the Aleutians and then sailed northwards.

South of Bering Strait, Cook reached a large, previously unmapped sound, which he named after the Speaker of the House of Commons, Sir Fletcher Norton. As the ships sailed up the sound, Cook noted a shoaling of the water that made him realize it was unlikely to be a passage. Nevertheless, it was explored and found not to divide Alaska from the rest of the coast.

On 9 August 1778, Cook reached the northwestern extremity of North America, which he named Cape Prince of Wales, after the heir to the British throne, despite the fact that it was already marked on Müller's maps of 1754 and 1758 (see pages 78–79), which he carried with him, as "coast surveyed by surveyor Gvozdev in 1730," actually 1732 (see page 65).

Cook then sailed through Bering Strait and reached 70° 44´ N before he was stopped by ice. This latitude was almost as far north as the equivalent southern latitude he had reached during his second voyage, 71° 10´ S, in January 1773.

On 29 August he decided to return to Hawaii to refit for a second season. While mapping some of the Aleutian Islands, Cook wrote in his journal:

In justice to Behrings Memory, I must say he has delineated this Coast very well and fixed the latitude and longitude of the points better than could be expected from the Methods he had to go by.

On his way he called at the island of Unalaska, where he met Russian fur traders. Unalaska was the site of the first permanent Russian settlement in North America. The senior Russian officer there, Gerasim Ismailov, allowed Cook to copy two Russian charts, showing, Cook wrote, *all the discoveries made by the Russians to the Eastward of Kamtschatka towards America, which if we exclude the Voyage of Behring and Tcherikoff* [Chirikov]*, will amount to little or nothing.*

Cook in turn presented Ismailov with a map of his explorations to date.

The following day, 20 October 1778, Cook gave Ismailov a letter that contained a map, addressed to the British Admiralty, with the request that they be forwarded by him to London. Cook obviously felt that they had a good chance of reaching London overland via the Russians before he could otherwise get a communication through to the Admiralty. The letter and the map did in fact get through, arriving at the Admiralty on 6 March 1780, and the map, probably drawn by Cook himself, is shown on page 95 (Map 136). This was the first map from Cook's third voyage, and the most complete map of Alaska and the Northwest Coast to date. It was to be much copied.

At this time, an interesting comment appears in Cook's journal relating to a map drawn by Jacob von Stählin (Map 117, page 82), which Cook had been using, or trying to use, up to this point. Von Stählin's map showed the Alaskan region broken up into many islands, including one itself labeled Alaschka. Cook wrote:

[The Russians] *assured me over and over again that they k*[n]*ew of no other islands but what were laid down on this chart* [the second of the two charts presented to Cook]*, and that no Russian had ever seen any part of the Continent to the northward, excepting that part lying opposite the Country of the Tchuktschis* [across the Bering Strait]*. If M*ʳ *Staelin was not greatly imposed upon what could induce him to publish so erroneous a Map? in which many of these islands are jumbled in regular confusion, without the least regard to truth and yet he is pleased to call it a very accurate little Map? A Map that the most illiterate of his Sea-faring men would have been ashamed to put his name to.*

Second Lieutenant James King noted in his journal:

As far as we can judge, there never was a Map so unlike what it ought to be.

Cook also had Müller's map with him, but it proved to be not much better. King also wrote in his journal, on 23 July 1778:

As we have already Saild over a great space where Muller places a Continent, we can no longer frame any supposition in order to make our Charts agree with his.

Cook was killed by natives in Hawaii in February 1779, before he could return to complete the task he had been set. Captain Charles Clerke then assumed command, and the ships returned to Alaskan waters directly, principally to determine for sure that there was no practicable Northwest Passage through Bering Strait. Clerke was already ill by this time and he died in August 1779, command then being taken over by John Gore, who guided the expedition back to London. In this, both Clerke and Gore received a great deal of help from William Bligh, who was a brilliant navigator.

Map 140 (right).
During a stopover in Kamchatka in 1779, a midshipman, Edward Riou, surveyed the harbor and drew this superb map of what is now Avachinskaya Guba, Avatcha Bay, on which sits the modern Russian city of Petropavlovsk–Kamchatskiy.

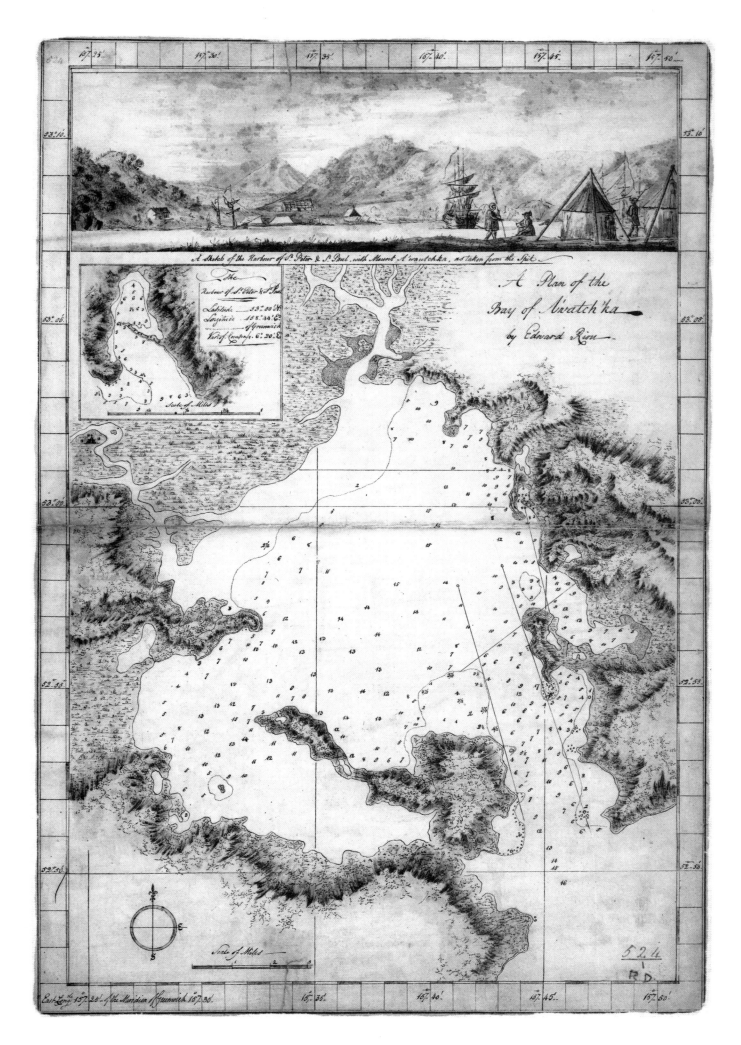

A Sketch of the Harbour of S.t Peter & S.t Paul, with Mount A'wautchka, as taken from the Spit.

The
Harbour of S.t Peter & S.t Paul

Latitude .... 53°. 00′ N.
Longitude ...... 158°. 44′ E.
.... of Greenwich
Var.t of Compass. 6°. 20′. E.

Scale of Miles

A Plan of the
Bay of A'vatch'ka
by Edward Riou

Scale of Miles

East Long.t 157. 25′. of the Meridian of Greenwich 157. 30′.

The Lovtsov Atlas of the North Pacific Ocean

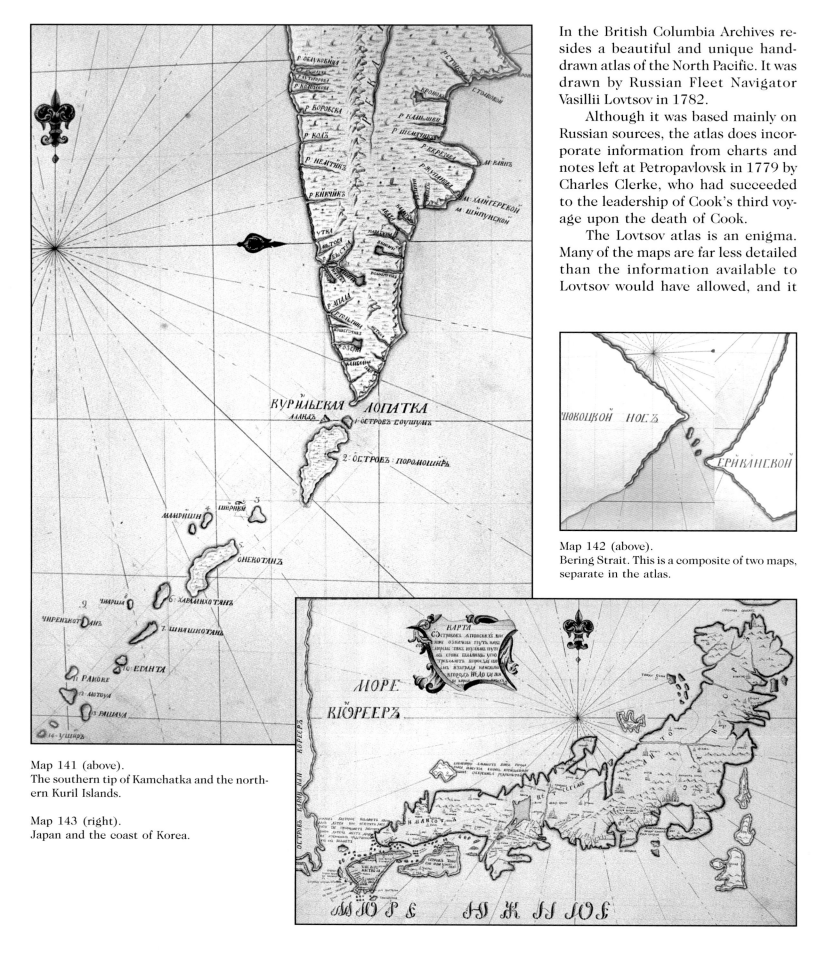

In the British Columbia Archives resides a beautiful and unique hand-drawn atlas of the North Pacific. It was drawn by Russian Fleet Navigator Vasillii Lovtsov in 1782.

Although it was based mainly on Russian sources, the atlas does incorporate information from charts and notes left at Petropavlovsk in 1779 by Charles Clerke, who had succeeded to the leadership of Cook's third voyage upon the death of Cook.

The Lovtsov atlas is an enigma. Many of the maps are far less detailed than the information available to Lovtsov would have allowed, and it

Map 142 (above).
Bering Strait. This is a composite of two maps, separate in the atlas.

Map 141 (above).
The southern tip of Kamchatka and the northern Kuril Islands.

Map 143 (right).
Japan and the coast of Korea.

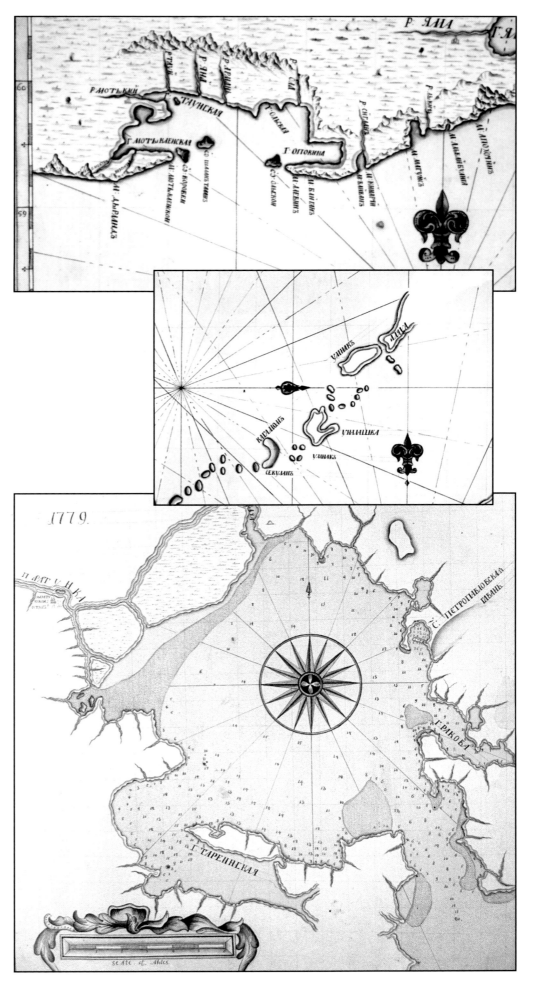

may be that some, particularly those of the west coast of North America, were simply drawn from memory, perhaps after being shown Cook's charts but not being allowed to retain them.

The atlas was drawn while overwintering "at the Bol'sheretsk ostrog" (fort), a Russian post on the west side of southern Kamchatka. Lovtsov is thought to have been in charge of supply vessels sailing from Okhotsk to Bol'sheretsk.

The eighteen charts in the atlas were drawn with pen and ink and finished with watercolors.

Maps from Vasilii Lovtsov's manuscript atlas (this page, top to bottom):

Map 145.
Northern part of the Sea of Okhotsk. This is Tauynskaya Guba, the bay on which the modern city of Magadan sits.

Map 146.
The easternmost Aleutians and the tip of the Alaska Peninsula.

Map 147.
Avatcha Bay on the Kamchatka Peninsula, site of modern Petropavlovsk. It is interesting to compare this map with Riou's (Map 140, page 99), with which it is contemporary.

Map 144 (below).
Part of the coast of the southern Alaska panhandle and northern British Columbia; the maps of the east Pacific are much less well defined than those of the west.

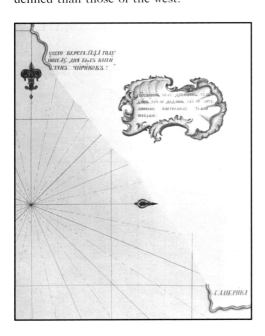

La Pérouse –
The French Answer to Cook

La Pérouse's ship, *Astrolabe*.

In the wake of Cook, the French organized a round-the-world scientific voyage designed to regain French prestige judged to have been lost to England.

Selected to command this expedition was Jean-François Galaup, Comte de la Pérouse, a highly regarded naval officer. Scientists from France and other countries, including Britain's Joseph Banks, assisted with the planning for the voyage. Banks even prevailed upon the British Board of Longitudes to lend the expedition two dipping needles (for measuring the direction of the Earth's magnetism) that had been used by James Cook.

Importantly, too, La Pérouse had some of the still scarce chronometers with him, including an English instrument.

La Pérouse sailed in August 1785 with two ships, *Boussole* and *Astrolabe*. In the North Pacific, La Pérouse was to determine the true position of the Aleutians and other islands to the west, whose positions were un-

known. He was also to survey the Kuril Islands, the coasts of Japan, and the Northwest Coast of America, altogether a massive undertaking which was to prove too much to achieve. His instructions stated:

We still lack a full knowledge of the earth and particularly of the Northwest coast of America, of the coast of Asia which faces it, and of islands that must lie scattered in the seas separating these two continents.

No less than eleven scientists and artists accompanied La Pérouse, and special quarters were added for them; this was a *scientific* voyage.

But there was more; La Pérouse was also instructed to determine just how far the Russians had pushed into North America. He was also to determine what kinds of furs received the best prices in China, and whether or not Japan might be tempted to open its doors to trade in furs. This was all a preliminary to a planned possible French commercial incursion into the North Pacific. Having lost their North American colonies in 1763, the French were on the lookout for new opportunities.

La Pérouse reached the North Pacific in July 1786, making a landfall near Mt. St. Elias on the Alaskan coast, then surveying southwards to Monterey. By keeping relatively close inshore, he was able to produce a superior chart to that of Cook, who, sailing northwards, had been forced to stay away from the coast more than he would have liked.

At Lituya Bay, which La Pérouse called Port des Français, his scientists went to work. A considerable record was made of native life and customs. But tragedy struck when twenty-one men drowned while carrying out a survey.

La Pérouse had been given three months to survey the entire Northwest Coast, a task that would consume three years of George Vancouver's life.

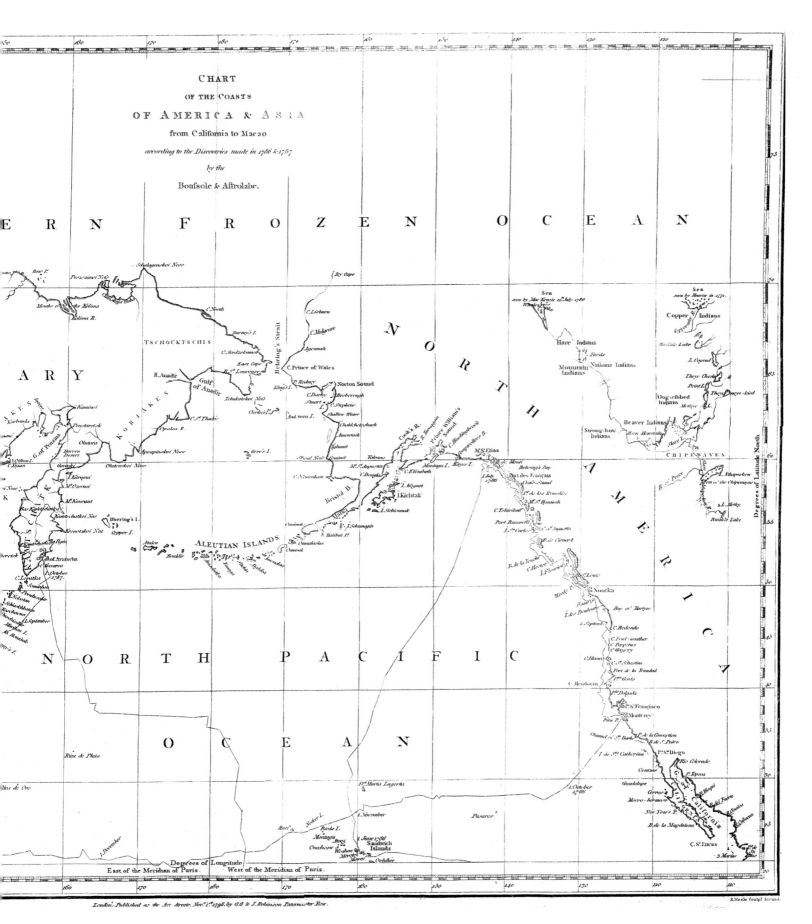

Map 148.
La Pérouse's summary map of the northern part of the Pacific Ocean, published in 1798, long after his disappearance. He had sent maps and data back to France from Australia, entrusting them to the British. Note that Sakhalin is shown as an island.

La Pérouse soon realized that his assignment was impossible. He gave up looking for a Northwest Passage, still thought perhaps to exist in these latitudes, and the quick survey he made of the coast led to the production of a remarkably accurate map.

Although he was well received in Monterey, the Spanish were alarmed that the French had arrived so soon after the British expedition of Cook.

After searching for lost islands in the central Pacific using a Spanish chart he had obtained (illustrated on page 19), La Pérouse visited Macao and then, in May 1787, sailed north into the East China Sea.

They surveyed the Korean coast, charting islands not already on the maps, and surveyed some of the coast of Japan, making no landings in either country due to their exclusion of foreigners.

Then the two ships sailed up the coast of Tartary, now part of Russia, into Tartar Strait, from approximately the position of modern Vladivostok.

La Pérouse sailed farther and farther north and the water became shallower and shallower. At Tomari natives informed him that Sakhalin was an island, not a peninsula. The illustration overleaf depicts this meeting. Another encounter confirmed the same thing. "I had gone too far not to want to explore this strait and ascertain whether it was passable," he wrote in his journal,

[but] *I was beginning to form an unfavorable opinion of it because the depth was lessening very quickly as one went north and the coast of Segalien Island was nothing more than drowned sand dunes almost level with the sea, like sand banks.*

Constant southerly winds presented a risk of being trapped at the north end of the strait, and so in the end La Pérouse decided not to risk his ships, turning south again without proving the insularity of Sakhalin, though he knew it to be an island and his charts show it as such.

Sailing south, hugging the west coast of Sakhalin, they found a strait – today called La Pérouse Strait – between Sakhalin and Hokkaido. Now

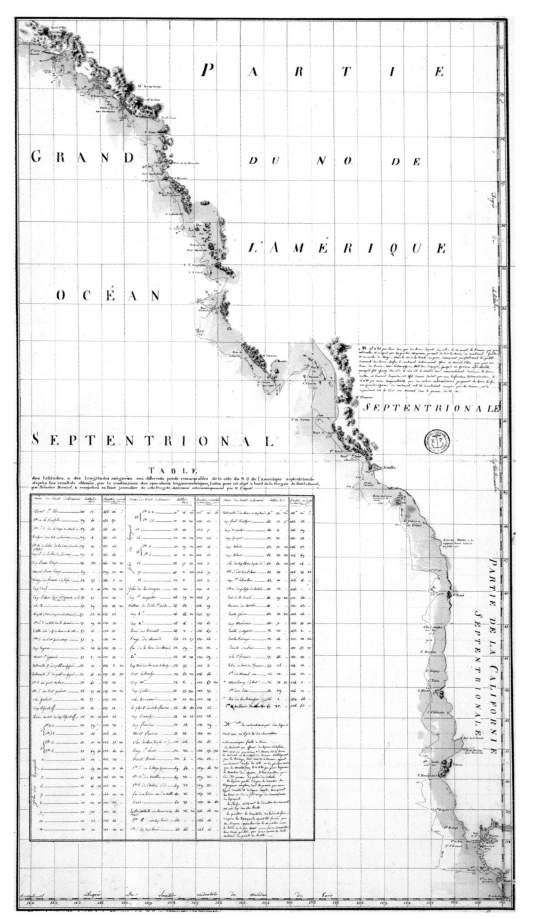

Map 149.

Map of the west coast of North America from Mt. St. Elias to Monterey, with the track of the La Pérouse expedition in 1786 and a table of positions prepared by two of the expedition's scientific staff, Gérault-Sébastien Bernizet, the surveyor, and Joseph Lapaute Dagelet, the senior astronomer. This survey was superior to Cook's or any other at the time; only Vancouver's exhaustive survey would prove more accurate. This is the original pen-and-ink map. It was not published until 1797.

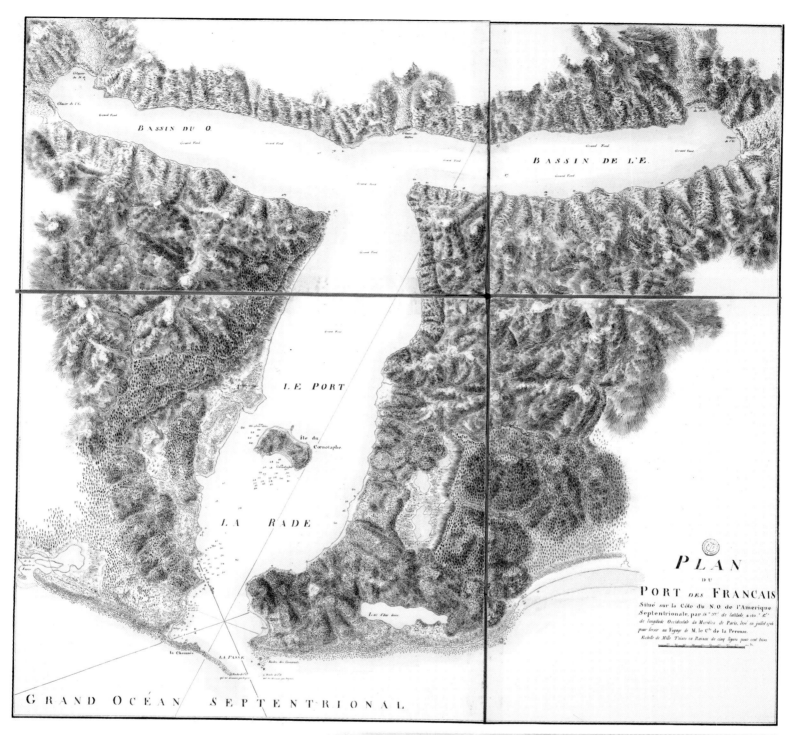

PLAN
DU
PORT DES FRANÇAIS
Situé sur la Côte du N.O de l'Amerique
Septentrionale, par 58°37' de latitude & 140°8'
de longitude Occidentale du Meridien de Paris, levé en juillet 1786
pour servir au Voyage de M. le Cte de la Perouse.
Echelle de Mille Toises en Raison de cinq lignes pour cent toises

BASSIN DU O.

BASSIN DE L'E.

LE PORT

Île du Cœnotaphe.

LA RADE

GRAND OCÉAN SEPTENTRIONAL

A spectacular view of Lituya Bay, Alaska (right), which La Pérouse called Port des Français, "drawn from nature by Duché de Vancy in July 1786." Gaspard Duché de Vancy had been appointed to *Boussole* as a "drawer of figures and landscapes." This inlet appeared on no chart and thus La Pérouse was interested in it as a potential base for any French fur trade establishment on the Northwest Coast. A map of the same inlet is shown above (Map 150). It was drawn by Gérault-Sébastien Bernizet and Paul Mérault de Monneron, *ingénieur en chef.* It was in attempting to determine soundings for this chart that disaster struck. A sounding party, which had been warned by La Pérouse not to go too close to the rocks at the entrance to the bay, did go too close and were caught by a strong tide. Twenty-one sailors lost their lives. In a sense this beautiful map lives on as their monument.

in seas mapped by Maarten Vries in 1643, they found a strait between two of the Kurils and sailed north to Avatcha Bay in Kamchatka, leaving there in September 1787 for the South Pacific.

By February 1788 they were in Botany Bay, Australia, and entrusted the British in Port Jackson, a few miles to the north, with their maps and journals, to be sent to France. It was just as well they did so, for after La Pérouse left Australia in March 1788, he was never heard from again.

The mystery of the disappearance of La Pérouse was solved in the 1960s, when the remains of both his ships were found on a reef on Vanikoro, in New Caledonia.

La Pérouse meets with natives of Sakhalin, who assured him of the island's insularity.

Map 151.

A map of La Pérouse's Castries Bay, now Zaliv Chikhacheva, on the coast of Siberia, drawn by Gérault-Sébastien Bernizet in July 1787. The name came from the French Minister of Marine, the Maréchal de Castries, and survives today in the town and port of De-Kastri, inside the bay. La Pérouse made many such detailed charts of bays and harbors. He had been specifically instructed "to draw careful plans of the coasts, bays, ports and anchorages he [was] in a position to inspect and explore; [and to] append to each plan instructions detailing everything relating to the approach and identification of the coast, the manner of anchoring and mooring and the best place to obtain water, the depths and the quality of the bottom; dangers, rocks and reefs; prevailing winds; breezes, monsoons, their duration and the dates of their changes; in short all the information that can be of use to navigators."

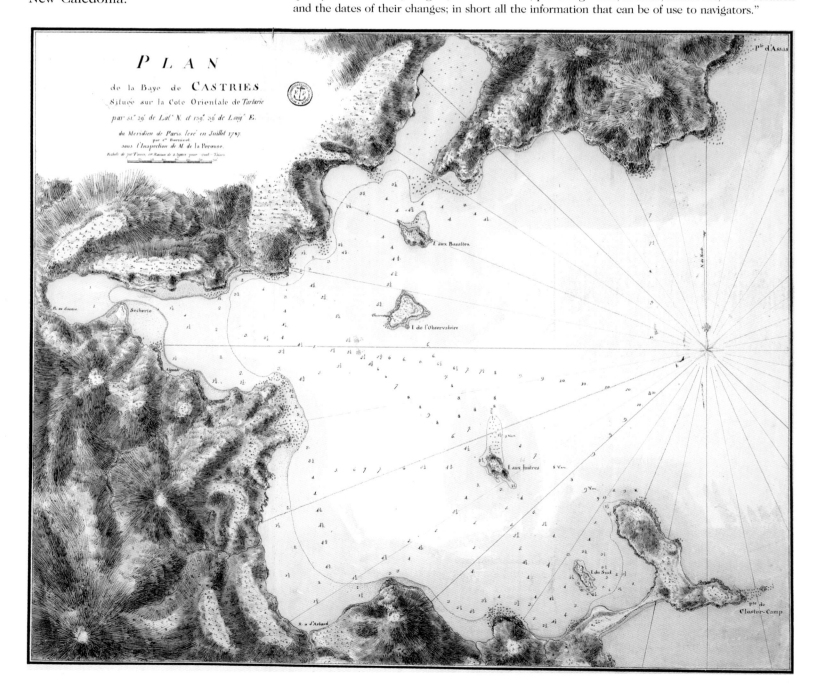

Billings and Sarychev

The publication in 1784 of James Cook's book on his third voyage was a matter of considerable interest to Russia's Catherine the Great. Here was documentary evidence of a major British incursion into what she regarded as her domain. There was also concern about Spanish northward voyages, and then, to cap it all, came news of the dispatch of the French expedition under La Pérouse.

In 1785, within a few weeks of La Pérouse's sailing, an expedition was organized to map "the numerous islands scattered in the eastern ocean, as far as the shores of America," and to obtain "a more accurate acquaintance with the seas separating the continent of Irkutsk from the coast of America."

To lead this expedition, who better than one of Cook's own? Joseph Billings had been a seaman, not an officer, with Cook, but he had offered his services to the Russians, who assumed that he would know what he was doing simply because he had sailed with Cook; such was the reverence in which Cook was held.

Fortunately for this expedition, a competent navigator and surveyor, Gavriil Sarychev, was appointed second-in-command. He would end his career an admiral and publish his own atlas.

Between 1787 and 1793, Billings and Sarychev sailed around the North Pacific, even marching overland at one point. Maps were drawn, and careful mapping allowed Sarychev to correct some of the mistakes made by Ivan Synd thirty years before, removing many islands from the charts.

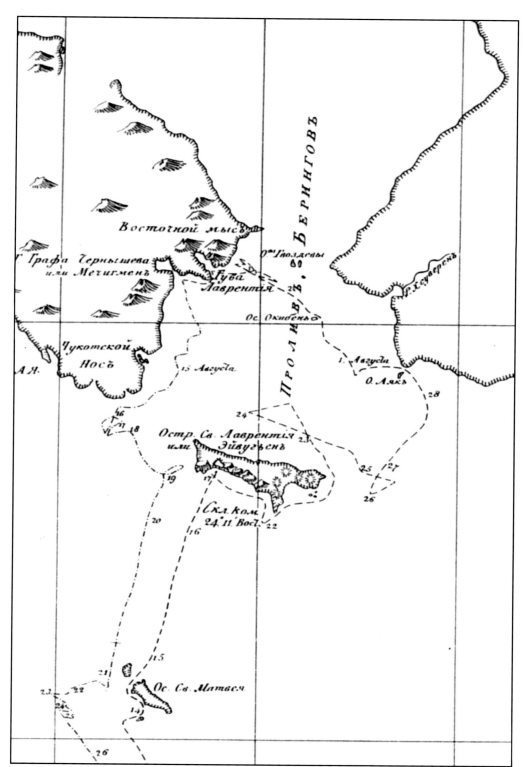

Map 152.
Part of Gavriil Sarychev's map of the North Pacific, showing Bering Strait, Bering Island, and St. Lawrence Island, 1802.

One grand impediment to [previous expeditions'] success was the size of their vessels, which were very well adapted for crossing the main on voyages of discovery, but could ill serve the purpose of passing through shallows, and making minute observations of the shores. By the removal of this evil I flatter myself that not a single bay, island, or mountain, has escaped our notice, on the coasts of which we have taken a survey, and that we have, in addition to this, been enabled to rectify the mistakes of former navigators.

– Gavriil Sarychev, in the preface to his book, 1806

Fur Traders of the Northwest Coast

Fur traders, who invaded the Northwest Coast after James Cook looking for sea otter furs, tended not to draw very detailed maps, generally being content with a map that would allow them to find again a harbor or trading ground that had proved lucrative.

Nevertheless, because there were quite a few of them, and their maps were gathered by Alexander Dalrymple, soon to be Britain's first Hydrographer of the Navy, the information they contained expanded the geographical knowledge of the coast in the period between Cook and Vancouver.

One of these traders, James Colnett, who had been with James Cook on his second voyage but not his third, was given command of two ships to compete in the fur trade. Colnett commanded *Prince of Wales* and his associate Charles Duncan *Princess Royal*.

They were on the Northwest Coast in 1787 and 1788. Colnett concentrated on the coast north of the Queen Charlottes, Duncan on the coast to the south. Colnett's map and Duncan's map of the Strait of Juan de Fuca are shown here.

The intervention of Joseph Banks resulted in Colnett having aboard a scientist, Archibald Menzies, who was principally a botanist. Menzies would later return to the Northwest Coast with George Vancouver.

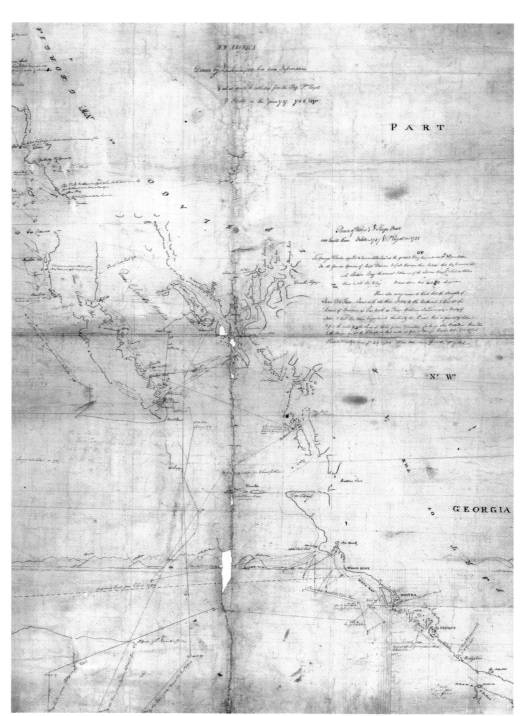

Map 154.
James Colnett's map of part of the coast of British Columbia and Alaska, 1788. Meticulously detailed, this map shows the considerable geographical knowledge of some British fur traders just prior to Vancouver's survey.

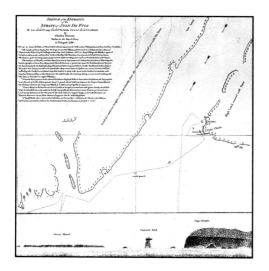

Map 153 (left).
The Strait of Juan de Fuca may have been discovered by the Greek pilot of a Spanish ship. He was born Apostolos Valerianos, but assumed the name Juan de Fuca when employed by the Spanish. However, no archival evidence of his discovery has ever been found. We do know that Charles Barkley, a British fur trader, rediscovered it in 1787. His chart of the strait is lost, and the earliest to survive is this one by Colnett's associate Charles Duncan. It is complete with a view, as a finding aid for this often missed strait. The Juan de Fuca account included a reference to pillars, at the entrance to the north side of the strait. There are pillars, but on the south side, as shown on Duncan's map.

The Sea That Never Was

John Meares was one of the fur-trading adventurers who followed in Cook's wake in search of the riches promised by the sea otter.

He also fancied himself a geographer-theorist, for when in 1790 he published a book about his voyages to the Northwest Coast, some of his maps contained a startling revelation. Meares drew an inland sea stretching from the Strait of Juan de Fuca northwards to a point approximating that of Dixon Entrance, north of the Queen Charlottes.

Not only did he show this sea on his maps, but also maintained that the American captain Robert Gray had sailed along this inland sea in his ship *Lady Washington* in 1789.

This was all a complete fabrication; not only did the sea not exist, but Gray did not sail there, and neither did he tell Meares that he had. George Vancouver was told this personally by Gray when he met him as he sailed towards the Strait of Juan de Fuca to begin his survey of the coast in 1792.

Nevertheless, at the time the story seemed quite feasible, and it misled many, even showing up on Russian maps soon after.

Map 155.
Part of Meares' map of the Alaska coast. Meares sailed here in 1788 and 1789.

Map 156.
One of John Meares' maps showing an inland sea stretching from the Strait of Juan de Fuca to Cross Sound. As the title suggests, Meares was also trying to promote the idea of a river route from the Pacific to Hudson Bay.

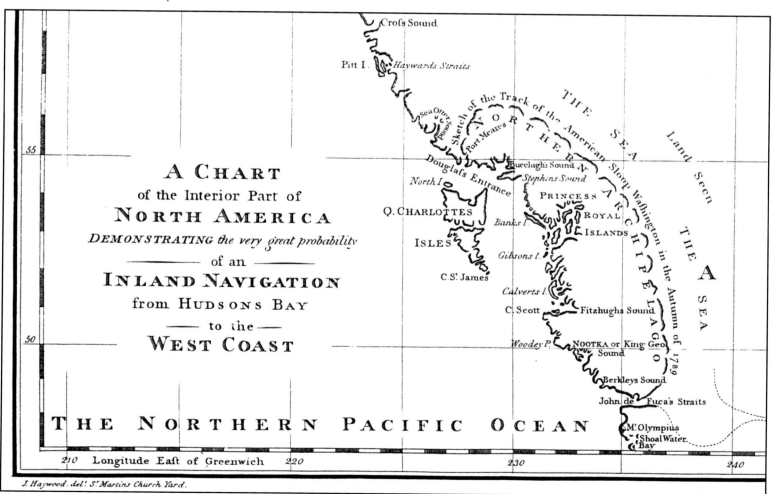

The Maps of Aaron Arrowsmith

Aaron Arrowsmith was the foremost mapmaker of his day, with a knack for collecting every bit of geographic information from whatever sources he could find. He managed to receive timely reports from many explorers, including most of the significant fur traders on the Northwest Coast of America, and from the Hudson's Bay Company, normally very secretive for competitive reasons. As a result, the maps he produced were by far the most accurate and comprehensive available.

Soon after Arrowsmith launched his own company producing and selling maps, he published a monumental map of the world. The 1790 first edition was followed in 1794 by an updated version, the Pacific part of which is shown below. Tracks are shown of voyages from Bering and Chirikov to Cook and the later fur traders. In the Pacific Northwest, the map shows the coastline as known to the British just before George Vancouver's arrival. The map shown here is an update published in 1794, a superb summary of all geographers knew about the Pacific up to that time.

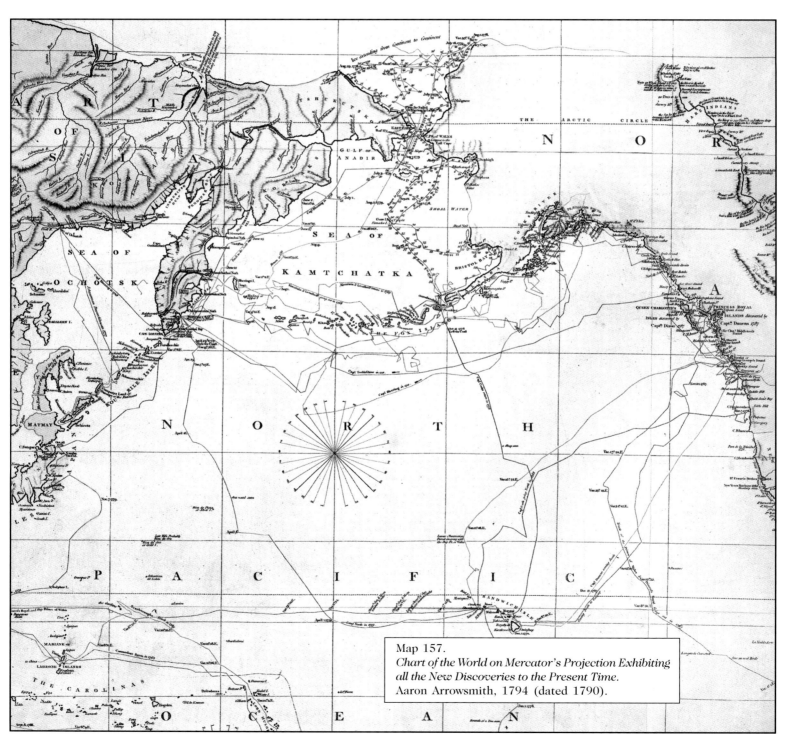

Map 157.
Chart of the World on Mercator's Projection Exhibiting all the New Discoveries to the Present Time.
Aaron Arrowsmith, 1794 (dated 1790).

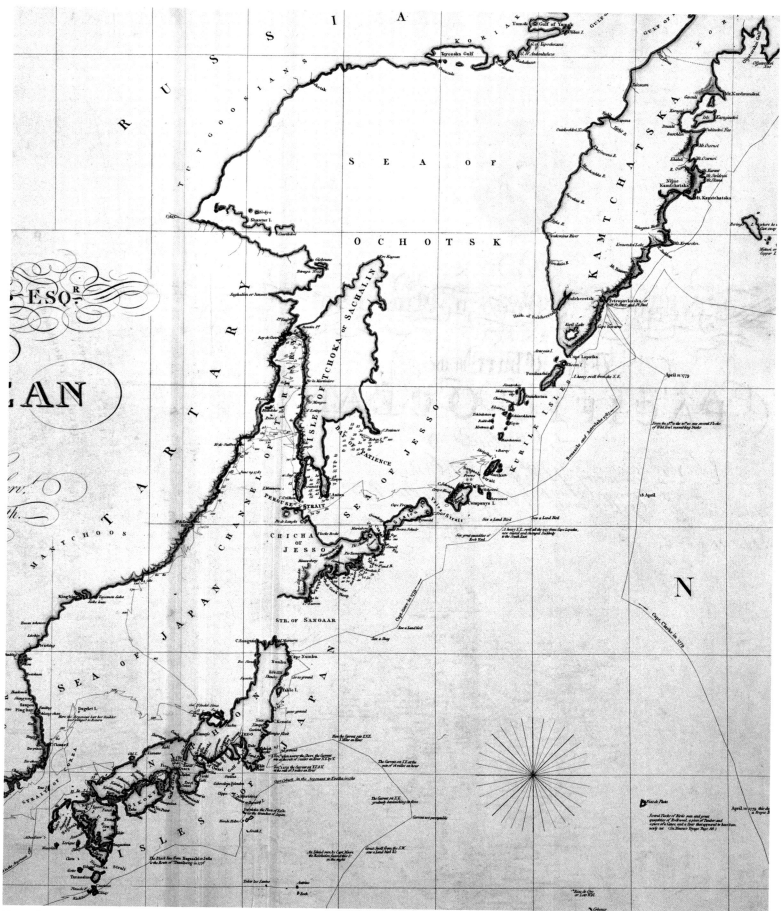

Map 158. Aaron Arrowsmith's map of the Pacific Ocean, published in 1798. Sakhalin is shown as an island, and the tracks of La Pérouse in 1787 are shown (see page 102). The latter's book had finally been published the year before Arrowsmith drew this map and thus the information was suddenly available. Hokkaido ("Chicha or Jesso") is undefined on its western side, and the southernmost two of the Kuril Islands are shown, after Maerten Vries' voyage of 1643, as "Staten Island" and "Companys Land," with Vries Strait between them. The southward track of John Gore in 1779 is also shown; Gore was in command of James Cook's third voyage after the demise of Cook and his second-in-command, Charles Clerke. Several imaginary islands are depicted, such as Rico de Oro (see page 59).

The Spanish Probe the Strait of Juan de Fuca

In 1790, the Spanish stepped up their pace of exploration in order to try to establish their claims to the Northwest Coast and at the same time make sure that no other nation discovered any possible Northwest Passage before them. Thus they began a series of voyages to determine the detail of the coast of the Pacific Northwest.

From a base at Friendly Cove in Nootka Sound, Spanish commander Francisco de Eliza dispatched an expedition to Alaska under Salvador Fidalgo. It was intended to counter any Russian presence.

Another expedition, under Manuel Quimper, was sent to probe the Strait of Juan de Fuca. In July 1790, just beyond the easternmost point

that they reached, pilot Juan Carrasco sighted an opening that he thought was a bay, naming it Ensenada de Caamaño, after Jacinto Caamaño, a naval officer. It was in fact Admiralty Inlet, the entrance to Puget Sound, which was to be discovered and named by George Vancouver two years later.

The following year, 1791, Eliza himself wanted to discover the remaining unknown parts of the Northwest Coast. Unable to sail north due to adverse winds, he entered the Strait of Juan de Fuca. Clayoquot Sound, Barkley Sound and Esquimalt Harbour were examined, and a longboat commanded by José Verdía was used to explore north into Haro Strait. Verdía found this opened out

into what the Spanish named the Canal de Nuestra Señora del Rosario, the Strait of Georgia. The Spanish name is still in use for the southern part of the strait, Rosario Strait.

Eliza then dispatched José María Nárvaez with pilot Juan Carrasco in *Santa Saturnina,* a small boat for exploring shallow waters, to accompany the longboat. Together they penetrated the Strait of Georgia as far north as Texada Island. They realized that this might lead to the open sea, and the presence of whales supported this idea. But their supplies were running low, and so they returned.

The superb map below is a summary map drawn by Nárvaez, the first map of the Strait of Georgia.

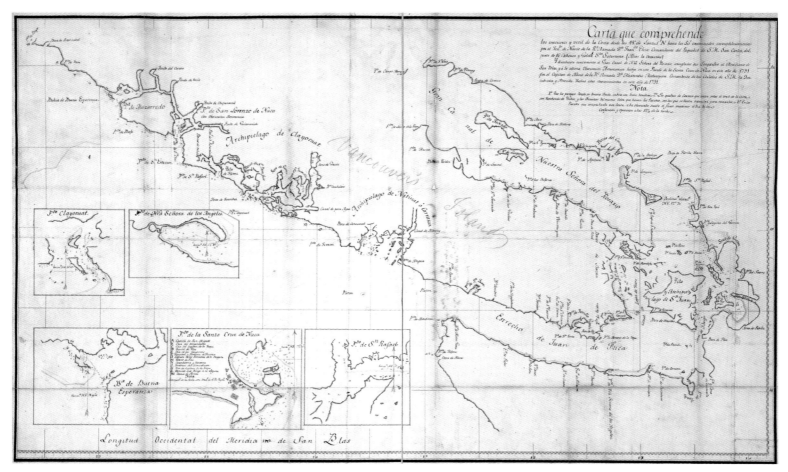

Map 159.
This *Carta que comprehende* – "Map of what is known" – of the Strait of Juan de Fuca and southern Strait of Georgia is the summary map drawn in 1791 after the probing expeditions of Manuel Quimper in 1790 and Francisco de Eliza in 1791. For the first time Vancouver Island is beginning to emerge as an island, but it is also becoming clear that it is unlikely these channels will lead to a Northwest Passage. This map graphically demonstrates the knowledge the Spanish possessed *before* George Vancouver began his survey the following year.

Malaspina's Voyage – The Spanish Answer to Cook

In the late 1780s Spain began to consider mounting a scientific round-the-world voyage to assert Spanish prestige after that of Cook for the British and in the immediate wake of the La Pérouse expedition for the French. This was encouraged by a seasoned naval captain, Alejandro Malaspina, who wanted to be the Spanish version of Cook and who managed to get himself selected for the task.

Not strictly just exploration, the voyage was to be principally one for more accurately charting the seas, using, for the first time comprehensively in a Spanish vessel, the new chronometers that had proven so successful for Cook.

Malaspina, like Cook, was sufficiently well regarded to be able to have a major say in his proposed route and objectives, though his actual instructions were brief and non-specific. "The project of circumnavigating the world has merited the acceptance of His Majesty, on the terms proposed by you," wrote the Minister of Marine.

That Malaspina considered his voyage a truly scientific one is witnessed by his behavior while in Alaska. Otter skins, the hot trading commodity of the day, and one with which they could have made money, were refused in favor of the deliberate collection of "artifacts for the Royal Museum," now part of the collection of the Museo de América.

Even the names of Malaspina's ships, *Descubierta* (*Discovery*) and *Atrevida* (*Audacious*) seem to be too close to Cook's *Discovery* and *Adventure,* on his second voyage, to be mere coincidence.

When Malaspina reached Acapulco, the Spanish government sent Malaspina orders to explore the Northwest Coast between 59° N and 60° N with particular care to ascertain whether an alleged Northwest Passage actually existed there, despite all the previous exploratory voyages that had not found such a passage. In 1770, a fictitious account of a voyage through the Strait of Anian had been published; it had been found in the archive of the family of one Lorenzo Ferrer Maldonado, who was later shown to have been an inventive charlatan. The strait was said to be between 59° N and 60° N.

Malaspina sailed directly from Acapulco to Yakutat Bay, at 60° N. This was Port Mulgrave, a name the Spanish accepted from fur traders. Here they stayed for more than a month, exploring channels and observing native customs. A map of Yakutat Bay was drawn. While the corvettes were anchored, two longboats were sent to determine whether some inlet contained a continental passage. Threading their way between the increasingly frequent pieces of ice in the water, they finally reached the front of a glacier (the Hubbard Glacier), from which large pieces of ice were breaking off. Malaspina named this Bahía del Desengaño, Disappointment Bay, because it was not a Northwest Passage.

The extensive research carried out by Malaspina's scientists meant that the report on the voyage would have been very large – seven volumes with seventy maps and seventy other illustrations – and correspondingly expensive. Nevertheless, the Spanish government approved the expenditure, because they wanted a work that would, in the eyes of the international community, surpass the British publication of Cook's voyages. It was never published, however, because on his return to Spain, Malaspina proposed that the king dismiss all his ministers, a plan that was judged seditious; he was thrown into jail, and his supporters and his work were scattered.

Map 160.
Malaspina's map of Yakutat Bay, which he called Bahía del Desengaño, Disappointment Bay. "Up to here the ice" is marked at the boundary of the glacier.

Above is a sketch of a Tlingit warrior with wood slat armor, by Tomás de Suria, an artist with Malaspina.

The Last Spanish Explorations

The last Spanish expeditions to the Pacific Northwest took place in the eventful year 1792, the same year that George Vancouver started his major survey.

The Spanish knew of the maze of islands and channels that are the Alaska panhandle of today and thought it possible that they might still hide a Northwest Passage. Jacinto Caamaño was dispatched in 1792 to explore the region, although his ship, *Aranzazu*, was really too large for the job.

Caamaño entered Clarence Strait, thinking it might be a Northwest Passage; today it is known as part of the Inland Passage. He followed Clarence Strait north to 55° 30´ N before being prevented by bad weather from going farther. He returned to Nootka in September.

Caamaño's voyage showed that much of what had previously been considered mainland was in reality an archipelago, today called the Alexander Archipelago.

As it turned out, the voyage of two of Malaspina's officers, Dionisio Alcalá Galiano and Cayetano Valdes, was the last Spanish exploration on the Northwest Coast. They had two ships specially built for exploration, *Sutil* and *Mexicana*.

They were to determine whether or not there was a Northwest Passage from the Strait of Juan de Fuca to Hudson Bay. At least that is what the Spanish government thought they were doing; the instructions they received from Malaspina and from the viceroy were less specific.

Galiano and Valdes entered the Strait of Juan de Fuca in June 1792, and anchored briefly at the newly established Spanish post of Núñez Gaona – Neah Bay. There they learned that two large ships had already passed into the strait. These were George Vancouver's two ships.

Galiano decided not to investigate Puget Sound, probably because it appeared to go the "wrong way" to that which they considered a Northwest Passage would have to run.

After entering the Strait of Georgia, they sighted William Broughton's ship *Chatham*. Broughton came aboard *Sutil*, and mutual assistance was offered.

On 14 June Galiano and Valdes found and entered the north arm of the Fraser River, anchoring there for the night. In so doing they became the first Europeans to find and enter the river.

A week later, Galiano finally met George Vancouver near today's city of Vancouver, B.C. Vancouver was shown Spanish maps, including the *Carta que comprehende* (page 112), revealing to him the fact that the Spanish had been here the year before.

Galiano and Valdes, like Vancouver, continued northwards, eventually circumnavigating Vancouver Island and establishing its insularity for the first time.

The summary map of Galiano and Valdes, as engraved and published in 1802, is shown here. It is detailed, accurate (they carried chronometers just as Vancouver did), and meticulously surveyed, a fitting end to Spanish efforts to define the Pacific Northwest Coast.

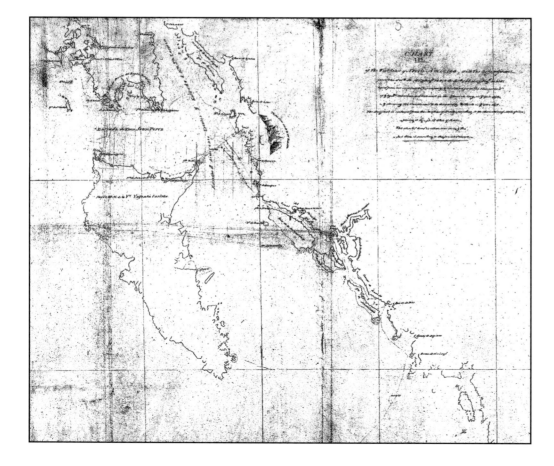

Map 161 (left).
An English copy of Caamaño's map of part of the Northwest Coast, showing the entrance to the strait he found. The Queen Charlottes are shown as a single island.

Map 162 (right).
This beautiful engraved map is a summary map of the voyage of Galiano and Valdes in 1792. It was not published until 1802, after Vancouver's book.

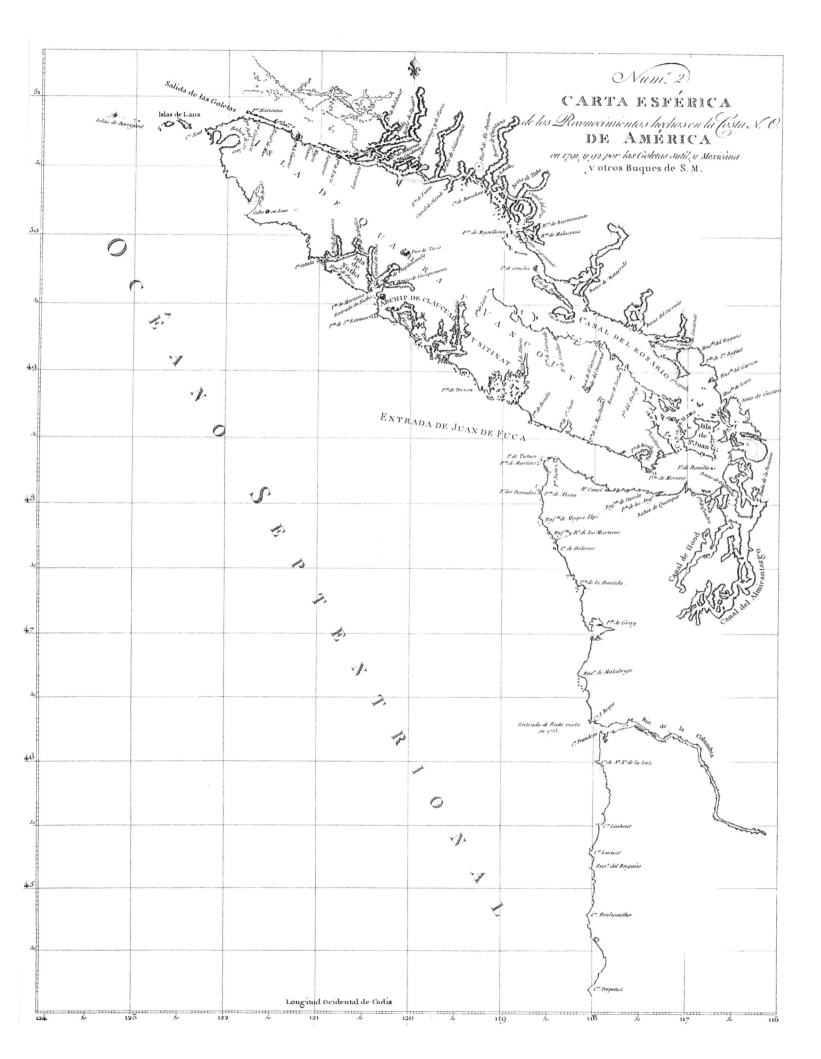

Num.º 2

CARTA ESFÉRICA

de los Reconocimientos hechos en la Costa N.O.

DE AMÉRICA

en 1791 y 92 por las Goletas Sutil y Mexicana

y otros Buques de S. M.

OCÉANO SEPTENTRIONAL

ENTRADA DE JUAN DE FUCA

Longitud Occidental de Cadix

The Spanish Define the West Coast

In the period from 1769 to 1792 the Spanish essentially defined the shape of the west coast of North America north of the current Mexico–U.S. border. Some information, such as Sebastián Vizcaíno's discovery of the harbor at Monterey, was known before, but the major sweep of the coast was not.

Although the Spanish incorporated information from non-Spanish sources, their definition of most of the coast was carried out independently of the efforts of any other nation.

One man was there almost at the beginning and there at the end, a brilliant navigator in his own right and a daring one too, who rose to the position of overall command, below the viceroy. He also possessed the ability to put the information he had gathered together with that of others to create the most superbly comprehensive maps of the west coast, by far the best available until the completion of George Vancouver's survey in 1794.

That man was Juan Francisco Bodega y Quadra, who would be better known but for the overshadowing of his achievements by Cook and Vancouver.

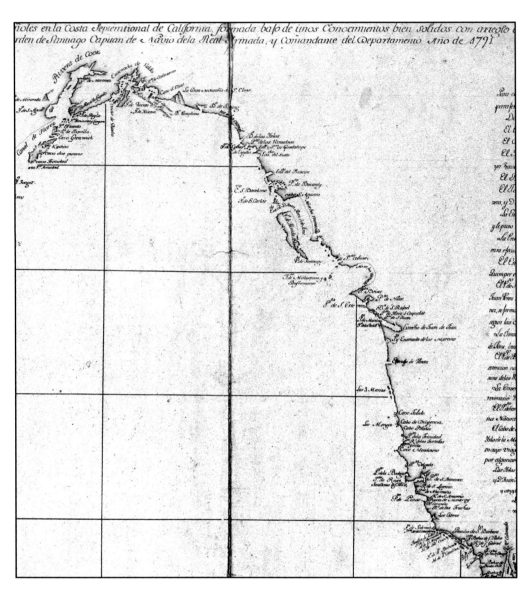

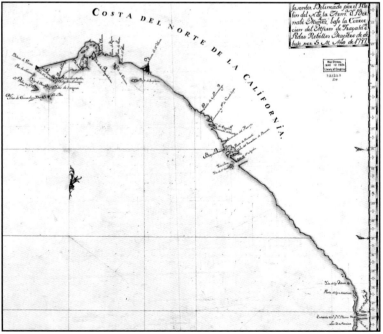

Map 163.
This map of the entire west coast of North America was drawn by Bodega y Quadra in 1791, before the Francisco Eliza expedition of that year revealed the Strait of Georgia; Vancouver Island is shown as part of the mainland. The mainland coast behind the Queen Charlotte Islands is tentative, perhaps holding the key to the elusive Northwest Passage. Jacinto Caamaño would be sent out the next year to investigate. The state of Spanish knowledge shown on this map can be compared with that later in the year, shown opposite. The vast improvement in knowledge in only sixteen years can be seen by a comparison with Bodega y Quadra's first map of the west coast of North America, shown on page 91.

Map 164 (left).
Spanish knowledge of the west coast before 1789 was limited to southern California and Alaska, the latter being the result of Bodega y Quadra's own explorations in 1775, on which others built. With one or two exceptions, much of the intervening coast was a blank. This map was drawn by Bernabe Muñoz in 1787.

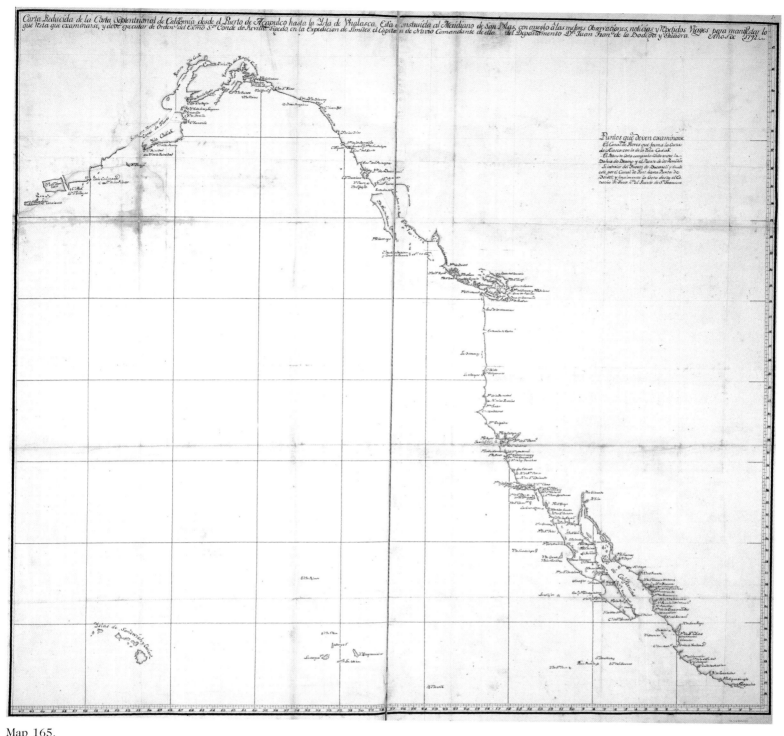

Map 165.
Bodega y Quadra's map of the west coast of North America drawn at the end of 1791 or beginning of 1792, before the explorations of Dionisio Galiano would demonstrate the insularity of Vancouver Island.

One of the reasons for this eclipse was the fact that the Spanish refused to present their findings to the world. The knowledge the world had of Spanish exploration was generally clandestine, except, notably, the cooperation with Vancouver. Spanish geographical knowledge otherwise seemed to surface in Britain in the hands of private individuals – Daines Barrington and Thomas Jefferys, for example.

Even Alejandro Malaspina's work, which was meant as a Spanish counterbalance to that of Britain's Cook, did not see the light of day because of internal political intrigues in Spain.

Only in 1802 would the Spanish government finally realize, somewhat belatedly, that their claims of sovereignty based on priority of discovery were in jeopardy because of the rest of the world's lack of knowledge of them. As a result they published in

that year the *Relación del Viage hecho por las goletas* Sutil *y* Mexicana *en al ano 1792 para Reconocer el Estrecho de Fuca,* ostensibly an account of only Galiano's voyage, but in fact a summary of all. The *Relación* contained an atlas with many of the significant Spanish maps in it, even Vizcaíno's map from as long ago as 1602.

Bodega y Quadra ended his days on the Northwest Coast at Nootka Sound, commandant at the Spanish

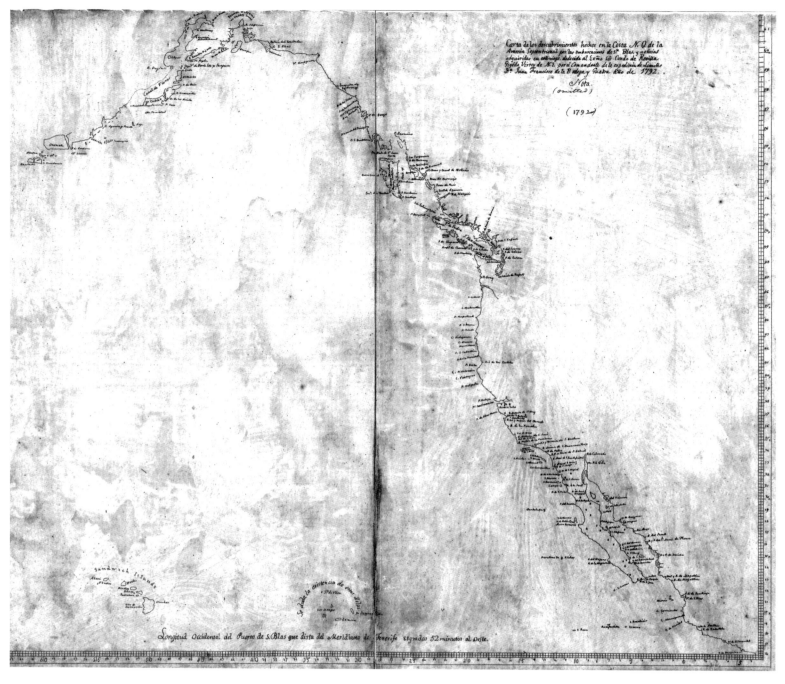

The handwritten text on the map reads:

Carta de los descubrimientos hechos en la Costa N.O. de la America Septentrional por las embarcaciones de S.r Blas y noticias adquiridas en estrivago deducida al Exmo S.or Conde de Revilla Gigedo Virrey de N.E. por el Comandante de la expedición de límites S.r Juan Francisco de la Bodega y Quadra. Año de 1792.

Nota.
(omitted)

(1792)

Sandwich Islands

Se duda la existencia de estas Islas

Longitud Occidental del Puerto de S. Blas que dista del Meridiano de Tenerife 83 grados 52 minutos al Oeste.

Map 166.

This map represents the cumulative peak of Spanish efforts to define the west coast of North America. It was drawn by Bodega y Quadra near the *end* of 1792, after the return of the expeditions of Caamaño and Galiano. Caamaño's strait (Clarence Strait) and Galiano's (and George Vancouver's) proof of the insularity of Vancouver Island are shown. The Spanish finally had a reasonably accurate map of the entire coast, though not without a lingering possibility that an entrance to a Northwest Passage could be found, a possibility that Vancouver would put to rest in the remaining two years of his survey. Spanish knowledge now extended from the tip of South America to halfway along the Aleutian chain.

headquarters there. It was in this capacity that he met with George Vancouver in 1792 in an attempt to finalize the wranglings over who owned the region contained in the Nootka Convention.

Bodega y Quadra was one of those all-too-rare individuals who seem to have been respected by all, whatever their nationality. When he finally left Nootka, one of Vancouver's men, the clerk of *Chatham,* Edward Bell, wrote:

Never was the departure of a man more regretted than that of Mr. Quadra's. He was universally belov'd and admired and the only consolation we had was that we should see him again at Monterrey.

Bodega y Quadra died in 1794, sparing him from the war between Spain and Britain that began in 1796. Others, like Dionisio Galiano, did not avoid this fate. He died fighting the British fleet at Trafalgar.

George Vancouver's Epic Survey

The distinguishing feature of George Vancouver's work, as compared with all others', is its comprehensiveness. It is hard to see how without Vancouver's tenacity the Northwest Coast of North America would ever have been surveyed properly, for it is a tangled web of islands, inlets, bays, and promontories sufficient to tax the proverbial patience of Job.

Yet the man has received scant enough recognition in these politically correct days, recognition he is absolutely entitled to if for no other reason than his superb surveying achievement.

George Vancouver surveyed the eastern shore of the Pacific in three seasons, in 1792, 1793, and 1794. His survey was part of a final thrust by the British to determine once and for all whether the Northwest Passage existed.

His instructions were to acquire

accurate information with respect to the nature and extent of any water communication which may tend in any considerable degree to facilitate an intercourse for the purpose of commerce between the North West coast and the countries upon the opposite side of the Continent.

He was specifically directed

not to pursue any inlet or river further than it shall appear to be navigable by vessels of such burthen as might safely navigate the Pacific Ocean.

Vancouver was also instructed to share any survey information with any Spanish subjects he might meet, a tacit acknowledgment that Spanish maps might contain useful information, certainly a justifiable assumption based on the Spanish maps existing as of 1792.

Discovery, commanded by Vancouver, and *Chatham,* commanded by Lieutenant William Broughton, made their first landfall

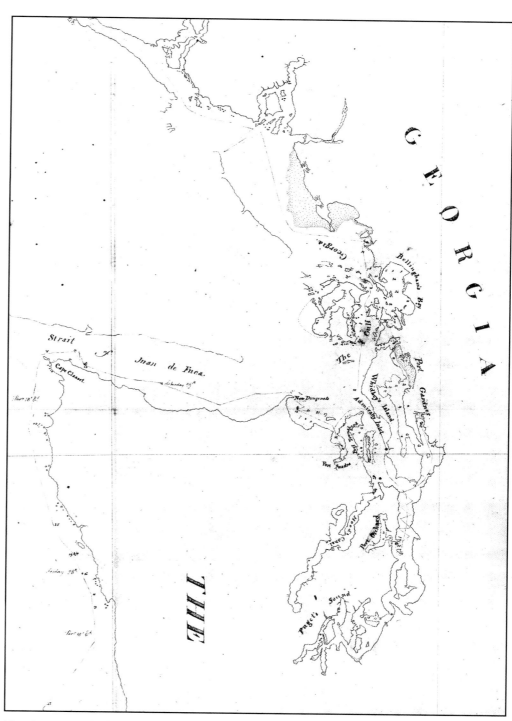

Map 167. Detail of George Vancouver's map of the west coast, showing Puget Sound and the southern part of the Strait of Georgia. Note the lack of detail for southern Vancouver Island.

about 175 km (110 miles) north of San Francisco, on 18 April 1792, on the coast of Drake's New Albion.

Sailing north, managing to stay inshore enough to survey, Vancouver somehow missed the mouth of the Columbia. Although he noted a change in the color of the water, he thought it the probable consequence of some streams flowing into the bay. He did recognize Cape Disappointment, the headland on the north side of the river named by John Meares when he too could not find the river.

But he did find the Strait of Juan de Fuca, having Charles Duncan's map with him. In May and June 1792 Vancouver explored and mapped

Puget Sound, the southern part of which was named after Peter Puget, the officer in charge of the ship's boat that surveyed it. Over time, the name came to refer to the whole inlet.

It was Vancouver who named the waters to the north the "Gulph of Georgia," after the British king, despite finding that it was a strait rather than a gulf.

Near the site of the city that now bears his name, Vancouver did meet Spanish surveyors, Captains Dionisio Galiano and Cayetano Valdes, and they did exchange information. Galiano showed him José Nárvaez's map of Spanish explorations the year before (page 112), and Vancouver wrote in his journal of the "mortification" he felt at having realized that he was not the first to survey the southern Strait of Georgia.

Vancouver continued north, for some time in company with the Spanish ships, perhaps the first example of international cooperation in Pacific Ocean waters. It is therefore unfortunate to note that four years later, Spain and Britain were at war.

Vancouver concentrated on what he referred to as the "continental shore," because of his instructions to look for any possible opening which might be a Northwest Passage.

One of Vancouver's officers, James Johnstone, master of the *Chatham,* led many mapping parties to map inlets and ensure that they were not passages to the interior.

Finally, on one such expedition, Johnstone discovered a channel, which was named Johnstone's Passage and is now called Johnstone Strait, which led to the open sea, at last proving the insularity of Vancouver Island.

That season, the coastal survey was continued northwards to about 52° 20′ N, stopping just short of today's Bella Coola. Then they went to Nootka Sound, where Vancouver had some diplomatic business to attend to with the Spanish commander, Bodega y Quadra, and then they sailed south, first to San

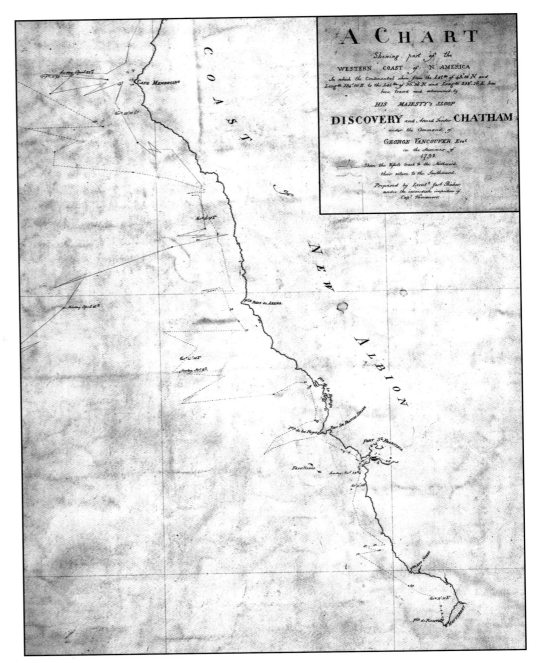

Map 168.
Part of George Vancouver's chart of the west coast of the United States, drawn in 1792 by Joseph Baker, one of his officers. The map shows the coast from Cape Mendocino south to Monterey.
© Crown Copyright 2000. Published by permission of the Controller of Her Majesty's Stationery Office and the U.K. Hydrographic Office.

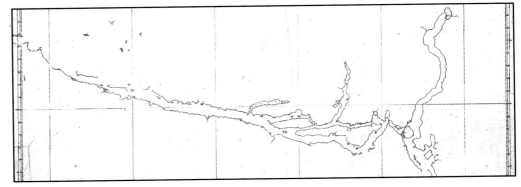

Map 169.
James Johnstone's original draft map of the passage he found and surveyed between Vancouver Island and the mainland, which established the insularity of Vancouver Island. The island is to the south, the "continental shore" to the north. The longest indentation shown in the coastline is Loughborough Inlet.

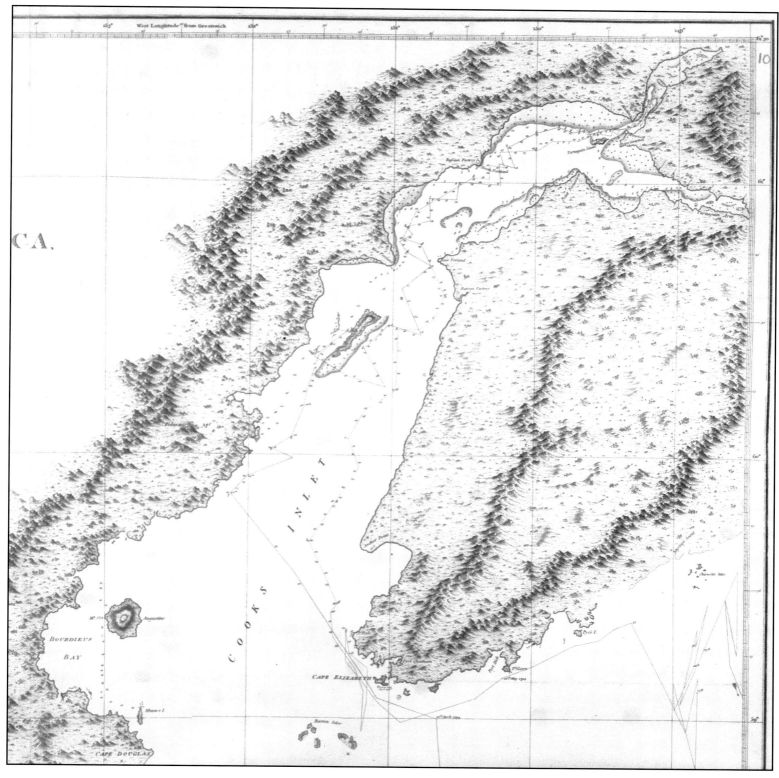

Map 170.

Vancouver's map of Cook Inlet, Alaska. He re-named it from Cook's River after determin-ing that there was no outlet at the north-eastern end. This map is from the atlas that accompanied his book, published in 1798. In the period between Cook and Vancouver, many speculative geographers, and notably North West Company fur trader Peter Pond, had considered that a large river which flowed from the western end of Lake Athabasca must reach the Pacific here. It was this river that Alexander Mackenzie explored in 1789 with the hope of reaching the Pacific Ocean. He didn't, of course, ending up in the Arctic Ocean instead; the river was the Mackenzie.

Francisco and then to Monterey. Vancouver was expecting further instructions from his government, which might have been sent to these places, but none were forthcoming.

After spending the winter in Hawaii, Vancouver was back again the next year, surveying northwards from the point he had left off the previous season. This time the coast to 56° N

was surveyed in four months – the intricately indented coastline of northern British Columbia and some of the Alaska panhandle, with too many islands to count.

They were back in Nootka by October. Then they surveyed the southern California coast until December, returning by January 1794 to Hawaii.

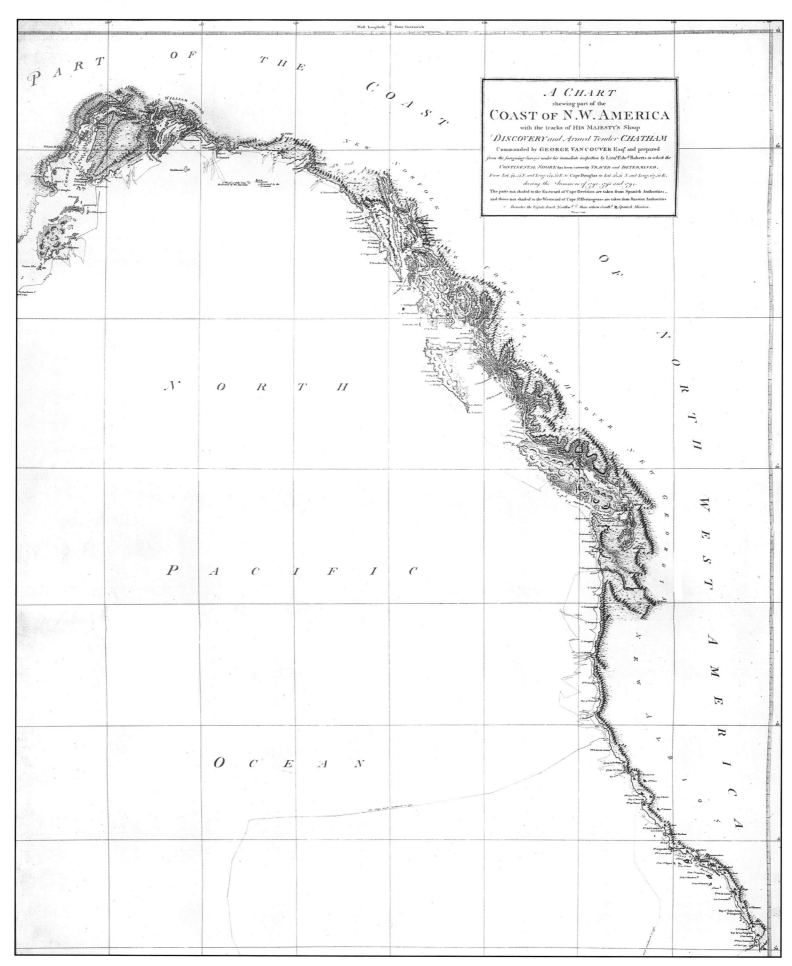

Map 171. The final result of George Vancouver's survey, the summary map of the west coast of North America. This was published in the atlas of his 1798 book. Most of the west coast is now shown accurately. Only relatively minor parts remain to be filled in.

Vancouver began his final season of survey, in 1794, from Cook Inlet in Alaska. They worked east and then south to join with the end of the 1793 survey.

One of the most significant results of this last survey was the determination that Cook Inlet, south of today's Anchorage, was indeed an inlet and not a river or other way to the interior. Cook had not explored the inlet to the very end and hence had left open the speculation that it was the mouth of a large river flowing from the interior. He similarly determined that Prince William Sound had no opening to the east.

Vancouver's superb three-season survey, much of it undertaken in small boats, for there was no other way to explore the detail of the deep inland indentations in the days of sail, was his magnum opus. He would not live even to see his work published; the job was finished by his brother John in 1798, achieving a worldwide recognition that has tended to overshadow the enormous contribution made by the Spanish in the years before Vancouver's arrival on the west coast.

Vancouver wrote:

I trust the precision with which the survey of the coast of North West America has been carried into effect will remove every doubt, and set aside every opinion of a north-west passage, or any water communication navigable for shipping, existing between the North Pacific, and the interior of the American continent, within the limits of our researches.

Pacific scholar J. C. Beaglehole noted that the Northwest Coast is

so remarkably complicated that Vancouver's systematic and painstaking survey ranks with the most distinguished work of the kind ever done.

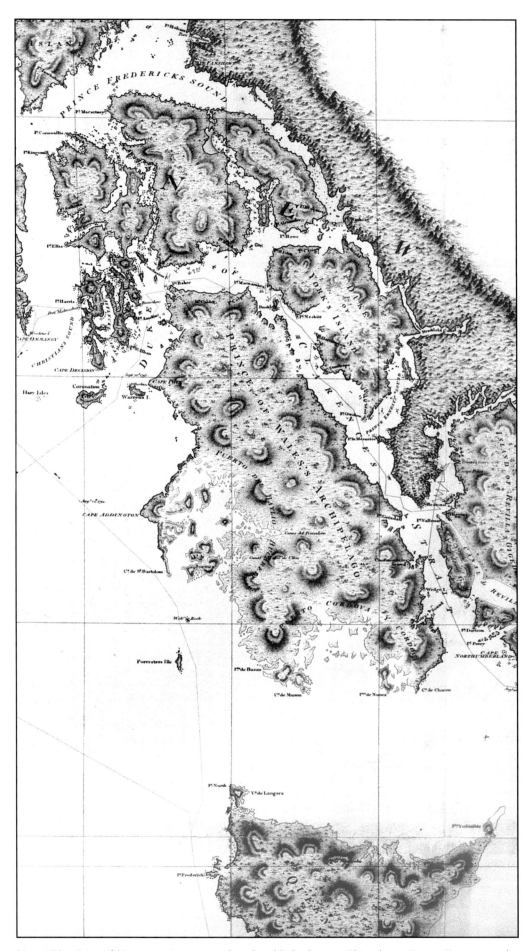

Map 172. Part of Vancouver's engraved and published map. This shows Dixon Entrance, the northern tip of the Queen Charlotte Islands, and the southern part of the Alaska panhandle. Juan Pérez's Langara Island is at the tip of the Queen Charlottes; Vancouver did not change its name, though many names that survive are his, not Spanish ones.

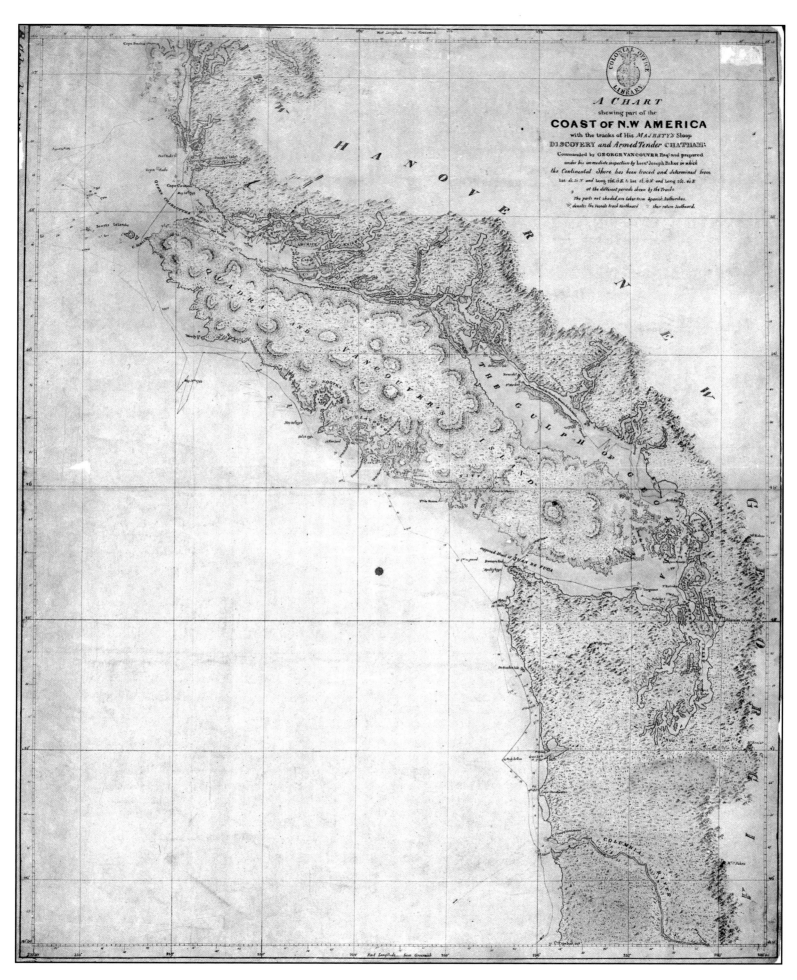

Map 173. This is one of the compilation charts for Vancouver's published atlas, showing Vancouver Island and adjacent coasts. It is a final manuscript map, which would have been sent to the engraver to make the plate for this sheet in the atlas.

Broughton Charts the West Pacific

Voyages of Discovery justly claim the public attention because they open new sources of knowledge and trade, and consequently are interesting to a scientific and commercial people.

– William Broughton, 1804

William Broughton was captain of *Chatham* for the first year of survey-ing on the Northwest Coast of America, 1792; he was sent back to England by Vancouver towards the end of that year to explain negotia-tions that had taken place with the Spanish. In 1793 Broughton was se-lected to conduct a survey of the southern part of the west coast of South America, which, it was as-sumed, Vancouver would not cover, despite it being in his orders. He was to proceed back to the Pacific by way of Nootka Sound, in case Vancouver was still on the Northwest Coast.

Broughton did not leave En-gland until February 1795, together with Zachary Mudge as second-in-command. Mudge had also been sent

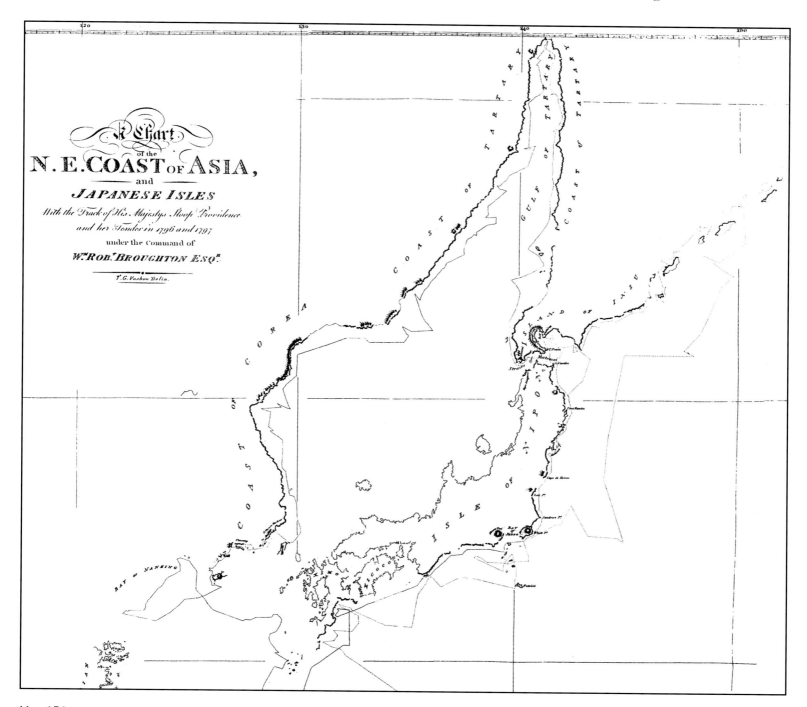

Map 174.
William Broughton's summary map of his voyage in 1796 and 1797. There is confusion between the northern islands of Japan and the Kuril Islands. Likewise, the insularity of Sakhalin is in doubt, with both the mainland and Sakhalin being labelled "Coast of Tartary."

home by Vancouver carrying information and maps.

The ship that Broughton commanded was *Providence,* the ship in which William Bligh, of mutiny on the *Bounty* fame, had returned to Tahiti to carry out the transportation of breadfruit to Jamaica, the task he had been trying to do in *Bounty.*

By spring 1796, Broughton was at Friendly Cove on the west coast of Vancouver Island. Because of the long time that had elapsed since Vancouver's original arrival on the Northwest Coast, Broughton assumed that Vancouver would have by this time carried out his instructions regarding the surveying of South America. Vancouver had not carried out this survey, but Broughton was unaware of this.

Broughton's instructions now left him to his own discretion; he could survey wherever he thought best "in such a manner as might be deemed most eligible for the improvement of geography and navigation."

Hence, in consultation with his officers, he decided to survey the only "blank" area left in the North Pacific at this time, the coast of Asia from Sakhalin, at 52° N, to the Nanking River at 30° N. He knew this area had been explored by La Pérouse, but his survey had not then been published.

Broughton arrived on the coast of Japan in September 1796 and charted the east coast of Hokkaido and Honshu. He determined that the rate of flow of the Kuroshio Current depended on the distance from the coast.

By the end of the year Broughton was at Macao. A smaller ship was purchased for surveying work in shallow waters, which was just as well, for the next year, *Providence* was wrecked south of Japan, the men being saved by the other ship.

After shipping some of his crew home from Canton, Broughton continued his survey, sailing up the east coast of Japan once more, through La Pérouse Strait separating Hokkaido from Sakhalin, and up the west coast of Sakhalin. Here he decided there was no passage northwards between Sakhalin and the mainland, so he returned southwards along the mainland coast to Quelpart Island, off the southern end of Korea.

At the northern end of Tatar Strait, called the Gulf of Tartary on Broughton's map, he found extensive shallows that led him to believe there was no navigable channel any farther north. Broughton's map drawn at this time (Map 176, below) clearly shows Sakhalin as an island, yet his published map (Map 174, previous page) shows it as part of the "Coast of Tartary."

The schooner was taken to Trincomalee and its crew paid off. The lieutenant who drew Broughton's maps was Lieutenant J. G. Vashon. But he was also the officer of the watch the night the *Providence* was wrecked. As a result he was "discharged as per sentence of court martial."

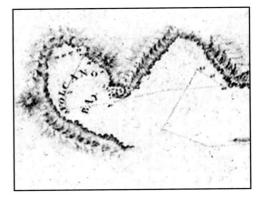

Map 175. Part of Broughton's 1796 survey of the east coast of Japan, showing Volcano Bay, on Hokkaido just north of Tsugaru Strait.

This illustration, entitled *Man and Woman of Volcano Bay,* appeared in Broughton's book. Note the smoking volcano in the background. The bay is on the southeast coast of Hokkaido.

Map 176.
Part of Broughton's map, showing the island of Sakhalin and the strait between it and the mainland, including the Amur River. The shape of Sakhalin is not correct, but the strait is relatively accurate.

© Crown Copyright 2000. Published by permission of the Controller of Her Majesty's Stationery Office and the U.K. Hydrographic Office.

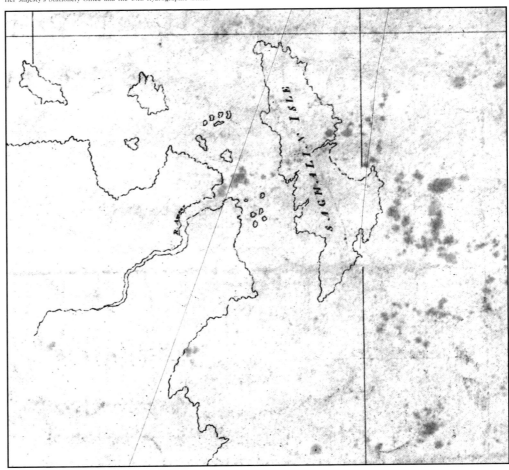

The First Russian Circumnavigation

The first Russian circumnavigation had a dual purpose. It was planned as a voyage to rather belatedly recoup some prestige lost to other nations, coming as it did after the scientific voyages of Britain's James Cook, France's La Pérouse, and Spain's Malaspina. It was also a practical venture encouraged by the new Russian-American Company, which was now esconced on the coast of Alaska complete with a monopoly on trade. Company officials had the idea that they could better supply their outposts with ships sailing from Russia's west coast outlet on the Baltic west around Cape Horn rather than overland through Siberia, which then still required a sea voyage.

The venture was approved by the new Tsar Alexander I as much because he was interested in expanding Russia's naval power in the North Pacific as for any scientific reason.

The voyage, which began in 1803 and lasted three years, did demonstrate the feasability of supply by sea, and numerous other Russian circumnavigations would follow, almost all calling at Sitka, the Russian settlement on Baranof Island in the Alaska panhandle, but food supply tended to be satisfied as much by traders of other nations as by Russian ships. A long series of Russian circumnavigations followed this first one, some of which were scientific. Accounts of

two of the more interesting ones follow (pages 132–35).

Ivan Fedorovich Kruzenstern and Urei Lisianskii were appointed captains of two ships, *Nadezhda* and *Neva,* respectively.

The two ships were destined to investigate different areas of the North Pacific, although at first they sailed in concert. Lisianskii spent more time in the eastern Pacific. At one point he helped the Russian-American Company retake a fort lost to the Tlingit natives; he assisted with cannon bombardment from the ship.

Map 177.
The North Pacific part of Urei Lisianskii's map of the world, published in 1812.

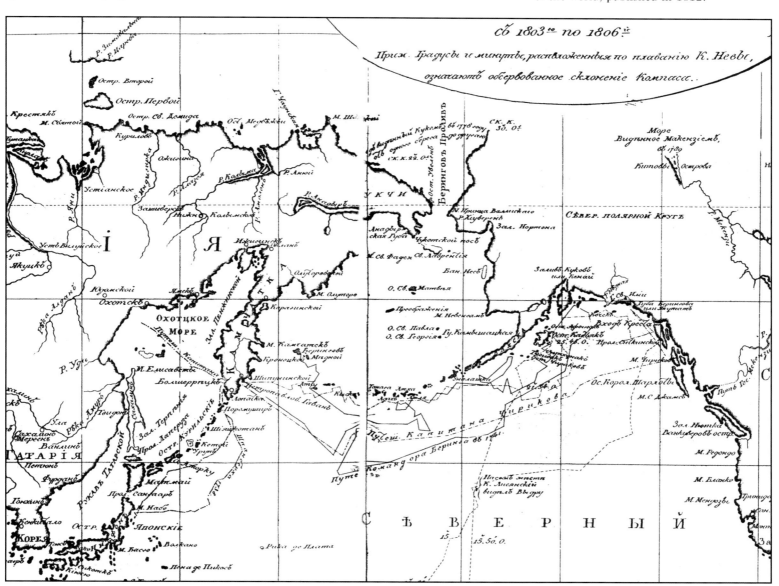

His account of the voyage, with maps, was published in 1812.

Ivan Kruzenstern spent more time in the western North Pacific and is best remembered for his explorations of the coast of Sakhalin.

Kruzenstern was the first to explore and map the north coast of Sakhalin. He wrote of the bay between Cape Elizabeth, the northeast point of the island, and Cape Maria, at the northwest point:

Should it ever be the intentions of Russia to plant a colony in the north of Sakhalin, this bay is the only spot calculated for such an undertaking.

Arriving at the north end of the strait between Sakhalin and the mainland, Kruzenstern sent out a boat to sound southwards, finding rapid shoaling to as shallow as three and a half fathoms (6 m). "I had every reason to believe we were near the mouth of the Amur," he wrote. He was right. In the middle of the channel, a bucket was used to sample the water. "It was perfectly sweet," Kruzenstern wrote. The ship's boat reported also that "the rapidity of the current from the southward had rendered the advance very laborious."

From these factors, Kruzenstern could not determine if there was a separation between Sakhalin and the mainland, although his map does show the island, but he could and did conclude that any passage wasn't safely navigable for *Nadezhda*.

Map 178.
Ivan Kruzenstern's explorations of Sakhalin, from his world map published with his book, 1813.

View of Nangosaki from Kruzenstern's book. The Japanese port of Nagasaki was visited, but the Russians were not well received.

Map 179.
Part of a map by Vasili Berkh, who was one of Urei Lisianskii's officers.

Mamiya and Sakhalin

La Pérouse, Broughton, and Kruzenstern were all undecided as to
whether Sakhalin was a peninsula or
an island, although all three had previously shown it as an island on their
maps. The confusion is understand-
able, for the water shoals dramatically
at the northern end of Tatar Strait
due to the sediments from the mouth
of the Amur River system. Here the
Sakhalin coast approaches that of the
mainland to within a few miles.

Japanese explorers were under-
standably interested in Sakhalin,
which they called Karafuto, as an extension of the islands that form their
own country. In 1785, ordered by the
shogun to explore northwards, an
expedition had sailed along the
western coast of Sakhalin almost to
48° N; in two subsequent attempts
they made it as far as 52° N, where
the Gulf of Tartary narrows, and
nearly 49° N on the eastern coast,
at Cape Terpeniya. They also surveyed as far as Ostrov Urup in the
Kuril Islands. Surveys by Mogami
Tokunai were made into maps and
submitted to the shogun.

Again by order of the shogun,
who was interested in Sakhalin for
reasons of defense, Matsuda Denjuro
and Mamiya Rinzo sailed north in
1808. Matsuda sailed up the west
coast, Mamiya up the east; near Cape
Terpeniya Mamiya crossed the mountains to join Matsuda on the west
coast. This convinced Mamiya that
Sakhalin was indeed an island.

The next year Mamiya sailed into
the mouth of the Amur River, reaching a Chinese trading post on the lower
part of the river. In so doing he finally
confirmed that there was a strait between Sakhalin and the mainland, and
thus that Sakhalin was an island.

Western knowledge of Sakhalin's
insularity did not come until considerably later. In 1852, Philipp Franz

Map 180.
Mogami Tokunai's maps of Sakhalin, published by Philipp Franz von Siebold in 1852.

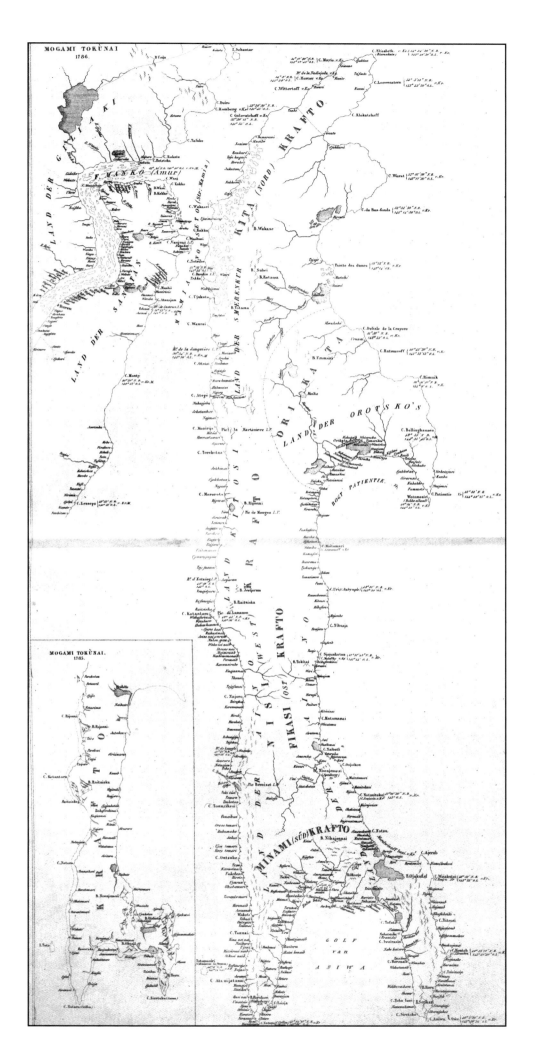

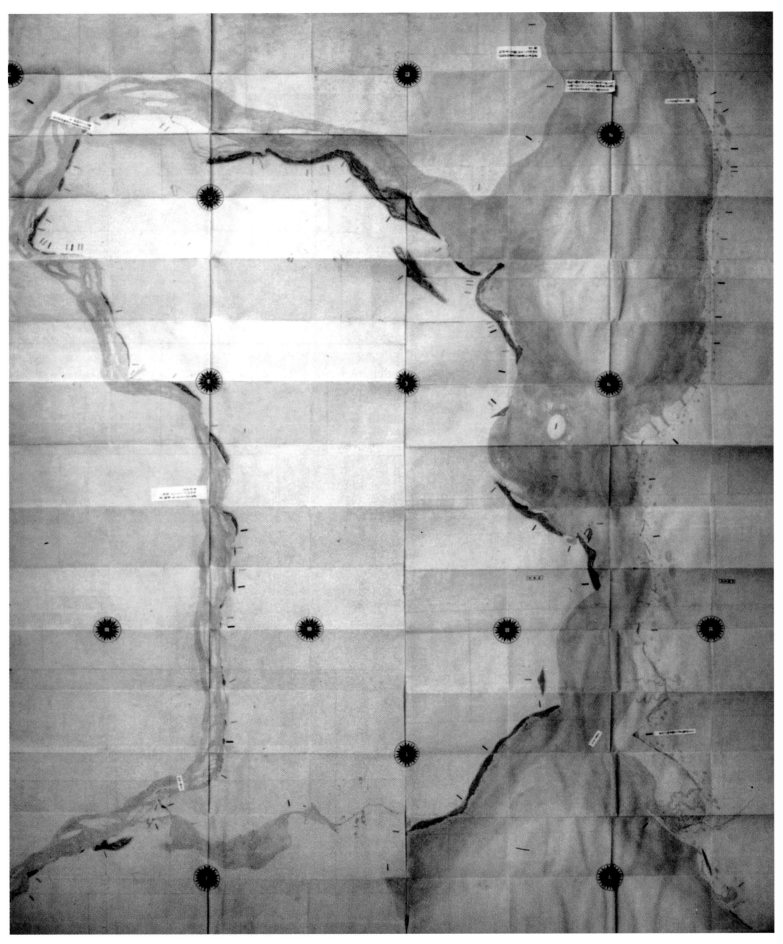

Map 181.
The strait between Sakhalin (Karafuto) and the mainland, as surveyed by Mamiya Rinzo in 1809. The Amur River enters the strait from the mainland side. Now part of Russia, the narrowest part of the strait is Proliv Nevel'skogo, and the wider part opposite the Amur is Amurskij Liman. The coast is highlighted by a band of blue, giving rise to the appearance on this map of an island opposite the mouth of the Amur, which was not intended.

von Siebold obtained copies of both Mogami's and Mamiya's maps and published a map incorporating their work. It was the first definitive proof of the insularity of Sakhalin based on actual penetration of the strait between the island and the mainland.

Map 182 (right).
Philipp Franz von Siebold's map of Sakhalin and adjacent coast, published in 1852, finally depicted Mamiya's survey of 1808 showing Sakhalin as an island. Although other maps had shown Sakhalin as an island, this was the first as the result of actual survey.

Map 183 (below, left).
A map by Jean Baptiste d'Anville published in 1737 shows that the idea of Sakhalin as an island had been around for some time.

Map 184 (below, right).
Aaron Arrowsmith's Pacific Ocean map of 1818 clearly shows Sakhalin as an island. The tracks are those of Ivan Kruzenstern.

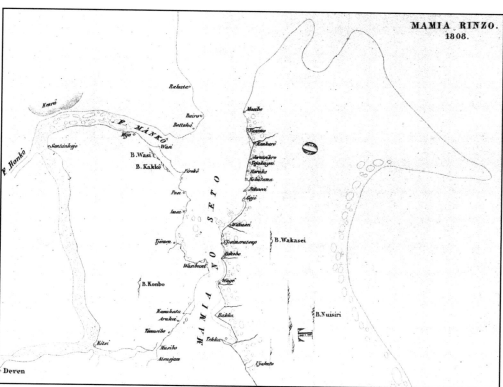

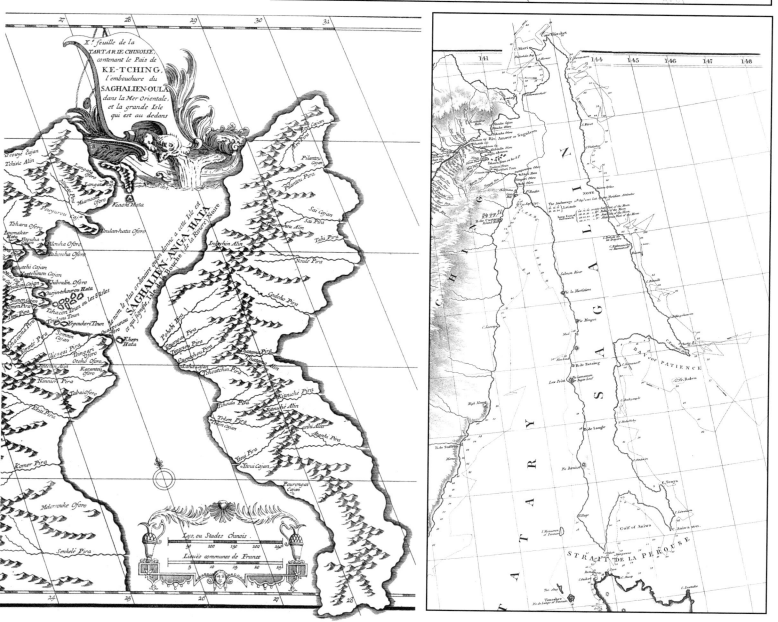

The Voyages of Otto Kotzebue

After the end of the wars against Napoleon, Russia was again able to turn its mind to round-the-world voyages of a scientific nature, although the first was initiated by a private individual, N. P. Rumiantsev. This voyage was to search for a Northeast Passage, which in this case meant that north of the North American continent usually referred to as the Northwest Passage. It was also to conduct scientific studies. Rumiantsev selected Otto Kotzebue, a naval lieutenant who had sailed with Kruzenstern on his round-the-world voyage in 1803–6.

Kotzebue took with him several scientists in his ship, *Riurik*. In the North Pacific in 1816, at a location given as 37° 30′ N and 199° 17′ (E; this is 160° 43′ W), Kotzebue made one of the first North Pacific measurements of temperature with depth, showing the following gradient:

6 June 1816	°F
Surface air temperature:	63.0
Surface water temperature:	61.0
At 10 fathoms:	59.5
At 25 fathoms:	56.8
At 100 fathoms:	52.7
At 300 fathoms:	43.0

Despite their value as pioneering efforts, these measurements were unfortunately not very accurate, due to poor instrumentation and research methods. Of the eight locations where Kotzebue measured temperature with depth, only the one noted above was in the North Pacific.

Proceeding northwards, Kotzebue thought he had discovered a fourth Diomede Island, which he named Ratmanoff Island "after the lieutenant of that name under whose command I was on the Voyage of Kruzenstern"; it is marked as such on his map (see facing page).

He thought it "singular that this island was neither seen by Cook or by Clark [Clerke], both having sailed close by it" and stated that he was "of the opinion that it has probably risen from the ocean." But Kotzebue in this instance was mistaken; there are only three islands in this location.

However, Kotzebue did make one major contribution to the knowledge of the geography of the coast of what is now Alaska. His own words tell the story best.

On 1st August, we observed that the coast took a direction to the east, the land continuing to be low. At eleven o'clock we were at the entrance of a large inlet . . . I cannot describe my feelings when I thought I might be opposite the long-sought-for N.E. Passage, and that fate had destined me to be its discoverer.

But the euphoria was not to last, for a week later Kotzebue recorded:

We had penetrated far enough to see that the land met everywhere . . . The depth had already decreased to five feet, and we gave up even the hope of finding a river.

Nevertheless, Kotzebue had discovered a hitherto unmapped bay which soon became known as Kotzebue Sound and is shown on his own map with this name.

The superb illustration of natives of Kotzebue Sound appears in Kotzebue's book, published in English in 1821. Kotzebue wrote that

they are above the middle size, of strong, vigorous, and healthy appearance; their motions are lively, and they seem much inclined to be jocose; their faces . . . are . . . distinguished by very small eyes and high cheekbones, and on both sides of their mouth they have holes, in which they wear morse-bone, ornamented with blue beads, which give them a terrific appearance.

Kotzebue's voyage also visited more tropical areas of the Pacific Ocean, and he is known for his observations and theories regarding coral atolls, some of which were later accepted by Charles Darwin.

Kotzebue was called upon to command the ship *Predpriatie* on another Russian round-the-world voyage in 1823–26, which again had scientists on board, including E. Lenz, a physicist. This time he made no new geographical discoveries in the North Pacific, but did add considerably to scientific knowledge.

Kotzebue visited the Russian-American Company's capital at New Archangel'sk, now Sitka, and made observations on the habits of the sea otter. Perceptively, Kotzebue noted, "It

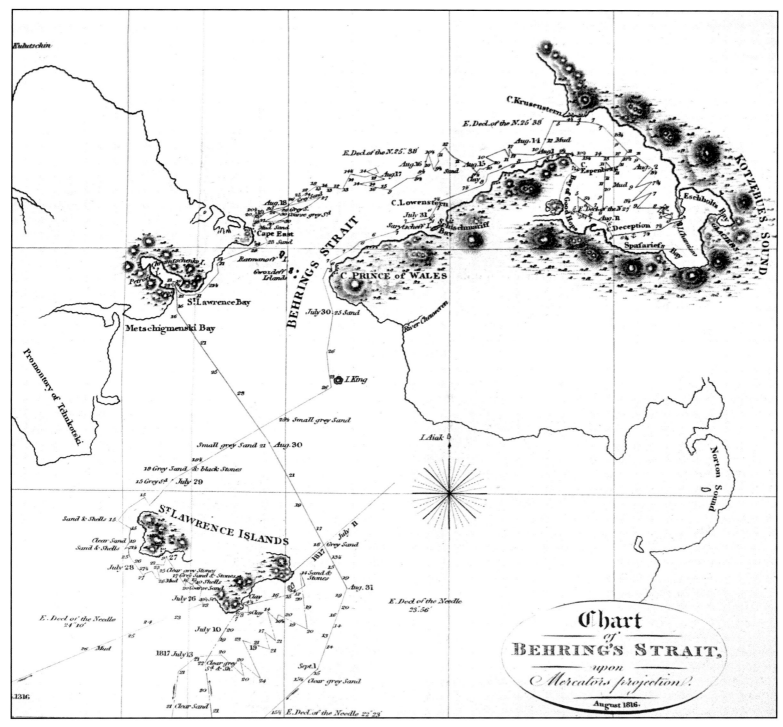

Map 185.
Otto Kotzebue's map of Bering Strait.
Most detail is concentrated on his discovery, Kotzebue Sound.

(above, left)
Inhabitants of Kotzebue Sound,
an illustration from Kotzebue's book.

will soon entirely disappear, and exist only in description to decorate our zoological works." The sea otter did indeed almost disappear in Alaskan waters until its reintroduction in the twentieth century.

Kotzebue's physicist, Lenz, tried to overcome the poor instrumentation that had plagued Kotzebue on his first voyage, and designed a bathometer, which sampled water at various depths, and a winched depth gauge for lowering the instrument to a specific depth. These two inventions have been considered by some to be the beginning of exact oceanographic technique.

From the data he collected with Kotzebue, Lenz formulated a theory of oceanic water circulation to explain the occurrence of lower temperatures at depth. Lenz was the first to establish the existence of lower salinity at the equator and higher salinity north and south of it, correctly explaining this as due to more intense evaporation in the area of the trade winds and less in the calmer regions around the equator.

Fedor Lütke's Scientific Voyage

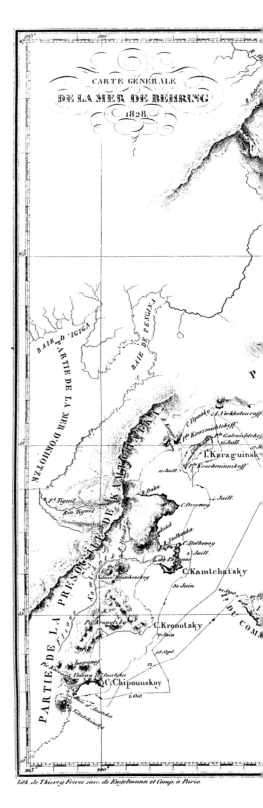

Of the approximately fifty Russian voyages around the world that were undertaken during the tenure of the Russian-American Company in Alaska, the voyage of Fedor Petrovich Lütke was one of the most successful from a scientific point of view.

Two ships, *Seniavin,* under Lütke, and *Moller,* commanded by M. N. Staniukovich, left the Baltic naval port of Kronstadt in August 1826 with instructions to survey the Northeast Coast of Asia and the Northwest Coast of America. After treaties signed with both the United States and Britain in 1824 and 1825, Russia no longer had to provide warships to patrol the coast of northwest America, hence the instructions for a more scientific voyage.

Once in the North Pacific, the two ships separated and went about their own tasks. Staniukovich had little scientific inclination and only surveyed the north coast of the Alaska Peninsula, producing routine reports. Lütke, on the other hand, accumulated a vast amount of scientific data, and produced and later published several books with his findings, including a historical section with an atlas and a nautical atlas with more than fifty maps and plans.

Three naturalists were with Lütke. All were masters at several branches of natural history, as was common in their day. Friedrich Hienrich Baron von Kittlitz specialized in ornithology, Aleksandr Filippovich Postels was a mineralogist-naturalist, and Karl-Heinrich Mertens was the ship's doctor and, of course, another naturalist. Together they produced more than 1,250 drawings and sketches. They also took meteorological observations.

In 1827 Lütke visited the Russian-American Company's headquarters at New Archangel'sk (Sitka) and surveyed some of the coast. The winter of 1827–28 was passed farther south, in the Caroline Islands, and in 1828 the expedition surveyed the eastern coast of Kamchatka Peninsula and measured the heights of some volcanoes.

The scientists took daily observations of the temperature of the water on the surface and attempted to measure the temperature in deeper water; however, the first time they tried to do this, three thermometers were found to be broken when they were retrieved. Lütke was of the opinion that this was caused by water pressure.

Three hundred species of fish were preserved in alcohol, and Postels painted some 245 of them. Many of these were entirely unknown to science at the time.

The scientists certainly were collectors. The expedition also gathered 100 amphibians; 150 species of crustaceans, a hundred of which Mertens painted while they were alive; 700 species of insects; a "considerable collection" of shells; and 300 species of birds represented by 750 specimens. Mertens collected 2,500 plant specimens, and Postels collected 330 rock samples. Lastly, the expedition collected a "rich collection" of costumes, arms, utentils, and ornaments, and "some skulls of savages."

When the expedition returned to Russia, the specimens were all deposited with the Imperial Academy of Sciences in St. Petersburg.

View of the Russian Colony of Novo-Arkhangel'sk. The view, according to Kittlitz, who drew this picture, is of the interior of the town in its most populous and important place, from the door of the citadel. A Tlingit native looks on.

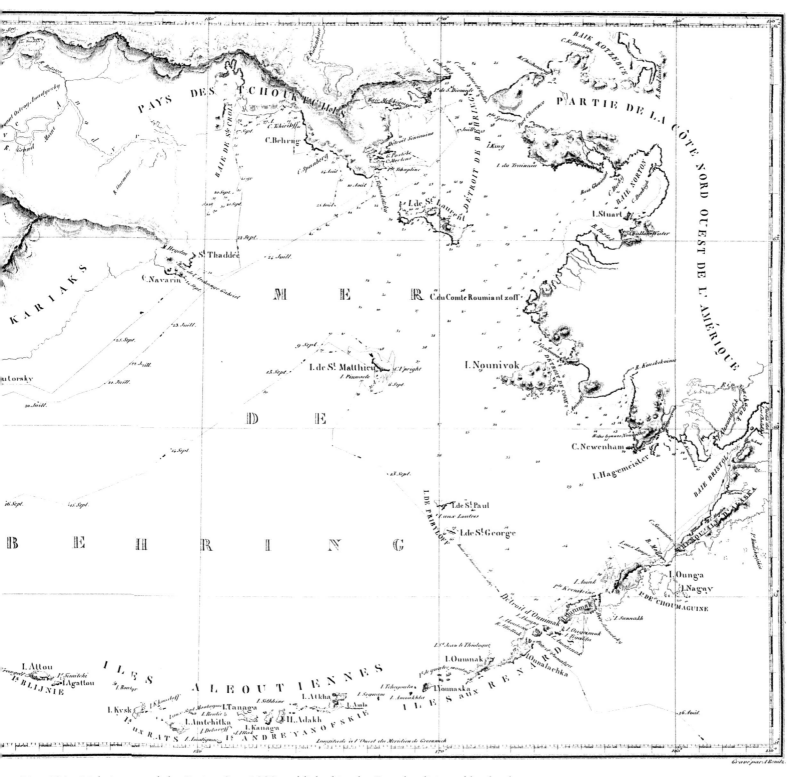

Map 186. Lütke's map of the Bering Sea, 1828, published in the French edition of his book.

(left)

Forest of Sitkha Island.
"In order to study as closely as possible the character of the vegetation we undertook an excursion to the summit of Mount Verstovaia, the highest of the island (3,000 English feet)," Postels wrote of this view from his own drawing. "The road through the forest . . . is represented in this picture."

(right)

Habitation at Unalaska, Aleutian Islands. Kittlitz drew this picture on Unalaska. He wrote:

The general appearance of the Aleutian Islands affords a striking contrast to that of Sitka. In place of the superb forest which covers the steep heights of this island from sea level, one does not see here the least small shrub; only the high grasses which extend to the arid region of a land composed likewise of high escarpments, presents an aspect more attractive than one might believe, like an immense carpet of velvet where the inequalities of the soil produce an infinity of nuances.

The United States Exploring Expedition

Porpoise.

In 1838 the United States Exploring Expedition, universally referred to as the U.S. Ex. Ex., was sent straggling round the world to collect scientific information both from lands and seas. It was a belated answer to the British and French expeditions of Cook and La Pérouse and, perhaps more immediately, that of Robert Fitzroy, with Charles Darwin in HMS *Beagle,* from 1831 to 1836.

Trade benefits were supposed to flow from this new expedition: new areas could be opened for trade, better routes found for New England whalers, and perhaps new islands would be discovered.

Charles Wilkes, though only a lieutenant, was appointed commander of the expedition. Wilkes had been appointed in 1833 the second superintendent of the U.S. Depot of Charts and Instruments, the predecessor of the U.S. Hydrographic Office. In twenty years of naval service Wilkes had proven himself scientifically. His affinity to the navy meant he preferred naval officers for scientific duties; "All the duties apertaining to Astronomy, Surveying, Hydrography, Geography, Geodesy, Magnetism, Meteorology, and Physics [are] generally to be confined to the

Navy officers," he directed, which subjects "are deemed the great objects of this expedition." Only nine positions were given to civilians.

Six ships sailed from Norfolk, Virginia, in August 1838. By the time they had done their work in the Atlantic, rounded Cape Horn, and were finally in the Pacific, half of them were out of commission, and

one, *Peacock,* was wrecked trying to cross the bar at the mouth of the Columbia River in 1842. All hands were saved, but the precious cargo of scientific specimens was lost. As a result, most of the work was done by two ships, *Vincennes* and *Porpoise.*

The expedition's most famous result was not achieved in the North Pacific but in the Antarctic, sailing within a mile of the coast of what Wilkes called "Termination Land," to this day named Wilkes Land. Wilkes claimed to have discovered Antarctica, a claim contested by Britain's James Clark Ross, whose own expedition sailed from 1839 to 1843.

Wilkes' expedition did not spend a large part of its time in the North Pacific. It visited Oregon and California in 1841, and Wilkes' reports were important in encouraging the United States to insist on holding the area that is now the states of Washington and Oregon against British demands.

Of importance were Wilkes' reports and survey of Puget Sound, which reemphasized the fact that it was the only significant harbor north of San Francisco.

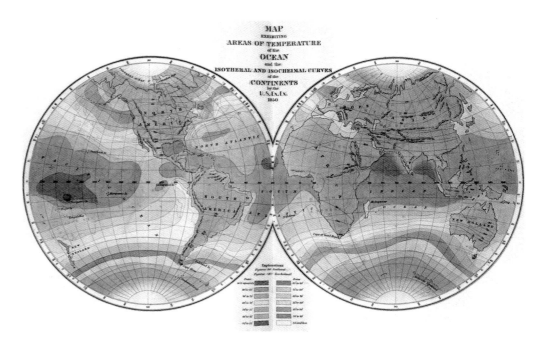

Map 187. *Map Exhibiting Areas of Temperature of the Ocean and the Isothermal and Isocheimal* [equal mean temperatures] *Curves of the Continents,* from a volume written by Wilkes himself, *Meteorology,* 1850.

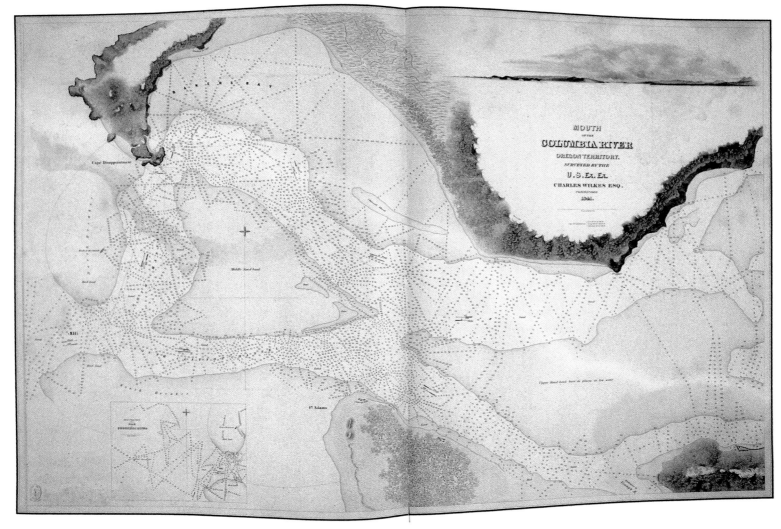

Map 188.
The survey of the treacherous mouth of the Columbia River, where one of the expedition's ships, *Peacock*, was destroyed trying to cross its notorious bar.

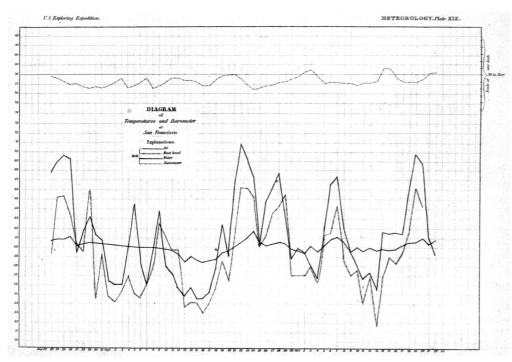

Graph of temperatures and air pressure recorded by the expedition while in San Francisco. The period covered is 22 August to 23 October 1841. Air temperatures at the surface and at the masthead were recorded, as was the surface water temperature.

Augustus Gould wrote the volume on *Mollusca and Shells*, from which these stunning engraved and hand-colored illustrations are taken. This plate, of *Pecten*, shows (at the top) two species from Puget Sound.

Many of the artifacts and specimens collected by the Wilkes expedition were sent to the National Institute, the forerunner of the Smithsonian, and promptly ruined. The curator also gave many away to his friends! Such was the respect for science. Plants from Oregon and California, neither at that time part of the United States, were shipped back to Washington on a ship which, after a voyage to China, was sold! The precious plants were dropped off in Havana, and did make it to Washington eventually.

Since his expedition was essentially a naval one, Wilkes needed government funds to process and publish the results of the voyage. Congress at first refused to pay, but due to Wilkes' persistence was at last persuaded to fund the preparation of some twenty-four volumes, twenty of which were ultimately published.

There was one catch: all had to be prepared by American scholars, which made it difficult for Wilkes to find appropriate scientists to do the job. He ended up writing several of the volumes himself, a task for which he was not unqualified. But it took a long time; Wilkes' volume of hydrography was not published until 1873, by which time new methods and better equipment had appeared.

In 1874, thirty-eight years after the start of the expedition, Congress cut funds for the remaining incomplete reports, and the United States Exploring Expedition was officially over.

Wilkes himself became a rear admiral and a significant backer of the new scientific oceanography. Towards the end of his days he toured the eastern United States with his sometimes unfinished reports urging scientists to consider "the vast space of our globe occupied by the great ocean . . . It cannot but strike every one," he maintained, "what a wide field is open for investigation and experiment."

In some respects Wilkes was ahead of his time, advocating an invention to

obtain an echo from the bed of the ocean by the explosion of a shell just beneath the surface, the depth to be measured through the propagation of reflected sound.

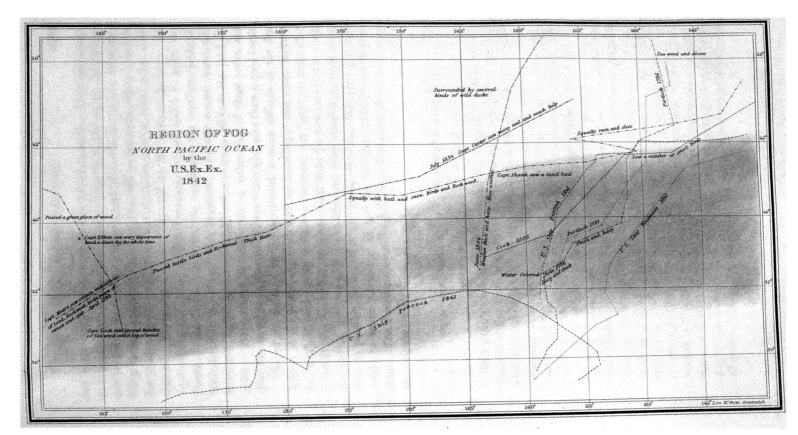

Map 189.
Wilkes wrote and published a book called *The Theory of the Winds*. This map of fog regions is taken from that book. Wilkes wrote: "All vessels may expect to meet with fogs and hazy atmosphere between latitudes 33° and 40°. This space might be very truly called the region of fog, the temperature of the water decreasing some 15°; and what is more remarkable, on a near approach to the coast, it again rises."

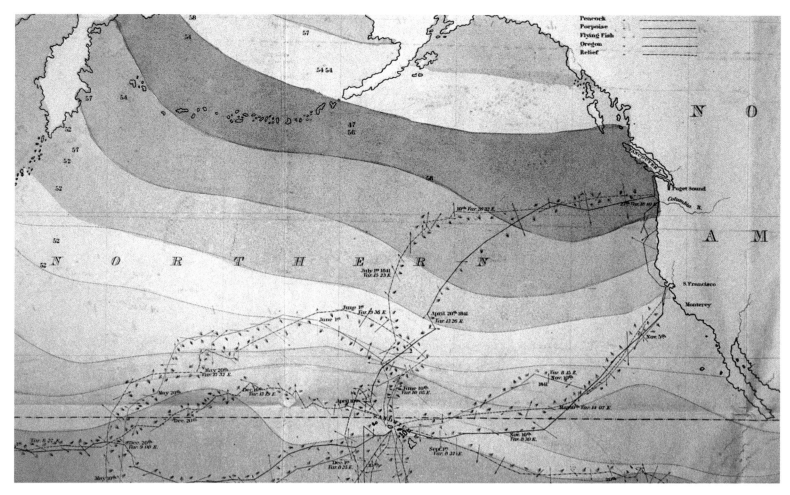

Map 190.
Track of the U.S. Exploring Expedition in the North Pacific. The map is from the *Narrative* of the voyage, published in 1845. The color bands are surface seawater temperatures. A lot of apparent information from so little actual data! Actually, the temperature distribution is not accurate, a consequence of too much extrapolation.

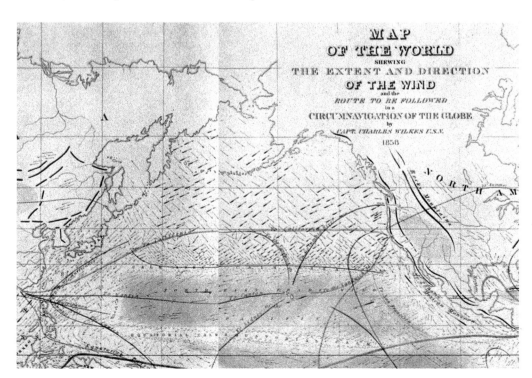

Map 191.
Part of a wind map of the world, from the volume *Hydrography*, written by Wilkes. The map was presented as a typical world map, running from 180° W to 180° E, but has here been cut and pasted to show the Pacific as a continuous sea.

Shells found in Puget Sound, from Augustus Gould's book *Mollusca and Shells*.

Mikhail Tebenkov's Atlas

Mikhail Dimitrievich Tebenkov's *Atlas of the Northwest Coasts of America from Bering Strait to Cape Corrientes and the Aleutian Islands* was published in St. Petersburg in 1852.

Tebenkov was a Russian naval officer who was manager of the Russian-American Company from 1845 to 1850. In 1831, he was responsible for building the Mikhailovskii re-doubt, St. Michaels, near the mouth of the Yukon River.

In the 1840s, before and during his tenure as manager, Tebenkov organized several expeditions to survey the coasts of Russian America.

Over a period of twenty-five years, he had collected hydrographic maps that he had drawn, and added them to maps from other sources, in particular those of George Vancouver.

He also used ships' logs for information and verification.

In 1852, Tebenkov consolidated maps from these sources and published an atlas, which represents a superb collection of maps of the Northwest Coast from Russian sources. Three selections from his atlas are shown here.

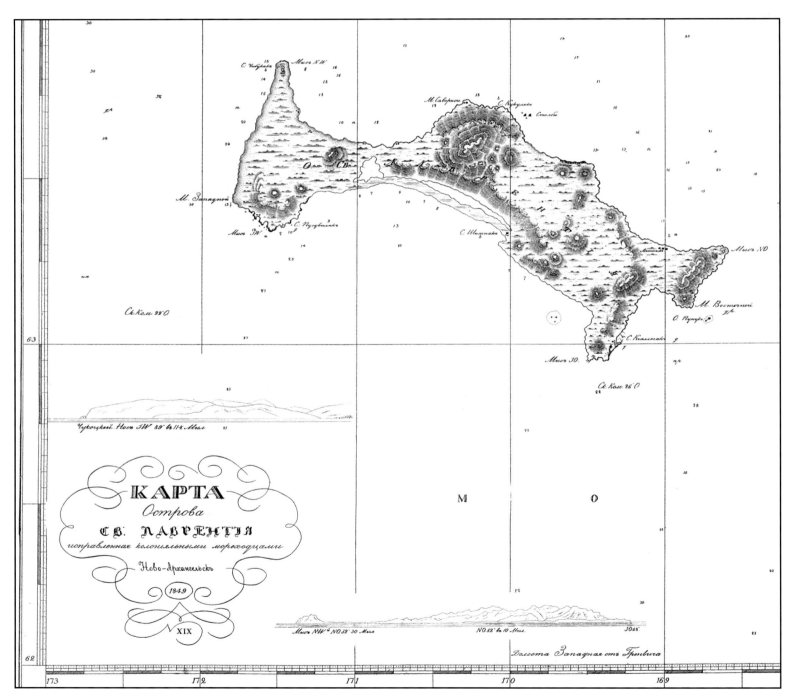

Map 192. Mikhail Tebenkov's map of St. Lawrence Island, in the Bering Sea, drawn in 1849. Note the soundings shown.

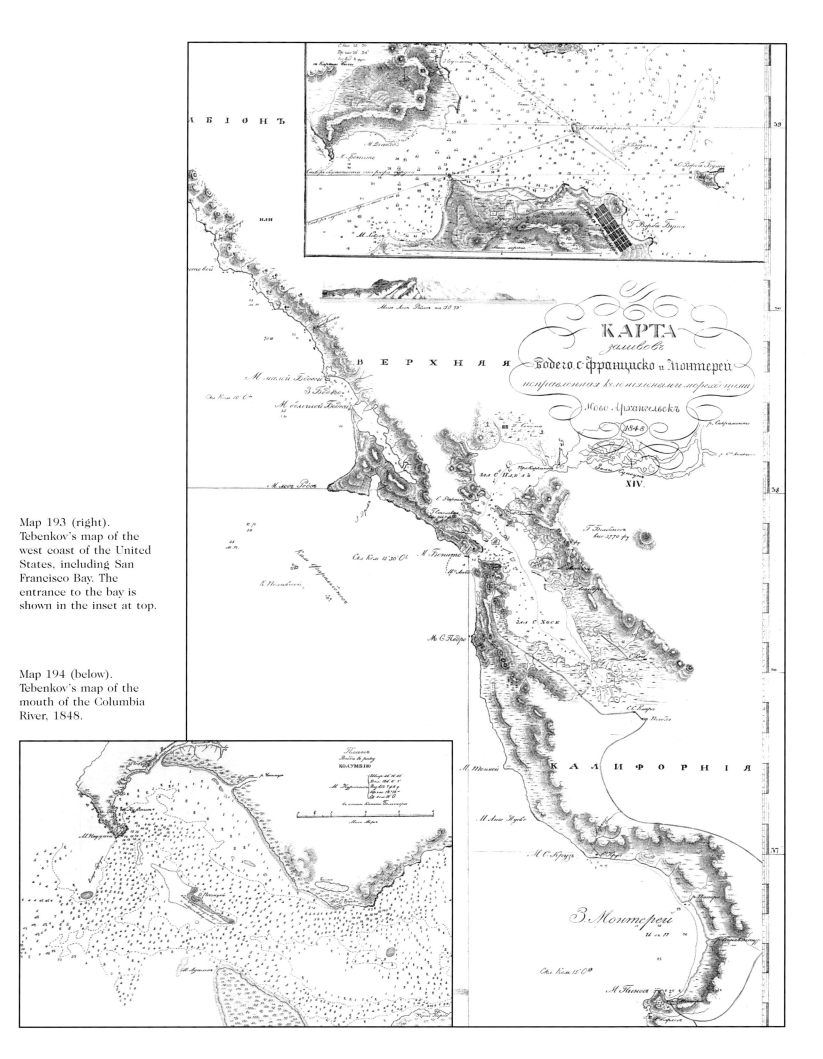

Map 193 (right).
Tebenkov's map of the
west coast of the United
States, including San
Francisco Bay. The
entrance to the bay is
shown in the inset at top.

Map 194 (below).
Tebenkov's map of the
mouth of the Columbia
River, 1848.

Commodore Perry's Black Ships – The U.S. Japan Expedition

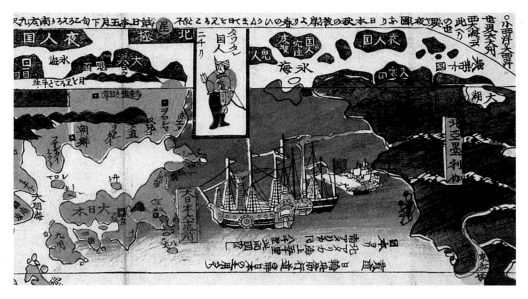

Map 195. Part of a mid-nineteenth-century Japanese world map showing the Pacific Ocean and Japan, with Perry's steamships – the "black ships."

The U.S. Japan Expedition under Commodore Matthew Calbraith Perry was an American effort to open Japan for trade. Japan was a closed society, where foreign ships that came within range had, by law, to be fired upon. The American government resolved to put an end to this situation, and Perry, with his squadron of what the Japanese called "black ships of the evil mien [main]," black smoke-belching ships, moving without the help of wind or the hand of man, arrived off the coast of Japan on 8 July 1853. The idea was to display a sufficient show of force that the Japanese would think it better to negotiate than fight.

The expedition was not intended to be a scientific one; Perry wrote that the expedition was

altogether of a naval and diplomatic character, and was never intended to embrace in its operations scientific researches.

But, he said,

Still I have determined that all shall be done under the circumstances to subserve the objects of science,

and so he issued orders that his officers collect hydrographical, meteorological, botanical, ichthylogical, zoological, ornithological, and other information. The result was that his expedition brought back many specimens and much information scientists could analyze.

There were few charts to guide the way; the American government purchased some inadequate ones from the Dutch for the astounding sum of $30,000.

The squadron steamed into Toyko Bay, repulsing all attempts to board them, until contact was made with a Japanese official who could speak Dutch. He had been brought from Nagasaki, the one place in Japan where Dutch merchants were allowed (see page 36). He was sent off with a copy of a letter from U.S. President Millard Fillmore to the Japanese emperor, but it seemed unlikely that it would actually be presented to the emperor.

While waiting for the Japanese to decide if the emperor would respond to their demands to negotiate, surveys and soundings were made in Tokyo Bay, protected by deployment of some of the squadron's ships.

At long length permission was given to meet a high official at Kurihama Bay, and Perry went ashore with as much pomp and circumstance as the Americans could muster, but at the same time defensively covered by his ship's guns. Here he met with Toda, the provincial governor, and officially delivered the letter to the emperor.

After more surveying, the squadron left, telling the Japanese that they would return the following spring for the emperor's reply.

Map 196 (right).
Perry's map of Tokyo wan (Tokyo Bay), which is here named "Jeddo Bay," from his first visit in 1853. The ships at anchor are named, and "Reception Bay" is shown. The land area on the map is today part of Yokohama.

Matthew Perry, commander of the U.S Japan Expedition.

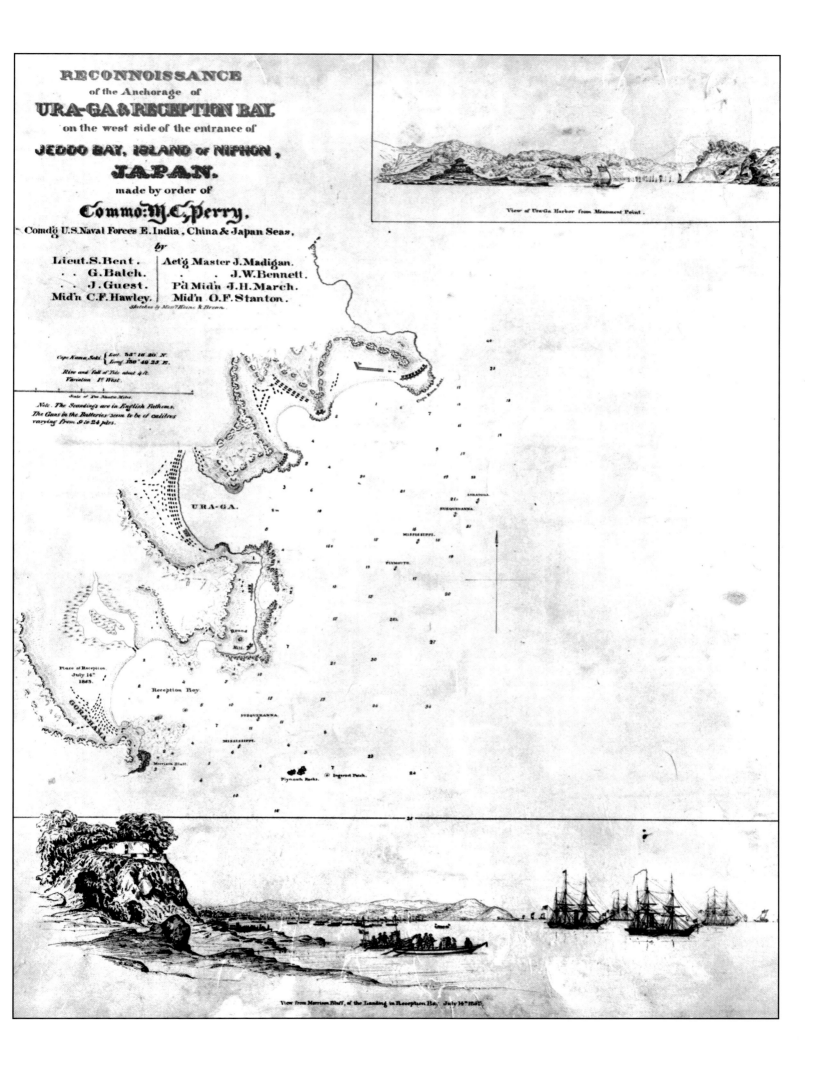

RECONNOISSANCE
of the Anchorage of
URA-GA & RECEPTION BAY
on the west side of the entrance of
JEDDO BAY, ISLAND OF NIPHON,
JAPAN.
made by order of
Commo: M. C. Perry,
Comd'g U.S. Naval Forces E. India, China & Japan Seas,

by

Lieut. S. Bent.	Act'g Master J. Madigan.
. . G. Balch.	. . J. W. Bennett.
. . J. Guest.	P'd Mid'n J. H. March.
Mid'n C. F. Hawley.	Mid'n O. F. Stanton.

Sketches by Mess'rs Heine & Brown.

Cape Kama Saki { Lat. 35° 16' 20" N.
{ Long. 130° 49' 25" E.

Rise and fall of Tide about 4 ft.
Variation 1° West.

Scale of Two Nautic Miles

Note. The Soundings are in English Fathoms.
The Guns in the Batteries seem to be of calibres
varying from 9 to 24 p'drs.

URA-GA.

SARATOGA.

SUSQUEHANNA.

MISSISSIPPI.

PLYMOUTH.

Round Hill.

Place of Reception
July 14th
1853.

Reception Bay.

SUSQUEHANNA.

MISSISSIPPI.

Morrison Bluff.

Plymouth Rocks.   Ingersol Patch.

View of Ura-Ga Harbor from Monument Point.

View from Morrison Bluff, of the Landing in Reception Bay, July 14th 1853.

In February the next year, 1854, they were back. This time they went ashore at Kanagawa, Yokohama. Accompanied by a well-armed retinue – even the band had pistols and swords – Perry went ashore, where he received the emperor's answer to President Fillmore's letter, in which he agreed to some of the American demands.

But Perry wanted more, and after weeks of further negotiations and military display, he got what he really wanted, a treaty.

The Treaty of Kanagawa between the United States and Japan was signed on 31 March 1854. It had twelve articles, including provisions that "there will be a perfect, permanent and universal peace, and a sincere cordial amnity, between the United States of America and Japan"; that the ports of Shimoda and Hakodate would be granted by the Japanese "as ports for the reception of American ships"; and that if U.S. ships were shipwrecked, Japan was to assist them, and shipwrecked sailors were not to be confined.

Although essentially forced upon the Japanese government, the treaty negotiated by Perry did in fact open up Japan to trade. For, once the Japanese started to trade with the outside world, there was no looking back.

Map 197 (top).
"Simoda Lt. Bents Survey with Topography," a pencil copy of a survey of the small port of Shimoda, at the tip of the Izu Hanto (Izu Peninsula) on the east coast of Honshu, a little south of Tokyo. Silas Bent, one of Perry's officers, surveyed this new treaty port in April 1854.

Map 198 (right).
Harbor of Hakodadi Island of Yesso Surveyed by order of Commodore M. C. Perry By Lieut. W. L. Maury, Lieut. G.H. Preble, Lieut J. Nicholson, Lieut A. Barbot 1854. A rough plotting sheet showing lines of soundings, shoreline features, settlement, and topography of the harbor of Hakodate, the other harbor opened by treaty to American ships. It is at the south end of Hokkaido, on Tsugaru-kaikyo (Tsugaru Strait).

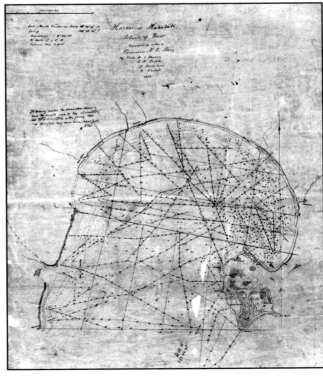

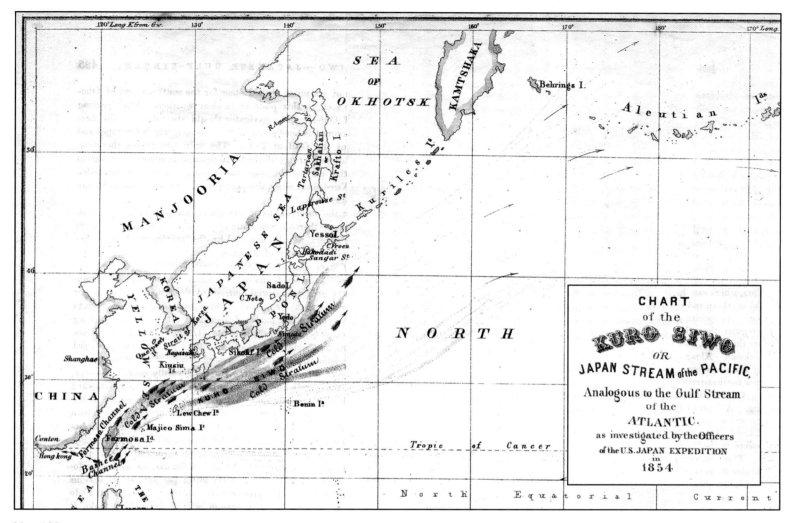

Map 199.
Chart of the Kuro Siwo or Japan Stream of the Pacific Analogous to the Gulf Stream of the Atlantic as investigated by the Officers of the U.S. Japan Expedition in 1854. From Perry's published reports, one of the first "scientific" mappings of the Kuroshio Current off the coast of Japan. An 1832 translation of a Japanese book Perry quoted in his journal noted the existence of a strong current between the islands of Mikura and Hachijojima "called Kouro se gawa (Kuroshio), or the black gulf current. It runs so rapidly that seamen regard it as the most difficult passage in these seas to get over."

Perry's book about the expedition was published in three large volumes in 1856–58. They contained a vast amount of information, sailing directions, illustrations of fish and other marine life, a whole volume of "observations of the zodiacal light," many maps and charts, reports on possible commercial features, such as coal deposits in Formosa, and even a copy of the treaty in Japanese.

Three fish caught and classified by the Perry expedition, beautifully illustrated and hand painted, from Perry's book. At left is (from Perry's descriptions) *Sebastes inermis*, 5¾ inches (142 mm) long, from Hakodadi (Hakodate). At right top is *Serranus tsirimenara* [*Epinephelus fasciatus*, blacktip grouper], 7¼ inches (181 mm) long, from Port Lloyd, Bonin Islands; and right bottom is *Serranus marginalis* [?], 8⅝ inches (216 mm) long, from Simoda (Shimoda).

The U.S. North Pacific Exploring Expedition

The U.S. North Pacific Exploring Expedition was authorized by Act of Congress in August 1852 for

the reconnaissance and survey for naval and commercial purposes of such parts of Behring's straits, of the North Pacific Ocean and of the China Sea as are frequented by American whaleships and by trading vessels in their routes between the United States and China.

The American government was trying to open the Orient, and especially Japan, to trade, and there was a need to test the treaty with Japan that Perry was expected to negotiate. In addition, the expedition was to chart the trans-Pacific routes to China. Whaling had become of considerable importance to the American economy at this time, and the uncharted islands of the Japan archipelago and farther north were a hazard to whaling ships.

Eager to acquire more information about the Pacific Ocean, Matthew Fontaine Maury, in charge of the Depot of Charts and Instruments (see page 152), undoubtedly had much to do with the decision to send out the expedition.

The expedition, the government explained to Cadwalader Ringgold, appointed to command it, was "not for conquest but discovery. Its objects are all peaceful, they are to extend the empire of commerce and of science; to diminish the hazards of the ocean."

Five ships formed the expedition, which left the United States in mid-1853. The flagship was *Vincennes*, the same as that of the Wilkes expedition fifteen years before (see page 136). Another was *Porpoise*, which had also been on the Wilkes expedition, under Ringgold. *Fenimore Cooper* was a smaller ship, intended as a tender. Only one of the ships, *John Hancock*, was a steamer.

Before the ships reached Hong Kong, Ringgold became ill and command devolved onto Lieutenant John Rodgers, who also took over command of *Vincennes*.

In September 1854 *Hancock* took American representatives to China to ask for revisions to treaties to open Chinese ports made in 1842–44. The

Map 200.
Straits of Tsugar Japan, 1855. This is the manuscript chart reduced for engraving. Tsugaru Strait is between Honshu and Hokkaido.

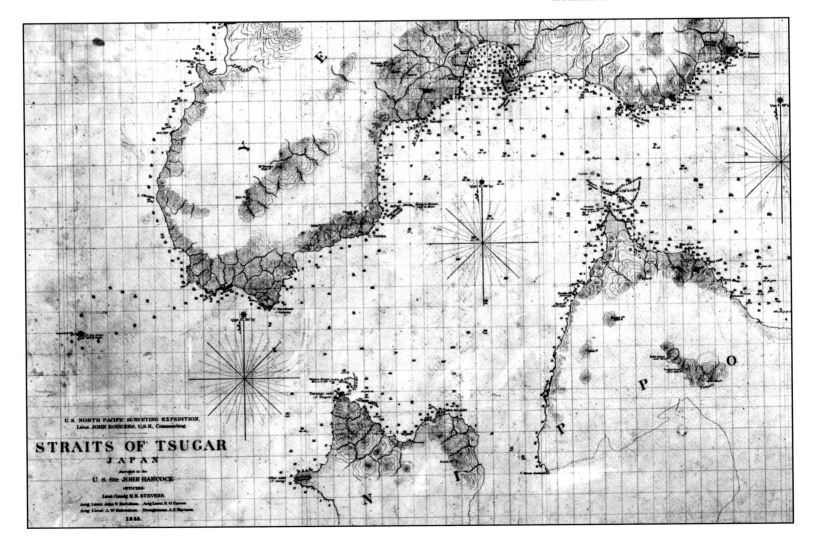

revisions were refused, but the opportunity was taken to sound around the mouths of several rivers, including the Yellow River and the Yangtze, and a survey was made in the Gulf of Chihli.

Meanwhile *Vincennes* and *Porpoise* had been surveying in the area south of Japan; *Porpoise* was lost, probably in a typhoon. Rodgers continued to chart islands between Okinawa (which they called Liu Ch'iu) and the Bay of Kagoshima, at the southern tip of the southernmost large Japanese island of Kyushu.

In 1855, the major surveying

Map 201 (top left).
Mouth of the Teen-Tsin-Ho (Yangtze-Kiang), surveyed by *John Hancock* and *Fenimore Cooper* in October 1854.

Map 202 (below).
Reconnoissance of the East Coast of Nippon, Empire of Japan, From Simoda to Hakodati By the launch of the United States Ship Vincennes, under the command of Lieutenant John M. Brooke, U.S.N., assisted by Edward M. Kern, Artist, and Richard Berry, Sailmaker. May 29th to June 17th 1855. Original Working Sheet. This is the map produced by Brooke from his epic voyage up the east coast of Japan in a small boat, *Vincennes Junior*.

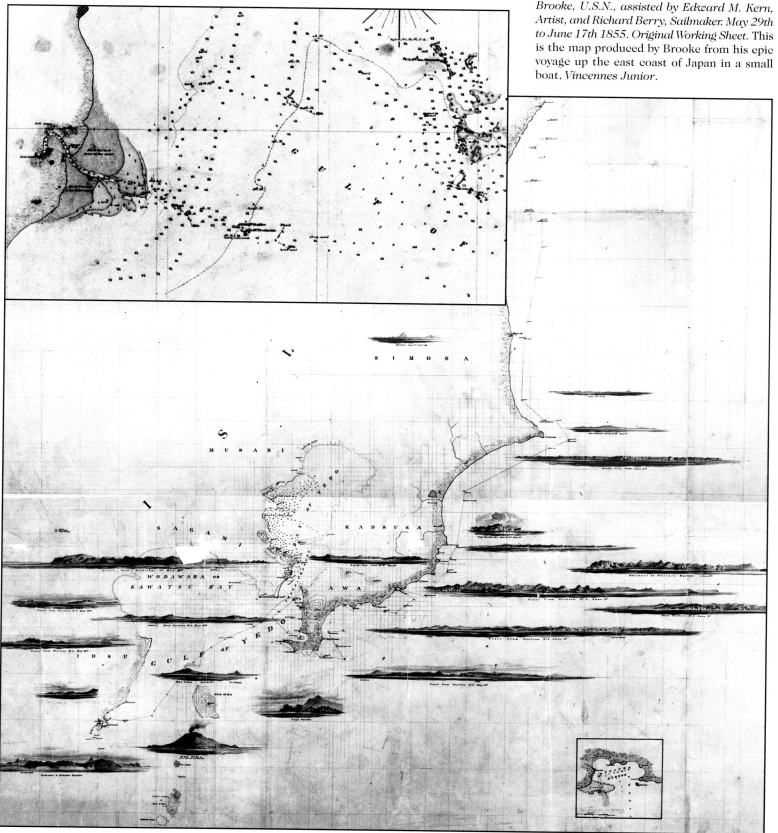

work began on the coasts of Japan. *Hancock* and *Vincennes* sailed north along the Ryukyu Islands and entered the new treaty port of Shimoda in May. Despite Japanese objections the two ships also visited the nearby port of Heda, charting into Suruga Bay.

At this time *Fenimore Cooper* surveyed parts of Kyushu and small islands, including the Goto Islands at the extreme western tip of Japan. Continuing northwards through the Korea Strait between Korea and Japan, *Cooper* surveyed the northwestern coast of Honshu and offshore islands such as the Oki Islands, meeting up with *Vincennes* and *Hancock* again at Hakodate, in Tsugaru Strait.

The southeastern coast of Honshu is often shrouded in fog, making it too hazardous to survey inshore with large ships, so men in one of *Vincennes'* boats, called *Vincennes Junior,* were ordered to survey the coast in detail from Shimoda to Hakodate. This somewhat epic voyage in an open boat, with fifteen men aboard, encountered some heavy weather in its 720-km or 450-mile survey. The boat was commanded by Lieutenant John M. Brooke, also the expedition's astronomer, who had two years before invented a new sounding apparatus that detached a weight used to sink a sounding line when it reached the seabed, allowing a relatively light line to be used to haul up the sampling tube. Now he put his sounding device to good work. This device would also be used to haul up seabed samples from 3,500 fathoms in the Japan Trench.

From Hakodate *Vincennes* surveyed north along the Kuril Islands to Petropavlovsk and the coast of Siberia to Bering Strait, and even farther, into the Arctic Ocean. Deep-sea soundings were made off the Aleutian Islands before the ship returned to San Francisco, which it reached on 13 October 1855.

Fenimore Cooper had arrived two days before. They had surveyed in the Aleutians and searched for places where coal might be found. Coal had been found by the Russians at vari-

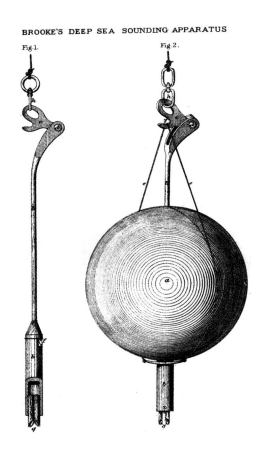

BROOKE'S DEEP SEA SOUNDING APPARATUS

Fig.1.   Fig.2.

ous places on the Alaska coast, notably in Cook Inlet, information which was given to the ship's captain William Gibson by the Russian-American Company governor at New Archangel'sk (Sitka), which they had also visited.

John Hancock charted Tsugaru Strait, between Honshu and Hokkaido, surveyed the northern part of Honshu, and then proceeded up the west coast of Hokkaido, charting La Pérouse Strait between Hokkaido and Sakhalin. Then the western coast of Sakhalin was surveyed, the approaches to the Amur River, the northern coast of the Sea of Okhotsk, and the western coast of Kamchatka. Here a search was made for coal to supply steamers, but only a small amount of inferior coal was found.

In September, surveying was finished and *Hancock* also made for San Francisco, arriving there on 19 October 1855.

Important information about the Great Circle route between the newly acquired west coast American ports (California was ceded to the United States in 1848) and Asia had been gained, at least, in addition to the surveys and the knowledge of the lack of coal sources.

In December 1855, Rodgers received orders to transfer the men and stores of *Fenimore Cooper* to *Vincennes* and return to the Atlantic coast. He was authorized to return by "any route as [he] may deem advisable," and in his letter of reply to the Secretary of the Navy is a very interesting observation.

An island has been reported to lie in Latitude 40° 40´ N, and in about Longitude 150° 50´ West. The report wears an appearance of authenticity. Should it accidentally contain a harbor, its examination before it has been landed upon or taken possession of may have political importance. In any case it is of consequence to know of its position. The probability is that the Island has no harbor; it is possible that it has a fine one. We shall look for it.

Look for it they may have; unfortunately for them not only did the island have no harbor, but the harbor had no island!

Although the work of the Perry expedition was published in three large volumes, that of the U.S. North Pacific Exploring Expedition was never published; it was in preparation when the American Civil War intervened. Disagreements between John Rodgers and Cadwalader Ringgold

We were rapidly clearing the land when a sea was observed to break about two points on our weather bow, a column of white foam high in the air. The helm put down, the sails lowered and the main quickly reefed to weather it, we were relieved in seeing the jet of a spouting whale in the hollow of the sea: it was upon his back that the sea had broken and not upon a rock.

– John Brooke, from his report to Commander John Rodgers on his small boat surveying between Shimoda and Hakodate, 22 June 1855 may have also contributed to delays; Rodgers thought Ringgold wanted to usurp his work.

John Brooke was involved in another foray into the North Pacific, however. The expedition had been intended to also survey proposed steamship routes from California to China, and this had not been done. Thus *Fenimore Cooper* was sent from San Francisco with Brooke in command in 1858 to chart this route. The purpose was to verify the existence or otherwise of reported reefs and shoals on the routes normally taken by steamers. Three months were spent surveying and correcting charts of islands and reefs northwest of Hawaii, and much deep-sea sounding was done using Brooke's invention. After surveying and sounding to Hawaii and to Hong Kong, a visit was made to Yokohama, Japan, in August 1859; ten days later *Fenimore Cooper* was destroyed in a typhoon. Her crew, instruments, and records were all saved, however. In February 1860 Brooke returned to the United States as a naval advisor on the *Kanrin Maru,* the first Japanese steamer to cross the Pacific Ocean.

The U.S. North Pacific Exploring Expedition was also active in collecting natural history specimens. A total of 5,211 species of vertebrates, insects, crustacea, annelids, molluscs, and radiates were collected, totalling over 12,000 specimens. When the botanical specimens were transferred to the Smithsonian Institution near the end of the nineteenth century, they took up more than 2.8 m³ or 100 cubic feet in their original packages.

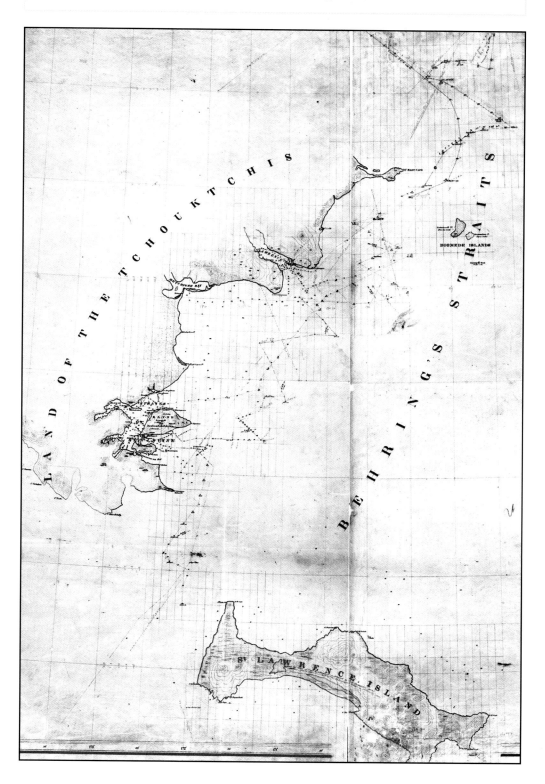

Map 203.
The Asiatic Coast of Behring's Straits. Surveyed in the U.S. Ship Vincennes July and August 1855. St. Lawrence Island is at the bottom.

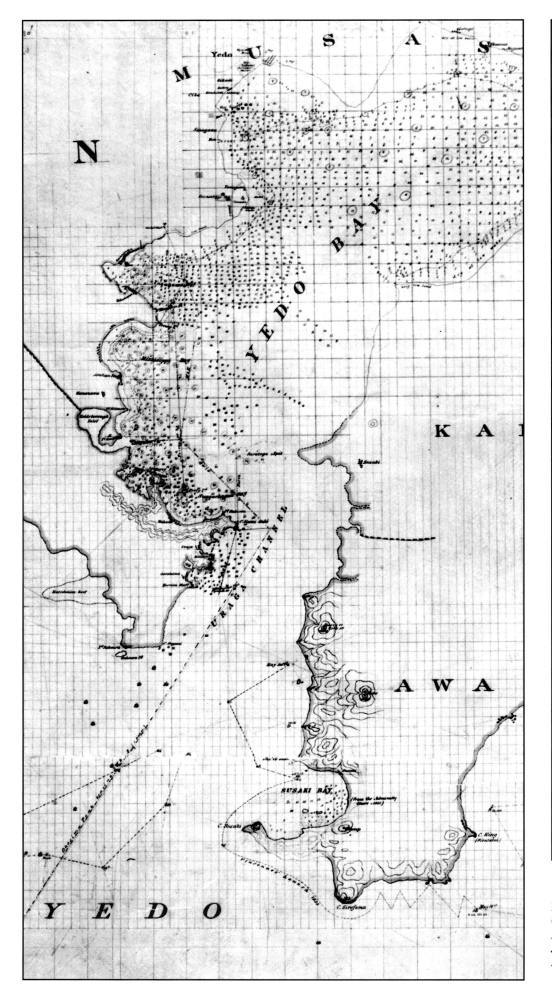

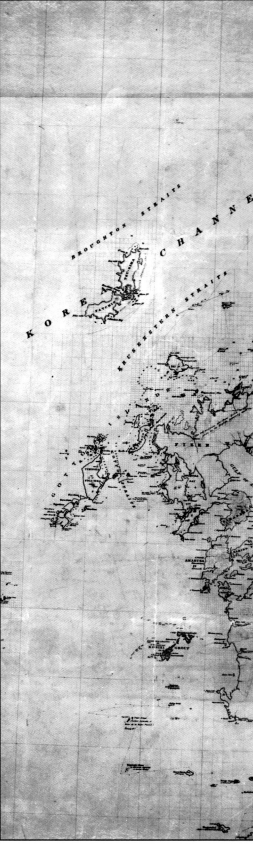

Map 204 (left).
Gulf of Yedo [Tokyo Bay] *and Approaches.*
A joint surveying effort by *Vincennes* and
John Hancock, May 1855, with additions by
John M. Brooke in *Fenimore Cooper,* 1859.

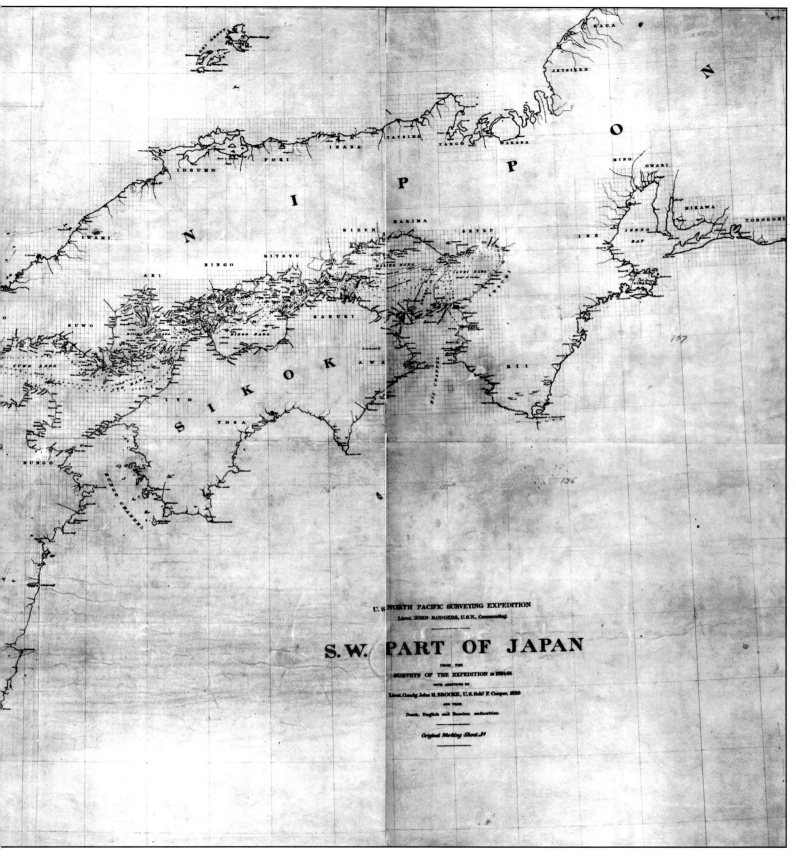

Map 205
S.W. Part of Japan from the Surveys of the Expedition in 1854–55 with additions by Lieut. Comdg.
John M. Brooke, U.S. Schr. F. Cooper, 1859, and from Dutch, English and Russian Authorities.
A smaller-scale map of the whole of southern Japan, nevertheless with a lot of detail. It is made up
of three large sheets.

Matthew Fontaine Maury's Wind and Current Charts

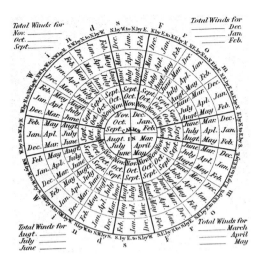

Maury's *Pilot Chart* key
(see Map 208, overleaf).

Matthew Fontaine Maury is widely regarded as being the father of modern ocean meteorology, if not oceanography as a whole.

After circumnavigating the globe between 1826 and 1830 as a midshipman in the U.S. Navy, Maury sailed around the Pacific Ocean extensively in the 1830s, and the information he gathered led to the publication in 1836 of a definitive book entitled *A New Theoretical and Practical Treatise on Navigation.*

In 1842 Maury was appointed Superintendent of the U.S. Navy Depot of Charts and Instruments (later the Hydrographic Office). Here he saw the potential in the mass of ships' logs and similar records gathered by ships crossing the world's oceans. The challenge was to gather the right information in a way it could be analyzed and used. He was responsible for a navy circular issued in late 1842 that invited ship owners and captains to send to the U.S. Bureau of Ordnance and Hydrography ten categories of hydrographical information that they might collect while at sea. Maury set copyists to work extracting the information these records contained. In the Pacific, information provided by whaling ships was valuable, because they tended to go where regular trading ships did not.

By 1847 Maury had enough information to begin to produce the *Wind and Current Charts* for which he is best known. They were an instant success; in a world of sailing vessels they were invaluable in reducing the time taken to sail from one point to another.

Simply knowing the locations of winds and currents enabled ships to sail an optimal route to take advantage of the winds or currents or both. This was particularly valuable for ships with time-sensitive cargoes, such as the clippers, which were built for speed. Even for the new-fangled steamships beginning to make their appearance on the world's oceans, the knowledge of currents made a big difference both in time saved and the amount of coal that had to be burned.

Maury's charts were soon in high demand. Five thousand were distributed, but they could not be bought except at the price of cooperation, which of course meant that more and more information flooded in to Maury. The U.S. Navy offered free charts to all who sent in data. A proud Maury was later to comment, "Never before was such a corps of observers known."

A pamphlet was prepared that told mariners not only how to use the charts but how to make observations at sea and how to record them. Maury knew that standardizing the format in which data was collected would increase the utility of the information.

The North Pacific Ocean chart was completed and issued in 1849.

In 1849 Maury began another method of plotting currents, one still in use by oceanographers today. He enlisted seamen on cooperating ships to mark their position and date on a piece of paper, and then seal it in a bottle and throw it overboard. Finders were asked to record the date and location the bottle was found, and send the information to Maury. Amazingly, the system worked, and

yet more information came to Maury. "In the absence of other information as to currents, that afforded by these mute little navigators is of great value," wrote Maury in 1855.

Maury then produced his so-called *Whale Charts,* which provided information on breeding habits, migrations, and the places where whales were most likely to be found from one season to the next. Naturally enough they proved a big success with the American whaling fleet, although Maury ran into some criticism from those who thought science should not assist commerce. But he was happy with his role as a practical scientist and laughed off the critics.

Also in 1849, Congress began to authorize the use of navy vessels for Maury's oceanographic investigations, a move prompted by the California gold rush, which meant that hordes of ships were in a big rush to get to California. The territorial designs of the American government on that region no doubt assisted Maury here. At the same time, Maury was advocating a railway across the

Map 206.
Maury's *Wind and Current Chart* for the middle of the North Pacific Ocean, 1849. The east coast of Japan's principal island, Honshu, is at top left, and the chart reaches eastwards to 170° E and south to the equator. The concentration of tracks in the trade winds is very apparent. Maury's charts were almost pictorial. In his words:

The winds are denoted by small brushes, the head of the brush pointing to the direction from whence the winds blow, the length of the brush showing the comparative force.
Currents are denoted by arrows, the length of the arrow being proportionate to the strength of the current: the figures beside the arrows show the number of knots.
The Roman numerals denote the degree of Magnetic Variation as recorded by the vessel near whose track they are placed.
The figures with a line drawn under them thus 80 show the temperature of the water.
The name of the ship which has supplied the route and the year of the voyage is recorded.

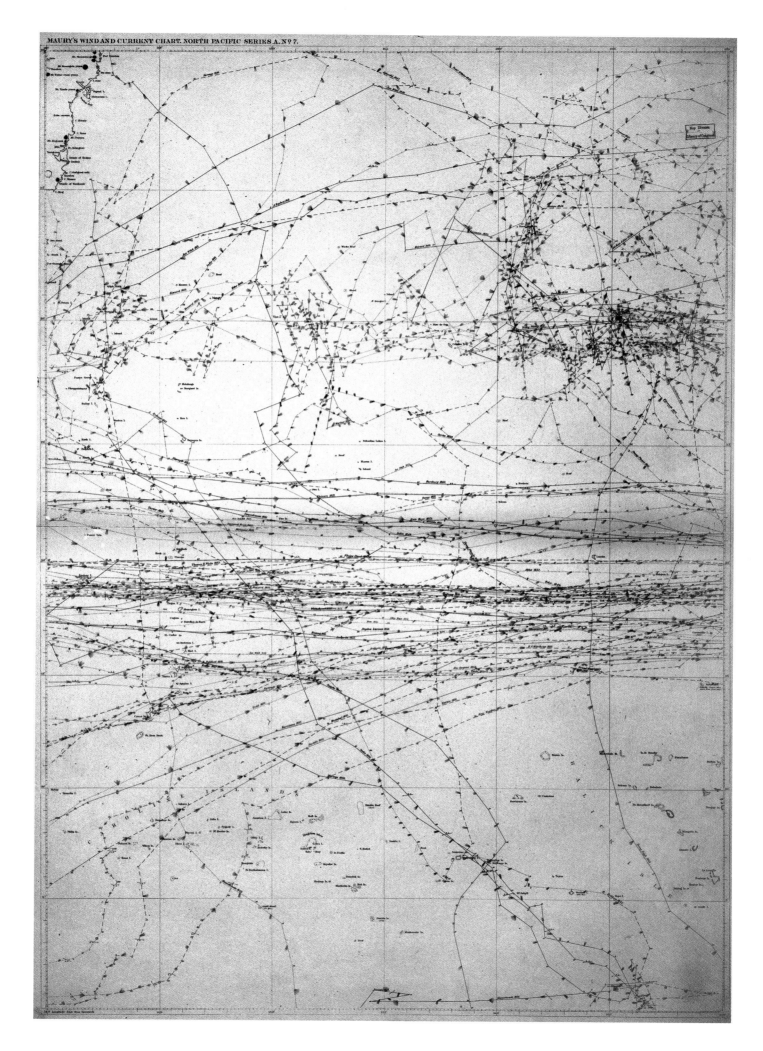

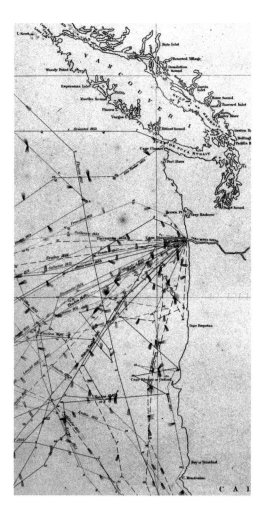

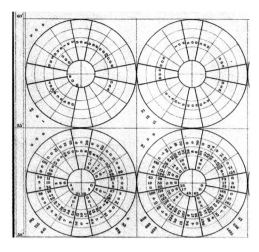

Map 207 (left).
Another of Maury's *Wind and Current Charts*, for the area off the Northwest Coast of North America. The concentration of tracks to and from the mouth of the Columbia River is distinct.

Map 208 (above).
Not looking like a map at all, Maury's 1851 *Pilot Chart* was a plotting of what were essentially glorified wind roses. A key is shown on page 152. This portion of the map of the North Pacific is for the area between 50° and 60° N and 155° and 165° W, for four 5° quadrants.

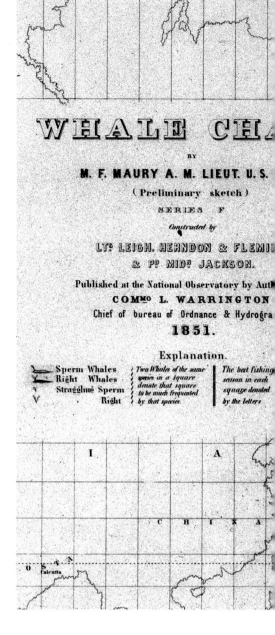

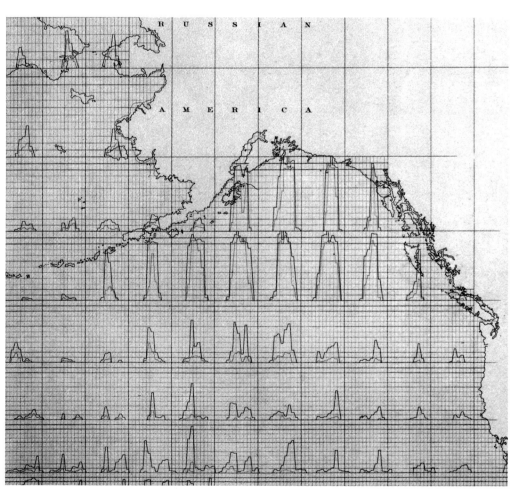

Map 209 (left).
Maury's *Whale Chart*, 1852. The data graphed refers to each square on the map. The top graph shows the number of days for which whales were searched, and the graphs below show the number of days when whales were sighted. A lot of information, all gathered from whaling ship logbooks, but a map that is not easy to interpret.

Map 210 (above).
A more pictorial version of Maury's *Whale Chart*, produced the year before, showing the distribution of sperm (red area) and right whales (green and blue), again by square. The map is printed but hand colored. Two whales per square indicates high frequency; a letter denotes season (see key).

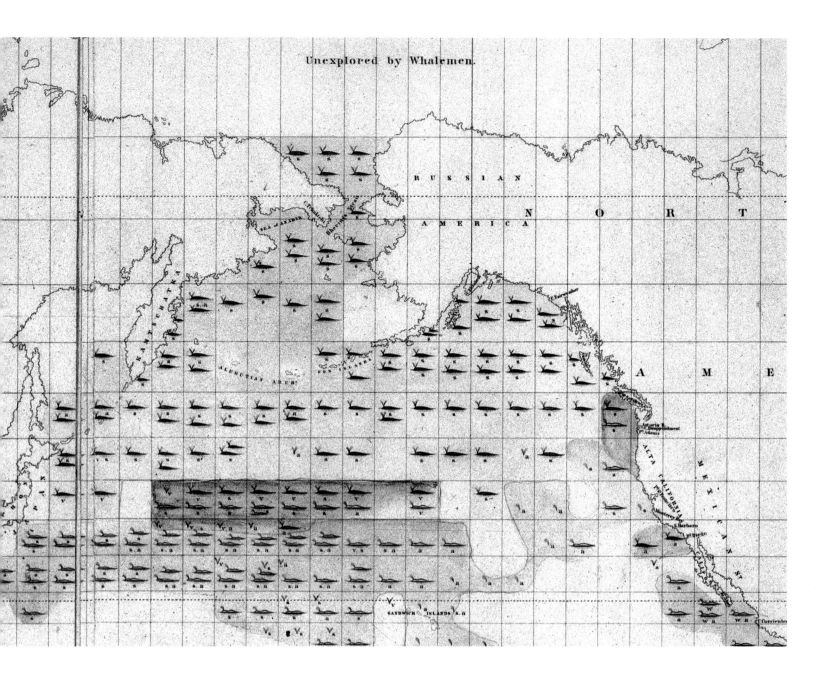

Isthmus of Panama and supported calls being made for the building of a canal.

By 1851, Maury's work had shortened the passage from New York to San Francisco by forty to forty-four days. The average time for ships *not* using the *Wind and Current Charts* was 187½ days, as compared to only 144½ days for those that did. In 1850 one ship sailed the 24 000 km or 15,000 miles in only ninety-seven days.

Also in 1851, Maury published the first edition – seven more would follow – of a voluminous work entitled *Explanations and Sailing Directions to Accompany the Wind and Current Charts,* which was distributed to the seamen who had helped compile his data.

In 1852 Maury played a major role in persuading the American government to send out the North Pacific Exploring Expedition (see page 146) and provided that expedition with charts and data to assist them.

In 1853 Maury's reputation was further enhanced by his correct prediction of the location to which a ship, disabled in a hurricane, would drift, enabling rescuers to find her.

The amount of money shipowners saved by following Maury's charts continued to mount; marine insurers also benefited, the latter presenting Maury with a handsome silver service and a check for $5,000 in 1853.

In 1854 Maury made another oceanographic "first"; he published a contour map of the North Atlantic

from Yucatan to the Cape Verde islands, using, as was his style, soundings from many ships. Though necessarily generalized, with data being available for only 200 points, and with contours only every 1,000 fathoms, it was the first contour bathymetric map to be drawn of an entire ocean basin. Not surprisingly, the map immediately attracted the attention of telegraph companies planning to lay cable across the Atlantic Ocean.

Utilizing the work on his *Wind and Current Charts,* in 1855 Maury published his *Physical Geography of the Sea,* a pioneering attempt to formulate a general theory of the circulation of the atmosphere. Although not accepted by many scientists, the book was immensely popular. It went

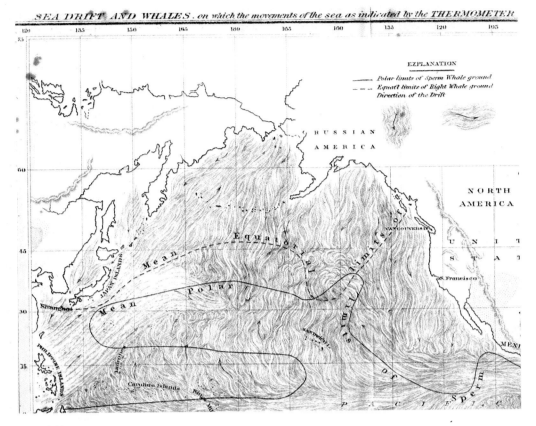

Map 211.
North Pacific Ocean part of Maury's map of *Sea Drift and Whales* from his
Physical Geography of the Sea, published in 1855.

Map 212 (below).
North Pacific part of Maury's map of *Winds and Routes,* also from his 1855
book. As published, these maps were world maps, with much condensed information from his larger charts, which were issued in sections.

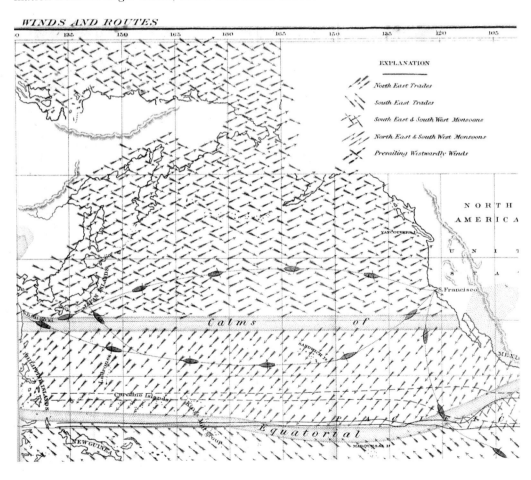

through eight editions at the time, and has been reprinted since.

Set out in the point-by-point deterministic format so common in the nineteenth century, Maury's text nevertheless provided an immense amount of information about the world's oceans for the first time. About the Pacific Maury wrote:

The currents of the Pacific are broad and sluggish, those of the Atlantic swift and contracted . . . [The Pacific] is a very much wider sea [than the Atlantic] and its Gulf Stream not so warm, nor so sharp, nor so rapid; therefore the broad Pacific does not, on the whole, present the elements of atmospherical disturbance in that compactness which is so striking in the narrow North Atlantic.

Under a heading "Average Depth of the North Pacific" he calculated, from tsunamis from an earthquake in Japan in 1854, the depth of the ocean over which the waves had traveled, concluding that

the average depth of the North Pacific between Japan and California, is, by the path of the San Francisco wave, 2149 fathoms, by the San Diego, 2034 (say 2½ miles).

Long after Maury's death in 1873, U. S. navigational charts bore the inscription

Founded upon the researches made in the early part of the nineteenth century by Matthew Fontaine Maury.

It was a fitting and long-lasting epitaph for a true oceanographic pioneer.

Becher's Navigation of the Pacific Ocean

Alexander Becher was a British Royal Navy captain working in the Admiralty Hydrographic Office. In 1860 he published a book entitled *Navigation of the Pacific Ocean with an Account of the Winds, Weather, and Currents Found Therein Throughout the Year*. Its purpose was stated in rhyme:

*That seamen may with steam or sail
Know where to meet the favoring gale;
May take instruction from the skies,
And find the path where swiftness lies.*

The book was clearly popular with Pacific navigators, going through several editions into the 1880s.

Essentially a generalized sailing directions manual, Becher's book compiled much of the known information into one easy-to-access source for practical use.

But there were still parts of the Pacific with insufficient information. "The Frigid Zone of the North Pacific Ocean has been little visited and the remarks consequently are few," wrote Becher. "Northward of 60° N the breadth of the ocean diminishes rapidly and it terminates in a basin of small extent. It is only during the fine season that these latitudes have been explored."

The striking thing about Becher's book to modern eyes is that although it is the essential authority of the late nineteenth century, much of the text is anecdotal, describing one captain or another's experiences in one place or another. It was not until Matthew Maury began the process of continuous surveying of the ocean (see page 152) that information began to be more comprehensive and based on much more available data.

Becher's book included a table of the "comparative mean rates of the currents in twenty-four hours":

North Equatorial Current	30 miles
Counter Equatorial Current	15 miles
Monsoon Current of the Carolines	3 miles
Japan Current	31 miles
Cold Current of the American and Californian Coast	16 miles
Kamtschatka Current	8 miles
Behring Current	14 miles

Map 213.
The general map of winds and currents in the Pacific Ocean, from Becher's book. There are a number of fictitious islands shown on this map.

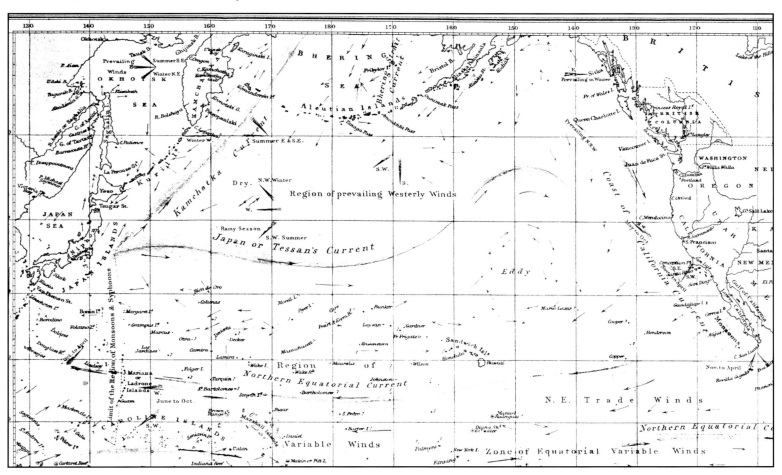

British Admiralty Hydrographic Surveying

British Admiralty charts have been used the world over for 175 years, and not just by British seamen; they have a deserved reputation for accuracy. These charts have been for sale to the merchant fleets of the world since 1823.

Some of the early charts were made by Frederick Beechey, who in his ship *Blossom* in 1825–28 completed a voyage of 117,000 km or 73,000 miles, principally in the Pacific Ocean, on his way to wait for the Franklin and Parry Arctic expeditions, which were expected to find their way to the coast north of Bering Strait. Beechey made surveys of most places he visited, including Avatcha Bay (Petropavlovsk Harbor) in Kamchatka, shown on the facing page.

In 1829, perhaps the most famous British hydrographer took over as Hydrographer of the Navy. He was Francis Beaufort, inventor of the Beaufort wind scale, and he oversaw the surveying efforts until 1855.

During his tenure, surveys were made all over the world, and there was a considerable increase in the number of charts available.

In the Pacific, Richard Collinson was surveying off the coast of China, and later, during a war with China that resulted in the British acquisition of Hong Kong, Collinson and fellow hydrographic surveyor Henry Kellett were able to pilot a British naval squadron 320 km or 200 miles up the uncharted Yangtze-Kiang River.

After this war, the ports of China, reluctantly opened to trade, were surveyed for the British Admiralty by William Bate.

Under Beaufort, there was increased precision in reproducing survey information. Every chart was scrutinized and checked by him before final printing and publication, improving the reliability of the charts.

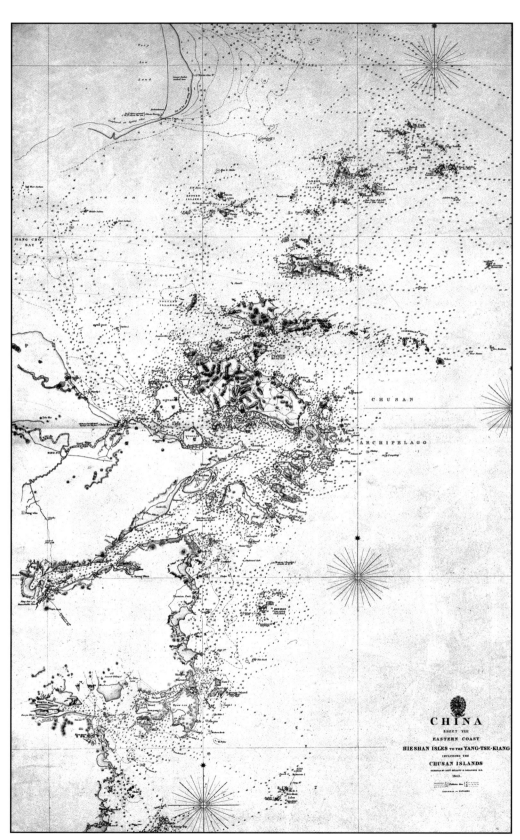

Map 214. The 1843 Admiralty Chart produced from the surveys of Captains Henry Kellett and Richard Collinson on the coast of China, including the mouth of the Yangtze-Kiang River (at top). The chart demonstrates with its incredible detail the amount of work that went into surveying an intricate coast such as this. The incongruity of names such as "Nimrod Sound" that the British bestowed on far-flung capes and bays did not seem to occur to them; they were British, and the British navy ruled the world!

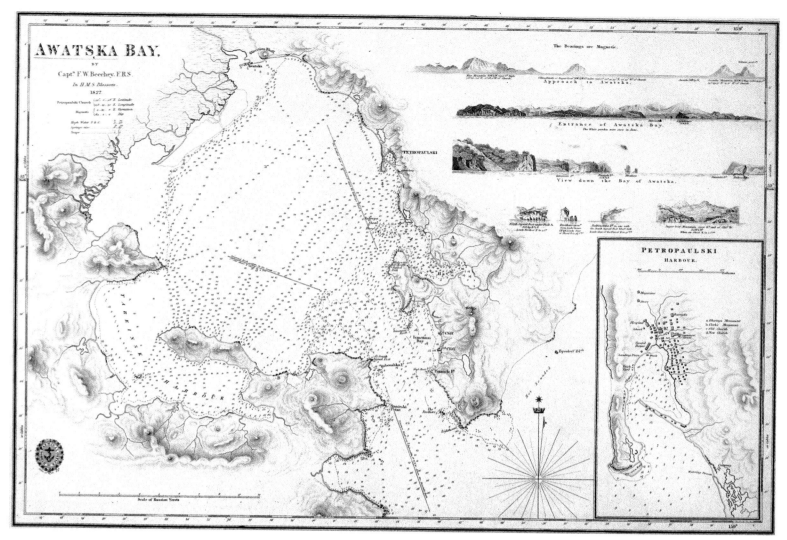

Map 215.
Early British Hydrographic Office chart, made by Frederick Beechey in 1827. This is Avatcha Bay ("Awatska Bay") or Avachinskaya Guba, the harbor of Petropavlovsk, in Kamchatka. Compare it with others made earlier by Vitus Bering (of the inner harbor only, page 69), Edward Riou in 1779 (page 99), and Vasillii Lovtsov in 1782 (page 101).

Map 216.
A map of the Point Roberts area of the Strait of Georgia, surveyed for a British Admiralty Chart in 1858 by Captain George Henry Richards. It is interesting to note that this British survey was being carried out at the same time as the American survey for the map on page162 (Map 218), which is slightly east of the area surveyed here. This is perhaps not surprising, since both countries were surveying their new mutual boundary at this time.

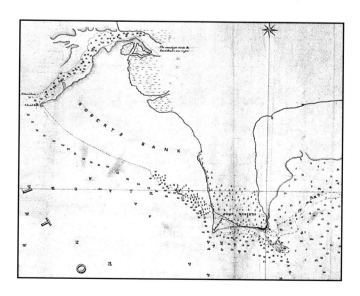

Coastal Surveys of the United States

The United States Coast Survey was created in 1807 primarily to assist in the navigation of the nation's merchant shipping.

In 1878 the organization's name was changed to the United States Coast and Geodetic Survey, responsible to this day for the production of navigational charts.

The United States just having acquired a west coast, Alexander Bache, the Coast Survey's first superintendent, initiated surveys of the Pacific coast in 1848 and 1849. William McArthur and George Davidson were responsible for beginning a proper triangulation of the coast. A chart of Point Pinos harbor was completed in 1851 and one of the rest of Monterey Bay in the following year. In 1851 the first map of the entire coast, at least from Monterey to the Columbia River, was produced. Part of this map is shown in Map 219, overleaf.

In 1853 accurate fixing of positions at close intervals along the coast was completed from San Diego to the Columbia, and surveys of all the main harbors were begun, this being of critical importance due to the relative dearth of proper harbors on the west coast. Lieutenants James Alden and George Davidson were responsible for much of this work.

In 1853 and 1854, enough surveying had been carried out to enable the production of a larger-scale reconnaissance map of the entire coast, issued in three sheets complete with coastal views. Half of one of the sheets is shown here (Map 217, above).

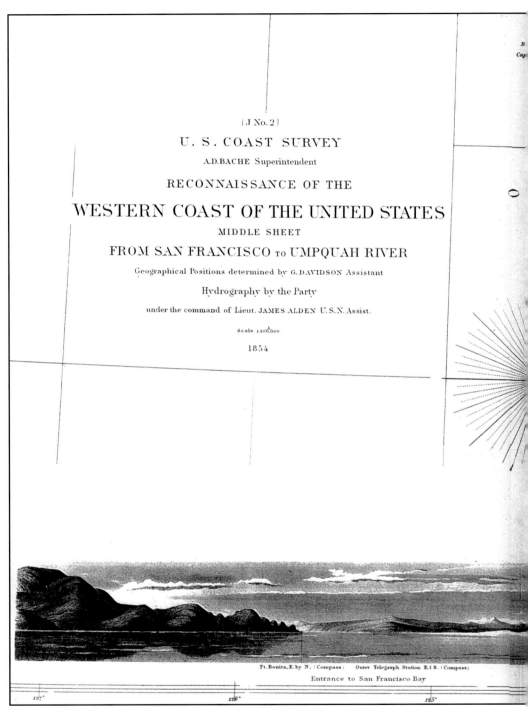

Permanent self-registering tide gauges were installed in 1854 at three places on the coast – Astoria, at the mouth of the Columbia; San Francisco; and San Diego. These revealed the large diurnal inequality in the tides characteristic of the west coast of North America.

Map 217.
A sheet of the *Reconnaissance of the Western Coast of the United States,* published in 1854, showing the coast from San Francisco to the Umquah River in southern Oregon. Complete with twelve engraved views, designed to aid mariners in recognizing where they were, the map was surveyed by James Alden. The bottom half only is shown here. Below, at right, is Cape Arago, from the same map.

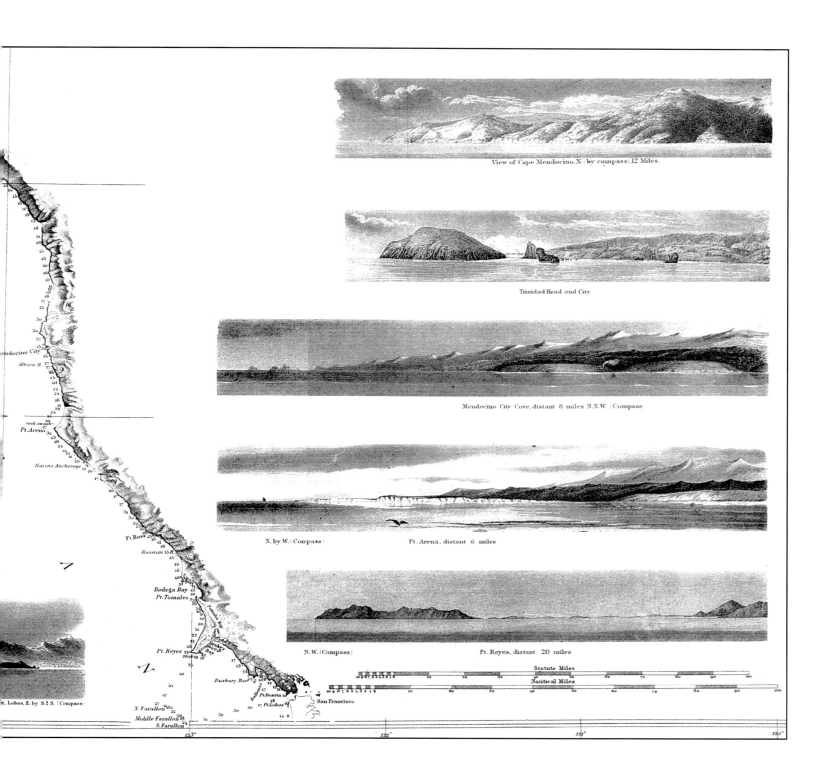

View of Cape Mendocino, N. (by compass) 12 Miles.

Trinidad Head and City

Mendocino City Cove, distant 8 miles N.N.W. (Compass)

N. by W. (Compass)   Pt. Arena, distant 6 miles

N.W. (Compass)   Pt. Reyes, distant 20 miles

Statute Miles

Nautical Miles

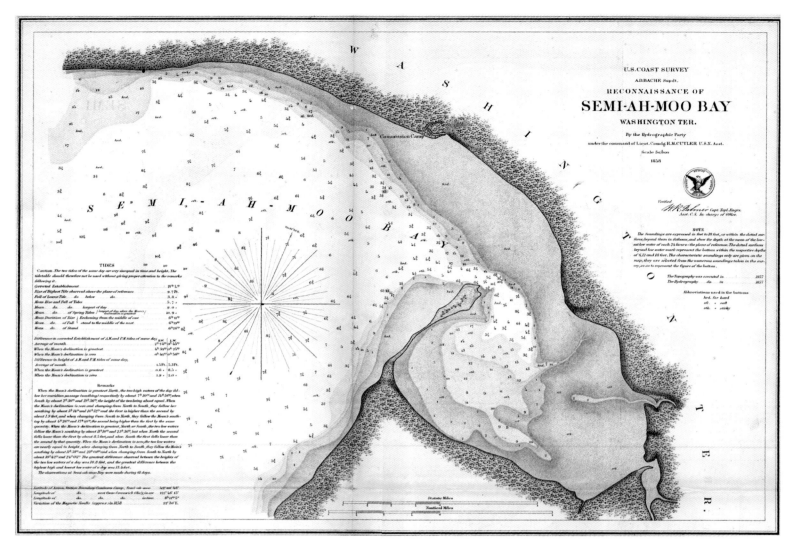

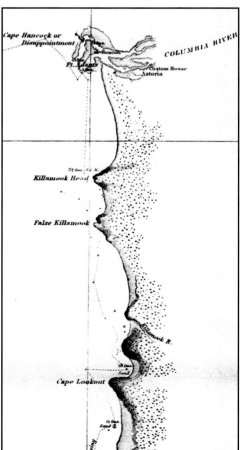

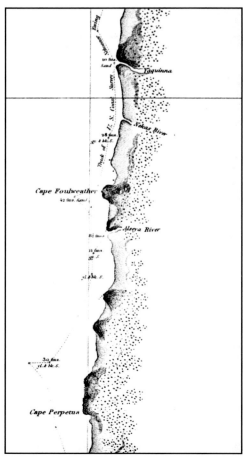

Map 218.
Surveying of harbors that could be used by shipping was a particular concern of the Coast Survey. This is a U.S. Coast Survey map of Semi-ah-moo Bay, Washington Territory, 1858, today's Drayton Harbor, Blaine, Washington State. The surveyed area actually crosses the 49th parallel, where the boundary between American and British territory had been drawn in 1846. You would never know it looking at this map, however. The "Commission Camp" is that of the Boundary Commission, which began surveying the boundary in 1858. Naturally, there is much more detail in the water area, with many detailed soundings.

Map 219.
These sections of an early U.S. Coast Survey map were produced by W. P. McArthur and W. A. Bartlett in 1851, as part of a three-sheet summary or reconnaissance map of the west coast of the United States from Monterey to the Columbia River. Shown here in two sections is the Columbia River to Cape Perpetua, on the Oregon coast.

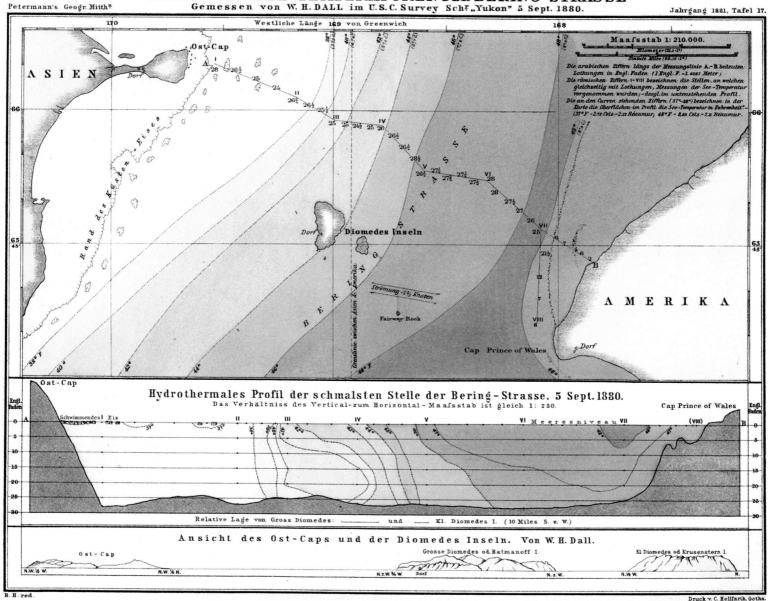

Map 220.

This map is a German edition of a hydrographic survey carried out by William Dall of the United States Coast Survey in the schooner *Yukon* in September 1880. It shows a depth profile across Bering Strait at its narrowest point, between East Cape and Cape Prince of Wales, and water temperatures with depth. The warmest and most ice-free channel is that nearest to the American shore. Lower water temperatures towards Siberia are manifested on the surface by pack ice.

Map 221.

Cortez Bank On the Western Coast of the United States By the Hydrographic Party under the command of Lieut. James Alden Assistant U.S.C.S. 1853. This is part of a U.S. Coast Survey map of 1853, showing the sounding and charting of Cortez Bank, about 200 km or 125 miles off the coast of southern California. This bank was in the path of steamers from Panama northwards. The shallowest water on the bank was 9 fathoms.

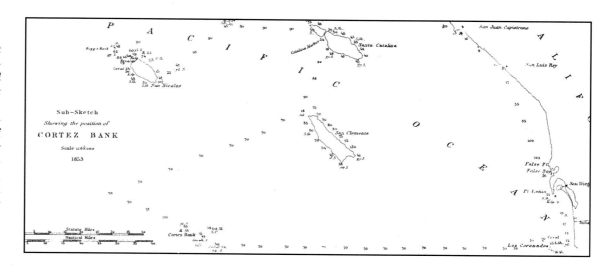

Tuscarora Discovers the Deeps

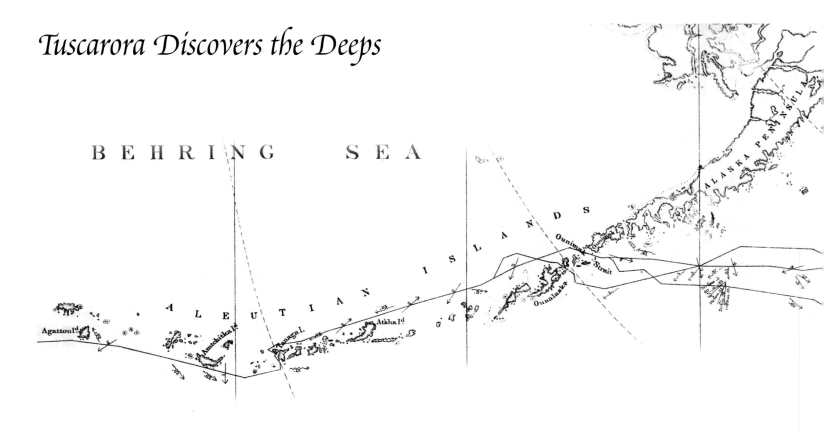

The success of a new submarine tele-graph cable across the Atlantic in 1866 spurred the idea that a similar cable could be laid across the Pacific. The U.S. Congress passed a special resolution allowing the use of naval vessels for survey work.

In 1873 George Belknap was given command of the U.S. steamer *Tuscarora* with instructions to survey a route from America to the Far East.

New sounding equipment was installed, and in particular a sound-ing machine that used piano wire rather than much more springy and bulky hemp rope. The use of piano wire had been incorporated into a sounding machine the year before by a British scientist, William Thomson. After a series of shake-down trials in 1873, Belknap began the survey in January 1874, which was to cover a north and south Great Circle route to Japan, a plan later abandoned as impractical due to water depths.

One hundred and thirty-five soundings later, they arrived in Yokohama. On 8 June they began the return survey, but after eighteen soundings they found the water too deep, having determined that it was over 4,600 fathoms (8 400 km or 27,600 ft) deep. This was not going

THE BROOKE-SAND'S SOUNDING APPARATUS AS FIRST MODIFIED BY COMDR. BELKNAP.

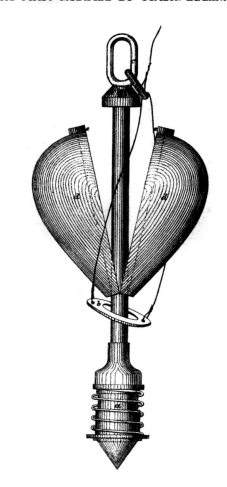

to be a possible route for any subma-rine cable. They had discovered the Japan Trench, one of the great ocean deeps.

In an attempt to avoid this trench, Belknap decided to try his luck on a more northerly route fol-lowing islands, where he thought there was less likelihood of encoun-tering such tremendous depths. Ac-cordingly, a survey was begun from Hakodate on 30 June via the Kurils to the Aleutians, Tanaga Island in the Andreanof Group, then to Unalaska, and thence to Cape Flattery. But in the process Belknap, trying hard to avoid ocean deeps, discovered yet another, the Aleutian Trench.

Belknap recorded that they had to run a line of soundings to the northwards and to the southwards of the first line of soundings "to ascer-tain how a deep hole of 3,359 fath-oms [6 150 m or 20,150 feet] might be avoided"; this was the Aleutian Trench.

(left and far right)
Sounding equipment used aboard *Tuscarora*.

(right)
Commander Belknap provided this rather daunting list of the equipment carried by *Tuscarora*.

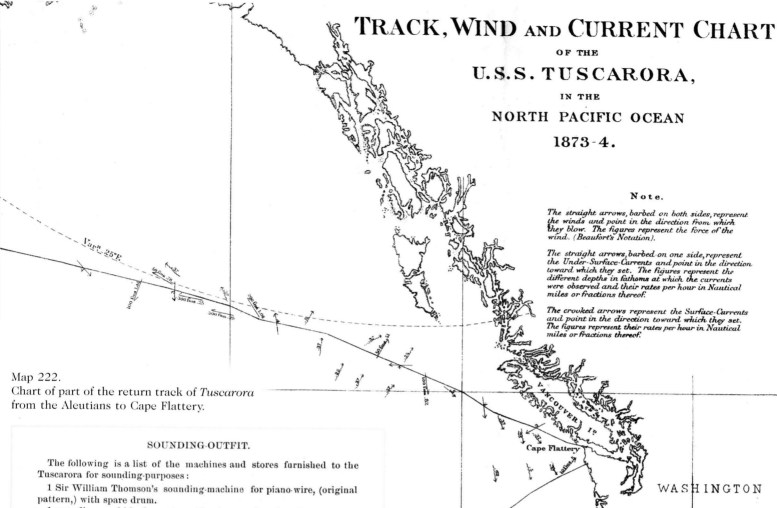

TRACK, WIND AND CURRENT CHART

OF THE

U.S.S. TUSCARORA,

IN THE

NORTH PACIFIC OCEAN

1873-4.

Map 222.
Chart of part of the return track of *Tuscarora*
from the Aleutians to Cape Flattery.

Note.

The straight arrows, barbed on both sides, represent the winds and point in the direction from which they blow. The figures represent the force of the wind. (Beaufort's Notation).

The straight arrows, barbed on one side, represent the Under-Surface-Currents and point in the direction toward which they set. The figures represent the different depths in fathoms at which the currents were observed and their rates per hour in Nautical miles or fractions thereof.

The crooked arrows represent the Surface-Currents and point in the direction toward which they set. The figures represent their rates per hour in Nautical miles or fractions thereof.

WASHINGTON

SOUNDING-OUTFIT.

The following is a list of the machines and stores furnished to the Tuscarora for sounding-purposes :

1 Sir William Thomson's sounding-machine for piano-wire, (original pattern,) with spare drum.

1 sounding-machine for rope, with steam-reel, and a dynamometer designed by Passed Assistant Engineer T. W. Rae, (originally fitted for the Juniata.)

10 Brooke's sounding-rods.

6 Brooke's sounding-rods, (long.)

15 Brooke's modified attachment and sinkers.

210 slings for Brooke's sounding-apparatus.

11 Sands' cups for sounding-purposes.

1 spare spring for sounding-purposes.

6 Fitzgerald's sounding-apparatus.

8 sounding-cylinders.

100 copper sleeves for sounding-rods.

1 Massey's registering-apparatus.

1 Trowbridge's registering-apparatus.

600 bored shot, VIII-inch, for sinkers.

50 bored shot, 32-pounder, for sinkers.

25 bored shot, XV-inch, for sinkers.

Square sinkers, 18 to 30 pounds, for the Fitzgerald apparatus.

Split sinkers, from 20 to 300 pounds.

1 200-pound sounding-lead.

2 150-pound sounding-lead.

2 100-pound sounding-lead.

6 90-pound sounding-lead.

1 80-pound sounding-lead.

1 50-pound sounding-lead.

180 pounds piano-wire, Birmingham gauge No. 22.

950 pounds Albacore line, (¾-inch untarred hemp, 9 thread.)

2,270 pounds 1¼-inch Manilla whale-line.

1,700 pounds 2½-inch Manilla carbolized line.

3,750 pounds 1¼-inch carbolized line.

2,800 pounds 1½-inch carbolized line.

1,575 pounds 1¾-inch carbolized line.

665 pounds 1¼-inch lead-line.

590 pounds 1½-inch lead-line.

9 dozen cod-line.

1 Burt's buoy and nipper.

3 accumulators.

3 iron dredge-frames.

22 swivels.

1 galvanized-iron tub.

12 Miller-Cassella thermometers.

BURT'S SOUNDING NIPPER.

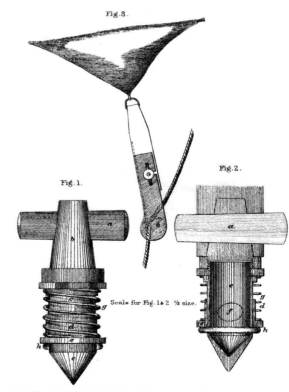

Fig.3.

Fig.1.

Fig.2.

Scale for Fig. 1 & 2 ⅓ size.

SAND'S SPECIMEN BOX FOR DEEP SEA SOUNDINGS.

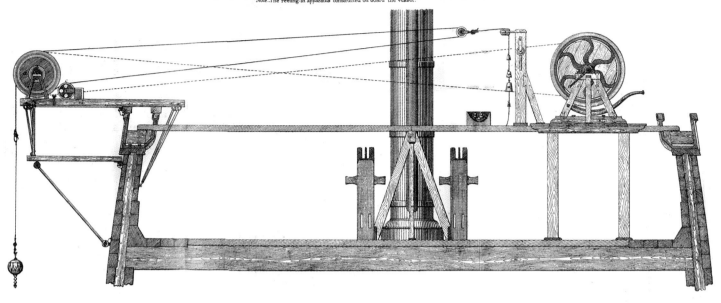

SIDE ELEVATION
OF THE
FLYING BRIDGE OF THE U.S.S. TUSCARORA.
Showing its position and the arrangement for reeling in, using Sir Wm Thomson's machine and piano wire
Note.-The reeling-in apparatus constructed on board the vessel.

Tuscarora was the first ship to use piano wire for sounding. This is the machine invented in 1872 by William Thomson and installed aboard the ship.

The voyage of *Tuscarora* was immensely fruitful; surveyors carried out nearly 500 soundings, to depths not before possible, which they were able to do because of the Thomson piano wire machine. As the direct result of this application of new technology, not one but two major submarine features of the Pacific Ocean were discovered. Bottom specimens of considerable zoological interest were also collected, and records obtained of water temperatures both at the surface and at immense depth.

(right)
This straightforward though hardly simple table records the discovery of the Japan Trench. It shows data recorded aboard *Tuscarora* on 17 June 1874, off the east coast of Japan. A depth of 4,356 fathoms (7 940 m or 26,136 feet) is recorded, using the piano wire machine. It took an hour and a half to reel the wire back in. The real discovery of the trench took place a few days before, on 11 June, when a depth of 4,643 fathoms (8 500 m or 27,850 feet) was reached without hitting bottom. Belknap's journal recorded: "Wire broke. Bottom not reached."

Journal of deep-sea soundings, North Pacific Ocean, by United States steamship Tuscarora,
Commander George E. Belknap, commanding;
Yokohama, Japan, to Cape Flattery,
via Aleutian Islands.

CAST No. 28.—JUNE 17, 1874.

Number	28.	Latitude, 42° 57' N., obs.	
Hour	9 h. 50 m. 54 s., a. m.	Longitude, 148° 23' E., chro.	
Wind	Variable.	Barometer, 30.18; ther. att'd, 55°.8.	
Force	0.5 to 1.	Temperatures: Air, 54°.6, D. B.; 55° W. B. Sea-surface, 49° 5.	
Weather	b c f clouds, cirrus. Prop. clear, 8.	Under-surface 700 fms., 34°—0°.49=33°.51. (18143.)	
Sea	Smooth.	Depth, 4,356 fms.	
Line	Piano-wire. No. 22.	Bottom, yellowish mud with sand and specks of lava.	
Sinker	8-inch shot and 19 lbs. lead weight on casting.	Surface-current, 3 fms.: N. E. Under-current: 10 fms., 3 fms. NE. by N.	
Weight	74 lbs.	20 fms., ¾ fms. N. W. 30 fms., 1 fm. W. 50 fms., 1½ fms. W.	
Machine	Sir William Thomson's.	100 fms., 2 fms. W. by S. 200 fms., 6 fms. SW. by S.	
App. for spec.	Belknap cylinder, No. 1.	Value of sounding, undoubtedly good.	

Current shown by observation during past 24 hours, N. 45° E., 3 fms. per hour.

Fathoms or revolutions.	Time. Hour.	Time. Min.	Time. Sec.	A. m. or p. m.	Interval. Min.	Interval. Sec.	2d Diff. Min.	2d Diff. Sec.	Time hauling in. Hour.	Time hauling in. Min.	Time hauling in. Sec.	Remarks.
	9	50	54	a. m.								Fine calm weather; engines moved occasionally; Lieutenant F. M. Symonds went out in whale-boat to try under-surface currents.
100	9	52	02	a. m.	1	08				1	12	
200	9	52	53	a. m.		51		17		1	08	
300	9	53	43	a. m.		50	1			2	02	Before beginning this cast, wound 706 fathoms more of wire on the reel. Reel so much strained by these deep casts that the wire will have to be wound upon a new one.
400	9	54	33	a. m.		50				1	23	
500	9	55	25	a. m.		52	2			1	29	
600	9	56	19	a. m.		54	2			1	26	
700	9	57	14	a. m.		55	1			1	29	At end of cast kept on course under fore and aft sail, foresail, and steam; wind very light.
800	9	58	10	a. m.		56	1			1	28	
900	9	59	07	a. m.		57	1			1	52	
1000	10	00	08	a. m.	1	01	4			1	59	SERIAL TEMPERATURES.
1100	10	1	11	a. m.	1	03	2			1	59	Surface, 49°.5.
1200	10	2	16	a. m.	1	05	2			1	48	10 fms., 42°.7—0°.00=42°.7. No. 18145.
1300	10	3	22	a. m.	1	06	1			1	54	15 fms., 36°.5—0°.01=36°.49. No. 18145.
1400	10	4	29	a. m.	1	07	1			2	02	25 fms., 33°.6—0°.02=33°.58. No. 18145.
1500	10	5	36	a. m.	1	07				2	07	50 fms., 32°.7—0°.03=32°.67. No. 18143.
1600	10	6	47	a. m.	1	11	4			2	19	100 fms., 33°.4—0°.07=33°.33. No. 18143.
1700	10	7	57	a. m.	1	10	1			2	20	300 fms., 33°.8—0°.21=33°.59. No. 18145.
1800	10	9	10	a. m.	1	13	3			2	00	500 fms., 34°.5—0°.35=34°.15. No. 18145.
1900	10	10	23	a. m.	1	13				2	04	700 fms., 34° —0°.49=33°.51. No. 18143.
2000	10	11	37	a. m.	1	14	1			2	08	
2100	10	12	53	a. m.	1	16	2			2	10	Weights on pulley. Dyn. ind.
2200	10	14	10	a. m.	1	17	1			2	18	125 lbs .... 48 lbs.
2300	10	15	28	a. m.	1	18	1			2	19	90 lbs ...... 44 lbs .... 50 fms.
2400	10	16	47	a. m.	1	19	1			2	11	65 lbs ...... 36 lbs .... 70 fms.
2500	10	18	07	a. m.	1	20	1			2	37	50 lbs ...... 30 lbs .... 90 fms.
2600	10	19	24	a. m.	1	17	3			2	43	25 lbs ...... 18 lbs .... 170 fms.
2700	10	20	43	a. m.	1	19	2			2	27	40 lbs ...... 18 lbs .... 970 fms.
2800	10	22	00	a. m.	1	17				2	15	90 lbs ...... 35 lbs ....3,390 fms.
2900	10	23	23	a. m.	1	23	6			2	14	112 lbs ...... 40 lbs ....3,600 fms.
3000	10	24	45	a. m.	1	22	1			2	51	150 lbs ...... 47 lbs ....3,985 fms.
3100	10	26	09	a. m.	1	24	2			2	49	Number of revolutions, 4,071.
3200	10	27	33	a. m.	1	24				2	47	
3300	10	29	01	a. m.	1	28	4			2	41	Number of measured fathoms 4,331
3400	10	30	43	a. m.	1	42	14			2	40	Stray line 25
3500	10	32	25	a. m.	1	42				2	56	Depth 4,356
3600	10	34	05	a. m.	1	40	2			2	54	
3700	10	35	55	a. m.	1	50	10			2	31	
3800	10	37	48	a. m.	1	53	3			2	50	
3900	10	39	46	a. m.	1	58	5			2	59	
4000	10	41	51	a. m.	2	05	7			2	51	
4071	10	43	30	a. m.	1	39				2	02	
Time going out		52	36	Com'g in	1	30	10					
Finished									12	17	51	p. m.
Total time of cast									2	26	57	

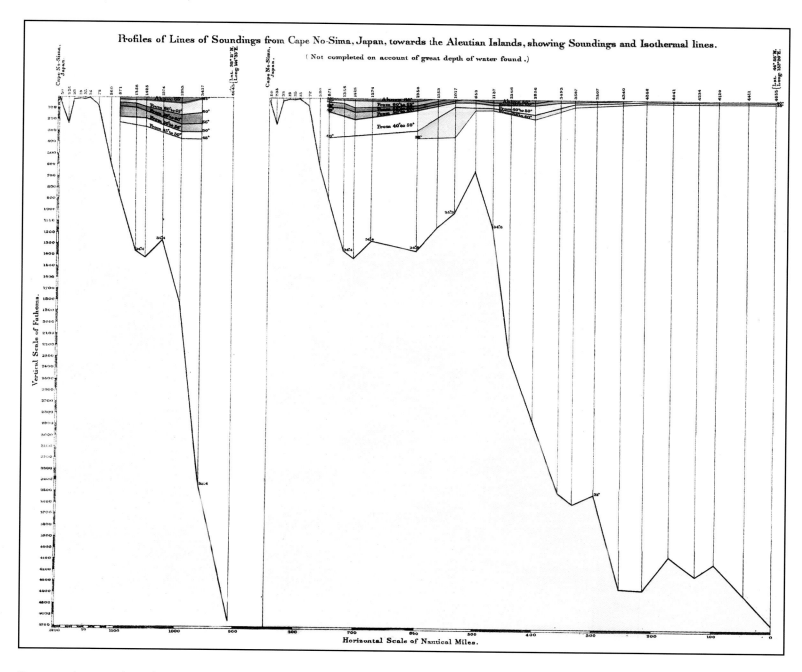

Profiles of Lines of Soundings from Cape No-Sima, Japan, towards the Aleutian Islands, showing Soundings and Isothermal lines.

(Not completed on account of great depth of water found .)

Horizontal Scale of Nautical Miles.

Tuscarora's survey lines from Japan towards the northeast had to be discontinued due to the inability to deal with the immense depths encountered. Above are two of the depth profiles, and at right (Map 223) is part of the track map with the tracks to which the profiles refer. Another part of this map is shown on the previous pages (164–65).

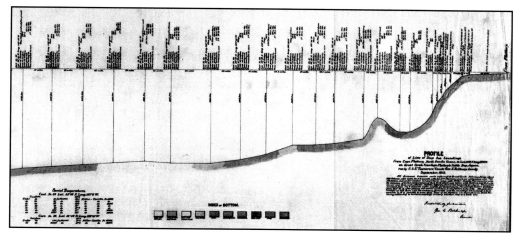

Part of the soundings profile approaching Cape Flattery.

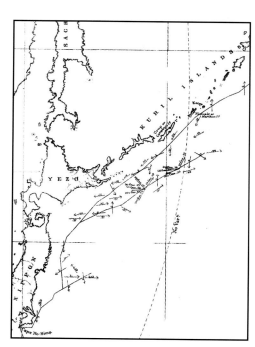

Exploring the Depths – The Challenger Expedition

Until the late 1850s, the common belief, which seemed eminently sensible, was that the "black abyss" of the deep sea below the reach of fishing nets could not possibly contain any life. What could be expected to live in such cold and completely dark conditions?

This concept changed dramatically in the 1860s, such that by the end of that decade the bottom of the ocean promised to become a cornucopia for the naturalist. An extensive sheet of living slime named *Bathybius* was thought to cover the seabed, forming the base of a food chain, a hypothesis that was to be disproved by *Challenger* while in the Pacific. It is therefore not surprising that in the 1860s oceanographic expeditions were proposed to explore these apparently newly alive deeps. By far the most famous and the most significant was that of *Challenger*.

The round-the-world voyage of the specially converted British ship HMS *Challenger* in 1873–76 is considered by many scientists to have inaugurated modern scientific research in the oceans. The Royal Society in Britain persuaded their government to outfit *Challenger* as a floating scientific laboratory.

After the voyage the scientific results were published in an enormous forty-volume report that was not completed until 1895.

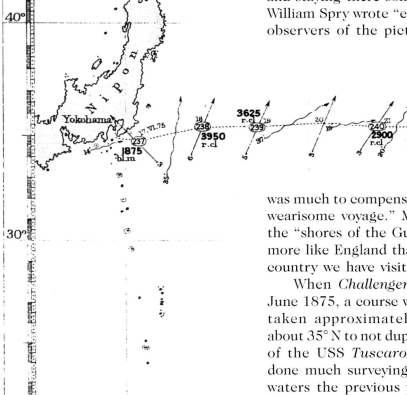

On 23 March 1875 at 11° 24′ N, 143° 16′ E, *Challenger* sounded the greatest depth ever before reached. This was the Mariana Trench, and the sounding was of 4,475 fathoms (8 190 m or 26,850 feet). Joseph Matkin, a young ship's steward, recorded the event in his diary.

The 23d was a great day on board, at 6 am we sounded at the enormous depth of 4,600 fms, but as there was a doubt about it, the line was hauled up again. It was sent down again more heavily weighted, & 2 patent Thermometers were attached. The depth was decided to be 4,550 fms (5 1/6 miles) – the greatest reliable depth ever obtained. One of the Therm'trs burst owing to the tremendous pressure on it.

Challenger entered the North Pacific in April 1875, arriving in Japan and staying there some two months. William Spry wrote "even to ordinary observers of the picturesque there was much to compensate for the long wearisome voyage." Matkin thought the "shores of the Gulf of Yedo look more like England than those of any country we have visited."

When *Challenger* left Japan in June 1875, a course was deliberately taken approximately due east at about 35° N to not duplicate the track of the USS *Tuscarora*, which had done much surveying work in these waters the previous year (see page 164). *Tuscarora* had found extraordinary depths; *Challenger* found even greater depths in the Mariana Trench, and almost as great depths in the Japan Trench.

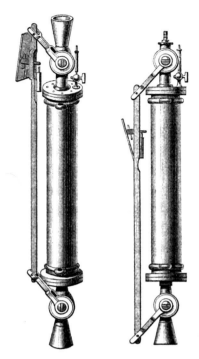

Water samplers used by *Challenger*. The top and bottom on the tube were open while being lowered (left), but as soon as the sampler was pulled up, both ends closed (right) and trapped a sample of water from that depth.

Map 224 (across page, below). Track of *Challenger* from Japan to Hawaii. Numbers in circles are sounding station numbers, bold number are depths in fathoms, and letters under the depth indicate bottom type (r. cl. is red clay; bl. m. is blue mud). Straight arrows are wind direction, with force according to the Beaufort scale; squiggly lines are surface current directions, with the number being rate in miles per 24 hours.

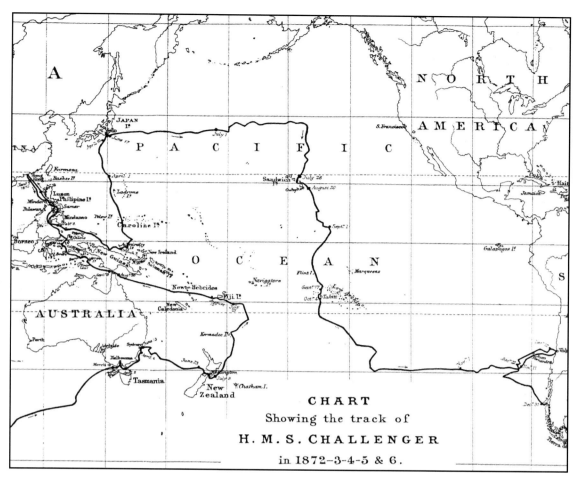

Map 225 (above). The track of *Challenger* in the Pacific Ocean.

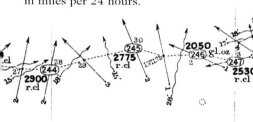

The day after leaving Japan, one of the sailors on board died, and on 18 July was buried at sea. Matkin noted that

directly after the funeral we took soundings at the enormous depth of 3,900 fathoms [7 140 m or 23,400 feet], 4½ miles, the second deepest sounding we have ever obtained.

The straight eastward track across the North Pacific after leaving the Japan Trench was relatively uneventful, even monotonous. Spry wrote that

very little of interest occurred from day to day, and the results of the trawling and additions to the natural history collection were very scanty.

They had crossed 180°; Matkin observed:

Last week with us contained 8 days, & we had two Sundays as the Admiralty allow us no pay for that day.

Generous lot, the British navy!

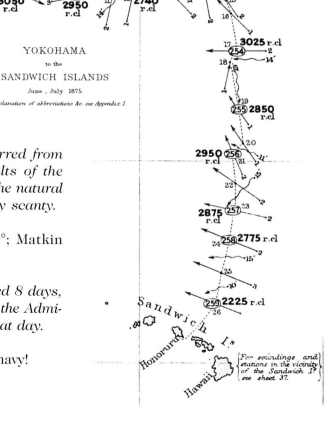

The observations and soundings made by *Challenger*, in conjunction with those made by *Tuscarora*, showed the Pacific to be different from other oceans. It was deeper, and much of the seabed was found to be covered with a characteristic deep-sea clay. Contained in this clay were larger mineral particles including quartz, mica, and pumice. This led John Murray to believe that its source was volcanic. Also present in large quantities were manganese nodules, precipitated around a nucleus of detritus.

By the time *Challenger* returned to Britain in May 1876, the ship had traveled 110 000 km or 69,000 miles, at an average speed, it has been pointed out, of little better than walking pace. She brought home an enormous scientific booty: 13,000 kinds of animals and plants, 1,441 water samples, and hundreds of sea bottom samples.

An animal called *Monocaulus imperator* retrieved from depth by *Challenger* in the North Pacific. In the report is the following:

Among the results of the Challenger dredgings must . . . be specifically recorded the discovery of a gigantic Tubularian, which was dredged in the North Pacific from depths of 1875 to 2900 fathoms. It is referable to the genus Monocaulus . . . One of the specimens whose dimensions were noted . . . was found to measure 9 inches from tip to tip of extended tentacles . . . while its stem rose from its point of attachment to a height of 7 feet 4 inches. This great Tubularian affords indeed an example of a Hydroid attaining dimensions far exceeding the maximum which would have been hitherto thought possible in Hydroid life – a character to which the vast depth whence it was obtained gives additional significance.

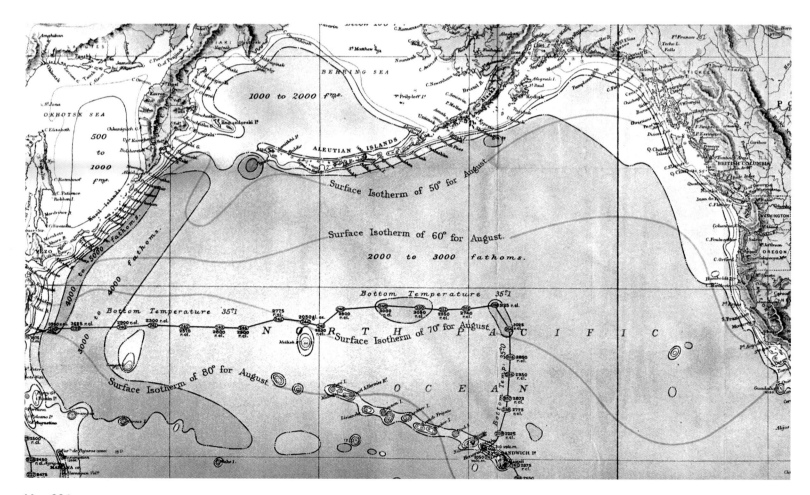

Map 226.

Map of the North Pacific Ocean showing information collected by *Challenger* augmented by that collected by others. It shows surface water temperatures (in °F) for August, bottom temperatures, and an elementary mapping of seabed depths, good enough to show the Japan Trench discovered by *Challenger*'s pioneering oceanographers.

William Spry wrote in his book about the expedition, published on its return in 1876:

When the deep sea dredge appears above the surface, there is usually great excitment amongst the "Philos", who are ever on the alert with forceps, bottles and jars, to secure the unwary creatures who may by chance have found their way into the net . . . We have no lack of wonderful things.

The method used for sounding is clear from the wonderful engraving of a deck scene on board *Challenger*, which was included in the expedition's report, and the diagram below.

Challenger's boat, complete with steam engine.

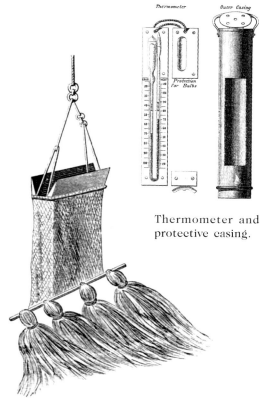

Thermometer and protective casing.

A deep-sea dredge. The brushes below the net were intended to sweep the seabed and bring up small animal life into the net.

East-west bottom profile obtained by *Challenger* from Japan, following the eastward track shown in Map 224 on pages 168–69. It shows the vast depth of the Japan Trench discovered by the expedition.

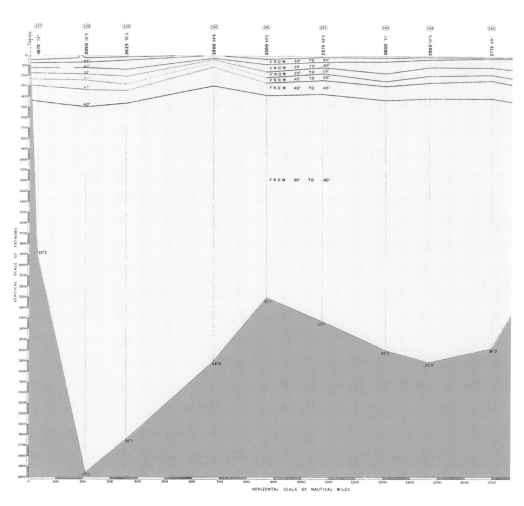

PACIFIC OCEAN

Longitudinal Temperature Section . Japan to a position in Lat. 35°49′N . Long. 180°

For explanation of symbols see Appendix 1.

171

The Maps of Sir John Murray

The historian will, in all probability, point to the oceanographical discoveries during the last forty years as the most important addition to the natural knowledge of our planet since the great geographical voyages . . . of Columbus, Da Gama, and Magellan.

— Sir John Murray, presidential address to the Geographical Section of the British Association, September 1899

John Murray, a geologist, was one of the scientists on *Challenger*. He and Alphonse Renard wrote the volume of the *Challenger Report* on marine deposits. But, not satisfied with data from *Challenger* alone, Murray embarked on a long-term project to gather, in Maury-like style, all available data from any ship.

Both scientific and telegraph-company ships sent him their samples. With each was information as to the location and depth from which it came, and Murray used this data to construct topographical maps of the world's oceans.

Maps of the Pacific, Atlantic, and Indian Oceans were published in 1886, based on about 6,000 soundings. The map shown below is part of a world map, not much revised, published in 1899.

Maps 228 and 229 (facing page).
John Murray also produced other maps based on data from the *Challenger* expedition and other data he collected later. At right are shown two maps of the Pacific he published in 1899. The top one shows the distribution of minimum surface water temperatures and the bottom one shows maximum surface water temperatures.

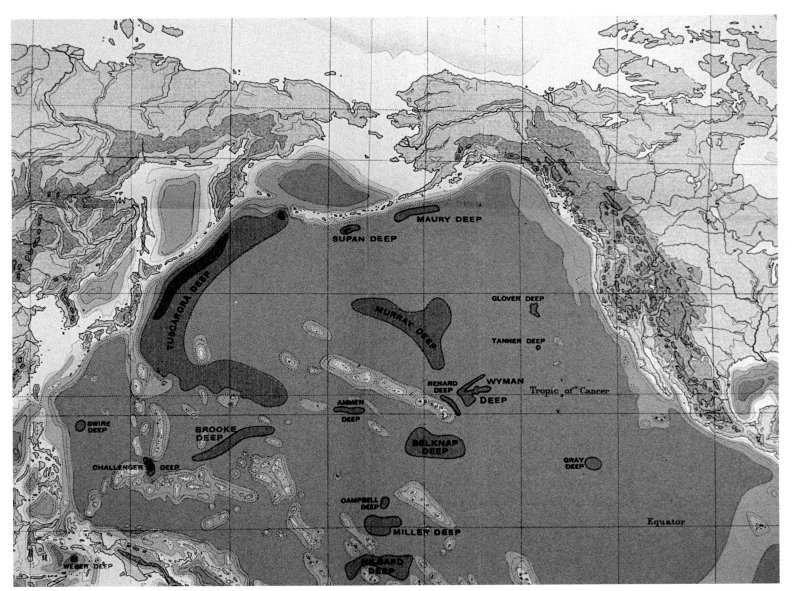

Map 227.
The 1899 edition of Murray's map, the first bathymetric map of the North Pacific that tried to be comprehensive in its scope. The recently discovered Aleutian and Japan Trenches are shown, but for all its apparent authority this map was very generalized, being based on remarkably few actual soundings considering the vast expanse of ocean covered.

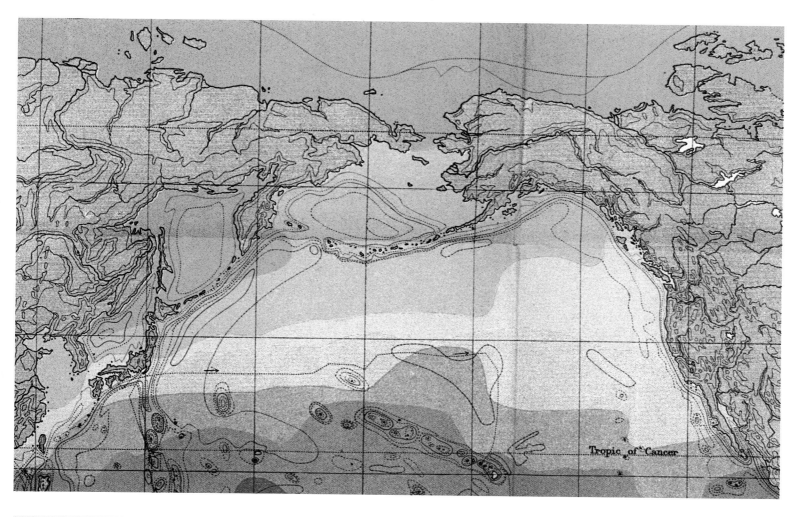

Tropic of Cancer

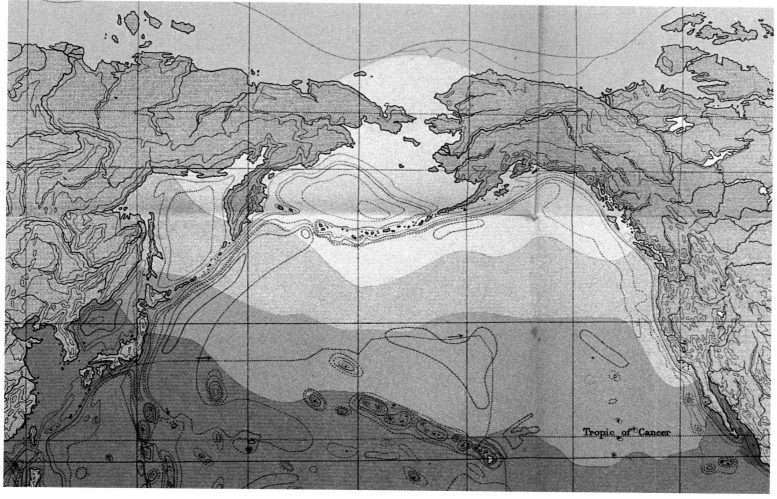

Tropic of Cancer

The Voyage of the Nero

Following the pioneering deep-sea surveying work of the *Tuscarora*, several other surveys were made to establish the best routes for trans-Pacific telegraph cables.

In 1899, the U.S. Navy fitted out a steam collier named *Nero* as a deep-sea surveying ship. The ship was to survey a route for a submarine telegraph cable between the United States, the Philippines, and Japan.

The route from the west coast of America to Hawaii was considered known by this time, so *Nero* began its survey from Honolulu.

The ship sailed to Midway, Guam, and the Philippines; back to Guam, then to Yokohama, Japan; back to Guam; then to Midway and back to Honolulu. Thus every part of the pos-sible route was surveyed twice. Over these routes, soundings were taken, on average, every ten miles.

The return route in each case was planned to cross the primary route zigzag at 45° angles with soundings taken at the change in di-rection; in this manner an examina-tion was made of a belt of ocean about 22 km or 14 miles wide and over 9 650 km or 6,000 miles in length. This detailed a survey had never before been attempted on any ocean.

About 50 km or 30 miles to the west and south of Midway a "very bold peak" was discovered, rising abruptly from the sea floor at 2,000 fathoms (3 650 m or 12,000 feet) to only 82 fathoms (150 m or 500 feet).

Nearing Guam, four soundings below 5,000 fathoms were made, one at 5,269 fathoms (9 650 m or 31,600 feet), the deepest ocean discovered at that time. This was a trench now known as the "Nero Deep," and its discovery is what the voyage of the *Nero* is most remembered for. The re-port of the voyage noted that this depth was "only 66 feet less than 6 statute miles."

An extract from the sounding log for the *Nero* on 17 September 1899, shown below, gives some idea of the level of detail and the work involved in making deep-sea soundings. The crew of *Nero* made a total of 2,074 soundings across the Pacific. Equipment was often lost, and in particular, the notation "thermometer failed to work" appears frequently. Given the huge changing pres-sures to which these relatively sensitive intruments were subjected, this is hardly surprising.

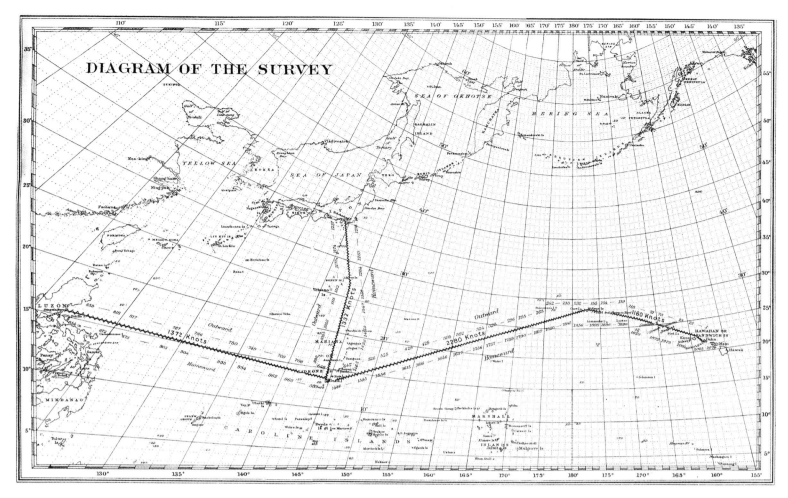

Map 230.

Map showing the track and the zigzag return track of the *Nero*.

Pacific

° 16·36 N Long. 141° 41'·15 E

.... Conradi U. S. N. _____, commanding.

.... hours .... minutes _____ Date, *Sept. 21*ˢᵗ 1899.

Abbreviated Cloud Definitions.

1. **CIRRUS (CI.)** — Isolated, feathery clouds, of fine fibrous texture; "Mares' tails."
2. **CIRRO-STRATUS (CI.-S.)** — Fine whitish veil, giving a whitish appearance to the sky; often produces halos; "Cirrus Haze."
3. **CIRRO-CUMULUS (CI.-CU.)** — Small, fleecy white balls and wisps, without shades, arranged in groups, and often in lines; "Mackerel Sky."
4. **ALTO-CUMULUS (A.-CU.)** — Larger white or grayish balls, with shaded portions, in flocks or rows, often so close that edges meet.
5. **ALTO-STRATUS (A.-S.)** — Thick veil of gray or bluish color, brilliant near sun or moon. May produce coronæ.
6. **STRATO-CUMULUS (S.-CU.)** — A succession of rolls of dark clouds which frequently cover the whole sky. The characteristic cloud of storm areas, especially of the fore part of those areas.
7. **NIMBUS (N.)** — Rain cloud. A thick layer of dark clouds, without shape, from which continuous rain is falling. Cirro-Stratus or Alto-Stratus is seen through the breaks. Low-flying fragments are known as "scud."
8. **CUMULUS (CU.)** — Thick clouds whose summits are domes with protuberances, but whose bases are flat. "Woolpack" clouds.
9. **CUMULO-NIMBUS (CU.-N.)** — Thunder-shower clouds. Mountainous clouds surrounded at top by veil or false cirrus, and below by nimbus-like masses of cloud.
10. **STRATUS (S.)** — Horizontal sheet of lifted fog.

The scale for recording amount of cloud varies from 0, clear blue sky, to 10, overcast.
For detailed information as to cloud forms and nomenclature, see Hydrographic Office Publication No. 112.

Symbols for State of Sea.

B—Broken or irregular sea.
C—Chopping, short or cross sea.
G—Ground swell.
H—Heavy sea.
L—Long rolling sea.
M—Moderate sea or swell.
R—Rough sea.
S—Smooth sea.
T—Tide-rips.

Abbreviations of Bottoms.

M. for Mud.	bk. for black.	hrd. for hard.	
S. " Sand.	wh. " white.	sft. " soft.	
G. " Gravel.	yl. " yellow.	fne. " fine.	
Sh. " Shells.	gr. " grey.	crs. " coarse.	
P. " Pebbles.	bu. " blue.	brk. " broken.	
Sp. " Specks.	dk. " dark.	stk. " sticky.	
C. " Clay.	gn. " green.	rky. " rocky.	
St. " Stones.	br. " brown.		
R. " Rock.	rd. " red.		
Co. " Coral.			

NOTE.—The principal materials and their qualities are represented by larger letters than the subsidiary.

+ Signifies Sunk Rock.   * Rock awash at Low-water.

Weather Symbols.

b—Clear blue sky.
c—Cloudy weather.
d—Drizzling or light rain.
f—Fog or foggy weather.
g—Gloomy or dark, stormy looking weather.
h—Hail.
l—Lightning.
m—Misty weather.
o—Overcast.
p—Passing showers of rain.
q—Squally weather.
r—Rainy weather or continuous rain.
s—Snow, snowy weather, or snow falling.
t—Thunder.
u—Ugly appearances or threatening weather.
v—Visibility of distant objects.
w—Wet or heavy dew.
z—Hazy.

To indicate greater intensity, underline the letter thus; r, heavy rain; r, very heavy rain, etc.

State of the Sea by Symbols.	Time of stopping to Sound.		Time of starting ahead after Sounding.		Time occupied in making distance from last Sounding.		COURSES.			DISTANCES.			Initials of Officer of the Deck.	REMARKS. Mention change of time, accidents, losses, failures of gear or apparatus to work satisfactorily, giving probable causes; give reasons for unusual delays; mention generally matters of importance or interest connected with the work.
							Compass Course from last Sounding.	Correction.	True Course from last Sounding.	Reading of Patent Log.	Distance from last Record of P. L.	Corrected Interval.		
	H.	M.	H.	M.	H.	M.								
m	1	06·2	1	04	1	12	N. J. E.	¼ W.	N. 7¼ E.	82.8	9.5	8.9	J.P.Mᶜᵈ	last good, wind tending N.
m	2	26·2	3	18	0	22	"	"	"	84.8	2.	2.	J.P.Mᶜᵈ	" up & down.
m	4	29·0	5	21	1	11	"	"	"	94.1	9.3	8.9	J.J.R.	"
m	5	58·0	6	13	0	14	"	"	"	96	1.9	2.	J.J.R.	" nearly
S.	7	20·	7	53	1	07	"	"	"	2.1	6.1	8.9	S.H.R.	" Log fouled by piece of wash, distu...
S.	8	18·1	4	35	0	20	"	"	"	4.	1.9	2.	J.H.R.	good wind tending slowly to E.
L.	10	63·0	10	35	1	08	"	"	"	13.6	9.6	8.9	J.H.R.	" up & down
L.	10	53·0	11	20	0	18	"	"	"	15.4	1.8	2.	J.H.R.	" nearly
L.	0	28·	1	05	1	08	"	"	"	24.9	9.5	9.25	M.J.	"
C.	1	20·	1	59	0	15	"	"	"	26.8	1.9	2.	M.J.	"

Whaling and Sealing in the North Pacific

WHALE FISHING

Although natives had hunted whales for centuries, whales were first commercially hunted in the North Pacific in 1835. It was the return to New England of Captain Barzillai Folger in his ship *Granges* loaded with whale oil and whalebone that first publicized the commerical possibilities of whale hunting in the region. After 1845, whaleships moved into the Bering Sea also, and soon up to 250 vessels each season were following the receding ice favored by the bowhead whale as a feeding ground. In 1848 the first whaler, now tracking rapidly diminishing whale stocks, entered the Arctic Ocean.

In the 1840s and 1850s, New England whale hunters killed bowhead whales by the thousands, outraging the Russians in the process. The hunt peaked in 1852, when 278 whaling ships were in the North Pacific, but by the 1860s the decline in whale numbers was such that fewer and

fewer ships found it economic to make the long voyage to the whaling grounds. A further spur to the decline of the whale hunt came from the new petroleum industry in the 1880s.

When whales were hard to find, the whalers often turned to the walrus, hunted both for its oil and its tusks. It has been estimated that 200,000 walruses were killed in the twenty years between 1860 and 1880. Out of the water, in particular, the walrus was no match for a rifle-toting gunman.

Russians had hunted the sea cow to extinction, and there had been no outcry over the decimation of the

whale and walrus stocks, but when the hunters turned to the fur seal, massive and complicated international controversies resulted. It is fair to say, however, that international difficulties developed as much for political and territorial reasons as for a concern for the seal herds, which were a convenient and nobler excuse for complaints.

Canadian intrusion into fur seal hunting led in short order to diplomatic incidents, as American naval vessels attempted to maintain their new sovereignty over Alaskan waters after the purchase of Alaska from the Russians in 1867.

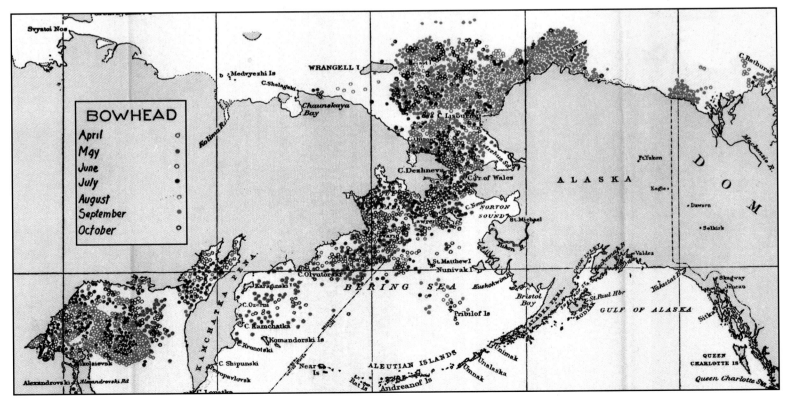

Map 231.
Distribution of bowhead whales by month of the year, as compiled from nineteenth-century whaleship logbooks by Charles Haskins, the director of the New York Aquarium, in 1935. The colored circles indicate the whale location and month.

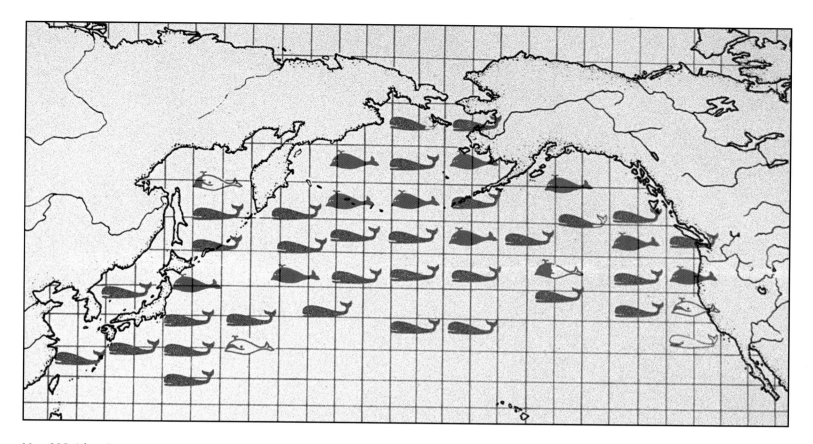

Map 232 (above).
Map of the whale catch in 1970, from the Food and Agriculture Organization of the United Nations, published in 1972. Blue whale symbols are sperm whales, red are baleen whales. Each completely colored symbol represents a catch of 500 whales. It may seem surprising to some today that the whale hunt was still going on as late as this.

(top left)
An engraving from the border decoration of a map entitled *British America,* drawn by John Tallis and published in 1851.

Map 233.
Map from the British counter case (see page 179) showing the places where seals were caught near the (Russian) Commander Islands in the Bering Sea in 1892.

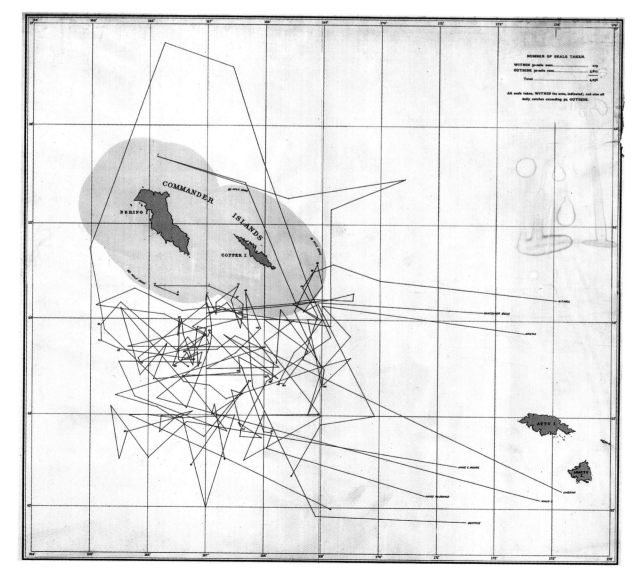

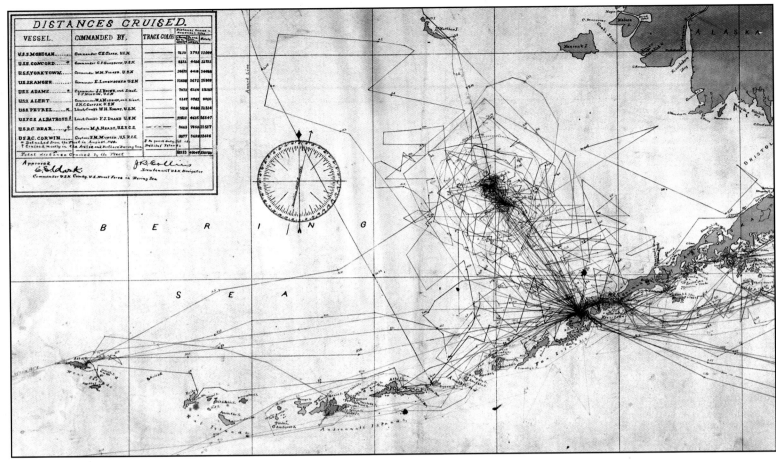

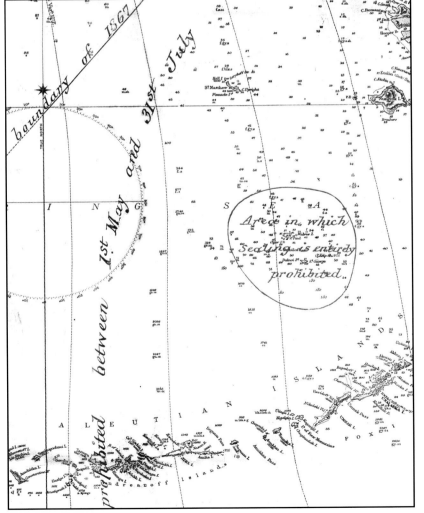

Map 234 (above).
Tracks of American naval vessels in the Bering Sea in 1894. This shows the incredible amount of patrolling that occurred as the U.S. Navy tried to prevent poaching of seals.

Map 235.
Map showing exclusion and restricted zones for sealing proposed in the 1892 arbitration.

In 1870, in order to protect an exclusive lease granted to the Alaska Commercial Company, the American government prohibited the killing of seals within its territory. The problem was in defining American territory. The 1867 treaty with Russia had appeared to give jurisdiction over much of the Bering Sea to the United States, but international law gave only a three-mile exclusion zone. American claims that the Bering Sea was a *mare clausum,* a closed sea surrounded by one country, did not carry much weight now that both Russian and American territory bordered that body of water. Nevertheless, there were significant economic reasons for arguing for total ownership. The British navy became involved, protecting Canadian and thus British interests, and the American navy sailed to protect its government's point of view.

Fur seals breed, now as then, in relatively few places in the Bering

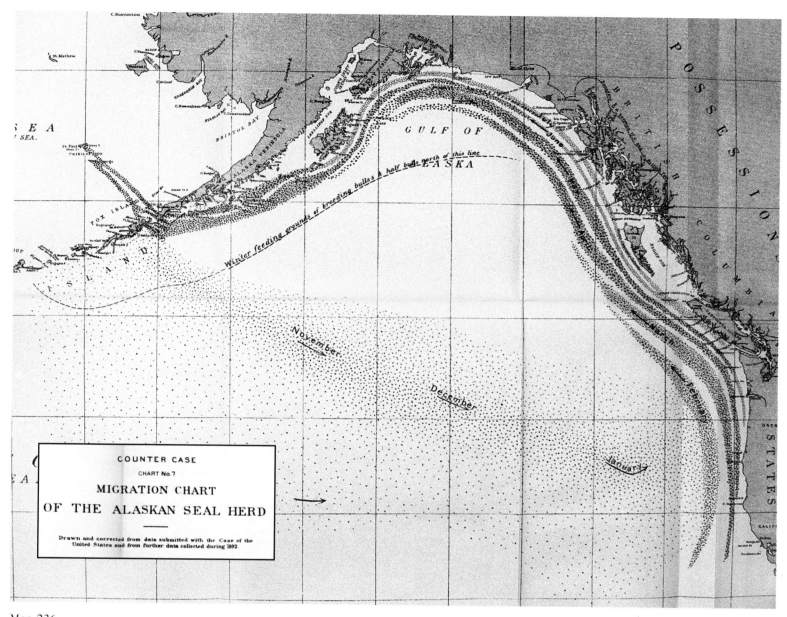

Map 236.
Map of seal migration for the 1893 arbitration, prepared in 1892.

Sea, most notably the Pribilof Islands and the Commander Islands. The Alaska Commercial Company had negotiated exclusive leases and rights to hunt seals on these islands first with the American government and then the Russian. The seals inhabit these islands during May, June, and July, but the rest of the year they migrate long distances southwards.

In 1874, Henry Elliott, who considered himself the premier scientist of the Bering Sea, even if others disagreed, had grossly overestimated the population of fur seals in the Pribilofs, and this was to lead to severe depletions of the rookeries in later years.

From 1879, ships began to engage in what was called pelagic seal-ing, the hunting of these migrating seals while they were at sea, an immensely wasteful hunt in which perhaps only 10 percent of the seals killed were actually recovered. So wasteful was this type of hunting that it rapidly threatened the survival of the Pribilof Islands herds.

In 1886, three Canadian ships were seized and taken to Sitka by a U.S. Revenue cutter, *Corwin*. Britain immediately protested this violation of the freedom of the seas, and the Bering Sea became for the next twenty years a focus of international attention.

The American government's claims of *mare clausum* were thrown out by an international arbitration tribunal in Paris in 1893. During the 1890s huge volumes of words and data were produced to buttress the claims of all sides. Heavy naval involvement, standoffs, and intimidation continued. The 1893 arbitration was ineffective, for by 1910 the Pribilof seal herd, which once numbered four million, was down to only one hundred thousand. Something had to be done, and fast. At the invitation of the United States, representatives of Britain, Russia and Japan met in Washington, D.C., to work out an agreement to save the herd from extinction. The result was the International Fur Seal Convention of 1911. Killing seals at sea was prohibited, and the Pribilof lessee, the Alaska Commercial Company, had to share furs with the Japanese, Canadians, and Russians.

The Prince Maps the Depths

John Murray compiled the first worldwide maps of the ocean floor in 1886 (page 172). In the ensuing years several others were produced, notably one in 1890 by James Dana, who had been Charles Wilkes' geologist, and another by Alexander Supan, in 1899. These were mainly based on the same sounding data.

In an attempt to coordinate bathymetric mapping, the International Geographical Congress in 1899 struck a commission to compile a general map of the world's oceans. Prince Albert of Monaco undertook this project and, perhaps as importantly, agreed also to bear the cost.

Prince Albert was one of the early benefactors of the science of oceanography, combining a personal interest with his own research, and funding all manner of others. He even had his own yacht fitted out for oceanographic work, and later he founded an oceanographic museum in Monaco.

Soundings from all over the world were again compiled, and by 1904 charts had been completed for all oceans, based now on some 18,400 locations. The result was the *Carte Generale Bathymetrique Des Oceans* (GEneral Bathymetric Chart of the Oceans, or GEBCO).

The task of keeping these maps up-to-date was later taken over by the International Hydrographic Bureau, with sixteen countries pooling data.

Four sheets of this map, shown here in part, form the North Pacific portion of the *Carte Generale*. The division of sheets is at 46° N and 180°.

The striking thing about the North Pacific sheets is how little actual information is recorded, as there are still relatively few sounding paths. Generalizations yet hide the unknown.

A new international effort was launched in the 1970s to bring the GEBCO up to modern standards, and

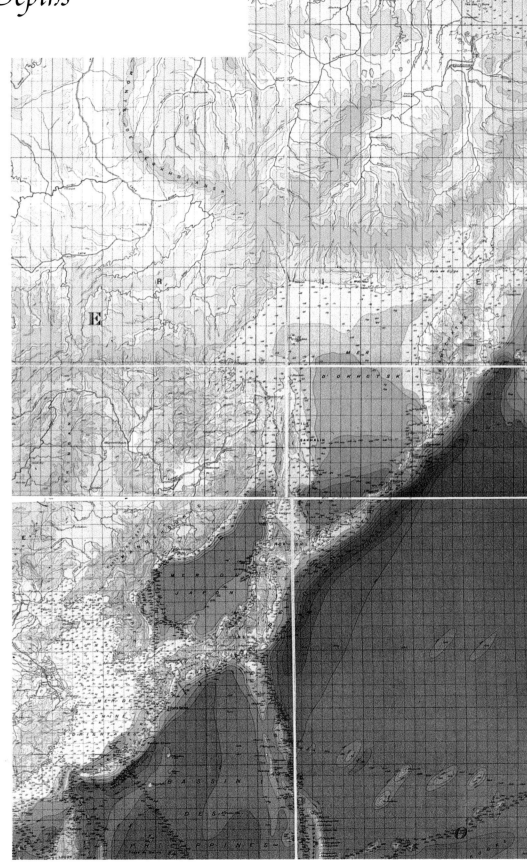

a new map appeared in 1982. Now the map has been digitized, following the release of a digital version of the map in 1994 on CD–ROM, and is much more regularly updated.

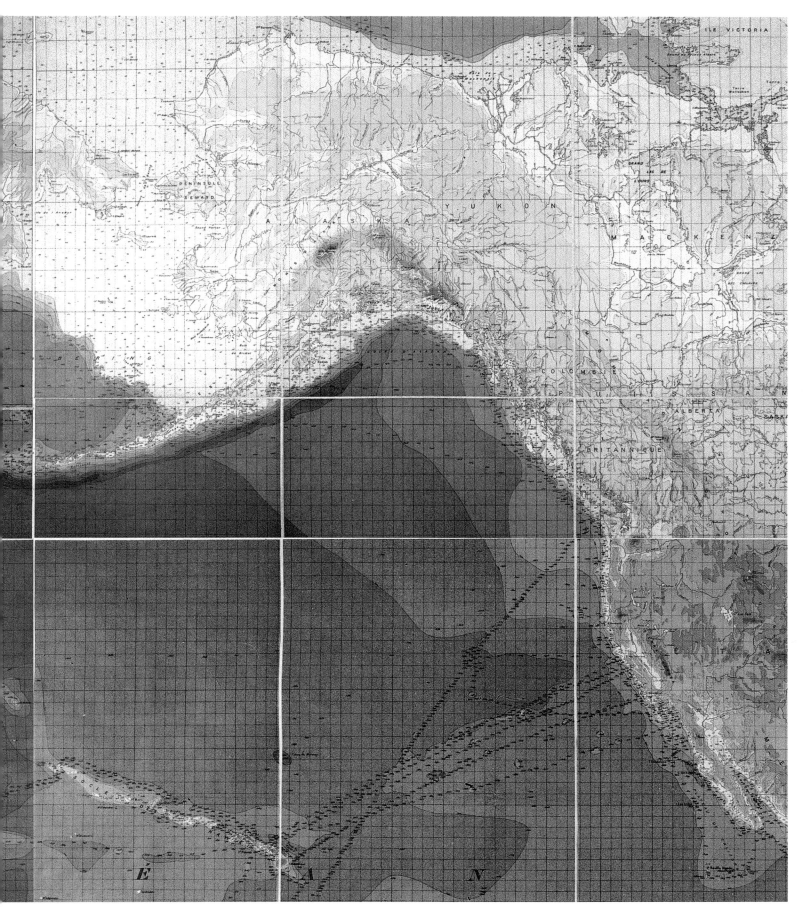

Map 237.
Part of four sheets of the *Carte Generale Bathymetrique Des Oceans*, the GEneral Bathymetric
Chart of the Oceans, or GEBCO. The regime of constant updating meant that sheets were
usually of different dates. Here the northeast (top right) sheet is dated 1 July 1927; the northwest (top left) sheet 1 July 1923; the southeast sheet (bottom right) 1 May 1912; and the
southwest (bottom left) sheet 31 December 1912.

The Coming of Sonar

The electronic sound-generating and echo-recording apparatus today known as sonar (for "SOund Navigation And Ranging") was invented by Canadian-born American physicist and electrical engineer Reginald Fessenden. He is known for his early work in wireless communication. A prolific inventor, he gathered over 500 patents in his lifetime.

One of these patents was for the "fathometer," a device for measuring the depth of water under a ship. It had originally been developed to detect icebergs following the *Titanic* tragedy in 1912. By 1914 Fessenden was able to successfully test his "Iceberg Detector and Echo Depth Sounder," and by 1915 his device had been installed in British submarines and warships.

After the war, the application of Fessenden's invention to oceanography was recognized. A physicist, Harvey Hayes, developed an improved model called the "Hayes Sonic Depth Finder," which used Fessenden's sound-generating oscillator. In June 1922 this was used aboard the U.S. Navy vessel *Stewart* to make the first continuous depth profile across an ocean, the Atlantic, drawn from the 900 soundings made in *eight days* during the crossing. To put this in perspective, *Challenger* in 1873–76 had made a total of less than 300 soundings in *three years*.

Suddenly, the view that the sea floor was flat and featureless changed dramatically. Now any ship equipped with a depth finder could produce contour profiles of the seabed. The first bathymetric charts based on sonic soundings appeared in 1923, after which they were produced regularly as new information was collected and processed.

The first use of the new "Sonic Depth Finder" in the Pacific was made towards the end of 1922, when the naval vessels *Corry* and *Hull* made sonic soundings for a deep-sea contour map off the coast of California.

At the end of 1923, the U.S. Coast and Geodetic Survey ship *Guide* sailed from New England to San Diego, after testing the sonic depth finder in the Atlantic. The results were satisfactory except that some interference with radio broadcasts of the World Series had been reported!

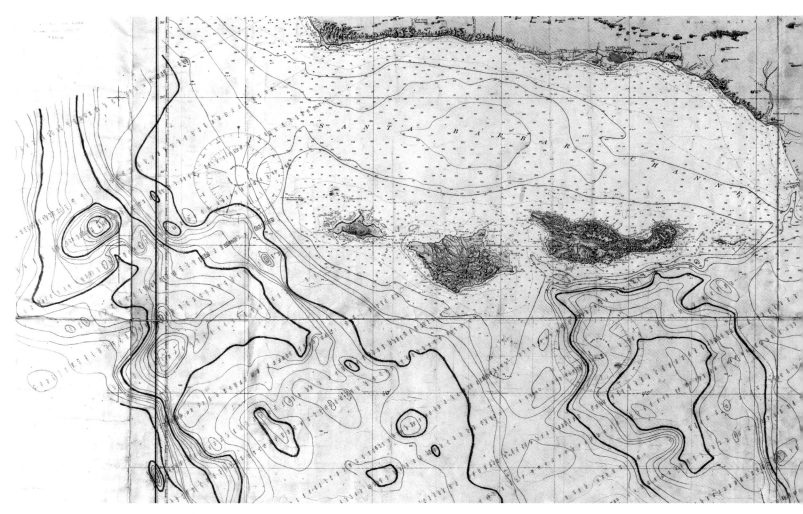

Map 238.
The first sonar map of any part of the Pacific Ocean.

On her voyage, via the Panama Canal, *Guide* compared sonic soundings with conventional wire soundings so that the accuracy of the new equipment could be assessed. It was found that the two types of soundings did not always agree, and it was recognized that variations in water temperature, salinity, and pressure could affect the speed at which sound traveled through water.

Off the Californian coast, further surveys were made while at the same time testing the water for temperature and salinity. Approximate corrections were made, and with further research into the way these factors affected sound transmission, the sonic method soon gained accuracy and, with it, acceptance.

In 1929 the U.S. Naval Hydrographic Office began regularly using this method to make bathymetric maps. Then, suddenly, map accuracy and detail improved dramatically.

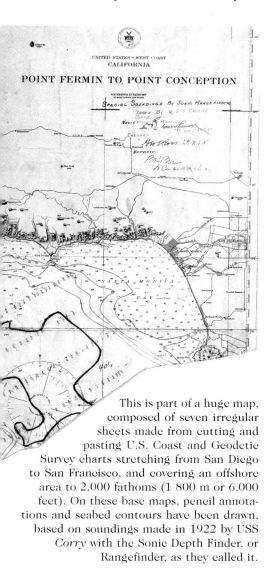

This is part of a huge map, composed of seven irregular sheets made from cutting and pasting U.S. Coast and Geodetic Survey charts stretching from San Diego to San Francisco, and covering an offshore area to 2,000 fathoms (1 800 m or 6,000 feet). On these base maps, pencil annotations and seabed contours have been drawn, based on soundings made in 1922 by USS *Corry* with the Sonic Depth Finder, or Rangefinder, as they called it.

The Last Cruise of Carnegie

Variation of the compass, the difference between geographical north and magnetic north, is influenced by magnetic anomalies all over the Earth's surface. It had therefore long been considered useful to know how the Earth's magnetic field varied from place to place, in order to be able to compensate for compass errors. It was on the oceans that the data was most urgently needed, but there also that it was hardest to collect.

In 1904 the Carnegie Institution set up a Department of Terrestrial Magnetism to study this problem, and in 1909 built *Carnegie*, a specially constructed ship with a bronze engine, and wood and bronze nails. A ship without iron was required or else the very nails of its body could influence a compass and make observation of the magnetic field impossible. The crew even wore non-magnetic belt buckles and ate their meals with aluminum flatware.

Carnegie spent many years traversing the seas and in 1928 was also outfitted to carry out other oceanographic observations; in that year she sailed on a round-the-world cruise.

As part of that voyage she was in the North Pacific in 1929. In May of that year she discovered the Fleming Deep, 8 350 m (27,485 feet) deep, at 24° N, 144° E.

Carnegie – a seagoing non-magnetic observatory.

But the voyage was not to be completed. In November *Carnegie* was at Apia, Samoa, and a spark from an electrical switch thrown after refueling caused an explosion and a fire that killed the captain and destroyed the ship.

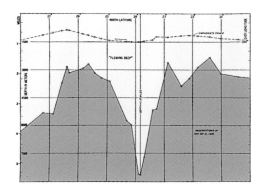

Chart showing the bottom profile and track of the *Carnegie* revealing the discovery of the Fleming Deep, the location of which is marked on the track chart below.

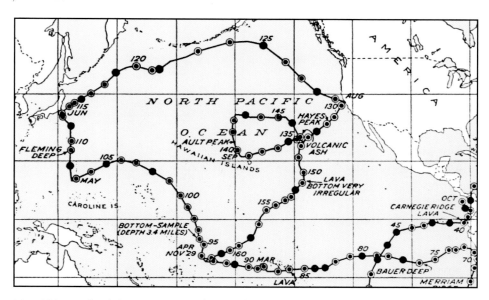

Map 239. Track of the *Carnegie* in the Pacific Ocean.

The Great Cooperative Effort – NORPAC

During the Second World War and in the period thereafter, the number of ships and scientists involved in oceanographic research increased dramatically, and in 1953 it was realized that if all the resources then available were combined at one time, better results might be achieved because a more complete and comprehensive "snapshot" of the state of the ocean might be obtained.

In 1953 Joseph Reid, an oceanographer at Scripps Institution of Oceanography, proposed a cooperative synoptic survey of the North Pacific Ocean be jointly undertaken in the summer of 1954 by ships from Canada and the United States. Although the project did not materialize in 1954, it did the following year, and with the additional resources of oceanographic institutions in Japan.

In total, some nineteen oceanographic research vessels took part. They did not stay in one location, for the belief was, partly correctly, that because of the greater amount of inertia inherent in ocean waters, simultaneity was less important than it would be in the atmosphere. Hence these nineteen ships covered some 1,002 hydrographic stations, or observation points, almost all during the course of three months, July, August, and September 1955. Fourteen oceanographic research institutions took part.

The venture became known as the NORPAC Expeditions. The area covered was the Pacific Ocean between 20° and 60° N.

For each oceanographic station, temperature, salinity, dissolved oxygen (a measure of productivity of the ocean), inorganic phosphate and phosphorus levels, and some other properties were all measured at standard depths, so that all the data would be comparable. In addition, biological data such as quantities and types of phytoplankton (microscopic plants that are the beginning of the food chain) and zooplankton (microscopic

animals) were collected. Some geophysical data was also obtained.

Nearly half of the observations were made during the month of August 1955. The result was a far more comprehensive one-time look at the state of the North Pacific than had ever been achieved – or even attempted – before.

The data collected was published in two special tomes of a publication, published each year, known as *Oceanographic Observations of the Pacific*, which was the way information on oceanographic work was disseminated to other scientists in the days before the Internet. These were the *NORPAC Data* and the *NORPAC Atlas*. The maps shown here illustrate the vastness of the project's size and scope.

The information collected was used in applications ranging from fisheries to the understanding of ocean circulation and climate.

The project was considered so successful that a similar one, dubbed EQUAPAC, explored the equatorial region of the Pacific Ocean the next year.

Nowadays oceanographers can obtain a near-simultaneous comprehensive view of many of the parameters measured by NORPAC using satellites, but at the time the project was the most extensive ever attempted.

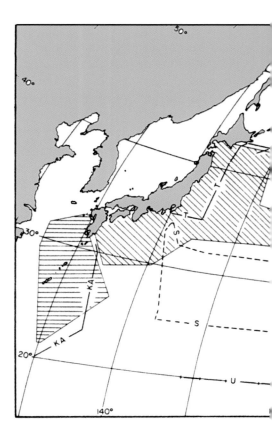

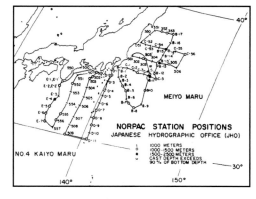

Map 240. Detail of the data collection points of one of the ships involved in NORPAC, *No. 4 Kaito Maru*, from the Japanese Hydrographic Office.

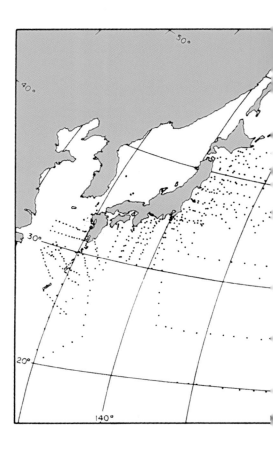

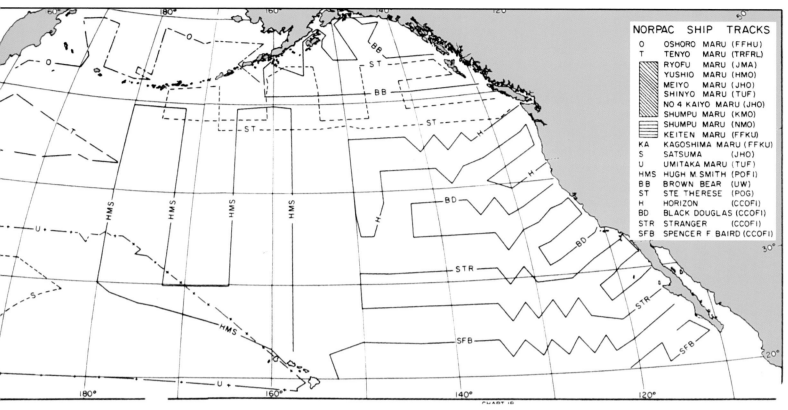

Nineteen ships from fourteen oceanographic institutions in three countries took part in NORPAC. It was the largest and most comprehensive attempt at near-simultaneous ocean data collection ever. The map above (Map 241) shows the actual tracks of the ships involved, and the one below (Map 242) shows the distribution of locations where data was gathered. The result of the rather haphazard-looking set of ship tracks above resulted, as planned, in the systematic distribution of data points below.

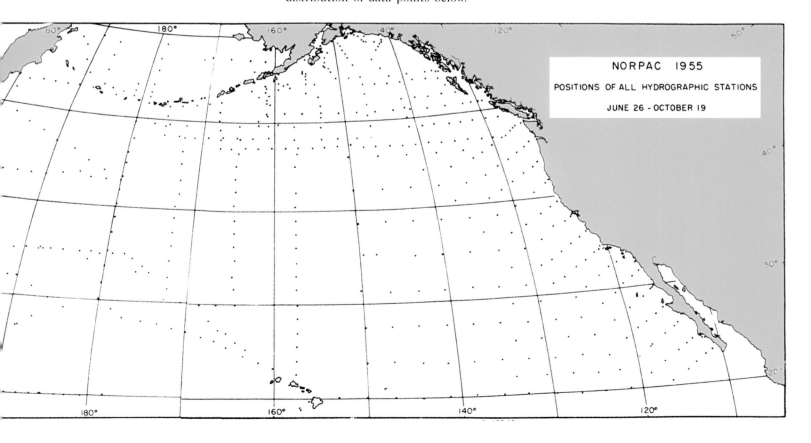

NORPAC 1955

POSITIONS OF ALL HYDROGRAPHIC STATIONS

JUNE 26 - OCTOBER 19

The Voyages of Vityaz

Vityaz has been a name for a succession of Russian oceanographic research vessels since the 1870s. The voyage of Stefan Makarov in the *Vityaz* of 1886–89 advanced knowledge of oceanography and the Pacific considerably.

In the period 1949 to 1955, a new *Vityaz* carried out more detailed surveys than had ever been done before in the northwestern part of the Pacific Ocean, as shown on Map 244 (right). The overwhelming coverage of the Russian ship is shown on the map that compares the tracks of that ship with those of other nations (Map 243, below).

A study of deep-sea fauna showed that life was possible at great depths despite their enormous pressures. A plot was made of the vertical distribution of animals in water 10 km (6 miles) deep.

After 1955 the *Vityaz* embarked on a survey of the whole North Pacific and was responsible for the discovery of a number of new trenches and seamounts. Map 245 (far right) shows some of the undersea features discovered by the ship.

In 1957 a new world record sounding of 10 990 m (36,056 feet) proved that the Mariana Trench was deeper than had previously been thought.

Bottom profile made by *Vityaz* from Tsugaru Strait, between Honshu and Hokkaido, and Adak Island, in the Aleutian chain. The two deeps are shown: the Japan Trench and the Aleutian Trench. Vertical exaggeration is 37x.

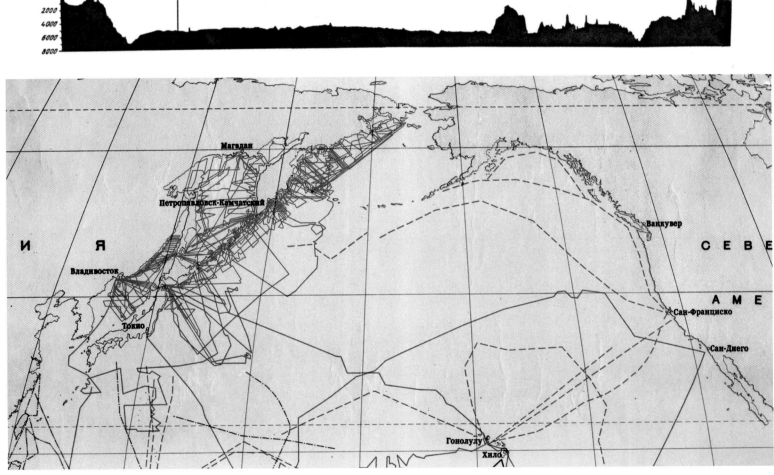

Map 243.
A Russian map dating from about 1960 showing the tracks of oceanographic vessels since *Nero* in 1899. The red lines are the tracks of *Vityaz*. The map shows dramatically, as it was no doubt supposed to, how much more comprehensive the Russian effort was to survey the oceans.

Map 244.
Map of the tracks of *Vityaz* in 1949–55.

Map 245 (right).
Summary map of Russian discoveries by *Vityaz* expeditions in the western Pacific.

Map 246 (below).
A simplified Russian bathymetric map produced as a result of the data collected from the intense activity of *Vityaz* in the northwest Pacific.

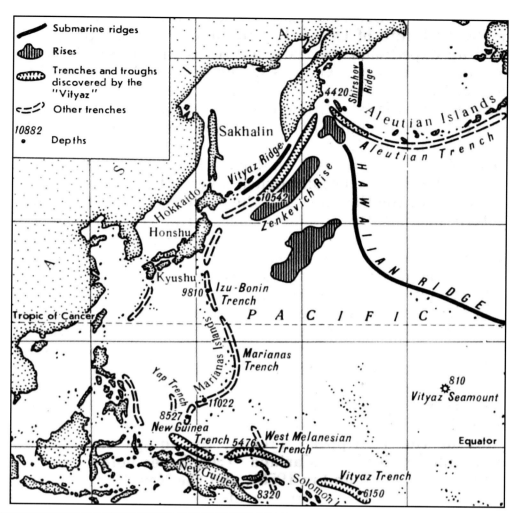

Envisioning the Sea Floor

This wonderfully artistic map is part of a map drawn by American marine geologist Bruce Heezen and his colleague Marie Tharp in 1971, as part of a continuing series of maps they drew of ocean floors.

Starting with the Atlantic Ocean in the early 1950s, Heezen and Tharp drew what they termed, with good reason, "physiographic diagrams" rather than maps, for the reality was that there was a good deal of imagination or at least informed guesswork that went into their construction, so limited was the data from which they were drawn relative to the detail that they show.

In 1953, Marie Tharp was working for Bruce Heezen. Tharp was laboriously plotting profile data from the Atlantic when she noticed a V-shaped notch in the crest of the Mid-Atlantic Ridge, a rift valley just like the one in East Africa. The theory of continental drift was not in vogue in those days, yet here was evidence for it. In addition, Heezen plotted records of earthquake epicenters, and most turned out to lie within Tharp's V-shaped notch.

As a result of this discovery, Heezen and another geologist, Maurice Ewing, made a logical leap. While they did not have detailed enough information as to the shape of the seabed for much of the world beyond the Atlantic, they did have earthquake records.

Thus they proposed that a continuous ridge, with a rift valley at its center, extended around the world, following the pattern of earthquake epicenters. It was the line from which the sea floor was wrenching apart, and generating earthquakes in the process.

In the Pacific it ran up the west coast of the Americas, in the north separating the North American Plate from the Pacific Plate, and across the Aleutians and south through the Kurils and Japan, separating the Pacific Plate from the Eurasian Plate.

Heezen and Tharp produced maps of the three major oceans of the world based on a painstaking plotting of any and all bathymetric data available at the time. But there were still huge holes in the vast expanses to be covered, and so Marie Tharp used her judgment to draw undersea mountains where she was sure they would be; she knew there was a range of mountains in a given location, but not the location of individual ones.

Thus the result they termed a "physiographic diagram" rather than a map, to admit the guesswork involved in some parts of the ocean.

The result was a series of artistically drawn maps that nevertheless gave an excellent impression of submarine topography. But the seabed was "envisioned," not mapped.

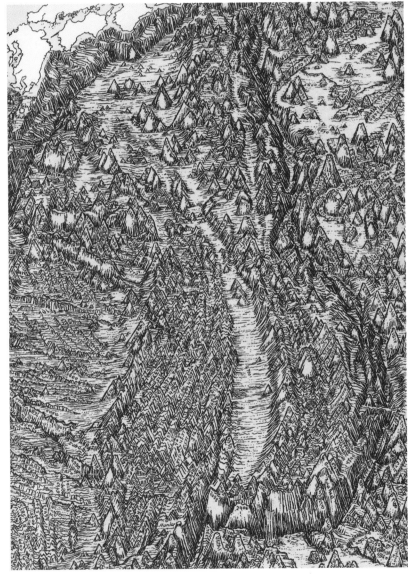

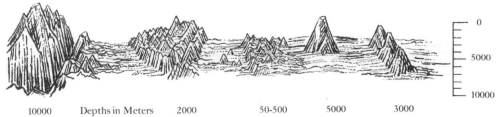

10000   Depths in Meters   2000   50-500   5000   3000

0

5000

10000

Map 248.
Part of a French world map of the oceans, drawn in 1979 based on the work of Bruce Heezen and Marie Tharp.

Map 247 (left).
Part of Bruce Heezen and Marie Tharp's "physiographic diagram" of the western Pacific Ocean, from a revised edition published in 1971. Shown is the area south of Japan (the land at the top of the map), including South Honshu Ridge (running down the middle); the Mariana Trench (bottom right); and the Bonin Trench (top right center, continuing northwards from the Mariana Trench). The ridge running down the left side of the map is the smaller Kyushu-Palau Ridge. Below is the map key.

The U.S. Navy's Climatic Atlas

During and after the Second World War, the use of the airplane revolutionized the collection of meteorological data in hitherto inaccessible places such as the North Pacific Ocean. Now information could be collected not only at sea level but at altitude.

Nevertheless, most data was still gathered at a finite number of "ocean station networks" established by the U.S. Navy, who had nine points only, and by other countries for the continuous observation of the weather. These locations were necessarily limited in number, but did allow collection of a time series of data from a single point, as on land. The rest of the information still came from transient shipping.

In the mid-1950s the U.S. Navy published a massive climatic atlas covering all the world's oceans; shown here are parts of just two of the many maps showing monthly conditions.

This situation was not to continue; the coming of satellites changed the observation of weather over the oceans forever. Now weather ships are gone, but the quality of information, now gathered remotely, has improved immensely.

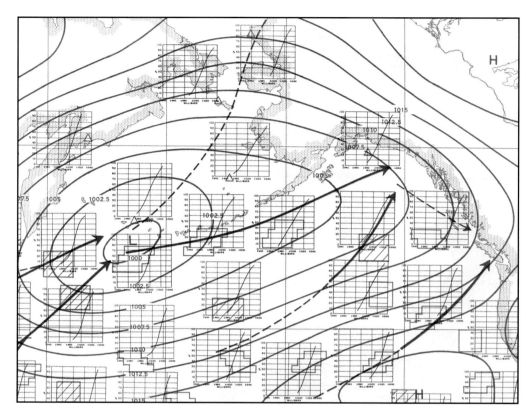

Two maps from the 1956 edition of the *U.S. Navy Marine Climatic Atlas of the World, Volume II, North Pacific Ocean*. Map 249, above, shows sea level pressure in January; storm tracks sweep towards the North American coast. Map 250, below, shows surface-level winds for April. The latter illustrates why it was difficult for Spanish and English voyages of exploration to sail close to the coast as they proceeded northwards in the springtime; the winds were contrary. The information shown on these maps is not as comprehensive as it looks, being based on a limited number of observation points. This was all about to change with the advent of satellites.

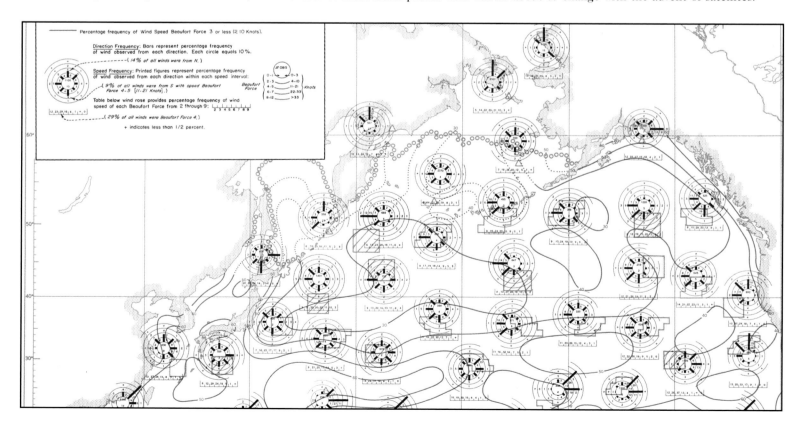

The Bathymetry of the North Pacific

In 1970, spurred by a considerably greater amount of information that had by then become available, scientists from Scripps Institute of Oceanography and Institute of Marine Resources compiled a large, multi-section bathymetric map of the North Pacific Ocean.

The map was intended for use by scientists who were studying the emerging geological theories of sea floor spreading and plate tectonics and the various ocean sciences. Scientists on land had good geological maps, but those working on the ocean did not.

The maps were stated to be *an interpretation* of sea floor relief, and indeed they were, but nevertheless a much better interpretation than anything before. The map below shows the tracks of ships that contributed data to these maps; there are a huge number of tracks now. The basic contour interval was 200 fathoms (365 m or 1,200 feet), with contours at 100 fathoms where the quality of the data allowed.

These charts showed many previously uncharted submarine features such as seamounts and trenches. Aside from their obvious scientific value, these maps are works of art as well.

Map 251 (above).
A portrayal of part of the Japan Trench, off the southeast coast of Japan. The map key is shown overleaf.

Map 252 (below).
Key map showing the tracks of ships whose information was used to construct the Scripps bathymetric map.

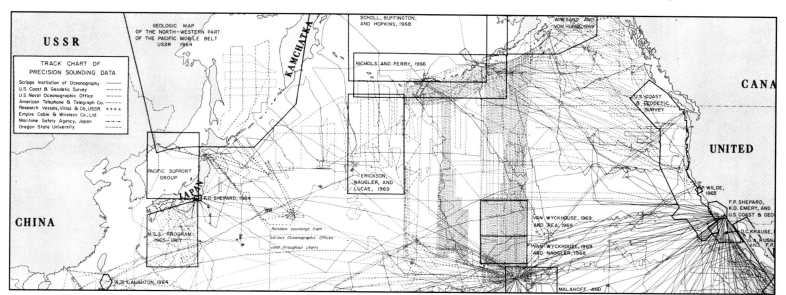

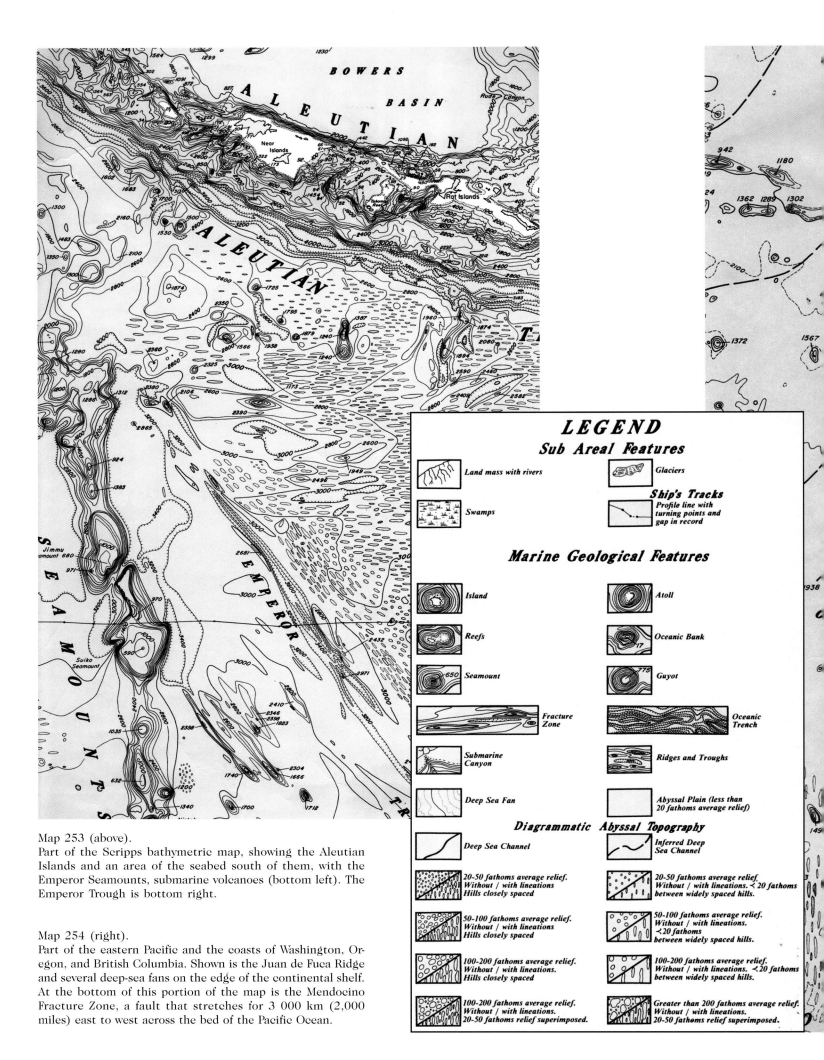

Map 253 (above).
Part of the Scripps bathymetric map, showing the Aleutian Islands and an area of the seabed south of them, with the Emperor Seamounts, submarine volcanoes (bottom left). The Emperor Trough is bottom right.

Map 254 (right).
Part of the eastern Pacific and the coasts of Washington, Oregon, and British Columbia. Shown is the Juan de Fuca Ridge and several deep-sea fans on the edge of the continental shelf. At the bottom of this portion of the map is the Mendocino Fracture Zone, a fault that stretches for 3 000 km (2,000 miles) east to west across the bed of the Pacific Ocean.

LEGEND
Sub Areal Features

Land mass with rivers

Glaciers

Ship's Tracks
Profile line with turning points and gap in record

Marine Geological Features

Island

Atoll

Reefs

Oceanic Bank

Seamount

Guyot

Fracture Zone

Oceanic Trench

Submarine Canyon

Ridges and Troughs

Deep Sea Fan

Abyssal Plain (less than 20 fathoms average relief)

Diagrammatic Abyssal Topography

Deep Sea Channel

Inferred Deep Sea Channel

20-50 fathoms average relief. Without / with lineations Hills closely spaced

20-50 fathoms average relief. Without / with lineations. < 20 fathoms between widely spaced hills.

50-100 fathoms average relief. Without / with lineations Hills closely spaced

50-100 fathoms average relief. Without / with lineations. <20 fathoms between widely spaced hills.

100-200 fathoms average relief. Without / with lineations. Hills closely spaced

100-200 fathoms average relief. Without / with lineations. < 20 fathoms between widely spaced hills.

100-200 fathoms average relief. Without / with lineations. 20-50 fathoms relief superimposed.

Greater than 200 fathoms average relief. Without / with lineations. 20-50 fathoms relief superimposed.

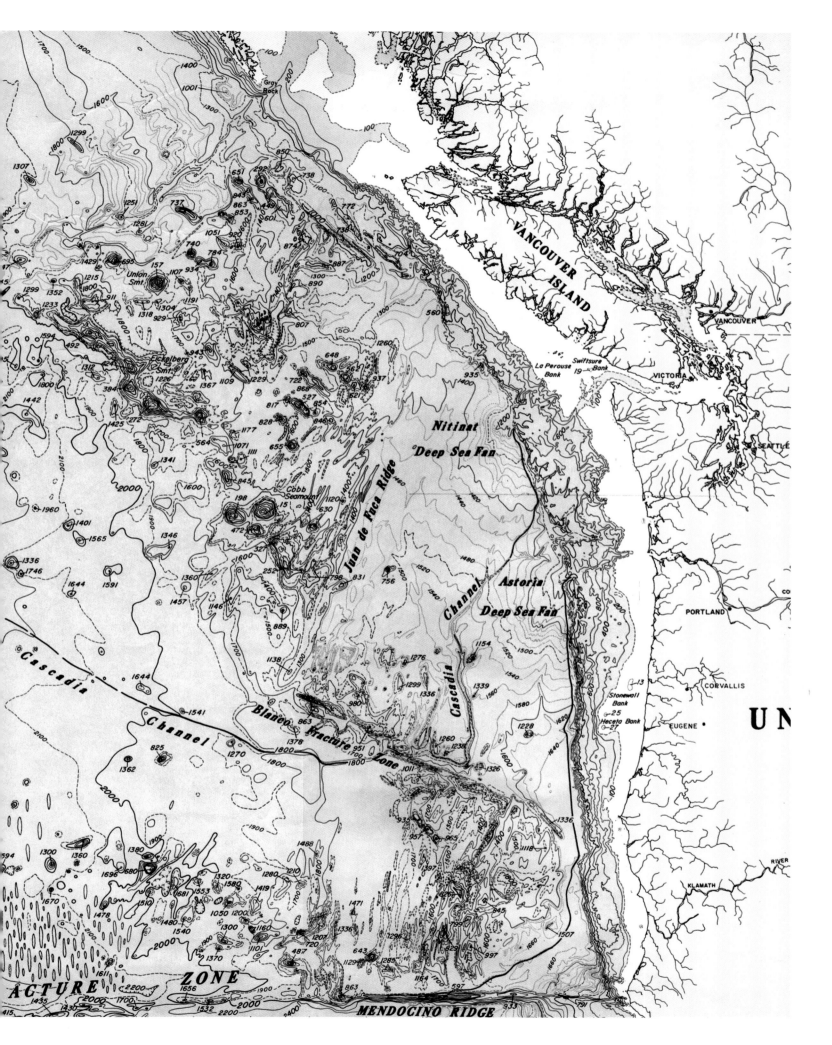

The Ocean Drilling Program

In 1957 the American Miscellaneous Society, a group of prominent ocean scientists, wanted to determine the physical properties of the discontinuity that exists between the Earth's crust and the underlying mantle, the Mohorovicic seismic discontinuity, as it is called. The scientists proposed to the U.S. National Science Foundation the aptly named Mohole Project, which was to drill a hole through the crust to the discontinuity and retrieve rock samples.

JOIDES Resolution, successor drilling ship to *Glomar Challenger.*

This project, though much promoted, never came to fruition, but it did generate interest in the idea of deep drilling, and in 1964 JOIDES (Joint Oceanographic Institutions for Deep Earth Sampling) was created to drill deep into the seabed, to help decipher the geologic history of the planet and look for evidence of ongoing processes such as sea floor spreading.

The thickness of the Earth's crust under the oceans is about 5 km or 3 miles, much less than it is under the continents, and so the record held in the crust could hopefully be accessed with considerably less drilling. However, the only way this could be done was from a ship, and the drill would first have to traverse the waters to the sea floor. A major challenge would be to keep the drilling platform in position.

In 1966, the U.S National Science Foundation, at the urging of JOIDES, approved construction of a specially designed ship. The Deep Sea Drilling Project, as the program was now called, contracted with Global Marine Inc., a commercial marine drilling company, to supply the ship, which was christened *Glomar Challenger,* in honor of the nineteenth-century pioneering oceanographic research vessel *Challenger* (see page 168).

Glomar Challenger went first to the Atlantic, where the cores drilled supported the new sea floor spreading hypothesis.

In the Pacific the crust far from centers of sea floor spreading was investigated, and from sediment-thickness data, epoch by epoch, a quantitative estimate of the rate of plate motion could be made.

Changes in the composition of sediments reflect changes in the productivity of the ocean above them, changes in the temperature of deep waters, and changes in large ocean-scale currents. Information from drill cores has been used to reconstruct the history of the Earth's climate. It has also provided records of cataclysmic events such as volcanic eruptions.

The Deep Sea Drilling Project was restructured in 1975 and with international participation became the International Ocean Drilling Program, with more than ten countries involved.

By the end of the program in 1983, *Global Challenger* had drilled a total of 325 km (200 miles) at 624 sites worldwide, and had penetrated as deep as 1 741 m (5,700 feet); the ship had traveled a total of nearly 700 000 km, or 435,000 miles.

But the drilling program was not finished; in 1985 a new ship was commissioned. This ship has been renamed *JOIDES Resolution,* this time named after James Cook's ship *Resolution.*

The deepest hole drilled by the new ship was one of 2 111 m (6,926 feet), in the eastern Pacific. The greatest water depth encountered at a drill site was 5 980 m (19,620 feet), in the western Pacific. Over 1,400 holes have been drilled.

Drilling in the modern era is made easier by the use of satellite technology to locate drill sites, and seabed sonar transmitters are used to maintain the ship in exactly the same position in all weathers.

Drilling today continues to explore the evolution and structure of the Earth below the world's oceans.

Map 255.
Drill sites of *Glomar Challenger* (blue) and *JOIDES Resolution* (red).

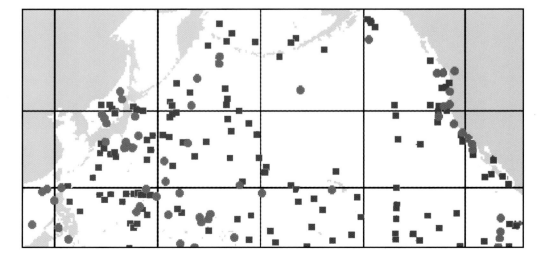

The International Decade of Ocean Exploration

The success of the International Geophysical Year in 1957–58 was the inspiration for a number of other scientific projects involving international cooperation. The International Decade of Ocean Exploration (IDOE) was sponsored by the Intergovernmental Oceanographic Commission and lasted from 1970 to 1980. It was an umbrella for an array of cooperative projects designed to further understanding of the processes that were taking place in the world's oceans and how these processes affected the environment.

Exploration of the sea was to be sustained rather than episodic and planned in a global context rather than as a collection of individual projects.

One project was termed the North Pacific Experiment, or NORPAX, and it was concerned with large-scale ocean-atmosphere interactions. Compared to the atmosphere, the ocean has an enormous capacity to store heat and energy, which can have a time-delayed effect on climate. NORPAX scientists discovered that they could predict El Niño (a warming of part of the ocean that materializes only once every four or five years) with tide-gauge measurements on certain islands near the equator. Just prior to an El Niño, mean sea level drops in the eastern Pacific and rises in the western Pacific, a change associated with a failure of equatorial trade winds. The ability to predict El Niño assists in the forecasting of anomalous weather patterns that are typically associated with it.

Another IDOE project, partly in the North Pacific, was the Coastal Upwelling Ecosystems Analysis, or CUEA, whose observations included the waters off Oregon and Baja California as well as those in analogous areas off Peru and northwest Africa. These studies were directed towards predicting the biological productivity of upwelling ecosystems from observations of critical air-sea processes, mainly wind and currents.

Yet another program was the Geochemical Ocean Sections Study, or GEOSECS. This program was the idea of Henry Stommel, who thought that deep ocean currents and the whole thermohaline circulation of the oceans (large-scale water circulation driven by differences in temperature and salinity in three dimensions) could be tracked by the use of trace chemicals, introduced into the ocean at one point, either naturally or artificially, and sampled at many other points. He realized that this would require a large-scale collaborative scientific effort.

Thus a global, three-dimensional survey of chemical, isotopic, and radiochemical tracers was initiated. Overall, the program lasted from 1972 to 1978, but in the Pacific the studies were carried out from August 1973 to June 1974. The Pacific survey was carried out by the research vessel *Melville*, from Scripps Institution of Oceanography.

GEOSECS was able to determine the rate and speed at which water sank, welled up, and moved laterally as currents in the deep ocean. In the process, it was found that in the northeast Pacific there was water at depth that had not been in contact with the atmosphere for a thousand years.

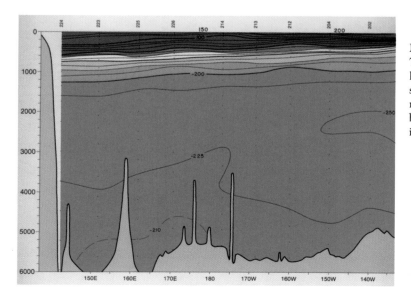

Map 256.
Track of Scripps' Research Vessel *Melville* in the Pacific Oceans during the GEOSECS project.

Map 257 (right, bottom).
The path of *Melville* while sampling water to compile the profile at left, which shows the vertical distribution of Carbon 14. The profile shows a very high surface maximum and a steep drop-off to a minimum in deep water. The high surface values are derived from nuclear bomb tests. The large area of minimum Carbon 14 represents water isolated from the surface for a long time.

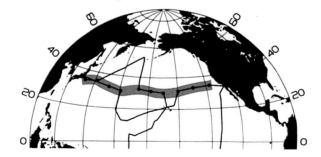

The Pacific Salmon

One of the great mysteries of evolution is how the salmon became anadromous, that is, living part of its life cycle in the salt of the sea and part, the beginning and end of its life, in the freshwater of the land.

Perhaps this was an adaptation to being driven from its streams by advancing ice during one of the ice ages. However it evolved, there is no doubt that the salmon has for millennia played a significant role in the diet and the culture of the peoples of the Pacific Rim.

In the nineteenth century, with the development of safe canning practices, the salmon spawned a major industry based on its capture and processing. More recently, there have been concerns about the maintenance of the resource for future generations.

As we have seen (page 70), it was Georg Steller who first described the life cycle of the Pacific salmon and identified the various species. But most of the major discoveries about salmon occurred two hundred years later as commercial salmon fisheries became an important economic force.

The first clear evidence that sockeye salmon returned to the stream where they hatched came at the beginning of the twentieth century. In 1903, an inquisitive technician at the Fortmann Hatchery on the Naha River, Alaska, removed some fins from 1,600 sockeye fry before they migrated seaward, and the fish reappeared as adult salmon in the same river in 1906 and 1907. But no one understood salmon behavior in the sea or the extent of their migrations until the middle of the century.

Following from a clause in the Peace Treaty of 1951 between the Allied Powers and Japan, the International Convention for the High Seas Fisheries of the North Pacific Ocean was signed in 1952 by Canada, Japan, and the United States. This led to the creation of the International North Pacific Fisheries Commission (INPFC) in 1953.

Between 1956 and 1958 scientists involved in INPFC began tagging salmon on the high seas to determine what line or lines at sea would best separate salmon originating in North America from those originating in Asia. This research led to the discovery that Pacific salmon and steelhead trout from Asia and North America migrate great distances and intermingle over broad areas of the North Pacific Ocean at certain times during their life. Tagging experiments now use more sophisticated tags that record depth, temperature, and even swimming speed.

During the twentieth century, humans have intervened increasingly in the natural life cycle of salmon. Eggs and milt are taken from returning spawning fish and incubated in hatcheries before being released to the ocean. Salmon production in Japan, largely chum salmon and pink salmon, relies almost entirely on hatcheries, while other nations have maintained both wild and hatchery production.

Map 258.
Distribution of recoveries of immature chum salmon, from a pioneer experiment carried out by American scientists in 1956–57. The salmon were tagged near Adak Island, in the Aleutians, in 1956, and caught at various locations in 1957, allowing plotting of the tracks they had taken.

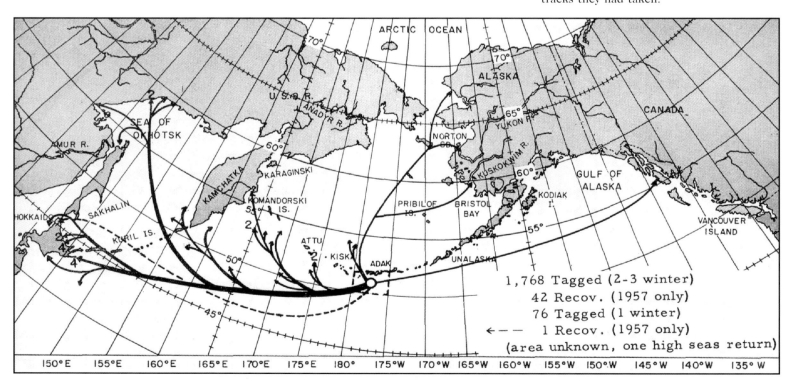

1,768 Tagged (2-3 winter)
42 Recov. (1957 only)
76 Tagged (1 winter)
← — 1 Recov. (1957 only)
(area unknown, one high seas return)

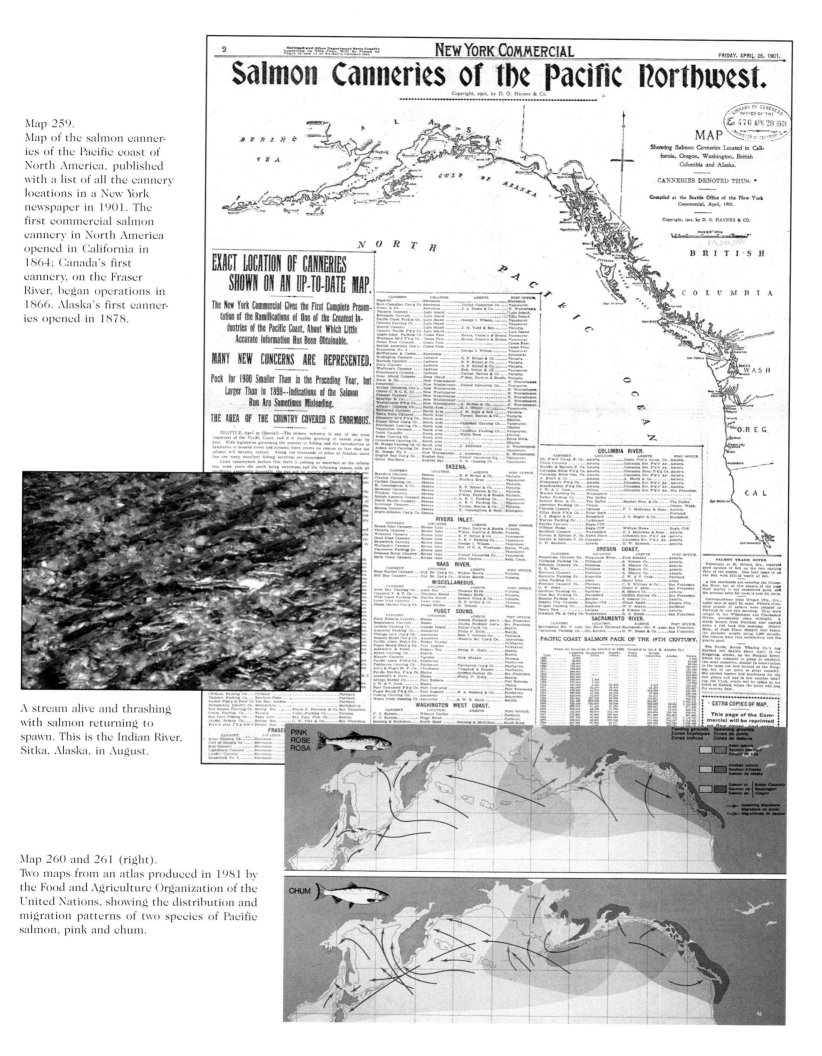

Map 259.
Map of the salmon canneries of the Pacific coast of North America, published with a list of all the cannery locations in a New York newspaper in 1901. The first commercial salmon cannery in North America opened in California in 1864; Canada's first cannery, on the Fraser River, began operations in 1866. Alaska's first canneries opened in 1878.

A stream alive and thrashing with salmon returning to spawn. This is the Indian River, Sitka, Alaska, in August.

Map 260 and 261 (right).
Two maps from an atlas produced in 1981 by the Food and Agriculture Organization of the United Nations, showing the distribution and migration patterns of two species of Pacific salmon, pink and chum.

The Origin of the Continents and Oceans

Two hundred million years ago there was only one continent, dubbed Pangaea, and one ocean surrounding it. The movement of the landmass and its breakup into separate continents formed the world's oceans, including the Pacific.

It was in 1915 that Alfred Wegener first proposed that the continents were originally one landmass, and that they are slowly drifting apart. In 1928 Arthur Holmes theorized that they moved because of convection currents in molten rock powered by radioactivity, thus laying the foundation from which modern ideas developed.

After more intensive surveying of the sea floor in the 1950s had revealed undersea topography to a previously unprecedented degree, a mechanism of sea floor spreading was proposed to explain the midocean ridges that had been identified in the world's oceans. In the process it explained continental drift,

continents moving away from each other because the ocean basins were expanding.

In the North Pacific, the mid-ocean ridge comes inland at Baja California and is otherwise limited to a short stretch off the coast from Cape Mendocino to the northern tip of Vancouver Island. Here the Pacific Plate is expanding away from the Juan de Fuca Plate, which is in turn plunging under the North American Plate (see Map 264, pages 200–201).

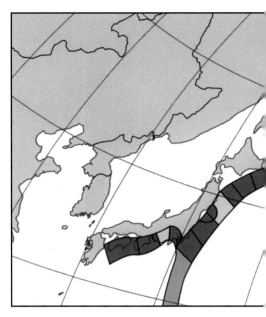

Map 262 (right, top).
Earthquake probability clearly follows the Pacific Rim and the active zone of spreading or subduction.

Map 263 (right, bottom).
Part of a map showing the tectonic features of the Pacific Ocean, vividly demonstrating the Asian part of the "Rim of Fire." The key for this map and the eastern Pacific portion on the next page is shown below.

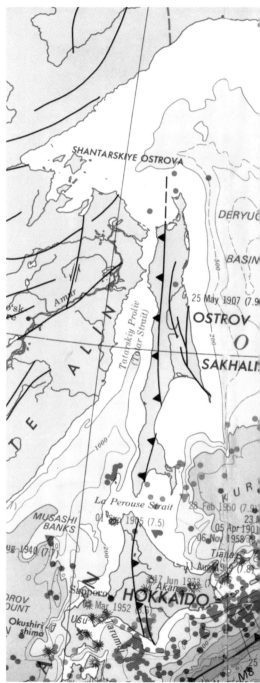

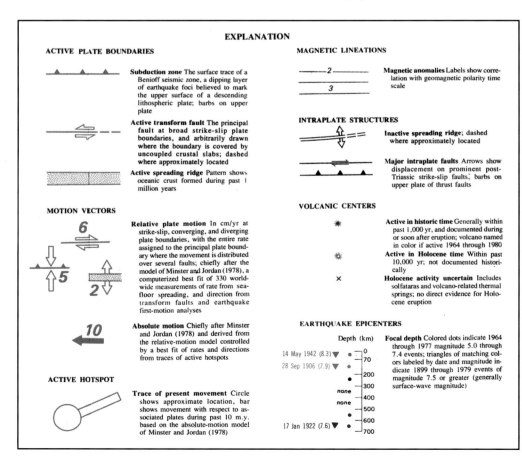

EXPLANATION

ACTIVE PLATE BOUNDARIES

Subduction zone The surface trace of a Benioff seismic zone, a dipping layer of earthquake foci believed to mark the upper surface of a descending lithospheric plate; barbs on upper plate

Active transform fault The principal fault at broad strike-slip plate boundaries, and arbitrarily drawn where the boundary is covered by uncoupled crustal slabs; dashed where approximately located

Active spreading ridge Pattern shows oceanic crust formed during past 1 million years

MOTION VECTORS

6

5 **2**

Relative plate motion In cm/yr at strike-slip, converging, and diverging plate boundaries, with the entire rate assigned to the principal plate boundary where the movement is distributed over several faults; chiefly after the model of Minster and Jordan (1978), a computerized best fit of 330 world-wide measurements of rate from sea-floor spreading, and direction from transform faults and earthquake first-motion analyses

10

Absolute motion Chiefly after Minster and Jordan (1978) and derived from the relative-motion model controlled by a best fit of rates and directions from traces of active hotspots

ACTIVE HOTSPOT

Trace of present movement Circle shows approximate location, bar shows movement with respect to associated plates during past 10 m.y. based on the absolute-motion model of Minster and Jordan (1978)

MAGNETIC LINEATIONS

——— 2 ———
——————————
——— 3 ———

Magnetic anomalies Labels show correlation with geomagnetic polarity time scale

INTRAPLATE STRUCTURES

Inactive spreading ridge; dashed where approximately located

Major intraplate faults Arrows show displacement on prominent post-Triassic strike-slip faults; barbs on upper plate of thrust faults

VOLCANIC CENTERS

✳ **Active in historic time** Generally within past 1,000 yr, and documented during or soon after eruption; volcano named in color if active 1964 through 1980

✸ **Active in Holocene time** Within past 10,000 yr; not documented historically

✕ **Holocene activity uncertain** Includes solfataras and volcano-related thermal springs; no direct evidence for Holocene eruption

EARTHQUAKE EPICENTERS

Depth (km)

14 May 1942 (8.3) ▼ ● ┬ 0
28 Sep 1906 (7.9) ▼ ● ┼ 70
                      ┼ 200
              none ┼ 300
              none ┼ 400
                   ● ┼ 500
                   ● ┼ 600
17 Jan 1922 (7.6) ▼ ┴ 700

Focal depth Colored dots indicate 1964 through 1977 magnitude 5.0 through 7.4 events; triangles of matching colors labeled by date and magnitude indicate 1899 through 1979 events of magnitude 7.5 or greater (generally surface-wave magnitude)

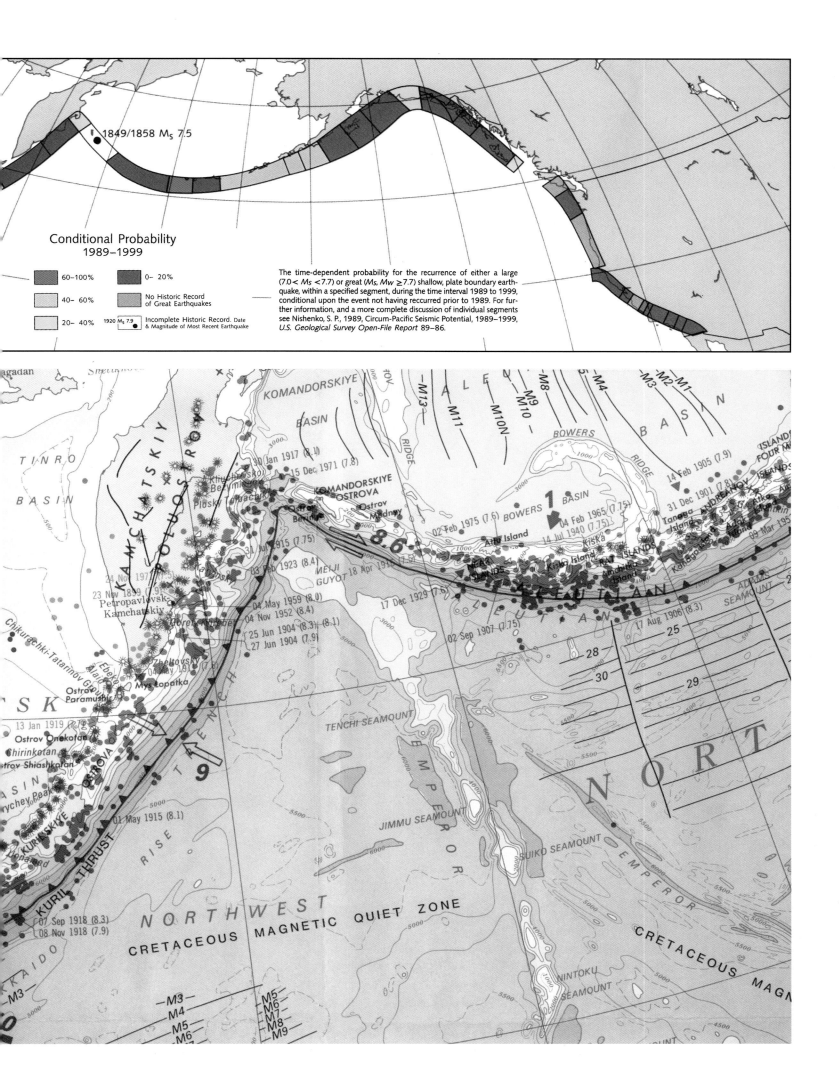

Conditional Probability
1989–1999

60–100%	0– 20%
40– 60%	No Historic Record of Great Earthquakes
20– 40%	Incomplete Historic Record. Date & Magnitude of Most Recent Earthquake

1920 M$_S$ 7.9

The time-dependent probability for the recurrence of either a large (7.0< M$_S$ <7.7) or great (M$_S$, M$_W$ ≥7.7) shallow, plate boundary earthquake, within a specified segment, during the time interval 1989 to 1999, conditional upon the event not having reccurred prior to 1989. For further information, and a more complete discussion of individual segments see Nishenko, S. P., 1989, Circum-Pacific Seismic Potential, 1989–1999, *U.S. Geological Survey Open-File Report 89–86.*

1849/1858 M$_S$ 7.5

The theory of sea floor spreading was confirmed in 1963–66 by studies of the direction of ancient magnetism in rocks surrounding the ridges. This confirmation paved the way for modern theories of plate tectonics, which envision the Earth's crust as consisting of a series of plates that move relative to one another.

Around the Pacific Rim is the corollary of the expanding midocean ridge, the subduction zone, where plates grind together and one is dragged under the other. Under California and in a vast arc from the Alaska panhandle through the Aleutians and Kurils to Japan is a major subduction zone where ocean floor is being dragged under the North American and Eurasian Plates. In the process, ocean trenches such as the Aleutian Trench, the Japan Trench, and the Mariana Trench are formed.

The majority of volcanic activity occurs at these plate margins, as do earthquakes, hence the name "Pacific Rim of Fire."

However, some volcanic activity also occurs in the interiors of plates, over "hot spots," or weak points in the underlying crust. But the plate above the crust continues to move as a result of continuous sea floor spreading, and so volcanoes migrate away from the hot spots that gave rise to them, forming chains of seamounts such as the Emperor Seamounts and, eventually, islands such as the Hawaiian Islands.

Fracture zones of various magnitudes cover the sea floor of the northeast part of the Pacific Ocean (map at right). These are thought to be caused by slight changes in sea floor spreading direction, over a long period of time, which cause stresses between one part of a plate and another that eventually lead to cracking.

Along the line where the Pacific Plate and the Juan de Fuca Plate meet is a midocean ridge, at which upwelling is creating new sea floor and in the process pushing the two plates apart. Here geologists have found a number of hot vents, a form of volcanic activity. At what are essentially hot springs, superheated water is vented into the colder ocean water. The difference in temperatures causes an immediate precipitation of minerals, metal sulfides, held in solution, giving the appearance of dense black smoke. The rapid precipitation causes a solid chimney of rock to be built up from the seabed.

These "black smokers" have now been discovered all over the world, but one of the largest is on the Juan de Fuca Ridge; dubbed "Godzilla," it is sixteen storeys high.

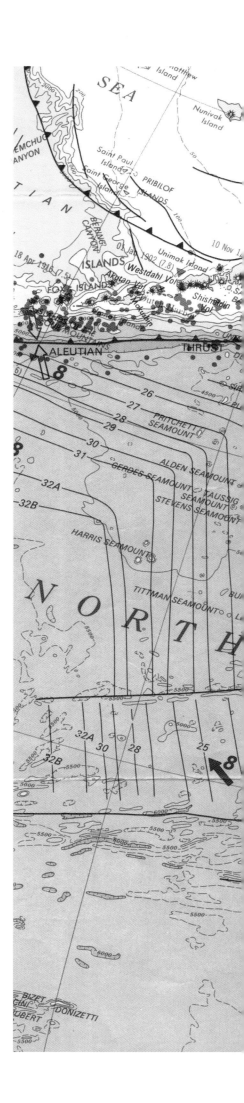

Map 264.
The eastern part of the tectonic map of the Pacific. The fracture zones are a nearly ubiquitous feature. The junction of the relatively small Juan de Fuca Plate with the much larger Pacific Plate to its west is the site of a midocean ridge, that is, a rift-type valley in the middle of a ridge, from which the plates are being propelled away from each other by the addition of new sea floor welling up from below. It is also the site of a line of volcanic activity, in this case hot vents. The red line with red triangles along the western coast of North America is a major subduction zone, where the Pacific and Juan de Fuca Plates are being dragged under the North American Plate.

Destructive Waves – Pacific Tsunamis

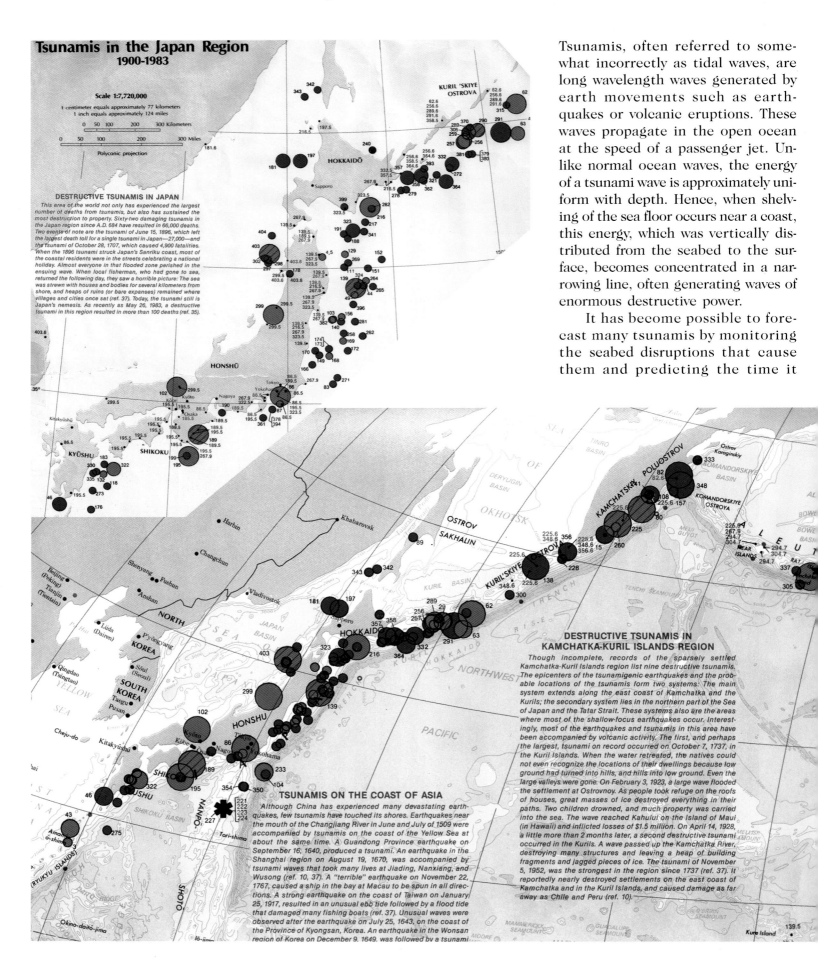

Tsunamis in the Japan Region
1900-1983

1 centimeter equals approximately 77 kilometers
1 inch equals approximately 124 miles

0 50 100   200   300 Kilometers

0   50   100   200   300 Miles

Polyconic projection

DESTRUCTIVE TSUNAMIS IN JAPAN

This area of the world not only has experienced the largest number of deaths from tsunamis, but also has sustained the most destruction to property. Sixty-two damaging tsunamis in the Japan region since A.D. 684 have resulted in 66,000 deaths. Two events of note are the tsunami of June 15, 1896, which left the largest death toll for a single tsunami in Japan—27,000—and the tsunami of October 28, 1707, which caused 4,900 fatalities. When the 1896 tsunami struck Japan's Sanriku coast, most of the coastal residents were in the streets celebrating a national holiday. Almost everyone in that flooded zone perished in the ensuing wave. When local fisherman, who had gone to sea, returned the following day, they saw a horrible picture: The sea was strewn with houses and bodies for several kilometers from shore, and heaps of ruins (or bare expanses) remained where villages and cities once sat (ref. 37). Today, the tsunami still is Japan's nemesis. As recently as May 26, 1983, a destructive tsunami in this region resulted in more than 100 deaths (ref. 35).

Tsunamis, often referred to somewhat incorrectly as tidal waves, are long wavelength waves generated by earth movements such as earthquakes or volcanic eruptions. These waves propagate in the open ocean at the speed of a passenger jet. Unlike normal ocean waves, the energy of a tsunami wave is approximately uniform with depth. Hence, when shelving of the sea floor occurs near a coast, this energy, which was vertically distributed from the seabed to the surface, becomes concentrated in a narrowing line, often generating waves of enormous destructive power.

It has become possible to forecast many tsunamis by monitoring the seabed disruptions that cause them and predicting the time it

DESTRUCTIVE TSUNAMIS IN KAMCHATKA-KURIL ISLANDS REGION

Though incomplete, records of the sparsely settled Kamchatka-Kuril Islands region list nine destructive tsunamis. The epicenters of the tsunamigenic earthquakes and the probable locations of the tsunamis form two systems: The main system extends along the east coast of Kamchatka and the Kurils; the secondary system lies in the northern part of the Sea of Japan and the Tatar Strait. These systems also are the areas where most of the shallow-focus earthquakes occur. Interestingly, most of the earthquakes and tsunamis in this area have been accompanied by volcanic activity. The first, and perhaps the largest, tsunami on record occurred on October 7, 1737, in the Kuril Islands. When the water retreated, the natives could not even recognize the locations of their dwellings because low ground had turned into hills, and hills into low ground. Even the large valleys were gone. On February 3, 1923, a large wave flooded the settlement at Ostrovnoy. As people took refuge on the roofs of houses, great masses of ice destroyed everything in their paths. Two children drowned, and much property was carried into the sea. The wave reached Kahului on the Island of Maui (in Hawaii) and inflicted losses of $1.5 million. On April 14, 1928, a little more than 2 months later, a second destructive tsunami occurred in the Kurils. A wave passed up the Kamchatka River, destroying many structures and leaving a heap of building fragments and jagged pieces of ice. The tsunami of November 5, 1952, was the strongest in the region since 1737 (ref. 37). It reportedly nearly destroyed settlements on the east coast of Kamchatka and in the Kuril Islands, and caused damage as far away as Chile and Peru (ref. 10).

TSUNAMIS ON THE COAST OF ASIA

Although China has experienced many devastating earthquakes, few tsunamis have touched its shores. Earthquakes near the mouth of the Changjiang River in June and July of 1509 were accompanied by tsunamis on the coast of the Yellow Sea at about the same time. A Guangdong Province earthquake on September 16, 1640, produced a tsunami. An earthquake in the Shanghai region on August 19, 1670, was accompanied by tsunami waves that took many lives at Jiading, Nanxiang, and Wusong (ref. 10, 37). A "terrible" earthquake on November 22, 1767, caused a ship in the bay at Macau to be spun in all directions. A strong earthquake on the coast of Taiwan on January 25, 1917, resulted in an unusual ebb tide followed by a flood tide that damaged many fishing boats (ref. 37). Unusual waves were observed after the earthquake on July 25, 1643, on the coast of the Province of Kyongsan, Korea. An earthquake in the Wonsan region of Korea on December 9, 1649, was followed by a tsunami.

will take for the tsunami to propagate from the source region to distant coastlines. This does not work, however, when the source is so near to a coastline that the tsunami arrives too quickly.

It is more difficult, however, to predict the height of tsunami waves, and sometimes alerts have been issued for massive evacuations of coastal areas only to find that the height of the arriving tsunami is inconsequential.

The solution to this problem lies in a network of moored ocean buoys supporting recording instruments on the seabed. Instruments are submerged, not on the buoy, because on the open ocean the unconcentrated tsunami wave can sometimes hardly be detected at the surface. The instruments detect the wave and send the information to the buoy, from where it is transmitted to a satellite.

Map 265.
The map on this page tells its own story. In several sections, the map shows the sources of tsunami-generating events around the Pacific Rim.

(inset)
A rare photograph of a tsunami coming ashore. This was the 1946 tsunami hitting Coconut Island, Hilo, Hawaii, an amazing image made by a no doubt fleeing photographer.
Pacific Tsunami Museum.

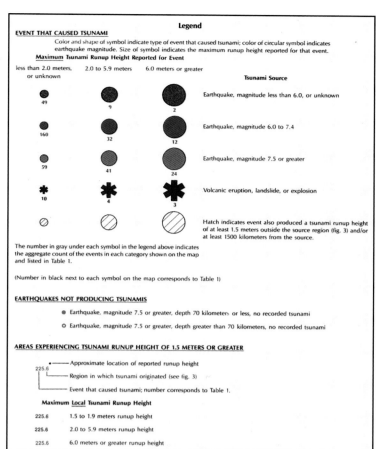

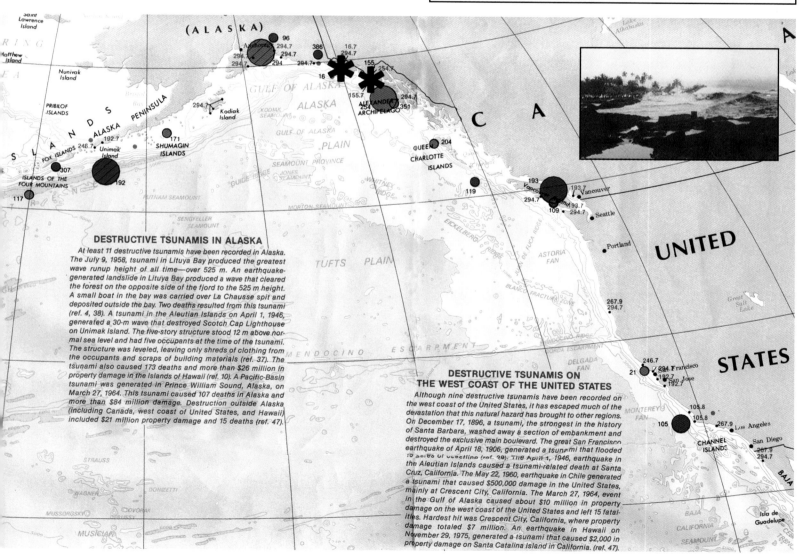

DESTRUCTIVE TSUNAMIS IN ALASKA

At least 11 destructive tsunamis have been recorded in Alaska. The July 9, 1958, tsunami in Lituya Bay produced the greatest wave runup height of all time—over 525 m. An earthquake-generated landslide in Lituya Bay produced a wave that cleared the forest on the opposite side of the fjord to the 525 m height. A small boat in the bay was carried over La Chausse spit and deposited outside the bay. Two deaths resulted from this tsunami (ref. 4, 38). A tsunami in the Aleutian Islands on April 1, 1946, generated a 30-m wave that destroyed Scotch Cap Lighthouse on Unimak Island. The five-story structure stood 12 m above normal sea level and had five occupants at the time of the tsunami. The structure was leveled, leaving only shreds of clothing from the occupants and scraps of building materials (ref. 37). The tsunami also caused 173 deaths and more than $26 million in property damage in the Islands of Hawaii (ref. 10). A Pacific-Basin tsunami was generated in Prince William Sound, Alaska, on March 27, 1964. This tsunami caused 107 deaths and more than $84 million damage. Destruction outside Alaska (including Canada, west coast of United States, and Hawaii) included $21 million property damage and 15 deaths (ref. 47).

DESTRUCTIVE TSUNAMIS ON THE WEST COAST OF THE UNITED STATES

Although nine destructive tsunamis have been recorded on the west coast of the United States, it has escaped much of the devastation that this natural hazard has brought to other regions. On December 17, 1896, a tsunami, the strongest in the history of Santa Barbara, washed away a section of embankment and destroyed the exclusive main boulevard. The great San Francisco earthquake of April 18, 1906, generated a tsunami that flooded to acres of coastline (ref. 39). The April 1, 1946, earthquake in the Aleutian Islands caused a tsunami-related death at Santa Cruz, California. The May 22, 1960, earthquake in Chile generated a tsunami that caused $500,000 damage in the United States, mainly at Crescent City, California. The March 27, 1964, event in the Gulf of Alaska caused about $10 million in property damage on the west coast of the United States and left 15 fatalities. Hardest hit was Crescent City, California, where property damage totaled $7 million. An earthquake in Hawaii on November 29, 1975, generated a tsunami that caused $2,000 in property damage on Santa Catalina Island in California. (ref. 47).

Multibeam Bathymetry Reveals the Details

The most detailed mapping possible is done with a camera. Over land, cameras can be mounted on planes, but in the ocean, lack of light means that cameras can only be used over extremely small areas that can be illuminated.

For larger areas, sonar mounted on a sled float at depth is towed behind a ship. The sonar scans the sea bed obliquely, producing a detailed topographical map. This is side-scan sonar.

A further method, utilized for larger areas, uses an array of sound sources and listening devices mounted on the hull of a ship. Every few seconds a strip of seabed perpendicular to the ship's direction is scanned. Because the ship is moving, a slightly different strip is scanned each time, building up a sort of stereoscopic picture of the sea floor. This is multibeam sonar, and it can produce remarkably detailed images of the seabed over a large area. It has been extensively used in the United States to map the undersea topography of the 200 mile (320 km) exclusive economic zone.

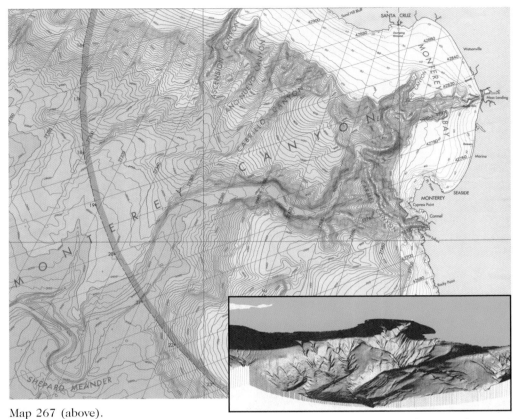

Map 267 (above).
Multibeam sonar allows the construction of very detailed maps of the sea floor, as this 1992 map of Monterey Canyon shows. The area is now the Monterey Bay National Marine Sanctuary. It covers an area the size of the state of Connecticut. Monterey Canyon cuts into the continental shelf on the scale of the Grand Canyon. Beginning just 100 m (300 feet) offshore, it extends westwards about 72 km (45 miles) and reaches depths of 3,000 m (10,000 feet). A three-dimensional view of the canyon is also shown above (Map 268).

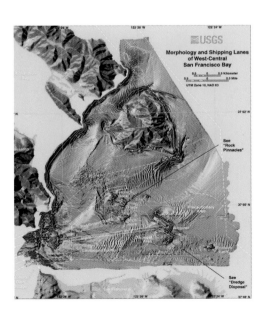

Map 266.
U.S. Geological Survey multibeam sonar image of part of San Francisco Bay.

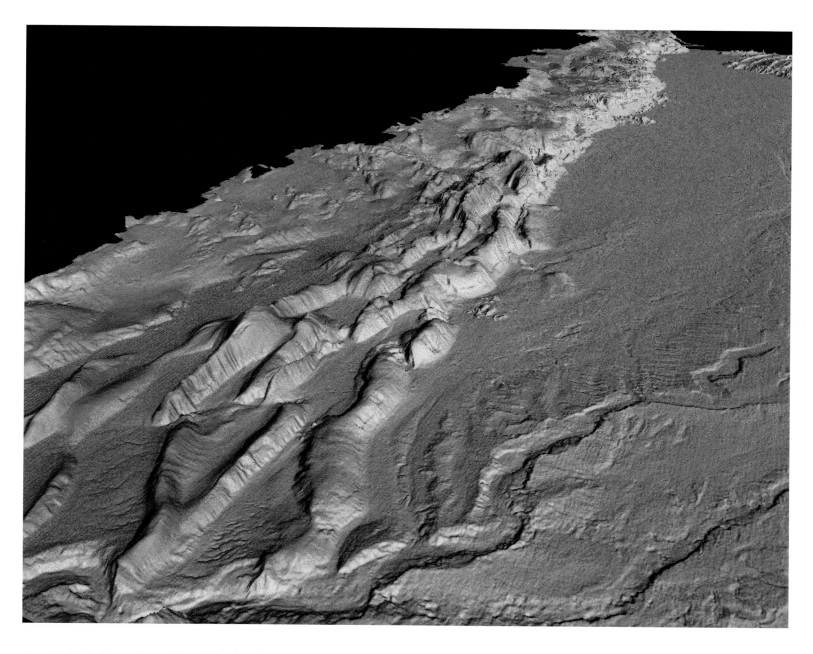

Map 269 (left, bottom) and Map 270 (above).

In 1981, the United States declared the waters and sea floor within 200 miles (320 km) of the shoreline to be an "exclusive economic zone." Between 1983 and 1993, NOAA, the National Oceanic and Atmospheric Administration, carried out detailed surveys of this zone using multibeam sonar. Computer-generated images like the two shown here allow the data to be interpreted as a three-dimensional "aerial view," producing revealing vistas of great beauty and detail. They were produced in 1996 by two geophysicists, Lincoln Pratson and William Haxby. Map 269, at left, is a view of the California coast, looking north from just south of Monterey. The Monterey Canyon shown in Map 267, above left, can also be seen in this view. Map 270, above, is a view of the Oregon coast, looking south, with the junction of the Juan de Fuca Plate, to the right, as it is dragged, or subducted, under the North American Plate, to the left. The ridges are the sediments that were on top of the Juan de Fuca Plate; they have been scraped off the sea floor by the North American Plate and accumulate as ridges. The vertical exaggeration in these images is 4x. A key for depths is given below.

| 3000 | 2000 | 1000 | Depth (m) |

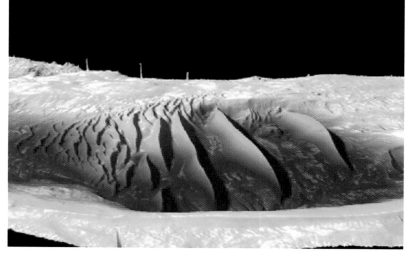

Map 271.
Multibeam imagery of a dune field off the coast of southern Vancouver Island, in the Strait of Juan de Fuca, off Victoria. The largest of these vertically exaggerated dunes is 8 m (25 feet) high.

The Satellite Sees All

The first Earth-observing satellites were launched in the 1960s and 70s. Since then, the capability of satellite sensors has increased dramatically, with a wide variety of instruments now covering almost all usable wavelengths of the spectrum, from ultraviolet light to microwaves. Nowadays, satellites play a key role in efforts directed at a better understanding of the ocean and climate.

Sea surface temperatures can be mapped to 1 000 m (3,300 feet) resolution by the thermal scanners carried by many weather satellites. Resolution of global composites is reduced to simplify processing and because features are in any case blurred from the month-long period typically chosen to allow all areas to be imaged be-

tween clouds (Maps 273 and 274). Periods of fine weather sometimes allows composite images to be made over a shorter time, in which smaller features are preserved (Map 272, below).

Sensitive optical instruments on the U.S. NASA *SeaWiFS* and Japanese NASDA *ADEOS* satellites have been designed to detect the colour change from clear blue to blue-green caused by chlorophyll in microscopic ocean plants – phytoplankton. Phytoplankton form the basis for the ocean food chain, and their distribution is an indicator of ocean productivity. Since life in the oceans affects many economic activities, such as fishing, being able to detect areas of increasing or decreasing productivity is very useful (Maps 275, 276, and 277).

Unlike visible imagers that are blocked by clouds and can operate only during the day, radar works day and night, and can "see" through cloud cover. High-resolution radar images of the ocean surface show roughness patterns due to winds, waves, oil slicks, current boundaries, and eddies, and are often used to track ships, especially those involved in commercial fishing. A more specialized radar scatterometer is now used to measure both wind speed and direction by looking at the sea surface from a variety of directions (Maps 278 and 279, page 208).

Most satellite data relate only to the ocean surface. Thermal measurements relate to less than the top millimeter of the sea; radar pen-

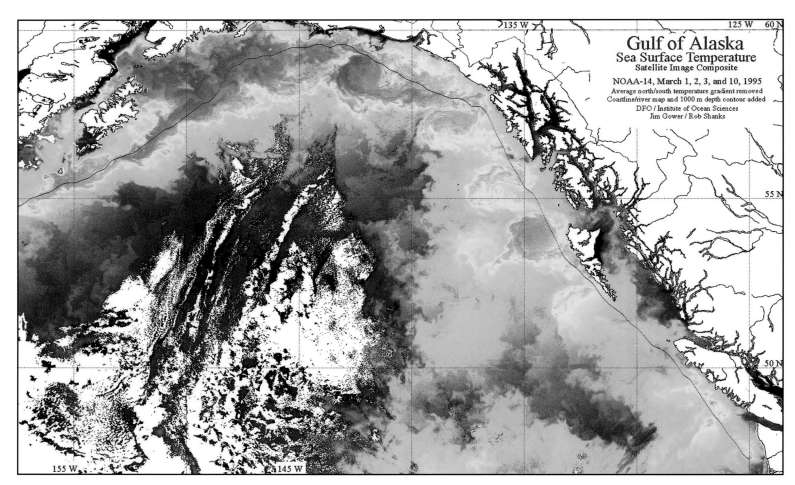

Map 272. This composite satellite image of sea surface temperature in the northeastern Pacific, obtained during early March 1995, shows a string of eddies along the B.C.–Alaska coast. At the top left of the image, the warmer water of the Alaska Stream can be seen moving westwards along the continental slope. The temperature differences in the image are about 4°C from the coolest (dark blue) to the warmest (red). An adjustment has been made to remove the effect of the normal north-to-south temperature gradient. The image was prepared by James Gower, Institute of Ocean Sciences, Fisheries and Oceans Canada.

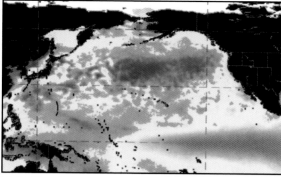

Map 273 (top) and Map 274. These images show the differences from the average sea surface temperature for the month, in the range ± 5°C. The top image is for November 1997, at the height of an El Niño, and the one below it is for November 1998, when warmer temperatures (red) along the equator have been replaced by colder (blue) La Niña conditions.

etrates a few centimeters. Visible radiation can "see" deeper, to a few meters, but this is still much less than the average 5-km (3 mile) depth of the ocean. Although unable to penetrate water to view the seabed directly, radar from, for example, the U.S. Navy's *Geosat* satellite can measure the distance to the sea surface to within 5 cm (2 inches). Sea surface height, which can vary as much as 200 m (650 feet), reflects small differences in the Earth's gravity caused by variations in undersea topography. For example, an underwater volcano 2 000 m (6,500 feet) high and 40 km (25 miles) wide will produce a bulge 2 m (6 feet) high in the seawater above it, due to its large mass and consequent increased gravitational attraction. But features less than 10 km (6 miles) across will not have sufficient mass to be detected. Sea surface elevation is measured over an area a few kilometers across, and this averages out the effects of waves.

Geosat satellite data was not declassified until 1995, but within two

Map 275.
Coccolithophores, a type of phytoplankton, bloom in the Bering Sea in this NASA *SeaWiFS* satellite image. The sea has been turned whiter by the *coccolithophores* shedding their little chalk shields, the coccoliths.

Map 276.
Monthly mean chlorophyll distribution in the North Pacific, May 1997. The *Advanced Earth Observing Satellite (ADEOS)*, carrying the Ocean Color and Temperature Scanner (OCTS), which made this image, was launched by the National Space and Development Agency of Japan (NASDA) in 1996. Phytoplankton distribution is shown by the production of chlorophyll and is an indicator of ocean productivity. The image shows remarkable differences between the eastern and western subarctic circulation systems, or gyres. The map was prepared by Sei-ichi Saitoh and Kosei Sasaoka, Hokkaido University, Japan.

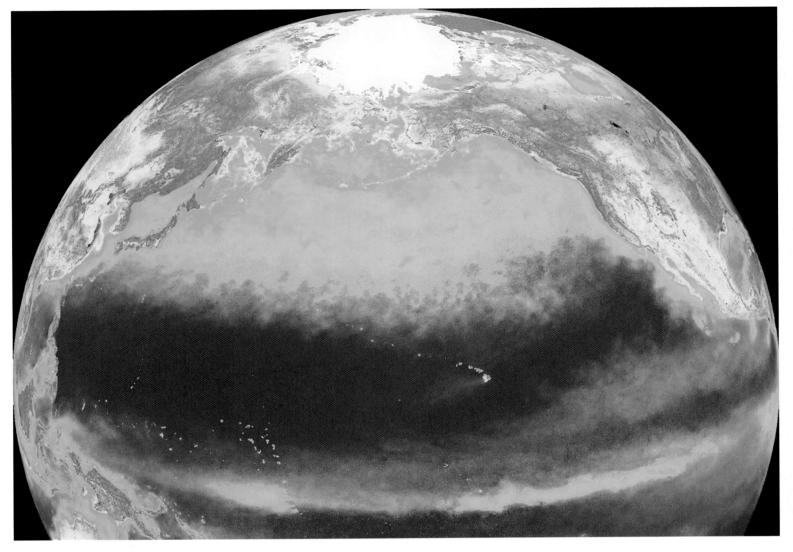

Map 277 (above). A composite image from the *SeaWiFS* satellite. The change in water color from clear blue to blue-green is caused by an increasing concentration of phytoplankton. A line of greener water can be seen along the equator, where a combination of wind and the Earth's rotation brings nutrients to the surface, and north of about 30 degrees latitude. The areas of highest productivity are the Sea of Okhotsk and the Bering Sea, where extraordinary "blooms" such as that shown on Map 275 sometimes occur.

Map 280 (right).
This phenomenal view of the Earth was computer generated using several different sets of satellite data by Rudolf B. Husar, Washington University, St. Louis. Sea surface temperatures are shown particularly well here (yellow-orange-red being warmer water), with El Niño flaring eastwards across the Pacific to the South American coast. Data used were: a true-color image for the land from NASA-GSFC *SeaWiFS;* fire maps from the European Space Agency; aerosols from *NOAA-NESDIS* AVHRR data; plus clouds from four geostationary satellites, *GOES 8, GOES 9, METEOSAT,* and *GMS5,* from the University of Wisconsin SSEC KidSat Project.

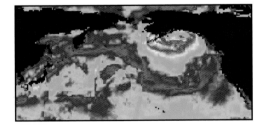

Map 278 (center) and
Map 279 (right, bottom).
Images from a new NASA satellite called *QuickScat*, with a radar scatterometer which measures wind speed and direction twice a day. Map 278 shows wind speeds during a storm in the Gulf of Alaska on 8 October 2000. The red area is the storm. Map 279 was recorded at the same time and shows wind stream lines in the entire North Pacific, indicating direction as well as speed.

W. Timothy Liu and Wenquing Tang, NASA/NOAA-sponsored data system Seaflux at JPL, U.S.A.

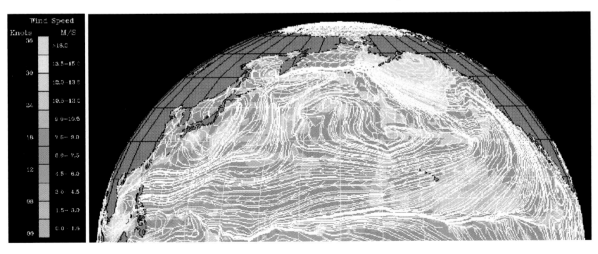

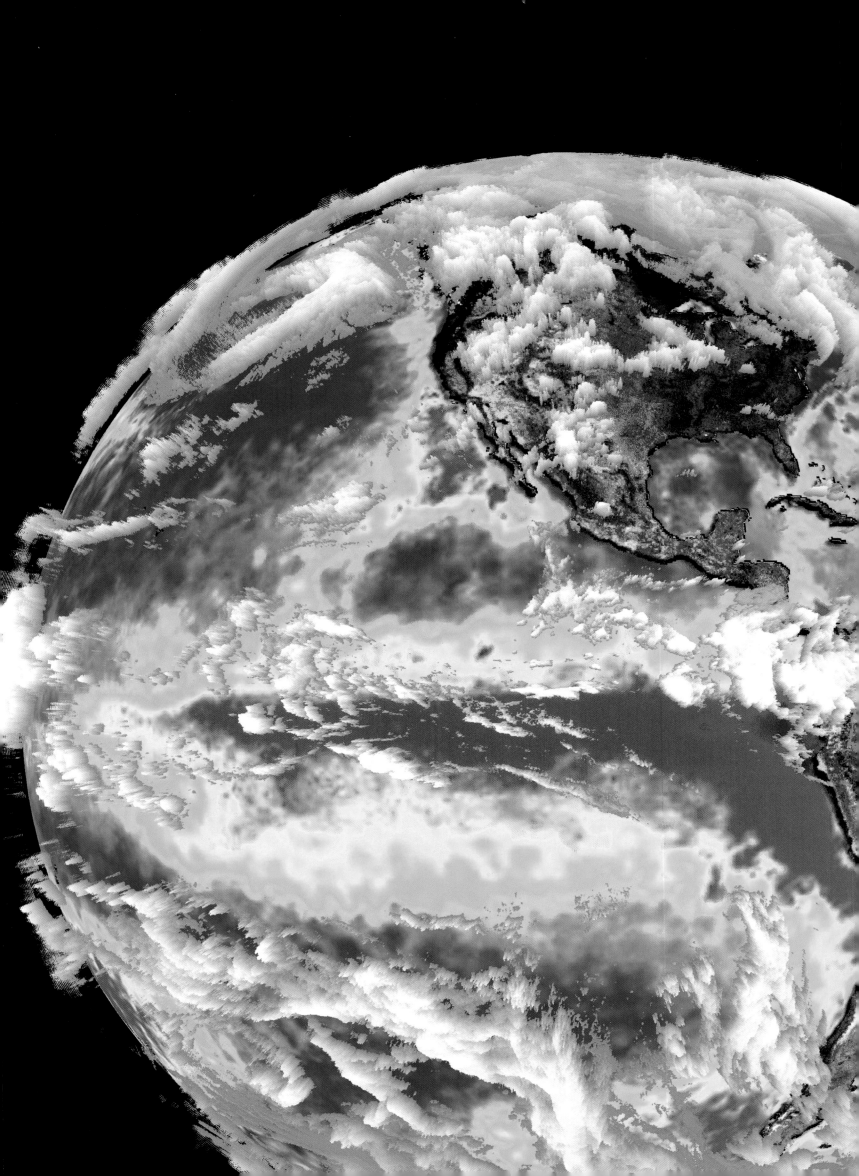

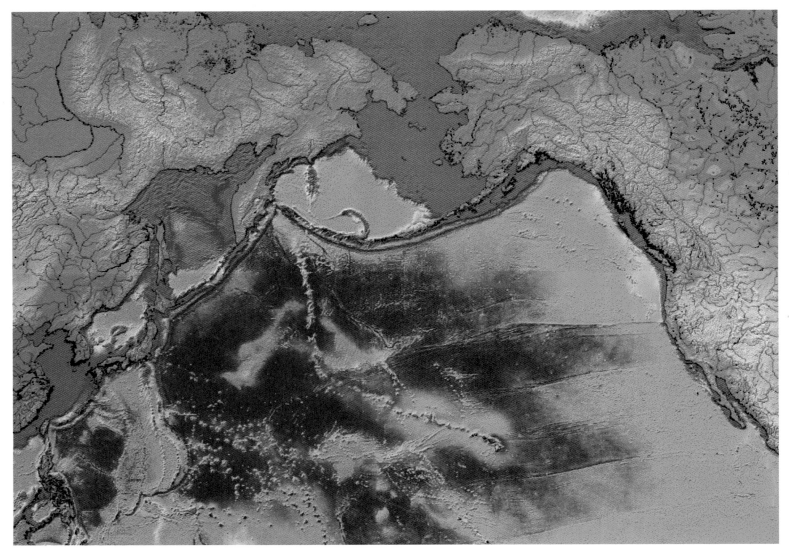

Map 281 (above).

A map of sea floor topography made from satellite gravity measurements supplemented with ship-based soundings, by Walter Smith of NOAA and David Sandwell of Scripps, published in 1997. The relatively shallow continental shelves are pink-orange; midocean ridges and seamounts are green and yellow; the abyssal plains, with fracture zones and deeper trenches, are blue and purple. This map showed thousands of seamounts worldwide that were not on the charts before.

months two geophysicists, David Sandwell of Scripps and Walter Smith of NOAA, had converted the data into a map. In order to improve its accuracy, they then correlated the data with known ship soundings. This eliminated errors due to, for example, increased gravitational pull that was due not to increased volume but to increased mass, that is, higher rock density. They also supplemented the map with data from a similar European satellite, *ERS-1*. The result is the rather beautiful map shown above (Map 281).

Radar altimeters have become an important source of data on water movement. Altimeters on U.S. *TOPEX/Poseidon* and European *ERS-2* satellites are more precise than *Geosat*, and are in orbits designed to detect changes in the height of the ocean surface to an accuracy that allows detection and tracking of eddies and other dynamic features.

Map 282. Radar altimeter map of the northeastern Pacific, from *TOPEX/ Poseidon* and *ERS-2* satellites. This map is an average for a 90-day period from November 1997 to February 1998, at the time of an El Niño. Sea level is 10 to 30 cm above normal

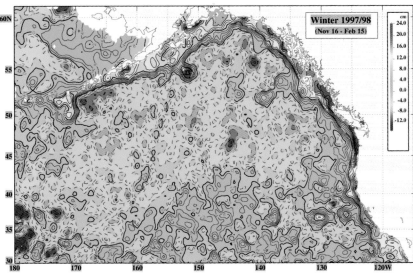

along the coast and in eddies, seen as areas 200 to 300 km wide. As this is the northern hemisphere, water in these eddies is slowly circulating in a clockwise direction. Images such as this are built up over a period of time as the satellite tracks overhead. Prepared by Josef Cherniawsky, Institute of Ocean Sciences, Fisheries and Oceans Canada.

Concerns about the impact of increasing levels of carbon dioxide in the Earth's atmosphere, first documented in the 1960s, coupled with advances in weather prediction techniques, led in 1980 to the establishment of the World Climate Research Program (WCRP). The mission of the WCRP is to carry out the research needed to predict climate on time scales ranging from months to decades.

The oceans are an important part of the world's climate system, capable of storing and transporting large quantities of heat; they also contain 96 percent of the Earth's water. The lack of reliable models of ocean circulation was seen as a major obstacle to climate prediction.

In response, scientists from more than thirty countries planned, managed, and carried out the World Ocean Circulation Experiment (WOCE), with the goal of developing models useful for predicting climate change and to find methods for determining long-term changes in ocean circulation.

Observations for WOCE were carried out between 1990 and 1997, and these were followed by an interpretation, analysis, modelling, and synthesis phase, planned to end in 2002. However, the work of scientific interpretation of the data is expected to go on for many years.

One major component of the observing program was a global one-time ship-based survey of the distribution of ocean temperatures, salinity, and chemical tracers including nutrients, dissolved oxygen, chlorinated fluorocarbons, tritium, helium, and Carbon 14. The tracks of ships during this survey are shown criss-crossing the Pacific in the map below.

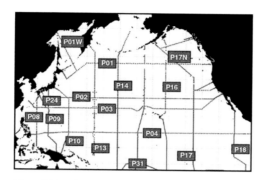

Map 283. The network of observational tracks made by research ships in the North Pacific during WOCE.

Specially launched satellites played an important part by making global observations of sea level, accurate to 5 cm, and the slope of sea level, which allowed changes in surface currents to be determined repeatedly over several years. Satellites also provided observations of sea surface temperature and winds and allowed precise navigation.

In addition, "repeat hydrography" was carried out; that is, multiple observations of temperature, salinity, and nutrients were made several times along the same ship track, in order to measure changes. Upper-ocean thermal structure was measured, in an interesting extension of work begun by Matthew Fontaine Maury in the mid-nineteenth century (see page 152), by merchant ships dropping expendable probes.

Satellite-tracked drifting buoys measured surface currents and temperature, acoustically tracked floats recorded conditions at various depths, anchored arrays of current meters measured ocean currents over time, and a network of tide gauges measured sea level.

With all this activity, naturally enough WOCE produced a massive amount of data that will be a scientific resource for many years to come.

One of its major achievements was developing a way of consolidating and storing this data, and distributing it over the Internet.

By the end of the observing phase, data from WOCE had already been used to improve estimates of the circulation of heat and water in the world's oceans. Another major result was a greatly improved understanding of the role of large eddies in the movement and mixing of heat (Map 272, page 206). A further important legacy of WOCE was the development of new techniques and equipment for ocean observation.

This WOCE profile is of water salinity in the North Pacific north-south along 179° E. It shows that nearer the surface, the northern part of the ocean is less salty than the rest.

Prepared by Alex Kozyr, CDIAC, University of Tennessee, using *Ocean Data View*, Version 5.1 - 2000, by Reiner Schlitzer, http://www.awi-bremerhaven.de/GEO/ODV.

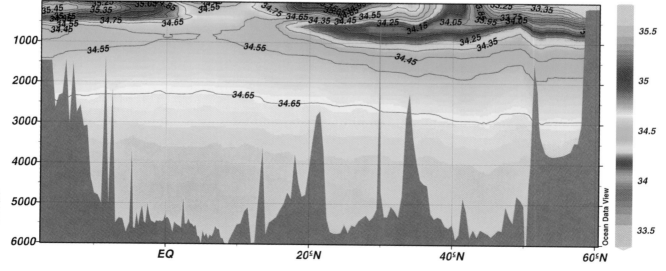

The Future – Project Argo

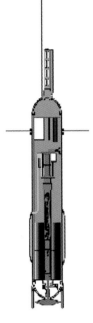

Project Argo, which is currently under way, aims to deploy floating observation robots at depth in the oceans around the world.

The idea of obtaining information on currents using floats was not new. The basic circulation, or gyre, of the Atlantic was determined in 1885–87 by Prince Albert of Monaco, who had released 1,675 bottles each with a polite message for the finder in ten languages, 227 of which were recovered.

Then in 1948 Henry Stommel, whom we have already met in our section on lost islands (page 59), produced a major theory explaining ocean circulation, which in the Atlantic predicted a southward counterflow of cold water *under* the northward-flowing Gulf Stream. British oceanographer John Swallow had invented a device that would prove Stommel correct, a variation of one Stommel himself had suggested.

The device consisted of two aluminum scaffolding tubes, each 3 m (10 feet) long, bound together. One tube provided flotation and was designed to hold the other tube, which contained batteries and a transducer, at a specific depth. The transducer emitted a sound that could be picked up by a nearby ship and its position thus determined.

In this way, Stommel's revelatory abyssal circulation theory, the precursor of the modern theory of thermohaline circulation of the oceans (that ocean circulation is caused by differences in temperature and salinity, and requires deep counter currents as well as surface currents) was proven.

The floating devices being deployed as part of Project Argo are the modern high-tech descendants of Stommel and Swallow's tubes. They are called PALACE floats, an acronym for Profiling Autonomous LAgrangian Current Explorer.

The Pacific Ocean has a profound effect on the climate of many areas of the Earth, and changes in currents and water temperatures at depth as well as at the surface often are behind changes in climate on land. The Argo floats will provide, it is hoped, vital information in a much more comprehensive fashion than was possible before.

When a PALACE float is deployed, mainly from the air, it will sink to 2 000 m (6,500 feet) and drift at that depth for ten days. It will then rise to the surface, transmit its data to a satellite, and then dive again. On the way up it will profile water temperature and salinity. Each float is expected to be able to dive two hundred times; thus each has a life of over five years, although it is expected that replacement floats will be deployed as required.

The difference in the position of the float from one dive to the next shows the ten-day drift at depth, and thus the average deep current speed. Going up and diving, the float will give information on the complete internal dynamics of the top 2 000 m of the ocean, every ten days on a continuing basis. Such data will be used to initialize climate forecast models and, it is hoped, thus provide much-improved seasonal weather forecasts. All this data is to be made available on the Internet within twenty-four hours.

By the end of 2003 it is expected that 3,000 PALACE floats will have been deployed worldwide, 850 of which will be in the North Pacific. This will create an internationally-sponsored global ocean climate observatory of unprecedented proportions.

Map 284.
Map showing the proposed deployment of PALACE floats.

(above, right)
Cross-section of a PALACE float.

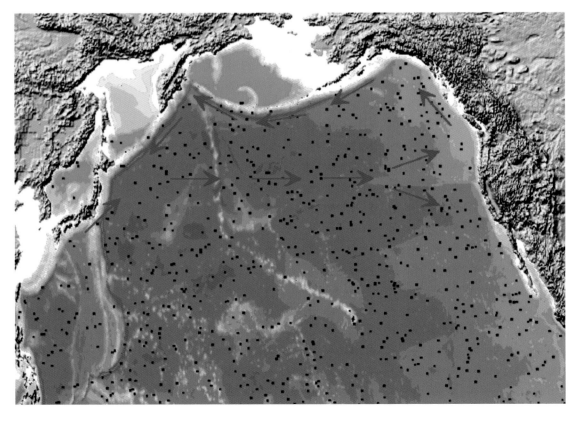

Map Sources

Map Catalog

Sources for maps are stated in the individual listings in the map catalog. Where none is given, the map is from the author's or another private collection, or an original source is untraceable. All efforts were made to ensure proper credit for sources, and I apologize if any have been missed.

Abbreviations used in the map catalog:

AN	Archives nationales, Paris
ARA	Algemein Rijksarchief, Hague
ARSI	Archivum Romanum Societatis Iesu (Jesuit Archives), Rome
Bancroft	Bancroft Library, University of California
BCA	British Columbia Archives
Beinecke	Beinecke Rare Book Library, Yale University
BL	British Library
BNF	Bibliothèque nationale, Paris
Cabinet Library	Cabinet Library, Tokyo, Japan
Huntington	Huntington Library, San Marino, CA
JCBL	John Carter Brown Library, Brown University, Providence, RI
JFBL	James Ford Bell Library, University of Minnesota
KB	Kungl. Biblioteket (Royal Library), National Library of Sweden, Stockholm
Kobe Public Library	Kobe Public Library, Kobe, Japan
LC	Library of Congress
MMPH	Maritiem Museum Prins Hendrick, Rotterdam
NAC	National Archives of Canada
NARA	National Archives and Records Administration (U.S. National Archives)
NLC	National Library of Canada
NMM	National Maritime Museum, Greenwich
NYPL	New York Public Library
OHS	Oregon Historical Society, Portland
Princeton	Princeton University Library
PRO	Public Record Office, Kew, U.K.
UBC	Special Collections, University of British Columbia, Vancouver
UKHO	United Kingdom Hydrographic Office, Taunton, U.K.
VPL	Special Collections, Vancouver Public Library
Yale	Yale University Library

Maps are listed by map number.

1   (Frontispiece)
    [Map of the North Pacific Ocean]
    Girolamo de Angelis, 1621
    ARSI

2   *Asia Novissima Tabula*
    Gerard de Jode, 1578. From: *Speculum Orbia Terrarum*, Plate #4.
    LC G1015.J6 1578 vault

3   *Carte Universelle du Monde*
    Pierre Du Val, 1684
    LC GM Neg. 259

4   *Carte de la partie Septentrionale et Orientale de l'Asie*
    Samuel Engel, 1764. From: *Extraits Raissonnés Des Voyages*, 1779.
    NLC G606 E53 1779 Fol. Res.

5   *Geographische Vorstelling eines Globi, welchen Anno 1492. Herr Martin Behaim*
    Johan Doppelmayer copy of Behaim globe, 1730
    Nordenskiöld, 1889

6   [World map]
    Giovanni Contarini and Francesco Rosselli, 1506
    BL Maps.C.2.cc.4

7   [Gores for a world globe]
    Martin Waldseemüller
    JFBL

8   [World map, west sheet]
    Diogo Ribiero, 1529. Copy made in 1886 or 1887.
    LC G3200 1529.R5 1887 MLC

9   [World map]
    Sebastian Münster, 1546
    JFBL

10 [1520 Schöner Globe redrawn by Kohl]
    LC Kohl Collection

11 [Map of East China Sea]
    Cheng Ho, no date. From: *Ying Yai Sheng Lan.*
    LC

12 [World map]
    Battista Agnese, 1542

13 [Chart of the Patagonian Region]
    Antonio Pigafetta, from his manuscript account of Magellan's voyage, c1525.
    Beinecke Folio 21, recto

14 [World map]
    Sebastian Cabot, 1544
    BNF RES Ge AA 582 Re C 2486

15 *Descripcion de las Indias Ocidentalis*
    After Juan López de Velasco, 1601.
    From: Antonio Herrera, 1622 edition.
    LC G1100.H42 1622 vault

16 *Descripcion de las Indias Del Poiniente*
    After Juan López de Velasco, 1601.
    From: Antonio Herrera, 1622 edition, between folio 78 and folio 79.
    LC G1100.H42 1622 vault

17 [Map of the Pacific Ocean showing galleon routes]
    Juan López de Velasco, c1575
    JCBL

18 *Part of the Pacific Ocean between California and the Philippine Islands*
    La Pérouse, 1798, atlas, English edition.

19 *Nova Totius Terrarum Orbis Ivxta Neotericorum Traditiones Descriptio*
    Abraham Ortelius, 1564
    BL Maps.C.2.a.6

20 [Southeast Asia, part of world map]
    Emery Molyneux, 1599. From: *Principall Navigations*, Richard Hakluyt, 1599 edition.

21 [Map of Southeast Asia]
    Fernão Vaz Dourado, 1570
    Huntington Library

22 *Asiae Novo Descriptio*
    Abraham Ortelius, 1570
    From: *Theatrum Orbis Terrarum.*
    LC G1006.T5 1570b vault

23 *Universale Descrittione di tutta la terra conosciuta fin qui*
    Paolo Forlani, c1562
    LC G3200 1565 .F6 vault

24 [World map]
    Giovanni Gastaldi, 1562

25 [World map]
    Bolognini Zalterii or Paolo Forlani, 1566

26 [Map of California, Japan, and the Pacific]
    Joan Martines, 1578
    BL Harley MS 3450, Map 10 in atlas

27 *Tartariae Sive Magni Chami Regni*
    Abraham Ortelius, 1570
    From: *Theatrum Orbis Terrarum.*
    LC G7270 1570.O7 vault

28 [Map of the world in two hemispheres]
    Title page to *Purchas His Pilgrimes*, Samuel Purchas, 1625.

29 *La Herdike* [sic, Heroike] *Enterprinse Faict par de Signeur Draeck d'avoir Circuit Toute la Terre* ("The French Drake Map")
    Nicola van Sype, c1583
    BL Maps Cs.a7(1)

30 *Carta particolare della stretto di Iezo Pra l'America e l'Isola Iezo D'America Carta XXXIII*
    Robert Dudley, 1647. From: *Dell' Arcano del Mare*, Florence, 1647.
    Engraved by Antonio Francesco Lucini.

31 *Vera Totius Expeditionis Nauticae descriptio D. Franc. Draci . . . Addita est etiam viva delineatio navigationes Thomea Caundish . . . Iudocus Hondius*
    Joducus Hondius, Amsterdam, 1589
    MMPH

32 *Portius Nova Albionis*
    Inset on Hondius, Map 31.
    MMPH

33 *Carta XVIII della parte Orientale del di Iezo con li Stretto fram America è la della Isola*
Robert Dudley, 1647
From: *Dell' Arcano del Mare*, Florence, 1661.
Engraved by Antonio Francesco Lucini.

34 *Carta particolare Grande Isola del Giapone è di Iezo xon il Regro di Corai el alt re Isole intorno*
Robert Dudley, 1647
From: *Dell' Arcano del Mare*, Florence, 1661.
Engraved by Antonio Francesco Lucini.

35 [Santa Barbara and Santa Catalina]
Attrib. Fray Antonio de la Ascension, copied by Enrico Martínez, 1602.

36 [Monterey Bay and adjacent coast]
Attrib. Fray Antonio de la Ascension, copied by Enrico Martínez, 1602.

37 *Carta de los reconociemientos hechos en 1602 por El Capitan Sebastian Viscayno Formaoa por los Planos que hizo el mismo durante su comision*
From: *Relación del Viage . . .*, atlas, No. 4, 1802.

38 [Part of a Map of California]
Joan Vinckeboons, c1650
LC G3291.S12coll.H3 Harrisse No. 10

39 [Map of Southeast Asia, 1596]
From: *Discours of Voyages into ye Easte of Weste Indies*, Jan Huighen van Linschoten, 1598.
LC

40 [Goto Islands and Nagasaki]
Dutch manuscript map, no date [c1680?]
UKHO c631 on Ba3
© Crown Copyright 2000. Published by permission of the Controller of Her Majesty's Stationery Office and the U.K. Hydrographic Office.

41 [Map of the Pacific Ocean]
Hessel Gerritz, 1622
BNF S.H. Arch. No. 30 Rc C 1239

42 [Japanese map of Nagasaki]
Japanese manuscript map, c1680
BL Oriental and India Office Collections, Or.75.g.25

43 *A New and Correct Map of the Whole World*
Hermann Moll, 1719
LC G3200 1719.M6 TIL vault

44 *Carte Tres Curieuse de la Mer du Sud, Contenant des Remarques Noui\velles et Tres Utiles non Seulement sur les Ports et Iles de cette Mer*
Henri Chatelain, 1719
LC

45 [Map of Japan and the Kuril Islands, including Company Land]
Maerten Vries, 1643
ARA

46 [Map of Vries' discoveries]
Isaak de Graaf, c1644
ARA

47 *Aenerkkinge op de Raise*
(Map to accompany a published account of the voyage of Maerten Vries), 1669
JFBL

48 *Nova et Accuratissima Totius Terrarum Orbis Tabula*
Joan Blaeu, 1664
LC G3200 1664.B5 TIL vault

49 [Map of Southeast Asia]
Diogo Homem, 1558
BL Add MS 5415.A Map 17–18

50 *Japoniae Insulae Descriptio*
Luis Teixeira, 1595

51 [Korea]
Martino Martini, 1655

52 [Chinese world map]
Anonymous, 1743
BL Oriental and India Office Collections, Ch.S.5a

53 [Chinese globe]
Manuel Dias and Nicolo Longobardi, 1623
BL Maps G.35

54 *Yudi shanhai quantu*
From: Zhang Huang, *Tushu bian*, 1613 (copy).

55 *Huatyi tu*
Anonymous, 1040/1136 (copy)

56 [Map of Eastern Siberia]
Anonymous, commissioned by Petr Godunov, 1667
From: A. V. Efimov, 1964, Map 28.

57 [Map of Eastern Siberia]
Gerhard Müller based on Semen Dezhnev's reports, 1736
From: A. V. Efimov, 1964, Map 79.

58 *Niewe Lantkaerte van het Noorder en Ooster deel van Asia* (northeast sheet)
Nicholaas Witsen, 1687
JFBL

59 [Russian map of Kamchatka]
Anonymous, 1701

60 [Map of Kamchatka]
Semen Remezov, c1712
From: A. V. Efimov, 1964, Map 48.

61 [Map of Kamchatka]
Ivan Evreinov, c1722
From: A. V. Efimov, 1964, Map 61.

62 *The island which the Marques del Valle discovered* from an official *islario*, by Alonso de Santa Cruz, 1542. From a facsimile.
LC

63 [Map of California]
Joan Vinckeboons, c1650
LC G3291.S12coll.H3 Harrisse No. 10

64 [Map of Pacific]
Henri Chatelain, 1719
From: *Atlas historique.*

65 *Recentissima Novi Orbis sive Americae Septentrionalis et Meridionalis Tabula*
Carolus Allard, 1700

66 *Totius Americae*
Johann Baptist Homann, 1731
From: *Neuer Atlas bestehend in einig curieusen astronomischen . . .*
LC G105.H59 1731 vault

67 [Part of a map of America]
Nicolas Sanson, 1696
LC

68 *A New and Correct Map of the whole World*
Herman Moll, 1719
LC G3200 1719.M6 TIL vault

69 [Three maps of California]
Philippe Buache, 1752 (1755)
From: *Considerations Geographiques et Physiques.*
LC G2860.B9 1755 copy 2 vault

70 *Nieuwe Pascaart Oost Indien*
Johannes van Keulen, 1680
BL Maps 7.TAB.126, Map No. 38

71 [Map of the North Pacific Ocean]
Gerard van Keulen, 1728
BL Maps 13.TAB.2, Map No. 87

72 *Bankoku-sozu*
Anonymous, Japanese, 1645
BL Maps *920.(485)

73 [Map of the Pacific]
From: Tsunenori Iguchi, *Temmon Zukai*, Osaka, 1689. Engraved by Balkado Gisetsu (copy).

74 [Map of junks drifting in the Pacific]
Charles Brooks, 1876
From: *Early Migrations: Japanese Wrecks Stranded and Picked Up Adrift in the North Pacific Ocean*, 1876.
UBC Special Collections

75 *Generalis Totius Imperii Moscovitici*
Johann Baptist Homann, 1704 (1731)
From: *Neuer Atlas bestehend in einig curieusen astronomischen . . .*
LC G105.H59 1731 vault

76 *Carte de Tartarie*
Guillaume de L'Isle, 1706
LC G7270 1706.L5 TIL vault

77 *Carte Generale de Toutes les Costes du Monde*
Nicolas Sanson
Published by Pierre Mortier, 1708.
From: *Le Neptune Francois, ou Atlas Nouveau des Cartes Marines*, 1708.
NMM D8171

78 *Asiae Recentissima Delineatio*
Johann Baptist Homann, 1707
JFBL

79 *A New and Correct Map of the whole World*
Herman Moll, 1719
LC G3200 1719.M6 TIL vault

80 *Generalis Totius Imperii Russorum*
Johann Baptist Homann, 1723
JFBL

81 *Das Land Kamtzedelie soust Jedso*
Johann Baptist Homann, 1725
From: *Grösser atlas uber die gantze welt*, Johann Gabriel Doppelmayr, 1725.
Princeton Rare Books (Ex) 1009.475e

82 *Kamtschatka quae Japonum Okv Jeso Ex recentissima Russia Impery Mappa*
Engelbert Kaempfer, 1727
From: *Historia Imperii Japonici*, Vol. 1, Plate VIII, 1727.
JFBL

83 [Map of Kamchatka and the Kuril Islands]
Afanasii Shestakov, c1730 (French copy)
BNF S.H. PF 177 Div. 2 84 C 122489

84 [Map of the North Pacific]
Anonymous, c1702
NAC NMC133187 H3 1-4000 1702

85 [Donna Maria Laxara Island]
John Green, 1776
From: *Chart containing part of the Icy Sea with the adjacent coasts of Asia and America.* Published by Thomas Jefferys, London, 1776.

86 *Nova et Accuratissima Totius Terrarum Orbis Tabula*
Reinier and Joshua Ottens, 1745
From: *Atlas van Zeevaert en Koophandel door de Geheele Weereldt,* 1745.

87 *Mar Del Zur Hispanis Mare Pacificum*
Joannes Jansson, 1650

88 *Mappe Monde ou Globe Terrestre en deux Plans Hemispheres. Dressee sur les observations de Mrss de L'Academie Royal Des Sciences*
Jean Covens and Corneille Mortier, c1780

89 *Carte Generale Des Découvertes de l'Amiral de Fonte et autres navigateurs Espagnols Anglois et Russes pour la recherche du passage a la Mer du Sud par M. De L'Isle del'Academie des Sciences etc.*
Robert de Vaugondy, 1755
Thought to be from Diderot's *Encyclopedié.*

90 *A Chart Containing the Coasts of California, New Albion, and Russian Discoveries to the North with the Peninsula of Kamschatka, Asia, opposite thereto And Islands dispersed over the Pacific Ocean to the North of the line*
Thomas Jefferys, 1775
From: *An American Atlas Engraved on 48 copper plates by the late Thomas Jefferys Geographer to the King, and others.*
BCA NW912.7 J45am

91 *La America Septentrional desde su extremo Norte hasta 10° de Latitud.*
Isidoro de Antillon, 1802

92 *Carte des Terres Aux Environs du Japon . . .*
Philippe Buache, 1752
From: *Considerations Geographiques et Physiques,* 1755.
LC G2860.B9 1755 copy 2 vault

93 *Carte du Geometrique . . .*
Philippe Buache, 1752
From: *Considerations Geographiques et Physiques,* 1755.
LC G2860.B9 1755 copy 2 vault

94 *Atlas Général a L'Usage Des Colleges et Museums D'Éducation . . . de J. B. Nolin*
Jean B. Nolin, 1783
From: *Amerique Septentrionale,* Plate 33.
LC G1015 .N68 1783

95 *A Map of the Country which Captⁿ Beerings past through in his Journey from Tobolsk to Kamtschatka*
Joseph-Nicolas de L'Isle, based on a map by Jean-Baptiste Bourguignon d'Anville
From: *The General History of China,* Jean Baptiste du Halde, 1736.

96 [Map of Bering's 1728 voyage]
Anonymous, c1728
KB

97 [Sketch illustrating Bering's first voyage, in 1728]
Joseph-Nicolas de L'Isle, based on his conversation with Bering, c1732

98 [Map of Mikhail Gvozdev's voyage]
Martin Spanberg, c1734
From: A. V. Efimov, 1964, Map 69.

99 [Kamchatka and the Kuril Islands]
Martin Spanberg, 1739
From: A. V. Efimov, 1964, Map 105.

100 *Carte Dressee en 1731 Pour Servir a la recherche des Terres et des Mers Situees Au Nord de la Mer du Sud*
Joseph-Nicolas de L'Isle, 1731
From: A. V. Efimov, 1964, Map 78.

101 [St. Elias (Kayak) Island]
Sofron Khitrov, 1741
From: F. A. Golder, 1922/25

102 [Shumagin Islands]
Sofron Khitrov, 1741
From: F. A. Golder, 1922/25

103 [Map of Bering's 1741 voyage]
Probably by Sven Waxell, 1742
From: A. V. Efimov, 1964, Map 101.

104 [Petropavlovsk Harbor, Kamchatka]
Vitus Bering, 1741
From: F. A. Golder, 1922/25

105 [East coast of Kamchatka and Bering Island]
Sven Waxell, c1742
From: F. A. Golder 1722/25

106 [Map of Alexei Chirikov's voyage]
Ivan Elagin, c1742
From: A. V. Efimov, 1964, Map 98.

107 [Map of Second Kamchatka Expedition (1)]
Anonymous, c1742
From: A. V. Efimov, 1964, Map 93.

108 [Map of Second Kamchatka Expedition (2)]
Anonymous, c1742
From: A. V. Efimov, 1964, Map 117.

109 *Carte de Nouvelles Decouvertes*
Joseph-Nicolas de L'Isle, 1752
NAC NMC 210056

110 *Carte des Nouvelles Decouvertes entre la partie Orientᵉ de Asie et Occidᵉ de L'Amerique*
Philippe Buache, 1755
From: *Considerations Geographiques et Physiques,* 1755.
LC G2860.B9 1755 copy 2 vault

111 *Chart containing part of the Icy Sea with the adjacent coasts of Asia and America*
John Green, 1753. Published by Thomas Jefferys, London, 1753.

112 *Chart containing the Coasts of California, New Albion, and Russian Discoveries to the North with the Peninsula of Kamchatka, Asia, opposite thereto; And Islands, dispersed over the Pacific Ocean, to the North of the Line*
John Green, 1753
Published by Thomas Jefferys, London, 1753.

113 *L'hydrographie françois: recueil des cartes générales et particulières qui ont ête faites pour le service des vaisseaux du roy, par ordre des Ministres de la marine, depuis 1737, jusqu'en 1765*
Jacques Nicolas Bellin, c1766
LC G1059.B43 1772

114 *Nouvelle Carte de decouvertes faites par de vaisseaux Russiens aux côtes inconnues de l'Amerique Septentrionale avec les pais adjacents*
Gerhard Müller, 1754
JCBL

115 [Map of Ivan Synd's voyage]
Ivan Synd, 1768

116 [Geographical map showing discoveries of Russian seagoing vessels on the northern part of America]
Gerhard Müller, Imperial Academy of Learning, St. Petersburg
Russian edition, c1773.

117 *A Map of the New Northern Archipelago discover'd by the Russians in the Seas of Kamtschatka & Anadir*
Jacob von Stählin, 1774
From: *Account of a New Northern Archipelago Lately Discovered by the Russians,* 1774.

118 *Chart of Synd's Voyage towards Tchukotskoi Nos*
From: William Coxe, *An Account of the Russian Discoveries between Asia and America,* London, 1780.
VPL

119 *Map of Krenitsin and Levashev's Voyage to the Fox Islands in 1768 and 1769.*
Published April 13th 1780 . . . by T. Cadell. Engr by T. Kitchin.
From: William Coxe, *An Account of the Russian Discoveries between Asia and America,* London, 1780.
VPL

120 [Potap Zaikov's map of the Aleutians]
1779
From: A. V. Efimov, 1964, Map 161.

121 [Map of the North Pacific Ocean]
Grigorii Shelikov, 1787
Yale °23 1787

122 *Magnum Mare del Zur cum Insula California*
Reinier and Joshua Ottens, 1750
LC G9230 1750 .R2 vault

123 *Plano del Puerto de S Diego . . .*
Anonymous, Spanish, no date
LC G3351.P5 1799.C vault

124 *Carta Reducida del Oceano Asiatico ō Mar del Sur que contiene la Costa de la California comprehendida desde el Puerto de Monterrey. hta la Punta de Sᵗᵃ Maria Magdelena hecha segun las observaciones y Demarcasiones del Aljerez de Fragata de la Rᵗ Armada y Primer Piloto de este Departamento Dⁿ Juan Perez por Dⁿ Josef de Cañizarez.*
Josef de Cañizarez, 1774
NARA

125 *Plano del Puerto de Sn Francisco*
Josef Camacho, Spanish, c1779 or later copy
LC G3351.P5 1799.C vault

126 *Plano del Puerto de Sn Francisco*
Josef de Cañizarez, 1774
Bancroft

127 *Plano del Puerto de los Dolores*
Jacinto Caamaño, 1792, or anonymous later copy
LC G3351.P5 1799.C vault

128 *Plano de la Rada de Bucareli situado . . .*
Bruno de Hezeta y Dudagoitia, July 1775.
Archivo General de Indias, Seville

129 *Plano de la Bahia de la Asunciōn . . .*
Bruno de Hezeta y Dudagoitia, August 1775
Archivo General de Indias, Seville

130 *Carta que contiene parte de la costa de la California*
Bernabe Muñoz, 1787
LC G4362.C6 1787.M8 TIL vault

131 *Plano de la Entrada de Ezeta*
Esteban José Martínez, Spanish, 1793
LC G3351.P5 1799.C vault

132 *Carta reducida de las costas, y mares septentrionales de California construida bajo las observaciones, y demarcaciones hechas por de Fragata Don Juan Francisco de la Vodega y Quadra commandante de la goleta Sonora y por el piloto Don Francisco Antonio Maurelle . . . , 1775*
Archivo General de Indias, Sevilla
MP, Mexico 581

133 *Carte de L'Ocean Pacifique au Nord de l'Equateur, et des Cotes qui . . . Espagnols, les Russes, et les Anglois, jusqu'en 1780*
Tobie Conrad Lotter, 1781
NAC NMC 8607 H2 1-4000 [1781?]

134 *Esquisse d'une Carte* and *Extrait de la Carte*
Samuel Engel, 1781
Beinecke Zc86 781en

135 *Track from first making the Continent, March 7th, to Anchoring in King George's Sound*
From: Journal of James Burney, 1778.
PRO ADM 51/4528

136 *Chart of part of the N W Coast of America Explored by Capt. J. Cook in 1778*
James Cook, 1778
PRO MPI 83 (removed from ADM 1/1621)

137 *Chart of the NW Coast of America and the NE Coast of Asia explored in the years 1778 and 1779. The unshaded parts of the coast of Asia are taken from a MS chart received from the Russians.*
From: James Cook, *Voyage to the Pacific Ocean,* 1784.

138 *Chart of Norton Sound and of Bherings Strait made by the East Cape of Asia and the West Point of America, 1778/1779*
From: James Cook, *Voyage to the Pacific Ocean,* 1784.

139 *General Chart exhibiting the discoveries made by Capt. James Cook in this and his preceding two voyages, with the tracks of the ships under his command.*
Henry Roberts. Wm. Faden, 1784
BCA CM B1189

140 *A Plan of the Bay of A'vatch'ka by Edward Riou*
Edward Riou, 1779
UKHO 524/1 on Rd
© Crown Copyright 2000. Published by permission of the Controller of Her Majesty's Stationery Office and the U.K. Hydrographic Office.

141–147 (seven maps)
From: *Atlas, by Navigator Lovtsov composed by him while wintering at the Bol'sheretsk ostrog in the year 1782*
Seven watercolor plates from MS atlas.
Vasilii Fedorovich Lovtsov, 1782
BCA NW 912.722 L922

148 *Chart of the Coasts of America & Asia from California to Macao according to the Discoveries made in 1786 & 1787 by the Boussole & Astrolabe*
G. G. and J. Robinson, November 1797

149 [Carte de la Côte Ouest de l'Amérique du Nord, de Mt. St. Elias à Monterey, avec la trajectoire l'expédition de La Pérouse et la table des données de longitude compilées par Bernizet and Dagelet]
Joseph Dagelet and Gérault-Sébastien Bernizet, 1786
AN 6 JJ1: 34B

150 *Plan du Port des Français Située sur la Côte du N.O. de l'Amerique Septentrionale*
Gérault-Sébastien Bernizet and Paul Mérault de Monneron, July 1786
AN 6 JJ1: 30

151 *Plan de Baye de Castries Située sur la Côte Orientale de Tartarie*
Gérault-Sébastien Bernizet, July 1787
AN 6 JJ1: 41B

152 [Northeast Portion of Siberia, the Arctic Ocean, Eastern Ocean, and Northwest Coasts of North America]
Gavriil A. Sarychev, 1802
From: *Puteshesvie flota kapitana Sarycheva po severovostochnoi chasti Sibiri. . . flota kapitana Billingsa s 1785 po 1793 god,* 2 volumes, St. Petersburg, 1802.
UBC Special Collections G9285 S2 1954 loc4

153 *Sketch of the Entrance of the Strait of Juan de Fuca by Charles Duncan Master in the Royal Navy 15th August 1788 Alexander Dalrymple, publ.*
LC

154 *N. W. America Drawn by J.C. from his own Information & what could be collected from the Sloop Pr Royal & Boats in the Years 1787 1788*
James Colnett, 1788
UKHO p24 on 87
© Crown Copyright 2000. Published by permission of the Controller of Her Majesty's Stationery Office and the U.K. Hydrographic Office.

155 *Chart of the N.W. Coast of America and the N.E. Coast of Asia, explored in the Years 1778 and 1779 by Capt Cook and further explored, in 1788, and 1789.*
From: John Meares, *Voyages made in the years 1788 and 1789 from China to the North West Coast of America,* 1790.

156 *A Chart of the Interior Part of North America Demonstrating the very great probability of an Inland Navigation from Hudson's Bay to the West Coast*
From: John Meares, *Voyages made in the years 1788 and 1789 from China to the North West Coast of America,* 1790.

157 *Chart of the World on Mercator's Projection Exhibiting all the New Discoveries to the Present Time*
Aaron Arrowsmith, 1794 (dated 1790)

158 *Chart of the Pacific Ocean drawn from a great number of printed and ms journals*
A. Arrowsmith, 1798, Sheet 11/9 [sic, 1/9]
LC G9230 1798.A72 vault

159 *Carta que comprehende los interiers y veril de la costa desde los 48° de Latitud N hasta los 50°. 1791*
José María Nárvaez, 1791
LC G3351.P5 1799.C vault, Map 12

160 *Num 9 Plano del Puerto del Desengaño Trabasado de Orden del Rey*
From: *Relación,* atlas, 1802.
VPL SPA 970P E77r2

161 *Chart of the West Coast of North America, with the Isles adjacent from the Latde 50 45'N & Longde. 30 [sic] copied from one constructed . . . by Dn. Caamano . . . in . . . 1792*
Traced by an English draughtsman.
UKHO 355/3 on Ac 1

162 *Num. 2 Carta Esférica de los Reconocimientos hechos en la Costa N.O. De América en 1791 y 92 por las Goletas Sutil y Mexicana y otros Bruques de S.M.*
Dionisio Galiano, 1792
From: *Relación,* atlas, 1802.

163 *Carta general de quanto asta hoy se ha descubierto y examinado por los Espanoles en la Costa Septentrional de California, formada . . . por D. Juan Francisco de la Bodega y Quadra Ano de 1791*
Museo Naval, Madrid

164 *Carta que contiene parte de la costa de la California. . .*
Bernabe Muñoz, 1787
LC G4362.C6 1787.M8 TIL vault

165 *Carta Reducida de la Costa Septentrional de California . . .*
Juan Francisco de la Bodega y Quadra, 1791 or 1792
LC G3351.P5 1799.C vault, Map 1

166 *Carta de los Descubrimientos hechos en la Costa N.O. America Septentrional*
Juan Francisco de la Bodega y Quadra, 1792
LC G3350 1792.B6 TIL vault

167 [Preliminary chart of N.W. Coast of America from George Vancouver's landfall to Cape Mudge, including the first mapping of Puget Sound]
PRO MPG 557 (4), removed from CO 5/187

168 *A Chart Showing part of the Western Coast of North America . . . George Vancouver in the Summer of 1792. Prepared by Lieut Josh Baker under the immediate inspection of Capt Vancouver.*
UKHO 226 on Ac1
© Crown Copyright 2000. Published by permission of the Controller of Her Majesty's Stationery Office and the U.K. Hydrographic Office.

169 [James Johnstone's first survey of Johnstone Strait and Loughborough Inlet, 1792]
UKHO 231/4 Ac 1

170 *A Chart shewing part of the Coast of N.W. America with the tracks of His Majesty's Sloop Discovery and Armed Tender Chatham Commanded by George Vancouver Esq. . . . The parts not shaded are taken from Russian Authority. [Cook Inlet]*
From: George Vancouver, *A Voyage of Discovery to the North Pacific Ocean and Around the World,* Plate 12 of atlas, 1798.

171 *A Chart shewing part of the N.W. Coast of North America with the Tracks of His Majesty's Sloop Discovery and Armed Tender Chatham.*
[Summary map of west coast]
From: George Vancouver, *A Voyage of Discovery . . .,* Plate 14 of atlas, 1798.

172 *A Chart shewing part of the N.W. Coast of North America with the Tracks of His Majesty's Sloop Discovery and Armed Tender Chatham . . .*
From: George Vancouver, *A Voyage of Discovery . . .,* Plate 7 of atlas, 1798.

173 *A Chart shewing part of the Coast of N.W. America with the tracks of His Majesty's Sloop Discovery and Armed Tender Chatham Commanded by George Vancouver Esq. and prepared under his immediate inspection by Lieut. Joseph Baker . . . The parts not shaded are taken from Spanish Authorities.*
Compilation chart for Plate 5 of the atlas for *A Voyage of Discovery . . .*
George Vancouver, 1798
PRO CO 700 British Columbia 1

174 *A Chart of the N.E. Coast of Asia, and Japanese Isles . . .*
William Broughton, 1797
From: William Broughton, *A Voyage of Discovery to the North Pacific Ocean*, 1804.

175 *A Chart of the East Coast of Japan with the Kurile and Liquieux Is. explored by Captn Broughton in His Majesty's Sloop Providence 1796* [Volcano Bay portion, 1796]
William Broughton, 1796–97
UKHO 514/2 on Se
© Crown Copyright 2000. Published by permission of the Controller of Her Majesty's Stationery Office and the U.K. Hydrographic Office.

176 *A Chart of the East Coast of Japan with the Kurile and Liquieux Is. explored by Captn Broughton in His Majesty's Sloop Providence 1796* [with 1797 additions]
William Broughton, 1797
UKHO 514/2 on Se
© Crown Copyright 2000. Published by permission of the Controller of Her Majesty's Stationery Office and the U.K. Hydrographic Office.

177 *Map of the Globe, incorporating the latest descriptions from the Lisianskii fleet, with a display of the route of the Neva from 1803–1806*
From: *Collection of Maps and Drawings Relating to the Voyage of the Fleet of Captain (1st Order) and Gentleman Urei Lisianskii of the ship Neva*, St. Petersburg, 1812.

178 *Chart of the Northwest Part of the Great Ocean. Drawn by D.F. Sotzmann 1811. Reduced from Captⁿ Krusenstern's Original Chart*
VPL 910.4R K94, Vol. 1

179 [Map of Russian possessions in North America]
From: Vasili Nikolayevich Berkh, *Atlas geograficheskikh otkrytii v Sibiri i v Severo Zapadnoi Ameriki*, 1821.

180 *Die Insel Krafto (Seghalien) und die Mundung Des Manko (Amur) Nach Original Karten von Mogami Tokunai und Mamia Rinzo* [Tokunai map]
Philipp Franz von Siebold, 1852
BL 14001.i.44, Vol. 7, Plate XXV

181 [Map of strait between Sakhalin and the mainland, with the Amur River]
Mamiya Rinzo, 1809
Cabinet Library, Tokyo

182 *Die Insel Krafto (Seghalien) und die Mundung Des Manko (Amur) Nach Original Karten von Mogami Tokunai und Mamia Rinzo* [Mamiya map]
Philipp Franz von Siebold, 1852
BL 14001.i.44, Vol. 7, Plate XXV

183 *Xᵉ feuille de la Tartarie Chinoise contenent le Païs de Ke-Tching l'embouchure du Saghalien-Oula dans al Mer Orientale et la grande Isle qui est au dedans*
Jean Baptiste d'Anville, 1737
From: *Nouvelle Atlas.*

184 *Chart of the Pacific Ocean drawn from a great number of printed and ms journals*
Aaron Arrowsmith, 1818

185 *Chart of Behring's Strait.*
Otto Kotzebue, August 1816

186 *Carte Générale de la Mer de Behring 1828*
Fedor Lütke, 1828

187 *Map Exhibiting Areas of Temperature of the Ocean and the Isothermal and Isocheimal Curves of the Continents by the U.S. Ex. Ex. 1850*
From: Charles Wilkes, *Meteorology*, 1850.
LC Q115.W6 folio

188 *Mouth of the Columbia River Oregon Territory Surveyed by the U.S. Ex. Ex. Charles Wilkes Commander. 1841*
Sheet #1
LC G2860.W52 1850 copy 2 fol., Vol. 2, Map #68

189 *Region of Fog North Pacific Ocean by the U.S. Ex.Ex., 1842*
From: Charles Wilkes, *Theory of the Winds*, 1856.
LC Toner QC931 W68 Copy 3 1856, between pages 102 and 103

190 *Chart of the World Shewing the Tracks of the United States Exploring Expedition*
Charles Wilkes, 1845
From: Charles Wilkes, *Narrative of the United States Exploring Expedition during the years 1838, 1839, 1840, 1841, 1842, 1845.*
VPL

191 *Map of the World Shewing the Extent and Direction of the Wind . . . 1856*
From: Charles Wilkes, *Hydrography*, 1856.
LC Q115.W6 vol 23, foldout map between pages 364 and 365

192 [Map of St. Lawrence Island, Bering Sea] 1849
From: Mikhail D. Tebenkov, *Atlas Severozapadnikh beregov Ameriki ot Beringova proliva do mysa i ostrov Aleutskikh*, 1852.

193 [Map of the coast of California, with inset of Golden Gate, San Francisco] 1848
From: Mikhail D. Tebenkov, atlas, 1852.

194 [Map of the mouth of the Columbia River] 1848
From: Mikhail D. Tebenkov, atlas, 1852.

195 *Sekai Bankoku Yori Kaijō Risu Kokuin Ōjō Jimbutsuzu* [Map of the world showing the distances of the various countries from Japan, their names, and inhabitants of their capitals; undated]
Kobe Public Library

196 *Reconnoissance of the Anchorage of Ura-Ga & Reception Bay, on the west side of the entrance of Jeddo Bay, Island of Niphon, Japan, made by order of Commo. M.C. Perry, Comd'g U.S. Naval Forces E. India, China & Japan Seas*
1853
NARA Record Group 37, 451.36 #40

197 "Simoda Lt. Bents Survey with Topography"
NARA Record Group 37, 451.36 #34b

198 *Harbor of Hakodadi Island of Yesso Surveyed by order of Commodore M.C. Perry By Lieut. W.L. Maury, Lieut. G.H. Preble, Lieut J. Nicholson, Lieut A. Barbot 1854*
NARA Record Group 37, 451.36 #31

199 *Chart of the Kuro Siwa or Japan Stream of the Pacific . . .*
Matthew Perry, 1854

200 *Straits of Tsugar*
MS chart reduced for engraving.
NARA Record Group 37, 451.36 #36

201 *Mouth of the Teen-Tsin-Ho And Approach to the Sha-lui-tien Banks By the U.S. Str. John Hancock & U.S. Schr. Fenimore Cooper October 1854*
NARA Record Group 37, 451.36 #28

202 *Reconnoissance of the East Coast of Nippon, Empire of Japan, From Simoda to Hakodati By the launch of the United States Ship Vincennes, under the command of Lieutenant John M. Brooke, U.S.N., assisted by Edward M. Kern, Artist, and Richard Berry, Sailmaker. May 29th to June 17th 1855. Original Working Sheet.*
NARA Record Group 37, 451.36 #13; Yedo (Tokyo) Bay and coast north and south: #1/5 and #2/5

203 *The Asiatic Coast of Behring's Straits. Surveyed in the U.S. Ship Vincennes July and August 1855*
NARA Record Group 37, 181.36 #67

204 *Gulf of Yedo and Approaches By the U.S. Ship Vincennes, Lieut. John Rodgers Commanding U.S. Str. John Hancock, Lieut. Commanding H. K. Stevens May 1855. Additions by Lieut. Commdg. John M. Brooke, U.S. Schr. Fenimore Cooper, 1859.*
NARA Record Group 37, 451.36 #19, Sheet 2 of 4

205 *S.W. Part of Japan From the Surveys of the Expedition in 1854–55 with additions by Lieut. Comdg. John M. Brooke, U.S. Schr. F. Cooper, 1859, and from Dutch, English and Russian Authorities*
NARA Record Group 37, 451.36 #20, 3 sheets

206 *Wind and Current Chart North Pacific No. 7 Series A*
Matthew Fontaine Maury, 1849
LC G9096.C7 svar.M3 vault

207 *Wind and Current Chart North Pacific No. 5 Series A*
Matthew Fontaine Maury, 1849
LC G9096.C7 svar.M3 vault

208 *Pilot Chart of the North Pacific Sheet No. 5, Series C*
Matthew Fontaine Maury, 1851
LC G9096.C7 svar.M3 vault

209 *Whale Chart of the World*
Matthew Fontaine Maury, 1852
LC G9096.C7 svar.M3 vault

210 *Whale Chart by M. F. Maury A. M. Lieut. U.S. Navy* (Series F)
Matthew Fontaine Maury, 1851
LC G9096.C7 svar.M3 vault

211 *Sea Drift and Whales*
Matthew Fontaine Maury
From: *The Physical Geography of the Sea and Its Meteorology*, 1855.

263 *Plate-Tectonic Map of the Circum-Pacific Region* (Northeast and Northwest Quadrants) Circum-Pacific Council for Energy and Mineral Resources, 1981. American Association of Petroleum Geologists.

264 *Plate-Tectonic Map of the Circum-Pacific Region* (Northeast Quadrant) Circum-Pacific Council for Energy and Mineral Resources, 1981. American Association of Petroleum Geologists.

265 *Tsunamis in the Pacific Basin 1900–1983* National Geophysical Data Center and World Data Center A for Solid Earth Geophysics, 1984

266 *Morphology and Shipping Lanes of West-Central San Francisco Bay* U.S. Geological Survey, 2000

267 *Monterey Bay National Marine Sanctuary Bathymetric Map MS-2* National Oceanic and Atmosphere Administration, National Ocean Service, Coast and Geodetic Survey, 1992

268 [Three-dimensional view from] *Monterey Bay National Marine Sanctuary Bathymetric Map MS-2* National Oceanic and Atmosphere Administration, National Ocean Service, Coast and Geodetic Survey, 1992

269 [Computer-enhanced multibeam sonar view of the California coast, looking northwards] Lincoln F. Pratson, Earth and Ocean Sciences, Duke University; and William F. Haxby, Lamont-Doherty Earth Observatory, 1996

270 [Computer-enhanced multibeam sonar view of the Oregon coast, looking southwards] Lincoln F. Pratson, Earth and Ocean Sciences, Duke University; and William F. Haxby, Lamont-Doherty Earth Observatory, 1996

271 [Multibean sonar view of dunes in the Strait of Juan de Fuca] Geological Survey of Canada, Pacific Geoscience Centre, Sidney, B.C. © Natural Resources Canada, 1998.

272 *A composite thermal (sea surface temperature) image for the Gulf of Alaska following removal of the average north-south temperature gradient* James F. R. Gower, Institute of Ocean Sciences (Fisheries and Oceans Canada), Sidney, B.C., 1998

273 [Differences from monthly average sea surface temperatures] November 1997 NOAA

274 [Differences from monthly average sea surface temperatures] November 1998 NOAA

275 [Satellite view of the Bering Sea showing *Coccolithophore* bloom, 1999] *SeaWiFS* satellite image supplied by James F. R. Gower, Institute of Ocean Sciences (Fisheries and Oceans Canada), Sidney, B.C.

276 [Satellite image of chlorophyll distribution in the North Pacific] OCTS/*ADEOS* satellite image from Sei-ichi Saitoh and Kosei Sasaoka, Hokkaido University, Japan. Image date May 1997.

277 Composite *SeaWiFS* satellite image, September 1997 to July 1998.

278 NASA *QuickSat* satellite image, 8 October 2000. Image from the NASA/NOAA sponsored data system Seaflux at JPL, courtesy W. Timothy Lui and Wenqing Tang.

279 NASA *QuickSat* satellite image, 8 October 2000. Image from the NASA/NOAA sponsored data system Seaflux at JPL, courtesy W. Timothy Lui and Wenqing Tang.

280 [Synthetic Earth image from composite satellite data] Rudolf B. Husar, Washington University, St. Louis, 2000

281 [Map of the world showing sea floor topography derived from satellite gravity measurements correlated with ship soundings] Walter Smith, NOAA, and David Sandwell, Scripps, c1999

282 Satellite radar altimeter image. Image supplied by Josef Cherniawsky. Altimeter data processed by Brian Beckley, Raytheon/GSFC (NASA Ocean Altimeter Pathfinder Project), and Josef Cherniawsky, Institute of Ocean Sciences (Fisheries and Oceans Canada), Sidney, B.C.

283 [Ship track map for WOCE project]

284 [Proposed distribution of PALACE floats, Project Argo] Howard Freeland, Institute of Ocean Sciences (Fisheries and Oceans Canada), Sidney, B.C., 2001

285 "Map with Ship" Anonymous; attributed as derived from Marco Polo, c1300. Date questionable. LC G7800 coll .M3 copy 1 Marcian F. Rossi Collection

Map 285.
During my searches for maps for this book I came across this intriguing manuscript on vellum map in the Library of Congress, where it is attributed to c1300. A palimpsest, the faintly visible and very hard to reproduce map is called "Map with Ship," from the ship on the left. It has been attributed in the past to some derivation of Marco Polo. Immediately suspicious because of the considerable geographical knowledge of the Pacific it shows (though it may have been added to later), it has been presumed by some to be a fake, though has not actually proven to be so. Not only does the map show China and Japan, but also what must be Kamchatka and eastern Siberia, the Kuril and Aleutian Islands, and Alaska. The map has a history all of its own; included in its file is a letter from J. Edgar Hoover of the FBI, to whom the map was at one time entrusted in order to have the inks tested. Unfortunately this analysis yielded little definite information, and the map, at least for now, remains an enigma.

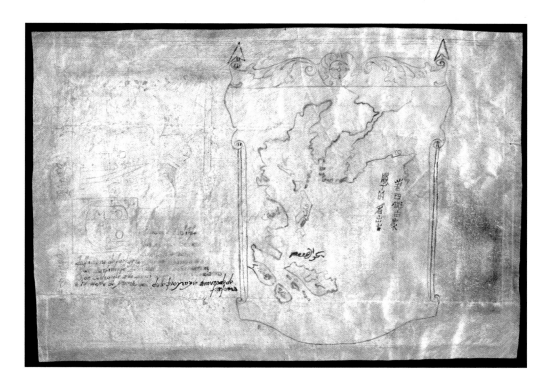

Bibliography

Bancroft, Hubert Howe
History of Alaska, 1730–1885
Bancroft & Co., San Francisco, 1886

Barkan, Frances B. (ed.)
The Wilkes Expedition:
Puget Sound and the Oregon Country
Washington State Capital Museum, Olympia, WA, 1987

Barratt, Glynn
Russia in Pacific Waters, 1715–1825
UBC Press, Vancouver, 1981

Beaglehole, John C.
The Exploration of the Pacific
Stanford University, Stanford, CA, 1966, third edition

Beaglehole, John C.
The Life of Captain James Cook
Hakluyt Society, London, 1974

Beaglehole, John C. (ed.)
The Journals of Captain James Cook on His Voyages of
Discovery: The Voyage of the Resolution *and the* Discovery,
1776–1780, Vol. 3
Hakluyt Society, Cambridge, 1967

Beals, Herbert K. (trans. and notes)
For Honor and Country: The Diary of Bruno De Heseta
Oregon Historical Society Press, Portland, 1985

Beals, Herbert K. (trans.)
Juan Pérez on the Northwest Coast.
Six Documents of His Expedition in 1774
Oregon Historical Society Press, Portland, 1989

Belknap, George E.
Deep-Sea Soundings in the North Pacific Ocean Obtained
in the United States Steamer Tuscarora
U.S. Hydrographic Office No. 54. Government Printing
Office, Washington, DC, 1874

Bishop, R. P.
"Drake's Course in the North Pacific"
British Columbia Historical Quarterly, 3, 1939

Black, Lydia (trans. and intro.)
The Lovtsov Atlas of the North Pacific Ocean
by Vasilii Fedorovich Lovtsov
Limestone Press, Kingston, ON, 1991

Breitfuss, L.
"Early Maps of North-Eastern Asia and of the Lands
around the North Pacific: Controversy between G. F.
Müller and N. Delisle"
Imago Mundi, 3, pp. 87–101, 1939

British Library
Sir Francis Drake: An Exhibition to Commemorate
Francis Drake's Voyage around the World, 1577–1580
Exhibition catalog.
British Museum Publications, London, 1977

Broughton, William Robert
A Voyage of Discovery to the North Pacific Ocean
Cadell and Davies, London, 1804

Challenger Office
Report on the Scientific Results of the Voyage of H.M.S.
Challenger *during the Years 1873–1876*
40 volumes in 44, London, 1880–95

Cortazzi, Hugh
Isles of Gold: Antique Maps of Japan
Weatherhill, New York, 1983

Cutter, Donald C.
Malaspina and Galiano: Spanish Voyages
to the Northwest Coast, 1791 and 1792
Douglas & McIntyre, Vancouver, 1991

Deacon, Margaret
Scientists and the Sea, 1650–1900:
A Study of Marine Science
Academic Press, London, 1971

Dickson, H. N.
"Prof. Pettersson on Methods of Oceanographic Research"
Geographical Journal, 14, No.2, pp. 185–90, August 1899

Divin, Vasilii A.
The Great Russian Navigator, A. I. Chirikov
Translated and annotated by Raymond H. Fisher.
University of Alaska Press, Fairbanks, 1993

Dmytryshyn, Basil, and E. A. P. Crownhart-Vaughan
(trans. and notes)
Colonial Russian America:
Kyrill T. Khlebnikov's Reports, 1817–1832
Oregon Historical Society Press, Portland, 1976

Efimov, A. V. (ed.)
Atlas geograficheskikh v Sibiri i severo-zapadnoy Amerike
XVII–XVIII vv. [Atlas of geographical discoveries in Siberia
and northwestern America in the 17th–18th centuries]
Nauka, Moscow, 1964

Erickson, Jon
Plate Tectonics: Unraveling the Mysteries of the Earth
Facts on File, New York, 1992

Falk, Marvin W.
"Mapping Russian America"
In *Russia in North America.* Proceedings of 2nd
International Conference on Russian America, Sitka,
Alaska, 19–22 August 1987

Fisher, Raymond H.
Bering's Voyages: Whither and Why
University of Washington Press, Seattle, 1977

Fisher, Raymond H.
The Voyage of Semen Deshnev in 1648:
Bering's Precursor; With Selected Documents
Hakluyt Society, London, 1981

Fisher, Robin
Vancouver's Voyage:
Charting the Northwest Coast, 1791–1795
Douglas & McIntyre, Vancouver; University of Washington
Press, Seattle, 1992

Fisher, Robin, and Hugh Johnston (eds.)
From Maps to Metaphors:
The Pacific World of George Vancouver
UBC Press, Vancouver, 1993

Flint, James M.
A Contribution to the Oceanography of the Pacific
[The voyage of the *Nero*]
United States National Museum Bulletin, 55, 1902

Ford, Corey
Where the Sea Breaks Its Back: The Epic Story of a Pioneer
Naturalist and the Discovery of Alaska
Little, Brown, Boston, 1966

Friis, Herman R. (ed.)
The Pacific Basin:
A History of Its Geographical Exploration
American Geographical Society, New York, 1967

Frost, Alan, and Jane Samson (eds.)
Pacific Empires: Essays in Honour of Glyndwr Williams
UBC Press, Vancouver, 1999

GEOSECS Executive Committee
GEOSECS Atlantic, Pacific, and Indian Ocean Expeditions
Vol. 7, Shorebased Data and Graphics
National Science Foundation, Washington, DC, 1987

Goetzmann, William H., and Glyndwr Williams
The Atlas of North American Exploration:
From the Norse Voyages to the Race to the Pole
Prentice Hall, New York, 1992

Golder, Frank A.
Russian Expansion in the Pacific, 1641–1850
Arthur H. Clark, Cleveland, 1914

Golder, Frank A.
Bering's Voyages: An Account of the Efforts of the Russians
to Determine the Relation of Asia and America, 2 vols.
American Geographical Society, New York, 1922 and 1925

Gough, Barry M.
The Northwest Coast:
British Navigation, Trade and Discoveries to 1812
UBC Press, Vancouver, 1992

Gvozdetsky, N. A.
Soviet Geographical Explorations and Discoveries
Progress Publishers, Moscow, 1978

Hayes, Derek
Historical Atlas of the Pacific Northwest
Sasquatch Books, Seattle, 1999
Also published as *Historical Atlas of British Columbia*
and the Pacific Northwest
Cavendish Books, Vancouver, 1999

Hayes, Derek
"Hydrographic Surveying in British Columbia
from 1774 to 1870"
Resolution: The Journal of the Maritime Museum of British
Columbia, No. 48, pp. 3–6, Spring 2000

Hough, Richard
Captain James Cook: A Biography
Hodder and Stoughton, London, 1994

Hunt, William R.
Arctic Passage: The Turbulent History of the Land
and People of the Bering Sea, 1697–1975
Charles Scribner's Sons, New York, 1975

Kearey, Philip, and Frederick J. Vine
Global Tectonics
Blackwell Science, Oxford, 1996

Kendrick, John
The Men with Wooden Feet:
The Spanish Exploration of the Pacific Northwest
NC Press, Toronto, 1986

Kendrick, John
Alejandro Malaspina: Portrait of a Visionary
McGill–Queen's University Press, Montreal, 1999

Kendrick, John (trans. and intro.)
The Voyage of Sutil *and* Mexicana *1792: The Last Spanish*
Exploration of the Northwest Coast of America
Arthur H. Clark, Spokane, WA, 1991

Kerr, Adam J. (ed.)
"The Dynamics of Oceanic Cartography"
Cartographica, Vol. 17, No. 2, Summer 1980
Monograph 25.

Kohl, J. G.
History of Discovery and Exploration on the Coasts
of the United States
U.S. Coast and Geodetic Survey, Washington, DC, 1885

Kunzig, Robert
Mapping the Deep: The Extraordinary Story
of Ocean Science
Sort of Books, London, 2000

Kushnarev, Evenii G., and E.A.P. Crownhart-Vaughan
(ed. and trans.)
Bering's Search for the Strait:
The First Kamchatka Expedition, 1725–1730
Oregon Historical Society Press, Portland, 1990

La Pérouse, Jean-François de Galaup de
The Journal of Jean-François de Galaup de la Pérouse,
1785–1788, 2 vols.
Translated and edited by John Dunmore.
Hakluyt Society, London, 1984

Litke, Frederic [Lütke, Fedor]
A Voyage Around the World, 1826–1829
English translation of French edition,
Voyage Autour de Monde, Paris, 1835
Limestone Press, Kingston, ON, 1987

Longenbaugh, Dee
"From Anian to Alaschka:
The Mapping of Alaska to 1778"
Map Collector, No. 29, p. 28, December 1984

McConnell, Anita
Historical Instruments in Oceanography:
Background to the Oceanography Collection
at the Science Museum (London)
Her Majesty's Stationery Office, London, 1981

McDougall, Walter A.
Let the Sea Make a Noise: A History of the North Pacific
from Magellan to MacArthur
Harper Collins, Basic Books, New York, 1993

McEvedy, Colin
The Penguin Historical Atlas of the Pacific
Penguin Putnam, New York, 1998

Mathes, W. Michael
Vizcaíno and Spanish Exploration
in the Pacific Ocean, 1580–1630
California Historical Society, San Francisco, 1968

Matkin, Joseph
At Sea with the Scientifics:
The Challenger *Letters of Joseph Matkin*
Edited by Philip F. Rehbock.
University of Hawaii Press, Honolulu, 1992

Maury, Matthew Fontaine
The Physical Geography of the Sea and Its Meteorology
Harvard University Press, Belknap Press, Cambridge, MA,
1963. First edition 1855.

Meares, John
Voyages Made in the Years 1788 and 1789
from China to the North West Coast of America
Logographic Press, London, 1790

Menard, H. W.
Marine Geology of the Pacific
McGraw-Hill, New York, 1964

Ministerio de Defensa, Museo Naval
La Expedición Malaspina 1789–1794, 2 vols.
Barcelona, 1987/1993

Mourelle, Francisco Antonio
Voyage of the Sonora from the 1775 Journal
Translated by the Hon. Daines Barrington.
From Daines Barrington, *Miscellanies,* 1781, reprinted by
Thomas C. Russell, San Francisco 1920; also reprint of
this edition by Ye Galleon Press, Fairfield, WA, no date.

Müller, Gerhard Friedrich
Bering's Voyages: The Reports from Russia
Trans. of *Nachricten von Seareisen,* St. Petersburg, 1758.
Commentary by Carol Urness.
University of Alaska Press, Fairbanks, 1986

Müller, Gerhard Friedrich
Voyages from Asia to America, for Completing the
Discoveries of the North West Coast of America
Trans. by Thomas Jefferys, London, 1764.

Murray, Sir John
"On the Temperature of the Floor of the Ocean,
and of the Surface Waters of the Ocean"
Geographical Journal, 14, No. 1, p. 34–51, July 1899

Murray, Sir John
"Oceanography"
Geographical Journal, 14, No. 4, pp. 426–39, Oct. 1899

Needham, Joseph "Geography and Cartography"
In *Science and Civilization in China,* Cambridge
University Press, Vol. 3, pp. 497–590, 1959

Pallas, Peter Simon
Neue nordische Beyträge 1781-3
Trans. by James R. Masterson and Helen Brower.
In *Bering's Successors, 1745–1780: Contributions of Peter*
Simon Pallas to the History of Russian Exploration toward
Alaska
University of Washington Press, Seattle, 1948

Parry, J. H.
The Discovery of the Sea: An Illustrated History of Men,
Ships and the Sea in the Fifteenth and Sixteenth Centuries
Dial Press, New York, 1974

Paul, J. Harland
The Last Cruise of the Carnegie
Williams and Wilkins, Baltimore, 1932

Pethick, Derek
First Approaches to the Northwest Coast
J. J. Douglas, Vancouver, 1976

Pethick, Derek
The Nootka Connection:
Europe and the Northwest Coast, 1790–1795
Douglas & McIntyre, Vancouver, 1980

Pigafetta, Antonio
The First Voyage around the World:
An Account of Magellan's Expedition
Edited by Theodore Cachey. Originally published as
Viaggio intorno al mondo in 1522.
Marsilio Publishers, New York, 1995

Pineau, Roger (ed.)
The Japan Expedition, 1852–1854:
The Personal Journal of Commodore Matthew C. Perry
Smithsonian Institution Press, Washington, DC, 1968

Riesenberg, Felix
The Pacific Ocean
McGraw-Hill, New York, 1940

Ritchie, G. S.
The Admiralty Chart: British Naval Hydrography
in the Nineteenth Century
Hollis and Carter, London, 1967

Sarychev, Gavriil
Account of a Voyage of Discovery to the North-East of
Siberia, the Frozen Ocean, and the North-East Sea
Richard Phillips, London, 1806

Schlee, Susan
The Edge of an Unfamiliar World:
A History of Oceanography
E. P. Dutton, New York, 1973

Sherry, Frank
Pacific Passions: The European Struggle for Power
in the Great Ocean in the Age of Exploration
William Morrow, New York, 1994

Smith, Richard J.
Chinese Maps
Images of Asia series
Oxford University Press, Oxford, 1996

Spry, William J. J.
The Cruise of Her Majesty's Ship Challenger:
Voyages over Many Seas, Scenes in Many Lands
Marston Searle and Rivington, London, 1876

Stanton, William
The Great United States Exploring Expedition
University of California Press, Berkeley, 1975

Stejneger, L. H.
Georg Wilhelm Steller: The Pioneer
of Alaskan Natural History
Cambridge, MA, 1936

Stommel, Henry
Lost Islands: The Story of Islands
That Have Vanished from Nautical Charts
UBC Press, Vancouver, 1984

Svet, Yakov M., and Svetlana G. Fedorova
"Captain Cook and the Russians"
Pacific Studies, Vol. 2, No. 1, pp. 1–19, Fall 1978

Sysoev, N. N. (ed.)
"Oceanographic Research by the 'Vityaz' in the North
Pacific under the I. G. Y. Program"
Transactions of the Institute of Oceanology, Vol. 45,
Academy of Sciences of the U.S.S.R.
Israel Program for Scientific Translations, Jerusalem, 1969

Thrower, Norman J. W. (ed.)
Sir Francis Drake and the Famous Voyage
1577–1580
University of California Press, Berkeley, 1984

Tompkins, S. R., and M. L. Moorhead
"Russia's Approach to America"
B.C. Historical Quarterly, 13,
April, July, and October 1949

Tooley, R. V.
Maps and Map-Makers
Dorset Press, 1987, seventh edition

United Nations Food and Agriculture Organization
Atlas of the Living Resources of the Sea
UNFAO, first edition 1971; second edition 1981

U.S. Navy. Chief of Naval Operations
U.S. Navy Marine Climatic Atlas of the World,
Vol. 2, *North Pacific Ocean*
U.S. Government Printing Office, Washington, DC, 1956

Vancouver, George
A Voyage of Discovery to the North Pacific Ocean
and Round the World, 1791–1795, 4 vols.
Edited by W. Kaye Lamb.
Hakluyt Society, London, 1984
Also original edition, London, 1798

Vaughan, Thomas, E. A. P. Crownhart-Vaughan,
and Mercedes Palau de Iglesias
Voyages of Enlightenment:
Malaspina on the Northwest Coast 1791/1792
Oregon Historical Society Press, Portland, 1977

Wagner, Henry R.
Spanish Voyages to the Northwest Coast
in the Sixteenth Century
California Historical Society, San Francisco, 1929

Wagner, Henry R.
Spanish Explorations in the Strait of Juan de Fuca
Santa Ana, 1933. Reprint AMS Press, New York, 1971

Wagner, Henry R.
Cartography of the Northwest Coast to the Year 1800
University of California Press, 1937. Reprint 2000

Walworth, Arthur
Black Ships Off Japan:
The Story of Commodore Perry's Expedition
Archon Books, Hamden, CT, 1966

Whitfield, Peter
The Image of the World: 20 Centuries of World Maps
Pomegranate Artbooks, San Francisco;
British Library, 1994

Wilkes, Charles
Narrative of the United States Exploring Expedition
during the Years 1838, 1839, 1840, 1841, 1842
Lea and Blanchard, Philadelphia, 1845

Williams, Frances Leigh
Matthew Fontaine Maury, Scientist of the Sea
Rutgers, State University, 1963

Williams, Glyndwr
The British Search for the North West Passage
in the Eighteenth Century
Longmans, Green, London, 1962

Wroth, Lawrence C.
"The Early Cartography of the Pacific"
Bibliographical Society of America Papers, Vol. 38,
No. 2, pp. 87–268, June 1944

Index

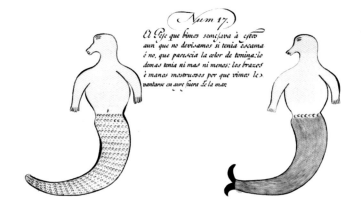